Pro Exchange 2013 SP1 PowerShell Administration

For Exchange On-Premises and Office 365

Jaap Wesselius

Michel de Rooij

Apress®

Pro Exchange 2013 SP1 PowerShell Administration: For Exchange On-Premises and Office 365

ISBN-13 (pbk): 978-1-4302-6848-2

ISBN-13 (electronic): 978-1-4302-6847-5

Managing Director: Welmoed Spahr
Acquisitions Editor: Gwenan Spearing
Development Editor: James Markham
Technical Reviewers: Maarten Piederiet, Shay Levy
Editorial Board: Steve Anglin, Mark Beckner, Gary Cornell, Louise Corrigan, James DeWolf, Jonathan Gennick, Robert Hutchinson, Michelle Lowman, James Markham, Matthew Moodie, Jeff Olson, Jeffrey Pepper, Douglas Pundick, Ben Renow-Clarke, Gwenan Spearing, Matt Wade, Steve Weiss
Coordinating Editor: Rita Fernando
Copy Editor: Carole Berglie
Compositor: SPi Global
Indexer: SPi Global

Distributed to the book trade worldwide by Springer Science+Business Media New York, 233 Spring Street, 6th Floor, New York, NY 10013. Phone 1-800-SPRINGER, fax (201) 348-4505, e-mail orders-ny@springer-sbm.com, or visit www.springeronline.com. Apress Media, LLC is a California LLC and the sole member (owner) is Springer Science + Business Media Finance Inc (SSBM Finance Inc). SSBM Finance Inc is a Delaware corporation.

For information on translations, please e-mail rights@apress.com, or visit www.apress.com.

Apress and friends of ED books may be purchased in bulk for academic, corporate, or promotional use. eBook versions and licenses are also available for most titles. For more information, reference our Special Bulk Sales–eBook Licensing web page at www.apress.com/bulk-sales.

Any source code or other supplementary material referenced by the author in this text is available to readers at www.apress.com. For detailed information about how to locate your book's source code, go to www.apress.com/source-code/.

Contents at a Glance

Contents

About the Authors

Jaap Wesselius is an independent consultant based in The Netherlands, focusing on Microsoft Unified Communications solutions, and in particular, Exchange Server, Lync Server, and Office 365. Jaap is also involved with private cloud solutions, especially Windows Azure Services and, to a lesser extent, VMWare.

Jaap learned Unified Communications, including Microsoft Exchange Server, in his years at Microsoft. He worked at Microsoft from 1997 to 2006, both in support as a Technical Account Manager and in MCS as an Infrastructure Consultant.

Besides work, Jaap spends a lot of time in the Exchange community, such as with the Dutch UC User Group and the Dutch Network User Group NGN. He is a frequent blogger on his own site www.jaapwesselius.com, but you can also find an extensive selection of his articles on Simple-Talk (www.simple-talk.com). And if that's not enough, Jaap is a regular speaker at major events like Microsoft TechEd, the Microsoft Exchange Conference, the Quest Experts Conference, and the IT/Dev Connections conferences. For his work in the community, Jaap was awarded with the Exchange Server MVP award in 2007, an award that he has held annually ever since.

When time permits (it never permits enough, so spare time has to be created), Jaap savors life with his wife and three sons, and also enjoys doing some serious hiking and cycling—the best way, he feels, for one to free one's mind. An ongoing dream is to cycle across Europe, but most likely this will remain a dream as long as he spends a good part of his time working, writing, and giving speeches.

Michel de Rooij is a consultant at Conclusion FIT, an IT company from The Netherlands offering a wide range of IT services. His primary focus is on helping customers with their Exchange or Office 365 related challenges, but it may also touch on similar technologies like Active Directory or Lync.

Michel started his professional career as a developer in the mid-90s, but quickly switched to working on infrastructure-related projects, such as office automation and desktop/server migration projects. In 2004, he got a chance to do dedicated work on Exchange and related technologies for a large multinational, and since then Exchange has become his main specialization. He finds the heritage of being a former developer a great asset for dealing with all PowerShell-enabled products.

Michel is also very active in the Exchange communities, like TechNet or the Dutch Network User Group NGN. He authors articles for his own Exchange blog www.eightwone.com, and TechTarget (searchexchange.techtarget.com). He is also guest author for companies like ISV ENow Software (enowsoftware.com) and is active on Twitter at @mderooij.

Apart from speaking at local events and co presenting a PowerShell for Exchange admins session at Exchange Connections in 2014, he is a contributor to The UC Architects (theucarchitects.com), a bi-weekly community podcast by people with a passion for Unified Communications, focused on Exchange, Lync, and related topics. For his community work, Michel was awarded the Exchange Server MVP award in 2013 and again in 2014.

In his spare time, Michel loves to spend time with his partner and two kids, ride his motorcycle, or watch a movie.

About the Technical Reviewers

Maarten Piederiet is a Senior Consultant at Conclusion FIT in The Netherlands. He has been working in IT since he graduated as Software Engineer in 1999. Since then, he has gradually switched his focus to IT infrastructure projects. Maarten's background as a programmer, combined with his infrastructure experience, has fed his passion for PowerShell and scripting. He has over 12 years' experience with Exchange Server and is a Microsoft Certified Master in Exchange Server 2010. He also managed to achieve the Microsoft Certified Solutions Master: Messaging (Exchange 2013) title, which he was awarded just before the Master's program was retired by Microsoft. Maarten has very strong troubleshooting skills, and takes on any technology-related challenge, be it Microsoft or any new technology that triggers his interest. He's eager to help customers with Active Directory, Exchange, Lync, Office 365, and Windows Server migration challenges or with designs and implementations. He's known for his positive energy and always contributes his great sense of humor!

In his spare time, Maarten enjoys spending time with his partner and young daughter, and relishes a beer (or two) with friends.

Shay Levy works as a Senior Systems Engineer for a government institute in Israel. He has over 20 years of experience, focusing on Microsoft server platforms, especially on Exchange and Active Directory.

Shay is a Microsoft Certified Trainer (MCT). He is a world-known knowledgeable figure in the PowerShell scripting arena.

He is the Co-Founder and Editor of the PowerShellMagazine.com website. He often covers PowerShell-related topics on his blog http://PowerShay.com, and you can also follow him on Twitter @ShayLevy.

For his community contributions he has been awarded the Microsoft Most Valuable Professional (MVP) award for seven years in a row.

Acknowledgments

Yet again I am surprised by the amount of work it takes to write a book like this, even with a co-author. Numerous times I have thought that this is going to be my last book ever! But now that this book is finished, I automatically start thinking about writing a new book, although I don't even know the topic yet.

Every time I write I'm amazed by the number of people who contribute to the project. First, there's co-author Michel de Rooij, with whom I not only wrote this book but also did a presentation at IT/Dev Connections 2014 in Last Vegas; we had a good time. Second, there are the reviewers of this book, in particular Maarten Piederiet, who was always willing to answer my questions and point me in the right direction.

Third, I thank a lot of people at my publisher, Apress, and our coordinator Rita Fernando, who was chasing us all the time, especially when we were approaching a deadline.

And I acknowledge the help of my fellow MVPs, MCMs around the world, with whom I have had solid discussions with, as well as everybody else I forgot, I thank you!

The last persons I thank are my wife and sons, who always had a hard time when I needed to do some research, jot down some notes, do the initial writing, or review the chapters for submission. It will sound familiar to most authors when I tell my wife, "Yes, this is the last book I'm gonna write!" Thank you all for your tremendous support during the past year.

—Jaap

A book! When Jaap asked me if I wanted to join him in writing the successor to *Pro Exchange Server 2013 Administration for Exchange 2013 Service Pack 1* at the end of December 2013, I immediately got enthusiastic. And now, after almost a year, I must say it has been an interesting and rewarding experience. I'd not been involved in the book-creation process before, but having something tangible to hold, after putting in lots of blood, sweat, and tears, feels great; I look forward to new writing opportunities and future collaborations.

A word of thanks to Jaap Wesselius for getting me on board this project. Jaap is great for sparring with and exchanging ideas, with his practical approach, vast amount of experience, and healthy sense of humor. I also extend my thanks to our technical reviewer, my co-worker and buddy Maarten Piederiet. His attention to detail, ability to focus, and sense of humor are unparalleled. To the people of Apress, especially Rita, I am appreciative for keeping us on track throughout this project. To fellow Exchange MVPs, MCMs, and the Exchange PG, I'm grateful to them for sharing their experiences and ideas, and having lots of interesting discussions. Finally, I send my gratitude to my family and friends, who saw me a lot less in the evenings and weekends in recent months when I was doing the research, writing, or reviewing. To you and everybody else I forgot, I say thank you for your support and patience.

—Michel

Introduction

The Microsoft UC solutions are changing rapidly, especially from on-premises operations to cloud solutions. This makes it hard to write a book about Exchange 2013. Changing the subject to PowerShell Administration makes it a bit more version independent, but even during this writing, we found the applications were changing rapidly. The book is based on Exchange 2013 SP1, but you'll find some information regarding subsequent cumulative updates, as these are released on a quarterly basis.

This book is aimed at IT Pro's, the Exchange administrators with a couple of years experience who need guidance in deploying and managing Exchange Server 2013 on-premises, especially when it comes to managing PowerShell. Inside these pages are eleven chapters that cover the following topics:

- Chapter 1 - Introduction to Exchange 2013. This is an overview of Exchange Server 2013, including new and discontinued features, integration with Active Directory, and an architectural overview of the product.

- Chapter 2 - Installing Exchange Server 2013. The first part of this chapter covers the installation of Exchange Server 2013, both on Windows Server 2008 R2 and on Windows Server 2012 R2. The normal graphic setup is discussed; also here is the unattended setup with all the command-line switches that are available, including the post-installation configuration options. The second part includes information regarding coexistence with Exchange 2010 or Exchange 2007.

- Chapter 3 - Client Access Server. This covers the Client Access server, Client Access technologies, and all available clients for use with Exchange 2013. Namespaces, SSL certificates, load balancing, and Publishing Exchange 2013 Client Access server are the most important topics here.

- Chapter 4 - Mailbox Server. This covers the Mailbox server, including the available recipients like mailboxes, distribution groups, and public folders, as well as how to manage them. Except for mailboxes, another important part of the Mailbox server is message transport, which is also covered here.

- Chapter 5 - High Availability. High Availability is an important and complex aspect of every Exchange 2013 deployment. This chapter covers the basics of the database availability group and how to build and configure it. The chapter covers also Client Access High Availability and Transport High Availability.

- Chapter 6 - Message Hygiene. This topic is new in Exchange 2013 SP1, and so the chapter discusses the Edge Transport server and how to implement all available anti-spam features, plus how it integrates with the Exchange 2013 Mailbox server.

- Chapter 7 - Backup, Restore, and Disaster Recovery. This discusses backup technologies and how backup technologies interact with Mailbox database technologies. Other topics in this chapter are restore technologies and the Microsoft Native Data Protections, sometimes also referred to as "backup-less environment."

- Chapter 8 - Unified Messaging. This explores the UM feature set, shows how to configure Exchange UM for supported IP telephony solutions, and explains how to integrate Exchange UM with Lync. Other topics are UM mailbox policies, UM auto attendants, Unified Contact Store, call answering rules, and voice-mail preview.

- Chapter 9 - Compliance. This discusses the compliance-related features of Exchange 2013, such as in-place archiving to manage the primary mailbox, in combination with message records management and in-place discovery that, in conjunction with in-place hold, can be used to support legal investigations or other purposes. Data loss prevention and fingerprinting are discussed as features to prevent data leakage. Other topics are administrator and mailbox auditing.

- Chapter 10 - Security. This explores the role-based access model and all its components, such as management roles, scopes, role groups, and special-purpose features like unscoped top-level management groups. Other topics are the split-permissions model for organizations with separated management of Active Directory and Exchange, and S/MIME.

- Chapter 11 - Office 365 and Exchange Online. This shows how to connect to Office 365, and discusses Autodiscover, as well as how to federate organizations to share information such as calendaring. It also covers how to configure directory synchronization with Azure Active Directory and how to configure Active Directory Federation Services and Multi-Factor Authentication. Additionally, it explains how to move mailboxes between on-premises and Office 365, Exchange Online Archiving, and how to reconfigure mail flow when using Exchange hybrid.

CHAPTER 1

■ ■ ■

Introduction to Exchange 2013 SP1

In October 2012, Microsoft released the eighth major version of its messaging and collaboration server, Exchange 2013. This version of Exchange 2013 is referred to as *Exchange 2013 RTM*, the lattermost which stands for "Release To Manufacturing." In early 2014, this release was followed by the release of Exchange 2013 Service Pack 1 (SP1). As usual, SP1 brings a lot of hotfixes, but also a lot of new features, both completely new features and features (including some that were available in Exchange 2010) that did not make it into Exchange 2013 RTM, mostly because of time constraints during development.

With the new servicing model that Microsoft introduced with Exchange 2013, cumulative updates (CUs) are released on a quarterly basis. A CU contains hotfixes, of course, but each CU also introduces new functionality. A CU is also a full package of Exchange 2013, so there's no longer a need to install Exchange 2013 RTM followed by the subsequent updates, as was common practice in earlier versions of Exchange Server.

After releasing three CUs in a row, Microsoft released CU4 on February 25, 2014, which was equivalent to Exchange 2013 SP1. Is Exchange 2013 SP1 a new major release? The answer is yes and no. Exchange 2013 gradually evolved into SP1, but Microsoft has also released a lot of new features in SP1. An example of one of these features is the Edge Transport server role. This was available in Exchange 2007 and Exchange 2010, but not in Exchange 2013 RTM. The Edge Transport role has returned in Exchange 2013 SP1. Another example is support for SSL Offloading, which was available in Exchange 2010 but not in Exchange 2013 RTM. This is an example of that time constraint: during development of Exchange 2013 RTM there wasn't enough time to test this feature properly and thus support it sufficiently.

Looking at the new servicing model with the cumulative updates you might ask why Microsoft is calling CU4 "SP1" instead of continuing the CU numbering. A new version, such as SP1, is a major milestone in a product's lifecycle and as such is supportable. Exchange 2013 RTM will be supported for 10 years, and Exchange 2013 SP1 will be supported for 12 months after the release of the next Service Pack.[1] When it comes to supporting Cumulative Updates, Microsoft only supports the current CU version and the previous CU version. So, it's purely a matter of supportability. The quarterly releases of CUs will continue, starting with the release of CU5 in the first quarter after release of SP1.

At first glance, Exchange 2013 RTM didn't seem like a revolutionary change, but there was more than met the eye. Exchange 2013 is the first version from Microsoft to be designed from the ground up with the cloud in mind—in particular, Office 365. This is an area where Microsoft is facing tough competition from others, such as Google. Google Mail and Google Apps have a slick underlying infrastructure that makes it possible for users to add new features quickly and have good performance figures at the same time. This ability was something that hasn't been Microsoft's strongest point in the last couple of years, and therefore Microsoft decided to invest heavily in its cloud infrastructure. At the same time, Exchange Server was being redesigned to take advantage of these cloud developments.

---

[1]The *Microsoft Product Lifecycle for Exchange 2013* states: "Support ends 12 months after the next service pack releases or at the end of the product's support lifecycle, whichever comes first. For more information, please see the service pack policy at http://support.microsoft.com/lifecycle/#ServicePackSupport."

What's important in a public cloud environment like Office 365? It's the scalability, architecture, and manageability of the platform. You'll see these in the new front- and back-end architecture, in which the front end is the Client Access server acting as a protocol proxy. This is important in an environment with multiple data centers, perhaps in combination with a geographically dispersed DNS solution, in which you want your application to run with as few administrators and as little administrator input as possible. A solid monitoring situation with predefined actions and solutions is key to achieving such an environment.

Look at the JBOD (just a bunch of disks) solutions that Microsoft has been promoting since its introduction of Exchange Server 2010. This is a development driven by a need to lower the price of storage per GB. Running multiple copies of a mailbox database on simple SATA disks is easy to manage and has low replacement cost. That is, when a disk fails, which is not uncommon with cheap SATA disks, the Exchange server automatically moves over to another mailbox database on another disk. Exchange 2013 has the ability to automatically create mailbox database copies when spare disks are available, a feature called *auto reseed*. Later on, it's a simple matter to rip and replace the faulty disk, and you're back in business. This both decreases the cost of maintaining the disk infrastructure and lowers the operational cost of administrative staff.

Manageability is also an important factor when running a huge infrastructure in a data center. You don't want to see an alert in your management console for every minor issue in your Exchange 2013 environment. This is where Managed Availability comes in; it will continuously monitor your Exchange 2013 environment and take appropriate action when needed. This action can include restarting an application pool in IIS, taking a process or service offline, or even rebooting a server. You can see this as a "self-healing" feature of Exchange 2013.

These are just a few key features for Microsoft data centers running Office 365, and you'll see these features in the new Exchange 2013 as well. Does this mean that Exchange 2013 is targeted to large, multinational organizations? Well, yes and no. It's yes in the sense that large, multinational organizations will certainly benefit from the new architecture with its front- and back-end technologies. But smaller organizations, perhaps with data-center resiliency, will certainly also benefit from Exchange 2013.

Larger organizations can create a combination of Exchange 2013 on premises and Office 365. This is called a "hybrid environment," where the two are tightly integrated. Together they form one namespace with one address book, and yet they are independent where the actual mailboxes are located. Also, email sent between Exchange 2013 on premises and Office 365 is fully secure because of the configuration changes made by the hybrid configuration wizard.

This book is just like the product it describes. Originally it was written for Exchange 2013 RTM, but then it was updated for Exchange 2013 SP1, with additional content. A lot of the material applies to both versions, but when something only applies to SP1, it is noted as such.

Getting Started

To begin, let's take a general look at Exchange 2013. First, we'll consider the two Exchange 2013 editions and review their features. Then, we'll look at their features compared to Exchange Server 2010, noting in particular which features are not part of Exchange 2013.

The Editions

Exchange 2013 is available in two editions:

- **Exchange 2013, Standard Edition.** This is a "normal" Exchange 2013, limited to five (5) mailbox databases per Mailbox server. This edition can also be used for Client Access servers.

- **Exchange 2013, Enterprise Edition.** This version can host up to 100 mailbox databases per Mailbox server. In Exchange 2013 RTM, the number of mailbox databases was limited to 50, but this was increased to 100 with the release of Exchange 2013 CU2. Just like the Standard Edition, this version can be used for Client Access servers. Considering the additional cost of an Enterprise Edition, it doesn't make sense to use it for a single Exchange 2013 Client Access server.

Except for the number of mailbox databases per Exchange server, there are no differences between the two versions; the binaries are the same.

Entering the Exchange 2013 license key changes the limit of maximum mailbox databases for that server. Besides the Exchange 2013 server license, there's also a Client Access license (CAL), which is required for each user or device accessing the server software.

There are two types of CALs available:

- **Standard CAL.** This CAL offers standard email functionality from any platform. The license is for typical Exchange and Outlook usage.

- **Enterprise CAL.** This more advanced CAL offers functionality such as integrated archiving, compliance features, and information-protection capabilities. The CAL is an add-on to the Standard CAL, so both licenses need to be purchased!

This is not a complete list of all available features for the different CALs. For a complete overview, visit the Microsoft licensing page at `http://bit.ly/exlicense`.

What's New in Exchange 2013 SP1?

So, what are the new features and improvements in Exchange 2013? There are a lot of new features, valuable both from an administrator's point of view and from that of an end-user. In Exchange 2013 SP1, a new set of features is introduced as well, but let's discuss the most important changes here:

- **Support for Windows Server 2012 R2.** Long awaited in the Exchange community, Exchange 2013 SP1 now supports Windows Server 2012 R2. Please note that this only applies to Exchange 2013 SP1; unfortunately, Exchange 2013 RTM up to CU3 does *not* support Windows Server 2012 R2.

- **Edge Transport server.** This server role was available in both Exchange 2007 and Exchange 2010, but not in Exchange 2013 RTM. Thankfully the Edge Transport server role is again included in Exchange 2013 SP1, allowing companies standardizing on Exchange Server 2013 or Windows Server 2012 R2 to utilize the desired platform or product version. The Edge Transport server role functionality is "message hygiene," which means its primary purpose is anti-spam and anti-virus. Related to this is Exchange Online Protection, which is Microsoft's similar solution in the cloud. Both the Edge Transport server role and Exchange Online Protection are explained in detail in Chapter 6.

- **SSL Offloading.** SSL Offloading is another feature that was supported in Exchange 2010 but not in Exchange 2013 RTM. It has now been returned and Exchange 2013 SP1 supports SSL Offloading.

- **A new look and feel for client interfaces.** Exchange 2013 has a new appearance and tone across all messaging clients. Outlook 2013 has a new interface based on the new Microsoft design language. It's not an overloaded amount of information but, rather, offers a consistent view of all information, is easy to find, and is a snap to use. This interface can also be found in the Outlook Web App (OWA), as shown in Figure 1-1, and it's obvious that the OWA team and the Outlook 2013 team have worked closely together. This new design can be seen on all kinds of devices, with all types of clients or browsers. Use Windows 8 with Outlook 2013, or Windows 7 with OWA, or Windows Phone 8 with the Outlook mobile mail client, and they all offer this consistent view and user experience.

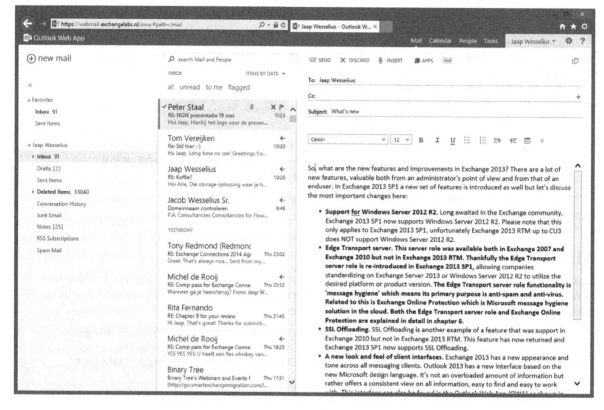

Figure 1-1. The new look and feel of Outlook Web App (OWA)

OWA also has a great new feature: When using Internet Explorer 10 or later (or Firefox 12, Safari 5.1, or Chrome 18, or later), you'll find OWA can be made available in offline mode, thereby giving you the option of working with OWA in an airplane, for example. Not all information is cached within the browser; it is comparable to a mobile client's use of ActiveSync, where only a few days' worth of data is stored. Only the default settings differ between ActiveSync and OWA offline.

Exchange 2013 SP1 has added three features to OWA:

- A rich text editor that make it possible to change the layout of newly created messages—for example, with other fonts, or to use bold or italic.

- An S/MIME control for Internet Explorer, making it possible to use secure messaging through S/MIME in OWA.

- DLP Policy tips.

- **Exchange Admin Center.** The Exchange Admin Center (EAC) is the new web-based management interface for Exchange 2013 (see Figure 1-2). Built on the new design for mail clients, it offers a management interface across various types of clients and web browsers and integration with Office 365 management.

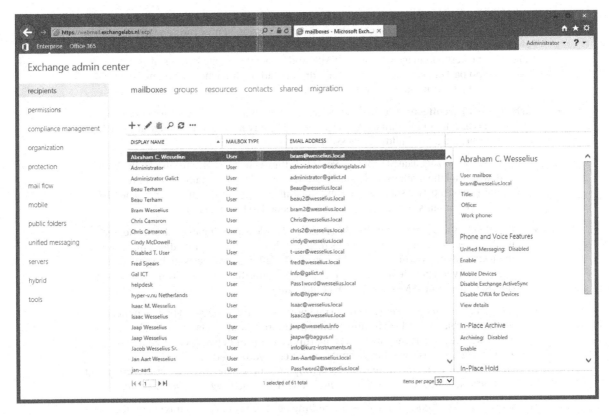

Figure 1-2. The new Exchange Admin Center (EAC) in Exchange 2013

Under the hood, EAC is using role-based access control (RBAC) so that only the management options enforced by RBAC are visible to the administrator. Just like the Exchange Management Console in Exchange Server 2010, not all the nitty-gritty details are available in the EAC; only the basic management functions are present. For all other management functions, the Exchange Management Shell (EMS) is available.

Exchange 2013 SP1 offers a new feature in EAC: cmdlet logging. That is, each action that's performed using EAC is translated under the hood in an Exchange Management Shell command, and this command is now shown in the cmdlet logging option. Yes, this feature was also available in Exchange 2007 and Exchange 2010, but it was *not* available in Exchange 2013 RTM.

The cmdlet logging is an extremely interesting feature for Exchange administrators because it allows us to learn PowerShell in a quick and easy way. Let's face it, as Exchange administrators we've been used to the GUI for so many years, but when we want to learn PowerShell and take advantage of its strength, we look for the easiest way to learn it. And that's using a cheat sheet like this.

- **Exchange Management Shell.** It's not really new in Exchange 2013, but the Exchange Management Shell (EMS) is strongly enhanced in this version. It now runs on top of PowerShell 3.0 (by default, in Windows Server 2012), with approximately 300 new cmdlets making it a powerful management tool. "EMS" and "PowerShell" are both used as names in this book, and part of its title is "PowerShell Administration," but when the name "PowerShell" is used in the text, we automatically mean the EMS.

- **Exchange 2013 architecture.** There's a new architecture when it comes to server roles. Only two server roles in Exchange 2013 RTM and three server roles in Exchange 2013 SP1, sometimes referred to as "building blocks," are available:

  - *Mailbox server role*: The Mailbox server role is the Exchange 2013 running in the back end, where all the mailboxes are stored. At the same time, the Mailbox server role contains the Hub Transport service and the unified messaging components. The Mailbox server role contains all the application logic needed to host a mailbox.

  - *Client Access server role*: The Client Access server role is running in the front end and is the server all clients connect to. It is responsible for authenticating the connection requests and proxies (or redirects, in case of SIP traffic) the requests to the appropriate Mailbox server. The Client Access server also contains the Front End Transport service (FETS) and a Unified Messaging (UM) Call Router.

  - *Edge Transport server role*: The Edge Transport server role is situated between the internal Exchange 2013 environment and the Internet, and it acts as an SMTP gateway. Typically, the Edge Transport servers are running in your network's demilitarized zone (DMZ), and as such they are not a member of your internal Active Directory environment. They commonly are workgroup members. The Edge Transport servers get their information via a synchronization mechanism called *edge synchronization.*

- **Managed store.** The "store" is the process running on the Exchange Mailbox server that's responsible for processing the mail transactions and storing the transactions in the mailbox databases. In Exchange 2013, the store process is completely rewritten in "managed code"— that is, C#, using the .NET Framework. More important, every mailbox database now has its own store process. So, even if one store process stops working, resulting in that particular mailbox database (copy) to stop working, the other mailbox databases on the same Mailbox server are unaffected. Earlier, in Exchange 2010, there was only one store process on a Mailbox server. When problems arose with the store process, all those mailbox databases were affected. This managed store is a great improvement in system stability.

- **Managed Availability.** One of the best new features of Exchange 2013 is its Managed Availability. It looks like some sort of "self-healing" feature, and it is responsible for monitoring all critical services on Exchange 2013. When needed, it takes appropriate action. Managed Availability consists of probes, monitors, and actions. *Probes* are constantly checking for certain services, and they feed the results into the monitors. The *monitors* evaluate the results from the probes. When needed, Managed Availability can perform certain *actions*. For example, it can check if OWA is up and running; if it's not, it can start or recycle the application pool where OWA is running or reset the Internet Information Services (IISRESET). Similarly, Managed Availability has probes for mailbox databases; if a mailbox database is found to be corrupted, Managed Availability can take action to automatically fail-over that mailbox database to another Mailbox server in the DAG and perform an automatic reseed of the corrupted mailbox database. This way, problems can be resolved even before end-users notice the failures, thereby reducing the number of calls to the help desk.

- **Outlook Anywhere.** This feature is not really new, but what's new in the Exchange 2013 environment is the fact that Outlook clients no longer connect using RPC over TCP (the traditional MAPI way). All Outlook clients now use RCP over HTTPS (i.e., Outlook Anywhere, or OA). This is true for both internal and external clients. So even an internal Outlook client automatically connects to the Exchange 2013 Client Access server (CAS) using RPC/HTTPS. The Outlook client is authenticated on the Exchange 2013 CAS, and after authentication, the request is proxied (again using RPC/HTTPS) to the Mailbox server where the mailbox is located.

- **MapiHttp.** Mapi over HTTP, codename Alchemy, is a new protocol in Exchange 2013 SP1, based on HTTP and positioned as a replacement for the RPC over HTTPS protocol. The idea behind this protocol is to remove the dependency on Remote Procedure Calls (RPC) when Outlook is communicating with the Exchange 2013 SP1 server. MapiHttp is only running on Exchange 2013 SP1 or later, and initially only Outlook 2013 SP1 will support it. Outlook 2010 will start supporting MapiHttp in a future update.

- **Anti-malware protection.** Exchange 2013 has built-in anti-malware protection available, but unfortunately it is not as feature-rich as the former Forefront Protection for Exchange (FPE), nor does it have the features that were available in the Exchange Server 2010 Edge Transport server. The anti-malware in Exchange 2013 is running one engine, and it scans messages that enter or leave the Exchange organization. If malware is found, it can remove the entire message or strip only the attachment if the malware is just in the attachment. For anti-spam and anti-virus solutions for SMTP in transit, Microsoft relies heavily on Exchange Online Protection (EOP), the successor to Forefront Online Protection for Exchange (FOPE), Microsoft's cloud solution for anti-spam and anti-virus. The good news is that both the Exchange Server 2010 and the Exchange Server 2007 Edge Transport server are running fine and are fully supported in combination with Exchange 2013, including Edge synchronization. For this to work correctly, though, you need Exchange 2007 SP3 RU10 or Exchange Server 2010 SP3.

- **"Modern" public folders.** Microsoft has invested heavily in public folders after years of uncertainty. They are calling the new version "modern public folders." The traditional public folders database has been discontinued in Exchange 2013, and it has been moved to the mailbox database. Because of this, the public folders are now protected by means of the database availability group (DAG) so that multiple copies of the public folders can exist in a DAG. Public folders themselves consist of the hierarchy (i.e., the folder structure) and the actual content. A writeable copy of the hierarchy is stored in a primary hierarchy mailbox, and there's only one writeable copy. The public folder content is stored in secondary hierarchy mailboxes; this is a new type of mailbox introduced in Exchange 2013. Besides public folder content, the secondary hierarchy mailboxes also contain a read-only copy of the hierarchy. Although public folders have migrated into these special mailboxes, Outlook clients and Outlook show them as "normal" public folders. Therefore, users will not notice the difference between the traditional public folders and the modern public folders.

- **Site mailboxes.** Site mailboxes are another new mailbox type in Exchange 2013, and they are a combination of Exchange 2013 and SharePoint Server 2013. That is, site mailboxes are designed for (temporary) project teams, where lots of Office documents are sent back and forth among members of the groups. Under the hood, these site mailboxes are actually a SharePoint team site that is much more capable of storing document-type information. For an Outlook client, it is fully transparent and the site mailbox is visible as a normal mailbox. This is a great example of "Exchange and SharePoint: Better Together."

- **Data Loss Prevention.** Data Loss Prevention, or DLP, is a new security feature in Exchange 2013. It's designed to prevent sending out messages that contain confidential information, based on Transport rules. For example, DLP can be used to filter messages that contain credit card numbers or Social Security numbers. It does this by checking the messages as they are submitted against certain predefined templates. If there's a match, a warning is displayed—much like mail tips—about what DLP has found to be a security issue. This is fully configureable so it can match your security requirements. A number of predefined DLP policies are included in Exchange 2013, and the policies are customizable to fit company policies.

Of course, there are many more new features in Exchange 2013, but these are the most important ones.

What Has Been Removed from Exchange Server

Every new version of Exchange Server introduces new features, but at the same time other features are discontinued, deprecated, or available only in some other form or scenario. The most important changes or discontinued features in Exchange 2013 are:

- **Support for Outlook 2003.** Outlook 2003 is not supported in Exchange 2013. Not only is it unsupported, it is not working. Outlook 2003 depends on system folders, free/busy, and offline address book distribution folders in public folders, and these system folders have been discontinued. Unfortunately, there is still a huge installed base for Outlook 2003, so this could be a major showstopper in the deployment of Exchange 2013.

- **RPC/TCP access for Outlook clients.** The traditional RPC/TCP access for Outlook clients is no longer supported in Exchange 2013. All Outlook clients will connect using Outlook Anywhere (OA, formerly known as RPC/HTTPS), whether they are on the internal or the external network. The reason is obvious; RPC/HTTPS is easier to route via the networks because it requires only port 443 to be open on firewalls. For RPC/TCP this is not the case and most firewalls block RPC traffic.

- **Hub Transport Server role.** The dedicated Hub Transport server that was used in Exchange Server 2007 and Exchange Server 2010 is no longer available as a dedicated server. Instead, it is integrated into the Mailbox server role, so that every Mailbox server automatically has a transport service installed. This transport service is responsible for routing SMTP messages, both inside the Exchange Service organization and to the Internet. The Exchange 2013 CAS is a protocol proxy for the transport service on the Mailbox server; the service on the Exchange 2013 CAS is called Front End Transport (FET). External SMTP hosts connect to the FET on the Exchange 2013 Client Access server, which proxies the request to the transport service running on the Mailbox server where the recipient's mailbox is located. The Mailbox server can route SMTP messages directly to the Internet, but it can also use the Exchange 2013 CAS as a front-end proxy for outbound messages.

- **Unified Messaging server role.** The dedicated Unified Messaging (UM) server role is no longer available as a dedicated server. Just like the Hub Transport server, it is now integrated with the Exchange 2013 Mailbox server. When you are installing an Exchange 2013 Mailbox server, the UM service is automatically installed. For SIP traffic, the Exchange 2013 CAS does not act as a proxy, but the UM Call Router service redirects the SIP request to the UM service on the Mailbox server where the recipient's mailbox is located.

- **Exchange Management Console and Exchange Control Panel.** In previous versions of Exchange Server, the Exchange Management Console (EMC) was the primary graphical UI for managing the entire Exchange environment. While this worked fine in a smaller environment, it was less usable in large, multi-center environments. In Exchange 2013, Microsoft has discontinued the EMC and it is replaced by the Exchange Admin Center (EAC). The same is true for the Exchange Control Panel (ECP). It has been discontinued in Exchange 2013, and user self-management is now performed by the EAC.

- **Managed folders.** Managed folders were introduced in Exchange Server 2007 as Microsoft's solution for information management and compliance. In Exchange Server 2010, Microsoft introduced the personal archive and retention policies; as a result, managed folders in Exchange Service 2010 were deprecated. This was clearly visible in Exchange Server 2010 SP1, where managed folders were manageable only from the EMS and were not compatible with the personal archive. In Exchange 2013, managed folders have been decommissioned.

- **Anti-spam agent management.** Anti-spam functionality as we knew it in Exchange Server 2010 is not available in Exchange 2013. The Exchange Service 2013 CAS does not perform any anti-spam duties, so all SMTP messages are proxied to the transport service on the Exchange 2013 Mailbox servers. These do have some anti-spam functionality, but compared to the Exchange Server 2010 Hub Transport server or the Exchange 2013 SP1 Edge Transport server, they are very limited.

- **Forefront Protection for Exchange.** The anti-malware built into Exchange 2013 is limited and absolutely not comparable to Microsoft's Forefront Protection for Exchange (FPE), which was previously available. Now, anti-malware is available only on the Mailbox server in the back end. There are no options for managing the anti-malware solution other than to turn it on or off or to change the notification text.

A bit beyond the scope of this book is the Forefront Threat Management Gateway (TMG) 2010. At the end of 2012, Microsoft announced the end of life for TMG 2010. While TMG will be supported for a couple of years, it will continue to work with Exchange Server 2010—and with some minor adjustments, it will also work with Exchange 2013. For the long term, however, it is recommended you start looking for alternatives to this firewall and pre-authentication functionality. Right after the end-of-life announcement, the official Microsoft alternative was to use its Forefront Unified Application Gateway (UAG), but then Microsoft announced the end of its life as well.

When publishing Microsoft services toward the Internet, using some sort of reverse proxy, you have to look for other alternatives. When it comes to reverse proxy, the Application Request Routing (ARR) module is available for running on top of the Internet Information server (IIS) or the Web Application Proxy (WAP) in Windows Server 2012 R2, but other third-party hardware vendors (like Cisco, Juniper, Kemp, or F5) can deliver the same functionality, sometimes combined with load-balancing functionality.

Integration with Active Directory

Active Directory is the foundation for Exchange 2013, as it has been for Exchange Server since Exchange 2000 was released 14 years ago. Earlier versions of Exchange Server—that is, Exchange 5.5 and earlier—relied on their own directory, which was separate from the (NT4) user directory. Active Directory stores most of Exchange's configuration information, both for server/organization configuration and for mail-enabled objects.

A Microsoft Windows Active Directory Directory Service (ADDS) is best described as a forest; this is the highest level in the Directory Service and is the actual security boundary. The forest contains one or more Active Directory Directory domains; a domain is a logical grouping of resources, such as users, groups, and computers. An Exchange 2013 organization is bound to one forest, so even if you have an environment with over 100 domains, there can be only one Exchange organization.

Active Directory sites also play an important role in Exchange deployment. An Active Directory site can be seen as a location, well connected with high bandwidth and low latency—for example, a data center or an office. Active Directory sites can contain multiple Active Directory domains, but an Active Directory domain can also span multiple Active Directory sites.

Exchange 2013 depends heavily on ADDS, and these need to be healthy. The minimum levels in ADDS need to be Windows 2003 Forest Functional Level (FFL) and Windows 2003 Domain Functional Level (DFL). The Domain Controllers need to be at a minimum level of Windows Server 2003 SP1.

Active Directory Partitions

A Microsoft Windows ADDS consists of three system-provided partitions:

- **Schema partition.** The schema partition is the blueprint for all objects and properties that are available in Active Directory. For example, if a new user is created, a user object is instantiated from the schema, the required properties are populated, and the user account is stored in the Active Directory database. All objects and properties are in the schema partition, and therefore it depends which version is used. Windows 2012 R2 Active Directory has much newer objects and newer (and more) properties than, for example, Windows 2003 Active Directory. The same is true, of course, for applications like Exchange Server. Exchange 2013 adds a lot of new objects and attributes to Active Directory that make it possible to increase functionality. Therefore, every new version of Exchange Server, or even the cumulative updates or service packs, needs to make schema changes.

  There is only one schema partition in the entire Active Directory forest. Even if you have an Active Directory forest with 100 domains and 250 sites worldwide, there's only one schema partition. This partition is replicated among all Domain Controllers in the entire Active Directory forest. The most important copy of the schema partition is running on the schema master, which is typically the first Domain Controller installed in the forest. This copy is the only read-write copy in the entire Active Directory forest.

- **Configuration partition.** The configuration partition is where all nonschema information is stored that needs to be available throughout the Active Directory forest. Information that can be found in the configuration partition is, for example, about Active Directory sites, about public key infrastructure, about the various partitions that are available in Active Directory, and of course about Exchange Server. Just like the schema partition, there's only one configuration partition. It replicates among all Domain Controllers in the entire Active Directory environment so that all the Exchange servers have access to the same, consistent set of information. All information regarding the Exchange server configuration, like the Exchange servers themselves, the routing infrastructure, or the number of domains that Exchange Server is responsible for, is stored in the configuration partition.

- **Domain Partition.** The domain partition is where all domain-specific information is stored. There's one partition per domain, so if you have 100 domains in your Active Directory forest, you have 100 separate domain partitions. User objects, contacts, and security and distribution groups are stored in the domain partition.

The best tool for viewing the three Active Directory partitions is the ADSI Edit MMC (Microsoft Management Console) snap-in, which is shown in Figure 1-3.

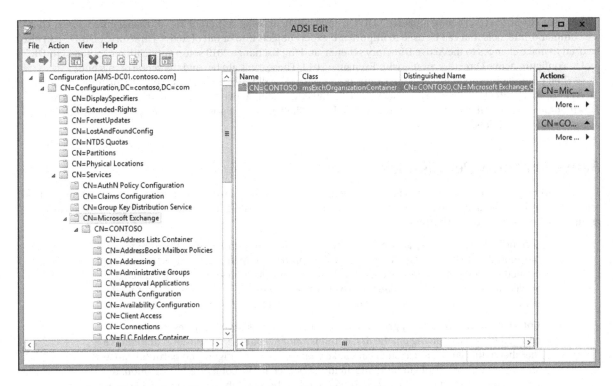

Figure 1-3. *The Exchange information is stored in the configuration partition*

■ **Warning** There's very little safeguarding in this tool, so it's easy to destroy critical parts in Active Directory when you're just clicking around!

The Active Directory Users and Computers (ADUC) MMC has a focus on the domain partition. In Windows Server 2012, the Active Directory Administrative Center (ADAC) is the preferred tool to manage the Active Directory environment. But using either tool is relatively safe, since the tool prevents messing around with objects in a way that Active Directory does not like. The Active Directory Sites and Services (ADSS) MMC snap-in reads and writes information from the configuration partition. All changes made here are visible to all domains in the forest; the same is true for the Active Directory domains and trusts MMC snap-in.

A very powerful tool regarding Active Directory is the Schema MMC snap-in, which is usually run on the Domain Controller that holds the schema master role. Using the Schema MMC snap-in, it is possible to make changes to the Active Directory schema partition.

■ **Warning** Only do this when you're absolutely sure of what you're doing, and when you have proper guidance—for example, from Microsoft support. Changes made to Active Directory can be irreversible!

Domain Controllers also have tools like LDIFDE and CSVDE installed as part of the AD management tools. These are command-line tools that can be used to import and export objects into or out of Active Directory. LDIFDE can also be used to make changes to the Active Directory schema, and the Exchange 2013 setup application uses the LDIFDE tool to configure Active Directory for use with Exchange 2013. These tools are beyond the scope of this book.

When promoting a server to a Domain Controller, or when installing the Remote Server Administration Tools (RSAT) for Active Directory Directory Services (ADDS), the PowerShell Active Directory module is installed as well. This module enables Active Directory functionality in PowerShell, making it possible to manage Active Directory using PowerShell cmdlets.

Active Directory Permissions

There are three partitions in Active Directory. Each of these partitions has separate permissions requirements, and not everybody has (full) access to these partitions. The following are the default administrator accounts or security groups that have access to each partition.

- **Schema Admins security group.** The Schema Admins have full access to the schema partition. The first administrator account is the top-level domain, which is the first domain created. To make the necessary changes to the schema partition for installing Exchange Server, the account that's used needs to be a member of this security group. Any other domain administrator in the forest is, by default, not a member of this group.

- **Enterprise Admins security group**. The Enterprise Admins have full access to the configuration partition. Again, the first administrator account in the top-level domain is a member of this group and as such can make changes to the configuration partition. Since all Exchange Server configuration information is stored in the configuration partition, the account used for installing Exchange Server needs to be a member of this group. Please note that the Enterprise Admins security group does not have permission to make changes to the schema partition.

- **Domain Admins security group**. The Domain Admins have full access to the domain partition of the corresponding domain. If there are 60 domains in an Active Directory environment, there are 60 domain partitions and thus 60 different Domain Admins security groups. The first administrator account in the top-level domain is a member of the Domain Admins security group in this top-level domain.

Why is this important to know? In the early days of Active Directory, Microsoft recommended using multiple domains in an Active Directory forest, preferably with an *empty root* domain. This empty root domain is a domain without any resources, and its primary purpose was for Active Directory management. All resources like servers, computers, users, and groups were located in child domains. Needless to say, this has some implications for the use of various administrator accounts. It is a delegated model, where the administrator accounts in the top-level domain have control over all Active Directory domains, whereas the administrators in the other domains have administrative rights only in their respective Active Directory domains. These other administrators do not have administrative privileges in other domains, let alone permission to modify the configuration partition or the schema partition.

But things have changed, and although an empty root Active Directory domain environment can still be used, it is no longer actively recommended. Mostly recommended these days is a "single forest, single domain" environment unless there are strict legal requirements that dictate using another Active Directory model.

Chapter 10 will explain about security in great detail and will explore the various options available for delegated administration and split permissions. But in short, the default administrator account that's created in the top-level Active Directory domain has enough permissions for installing Exchange 2013.

Active Directory Sites

Active Directory sites play an important role in the larger Exchange 2013 deployments. As stated earlier, an Active Directory site can be seen as a (physical) location with good internal network connectivity, high bandwidth, and low latency—that is, a local LAN. An office or data center is typically a good candidate for an Active Directory site.

An organization can have multiple locations or multiple data centers, resulting in multiple Active Directory sites. Sites are typically interconnected, with lower bandwidth, higher latency connections. An Active Directory site can also have multiple domains, but at the same time an Active Directory domain can span multiple sites.

An Active Directory site also is a replication boundary. Domain Controllers in an Active Directory site replicate their information almost immediately among Domain Controllers in the same site. If a new object is created, or if an object is changed, the other Domain Controllers in that same site are notified immediately and the information is replicated within seconds. All Domain Controllers in an Active Directory site should contain the same information.

Information exchanged between Domain Controllers in different Active Directory sites is replicated on a timed schedule, defined by the administrator. A typical timeframe can be 15 minutes, but depending on the type of connection or the bandwidth used to a particular location (you don't want your replication traffic to interfere with normal production bandwidth), it can take up to several hours. This means that when changes are made to Active Directory—for example, when installing Exchange 2013—it can take a serious amount of time before all the information is replicated across all the Domain Controllers and the new changes are visible to the entire organization.

Active Directory sites are created using the Active Directory Sites and Services MMC snap-in (see Figure 1-4). The first step is to define the network subnets in the various locations in the snap-in, and then tie the actual Active Directory site to the network subnet. For example, a data center in the Amsterdam site has IP subnet 10.38.96.0/24, while the data center in the London site has IP subnet 10.38.97.0/24.

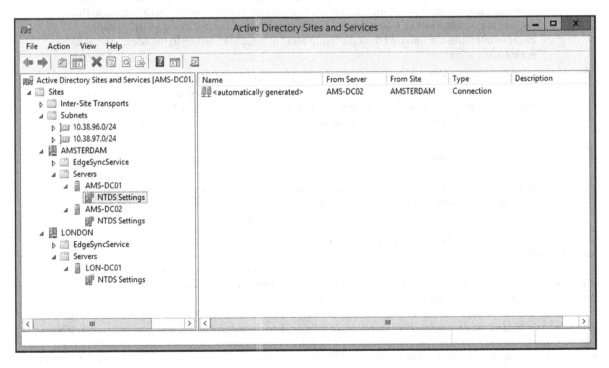

Figure 1-4. *Two different subnets and sites, as shown in Active Directory Sites and Services*

A location like a data center in London or in Amsterdam (which corresponds with the Active Directory sites) can be "Internet facing" or "non-Internet facing," a descriptor that indicates whether the location has Internet connectivity or not. This is important for Exchange 2013, since it determines how namespaces are configured and thus how external clients are connected to their mailboxes in the different locations.

For example, the environment in Figure 1-4 has two Active Directory sites. If the data center in Amsterdam has an Internet connection and the data center in London does not, all clients from the Internet are connected initially to the Exchange 2013 servers in Amsterdam. If a user's mailbox is located in London, the client request is proxied to the Exchange 2013 servers in London.

But, if the data center in London also has an Internet connection and the Exchange servers are configured accordingly, the London-based clients can access the Exchange 2013 servers from the Internet in Amsterdam, though the request will be redirected to the Exchange 2013 servers in London and thus connect directly to the servers in London.

Also, the routing of SMTP messages through the Exchange organization is partly based on Active Directory sites. In the example just given, it is not that difficult to do, but if you have an environment with dozens of Active Directory sites, the SMTP routing will follow the Active Directory site structure unless otherwise configured.

Exchange 2013 Architecture

Exchange 2013 is using what they have termed "building blocks"; there are three such building blocks:

- **Client Access server.** The Client Access server (CAS) is the server where all clients connect. The CAS consists of three parts: Client Access Front End (CAFE), Front End Transport Service (FETS), and the UM Call Router (UMCR). The CAS performs authentication of a client request, it locates the location of the client's mailbox, and it proxies or redirects the client request to the appropriate Mailbox server, where the actual client mailbox is located. The CAS in Exchange 2013 is sometimes also referred to as the "front end," although according to the book, UMCR is not officially a front end.

- **Mailbox server.** The Mailbox server is the server where the actual mailbox data is stored. Clients do not access the Mailbox server directly; all requests are routed through the CAS. The Mailbox server in Exchange 2013 is sometimes also referred to as the "back end." Rendering for clients like OWA, transport trancoding for SMTP, or voice processing for the UM role *always* takes place on the Mailbox server.

- **Edge Transport server.** The Edge Transport server is used for message hygiene purposes and acts as an SMTP gateway between your internal Exchange environment and the Internet. When an Edge Transport server is used, all messages are routed through this server. Using an Edge Transport server is not mandatory; there are lots of customers who have decided not to use an Edge Transport server and use a third-party solution instead.

In Exchange Server 2007 and Exchange Server 2010, the Hub Transport server and the Unified Messaging server were also dedicated server roles, next to the Client Access server and the Mailbox server. These four server roles were tightly coupled and they used RPC for inter-server communication. Although this works fine, it presents some challenges when it comes to an environment with multiple data centers and to site resiliency. One of the design goals for Exchange 2013 was to remove the tight coupling of the server roles and replace them with a more loosely coupled mechanism.

Hence, the four server roles are no longer available in separate server roles. The Client Access server continues to exist as a dedicated server, but the other three server roles are incorporated into the Mailbox server role. When installing the latter, the Hub Transport and Unified Messaging services are automatically installed as well. The Mailbox server contains most of the business logic of Exchange 2013, and this is the server where all the processing takes place for all mailboxes located on that Mailbox server. And since all business logic and processing takes place on the Mailbox server, the Client Access server has a relatively light service role.

Microsoft has a nice poster, which is a large PDF ready for printing, showing the entire Exchange 2013 architecture; it is available at http://bit.ly/ExPoster.

The Client Access Server

The Client Access server (CAS) performs only authentication of a client request; after authentication, the client request is proxied to the Mailbox server where the destination mailbox is located. The CAS in itself does not perform any processing with respect to mail data. Compared to previous versions of Exchange Server, the Exchange 2013 CAS is basically a "thin" server. According to Microsoft, its connections are stateless (not clueless, though). But the connections are not really stateless because the SSL connection is terminated at the CAS and then processed. If a CAS goes offline, all connections are terminated and they have to be set up again on another CAS (which would not be the case in a true stateless setup). The reason that Microsoft calls it "stateless" is that there's no persistent storage on Exchange 2013 CAS.

Unlike Exchange Server 2010 and Exchange Server 2007, the CAS no longer communicates with the Mailbox server using RPC; the original client request is instead proxied to the Mailbox server using the same protocol as was used when the connection reached the CAS server. If the initial request from the client to the Client Access server is from Outlook Web App (so HTTPS), the protocol between the CAS and the Mailbox server is also HTTPS. Note that the request from Internet to the CAS is using the regular port 443, but that the proxied request to the Mailbox server is using port 444.

The same is true for other protocols like POP3, IMAP4, and SMTP. After the Exchange 2010 Client Access server receives the request, the Client Access server proxies the request to the Exchange 2013 Mailbox server, as shown in Figure 1-5. An exception is the SIP protocol. When a SIP request is received from a Lync server, the Client Access server determines the appropriate Mailbox server, but instead of proxying the request, the Client Access server redirects the request to the appropriate Mailbox server. From this moment on the Lync server communicates directly with the Mailbox server. This is also clearly visible in Figure 1-5.

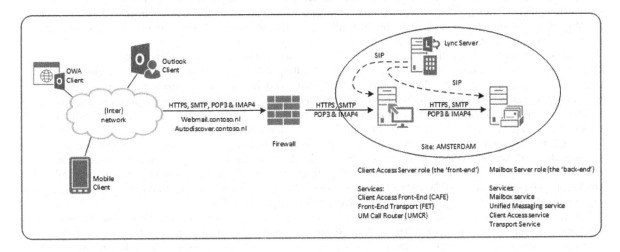

Figure 1-5. *The front-end and back-end architecture in Exchange 2013*

This architecture means that the actual Exchange 2013 servers are now loosely coupled, which offers huge advantages when multiple offices or multiple data centers are used.

As stated before, the CAS is a "thin" server and does not store any information from the sessions, except for the various protocol proxy logs like Autodiscover, Outlook Anywhere, or IIS logging. This is true for both regular client requests and SMTP requests. SMTP requests are accepted by the Client Access Front End service on the CAS, but the message itself is not stored or queued on the CAS, as it is on an Exchange 2010 Edge Transport server, for example.

The Front End Transport service that is responsible for handling SMTP messages on the CAS doesn't store messages on the server itself, but passes the SMTP messages directly to the appropriate Mailbox server where the intended recipient's mailbox is located, or to a down-level Hub Transport server if the recipient is located on a down-level Mailbox server. The Front End Transport service does not inspect message content.

Because of the stateless connections from clients, the load-balancing solution needed when multiple CAS are used doesn't have to be a layer 7 load balancer, as used to be the case in Exchange 2010; Exchange 2013 works fine with (much simpler) layer 4 load balancers.

The Mailbox Server

The Mailbox server is where all the processing regarding messages takes place. Clients connect to the CAS, but the requests are proxied or redirected to the appropriate Mailbox server or to another down-level CAS server. All message rendering takes place on the Mailbox server, in contrast to Exchange Server 2010, where all rendering took place on the CAS itself. To achieve this, there's also a CAS component on the Mailbox server.

SMTP Transport is now also located on the Mailbox server and consists of three separate services:

- The Transport service
- The Mailbox Transport Delivery service
- The Mailbox Transport Submission service

The Transport service can be seen as the successor to the "old" Hub Transport server, and it handles all SMTP message flow within the organization, such as routing, queuing, bifurcation, message categorization, and content inspection. Important to note is that the Transport service never communicates directly with the mailbox databases. Communication between the Transport service and the mailbox database is performed by the Mailbox Transport Delivery service and the Mailbox Transport Submission service. These services connect directly to the mailbox database (using RPC!) to deliver or retrieve messages from the mailbox database. As with the Front End Transport service, the Mailbox Transport Delivery and Mailbox Transport Submission services do not queue any messages on the Mailbox server; the Transport service (notice the absence of the word *mailbox*) does queue information on the Mailbox server. (The transport mechanism is covered in detail in Chapter 4.)

The most important part of this, of course, is the mailbox components that run on the Mailbox server. The information store, or store process, is responsible for handling all mailbox transactions and for storing these transactions in a mailbox database. The database is not a relational database like SQL server; it's running on its own engine, the extensible storage engine or ESE. The ESE database engine has been fully optimized for the past 15 years for use with Exchange Server, so it performs very well and is very reliable. The ESE database is a transactional database using a database, log files, and a checkpoint file. (I'll get back to database internals in Chapter 4.)

The Exchange Replication service is another important service running on the Mailbox server. This service is responsible for replicating mailbox data from one mailbox database on one Mailbox server to a mailbox database running on another Mailbox server. The collection of Mailbox servers replicating data between each other is called the Database Availability Group, or DAG. A DAG can take up to 16 Mailbox servers. Each mailbox database has one active mailbox database copy, and may have up to 15 passive mailbox database copies.

The database in Exchange 2013 has been greatly improved compared to earlier versions. For instance, Exchange 2013 now generates 50 percent fewer IOs per second (IOPS) compared with Exchange Server 2010, making it now possible to store multiple databases, including their log files, on one physical disk. This is something that Microsoft never recommended doing in the past, but now it is a viable solution. Of course, this is recommended only when there are multiple copies of a mailbox database available for redundancy purposes and after proper sizing to ensure that the disk will be able to handle the total number of IOPS.

Exchange 2013 Management

When it comes to Exchange 2013 Management, there are major changes compared to the previous versions of Exchange. There are two options for managing your Exchange 2013 environment:

- Exchange Admin Center – The HTML-based GUI that offers the most basic options for managing your Exchange 2013 environment

- Exchange Management Shell – The command-line interface running on top of Windows PowerShell and offering all nitty-gritty options when managing your Exchange 2013 environment

I'll discuss these in more detail, as follows.

Exchange Admin Center

The Exchange Admin Center (EAC) is the GUI for managing your Exchange 2013 environment. The EAC can be managed from the internal network as well as from the external network. The EAC is accessible via a URL like `https://webmail.contoso.com/ecp`, and when the EAC is opened, a window like the one shown in Figure 1-6 appears.

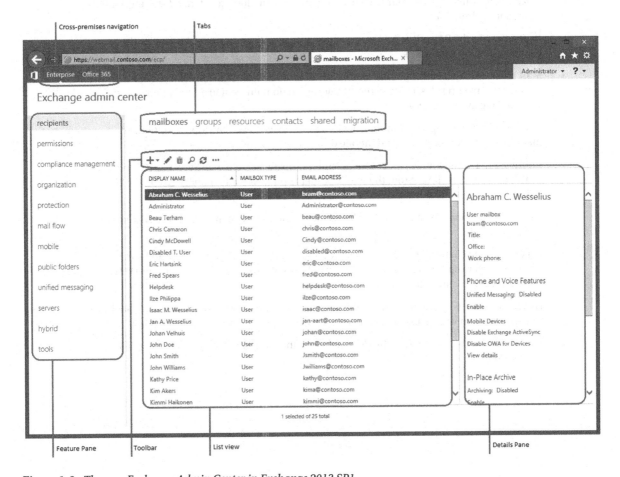

Figure 1-6. *The new Exchange Admin Center in Exchange 2013 SP1*

■ **Note**   There were little changes with respect to EAC in Exchange 2013 SP1. The tools section in the Feature pane is new.

In the left-hand menu, there are various components of Exchange 2013 that can be managed in the EAC. The left-hand menu is also called the "Feature pane" and consists of the following features:

- **Recipients**. All recipients, like mailboxes, groups, contacts, shared mailboxes, and resource mailboxes, are managed from the Recipients option.

- **Permissions**. In the Permissions option, you can manage administrator roles, user roles, and Outlook Web App policies. The first two roles are explained in more detail in the RBAC section later in this chapter.

- **Compliance Management**. In the Compliance Management option, you can manage In-Place eDiscovery, In-Place Hold, auditing, data loss prevention (DLP), retention policies, retention tags, and journal rules.

- **Organization**. The Organization option is the highest level of configuration, and this is the place where you'll manage your Exchange organization, including federated sharing, Outlook Apps, and address lists.

- **Protection**. In the Protection option, you can manage anti-malware protection for the Exchange 2013 organization.

- **Mail Flow**. The Mail Flow option contains all choices regarding the flow of messages, including transport rules, delivery reports, accepted domains, email address policies, and send and receive connectors.

- **Mobile**. All settings regarding mobile devices are managed from the Mobile option. You can manage mobile device access and mobile device mailbox policies.

- **Public Folders**. The Public Folder Management Console in Exchange Server 2010 is replaced by this feature in the EAC. From the Public Folders option you can manage Exchange 2013 public folders. Note that legacy public folders cannot be managed using the EAC.

- **Unified Messaging**. From the Unified Messaging option you can manage UM Dial Plans and UM IP Gateways.

- **Servers**. The Exchange 2013 servers, both Mailbox and Client Access server, can be managed from the Servers option. This also includes databases, database availability groups (DAGs), virtual directories, and certificates.

- **Hybrid**. Using the Hybrid option, it is possible to configure a hybrid organization—that is, you can connect your on-premises Exchange 2013 organization with an Office 365 tenant.

- **Tools**. This is new in Exchange 2013 SP1 and contains links to Exchange and Office 365 specific tools.

■ **Note** Just like the EMS, the functions available in the EAC are limited by the permissions enforced by RBAC.

In previous versions of Exchange Server, all the configuration changes made using the Exchange Management Console were translated to EMS under the hood. In the EAC, this is no different, and like the EMC, these commands are logged in a special section so you can check out the actual commands. Although small, this is one of the great improvements in Exchange 2013 SP1, as this feature was not available in Exchange 2013 RTM!

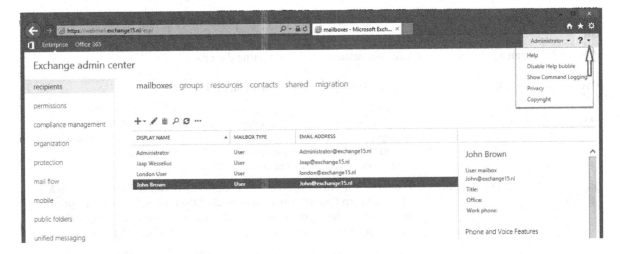

Figure 1-7. *The command log is available in the upper right menu in EAC*

The tabs in the top-level menu are context sensitive. In other words, they change when a different feature in the Feature pane is selected.

The toolbar can be compared to the Actions pane in the Exchange Server 2010 Management Console. All actions are associated with an icon. Table 1-1 describes each of the icons.

Table 1-1. *Available Options (icons) in the EAC Toolbar*

Icon	Name	Description
✚	Add, New	Use this option to create a new object. Some of these icons have an associated down arrow you can click to show additional objects you can create. For example, in Recipients and then Mailboxes, clicking the down arrow displays User Mailbox and Linked Mailbox as additional options.
✎	Edit	You can use this option to edit an object.
🗑	Delete	Use this option to delete one or more objects.
🔍	Search	Use this option to query for a particular object.
↻	Refresh	Use this icon to refresh the objects in the list view.
•••	More options	Use this icon to view more actions you can perform for that tab's objects. For example, in Recipients > Mailboxes, clicking this icon shows the following options: Disable, Add/Remove Columns, Export Data to a CSV File, Connect a Mailbox, and Advanced Search.
↑ ↓	Up and Down arrow	Use these icons to move an object's priority up or down. For example, in Mail Flow and then Email Address Policies, click the up arrow to raise the priority of an email address policy. You can also use these arrows to navigate the public folder hierarchy or to move rules up or down in the list view.
📑	Copy	Use this icon to copy an object so you can make changes to it without changing the original object. For example, in Permissions and then Admin Roles, select a role from the list view, and then click this icon to create a new role group based on an existing one.
▬	Remove	Use this icon to remove an item from a list. For example, in the Public Folder Permissions dialog box, you can remove users from the list of users allowed to access the public folder by selecting the user and clicking this icon.

The list view in EAC is designed to remove limitations that existed in ECP and EMC in Exchange 2010. The ECP is capable of listing up to only 500 objects in one page at the same time, and if you want to view objects that aren't listed in the Details pane, you need to use Search and Filter options to find those specific objects. In Exchange 2013, the viewable limit from within the EAC list view is approximately 20,000 objects for on-premises deployments and 10,000 objects in Exchange Online. In addition, paging is included so you can page to the results. In the Recipients list view, you can also configure page size and export the data to a CSV file.

When you select an object from the list view, information about that object is displayed in the Details pane. In some cases (for example, with recipient objects), the Details pane includes quick management tasks. For example, if you navigate to Recipients and then Mailboxes, and select a mailbox from the list view, the Details pane displays an option to enable or disable the archive for that mailbox. The Details pane can also be used to bulk-edit several objects. Simply press the CTRL key, select the objects you want to bulk-edit, and use the options in the Details pane. For example, selecting multiple mailboxes allows you to bulk-update users' contact and organization information, custom attributes, mailbox quotas, Outlook Web App settings, and more.

■ **Note**   Supported browsers for the EAC are Internet Explorer 8 or later, Firefox 11 or later, Safari 5.1 or later, and Chrome 18 or later.

Exchange Management Shell

The Exchange Management Shell (EMS) is the core of Exchange Server management and this is what this book is all about. This is the place where you can configure everything—every little, tiny tidbit of Exchange Server. The EMS is not new; its first version appeared with Exchange Server 2007 and EMS has become more and more important over the years.

EMS is running on top of the Windows PowerShell and as such it can use all functionality that's available in PowerShell, like pipelining, formatting output, saving to local disk, ordering the output, or using filtering techniques. We'll discuss the most important basics here but also at various points throughout this book.

PowerShell

Lots of Microsoft server applications have their own management shell and all are running on top of Windows PowerShell; and whether you like it or not, PowerShell is the future for Windows management and for applications that run on top of Windows. And it's not only Microsoft that's using PowerShell for managing their applications; third-party vendors are also writing PowerShell add-ons for their products. Examples of these are HP, for their EVA storage management solutions; Vmware, for their virtualization platform; and KEMP, for their load-balancing solutions.

The first version of PowerShell was a downloadable add-on for Windows 2003, but Windows Server 2008 was the first operating system that came with PowerShell built into the product.

PowerShell is a command-line shell and scripting environment, and it uses the power of the .NET Framework. But PowerShell is not text based, it is object based and as such it supports nice features such as pipelining, formatting, or redirecting the output. All objects have properties or methods and that's not different in PowerShell.

The last feature we're going to discuss is additional modules, such as the Server Manager, Active Directory, and the Exchange module.

Object Model

Although a command-line interface, PowerShell uses an object-oriented model. This means you are working with objects and not with normal text, as in a regular command prompt.

Since an object is returned, it can be manipulated or you can check certain attributes. For example, you can request information regarding an Exchange server with the following command:

```
Get-ExchangeServer -Identity AMS-EXCH01
```

Although it is returned as text on the console, it is actually an object being returned and you can treat is this way; for example:

```
(Get-ExchangeServer -Identity AMS-EXCH01).AdminDisplayVersion
```

This will return the AdminDisplayVersion property of the Exchange server. Or, when moving mailboxes and you want to check the number of mailboxes that are in the queue waiting to be processed, you can use the following command:

```
(Get-MoveRequest -MoveStatus Queued).count
```

So, the output of a command is an object and you can continue working with this object. This way you can use the output of one command as actual input for another command, a technique which is called pipelining. This technique is very often used in managing Exchange environments.

Pipeline

You can see a pipeline as a series of connected segments of pipe where all items or objects pass through each segment. Each segment has its own functionality or purpose and can alter the objects. To create a new pipeline the pipe operator "|" is used with the various commands. The simplest form of a pipeline is to use a Get command in conjunction with a Set command; for example:

```
Get-Mailbox | Set-Mailbox
```

In this command a pipeline is created between the Get-Mailbox and the Set-Mailbox commands. The Get-Mailbox command retrieves one or more mailbox objects, and these objects are sent through the pipeline to the Set-Mailbox command, which can make certain changes to the mailbox objects.

Personally, I use this pipelining a lot when administering Exchange server. You can use the various Get commands to retrieve objects from Exchange and you can actually see if you have the right objects. Then you can pipe them into the corresponding Set command and you're done. Very valuable!

Objects and Members

Each object in PowerShell has members, and members can be properties or methods. A property is something that has a value—for example, the name of a mailbox. A method is something that can be executed against an object—for example, to clone a mailbox.

To see all members of a particular mailbox you can use the following command:

```
Get-Mailbox –Identity Administrator | Get-Member
```

This command will result in an output similar to:

```
[PS] C:\>Get-Mailbox -Identity Administrator | Get-Member


   TypeName: Microsoft.Exchange.Data.Directory.Management.Mailbox

Name                     MemberType   Definition
----                     ----------   ----------
Clone                    Method       System.Object Clone(), System.Object...
Equals                   Method       bool Equals(System.Object obj)
GetHashCode              Method       int GetHashCode()
GetProperties            Method       System.Object[] GetProperties(System.Collections...
GetProxyInfo             Method       System.Object GetProxyInfo(), System.Object...
GetType                  Method       type GetType()
ResetChangeTracking      Method       void IConfigurable.ResetChangeTracking()
SetProxyInfo             Method       void SetProxyInfo(System.Object proxyInfoValue)...
PSComputerName           NoteProperty System.String PSComputerName=ams-exch01.contoso.com
PSShowComputerName       NoteProperty System.Boolean PSShowComputerName=False
RunspaceId               NoteProperty System.Guid RunspaceId=2e837bce-b1a8-4004-...
AcceptMessagesOnlyFrom   Property     Microsoft.Exchange.Data.MultiValuedProperty...
AddressBookPolicy        Property     Microsoft.Exchange.Data.Directory.ADObjectId...
```

```
AddressListMembership        Property      Microsoft.Exchange.Data.MultiValuedProperty...
AdminDisplayVersion          Property      Microsoft.Exchange.Data.ServerVersion...
ArchiveDatabase              Property      Microsoft.Exchange.Data.Directory.ADObjectId
ArchiveGuid                  Property      guid ArchiveGuid {get;}
ArchiveName                  Property      Microsoft.Exchange.Data.MultiValuedProperty[string]...
```

When you use PowerShell to retrieve an object, only a limited set of members is shown. This is purely practical; your console would be overwhelmed with data if all members were shown.

Formatting

It is possible to format the output as shown on the console using cmdlets that start with the *Format* verb. The following are used throughout this book:

- **Format-List**. This is abbreviated to FL and is used to show all properties of a certain object. To retrieve all properties of the Administrator mailbox you would use Get-Mailbox -Identity | FL

- **Format-Table**. This is abbreviated to FT and can be used to retrieve certain properties of an object. The Get-Mailbox command, for example, returns only the Name, Alias, ServerName, and ProhibitSendQuota properties. To retrieve the Name, Alias, Database, and ArchiveState, a command similar to Get-Mailbox -Identity Administrator | FT -Property Name, Alias, Database, ArchiveState can be used.

- **Format-Wide**. This command is abbreviated to FW and shows only one property of an object. Typically it shows only the default property of an object; for a mailbox this would be its name, but you can select another property using the -Property option.

In addition to these *Format* verbs you can use the -Wrap and -AutoSize parameters in PowerShell to format the output of the Format-Table command, as shown on the console. The -Wrap option does not truncate output in a column, but it wraps all output in its column, thereby showing the entire property. The -AutoSize option varies the width of the column, depending on the data that is shown in the column.

Important to note is that PowerShell expects the first column to be the most important, decreasing the importance with subsequent columns. As such, later columns can even be removed from the output when there's too much information to be shown. If this happens, you can change the order of information shown on the console by reordering the properties using the -Property option.

Normally the output of commands is shown on the console. It is possible to redirect the output elsewhere using the *Out* verb in PowerShell. The following options are available in PowerShell.

- **Out-Host**. The Out-Host option redirects the output to the console, which is the default option. You can use the -Paging option to show only a limited amount of information at one time. You can use the <SPACE> to view another page with information on the console.

- **Out-Null**. The Out-Null option immediately discards any information without showing it on the console. However, any error message or, more specifically, output from the error stream will be shown on the console.

- **Out-Printer**. The Out-Printer option redirects any output directly to the printer. The default printer is used if no printername is provided; otherwise, a command similar to Out-Printer -Name "HP LaserJet 1200 Series PCL 5" can be used.

- **Out-File**. The Out-File command is often used because it redirects any output to a (Unicode) file on the local hard disk. If a pure ASCII-coded file is needed, the -Encode ASCII option can be used—for example, Out-File -FilePath C:\Logging\Mailboxes.txt -Encode ASCII.

These methods and concepts are widely referenced throughout this book.

Grouping

Another useful parameter to organize output is the GroupBy control. Long output listings that are hard to view offer the option to group the output based on a property. For example, it is possible to retrieve all users from Active Directory and group the output by the value of their Company attribute, like this:

```
Get-User | Format-Table -Property Name,SamAccountName,Company -Sort Company -GroupBy Company
```

Filtering

It's also possible to filter the output of the Get-User command with the -Filter parameter. For example, to mailbox-enable all users whose company attribute is set to "Fourth Coffee," enter the following command:

```
Get-User -Filter {Company -eq "Fourth Coffee"}
```

■ **Note** Whenever possible you should use the –Filter option. This will only send the objects to the console that come out of the filter, resulting in much more efficient processing.

If you want to be even more specific—for example, to mailbox-enable all users whose company attribute is set to "Fourth Coffee" *and* whose department attribute is set to "Marketing," enter the following command:

```
Get-User -Filter {(Company -eq "Fourth Coffee") -AND (Department -eq "Marketing")}
```

In short, the following operations are available for the -Filter option:

- -and
- -or
- -not
- -eq (equals)
- -ne (does not equal)
- -lt (less than)
- -gt (greater than)
- -like (compare strings by using wildcard rules)
- -notlike (compare strings by using wildcard rules)

Conversion

It's possible to convert objects to a certain format—for example, HTML or CSV. This can be useful if you want to just collect data or you want to process it using applications like Excel. For instance, to collect a simple list of mailboxes and export that information to a CSV file that you can import in Excel, enter the following cmdlet:

```
Get-Mailbox | Select DisplayName, WindowsEmailAddress | Export-CSV -NoTypeInformation Mailboxes.csv
```

When exporting output into a CSV file, PowerShell writes the Type of Object onto the first line of the CSV file—something like #TYPE Selected.Microsoft.Exchange.Data.Directory.Management.Mailbox, as shown in Figure 1-8.

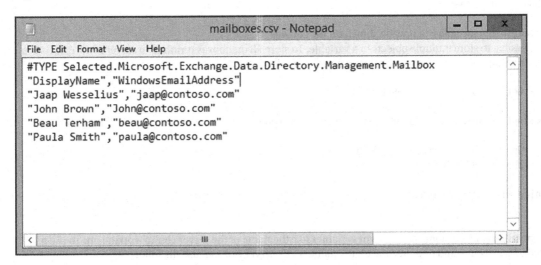

Figure 1-8. *The Export-CSV creates an additional #Type entry in the CSV file*

The -NoTypeInformation option prevents this line in the output file.

Conversion cmdlets also have an import counterpart—that is, Import-CSV—which allows you to import information that is stored in a certain format.

Variables

Using variables is not really specific for PowerShell, but every command-line interface or scripting engine can use variables, and that's no different in PowerShell.

As explained earlier, PowerShell is using objects, and you can store objects in variables so you can use them later on. This can be used in a PowerShell script, but also on the command line. An object is kept alive as long as the PowerShell window is open or until it is destroyed.

Variables are identified with a $ character, followed by any name you want. Of course, it is good practice to use an easy-to-identify name.

To create a variable called $AdminMailbox and store the Administrator mailbox object in it, you can use the following command:

```
$AdminMailbox = Get-Mailbox –Identity Administrator
```

The mailbox object is now stored in the variable $AdminMailbox and ready for use directly, or for later use. To view the contents of the variable, you can type in its name in the PowerShell window.

```
[PS] C:\Windows\system32>$AdminMailbox

Name                   Alias                  ServerName            ProhibitSendQuota
----                   -----                  ----------            -----------------
Administrator          Administrator          ams-exch01            Unlimited

[PS] C:\Windows\system32>
```

You can see that the output is identical to a normal Get-Mailbox command. To view all members of the object stored in this variable, you can request them, just like a normal object:

```
$AdminMailbox | Get-Member
```

All members of this variable will now be shown on the console.

It is also possible to store multiple objects in a variable. To store all mailboxes running on server AMS-EXCH01 in a variable called $Mailboxes, you can use the following command:

```
$Mailboxes = Get-Mailbox -Server AMS-EXCH01
```

To do "something" with all these mailboxes, you can create a conditional loop in PowerShell, along the line of:

```
$Mailboxes = Get-Mailbox -Server AMS-EXCH01
ForEach ($Mailbox in $Mailboxes)
  {
  Do Something with each mailbox
  }
```

It is also possible to use system environment variables like the name of the server you're working on. To use a variable called $ServerName and populate it with the name of the server, you can use the following:

```
$ServerName = $env:COMPUTERNAME
```

To retrieve the Active Directory domain name you're logged onto and to create the FQDN you will use to configure the OWA virtual directory, you can use the following commands:

```
$Domain = $env:UserDnsDomain
$FQDN = "webmail." + $Domain
```

■ **Note**   This example is based on the assumption that your Active Directory Domain name is identical to your external domain name.

If this is not the case in your environment, you can also user the Read-Host command to request user input on the PowerShell console and combine this with the "webmail" string to create the FQDN:

```
$Domain = Read-Host "Pleae enter your external domain name"
$FQDN = "webmail." + $Domain
```

By using these variables, it is possible to set the OWA virtual directory like this:

```
Get-OWAVirtualDirectory -Server $ServerName | Set-OWAVirtualDirectory -ExternalURL
https://$FQDN/owa -InternalURL https://$FQDN/owa
```

In this example you see the pipelining technology combined with the use of variables. In this book you'll learn how to use several kinds of these scripts to manage your Exchange 2013 environment.

Additional Modules

PowerShell is interesting to use, but it gets more interesting when you're using additional modules. The Server Manager module is used, for example, to use Server Manager features using PowerShell. When installing Exchange 2013, you need to install the prerequisite Server Roles and Features. You can do this using the Server Manager, but you can also load the Server Manager module in PowerShell, followed by the Server Role or Server Feature you want to install. For example, if you want to install the Remote Server Administration Tools, you can use the following commands:

```
Import-Module ServerManager
Install-WindowsFeature RSAT-ADDS
```

To install the IIS web server, you can use commands similar to the following:

```
Import-Module ServerManager
Install-WindowsFeature Web-Server
```

■ **Note**   If you have a PowerShell window open, you only have to run the Import-Module once. If you reopen a PowerShell window, you have to run this command again.

Another interesting module when administering your Exchange 2013 environment is the Active Directory module, which can be loaded using the following command:

```
Import-Module ActiveDirectory
```

When the Active Directory module is loaded, the following options will be available in PowerShell:

- Account management

- Group management

- Organizational unit management

- Search and modify objects in Active Directory

- Forest and Domain management

- Domain Controller management

- Operations Master management

To create a new user in Active Directory called "Joe Bloggs" in the OU=Contoso Organizational Unit in the Accounts Organization Unit, a command similar to the following can be used:

```
Import-Module ActiveDirectory
New-ADUser -SamAccountName Joe -Name "Joe Bloggs" -GivenName Joe -SurName Blogss -AccountPassword
(ConvertTo-SecureString -AsPlainText "Pass1word" -Force) -Enabled $TRUE -Path
"OU=Contoso,OU=Account,DC=CONTOSO,DC=COM"
```

> ■ **Note** The `ConvertTo-SecureString` is used because the `AccountPassword` parameter does not accept any clear text as input for a password. In addition, `AsPlainText` and `Force` are required to convert plain text to a secure string.

For a complete overview of all PowerShell administration in Active Directory, you can check the Microsoft TechNet pages *Active Directory Administration with PowerShell* on http://bit.ly/ADPowerShell

Another module that's often used in Exchange management using PowerShell is the Web Administration module. Using this module you can manage websites and their properties on your Exchange 2013 server. For example, to load the Web Administration module and clear the SSL offloading flag on the OWA Virtual Directory, you can use the following commands:

```
Import-Module WebAdministration
Set-WebConfigurationProperty -Filter //security/access -name sslflags
-Value "None" -PSPath IIS:\ -Location "Default Web Site/OWA"
```

The last module I want to discuss is the Exchange module. The Exchange System Manager (EMS) is best started using the EMS icon on the Start menu. This will make sure the binaries are loaded correctly. What basically happens is that PowerShell is started and a special Exchange management script is loaded, and the session is connected to an Exchange 2013 server. This can be the local Exchange server you're logged on to, but it can also be another server, as long as it is in the same Active Directory site. This is called Remote PowerShell, even when it's connected locally.

Remote PowerShell

When you open the EMS on the Exchange 2013 server, it is running on the local server and you need access to the console of the server. But, in Exchange 2013 it is possible to use a remote PowerShell as well, thereby making connection a local Windows PowerShell instance to an Exchange 2013 server at a remote location. The workstation doesn't have to be in the same domain; as long as the proper credentials and authentication method are used, it will work. With this kind of function, it's now as easy to manage your Exchange 2013 servers in other parts of the building as those servers in data centers in other parts of the country. Needless to say, if you are using a non-domain-joined client for remote PowerShell, you cannot use Kerberos. You have to change authentication on the PowerShell Virtual Directory to Basic Authentication for this to happen.

When the Exchange Management Shell is opened, it will automatically try to connect to the PowerShell virtual directory on the Exchange 2013 server you're logged onto. However, this is only true if you are logged onto an Exchange server (Console or RDP) at the time. If you are on a management workstation with the Exchange management tools installed, it will choose any Exchange server within your Active Directory site. Alternatively, by using the remote option it's possible to connect to a remote Exchange server at this stage.

To use the remote PowerShell with Exchange 2013, you need to log on to a Windows server or workstation that has the Windows Management Framework 3.0 installed. The Management Framework consists of PowerShell 3.0 and Windows Remote Management (WinRM) 3.0. Also, make sure that the workstation (or server) supports remote signed scripts. Owing to security constraints, this is disabled by default. You can enable the support by opening an elevated Windows PowerShell command prompt and entering:

```
Set-ExecutionPolicy RemoteSigned
```

The next step is to create a session that will connect to the remote Exchange server. When the session is created, it can be imported into PowerShell:

```
$Session = New-PSSession –ConfigurationName Microsoft.Exchange –ConnectionUri
https://ams-exch01.contoso.com/PowerShell -Authentication Kerberos

Import-PSSession $Session
```

The PowerShell on the workstation will now connect to the remote Exchange server using a default SSL connection and, RBAC permitting, all Exchange cmdlets will be available. It's incredibly easy, as can be seen in Figure 1-9. To end the remote PowerShell session, just enter the command:

```
Remove-PSSession $session
```

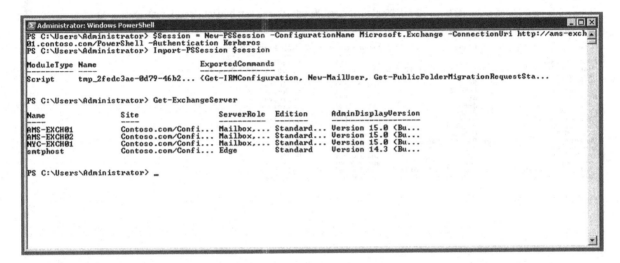

Figure 1-9. *Using remote PowerShell on a local workstation to manage Exchange 2013*

■ **Note**   It is also possible to setup an Exchange session using the `Add-PSSnapin Microsoft.Exchange.Management.PowerShell.E2010` command. While the result look similar it's not. This does connect, but it bypasses the RBAC configuration and it is not supported.

Admittedly, the example in Figure 1-9 is from a Windows 7 workstation that's also a member of the same Active Directory domain. To connect to a remote Exchange 2013 server that's available over the Internet, multiple steps are required. The first step is to create a variable in the PowerShell command prompt that contains the username and password for the remote session `$Credential = Get-Credential`. A pop-up box will appear, requesting a username and password for the remote Exchange environment. Once you've filled in the credentials, the following command will create a new session that will set up a connection to the Exchange environment. The `$Credential` variable is used to pass the credentials to the Exchange environment, and then the session is imported into PowerShell. See Figure 1-10.

```
$Credential = Get-Credential

$Session = New-PSSession –ConfigurationName Microsoft.Exchange –ConnectionUri
https://webmail.contoso.com/PowerShell -Authentication Basic -Credential $Credential

Import-PSSession $Session
```

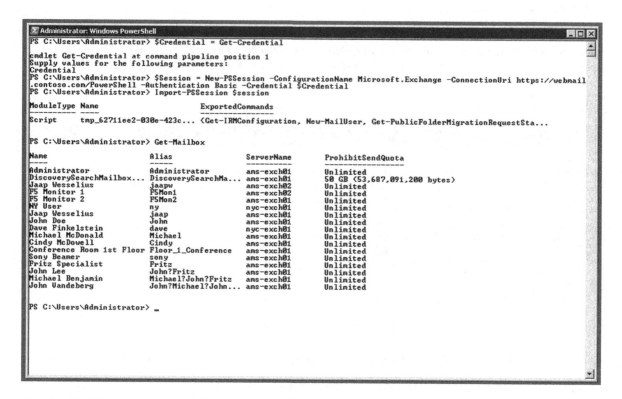

Figure 1-10. *Using remote PowerShell on a remote workstation to manage Exchange 2013*

■ **Note** If you want to connect to a remote Exchange 2013 server over the Internet, remember to enable Basic Authentication on the PowerShell virtual directory on the remote server, using the Exchange Management Shell and the Set-PowerShellVirtualDirectory command. When split-DNS is used, the authentication used for Internet connections can be used internally as well.

These examples were for the Active Directory domain administrator, who automatically has the Remote Management option enabled. To enable a non-domain administrator for remote management, just enter the Set-User <username> -RemotePowerShellEnabled $True command.

PowerShell ISE

When you want to create PowerShell scripts you can use a basic tool like Notepad or Notepad++ (downloadable via http://bit.ly/np-plus-plus) but you can also use the PowerShell Integrated Scripting Environment, or ISE. Using ISE, you can run single commands, but you can also write, test, and debug PowerShell scripts. ISE supports multi-line editing, tab completion, syntax coloring, and context-sensitive help. When debugging, you can set a breakpoint in a script to stop execution at that point. Windows PowerShell ISE can be found at the Administrative Tools menu, but when selecting a PowerShell script in Windows Explorer, you can also edit the script using ISE.

It is fully supported to use the remote PowerShell functionality and import Exchange sessions as explained in the previous section in ISE, making it possible to use all Exchange 2013-related cmdlets in ISE and to create your own Exchange 2013 scripts. This is shown in Figure 1-11.

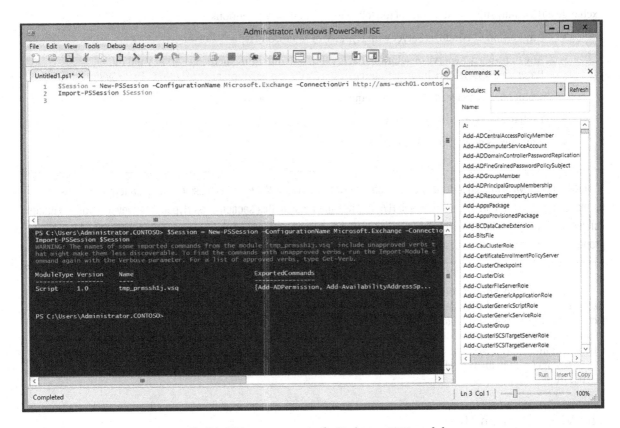

Figure 1-11. Using remote PowerShell in ISE to get access to the Exchange 2013 modules

There are more PowerShell script editors available. Another widely used one is PowerGui. PowerGui is available for download (free) at http://bit.ly/PowerGui.

If you want to read a lot more about Windows PowerShell in general, you can visit the Windows PowerShell User's Guide at http://bit.ly/WinPowershellGuide.

Virtualization

Running Exchange 2013 in a virtualized environment is not uncommon these days, and Microsoft fully supports running virtualized Exchange servers. This is true for all three server roles in Exchange 2013 SP1, as it was true for all five server roles in Exchange 2010.

When virtualizing Exchange 2013, there are some specific requirements for the virtualization solution (a.k.a. the Hypervisor), but these are more general requirements or recommendations. There are also more specific requirements for storage, memory, and high-availability solutions. We will discuss these in more detail.

Requirements for Hardware Virtualization

Exchange 2013 is fully supported on one of the following virtualization solutions:

- Any version of Windows Server with Hyper-V or Microsoft Hyper-V Server.

- Any third-party hypervisor solution that is validated under the Microsoft Server Validation Program (SVVP). More information regarding SVVP can be found at http://bit.ly/ExSVVP.

When it comes to Exchange, the following requirements are applicable:

- Exchange server 2013 or later is used

- Exchange is deployed on Windows Server 2008 R2 SP1 or later

---

■ **Note**   I've always managed to stay away from the Hyper-V versus VMware discussions, but as a former Microsoft employee I have a bit more experience with Hyper-V and the focus in this section is on Hyper-V. However, as an Exchange consultant, I really don't care which virtualization platform is used by a customer. As long as the virtualization platform is properly designed and operated, and the virtual Exchange servers are properly designed, I'm happy!

The most tested virtualization platform for Exchange Server is, of course, Hyper-V. Every day the Microsoft Exchange team is testing thousands of Exchange servers, all running on Hyper-V. Since it's the same company, there's a close ongoing cross-group engineering relationship and there's a direct feedback loop between the Exchange team and the Hyper-V team. A lot of the recommendations are directly targeted to Hyper-V, but they apply to other virtualization solutions as well.

When it comes to the virtualization platform, there are a couple of things you have to be aware of. Let's discuss these.

The Virtualization Host

The hosts running Hyper-V are designed to run Hyper-V and nothing else. Although it might be tempting to install other software on the Hyper-V host, especially when it's running a normal version of Windows as the host or parent partition, it is absolutely *not* supported and *not* recommended. It works and I've seen customers do it, but it's a good idea. The applications installed on the Hyper-V host consume valuable resources, especially memory, that are no longer available for virtual machines running on that host.

The only software that is supported and can be installed on the Hyper-V host is management software like a System Center Configuration Manager (SCCM) client, a System Center Operations Manager (SCOM) client, a backup client, or an anti-virus client. No other software should ever be installed on the virtualization host. Also, the Hyper-V host itself should never be configured as a Domain Controller!

Virtual Processors

When using server virtualization, there's a given number of processors and processor cores available on the virtualization host and virtually unlimited number of virtual processors. However, you cannot give away an unlimited amount of processor cycles so you have to be aware of the number of virtual processors—that is, the processors that are assigned to a virtual machines and the number of logical processors, or actual processors on the virtualization host.

The Microsoft Exchange product team supports a virtual to logical processor ratio of 2:1. In other words, when your virtualization host has eight processor cores installed, you should not use more than 16 virtual processor cores to virtual machines on that host. The ratio of 2:1 is officially supported by the Exchange product team, but their recommendation for the ratio is actually 1:1.

When it comes to processors on your virtualization host, there's also something called *hyperthreading*. This is Intel's implementation of Simultaneous MultiThreading (SMT), used to improve parallel processing of instructions within the processor. Although the number of cores double when hyperthreading is enabled, the performance is not doubled at the same time. It is true, however, that performance increases when hyperthreading is enabled, though not more than by 20 percent generally.

But there's a downside to enabling hyperthreading, especially when running Exchange on virtual machines. When a processor is added to a virtual machine running Exchange, the memory consumed by the Exchange server also increases, by approximately 2 GB per processor core.

So, when using hyperthreading and assigning additional processor cores to virtual machines running Exchange, note that the memory requirements increase as well, resulting in a strange scenario. Tests performed by the Microsoft Exchange product team have shown situations where the performance actually decreased after enabling hyperthreading. Therefore, the recommendation is to *not* enable hyperthreading when running Exchange on virtual machines on these hosts.

Storage Requirements for Virtual Machines

When it comes to storage, there are two ways of looking at it. There's the storage used on the virtualization host itself, which is where the virtualization host's operating system is installed, and there's the storage solutions used by the virtual machines. The latter are the virtual hard disks. I'll discuss both.

Virtualization Host Storage

There are multiple types of storage solutions used on a virtualization host. First, there are the disks used by the operating system running the virtualization software. Typically there are two disks for this operating system, configured in a RAID-1 setup so the disks are mirrored. These disks should be the fastest disks you can get—15k rpm disks or even better, and solid state disks (SSD) are the fastest you can get. At all times you must make sure this operating system is located on disks different from where the virtual machines are located.

Data disks are disks where the virtual machines are stored; these disks can be:

- **Direct Attached Storage** (DAS). When using DAS, the data disks are local to the virtualization host. These should also be fast disks, preferably in a RAID-10 configuration offering the best performance and redundancy.

- **iSCSI storage**. When iSCSI is used, the disks (LUNs) are presented to the virtualization software, which can access them just as local disks. Interesting to note is that iSCSI disks can also be accessed from within the virtual machine via a network connection.

- **SAN storage**. When a SAN is used, the virtualization host typically uses a Fibre Channel (FC) solution to access the disks (LUNs). This is a fast and redundant solution, but at the same time costly.

All three solutions are fully supported when running the virtualized Exchange 2013 server. These storage solutions are *block-level storage* solutions. The host "owns" the file system on the storage solution and therefore controls the storage solution.

I've seen numerous implementations of VMware where the virtual disks (.vmdk) are stored on an NFS volume, mostly NetApp solutions. This is a *file-level storage* solution. The operating system—that is, vmware—does not own and thus does not control the underlying file system where the virtual disks are stored. While this works fine in most scenarios, it can yield unpredictable results due to performance issues, especially when using other solutions that also access the NFS storage. Therefore, this is not a supported scenario.

■ **Note**   In this section I'm discussing the storage requirements, recommendations, and supported scenarios from a hypervisor point of view when it comes to running a virtualized Exchange. In the next chapter I will discuss designing Exchange 2013 and the storage requirements from an Exchange server point of view.

So, storing your VHD files on a NAS solution is not supported. Storing the VHD files on an SMB 3.0 share, which was new in Windows Server 2012, is supported, but only when the SMB 3.0 share is backed by a block-level storage solution. So block-level storage is key when it comes to virtual Exchange servers!

Here's one last remark regarding the separation of disk spindles. In a normal physical environment it is best practice to store the Windows operating system on one disk and the mailbox database files on another disk, or set of disks. Of course, this is not different when virtualizing the Exchange servers. But you have to be careful to store the actual virtual hard disks that contain the windows operating system and the mailbox database files on separate hard disks on the virtualization host. This gives the best performance within your virtualized Exchange servers; but in case of a disk failure, you'll lose only one, either the operating system or the mailbox database. If you lose one, it is always recoverable, although most likely quite a bit of work.

Virtual Hard Disks

Virtual machines are using virtual hard disks. In Hyper-V, these are the VHD or VHDX files; in Vmware, they are the VMDK files. These are large, single files holding the operating system or the data from the virtual machines and are stored on one of the three storage solutions just mentioned. Also noted, these files should be located outside of the disks holding the virtualization host operating system.

In Hyper-V, there are four types of virtual hard disks available:

- Fixed size

- Dynamically expanding

- Differencing disk

- Pass-through disk

I discuss these in more detail.

Fixed Size

A *fixed-size virtual disk* is a pre-created and fully allocated virtual disk. If you create a fixed-size virtual disk of 127 GB, a VHD file is created of 127 GB in size on the virtualization host's storage solution. Yes, it takes time to create the VHD file and fill it up with nothing but zeroes, but it saves you from experiencing performance issues later on. Also, since the disk is pre-created before creating the actual virtual machine, you will not run into "disk full" situations when using other types of VHD files, as explained in the next sections.

The fixed-size virtual hard disk is the only virtual hard disk supported in virtualized Exchange 2013 solutions.

Dynamically Expanding

A *dynamically expanding virtual disk* is also pre-created, but it doesn't contain any data at the time of creation and therefore has only a couple of megabytes after the initial creation.

When data is stored on this type of virtual disk—that is, when an operating system is installed or when a mailbox database located on this disk is expanding—it is automatically expanding. Although small, there's a performance penalty when the disk is expanding, however. More important, there a serious risk of overcommitting the underlying disk when you're using this type of virtual disk. You won't be the first, and certainly not the last, person to use a dynamically expanding disk to discover that it is completely filled and the virtual machines have stopped working.

Therefore, dynamically expanding disks are *not* supported for running Exchange 2013 in a production environment, but for a lab environment it is a great solution, as it will save you a lot of disk space.

Differencing Disk

A *differencing disk* is an interesting solution, as it consists of actually two virtual hard disks linked together in a parent-child relationship. The first disk is known as the "parent" disk and this is typically the most important one. This disk is used as read-only, which means that data is read from this disk and never written to this disk. Thus, it will never change and typically it is stored where the actual virtual hard disk is stored. In a differencing disk scenario, you cannot afford to lose this disk.

The second disk is known as the "child" disk, and this is a read-write disk. Data is read from the child disk, but data can also be stored on the disk. It is possible to create multiple differencing disks, based on the same parent disk. This is shown in Figure 1-12, with the Diff 1, 2, and 3 VHD. You can also create a chain of differencing disks, shown in Figure 1-12 with the Diff 2-2 VHD.

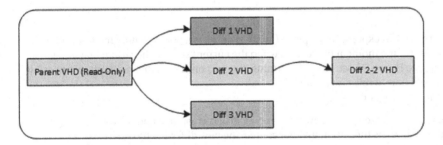

Figure 1-12. *Multiple differencing disks with one parent disk*

Why use a differencing disk? Imagine you create a virtual machine with Windows 2012 R2 installed, and it is fully configured and operational. You shut down the virtual machine, and based on this VHD, you create a new differencing disk. Your next step is to create a new virtual machine, based on this differencing disk. When the new VM is started, the configuration is read from the parent disk, but all changes are written to the child disk, leaving the parent disk untouched. This way it is possible to return to the point where you originally shut down the first virtual machine. You have created a point-in-time mechanism.

Even better, before you create the differencing disk, you can use the SYSPREP utility to prepare the virtual machine for a fresh "mini setup." When you create a new differencing disk based on the sysprepped VHD, you can create a new virtual machine based on the mini setup of sysprep. Since you can create multiple differencing disks based on the same sysprepped parent partition, you can create multiple new virtual machines in a matter of minutes. If you store the parent VHD file on one hard disk and the child VHD file on another, you get acceptable performance as well.

The downside of this is that differencing disks are *not supported* in Exchange Server scenarios by Microsoft. The main reason for this is that Exchange Server is unaware of what's going on in the background. When a differencing disk is removed, you can get back to a previous state, but Exchange Server is not aware of that.

Nevertheless, differencing disks are a great solution for lab and test environments because they allow you to quickly create multiple virtual machines for testing purposes.

▪ **Note**   As you might now understand, if you lose the child disk you lose data, but since you still have to parent disk, there's a situation you can return to. If you lose the parent disk, you lose everything. This is important to understand and to realize.

Pass-Through Disk

A *pass-through disk* is not really a virtual hard disk because it is not stored as a VHD or VMDK file, as with the previous types of virtual disks, but a pass-through disk can be used by a virtual machine.

A pass-through disk can be a physical disk, or a LUN on a SAN presented directly to the SCSI adapter of the virtual machine. Sometimes a pass-through disk is also referred to as a "raw disk." Since there isn't any overhead from any kind of virtual hard disk file, this solution offers the best performance.

There's only one catch here. Since a pass-through disk is presented directly to the SCSI adapter of the virtual machine, it is possible to use this solution only when the virtual machine is running. It is not possible to create a virtual machine that's bootable from a pass-through disk, because the SCSI adapter is not available during boot time.

This is only true for older Hyper-V environments. Windows Server 2012 R2 supports Generation 2 virtual machines. Generation 2 virtual machines are capable of booting from a SCSI disk, but the guest operating system inside the virtual machine must be at least Windows Server 2012.

Snapshots

A snapshot, sometime also referred to as "checkpoint" in Hyper-V (and VMware), is a point-in-time recovery method for virtual machines. A snapshot captures the moment of creation when the current state of the virtual machines memory and hard disk are stored on the Hyper-V host. Since everything is stored on disk at that moment, it is possible to return to this exact point in time and thus to this exact state.

When a snapshot is created, the following occurs:

- The current virtual hard disk is frozen and a new differencing disk is created, whereby the current virtual hard disk will act as the parent disk. Of course, the new differencing disk is linked to this parent disk.

- The state of the server memory inside the virtual machine and the processor state are frozen at the same time and stored on the virtual host.

When done, the virtual machine continues running normally, but all data will now be stored in the newly created differencing disk. It is possible to create multiple, consecutive snapshots, making it conceivable to return to multiple points in time. This is shown in Figure 1-13, where a snapshot is created at point T=1 and later another snapshot is created at T=2.

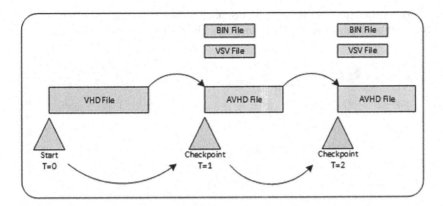

Figure 1-13. Two snapshots at different points in time

When reverting a snapshot, the following occur:

- The virtual machine is stopped. Since the situation at that moment will destroyed, the virtual machine is powered off.

- The differencing disk is deleted and a new differencing disk is created.

- The virtual machine is started, data is read from the original parent VHD disk, and the state of the server memory and processor state are read from the BIN and VSV file.

The server now continues running exactly as it had been when the snapshot was created.

Now, this is absolutely fine if you have a static server where changes are minimal to zero—for example, a file server or a web server. But if you have a dynamically changing server, or a server that's using replication techniques for redundancy as would an Exchange server, a SQL server, or a Domain Controller, things are different. These applications are not snapshot aware, so they have no clue what's actually happening in the background. When you revert to a snapshot, Exchange Server literally makes a time jump, and it's unpredictable how Exchange Server will react on this.

Therefore, use of snapshots is *not* supported in combination with Exchange Server in a production environment. But even in a test environment you have to be careful. If you restore a virtual machine from a snapshot, you might have to roll back multiple machines—for example, if the server is a DAG member or maybe even a Domain Controller—to prevent any issues with machines passwords and the like.

However, VSS snapshots can be used as a backup solution; this will be explained in detail in chapter 7.

Memory Requirements for Virtual Machines

In Windows Server 2008 R2, Hyper-V Microsoft introduced the concept of *dynamic memory*. Instead of assigning a fixed amount of memory to a virtual machine, memory is assigned to a virtual machine dynamically. That is, depending on the workload within the virtual machine, the amount of memory in use by the virtual machine can vary.

In Hyper-V dynamic memory, the following memory assignments are available:

- **Minimum RAM** – This is the amount of memory assigned to a virtual machine at boot time.

- **Maxiumum RAM** – This is the maximum amount of memory that can be assigned to a virtual machine when running. You can set this to an extremely high value, but it will never grow beyond the amount of physical memory in the Hyper-V host.

- **Memory buffer** – A small but configurable amount of memory that is reserved for the virtual machine, useful for memory bursts.

A fourth setting is about the memory weight. This determines the importance of the virtual machine when it comes to reassigning memory. A higher weight means more important and thus a better assignment of memory.

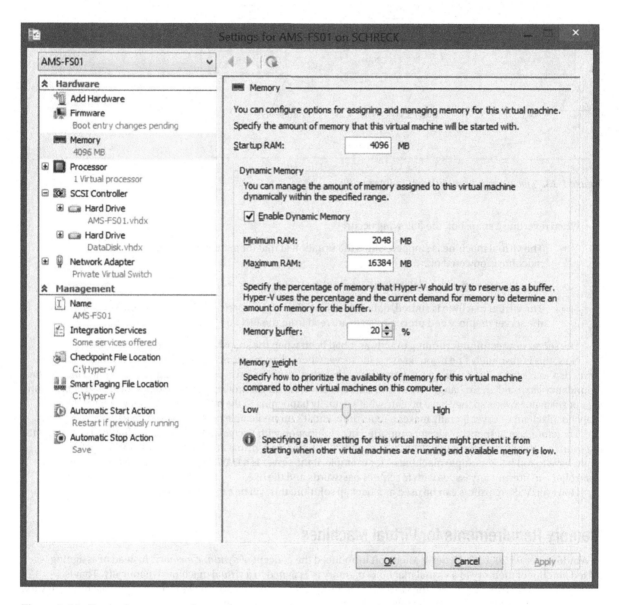

Figure 1-14. *Dynamic memory assignments*

When a virtual machine is started, it gets the minimum amount of RAM assigned, but as soon as it's needed, more RAM is assigned to the virtual machine; over time, you'll see the amount of memory stabilizing. But when other virtual machines need more memory, the hypervisor needs to reclaim memory from some virtual machines.

When the hypervisor reclaims memory, a process called *ballooning* takes place inside the virtual machine to reclaim any non-used memory pages inside the virtual machine. But when there aren't any pages available, the kernel inside the virtual machine start paging to disk to reclaim memory. As you might know, paging typically has a dramatic effect on server performance.

Tests within Microsoft have shown that when memory is reclaimed from an Exchange 2013 Mailbox server, the RPC Averaged Latency counter increases dramatically. When this happens, users experience performance issues immediately. In Figure 1-15, you can see the RPC Averaged Latency increase when the available bytes decrease. (This figure was part of a presentation delivered by Jeff Mealiffe, a Program Manager from the Microsoft Exchange product group at TechEd 2013. You can view his entire presentation on the MSDN Channel9 website, `http://bit.ly/TechedVirtualization`.)

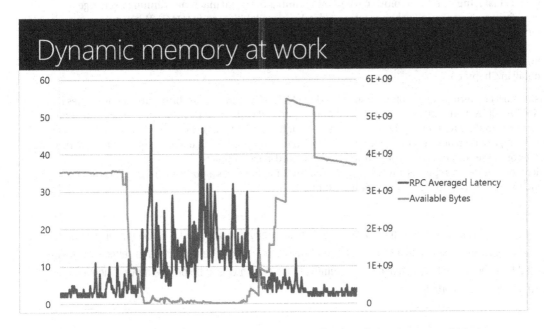

Figure 1-15. *The RPC Averaged Latency increases dramatically when dynamic memory kicks in*

Dynamic memory is useful for applications that need a memory boost on a temporary basis, like a web server or a file server. Exchange does not need a memory boost; it needs all its memory all the time. Therefore, the use of dynamic memory on an Exchange 2013 server is *not* supported in a production environment. The same is true for any solution that manipulates the memory inside virtual machines when running Exchange 2013, such as oversubscription of memory. (I have written an interesting article on dynamic memory some time ago. It was written for Windows Server 2008 R2 SP1, but the basic idea has not changed. You can find the article at `http://bit.ly/DynMemory`.

High-Availability Solutions

When it comes to high-availability solutions in a virtualized Exchange 2013 environment, there are basically two solutions:

- **Host clustering** – This is a solution whereby the virtualization hosts form a cluster where the virtual machines are created as a cluster resource. When a host fails, the virtual machine is moved to another host in the cluster. Please note that when a host fails, the virtual machine will crash as well and perform a cold boot on the other cluster node. When a planned migration occurs the virtual machine is gradually moved from one cluster node to another, preferably without any downtime.

- **Guest clustering** – This is a solution whereby a number of virtual machines running Exchange 2013 form a cluster, or in Exchange terms, a database availability group (DAG). When a virtualization host fails, the DAG member on that host will fail and another virtual machine that's part of the DAG will take over the Exchange service, most likely without any downtime for the users. Guest clustering—that is, the database availability group—will be discussed in detail in Chapter 5.

When using host clustering, Microsoft fully supports Live Migration and similar third-party technologies like VMware's VMotion. All Exchange 2013 server roles are fully supported with these technologies. Please note that all third-party vendors should have their solutions validated through the SVVP program, as stated earlier. Microsoft can support Exchange Server, but cannot support these third-party solutions, so you have to make sure that running Exchange Server on these solution is fully supported by these third-party vendors.

What Microsoft does *not* support is any other migration solution that uses a point-in-time or saved-state technology, including the Hyper-V quick migration solution.

■ **Note** A "saved state" is a state in which the virtual machine is "brought to sleep." The virtual machine is turned off and its memory contents are stored in a separate file on disk. When the machine is returned to service, the memory contents are read from the file and the virtual machine returns to the state it was in before the move. When it comes to Exchange 2013, this is not supported.

It is important to realize that when you're running an Exchange server on a host-based clustering solution, you still have one copy of an Exchange server. That is, there's redundancy on a host level, but not on the Exchange level. If the Exchange server fails inside the virtual machine, you end up with a high-availability virtual machine and an unwilling Exchange server. If redundancy in Exchange Server is important, it is recommended you use guest clustering—that is, a database availability group in a host-based clustering solution. This way you can survive failures on a hypervisor level as well as on an Exchange level.

Related to this, I've received several questions regarding the Hyper-V replica, and if this is a useful solution for Exchange Server. Unfortunately, it's not. The first thing to know is that Hyper-V replica is a disaster-recovery solution and not a high-availability solution. Hyper-V replica uses a special Hyper-V replication technology whereby special log files (*not* Exchange log files) are shipped asynchronously to a remote Hyper-V server. And with asynchronous replication technology, this introduces the most horrible situations with Exchange Server. Therefore, Hyper-V replica is *not* supported by Exchange Server.

There's a lot of information on Microsoft TechNet—for example, Exchange 2013 virtualization on http://bit.ly/ExVirtualization. There's also an excellent whitepaper "Best Practices for Virtualizing & Managing Exchange 2013" that you can find on http://bit.ly/VirtualizationWP

Sizing Virtual Exchange 2013 Servers

Virtualization is a pretty cool solution and very interesting for a lot of customers to use, but CPU resources don't appear out of thin air. What I mean is that there's overhead in the virtualization layer. For Hyper-V, for example, you have to calculate an additional 10 percent CPU overhead. For third-party solutions, you have to follow the vendor's guidance for processor overhead in their virtualization solutions.

The best recommendation when you are virtualizing is to use the Exchange 2013 Server Role Requirements Calculator. You'll find two options in this requirements calculator for virtualization: the Server Role Virtualization option and the Hypervisor CPU Adjustment factor. These are explained in the next chapter.

Other important factors to consider are the memory recommendations made earlier in this section; also, note that storage is as important as before. Storage should be optimized for IO latency and high availability, for both host clustering and guest clustering.

Virtualization has major advantages when it comes to networks. You can use the hypervisor networking flexibility to provide availability and performance. The general recommendation is to design a physical Exchange 2013 environment and apply it to a virtual Exchange 2013 environment. However, I have seen too many customers create virtual Exchange servers without enough memory, too many virtual machines using the same network interface, or too many virtual hard disks on the same set of physical disks. These combinations are recipes for disaster!

Summary

Exchange 2013 is the newest version of Microsoft's well-known messaging and collaboration solution. There are a lot of new features and a lot of changes as well. Exchange 2013 Service Pack 1 in turn adds more interesting features. The most important difference is the changes in architecture, resulting in three server roles: the Client Access server, the Mailbox server, and the Edge Transport server. These Exchange 2013 roles are now loosely coupled, and as a result it is much easier to implement an Exchange Server environment with multiple data centers.

There have been major changes in Exchange Server management as well. The Exchange Admin Center has replaced the Exchange Management Console, but the EAC is fairly limited. The most important management tool for Exchange 2013 is the Exchange Management Shell, running on top of Windows PowerShell.

Virtualization is becoming more and more important in Windows Server environments. Microsoft Windows Hyper-V is a virtualization solution, but VMware is an important player in this market segment as well. There are more virtualization vendors, but as long as their solutions are validated in the SVVP program, you should be fine. Implementing virtualization can introduce an additional layer of complexity, but when designed properly, both the hypervisor and the Exchange solutions should be fine. It all comes down to common sense when using a virtualization solution. Remember, you cannot produce resources out of thin air. Do not overcommit your production environment, as this will impact your Exchange server performance.

The next chapter is about designing your Exchange 2013 infrastructure and installing Exchange 2013. This will be explained in a greenfield scenario, as well as into an existing Exchange 2007 or Exchange 2010 environment.

CHAPTER 2

■ ■ ■

Installing Exchange Server 2013

Now that we've covered some of the new functions of Exchange Server 2013 SP1 and have provided some background information, it's time to move on to actually installing Exchange 2013 SP1 and getting it working. This chapter covers the design of an Exchange Server 2013 environment and the process of installing Exchange Server 2013 SP1.

The first section is about designing your Exchange 2013 environment. The Exchange 2013 role requirements calculator will be used to a design an environment for our 1,500-user fictitious company called Contoso.

Installing Exchange Server 2013 can be done in a clean and fresh Active Directory by what is called a *green-field installation,* covered in the second part of this chapter. While this is certainly useful, chances are you already have an existing, earlier version of Exchange Server running. In this case, you have to upgrade the environment, which is covered in the third part of this chapter.

The last part covers the update process of your Exchange Server 2013 environment with cumulative updates.

Designing Exchange Server 2013

When you want to deploy Exchange 2013 for a larger number of users you have to make a proper design of your Exchange Server environment. You have to do an inventory of all business and legal requirements and write these down in a design document. Together with the user requirements, such as the number of users (i.e., mailboxes), the mailbox sizing, and so on, you create a design of your Exchange 2013 environment based on the proper design decisions. If you fail to do so, most likely you will run into sizing issues when you run your Exchange 2013 environment.

Business, legal, and user requirements include answers to the following questions:

- What is the typical mailbox size?
- Do you have to create backups?
- If you will have backups, how long do you need to keep these backups and do you need to store the backups at an off-site location?
- What's the average message size used by your users?
- What are the normal business hours?

- What does your service-level agreement (SLA) look like? In your SLA you will define your answers to such questions as the following:

  - Is there a need for 24x7, or will 5x12 do as well?

  - How long does it take to create a backup and, more important, how long does it take to restore data?

  - How long does it take to restore a mailbox, a mailbox database, or an entire Exchange 2013 server?

  - Are there guaranteed delivery times for messages?

- What is the user concurrency? That is, how many users are online at the same time?

These are questions you need to answer when designing a proper Exchange 2013 environment. They are a different kind of question from the ones you, as an Exchange administrator, are accustomed to answering, such as "How much memory do I need in my server?" or "How about the disk configuration of my Exchange 2013 server?"

In our fictitious contoso.com company we have 1,500 users, we anticipate a 2 GB mailbox for each user, and we don't need any high availability at this point. (High availability will be discussed in Chapter 5.)

Exchange 2013 Server Role Requirements Calculator

One of the best tools to determine the sizing of your Exchange 2013 server is the *Exchange 2013 Server Role Requirements Calculator.* This is basically a spreadsheet created by the Microsoft Exchange product group that determines the sizing of an Exchange 2013 environment based on the requirements you have to enter as input. You can download the Exchange 2013 Server Role Requirements Calculator at `http://bit.ly/ExCalculator`.

When you open the calculator, you will see an Excel spreadsheet with eight tabs. The first tab is where you enter the requirements that will be used as input for the actual design.

Important requirements you have to enter here are, for example:

- **Which Global Catalog server architecture to use:** The choice is between a 32-bit Global Catalog server and a 64-bit Global Catalog server. A 64-bit Global Catalog server gives better performance owing to more efficient processor usage and the possibility of addressing more internal memory. Windows Server 2008 R2 and later are available only as 64-bits versions. Windows Server 2003 R2 is available as 32-bit and 64-bit versions.

- **If you are using a multi-role configuration:** Starting with Exchange 2010, Microsoft recommends using *multi-role servers*. These are Exchange servers whereby multiple roles are installed in one box. In Exchange 2013, this means that one server holds both the Mailbox server role and the Client Access server role. More information regarding this recommendation can be found on the Exchange Team blog at `http://bit.ly/MultiRole`. Though the article was written for Exchange 2010, it also applies to Exchange 2013.

- **If you are virtualizing your Exchange servers:** As explained in Chapter 1, virtualizing your Exchange 2013 servers is not a problem as long as the virtualization solution is validated in the SVVP program and the virtualization vendor supports running Exchange 2013 in its solution.

- **How many Mailbox servers you'll use:** This is a tricky matter; the number you choose depends on the number of mailboxes you will be hosting on your Mailbox server. You have to start somewhere, and as a rule of thumb I always start with approximately 2,500 mailboxes on one Mailbox server, so for 10,000 mailboxes I start with four Mailbox servers. Depending on the sizing that comes out of the Requirements Calculator, I can always adjust the number of Mailbox servers.

- **How many mailboxes in your environment:** This is a hard number to ascertain for setting your requirements, but when you're designing your Exchange 2013 environment, keep future growth in mind.

- **How many messages sent and received per mailbox each day:** This number is also known as the *usage profile* and it might be quite difficult to ascertain.

- **How large the mailbox size:** In our contoso.com environment we set this to 2 GB. Quite a lot of people still have doubts about large mailboxes, but Exchange 2013 does not have trouble with 25 GB mailboxes. If you're running Outlook 2010, though, you have to realize that when running cached mode, the OST file in Outlook can grow very large. As a result, performance on a user's workstation, especially when it's a laptop with a 5400 rpm hard disk, can be seriously impacted.

- **The backup architecture:** A traditional backup is VSS based, whether it is a hardware VSS solution or a software VSS one. There's a backup server running in your network and backup clients on your Exchange servers. Microsoft System Center DPM is an example of this, but there are a lot more from Symantec, IBM, HP, and others. The Exchange Native Data Protection is another way of safeguarding your information, sometimes also referred to as a "backup-less" environment.

In our contoso.com environment, the requirements fed into the Requirements Calculator are listed in Table 2-1.

Table 2-1. *Requirements Used as Input for the contoso.com Exchange Server Configuration*

Requirement	Value
Server multi-role configuration	Yes
Server role virtualization	Yes
High availability deployment	No
Number of Mailbox servers	1
Number of mailboxes	1500
Total send/receive messages per mailbox per day	100
Average message size	75 KB
Mailbox size limit	2 GB
Backup methodology	Software VSS backup/restore
Backup frequency	Weekly full /daily incremental
System and boot disk	320 GB, 10k rpm SAS
Database disk	2 TB 7200 rpm 3½ SAS disk
Log disk	2 TB 7200 rpm 3½ SAS disk
Restore volume	2 TB 7200 rpm 3½ SAS disk
Processor cores/server	8

These are the most important settings for the first page of the Requirements Calculator; all other requirements can be left at their default settings at this point. A screenshot of the first tab of the Requirements Calculator is provided in Figure 2-1.

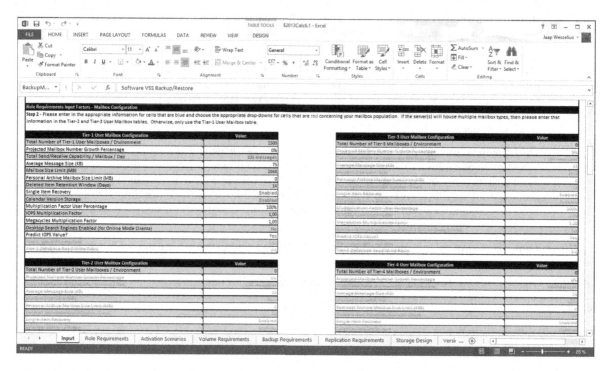

Figure 2-1. Entering the data into the Requirements Calculator

When you've entered all data into the Requirements Calculator, you can navigate to the second tab for viewing the Role Requirements. On this sheet, you'll find the sizing of the Exchange 2013 servers, based on the input you've just entered.

You'll find the number of mailboxes, the number of mailbox databases, the IOPS generated, and the amount of memory needed in the Exchange server, just to name a few. In our example, the most important results are listed in Table 2-2.

Table 2-2. *Calculated Requirements of Our contoso.com Exchange Environment*

Requirement	Value
Number of mailboxes	1,500
Number of mailboxes per database	83
Transaction logs generated per mailbox per dag	20
IOPS profile per mailbox	0.07
Number of mailbox databases	18
Available database cache per mailbox	8.19 MB
Recommended RAM configuration	48 GB
Server CPU megacycle requirements	87 66
Database space required (per database)	183 GB
Log space required (per database)	7 GB
Database space required (per server)	3287 GB
Log space required (per server)	121 GB
Total database required IOPS (per server)	121
Total log required IOPS (per server)	24

The megacycles estimate is based on the measurement of Intel E5-2650 2 GHz processors (2x8 core arrangement). A 2 GHz processor core equals 2000 megacycles of performance throughput, so at least five processor cores are needed in this environment.

As you can see, Exchange 2013 needs quite some resources according to the Requirements Calculator; on the other hand, it could be said that this calculation is a worst-case scenario in which all resources are stressed to the max. In real life, the resources used by Exchange 2013 are probably much less, but when your design is according to the Requirements Calculator, you know it is fully supported. When you assign fewer resources to your Exchange 2013 server, especially memory, there's a serious risk of experiencing performance issues.

So, 18 mailbox databases are used by this Exchange 2013 server. The fourth tab in the Requirements Calculator (Volume Requirements) shows the number of mailbox databases and the volumes used where the mailbox databases are stored. Since Exchange 2013 supports multiple mailbox databases on one volume, only three volumes are used and the mailbox databases are spread across these three volumes.

The seventh tab in the Requirements Calculator (Storage Design) tells you how many disks are used for each volume. For the mailbox database, six disks are used, two disks are in a RAID-1 configuration (mirroring) and are used by a volume. The transaction log files of all mailbox databases are stored on a separate volume, also consisting of two disks in a RAID-1 configuration.

A special volume is used for restore purposes. If you want to restore one or more mailbox databases from backup, a special volume is used for this. In our example, three disks in a RAID-5 configuration are used to create this restore volume.

So, in total, this Exchange 2013 server is using 11 physical disks of 2 TB each for storing 1,500 mailboxes of 2 GB in size. The server itself is using two disks in a RAID-1 configuration for the Operating System and the Exchange 2013 server software. A graphic representation of this distribution is shown in Figure 2-2.

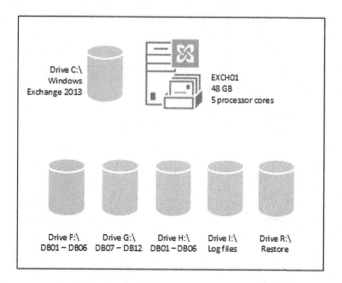

Figure 2-2. The Exchange 2013 server design for a 1,500-mailbox contoso.com environment

When designing your Exchange 2013 Mailbox server, note that this is the time to start thinking about drive letters. When you only have three physical disks in your environment, you can assign drive letters like F:\, G:\, and H:\ to these disks. Things get more complicated when you have 15 disks in your server, however. In this case, you don't want to assign drive F:\ to drive T:\ to these disks. Instead, you use *Mount Points* on your server. That is, when disks are formatted they are not assigned a drive letter and instead are mounted in a directory on the C:\ drive—for example, C:\MountPoints. If you have multiple disks on your server, then, these are available via C:\MountPoints\Disk1, C:\MountPoints\Disk2, C:\MountPoints\Disk3, and so on. This method gives you much more flexibility than simply using drive letters; it also makes available a feature called *Auto Reseed,* as this uses Mount Points. Auto Reseed is part of the Exchange 2013 high-availability solution, discussed in detail in Chapter 5.

Microsoft has an excellent white paper on sizing Exchange 2013, called "Ask the Perf Guy: Sizing Exchange 2013 Deployments"; it can be found at `http://bit.ly/ExSizing`.

Green-Field Installation of Exchange 2013

When you are installing Exchange 2013, you must meet a number of requirements regarding hardware, the operating system where Exchange Server will be installed, and the version of Active Directory Directory Services (ADDS) that will be used. There's also some prerequisite software that needs to be installed in advance, including Windows Server roles or features.

Hardware Requirements

Exchange 2013 has the following hardware requirements, but please note that these requirements seem to have been established by a marketing department. As we've seen in the previous section, the normal hardware requirements are a bit different, depending on the expected usage. The following are the bare-minimum requirements—just enough to start Exchange Server:

- X64 architecture-based processor (Intel Itanium IA-64 is not supported).

- 8 GB of RAM for the Mailbox server.

- 4 GB of RAM for the Client Access server.

- 8 GB of RAM for the combined Mailbox and Client Access servers.

- At least 30 GB of free space where Exchange 2013 will be installed. (Add 500 MB for every UM language pack. All disks have to be formatted with the NTFS file system.).

- An additional hard disk of 500 MB where the Transport Queue database is stored, although this is stored by default on the system and bootdisk (i.e., C:\ drive).

For a full and up-to-date overview of all Exchange 2013 requirements, visit the Microsoft TechNet site at `http://bit.ly/ExRequirements`.

■ **Note** The numbers listed above are the bare minimum for Exchange 2013, as published by Microsoft. These are sufficient to start an Exchange 2013 server, but for a regular production server you need to design your server as discussed in the first section of this chapter.

Software Requirements

Exchange 2013 SP1 can be installed on the following Windows operating systems:

- Windows Server 2012 R2 Datacenter Edition

- Windows Server 2012 R2 Standard Edition

- Windows Server 2012 Datacenter Edition

- Windows Server 2012 Standard Edition

- Windows Server 2008 R2 Datacenter Edition

- Windows Server 2008 R2 Enterprise Edition

- Windows Server 2008 R2 Standard Edition

■ **Note** Exchange Server 2013 RTM is supported on the same Windows operating systems, except for Windows Server 2012 R2 Datacenter and Standard Edition. Both versions of Exchange 2013 can be installed only on Windows Server with the full GUI. The Windows Server core is not supported on any version of Exchange 2013.

The Exchange 2013 Management Shell can be installed on the following Windows operating systems:

- Windows Server 2012 R2 Datacenter Edition

- Windows Server 2012 R2 Standard Edition

- Windows Server 2008 R2 SP1 Standard Edition

- Windows Server 2008 R2 SP1 Enterprise Edition

- Windows Server 2008 R2 RTM Datacenter Edition

- Windows Server 2012 Standard Edition

- Windows Server 2012 Datacenter Edition

- Windows 8.1 64-bit version (except home edition)

- Windows 7 SP1 64-bit version (except home edition)

When it comes to Active Directory, the following requirements can be identified:

- Schema master Windows Server 2003 SP2 or later

- Global Catalog server Windows Server 2003 SP2 or later

- Domain controller Windows Server 2003 SP2 or later

- Active directory Forest Functional Level at Windows Server 2003 or higher

A number of DNS namespace scenarios are supported in Exchange 2013, although these requirements haven't changed in years. The following namespaces can be used with Exchange 2013:

- **Contiguous namespace:** This is a normal namespace where all domain names in the environment are contiguous. For example, a root domain would be contoso.com and the child domains would be emea.contoso.com, na.contoso.com, or asia.contoso.com. Go one level deeper, and it would be prod.emea.contoso.com, and rnd.na.contoso.com.

- **Non-contiguous namespace:** This is a namespace where the different trees in an Active Directory forest do not have similar names. For example, one tree in the Active Directory forest can be contoso.com, while another tree in the same Active Directory forest can be Fabrikam.com, and a third tree can be FourthCoffee.com. They form separate domain trees in one forest. A special example of a non-contiguous namespace is where one tree would be contoso.com and another tree would be contoso.net. In this scenario, you would run into problems with the NetBIOS name of these domains. By default, the NetBIOS name of the domains would be contoso, but since you cannot have two identical NetBIOS names in one network, you have to another NetBIOS name for the second contoso domain.

- **Single-label domain:** A single-label domain is a domain name that does not contain a DNS suffix—for example, no .com, .net, .org, or .corp. A normal domain name would be contoso.com, but a single-label domain would be contoso. A single-label domain is supported by Exchange 2013, but the use of single-label domains is not recommended by Microsoft.

- **Disjoint namespace:** A disjoint namespace is a namespace where the primary DNS suffix of a server does not match the DNS name of the Active Directory domain. For example, you can have an Exchange server called LON-EXCH01 with a primary DNS suffix corp.contoso.com in the Active Directory domain emea.contoso.com.

For a complete overview of supported DNS namespaces and additional resources, you can check the support for DNS namespace planning in the Microsoft server products article at http://bit.ly/DNSNameSpace.

■ **Note** Installation of Exchange 2013 on domain controllers is supported but not recommended. The recommended way of installing Exchange 2013 is on a member server in an Active Directory domain.

Exchange 2013 SP1 installation

It is my personal recommendation that you install Exchange Server 2013 on the latest available version of Windows server that's being supported. For Exchange 2013 SP1, this means Windows Server 2012 R2 and Exchange 2013 RTM on top of Windows Server 2012. Both versions of Windows Server 2012 are more scalable than Windows Server 2008 R2, and their support lifecycle is better. Windows Server 2012 R2 will be supported for 10 years after the time of this writing. Also, upgrading an underlying operating system on an Exchange 2013 server is not supported, so when you are installing Exchange 2013 on Windows Server 2008 R2, there's no way to upgrade the operating system later on.

However, not all companies have raised Windows Server 2012 R2 to the company standard, and many are still running Windows Server 2008 R2 as their default operating systems. In this section, I start with installation of Exchange 2013 SP1 on Windows Server 2012 R2. When needed, I make some remarks regarding previous versions of the Windows server operating system. This book is a PowerShell administration book, so I start with the unattended setup of Exchange 2013 SP1; the GUI setup will be discussed later in this section.

Installing Exchange Server 2013 is relatively easy and consists of the following steps:

- Preparing Windows Server and installing prerequisite software.

- Preparing all partitions of Active Directory.

- Installing Exchange 2013.

- Performing post-configuration steps.

Preparing Windows Server

When installing Exchange Server 2013 SP1 on top of Windows Server 2012 R2, the following prerequisite software is needed on the Windows server:

- .NET Framework 4.5, which is available at `http://bit.ly/NETFramework45`

- Management Framework 3.0, which contains PowerShell 3.0 and is available at `http://bit.ly/ManagementFramework`

- Unified Communications Managed API 4.0, which is available at `http://bit.ly/ManagedAPI`

- Internet Information Server

The first two items are included in Windows Server 2012 and Windows Server 2012 R2 by default, so there's no need to install these manually. However, you have to download the Unified Communications Managed API 4.0 and install this on all Exchange 2013 servers.

One step not listed above is the installation of the Remote Server Administration Tools (RSAT). These are needed only on the first server where Exchange 2013 will be installed, because those tools are used to make the modifications to Active Directory. But installing RSAT also installs tools like Active Directory Users and Computers or Active Directory Sites and Services, and these can be useful on other servers as well.

To install the Remote Server Administration Tools, open a PowerShell window and enter the following commands:

```
Import-Module ServerManager
Install-WindowsFeature RSAT-ADDS
```

This is shown in Figure 2-3.

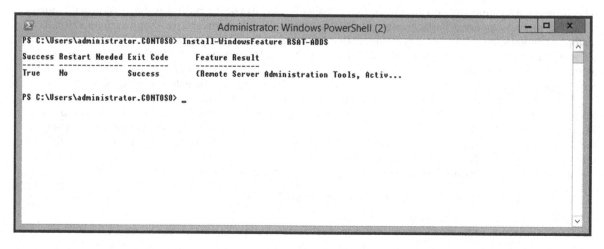

Figure 2-3. *Installing the Remote Server Administration Tools on Windows 2012 R2*

Internet Information Server can be installed using PowerShell. Import the Server Manager module in PowerShell and add the Windows Server Roles and Features. For a multi-role server, the following commands can be used:

```
Import-Module ServerManager
Install-WindowsFeature AS-HTTP-Activation, Desktop-Experience, NET-Framework-45-Features,
RPC-over-HTTP-proxy, RSAT-Clustering, RSAT-Clustering-CmdInterface, RSAT-Clustering-Mgmt,
RSAT-Clustering-PowerShell, Web-Mgmt-Console, WAS-Process-Model, Web-Asp-Net45, Web-Basic-Auth,
Web-Client-Auth, Web-Digest-Auth, Web-Dir-Browsing, Web-Dyn-Compression, Web-Http-Errors,
Web-Http-Logging, Web-Http-Redirect, Web-Http-Tracing, Web-ISAPI-Ext, Web-ISAPI-Filter,
Web-Lgcy-Mgmt-Console, Web-Metabase, Web-Mgmt-Console, Web-Mgmt-Service, Web-Net-Ext45,
Web-Request-Monitor, Web-Server, Web-Stat-Compression, Web-Static-Content, Web-Windows-Auth,
Web-WMI, Windows-Identity-Foundation
```

For a dedicated Client Access server, use the following commands:

```
Install-WindowsFeature AS-HTTP-Activation, Desktop-Experience, NET-Framework-45-Features,
RPC-over-HTTP-proxy, RSAT-Clustering, Web-Mgmt-Console, WAS-Process-Model, Web-Asp-Net45,
Web-Basic-Auth, Web-Client-Auth, Web-Digest-Auth, Web-Dir-Browsing, Web-Dyn-Compression,
Web-Http-Errors, Web-Http-Logging, Web-Http-Redirect, Web-Http-Tracing, Web-ISAPI-Ext,
Web-ISAPI-Filter, Web-Lgcy-Mgmt-Console, Web-Metabase, Web-Mgmt-Console, Web-Mgmt-Service,
Web-Net-Ext45, Web-Request-Monitor, Web-Server, Web-Stat-Compression, Web-Static-Content,
Web-Windows-Auth, Web-WMI, Windows-Identity-Foundation
```

■ **Note** For troubleshooting purposes, I always install the Telnet client on every Exchange server. This can be achieved by adding the `Telnet-Client` to the Windows features list mentioned above.

Figure 2-4 shows the command executed successfully for a multi-role server and the warning that a reboot is needed.

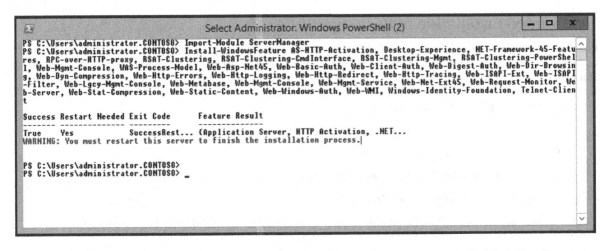

Figure 2-4. *Installing prerequisites Server Roles and Features in a PowerShell window, including the Telnet client feature*

When installing Exchange Server 2013 on Windows Server 2008 R2, the process is similar, but the following three additional hotfixes need to be added to the list of prerequisite software:

- Knowledge Base article KB974405 ("Windows Identity Foundation"), available at http://bit.ly/IdentityFoundation

- Knowledge Base article KB2619234 ("A hotfix is available to enable the association cookie/GUID that is used by RPC over HTTP to also be used at the RPC layer in Windows 7 and in Windows Server 2008 R2"), available at http://bit.ly/CookieGUID

- Knowledge Base article KB2533623 ("Insecure library loading could allow remote code execution"), available at http://bit.ly/InsecureLibrary

If you have been working with Exchange 2013 RTM, you might remember there was a prerequisite warning about the Office 2010 Filter Pack software. This software was not used by Exchange 2013 RTM (the warning was erratic), and was replaced by the Exchange 2013 FAST search technology. In Exchange 2013 SP1, this warning message is no longer shown.

The last piece of prerequisite software that needs to be installed is the Unified Communications Managed API 4.0 Runtime. This is relatively straightforward. You download the software, start the setup application, and follow the wizard. You then reboot the server when needed. Once the preparation of Active Directory is installed, part of the unattended installation can be started.

It is possible to download and install the Unified Communications Managed API 4.0 runtime using PowerShell by entering the following command:

```
Start-BitsTransfer -Source http://download.microsoft.com/download/2/C/4/2C47A5C1-A1F3-4843-B9FE-
84C0032C61EC/UcmaRuntimeSetup.exe -Destination c:\temp

c:\temp\UcmaRuntimeSetup.exe /q
```

The second command is not actually a PowerShell command, it just executes the setup application and runs it quietly without user interaction.

Unattended Installation of Exchange 2013

Installing Exchange 2013 can be achieved using the GUI mode of the setup application, or it can be done by using the unattended option of the setup application. My personal preference is to use the unattended setup. It is much more granular, the multiple installations are consistent, and there's no interaction with the server. You start the unattended setup, and after half an hour or so your Exchange server is up and running.

Unattended setup consists of the following steps:

- Preparing the Active Directory Schema partition.

- Preparing the Active Directory Configuration partition.

- Preparing the Active Directory Domain partition.

- Installing the actual Exchange 2013 software.

But before diving into this, let's take a closer look at the setup applications and the setup switches that are available for performing an unattended setup.

The Exchange 2013 Setup Application

If you want to install multiple Exchange 2013 servers, and you want to minimize your console interaction, it is possible to do an unattended installation. Also, for example, if your IT organization has multiple departments for Active Directory administration and Exchange Server administration, the unattended setup can be useful because it offers a granular way of configuring Active Directory and installing Exchange 2013.

The unattended installation is the same setup application as found on the installation media (setup.exe), but it is started from a command prompt and includes multiple setup switches.

■ **Note**   In Exchange 2013, the setup application is started using setup.exe. In Exchange 2007 and Exchange 2010, the setup application is started using setup.com.

Setup Switches

For installing Exchange 2013, the setup.exe application has a number of switches that can be used while executing the command. Table 2-3 lists these switches, with descriptions of their purposes.

Table 2-3. Exchange 2013 Setup Switches

Switch	Description
/IAcceptExchangeServerLicenseTerms	Mandatory switch for legal reasons
/PrepareSchema	Prepares the schema for Exchange 2013
/PrepareAD	Prepares the configuration partition in Active Directory and creates the Exchange 2013 organization in Active Directory
/OrganizationName	Defines the name of the configuration, used for preparing Active Directory. Used in conjunction with the /PrepareAD switch in a new Exchange environment
/PrepareDomain	Prepares the current domain for implementation of Exchange 2013
/PrepareAllDomains	Prepares all domains in the Active Directory forest for implementations of Exchange 2013
/Mode	Indicates installation mode, like Install, Uninstall, or Upgrade
/Roles	Defines the server roles that need to be installed, like Client Access or Mailbox
/InstallWindowsComponents	Installs the Windows roles and features needed for Exchange 2013
/Targetdir	Indicates the directory where the Exchange binaries will be installed
/Sourcedir	Indicates the directory where the installation files can be found
/Domaincontroller	Names a specific domain controller to be used during installation
/Answerfile	Indicates a file containing more specific configuration settings
/EnableErrorReporting	Enables or disables error reporting during setup
/CustomerFeedbackEnabled	Enables or disables the customer feedback option
/AddUMLanguagepack	Adds a specific unified messaging language pack
/RemoveUMLanguagepack	Removes a specific unified messaging language pack
/NewProvisionedServer	Provisions an Exchange Server object in Active Directory
/RemoveProvisionedServer	Removes an Exchange Server object from Active Directory
/Mdbname	Names the mailbox database that will be created during setup
/Dbfilepath	Locates the initial mailbox database
/Logfolderpath	Locates the mailbox database log files and checkpoint file
/ActiveDirectorySplitPermissions	Configures a split permissions model
/DoNotStartTransport	Does not start the Transport service (SMTP) during setup to prevent "strange" routing problems

Not all options are mandatory when installing Exchange 2013 unattended, but the more options you use, the more granular will be your setup application. I discuss some of these options in the following sections when preparing the Active Directory containers and installing the actual Exchange 2013 servers.

Prepare the Active Directory Schema Partition

The first step in an unattended installation is to update the schema. You do this by using the setup application with the /PrepareSchema switch. When it comes to permissions, make sure that the account you use for executing this step is a member of the Schema Administrators and Domain Administrators security groups in Active Directory. To make the necessary changes to the schema partition, open a command prompt and enter the following command:

```
Setup.exe /PrepareSchema /IacceptExchangeServerLicenseTerms
```

This is shown in Figure 2-5.

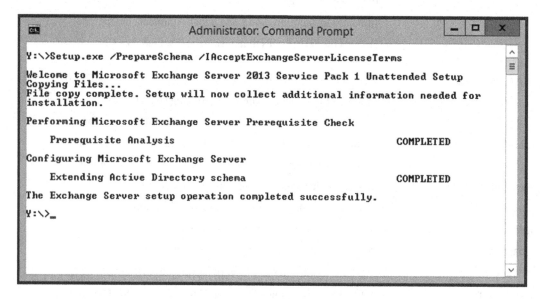

Figure 2-5. *Preparing the Active Directory schema for Exchange 2013*

You can check the version of the Active Directory schema by using the following PowerShell commands. This will bind the Active Directory to the variable called $root and use this variable to bind to the schema partition. From there the rangeUpper property, which holds the version of the Active Directory schema, is requested:

```
$root = [ADSI]"LDAP://RootDSE"
$Version = [ADSI]("LDAP://CN=ms-Exch-Schema-Version-Pt," + $root.schemaNamingContext)
$Version.rangeUpper
```

Every version of Exchange Server has its own value for the rangeUpper attribute, and this value even changes with the service pack. Table 2-4 lists all the values up until Exchange 2013 SP1.

Table 2-4. *Schema Values for Exchange Server Versions*

Exchange Server Version	Corresponding Value for rangeUpper Attribute
Exchange Server 2000	4397
Exchange Server 2000 SP 3	4406
Exchange Server 2003 RTM	6870
Exchange Server 2003 SP 2	6936
Exchange Server 2007	10628
Exchange Server 2007 SP 1	11116
Exchange Server 2007 SP 2	14622
Exchange Server 2007 SP 3	14625
Exchange Server 2010	14622
Exchange Server 2010 SP 1	14726
Exchange Server 2010 SP 2	14732
Exchange Server 2010 SP 3	14734
Exchange Server 2013	15137
Exchange Server 2013 CU1	15254
Exchange Server 2013 CU2	15281
Exchange Server 2013 CU3	15283
Exchange Server 2013 SP1	15292
Exchange Server 2013 CU5	15300
Exchange Server 2013 CU6	15303

After preparing the Active Directory schema partition, you have to wait until this update is replicated to all domain controllers in the entire organization. Once finished, you can continue with the next step.

Prepare Active Directory Configuration Partition

As explained in Chapter 1, the Exchange 2013 information is primarily stored in the Active Directory configuration partition.

Before Exchange 2013 can be installed, the configuration partition needs to be changed as well. This can be achieved by using the setup application with the /PrepareAD option. Since we create a new Exchange 2013 organization in this example, the /OrganizationName option followed by the name of the Exchange organization needs to be entered as well. The entire command to prepare the Active Directory configuration partition will be:

```
Setup.exe /PrepareAD /OrganizationName:CONTOSO /IacceptExchangeServerLicenseTerms
```

For this command to complete successfully you need to be logged on as a member of the Enterprise Admins group because this group will have sufficient permissions in the configuration partition. Preparing the configuration partition is shown in Figure 2-6.

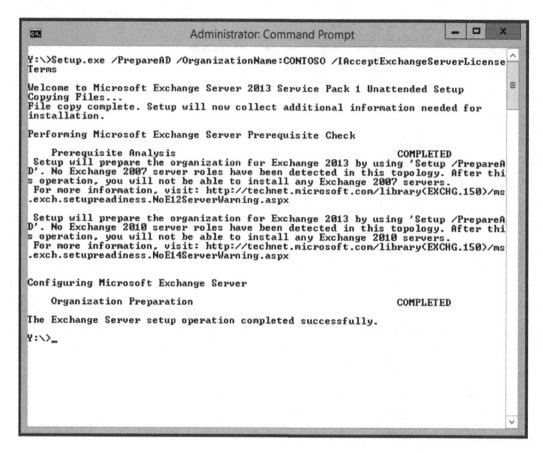

Figure 2-6. *Preparing the Active Directory configuration partition for Exchange 2013*

When you use ADSIEdit and open navigate to CN=Microsoft Exchange, CN=Services, CN=Configuration, DC=Contoso, DC=com (i.e., the Exchange organization leaf in the Active Directory configuration partition), you'll see the newly created Exchange organization CONTOSO. This is shown in Figure 2-7.

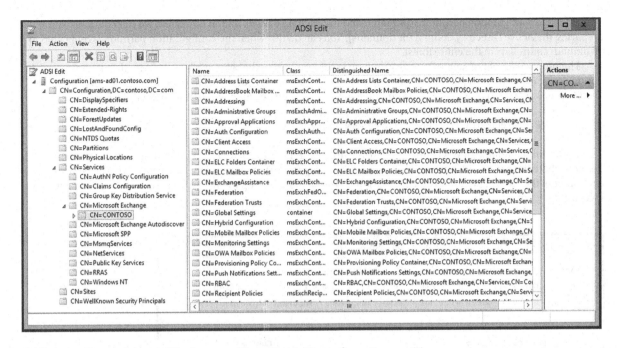

Figure 2-7. *The newly created Exchange configuration in the configuration partition*

When you open Active Directory Users and Computers, you'll see a new organizational unit (OU) in the root domain called "Microsoft Exchange Security Groups" and this OU contains 17 new universal security groups (USGs), all related to Exchange 2013. These groups will be the basis of Role Based Access Control, which will be explained in Chapter 10. Figure 2-8 shows the 17 USGs in the Microsoft Exchange Security Groups container.

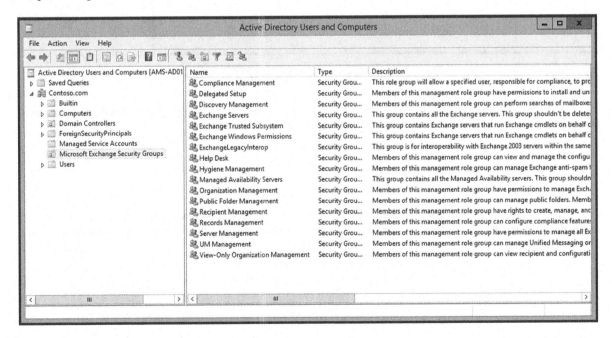

Figure 2-8. *The newly created Exchange 2013 universal security groups*

Once the configuration partition is prepared and the Exchange organization is created, we can continue with preparing the Active Directory domain (or domains). You can do this when the configuration partition is replicated to all domain controllers in the entire forest.

The preparation of the Active Directory domain is achieved using the setup application with the /PrepareDomain option. You can use the /PrepareAllDomains option if you have multiple domains in your Active Directory forest and want to prepare them in one step. The command to prepare the Active Directory domain will be like this:

```
Setup.exe /PrepareDomain /IAcceptExchangeServerLicenseTerms
```

To run this command, the account you're using must be a member of the Domain Admins security group in the domain where the command is executed. If you use the /PrepareAllDomains option, the account you're using must be a member of the Enterprise Admins security group. The command to prepare the Active Directory domain is shown in Figure 2-9.

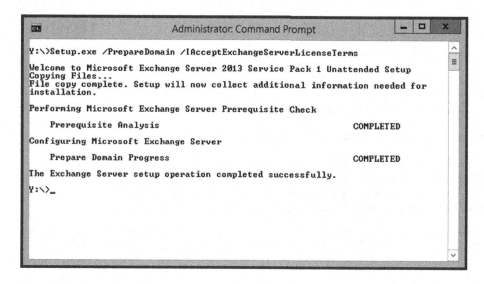

Figure 2-9. *Preparing the Active Directory domain for Exchange 2013 SP1*

The /PrepareDomain option creates a Microsoft Exchange System Objects container in the root domain in Active Directory and sets permission on this container for the following security groups:

- Exchange servers
- Exchange organization administrators
- Authenticated users

In this container, a security group called Exchange Install Domain Servers is created. Please note that you have to enable the View Advanced Features option in Active Directory Users and Computers to make this container visible. This is shown in Figure 2-10.

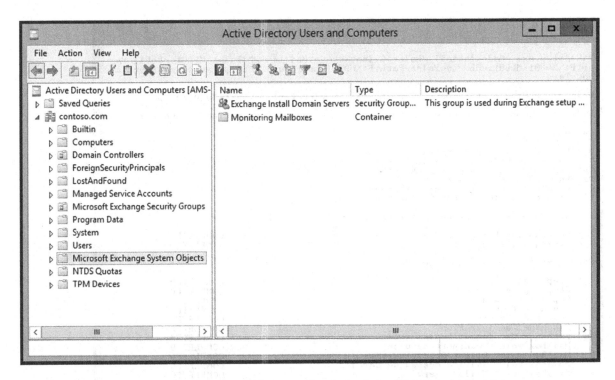

Figure 2-10. *The Microsoft Exchange System Objects container in the Active Directory root domain*

I've hardly ever seen these steps fail in the initial installation phase. If they do fail, it's most likely a permissions error or a replication error, which can be solved easily and the installation option tried again.

When the Active Directory domain is prepared and the information is replicated to all domain controllers in the entire forest, you can continue with installing the actual Exchange 2013 servers.

Install Exchange 2013

Once all Active Directory partitions are prepared, the actual Exchange 2013 servers can be installed. The easiest, most granular, and most consistent way to do this is to use the unattended setup. As you've seen in the first part of this section, the setup application accepts various options. For example, to install an Exchange 2013 server that:

- Is a multi-role server—that is, it contains both the Mailbox server role and the Client Access server roles

- Has an additional drive F:\ that will hold the mailbox database and its transaction log files

- Has a mailbox database called MDB01

You can use a command like this, also shown in Figure 2-11:

```
Setup.exe /Mode:Install /Roles:Mailbox,ClientAccess /Mdbname:MDB01 /DbFilePath F:\MDB01\MDB01.edb
/LogFolderPath F:\MDB01\LogFiles /IacceptExchangeServerLicenseTerms
```

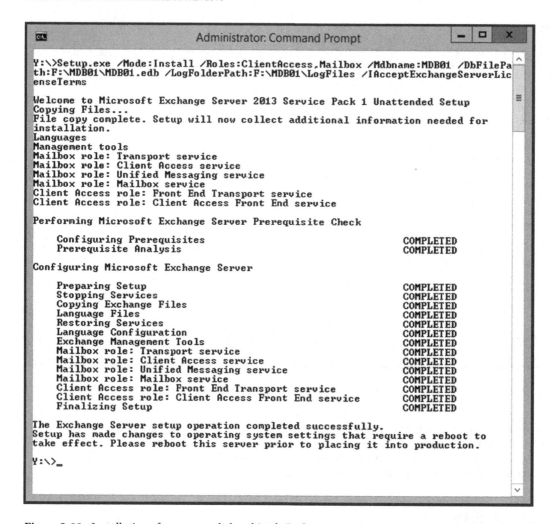

Figure 2-11. Installation of an unattended multi-role Exchange 2013 server

After the setup has finished, you reboot the server and continue with the post-installation tasks, as described in the next section.

Scripted Installation

The unattended installation of Exchange 2013 is a perfect candidate for scripting. Co-author Michel de Rooij wrote an installation script to be run on Windows Server 2008 R2 and Windows 2012 that will download, install, and configure the prerequisite software, prepare the Active Directory when needed, and install the Exchange servers—all from the command line! You can download his installation script from the Microsoft Technet gallery on http://bit.ly/UnAttendedSetup.

Post-Installation Tasks

After the initial installation of Exchange 2013, there is still quite some more work to be done before you have the server fully operational. Tasks that still need to be performed are:

- Creating accepted domains

- Creating an email address policy

- Configuring SSL certificates

- Configuring connectors

- Configuring Outlook Anywhere

- Enabling MapiHttp

Let's investigate each of these topics.

Accepted Domains

An *accepted domain* in Exchange 2013 is an SMTP domain for which an Exchange 2013 server is responsible. This means that it's going to accept mail for this SMTP domain, but it can also be used to send email. The initial accepted domain that's configured on the server is the domain name that's used in the Active Directory domain; in our example, this is the domain contoso.com. If this is the only domain that's going to be used, you're fine; but maybe you want to add additional SMTP domains?

When you want to create another accepted domain—for example, Fabrikam.com—you open the Exchange Management Shell and enter the following command:

```
New-AcceptedDomain -Name Fabrikam -DomainName Fabrikam.com -DomainType Authoritative
```

The command and its output are shown in Figure 2-12.

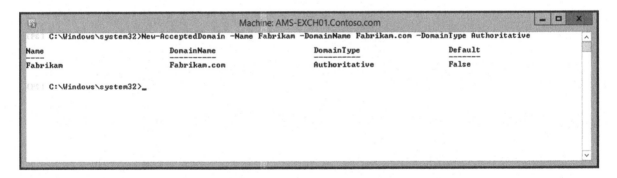

Figure 2-12. *Using the Exchange Management Shell to create an accepted domain*

Email Address Policies

An *email address policy* is a policy in Exchange 2013 that is responsible for assigning email addresses to recipients according to a predefined set of filters and formats. When a new recipient is created and it fits into such a filter, the accompanying email address is automatically assigned to the new recipient based on the defined format.

By default, there's one email address policy that filters all recipients and assigns the default accepted domain to all these new recipients. To create a new email address policy using the fabrikam.com SMTP domain, for users in the Fabrikam OU under the Accounts organizational unit, you open the Exchange Management Shell and enter the following command:

```
New-EmailAddressPolicy -Name Fabrikam -IncludedRecipients AllRecipients -RecipientContainer
"contoso.com/accounts/fabrikam" -EnabledEmailAddressTemplates "SMTP:%1@fabrikam.com"
```

This policy stamps an SMTP email address on each user that's within the reach of this policy with a format of %l@ fabrikam.com, where %l means the user's logon name in Active Directory.

To apply this newly created email address policy, you can use the following command:

```
Update-EmailAddressPolicy -Identity Fabrikam
```

Figure 2-13 shows the process completed successfully.

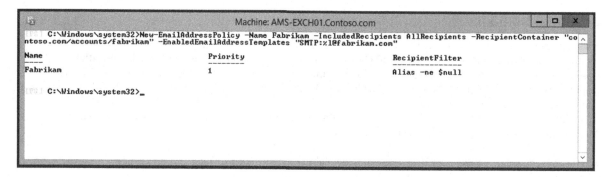

Figure 2-13. *Creating and applying an email address policy using the Exchange Management Shell*

SSL Certificates

By default, a self-signed certificate is installed on each Exchange server during installation of Exchange 2013. This self-signed certificate has the NetBIOS name of the server as its common name and the fully qualified domain name (FQDN) of the server configured in the Subject Alternative Name field of the certificate (see Figure 2-14).

***Figure 2-14.** The self-signed certificate of Exchange 2013*

The self-signed certificate works fine for *testing* OWA and the EAC, but it will cause headaches when you try to use it for Outlook Anywhere or other Web services of the Client Access server. To avoid these headaches you should always use a valid SSL certificate. Requesting an SSL certificate is next topic's subject.

Requesting an SSL Certificate Using EMS

To use the Exchange Management Shell to request, install, and configure an SSL certificate is a bit more complex. To do this, use the following commands:

```
$Data = New-ExchangeCertificate -FriendlyName "Contoso SSL Certificate" -GenerateRequest
-SubjectName "c=US, o=Contoso, cn=webmail.contoso.com" -DomainName webmail.contoso.com,
autodiscover.contoso.com -PrivateKeyExportable $true

Set-Content -path "\\ams-ad01\mgmtshare\SSLCertRequest.req" -Value $Data
```

■ **Note**   The universal security group Exchange Trusted Subsystem needs write permissions on the file share where the request will be stored.

You can use the contents of the SSLCertRequest.req file to request an SSL certificate from a certificate authority (CA). This can be an Active Directory certificate authority or a third-party certificate authority like Digicert or Comodo. A full list of Unified Communications certificate partners is in Microsoft knowledgebase article 929395, which can be found at http://bit.ly/UCCerts.

After ordering the certificate from your certificate authority, you store the new certificate on the same share and continue with the following commands:

```
Import-ExchangeCertificate –Server AMS-EXCH01 -FileData ([Byte[]]$(Get-Content -Path "\\ams-ad01\
management\certnew.cer" -Encoding byte -ReadCount 0)) | Enable-ExchangeCertificate
-Server AMS-EXCH01 -Services IIS
```

This step actually consists of three commands:

1. The Import-ExchangeCertificate, which imports the SSL certificate (the .cer file) that was returned from the CA into local certificate store of the Exchange 2013 server.

2. The Get-Content cmdlet, which actually reads the .cer file from disk and sends it as byte data to the Import-ExchangeCertificate cmdlet.

3. The Enable-ExchangeCertificate cmdlet, which receives its input from the Import-ExchangeCertificate cmdlet. This cmdlet enables the newly imported SSL certificate to be used with the Internet Information Service.

Importing an Existing SSL Certificate

There's also the possibility that you already have a valid and usable SSL certificate, perhaps from another deployment or another server, and you have exported it to a .pfx file (certificate export file). If so, then you can copy the .pfx file to the management share on the network share we used earlier.

If you want to import an existing SSL certificate on the Exchange 2013 server, you can use the following command:

```
Import-ExchangeCertificate –Server AMS-EXCH01 -FileData ([Byte[]]$(Get-Content -Path "\\ams-ad01\
management\webmail_contoso_com.pfx" -Encoding byte -ReadCount 0)) -Password:(Get-Credential).
password | Enable-ExchangeCertificate -Server AMS-EXCH01 -Services IIS
```

The `-Password:(Get-Credential).password` parameter shows a Windows popup in which you enter the password while exporting the certificate. The output of the `Import-ExchangeCertificate` command is piped directly to the `Enable-ExchangeCertificate` command to assign the IIS service to the imported SSL certificate.

Connectors

In Exchange 2013, connectors are used for sending and receiving messages. These are called *send connectors* and *receive connectors*.

Send Connector

An Exchange server by default is unable to send messages to any other server except other Exchange servers in the same organization. To achieve this functionality, a send connector has to be created. The send connector is a connector in Exchange 2013 with a namespace, cost, permissions, and one or more source Transport servers. For example, the Exchange server uses this to route messages to the Internet.

To create a new Internet send connector using the Exchange Management Shell, use the following command:

```
New-SendConnector -Name "Internet Send Connector" -Internet -AddressSpaces "*"
-DNSRoutingEnabled:$TRUE -SourceTransportServers "AMS-EXCH01"
```

Receive Connectors

Besides send connectors, Exchange 2013 also has receive connectors. A receive connector is configured as part of the Front End Transport service on the Client Access server, as well as on the Transport service of the Mailbox server and is capable of receiving SMTP messages. There are default receive connectors for receiving messages from other SMTP hosts, and there are client receive connectors used so that authenticated clients can send SMTP messages. The latter may sound strange, but the Exchange 2013 server is actually receiving messages from the client and, when needed, routes those messages to the Internet.

An out-of-the-box Exchange 2013 Client Access server has the following receive connectors:

- **Client proxy** <<ServerName>> Listening on port 587, this receive connector is used by clients like Outlook Express or Mozilla Thunderbird that want to use SMTP to send email. This port needs users to authenticate so as to use the service.

- **Default** <<ServerName>> Listening on port 25, this is the SMTP service listening "on the Internet" for SMTP messages to arrive from other hosts. This is unauthenticated access, but it is not possible to use this port to relay SMTP messages to other environments. Only messages destined to internal accepted domains are accepted.

- **Outbound proxy front end** <<ServerName>> This connector, which is only available on the Exchange 2010 Client Access server accepts messages from a send connector on a back-end server, with the front-end proxy option enabled.

The Exchange 2013 Mailbox server has the following receive connectors:

- **Client proxy** <<ServerName>> Listening on port 465, this connector receives the client's messages from the Client Access server.

- **Default** <<ServerName>> Listening on port 25, this is the receive connector used by the Mailbox server to receive SMTP connections from the Client Access server, SMTP messages from other Mailbox servers in the Exchange organization, or messages from down-level Exchange Hub Transport servers. If an Edge Transport server is used, this port receives SMTP messages from this server. The port is not used to receive message from external (i.e., the Internet) hosts.

If there's a multi-role Exchange 2013 server, the connections are a bit different. It's not possible to combine both default receive connectors, as both use the same TCP port 25. When installing an Exchange 2013 multi-role server, the default receive connector for the Mailbox server is configured to use port 2525 instead.

When installing Exchange 2013 out of the box, there's no need to configure anything on the receive connector; it just works. You configure the firewall to forward SMTP to TCP port 25 on the Exchange 2013 Client Access server, and you're ready to go.

Outlook Anywhere

On the Exchange 2013 Client Access server, Outlook Anywhere is enabled by default. The only step an administrator needs to take is to install a valid (third-party) SSL unified communications certificate and to configure an external hostname—that is, the name of the proxy server that the Outlook clients connect to. In a typical deployment, this is the same FQDN as used for OWA—that is, webmail.contoso.com.

Installing and configuring the SSL certificate has been explained earlier in this section. To configure Outlook Anywhere on the Client Access server, you open the Exchange Management Shell and enter the following command:

```
Get-OutlookAnywhere -Server AMS-EXCH01 | Set-OutlookAnywhere
-ExternalHostname webmail.contoso.com -ExternalClientsRequireSsl:$true
-ExternalClientAuthenticationMethod:Basic -InternalHostName webmail.contoso.com
-InternalClientsRequireSsl:$true -InternalClientAuthenticationMethod:Basic
```

MapiHttp

MapiHttp is the new protocol for Outlook that was introduced in Exchange 2013 SP1. For Outlook, you need to use Outlook 2013 SP1 as well, but it might be possible that this new protocol will be introduced in a future service pack or cumulative update for Outlook 2010.

MapiHttp is enabled on an organizational level, so it's turned on or off for the entire environment. To enable MapiHttp for Exchange 2013 SP1, you open the Exchange Management Shell and enter the following command:

```
Set-OrganizationConfig -MapiHttpEnabled $true
```

Please note that it can take up to three hours for the changes to take effect.

Virtual Directories

When you're deploying Exchange 2013, all virtual directories on the server are configured with their local FQDN, followed by the short name of the virtual directory—that is, https://ams-exch01.contoso.com/owa. While this works fine if there's only one Exchange server, it becomes challenging when multiple Exchange servers are installed. In this more complex scenario, you use one namespace spanning multiple Exchange servers. For example, you would use https://webmail.contoso.com/owa to cover all Client Access servers in your organization, both internally and externally.

Microsoft recommends that you use one namespace for both external URLs and internal URLs for all virtual directories. This means that webmail.contoso.com on the Internet points to your public IP address on the Internet; but at the same time, webmail.contoso.com points to the private IP address on the internal network. This is called a "split-brain DNS" configuration.

In Exchange 2013, the following directories need to be configured:

- OWA virtual directory
- ECP virtual directory
- EWS (web services) virtual directory
- Activesync virtual directory
- OAB (offline address book) virtual directory
- PowerShell virtual directory
- MapiHttp virtual directory

To begin, you open the virtual directory by double-clicking it and then changing both the internal and external URLs according to Table 2-5.

Table 2-5. *Virtual Directory Settings (note from author: I don't understand what's happening with this formatting)*

Virtual Directory	Internal URL	External URL
OWA virtual directory	https://webmail.contoso.com/owa	https://webmail.contoso.com/owa
ECP virtual directory	https://webmail.contoso.com/ecp	https://webmail.contoso.com/ecp
Activesync virtual directory	https://webmail.contoso.com/Microsoft-Server-ActiveSync	https://webmail.contoso.com/Microsoft-Server-ActiveSync
EWS virtual directory	https://webmail.contoso.com/ews/exchange.asmx	https://webmail.contoso.com/ews/exchange.asmx
OAB virtual directory	https://webmail.contoso.com/oab	https://webmail.contoso.com/oab
PowerShell virtual directory	https://webmail.contoso.com/powershell	https://webmail.contoso.com/powershell
MapiHttp virtual directory	https://webmail.contoso.com/mapi	https://webmail.contoso.com/mapi

When you look closely at Table 2-6, you'll notice that the Autodiscover virtual directory is not mentioned. This is correct because there is no need to set the internal URL and external URL property of this virtual directory. Autodiscover functionality and how to configure Autodiscover are discussed in more detail in Chapter 3.

You can change these virtual directory settings using EMS commands like Set-OWAVirtualDirectory, Set-ECPVirtualDirectory, or Set-MAPIVirtualDirectory. I find it easier to combine the Set- commands with the corresponding Get- command; for example:

```
Get-OWAVirtualDirectory –Server AMS-EXCH01 | Set-OWAVirtualDirectory –InternalURL
https://webmail.contoso.com/owa -ExternalURL https://webmail.contoso.com/owa
```

or

```
Get-MAPIVirtualDirectory –Server AMS-EXCH01 | Set-MAPIVirtualDirectory –InternalURL
https://webmail.contoso.com/mapi -ExternalURL https://webmail.contoso.com/mapi
```

You can combine the commands to configure all virtual directories in one small script whereby the script takes the domain name as a parameter and where all the URLs are automatically constructed. Such a script would look like this:

```
<#
    .SYNOPSIS
    Change_vdir_Settings.ps1
    Jaap Wesselius
    mail@jaapwesselius.com

    THIS CODE IS MADE AVAILABLE AS IS, WITHOUT WARRANTY OF ANY KIND. THE ENTIRE
    RISK OF THE USE OR THE RESULTS FROM THE USE OF THIS CODE REMAINS WITH THE USER.

    .PARAMETER DomainName
    Specifies the domainname being used to construct all URL's

    .EXAMPLE
    .\Change_vdir_Settings.ps1 contoso.com

#>

$ServerName = $env:COMPUTERNAME
$Domain = $args[0]
$Server = "webmail"

$External = "$Server.$Domain"
$AutoD = "autodiscover.$Domain"

Write-Host "The following FQDN will be used for configuring the virtual directories: $External"
Write-Host "The following FQDN will be used for configuring autodiscover: $AutoD"

Set-OWAVirtualDirectory -Server $ServerName -ExternalURL https://$External/owa
-InternalURL https://$External/owa

Set-ECPVirtualDirectory -Server $ServerName -ExternalURL https://$External/ecp -InternalURL
https://$External/ecp

Set-ActiveSyncVirtualDirectory -Server $ServerName -ExternalURL https://$External/Microsoft-Server-
ActiveSync -InternalURL https://$External/Microsoft-Server-ActiveSync
```

```
Set-WebServicesVirtualDirectory -Server $ServerName -ExternalURL https://$External/ews/exchange.asmx
-InternalURL https://$External/ews/exchange.asmx

Set-OABVirtualDirectory -Server $ServerName -ExternalURL https://$External/OAB -InternalURL
https://$External/OAB

Set-PowershellVirtualDirectory -Server $ServerName -ExternalURL https://$External/Powershell
-InternalURL https://$External/Powershell

Set-ClientAccessServer -Server $ServerName -AutoDiscoverServiceInternalUri https://$AutoD/
autodiscover/autodiscover.xml

Set-OutlookAnywhere -Server $ServerName -ExternalHostname $External
-ExternalClientsRequireSsl:$true

Set-MAPIVirtualDirectory -Server $ServerName -InternalURL https://$External/MAPI -ExternalURL
https://$External/MAPI -IISAuthenticationMethods Ntlm, OAuth, Negotiate

Write-Host "Do not forget to issue an IISRESET command."
```

You can download this script from the Apress website, copy it to the server's local hard drive, and execute it from the Exchange Management Shell; for example, \change_vdir_settings.ps1 contoso.com.

Now, all your virtual directories will be configured with the correct internal and external URLs. Also, the Autodiscover service connection point will be correctly configured.

Installation and Configuration of Exchange 2013 Using the GUI

The main focus of this book is on administering your Exchange 2013 environment using PowerShell or the Exchange Management Shell. However, if you're a novice Exchange 2013 administrator, you might want to install and configure your first Exchange 2013 server using the Graphical User Interface (GUI) and then learn how to use PowerShell for managing your Exchange 2013 environment as you read through this book. Therefore, this section can help you easily install and configure your first Exchange 2013 server.

Install Exchange 2013

The installation and configuration steps of the prerequisite software are no different from those explained earlier in this chapter, so there's no need to review those here. When you run the GUI setup, it will automatically make the changes to Active Directory, so there's no need to run setup separately to achieve this result.

Now, to install Exchange 2013, you follow these steps:

1. Log on to the server as a member of the Enterprise Admins security group. Besides being a member of this security group, you also need to make sure the account is a member of the Schema Admins security group. You need to be a member of these groups in order to write to the configuration partition and the schema partition.

2. Navigate to the installation media. This can be a physical DVD, an ISO image mounted to a virtual machine, or the extracted binaries on a fileshare on the network. Start the setup application by double-clicking setup.exe.

3. Note that Microsoft has made significant changes to the Exchange Server setup process. The first window that's shown asks whether the setup application needs to check for updates. If updates are available, the setup application will download them and automatically install them. Leave the default settings (Connect to the Internet and Check for Updates), and click Next to continue and follow the wizard.

4. Setup will now start copying the files needed to install Exchange 2013. When the introduction screen appears, click Next to continue.

5. Read the license agreement, and if you agree with the terms, select I Accept the Terms in This License Agreement, and click Next to continue.

6. The window for recommended settings asks you to select whether or not you want to use the recommended settings. There's not much information on this screen, but when you select Use Recommended Settings, it enables the error reporting and the Customer Experience Improvement Program (CEIP), which collect information on your hardware and how you use Exchange Server. If you agree with this, select Use Recommended Settings; if not, select Don't Use Recommended Settings. Click Next to continue.

7. The next screen, shown in Figure 2-15, is the most important in the installation process, as it's here that you select which server roles to install. Select the Mailbox role and the Client Access role to have both installed on the server. Note the checkbox for Automatically Install Windows Server Roles and Features That Are Required To Install Exchange Server. This makes it possible to automatically install these prerequisites instead of installing them manually. Since this box is checked by default, leave it this way. Click Next to continue.

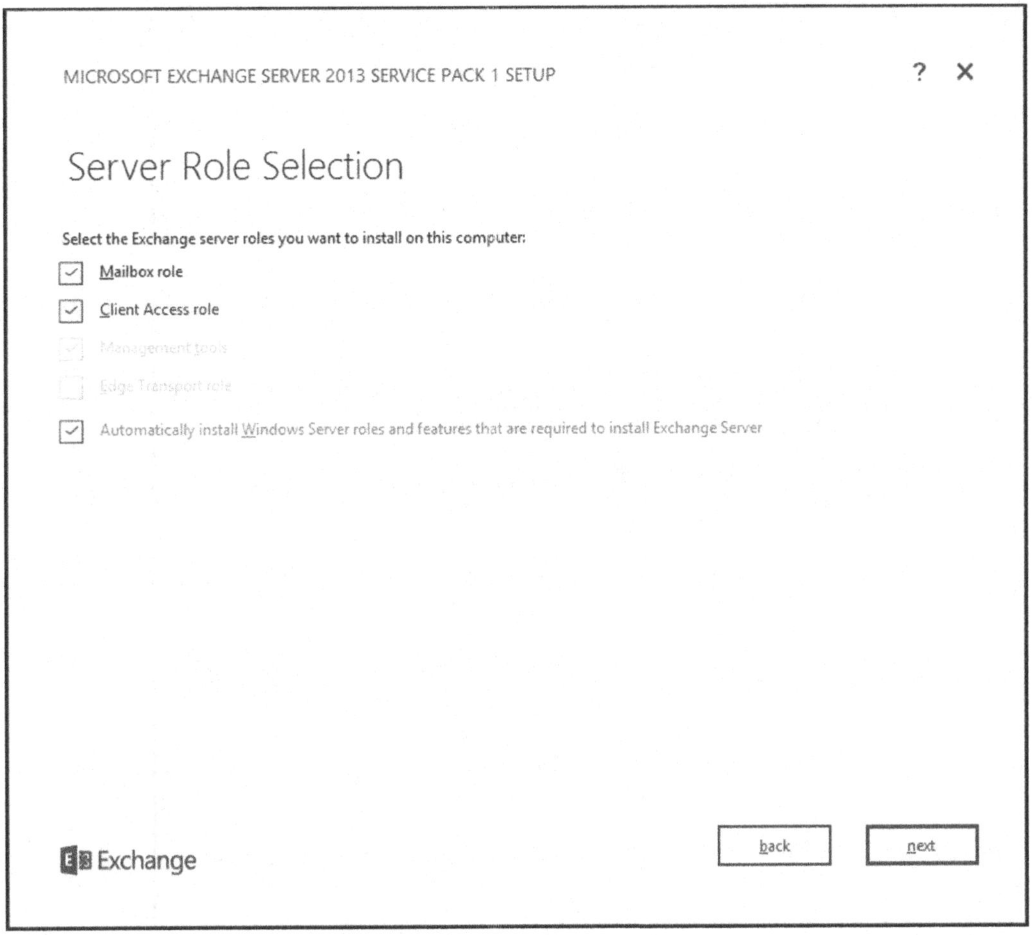

Figure 2-15. *Server role selection window during setup*

8. If you want to install only the Mailbox server, make sure *only* the Mailbox server role is selected. If you want to install a dedicated Client Access server, make sure *only* the Client Access server role is selected.

9. On the Installation space and location screen, you can change the location where the Exchange 2013 files are installed, if needed. Click Next to continue.

10. Since this is the first Exchange 2013 server in your environment, the name of the Exchange Organization needs to be entered. This is similar to the /OrganizationName discussed in the previous section. Enter the name of the new organization—in this example, this is CONTOSO. This is shown in Figure 2-16. In this same screen, there's also the option to configure your Active Directory for a split permissions security model. This is covered in more detail in Chapter 10; for now, just leave this checkbox unchecked. Click Next to continue.

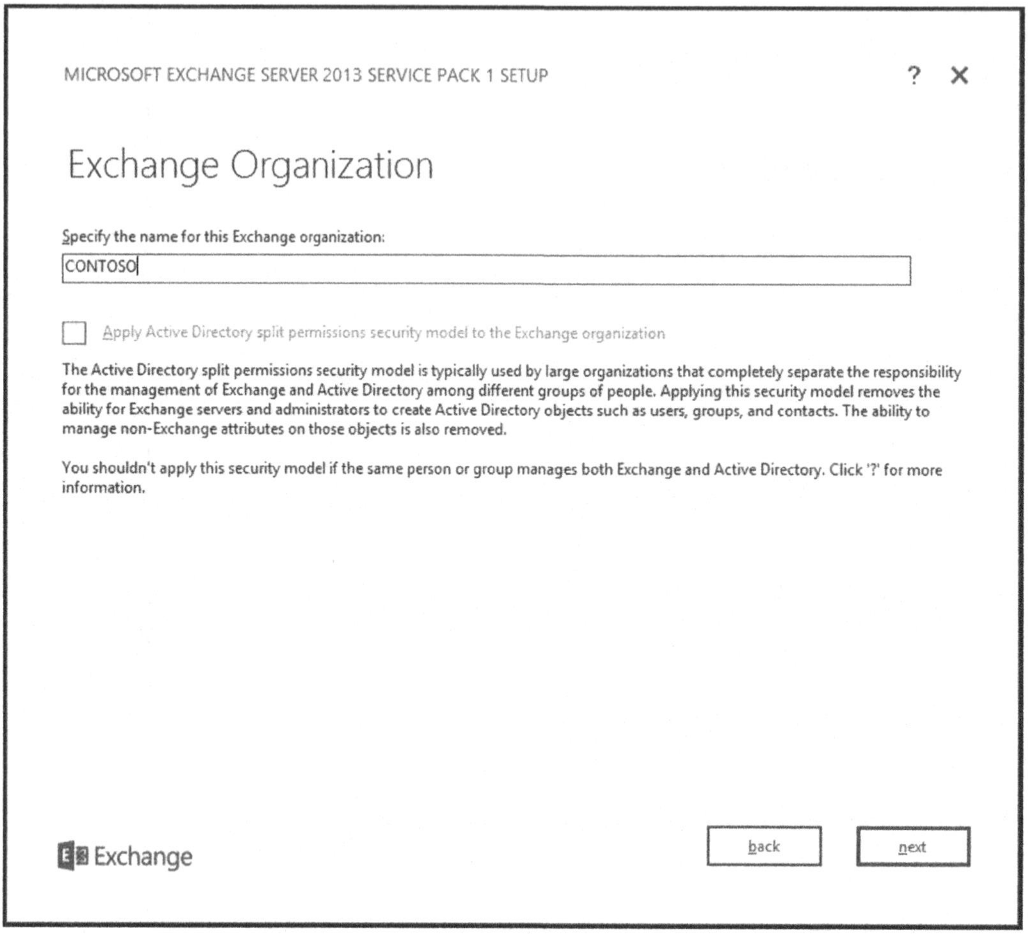

Figure 2-16. *Enter the name of the Exchange organization*

11. Exchange 2013 comes with a default anti-malware solution. It is not as complete as, for example, the earlier Forefront protection for Exchange Server, but it can certainly help keep your messaging environment clean. By default, the anti-malware is enabled; you can disable it if you want to use another (third-party) solution, but check with your anti-malware vendor first. Internet access is required to download the latest anti-malware updates. Click Next to continue.

12. The setup program has now gathered enough information to proceed with the installation and will perform a readiness check. In a green-field scenario you'll get a warning message that setup is going to perform an organization change using the /PrepareAD option and that no Exchange 2007 servers have been detected in this topology. If you think about this message, it makes sense and therefore you can continue with the installation process by clicking the Install button. Now it's time to wait. . . .

The setup consists of 15 different steps. The screen is updated with every step, and within every step, the progress is indicated by a blue bar, as shown in Figure 2-17.

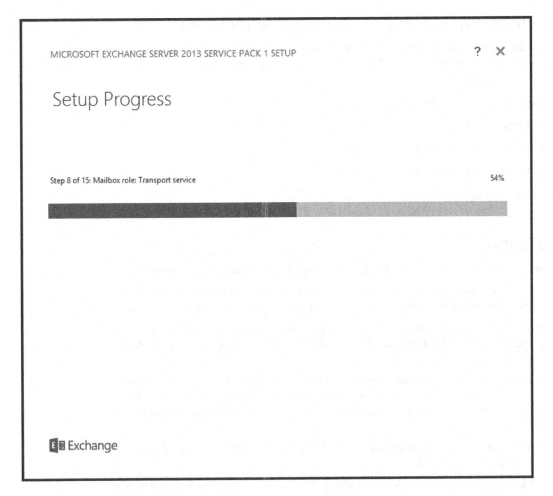

Figure 2-17. *The blue bar indicating progress in the setup application*

13. When setup is completed, you're given the option of selecting Launch Exchange Administration Center After Finishing Exchange Setup. Doing so will start the Exchange Admin Center (EAC), so that you can continue the post-configuration tasks. But whether you select this or not, click the Finish button to finish the setup application.

Post-Installation Tasks Using the Exchange Admin Center

Similar to an unattended setup of Exchange 2013, you have to perform some post-installation tasks using the GUI (i.e., the Exchange Admin Center). Again, the tasks that need to be performed are:

- Creating accepted domains

- Creating an email address policy

- Configuring SSL certificates

- Creating a send connector

- Configuring a receive connector

Let's cover each of these topics.

Accepted Domains

When you need to create another accepted domain—for example, `Fabrikam.com`—you follow these steps:

1. Log on to the new Exchange 2013 server as an administrator, open a browser, and navigate to the Exchange Admin Center (EAC)—that is, `https://localhost/ecp`.

    (For now you can ignore the SSL security warning; this is caused by the self-signed certificate, combined with the fact that you are accessing the server using the localhost name.)

2. On the logon page, use the domain administrator account to log on to the EAC. If this account is *not* the account that was used to install Exchange 2013, make sure that this account is also a member of the Organization Management security group in Active Directory.

3. To configure an accepted domain, select Mail Flow in the Features pane and then select the Accepted Domains tab.

4. Click the + icon to start the new accepted domain wizard. Give the new accepted domain a display name (this is just a cosmetic name; it's how the accepted domain will show up in the EAC), like "Fabrikam," and then enter the actual SMTP domain name—that is, `fabrikam.com`. Leave the new accepted domain as an authoritative domain and click Save to continue.

Email Address Policies

To create a new email address policy using the `fabrikam.com` SMTP domain, for users in the OU=Accounts organizational unit, you can follow these steps:

1. Assuming you're still logged on to the EAC, select Mail Flow from the Features pane and then the Email Address Policies tab, next to Accepted Domains. In the wizard, click the + icon to add a new email address policy.

2. Give the policy a name. As with the accepted domain, this is only for display purposes; enter something like "Fabrikam."

3. Click the + icon to select an SMTP domain. This is one of the accepted domains available on the Exchange 2013 server. Use the drop-down box to select the accepted domain `fabrikam.com`, which was configured in the previous section.

4. Select the proper format of the email address that will be assigned to users. When chosen, click Save to continue with the wizard.

5. By default, a new email address policy will be used for all recipients, but in the wizard it's also possible to select other recipients, such as mail users, resource mailboxes, or mail-enabled groups.

6. Scroll down and click the Add a Rule button. Here, you select a predefined set of rules that can be used to filter recipients. For example, you can select an organizational unit in Active Directory, or recipients with a certain value in the "company" attribute, or those with one of the 15 custom attributes. In our example, we select Recipient Container, and in the popup, we click on the correct container—that is, Accounts. Click OK to continue and click Save to finish the wizard.

SSL Certificates

Requesting an SSL certificate in EAC is a bit easier than using PowerShell, but storing the request file and the certificate on a file share are mandatory here as well. Use these steps to request an SSL certificate using EAC:

1. Assuming the EAC is still open in your browser, navigate to the Servers option in the Features pane and then click the Certificates tab.

2. Click the + icon to start a new certificate request. Select Create a Request for a Certificate From a Certification Authority and click Next to continue.

3. Enter a friendly name for the certificate—something like "Contoso SSL certificate" and click Next to continue.

4. A wild-card certificate is fully supported, but since we want to use a unified communications SSL certificate with a subject alternative name, leave this blank and click Next to continue.

5. Use the Browse button to select a Client Access server for this certificate and click Next to continue. This is an important step if you have multiple Client Access servers. If you request a new SSL certificate, the private key of this particular server is used. When you receive the certificate from the CA, it is important to finish the request on this same Exchange server to make sure the proper private key is used in the SSL certificate. If you try to finish the certificate request on another server, you'll end up with a certificate without a private key. Needless to say, this is useless for an Exchange 2013 server!

6. In the next screen, there's the option to specify an FQDN for every service offered by Exchange 2013. The most important ones are the FQDN for OWA (webmail.contoso.com) and the FQDN for Autodiscover (autodiscover.contoso.com). Scroll down to make sure you covered all the services. For services not used, or when using the same FQDN as OWA, you can empty the field using the small pencil icon. When done, click Next to continue.

7. When there are multiple accepted domains in the Exchange environment, the wizard will show them all, and there's the option to add them to the certificate as well. For a simple scenario, remove all additional names until only the autodiscover.contoso.com and webmail.contoso.com are left.

Figure 2-18 shows the names Contoso.com and Fabrikam.com that you need to remove.

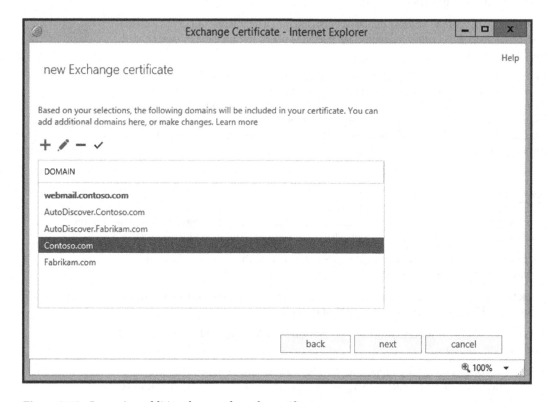

Figure 2-18. *Removing additional names from the certificate request*

8. Click Next to continue.

9. Fill in the required information, such as organization name, country, city, and so on, as shown in the WHOIS database where all the Internet domain details are stored. If there's a mismatch, the certification authority will most likely push back the certificate request. Click Next to continue.

10. Enter the location where the request file will be stored (see Figure 2-19). This location is a UNC path like \\ams-fs01\management\certrequest.req. Don't forget to enter the filename of the request file as well.

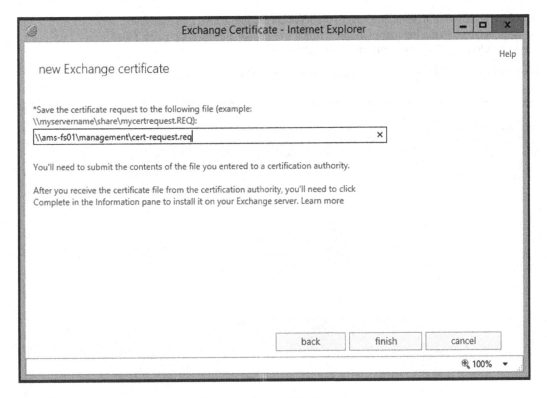

Figure 2-19. *Location of the request file, entered in UNC format*

■ **Note** The universal security group Exchange Trusted Subsystem needs Full Control permissions on the file share where the request will be stored.

11. Click Finish to save the request file and end the new Exchange Certificate wizard.

   The request file is a text file with a lot of characters in a fully random order, not readable by a normal human being. The content of this request file is used to request the SSL certificate from a certification authority (CA).

12. Once processed by the CA, the certificate is returned. Store this file in the same location or in another location that is accessible over the network, and return to the EAC.

13. In the EAC, select Servers in the left-hand menu and select Certificates in the top menu. Select the Contoso SSL Certificate request created earlier; you'll see that its status is "Pending request."

14. In the right-hand pane under Status, click Complete. In the popup screen, enter the location where the file that was returned by the CA is stored—that is \\ams-fs01\management\webmail-contoso.com-cer and click OK.

   The certificate is now imported onto the Exchange Server. If all goes well, it should be listed as "valid" and it's almost ready to use. The last step to accomplish this is to assign services like IIS to the certificate.

15. To assign services to the certificate, make sure it is selected in the EAC and then click on the pencil icon in the top menu. In the certificate details in the left-hand pane, select Services. Select the IIS service and click Save to continue.

The certificate should now have IIS listed as the assigned service (see Figure 2-20).

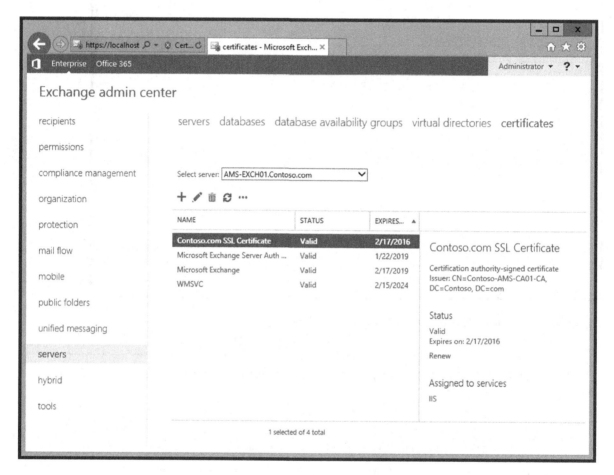

Figure 2-20. *IIS as now assigned to the new certificate*

Importing an Existing SSL Certificate

There's also the possibility that you already have a valid and usable SSL certificate, possibly from another deployment or another server, and you have it exported to a .pfx file (certificate export file). If so, you copy the .pfx file to the management share on the network share we used earlier.

1. Log on to the EAC, select Servers in the Features pane and click the Certificates tab.

2. Click on the three dots just above the list of certificates and select Import Exchange Certificate.

3. In the Import Exchange Certificate wizard, enter the location where the .pfx file is stored. This is a UNC path like \\ams-fs01\management\exported-certificate.pfx and enter the password used while exporting (see Figure 2-21). Click Next to continue.

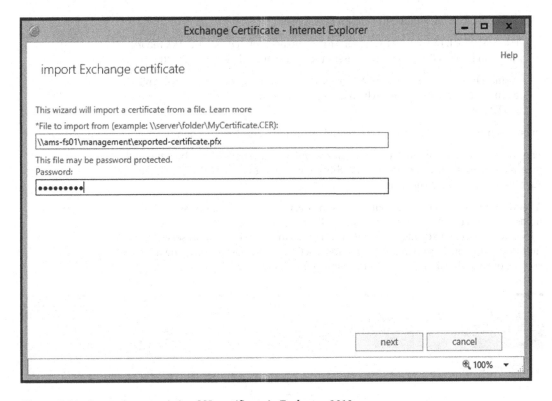

Figure 2-21. *Importing an existing SSL certificate in Exchange 2013*

4. Click on the + icon to add the Exchange 2013 server that you want to import the SSL certificate onto and click Finish to close the window. The SSL certificate is now imported and Exchange services can now be assigned to the SSL certificate, just as when you create new SSL certificates.

Connectors

In Exchange 2013, connectors are used for sending and receiving messages. These are called *send connectors* and *receive connectors*.

Send Connector

An Exchange server is by default not able to send messages to any other server. To achieve this function, however, a send connector has to be created. The send connector is a connector in Exchange 2013 with a namespace, cost, permissions, and one or more source Transport servers. The Exchange server uses this to route messages, for example, to the Internet.

To create a new connector that will send messages to the Internet, use the following steps:

1. Log on to the EAC and select Mail Flow in the Features pane and then click the Send Connectors tab.

2. Click on the + icon to start the new send connector wizard. Enter a name for the send connector—something like "Internet send connector"—and click the Internet radio button. Click Next to continue.

3. There are two ways the connector can send messages:

   a. Use MX, which means the Exchange Hub Transport service uses the MX records found in public DNS and then accesses the destination SMTP host directly.

   b. A smart host, which means all messages are delivered to one SMTP host, typically an Internet service provider, which in turn delivers the message to the destination SMTP host.

4. In our example we use MX, which is selected by default. Click Next to continue.

5. The address space for an Internet connector is typically an asterisk (*), which basically means all external SMTP domains. Click the + icon, type * in the FQDN field, and click Save, then click Next to continue.

6. A send connector also needs a source transport server. This is a Mailbox server (which also holds the Hub Transport service) that will deliver the messages to the Internet. Click the + icon and select an Exchange server that will act as the source transport server. Choose Add to add the source server to the list, and click OK. Click Finish to close the new send connector wizard and save all the information (see Figure 2-22).

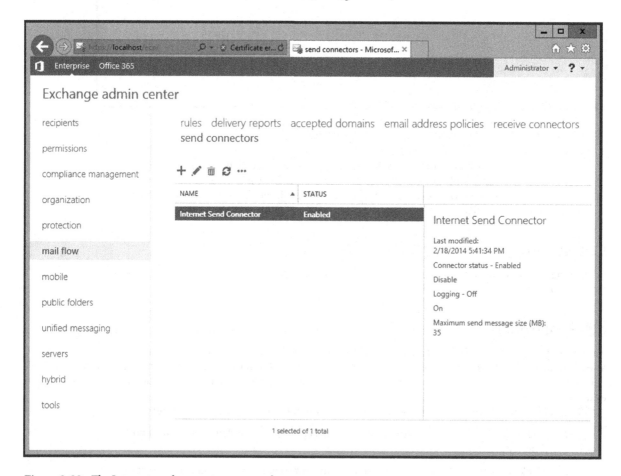

Figure 2-22. The Internet send connector, now ready to use

Receive Connector

Just as when installing Exchange 2013 unattended, there's no need to configure anything on the receive connector; it just works. You configure the firewall to forward SMTP to port 25 on the Exchange 2013 Client Access server, and you're ready to go.

Outlook Anywhere

Exchange 2013 does not have the option to configure Outlook Anywhere using the EAC, so you're stuck to configure this using EMS. To configure Outlook Anywhere on the Client Access server, open the Exchange Management Shell and enter the following command:

```
Get-OutlookAnywhere -Server AMS-EXCH01 | Set-OutlookAnywhere
-ExternalHostname webmail.contoso.com -ExternalClientsRequireSsl:$true
-ExternalClientAuthenticationMethod:Basic -InternalHostName webmail.contoso.com
-InternalClientsRequireSsl:$true -InternalClientAuthenticationMethod:Basic
```

MapiHttp

Just as with Outlook Anywhere, there's no way to configure MapiHttp using the EAC, so again you have to use EMS to enable this. To configure MapiHttp, open an EMS window and enter the following command:

```
Set-OrganizationConfig -MapiHttpEnabled $true
```

Please note that it can take up to three hours for the changes to take effect.

External URLs

As designed, all virtual directories in Exchange 2013 are configured with their local FQDN—that is, `https://ams-exch01.contoso.com/owa`. While this works fine if there's only one Exchange server, it becomes challenging when multiple Exchange servers are installed. In this scenario, you would use one namespace spanning multiple Exchange servers. For example, use `https://webmail.contoso.com/owa` to cover all Client Access servers in your organization.

Microsoft recommends that you use one namespace for both external URLs and internal URLs for all virtual directories. This means that `webmail.contoso.com` on the Internet points to your public IP address on the Internet; but at the same time, `webmail.contoso.com` points to your private IP address on the internal network. This is called a "split-brain DNS" configuration.

In Exchange 2013, the following directories need to be configured:

- OWA virtual directory

- ECP virtual directory

- EWS (web services) virtual directory

- Activesync virtual directory

- OAB (offline address book) virtual directory

- PowerShell virtual directory

- Autodiscover virtual directory

- Mapi virtual directory

In the EAC, click on the Servers in the Features pane and click the Virtual Directories tab. All virtual directories will be shown here (see Figure 2-23). If there are multiple servers, you can use the Select Server drop-down box to select a particular Exchange server to configure.

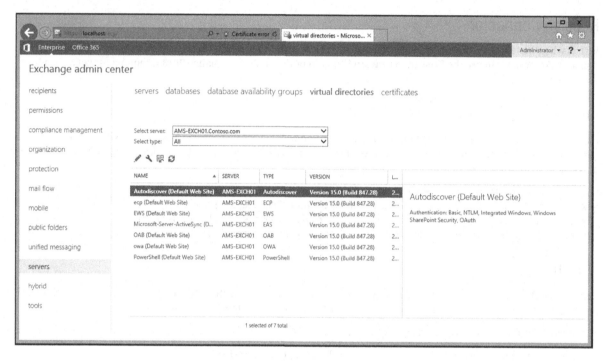

Figure 2-23. *Using the EAC to configure the virtual directories*

■ **Note** Unfortunately, the MapiHttp virtual directory cannot be configured using the EAC so you have to switch to EMS to configure this. At the time of this writing it is unknown if this will be changed by Microsoft in a later cumulative update or service pack.

To configure the virtual directories for use on the Internet, select Servers in the Features pane and click the Virtual Directories tab. Click on the wrench icon in the toolbar. In the Configure External Access Domain window, use the + icon to select one or more Client Access servers to configure. In the text box shown in Figure 2-24, you would enter the externally accessible domain name, such as webmail.contoso.com. When done, click Save and wait for the wizard to finish the configuration of the external domain name.

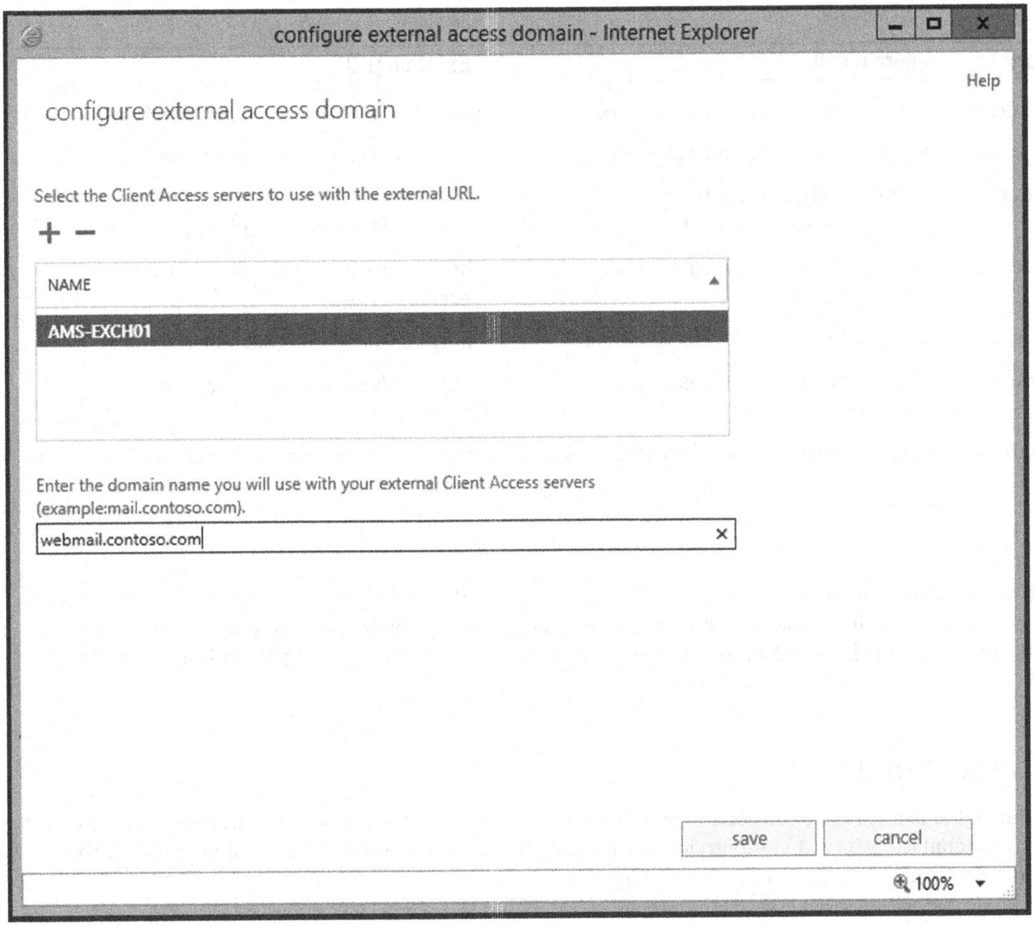

Figure 2-24. Configuring the external virtual directories

In EAC, it is unfortunately not possible to use a similar wizard to configure the virtual directories for internal usage, so these have to be configured manually, step by step.

To begin, open the virtual directory by double-clicking it and then changing both the internal and external URLs according to Table 2-6.

Table 2-6. *Virtual Directory Settings*

Virtual Directory	Internal URL	External URL
OWA virtual directory	`https://webmail.contoso.com/owa`	`https://webmail.contoso.com/owa`
ECP virtual directory	`https://webmail.contoso.com/ecp`	`https://webmail.contoso.com/ecp`
Activesync virtual directory	`https://webmail.contoso.com/` `Microsoft-Server-ActiveSync`	`https://webmail.contoso.com/` `Microsoft-Server-ActiveSync`
EWS virtual directory	`https://webmail.contoso.com/ews/` `exchange.asmx`	`https://webmail.contoso.com/ews/` `exchange.asmx`
OAB virtual directory	`https://webmail.contoso.com/oab`	`https://webmail.contoso.com/oab`
PowerShell virtual directory	`https://webmail.contoso.com/` `powershell`	`https://webmail.contoso.com/` `powershell`
Autodiscover virtual directory	`https://autodiscover.contoso.com/` `autodiscover`	`https://autodiscover.contoso.com/` `autodiscover`

Making all these changes manually using the EAC is quite some work and it's prone to error, so it's better to use the Exchange Management Shell to make all the settings, as explained in the unattended setup section earlier in this chapter. The `change_vdir_settings.ps1` PowerShell script as outlined in the unattended section is a nice tool to configure this.

Service Connection Point

Outlook 2007 and higher use a service connection point in Active Directory for Autodiscover purposes. (Autodiscover will be discussed in detail in Chapter 3.) The service connection point can only be configured using EMS. Use the following command to configure the service connection point:

```
Get-ClientAccessServer -Identity AMS-EXCH01 | Set-ClientAccessServer -AutoDiscoverServiceInternalUri
https://autodiscover.contoso.com/autodiscover/autodiscover.xml
```

This setting is included in the `change_vdir_settings.ps1` script.

Although very basic, your server is now fully configured to be used as a production server. If you want more information regarding recipients like mailboxes, public folders, or distribution groups, these will be discussed in Chapter 4.

Coexistence with Previous Versions of Exchange Server

The previous section was about installing a brand-new Exchange Server 2013 SP1 environment, called a green-field installation. While there's nothing wrong with this, the chances are you already have an older Exchange environment running in your organization. If this existing environment is based on Exchange Server 2007 or Exchange Server 2010, then it is possible to create a coexistence scenario into which the new Exchange Server 2013 SP1 can be installed, and you can gradually transition your mailboxes to Exchange Server 2013 SP1.

If your existing environment is based on Exchange Server 2003, however, then you'll run into difficulties. A coexistence scenario between Exchange 2003 and Exchange 2013 is impossible, blocked by hardcoding in the setup application. In this case, you will have to either (1) upgrade Exchange Server 2003 to Exchange Server 2010 and then move on to Exchange Server 2013 SP1; or (2) build a brand-new Active Directory with a green-field Exchange

Server 2013 SP1 and perform an *interorg migration*; that is, you move your user accounts and mailboxes to the new environment using a tool like Active Directory Migration Toolkit (ADMT) or a third-party migration tool. Migrating from Exchange Server 2003 using these options is beyond the scope of this book.

Here, we cover how to transition from either Exchange Server 2007 or Exchange Server 2010 to Exchange Server 2013 SP1. In the preparation and installation phases, the transitions from Exchange Server 2007 or Exchange Server 2010 to Exchange Server 2013 are similar. The differences occur when you start to implement Exchange Server 2013 SP1. That is, proxying and redirection differ greatly in an Exchange Server 2010/2013 scenario compared to an Exchange Server 2007/2013 scenario.

Therefore, we deal initially here with both scenarios up to the point when things start to be different, then each scenario is discussed individually. Also, when I talk about "previous versions of Exchange Server," I am referencing *both* Exchange Server 2007 and Exchange Server 2010 unless otherwise noted.

■ **Note** Creating a coexistence scenario with Exchange Server 2007 or Exchange Server 2010 is possible only with Exchange Server 2013 RTM CU1 or higher. So when implementing Exchange 2013 SP1, this should not be a problem.

Transition to Exchange Server 2013

Transitioning from Exchange Server 2007 or 2010 is relatively easy because Exchange 2013 is simply introduced *into* the current Exchange Server environment. This saves you the hassle of building a new Active Directory environment, moving all your resources to that new Active Directory, and working around any problems that might occur when you're keeping both directories in sync during the coexistence phase.

I deliberately say "relatively easy" because it still takes quite some time to accomplish this task and to work around some difficulties caused by incompatibilities between the previous versions and Exchange 2013. Just as in the past, it's not possible to have the Exchange 2013 Client Access server (CAS) work directly with an earlier version's Mailbox server. Even worse, an Exchange 2013 CAS won't work directly with an Exchange Server 2007 CAS (like proxying requests). As a result, in the coexistence scenario, all client requests need to be redirected to the 2007 CAS (except for Autodiscover). The client in this case creates a new connection with the 2007 CAS and continues working. This is the reason you need an additional namespace with a name like legacy.contoso.com. (This is discussed in more detail later on in this chapter.) If you have been working with Exchange Server for a long time, this requirement will probably sound familiar, as the same situation existed when you upgraded from Exchange Server 2003 to Exchange Server 2010.

Upgrading from Exchange Server 2010 to Exchange Server 2013 works better in this case. When you access an Exchange 2013 CAS while trying to retrieve information from an Exchange 2010 Mailbox server, the request will be proxied to the Exchange 2010 CAS, so there's no need for Exchange 2013 to redirect the request to the other CAS. In this case, the client keeps its connection with the Exchange 2013 CAS, and this server is responsible for communication with the Exchange 2010 CAS.

The upgrade steps to move from Exchange Server 2007 or Exchange Server 2010 to Exchange 2013 are as follows:

1. Preparing Active Directory.

2. Installing the first Exchange 2013 Mailbox server.

3. Installing the first Exchange 2013 Client Access server.

4. Configuring namespaces and client access redirection (only needed for Exchange Server 2007).

5. Changing client access to contact Exchange 2013 CAS directly.

6. Changing SMTP routing from the previous version of Exchange Server to Exchange 2013.

7. Moving resources from the previous version of Exchange Server to Exchange Server 2013.

8. Decommissioning the previous version of Exchange Server.

The first three steps are similar to the steps as described in the previous section so I won't go into detail about these here. Instead, I'll discuss the specific prerequisites when it comes to creating the coexistence scenario and then move on to the fourth step in the process.

Prerequisites

The prerequisites for introducing Exchange 2013 SP1 in an existing environment are similar to those described in the green-field scenario. The Domain Controllers need to be at least Windows Server 2003 R2 SP2, while the Forest Functional Level (FFL) and the Domain Functional Level (DFL) must both be at least at Windows 2003 level.

When you're running Exchange 2007, all your servers in the environment should be at least running Exchange 2007 Service Pack 3 and Update Rollup 10 or higher. If you're running Exchange 2010, all your servers in the environment should be at least Exchange 2010 Service Pack 3 or higher.

When these requirements are met, you can prepare the Active Directory for the introduction of Exchange 2013 SP1 using the following commands:

```
Setup.exe /PrepareSchema /IAcceptExchangeServerLicenseTerms
Setup.exe /PrepareAD /IAcceptExchangeServerLicenseTerms
Setup.exe /PrepareDomain /IAcceptExchangeServerLicenseTerms
```

Or, if you are using multiple Active Directory domains, you can replace this last command with the following command for easy deployment:

```
Setup.exe /PrepareAllDomains /IAcceptExchangeServerLicenseTerms
```

▪ **Note**   Please note the absence of the /OrganizationName in the second command. This is because an Exchange organization already exists in Active Directory so there's no need for a new organization name.

When Active Directory is fully prepared, you can introduce the first Exchange 2013 SP1 server into the existing organization. Please refer to the previous section to determine which method of installation fits your situation best.

Configuring the Namespaces and Coexistence

When installing Exchange Server 2013 into an existing Exchange Server 2010 or Exchange Server 2007 environment, you have to configure what are called *namespaces*. A namespace is a name that clients use to access the Exchange services, like webmail.contoso.com or autodiscover.contoso.com. As you will see in the following sections, there are differences in how Exchange Server 2007 and Exchange Server 2010 handle namespaces.

Namespaces and Coexistence with Exchange Server 2007

When you are installing Exchange 2013 into an Exchange Server 2007 environment, namespaces are extremely important because they determine how a particular client accesses the platform. Clients use these namespaces to make a distinct difference between accessing Exchange 2013 and accessing Exchange Server 2007. They use a technique called *redirection* to switch from Exchange 2013 to Exchange Server 2007.

Namespaces with Exchange Server 2007

In the original Exchange Server 2007 environment, two namespaces are typically used:

- `webmail.contoso.com` Used for all HTTPS-based services, including Outlook Anywhere

- `autodiscover.contoso.com` Used by external Outlook clients for discovering the internal Exchange configuration

In Exchange 2013, this namespace planning is not very different, but since Exchange Server 2007 and Exchange 2013 are not compatible, we have to come up with a solution for the coexistence scenario whereby both Exchange Server 2007 and Exchange 2013 are accessible. Needless to say, this does not work with a single namespace.

When Exchange 2013 is initially installed into an existing Exchange Server 2007 environment, nothing happens with regard to clients. At one point, the client access is changed from the Exchange Server 2007 CAS to the Exchange 2013 CAS. When the mailbox is located on an Exchange 2013 Mailbox server, this is fine, but when the mailbox is still located on the Exchange Server 2007 Mailbox server, things don't go so well. The client request is redirected from the 2013 CAS to the 2007 CAS to be processed there. You will see this happen in OWA, where the URL in the navigation bar changes from the 2013 CAS to the 2007 CAS.

Since the FQDN `webmail.contoso.com` is pointing to the 2013 CAS, a new FQDN has to be created to access the old 2007 CAS. Microsoft typically uses the FQDN `legacy.contoso.com` for this (see Figure 2-25).

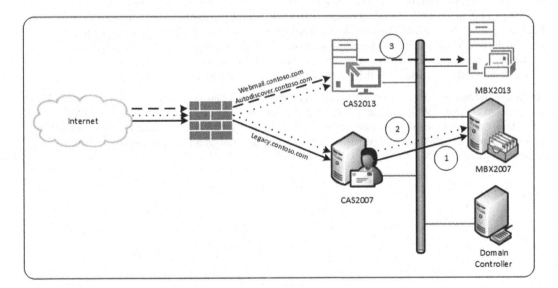

Figure 2-25. *Coexistence scenario with Exchange Server 2007*

In Figure 2-25, the three scenarios are clearly visible.

1. The solid line is the original situation, in which clients connect via `webmail.contoso.com` and `autodiscover.contoso.com` to the 2007 CAS. The CAS retrieves the information from the 2007 Mailbox server.

2. The dotted line is the coexistence scenario. Clients connect using `webmail.contoso.com` and `autodiscover.contoso.com` to the Exchange 2013 CAS. Requests for `webmail.contoso.com` are now redirected to the 2007 CAS using the `legacy.contoso.com` FQDN. The 2007 CAS retrieves the information from the 2007 Mailbox server and returns the information directly to the clients.

3. The dashed line is the final situation. Clients connect to the Exchange 2013 CAS using the `webmail.contoso.com` and `autodiscover.contoso.com` FQDN, and the requests are proxied directly to the Exchange 2013 Mailbox server.

Unfortunately this is not identical for all protocols:

- *Outlook Web App* is redirected from the Exchange 2013 CAS to the 2007 CAS. This conforms with the three bullets mentioned above.

- *Outlook Anywhere* is not redirected, but the client requests (HTTPS) are proxied from the Exchange 2013 CAS to the 2007 CAS. This server retrieves the information from the 2007 Mailbox server and the information is returned to the clients through the 2013 CAS.

- *Exchange activesync* and *Exchange web services* are proxied from the Exchange 2013 CAS to the 2013 Mailbox server, and then proxied to the 2007 CAS.

- *POP3 and IMAP4* are proxied from the Exchange 2013 CAS to the 2007 CAS.

- *Autodiscover* is a bit different. In an Exchange Server 2007/2013 coexistence scenario, the Autodiscover requests are sent to the Exchange 2013 CAS, which proxies them to (1) the 2013 Mailbox server if the user's mailbox exists on Exchange 2013; or (2) a down-level Client Access server if the user's mailbox exists on a previous version of Exchange Server. This is true both for internal clients who get the 2013 CAS from the service connection point (SCP) and for external clients who construct the URL based on the user's SMTP address.

Outlook clients in an Exchange Server 2007 environment on the internal network connect directly to the Mailbox server where the mailbox is hosted. When Exchange 2013 is introduced into the existing Exchange Server 2007 environment, this does not change the way Outlook clients connect to the Exchange Server 2007 mailbox. But as soon as the mailbox is moved to the 2013 Mailbox server, the Outlook client automatically switches to Outlook Anywhere and starts to connect to the 2013 CAS.

■ **Note** There's a distinct difference between *proxying* and *redirection*. In a proxy situation, the client keeps the connection with the Exchange 2013 server, which forwards the request to the Exchange 2007 server. This server returns the information to the Exchange 2013 server, which returns the information to the client. Thus, connection with the Exchange 2013 server never gets lost. In a redirection situation, the connection with the Exchange 2013 server is closed after the authentication request and the client sets up a new connection with the Exchange 2007 server.

Coexistence with Exchange Server 2007 and SSL Certificates

When configuring the Exchange 2007 CAS for coexistence scenario with the Exchange 2013 CAS, know that the SSL certificates need to be changed. The webmail.contoso.com and autodiscover.contoso.com names are used on the SSL certificate on the 2013 CAS, and the legacy.contoso.com name is used on the SSL certificate on the 2007 CAS.

The easiest and cheapest way to achieve this is to use one SSL certificate on both Client Access servers, whereby:

- webmail.contoso.com is used as the common name (CN).

- autodiscover.contoso.com is added to the subject alternative names (SAN) field.

- legacy.contoso.com is added to the subject alternative names (SAN) field.

An advantage of using the same SSL certificate on both the 2007 CAS and the 2013 CAS is that the moment of switching the FQDN from Exchange 2007 to Exchange 2013 is fully independent of the SSL certificate activities.

To request a new SSL certificate on the Exchange 2013 server, you open EMS and enter the following commands:

```
$Data = New-ExchangeCertificate -FriendlyName "Coexistence SSL Certificate" -GenerateRequest
-SubjectName "c=US, o=Contoso, cn=webmail.contoso.com"
-DomainName webmail.contoso.com,autodiscover.contoso.com,legacy.contoso.com
-PrivateKeyExportable $true

Set-Content -path "\\ams-ad01\mgmtshare\SSLCertRequest.req" -Value $Data
```

After ordering the certificate from your certificate authority, you store the new certificate on the same share and continue with the following commands:

```
Import-ExchangeCertificate –Server AMS-EXCH01 -FileData ([Byte[]]$(Get-Content
-Path "\\ams-ad01\management\certnew.cer" -Encoding byte -ReadCount 0)) |
Enable-ExchangeCertificate -Server AMS-EXCH01 -Services IIS
```

When you check the new certificate, using either the certificates MMC snap-in or your browser, and you navigate to the Exchange 2013 CAS, you'll see all entries, similar to those shown in Figure 2-26.

Figure 2-26. *The new SSL certificate with the subject alternative names entries*

The final step is to export this SSL certificate on the Exchange 2013 CAS and import it on the 2007 CAS. Don't forget to assign the services on the 2007 CAS to the newly imported SSL certificate.

Exchange Server 2007 and Virtual Directories

Now that there are two separate and different Exchange CAS servers, you need to take special care when it comes to configuring the virtual directories that are part of those Client Access servers.

In Exchange 2013, all virtual directories should point to the Exchange 2013 server, so this is no different from a normal green-field installation. All mailboxes that have been moved to Exchange 2013 will use these settings (see Table 2-7).

Table 2-7. *Virtual Directory Settings on the Exchange 2013 Client Access Server*

Virtual Directory	Internal URL	External URL
OWA virtual directory	`https://webmail.contoso.com/owa`	`https://webmail.contoso.com/owa`
ECP virtual directory	`https://webmail.contoso.com/ecp`	`https://webmail.contoso.com/ecp`
Activesync virtual directory	`https://webmail.contoso.com/` `Microsoft-Server-ActiveSync`	`https://webmail.contoso.com/` `Microsoft-Server-ActiveSync`
EWS virtual directory	`https://webmail.contoso.com/ews/` `exchange.asmx`	`https://webmail.contoso.com/ews/` `exchange.asmx`
OAB virtual directory	`https://webmail.contoso.com/oab`	`https://webmail.contoso.com/oab`
PowerShell virtual directory	`https://webmail.contoso.com/` `powershell`	`https://webmail.contoso.com/` `powershell`
Mapi virtual directory	`https://webmail.contoso.com/mapi`	`https://webmail.contoso.com/mapi`
Outlook Anywhere	`Webmail.contoso.com`	`Webmail.contoso.com`

To configure a virtual directory—for example, the OWA virtual directory—you can use a command like this in EMS:

```
Get-OWAVirtualDirectory –Server AMS-EXCH01 | Set-OWAVirtualDirectory –InternalURL
https://webmail.contoso.com/owa -ExternalURL https://webmail.contoso.com/owa
```

And repeat this command for other virtual directories using these commands in EMS:

- Set-EPCVirtualDirectory

- Set-ActiveSyncVirtualDirectory

- Set-WebServicesVirtualDirectory

- Set-OABVirtualDirectory

- Set-PowershellVirtualDirectory

- Set-MAPIVirtualDirectory

There's no need to configure the Autodiscover virtual directory with the –InternalURL and –ExternalURL properties. These are available on the virtual directory, but they not used by Exchange 2013.

As with the previous sections in this chapter, you can best use the PowerShell `Change_vdir_settings.ps1` script to configure all settings with just one command.

On the new 2013 CAS, Outlook Anywhere has to be configured as well. Remember that Outlook Anywhere is enabled by default on Exchange 2013, as all Outlook clients on Exchange 2013 use Outlook Anywhere. The internal hostname and the external hostname need to be configured as well as the SSL requirement parameter:

```
Set-OutlookAnywhere -Identity van-cas2013\rpc* -InternalHostname webmail.contoso.com
-InternalClientsRequireSSL $true -InternalClientAuthenticationMethod Basic
-ExternalHostname webmail.contoso.com -ExternalClientsRequireSSL $true
-ExternalClientAuthenticationMethod Basic
```

When a mailbox has not been moved to the Exchange 2013 Mailbox server, the 2013 CAS will detect this during the initial client request when the user is authenticated. The request will either be redirected or it will be proxied to the 2007 CAS, depending on the protocol being used.

The virtual directories on the 2007 CAS (see Table 2-8) either should point to the legacy URL when the request is redirected or should point to the 2013 CAS when the request is proxied or handled by the 2013 Mailbox server.

Table 2-8. *Virtual Directory Settings on the Exchange Server 2007 Client Access Server*

Virtual Directory	Internal URL	External URL
OWA virtual directory	`https://legacy.contoso.com/owa`	`https://legacy.contoso.com/owa`
ECP virtual directory	n/a	n/a
Activesync virtual directory	`https://webmail.contoso.com/Microsoft-Server-ActiveSync`	`https://webmail.contoso.com/Microsoft-Server-ActiveSync`
EWS virtual directory	`https://legacy.contoso.com/ews/exchange.asmx`	`https://legacy.contoso.com/ews/exchange.asmx`
OAB virtual directory	`https://legacy.contoso.com/oab`	`https://legacy.contoso.com/oab`
PowerShell virtual directory	`https://legacy.contoso.com/powershell`	`https://legacy.contoso.com/powershell`
Autodiscover virtual directory	`https://autodiscover.contoso.com/autodiscover`	`https://autodiscover.contoso.com/autodiscover`

■ **Note** When enabling Outlook Anywhere on Exchange Server 2007 in a coexistence scenario, you'll find the same settings apply as when enabled in a pure Exchange Server 2007 scenario. The Outlook clients who have a mailbox on Exchange Server 2007 and access 2013 CAS are proxied to the 2007 CAS.

Please note that it is not possible to manage Exchange Server 2007 settings from the EMS running on the Exchange 2013 environment, nor is it possible from the EAC. Exchange Server 2007 settings should be managed from the 2007 Exchange Management Console or the 2007 Exchange Management Shell. Since you are reading this, you should be familiar with Exchange Server 2007 and how to configure the virtual directories in the 2007 Exchange Management Console or the 2007 Exchange Management Shell, so I won't go into detail here.

■ **Note** Don't make changes to the Exchange 2007 virtual directories yet, because that will immediately change the client behavior. Make these changes at the moment when you are actually changing the access method, as explained in the next section, when all clients access the 2013 CAS and are redirected to the 2007 CAS.

Making the Change for Clients

If all servers have been installed and configured, it's time to change how these clients access the Exchange platform. This is an important moment because one mistake here can potentially have an impact on all clients.

I've said before that Outlook clients connect directly to the 2007 Mailbox server, and this does not change when you make the change to the 2013 CAS. While this is true, Outlook clients use Autodiscover and the Exchange web services at the same time, and these protocols are impacted by a change to the 2013 CAS.

For internal clients, it is just a matter of changing the internal DNS records for webmail.contoso.com and autodiscover.contoso.com to the 2013 CAS and of creating a new record for legacy.contoso.com pointing to the 2007 CAS. If there are multiple CAS in a load-balanced array, you have to change the IP address from the old load-balanced array to the new load-balanced array.

For external clients, the forwarding address on the firewall needs to be changed from the 2007 CAS to the 2013 CAS. If the Microsoft Threat Management Gateway (TMG) 2010 is used, more steps are involved. In this case, you do the following:

1. Import the new SSL certificate that includes the legacy.contoso.com domain name to the TMG server, and bind it to the web listener that's used by the Exchange servers.

2. Create a new web publishing rule in the TMG console for publishing the legacy.contoso.com Exchange 2007 server. The existing web listener can be used for this new web publishing rule.

3. Change the web listener for webmail.contoso.com so that it now points to the 2013 CAS. If the self-signed certificate is used on the CAS, make sure it is imported in the trusted root certification authority's store on the TMG server so that the self-signed certificate is trusted. This certificate is only used for communication between the TMG server and the CAS.

■ **Note** It is possible to create the legacy web publishing rule before making the actual network changes. This way you have the possibility of testing the new legacy rule.

---

4. Clients will use the webmail.contoso.com FQDN to connect to the 2013 CAS.

5. When the mailbox is still on Exchange Server 2007, the client will be redirected to 2007 CAS and the client will use the legacy.contoso.com FQDN to connect to the legacy CAS. Since one web listener is used by both web publishing rules, one authentication is sufficient.

Figure 2-27 outlines how clients connect in a coexistence scenario with Exchange Server 2007:

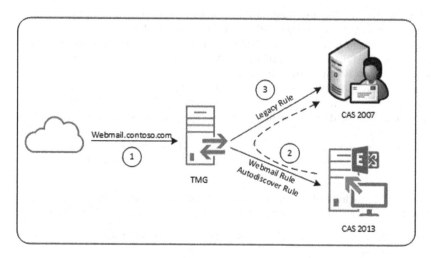

Figure 2-27. *TMG rules in a coexistence scenario*

■ **Note**   Make sure that the authentication settings on the TMG publishing rules match the authentication settings on the virtual directories in Exchange Server 2007 and Exchange Server 2013.

When these changes are made, the last step is to change the virtual directories on the 2007 CAS using the 2007 Exchange Management Console or the 2007 Exchange Management Shell, according to settings shown in Table 2-8. Then, you're ready to go.

A client will now use the http://webmail.contoso.com/owa URL to connect to the Exchange 2013 CAS and the Exchange 2013 logon form is presented. This is the first change for users! When the user's mailbox is on the Exchange 2013 Mailbox server, the mailbox is shown directly after authentication. When the user's mailbox is still on Exchange Server 2007, TMG redirects the request to the 2007 CAS, which will automatically authenticate the request and the client is shown the Exchange 2007 mailbox (see Figure 2-28).

Figure 2-28. *The mailbox is still on Exchange Server 2007; note the legacy URL in the navigation bar*

Once you've made this change, you've finished one the most important steps in the transition, and it's time to relax a bit and enjoy the Exchange 2013 CAS. Moving mailboxes is the next step in the transition process, and this will be explained after we've covered namespaces and coexistence with Exchange Server 2010.

■ **Note**   Make absolutely sure that the `legacy.contoso.com` namespace is configured as identical to the `webmail.contoso.com` namespace regarding proxy settings, the cookie/popup blocker, and the Trusted Sites setting.

Namespaces and Coexistence with Exchange Server 2010

Life is a little easier when you're installing Exchange 2013 into an existing Exchange Server 2010 environment. Exchange 2013 works quite well with Exchange Server 2010, making use of an additional namespace unnecessary. There's only one namespace, so there's not a lot of change needed.

Namespaces with Exchange Server 2010

In a typical Exchange Server 2010 environment, two namespaces are used:

- webmail.contoso.com Used for all HTTPS-based services, including Outlook Anywhere.

- autodiscover.contoso.com Used by external Outlook clients for discovering the internal Exchange configuration.

The namespace planning is identical in a native Exchange 2013 environment. Also, the Exchange 2013 CAS works smoothly with the 2010 CAS. Requests that hit the 2013 CAS for a mailbox running on Exchange Server 2010 are automatically proxied to the 2010 CAS (see Figure 2-29). For the end user, this is a seamless experience; his connection is set up to the 2013 CAS, and this connection is preserved as long as his session is kept alive. So, in this scenario there's no need for an additional namespace, as was needed for the Exchange Server 2007/2013 coexistence.

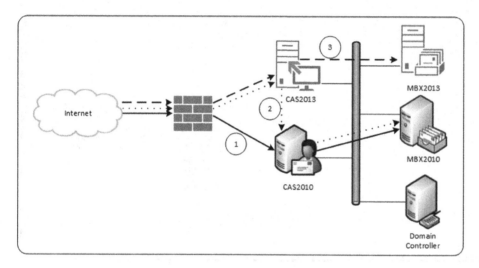

Figure 2-29. *Coexistence scenario with Exchange Server 2010*

Figure 2-29 shows what happens in an Exchange Server 2010/2013 coexistence scenario:

1. The solid line is the original situation, where clients connect via webmail.contoso.com and autodiscover.contoso.com to the Exchange Server 2010 CAS. The CAS retrieves the information from the 2010 Mailbox server.

2. The dotted line is the coexistence scenario. Clients connect using webmail.contoso.com and autodiscover.contoso.com to the 2013 CAS. Requests are proxied to the 2010 CAS, which retrieves the information from the 2010 Mailbox server and returns the information via the 2013 CAS to the client. No connection is set up between the client and the 2010 CAS, and this is fully transparent for the end user.

3. The dashed line is the final situation. Clients connect to the 2013 CAS using the webmail.contoso.com and autodiscover.contoso.com FQDN, and the requests are proxied directly to the 2013 Mailbox server.

In an Exchange Server 2010/2013 coexistence scenario, the following are true for all protocols:

- *Outlook Web App* is proxied from the 2013 CAS to the 2010 CAS when the mailbox is still on the 2010 Mailbox server. The interface for those mailboxes is still 2010 and will not benefit from the new 2013 Outlook Web App features.

- *Autodiscover* requests are proxied to the 2010 CAS when the user mailbox is still on the 2010 Mailbox server. This is true for both internal and external clients. Internal clients get the 2013 CAS via the service connection point (SCP) while external clients construct the URL from the SMTP email address of the user.

- *Outlook Anywhere* connections (HTTPS) from Outlook clients are proxied from the 2013 CAS to the 2010 CAS as long as the mailbox is on the 2010 Mailbox server.

- *Exchange activesync* and *Exchange web services* are proxied from the 2013 CAS to the 2010 CAS as long as the mailbox is running on the 2010 Mailbox server.

- *POP3* and *IMAP4* are proxied from the 2013 CAS to the 2010 CAS.

So, all requests are proxied from the 2013 CAS to the 2010 CAS. If there are multiple 2013 Client Access servers, they are load-balanced using a layer-4 load balancer. If there are multiple 2010 Client Access servers, though, there's no need for a load-balancer solution on Exchange Server 2010. The 2013 CAS picks a (healthy, available) 2010 CAS randomly from Active Directory so the load is automatically distributed across all 2010 Client Access servers in this particular site.

Outlook clients in an existing Exchange Server 2010 environment connect to the RPC ClientAccess service running on the Exchange Server 2010 Client Access server. If multiple Exchange 2010 Client Access servers are used, a load-balanced array of Client Access servers is used—the CAS array. When Exchange 2013 is introduced into the existing Exchange Server 2010 environment, nothing changes in the way internal Outlook clients connect to the CAS array. Only if the mailbox is moved from Exchange Server 2010 to Exchange 2013 does the Outlook client no longer connect to the CAS array; instead, the client starts using Outlook Anywhere and then connects to the 2013 CAS.

Coexistence with Exchange Server 2010 and SSL Certificates

In an Exchange Server 2010/2013 coexistence scenario, there's no need to worry about SSL certificates. The existing SSL certificate on the 2010 CAS in a typical environment should have domain names webmail.contoso.com and autodiscover.contoso.com. At one point, the clients connect to the 2013 Client Access servers using the same domain names, so it's just a matter of exporting the SSL certificate from the 2010 CAS to the 2013 CAS.

Client requests are proxied to the 2010 CAS, but the information is only encrypted using the SSL certificate; the SSL certificate is *not* used for server authentication. Since the 2010 CAS is a member of the same Active Directory environment, it is automatically trusted by the 2013 CAS.

To use an existing SSL certificate from the 2010 CAS, you follow these steps:

1. On the 2010 CAS, you use the Exchange Management Console to export the SSL certificate to a .pfx file and store this .pfs file on a network share—for example, \\ams-fs01\management\exported-certificate.pfx.

2. On the Exchange 2013 server, you open EMS and enter the following command to import the .pfx file:

```
Import-ExchangeCertificate -Server AMS-EXCH01 -FileData ([Byte[]]$(Get-Content
-Path "\\ams-ad01\management\exported-certificate.pfx" -Encoding byte -ReadCount 0)) |
Enable-ExchangeCertificate -Server AMS-EXCH01 -Services IIS
```

Exchange Server 2010 and Virtual Directories

Now that there are two separate and different Client Access servers, you need to take special care when it comes to configuring the virtual directories that are part of those Client Access servers.

In Exchange 2013, all virtual directories should point to the Exchange 2013 server, so this is no different from a normal green-field installation. All mailboxes that have been moved to Exchange 2013 will use these settings (see Table 2-9).

Table 2-9. *Virtual Directory Settings on the Exchange 2013 Client Access Server*

Virtual Directory	Internal URL	External URL
OWA virtual directory	https://webmail.contoso.com/owa	https://webmail.contoso.com/owa
EAC virtual directory	https://webmail.contoso.com/ecp	https://webmail.contoso.com/ecp
Activesync virtual directory	https://webmail.contoso.com/ Microsoft-Server-ActiveSync	https://webmail.contoso.com/ Microsoft-Server-ActiveSync
EWS virtual directory	https://webmail.contoso.com/ews/ exchange.asmx	https://webmail.contoso.com/ ews/ exchange.asmx
OAB virtual directory	https://webmail.contoso.com/oab	https://webmail.contoso.com/oab
PowerShell virtual directory	https://webmail.contoso.com/ powershell	https://webmail.contoso.com/ powershell
MAPI virtual directory	https://webmail.contoso.com/mapi	http://webmail.contoso.com/mapi
Outlook Anywhere	webmail.contoso.com	webmail.contoso.com

Just as in the previous sections, the best way to configure the virtual directories is to use the change_vdir_settings.ps1 PowerShell script to minimize the risk for errors. This script will set all the virtual directories and configure Outlook Anywhere as well.

■ **Note** As with Exchange Server 2007, make sure the internal URL is resolvable as well when making changes. When this is not resolvable, a warning message will be shown.

If a mailbox has not been moved to the 2013 Mailbox server, the 2013 CAS will detect this when the user is authenticated during the initial client request, and the request will be proxied to the 2010 CAS. In this situation, the same settings (see Table 2-10) are used, as all client requests are proxied from the 2013 CAS to the 2010 CAS. For the client, what happens on the Exchange Server level is fully transparent, so the same virtual directory settings apply as for mailboxes that are already on Exchange 2013. In the original environment, the namespaces used were the same as in the coexistence scenario, so if all is correct, there's no need to change anything on the Exchange Server 2010 virtual directory settings.

Table 2-10. *Virtual Directory Settings on the Exchange 2013 Client Access Server*

Virtual Directory	Internal URL	External URL
OWA virtual directory	`https://webmail.contoso.com/owa`	`https://webmail.contoso.com/owa`
ECP virtual directory	`https://webmail.contoso.com/ecp`	`https://webmail.contoso.com/ecp`
Activesync virtual directory	`https://webmail.contoso.com/` `Microsoft-Server-ActiveSync`	`https://webmail.contoso.com/` `Microsoft-Server-ActiveSync`

EWS virtual directory	`https://webmail.contoso.com/ews/`
	`exchange.asmx`
		`https://webmail.contoso.com/`
		`ews/`
		`exchange.asmx`

OAB virtual directory	`https://webmail.contoso.com/oab`	`https://webmail.contoso.com/oab`
PowerShell virtual directory	`https://webmail.contoso.com/` `powershell`	`https://webmail.contoso.com/` `powershell`

■ **Note**   Outlook Anywhere in a coexistence scenario is similar to Outlook Anywhere in a native Exchange 2010 environment, so no additional changes are necessary.

Please note that it is not possible to manage Exchange Server 2010 settings from the EMS running on the Exchange 2013 environment. Exchange Server 2010 settings should be managed from the 2010 Exchange Management Console or 2010 Exchange Management Shell.

Making the Change for Clients

If all servers have been installed and configured, it's time to make the change in how clients access the Exchange platform. This is an important moment; one mistake here can potentially have an impact on all clients.

Although this change is important, the effect is different for every client. Outlook clients, for example, will connect to the Exchange 2010 CAS array, and this will not change when the switch to the 2013 CAS is made. But those same Outlook clients also use Autodiscover and the Exchange web services, and these protocols are impacted during the change.

For internal clients, it is just a matter of changing the internal DNS records for `webmail.contoso.com` and `autodiscover.contoso.com` to the 2013 CAS. If there are multiple Client Access servers in a load-balanced array, you have to change the IP address from the old load-balanced array to the new load-balanced array. However, this is the case only for HTTP services; the CAS array IP address should not be changed, of course.

For external clients, the forwarding address on the firewall needs to be changed from the 2010 CAS to the 2013 CAS.

If Microsoft Threat Management Gateway (TMG) 2010 is used, an additional step is needed. The web listener for `webmail.contoso.com` needs to be changed so that it now points to the 2013 CAS. If the self-signed certificate is used (which shouldn't be the case if you have been following the steps in this book) on the CAS, you need to make sure it is imported in the trusted root certification authority's store on the TMG server so that the self-signed certificate is trusted. This certificate is used only for communication between the TMG server and the CAS. Figure 2-30 outlines how clients connect with an Exchange Server 2010/2013 TMG coexistence scenario:

1. Clients use the webmail.contoso.com FQDN to connect to the 2013 CAS.

2. When the mailbox is still on Exchange Server 2010, the client request is proxied to Exchange Server 2010 CAS. For the client, this step is fully transparent.

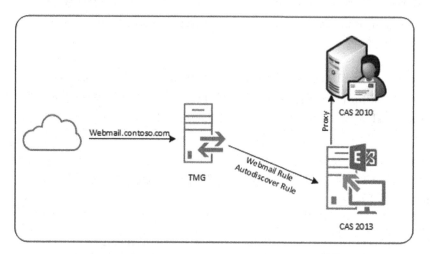

Figure 2-30. *TMG in an Exchange 2010/2013 coexistence scenario*

■ **Note**   Make sure that the authentication settings on the TMG publishing rules match the authentication settings on the virtual directories in both Exchange Server 2010 and Exchange Server 2013.

The client now uses the webmail.contoso.com FQDN to connect to the 2013 CAS and the Exchange 2013 logon form is presented. As with the Exchange 2007 coexistence scenario, this is the first change for users! When the user's mailbox is on the 2013 Mailbox server, the mailbox is shown directly after authentication. When the user's mailbox is still on Exchange Server 2010, the request is proxied to the 2010 CAS and the mailbox data is retrieved. No second logon attempt is needed. The end user with his mailbox doesn't see any difference at this point until his mailbox is moved to Exchange 2013.

SMTP Mail in a Coexistence Scenario

During the coexistence phase, SMTP mail flow has to be changed from the previous version of Exchange Server to Exchange 2013. It does not matter when the mail flow is changed, however. It can be changed in the beginning of the transition process, halfway through the process, or just before the previous version of Exchange Server is decommissioned. The Edge Transport server from the previous versions can also play a role in the Exchange 2013 environment.

Changing the SMTP Mail Flow

Initially, SMTP messages are delivered to the previous Exchange Hub Transport servers, and inbound SMTP messages are delivered to the recipients' mailboxes. When mailboxes are moved to Exchange 2013, the previous Hub Transport server sends inbound messages using SMTP to the Exchange 2013 Mailbox server, where they are delivered to the recipients' mailboxes.

Specifically, an inbound SMTP message is delivered to the 2013 Client Access server, which proxies the inbound SMTP connection to a 2013 Mailbox server. An inbound SMTP message intended for a recipient still on Exchange Server 2007 is sent from the 2013 Mailbox server using SMTP to an old Exchange Server Hub Transport server. From there it is delivered to the recipient's mailbox. Needless to say, if the mailbox is moved to Exchange 2013, the Hub Transport service on the 2013 Mailbox server delivers the message to the 2013 Mailbox server hosting the recipient's mailbox.

Is there a guideline or best practice for when to change the mail flow? I don't know. I have seen customers change the SMTP mail flow as their first step in the transition process so that they know their platform is running fine. At the same time, I have seen customers change the mail flow after the last mailbox move, a step that concludes their transition process. It depends on your own preferences.

Using an Edge Transport Server

In the previous versions of Exchange Server there was an additional server role called the Edge Transport server, a server typically located in the perimeter network. The Edge Transport server role was not available at the initial release of Exchange 2013, but it has been reintroduced with Exchange 2013 SP1.

The Edge Transport server is responsible for SMTP message hygiene. The MX records on the public DNS point to the Edge Transport servers, and therefore these Edge Transport servers accept messages from the Internet. They apply a set of anti-spam rules to the inbound messages, ensuring that only legitimate messages are sent to the internal Exchange organization. After cleaning, the messages are delivered to the internal Exchange Hub Transport server, which delivers the messages to the recipients' mailboxes. The Edge Transport server is tied to the internal Hub Transport server using the Edge subscription, a mechanism whereby information from the internal Exchange structure is pushed to the Edge Transport server.

In Exchange 2013 SP1, the process is similar; the difference is that the Edge 2013 is now tied to the Exchange 2013 Mailbox server.

In a coexistence scenario with an Exchange 2007 Edge server or an Exchange 2010 Edge server, mail continues to be delivered to the Exchange Server's Hub Transport server, and this server delivers the messages to an Exchange 2013 Mailbox server when the recipients' mailboxes are moved to Exchange 2013.

The good news is that the previous Exchange Edge Transport servers continue to work with the 2013 Mailbox server, including the Edge synchronization. The only thing you have to do is to create a new Edge subscription.

Another option is to introduce a new Exchange 2013 Edge Transport server into your organization and decommission the previous Edge Transport server. Here are the two options.

Continuing with the Previous Edge Transport Server

If you opt for the first option—using the previous Edge Transport server with the Exchange 2013 Mailbox server—it's just a matter of removing the existing Edge subscription between the Edge server and the previous Exchange Hub Transport server, then creating a new Edge subscription between the Edge Transport server and the 2013 Mailbox server. Mail from the Internet will then be delivered to the Exchange 2010 Edge Transport server and sent to the Exchange 2013 Mailbox server (see Figure 2-31).

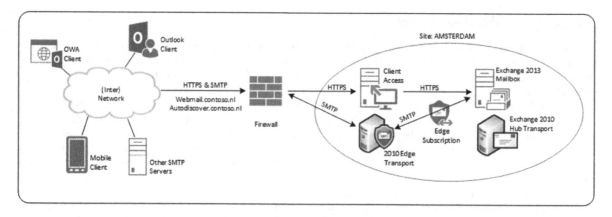

Figure 2-31. *The 2010 Edge Transport server in an Exchange 2013 environment*

■ **Note** The previous Edge Transport server needs to be at Exchange Server 2007 SP3 RU10 or Exchange Server 2010 SP3 level for coexistence to work.

To change the Edge synchronization from an Exchange 2007 or 2010 Hub Transport server to a new Exchange 2013 Mailbox server, you have to remove the existing Edge subscription and create a new one, then bind it to the Exchange 2013 Mailbox server.

To remove an existing Edge Subscription, open EMS and enter the following command:

```
Get-EdgeSubscription -Identity <<Name>> | Remove-EdgeSubscription
```

In this command, <<Name>> is the NetBIOS name of the previous Edge Transport server. Please note that at this stage you don't have any connection left between the previous Edge Transport server and the internal Exchange organization so you have to quickly to minimize downtime.

To create a new Edge Subscription, log on to the previous Edge Transport server, open EMS, and enter the following command:

```
New-EdgeSubscription -FileName C:\Temp\Edge01.xml
```

A warning message is shown, basically saying the subscription file is valid for 1440 minutes (which equals 24 hours). (If the subscription file is not processed within this time frame, a new subscription has to be created.) Enter "Y" to confirm your knowledge of the warning message, and the subscription file will be created.

Copy the Edge01.xml subscription file to a directory on the local disk of the 2013 Mailbox server. On this server, open the EMS and enter the following commands:

```
New-EdgeSubscription -FileData ([byte[]]$(Get-Content -Path "C:\Temp\edge01.xml"
-Encoding Byte -ReadCount 0)) -Site "Default-First-Site-Name" -CreateInternetSendConnector $true
-CreateInboundSendConnector $true
```

```
Start-EdgeSynchronization
```

The first command is an instruction to read the contents of the subscription file, import it, and bind it to the Mailbox server in the Active Directory site. Also, an Internet send connector and an inbound send connector are created. The second command starts the Edge synchronization process. It's as easy as that.

■ **Note**   The Exchange 2010 Edge Transport server should be able to resolve the Exchange 2013 Mailbox server, and vice versa. This can be achieved using DNS, but using a HOSTS file for resolving an Edge Transport server is quite common as well.

Introducing a new Exchange 2013 Edge Transport Server

The second option when working with Edge Transport servers is to introduce a new Exchange 2013 Edge Transport server next to the existing Edge Transport server.

You install a brand-new Exchange 2013 Edge Transport server in the perimeter network and make sure you have Internet connectivity (at least on port 25), and that name resolution works fine, both to the Internet and to the internal network, then you install the Exchange 2013 Edge Transport server role.

■ **Note**   Installing and configuring the Exchange 2013 Edge Transport server role is explained in detail in Chapter 6.

When the Exchange 2013 Edge Transport server is installed, you can create a new Edge Subscription. Log on to the Exchange 2013 Edge Transport server, open EMS, and enter the following command:

```
New-EdgeSubscription –FileName C:\Temp\Edge01.xml
```

When the file is created, you copy it to the local hard disk of the Exchange 2013 Mailbox server. On this server, you open EMS and enter the following commands:

```
New-EdgeSubscription -FileData ([byte[]]$(Get-Content -Path "C:\Temp\edge01.xml"
-Encoding Byte -ReadCount 0)) -Site "Default-First-Site-Name" -CreateInternetSendConnector $true
-CreateInboundSendConnector $true

Start-EdgeSynchronization
```

This will create the subscription between the Exchange 2013 Edge Transport server and the Exchange 2013 Mailbox server, and initiate the synchronization process. You now have a situation as shown in Figure 2-32.

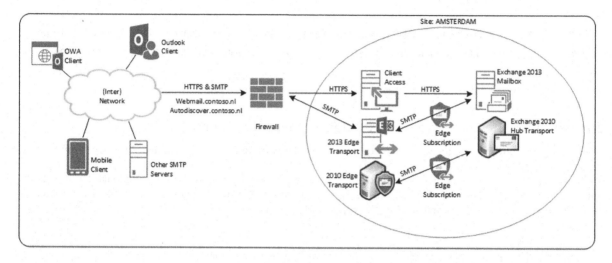

Figure 2-32. *Introducing a new 2013 Edge Transport server next to the downlevel Edge Transport server*

When you have rerouted incoming SMTP traffic from the firewall to the Exchange 2013 Edge Transport server, you can decommission the downlevel Edge Transport server. To remove the Edge Subscription between the downlevel Hub Transport server and the downlevel Edge Transport server, you log on to the downlevel Hub Transport server, open EMS, and enter the following command:

```
Get-EdgeSubscription –Identity <<Name>> | Remove-EdgeSubscription
```

where <<Name>> is the NetBIOS name of the downlevel Edge Transport server. When the old Edge Subscription is removed, you can remove the downlevel Edge Transport server.

Moving Resources to Exchange 2013

The most important step in this transition process is to move the mailboxes and other resources from the previous version of Exchange Server to the new Exchange 2013. "Other resources" in this respect are the address lists and the offline address book.

Moving Mailboxes to Exchange 2013

Moving the mailboxes to Exchange 2013 is an online process, which means the client stays connected to the mailbox until the very last step of the migration. Even when the contents are moved to Exchange 2013, the user can continue to work. This is called an *online migration*. When the migration process for a mailbox is finished, the user receives a message that the Outlook client needs to be restarted. At that point, the migration is finished and the user starts to connect to the Exchange 2013 environment.

The reason for restarting the Outlook client is basically that the client was connected to a particular Mailbox server in Exchange Server 2007 or to the CAS array in Exchange Server 2010. This was reflected in the Outlook profile where the server was shown. In Exchange 2013, though, this is no longer the case and the mailbox is no longer connected to that particular Mailbox server. You can see this in the Outlook profile, where there is no longer a server or CAS array shown; instead, the GUID of the mailbox is followed by the end user's primary SMTP address.

The process responsible for moving the Mailboxes is the Mailbox Replication service (MRS), a service that's running on the Exchange 2013 CAS or, better, on every 2013 CAS (see Figure 2-33).

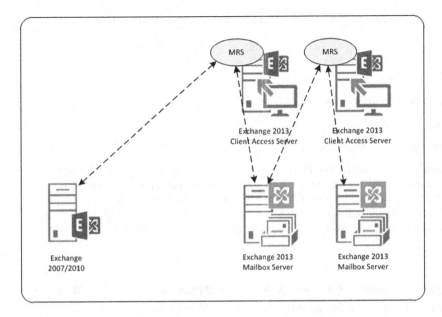

Figure 2-33. *The Mailbox Replication service*

When a mailbox needs to be moved from one mailbox database to another mailbox database, the actual mailbox move is initiated with a *move request*. With a move request, a flag is set in the system mailbox of the source mailbox database, and this flag is picked up by the MRS. The MRS then creates a copy of that mailbox in the target mailbox database, and it starts moving the mailbox data from the source to the target. This is an online and fully transparent mechanism; the recipient can be online and won't notice anything about moving data. When the MRS is about to finish the migration of data, the source mailbox is closed and all remaining data is written into the target mailbox; the properties in Active Directory are updated as well.

When the source mailbox is:

- Exchange Server 2007 or Exchange Server 2010: The user gets a warning message that the administrator has made changes to the mailbox that require the user to restart Outlook.

- Exchange 2013: The user won't notice anything. The source mailbox is closed, the Active Directory properties are updated, and there's no need to restart Outlook.

The MRS is running on every Exchange 2013 Mailbox server, so if there are five Mailbox servers, there are also five instances of MRS running in the Exchange environment. It is possible to tune the MRS on the 2013 Mailbox server. By default, very few mailboxes are moved concurrently, so as to prevent the Mailbox server from becoming overwhelmed as mailboxes are moved. This otherwise tremendous amount of traffic might impact users when mailboxes are being moved during business hours.

The configuration of the MRS is stored in a config file located in the `C:\Program Files\Microsoft\Exchange Server\V15\Bin` directory, called `MSExchangeMailboxReplication.exe.config`. When you open this file and scroll to the end, there's a section called "Mailbox Replication Service Configuration," where all the default, minimum, and maximum values are stored. There's also a section called "MRSConfiguration," where the actual settings are stored. You can changes the values stored in this config file, but don't be surprised if your Exchange servers are overwhelmed with move requests; it's best to leave the default values.

New in Exchange 2013 is the concept of "batch moves" whereby mailboxes are moved in (large) batches. Using these batches, it is possible to:

- Set email notifications.

- Set prioritization of mailbox moves.

- Set automatic retry options when mailbox moves fail.

- Set options for finalizing move requests.

- Use incremental syncs to update migration changes.

The move-request finalization is an interesting feature that was also available in Exchange Server 2010. It makes it possible to move mailboxes from a source mailbox database to a target mailbox database, but without finalizing the actual move. When the move is around 90 percent finished, the movement of mailbox data stops and the source and the target are kept in sync. It is then possible to finalize the actual move at a later time—for example, during off-business hours—so that the user doesn't receive the (disruptive) message about restarting the Outlook client at an inconvenient time.

■ **Note** Moving mailboxes is a "pull" mechanism, so the move process is initiated from the Exchange 2013 Mailbox server. To initiate a move request, the EAC or the 2013 Exchange Management Shell can be used.

To initiate a mailbox move for a user called joe@contoso.com, you log on to an Exchange 2013 server, open EMS, and execute the following command:

```
New-MoveRequest –Identity joe@contoso.com –TargetDatabase MDB01
```

You can also get a list of mailboxes on the previous Exchange Mailbox server—for example, based on a mailbox database called Mailbox Database 01—and use the pipeline feature to move all mailboxes to a mailbox database called MDB; for example,

```
Get-Mailbox –Database "Mailbox Database 01" | New-MoveRequest –TargetDatabase MDB01
```

You can monitor the move of the mailboxes with the Get-MoveRequest command, if needed you can add the Get-MoveRequestStatistics command, like this:

```
Get-MoveRequest | Get-MoveRequestStatistics
```

This will give you a quick overview of all move requests that are currently available, and whether their status is queued, in progress, or completed. To get an overview of all move requests that are running at a particular moment, you can make a selection based on the status of the move request, like this:

```
Get-MoveRequest | Where {$_.Status -eq "InProgress"}
```

Exchange Server 2010 has a mailbox for discovery search purposes. To move this mailbox, you need to use the EMS on Exchange 2013 with the following command:

```
get-mailbox -id discovery* | New-MoveRequest –TargetDatabase MDB01
```

Exchange Server also uses system mailboxes and arbitration mailboxes for approval functionality—for example, when messages need to be moderated before they are sent out. Messages that need moderation are stored temporarily in these mailboxes. The mailboxes are hidden, but they can be migrated only by using the EMS.

To retrieve a list of all system mailboxes on Exchange Server 2010, execute the following command in EMS:

```
Get-Mailbox -Server EX2010SRV -Arbitration
```

This action will return all system mailboxes on Exchange Server 2010. To move these mailboxes, you simply pipe the output of the Get-Mailbox command into the New-MoveRequest command:

```
Get-Mailbox -Server EX2010SRV -Arbitration | New-MoveRequest -TargetDatabase MDB01
```

If you don't specify a target database, Exchange 2013 will select a mailbox database automatically, based on the availability of mailbox resources. (This process will be explained in Chapter 4.)

When the regular mailboxes, the discovery mailbox, and the system mailboxes are moved to Exchange 2013, then the mailbox databases on the previous version of Exchange Server should be empty and ready for removal.

Moving Address Lists to Exchange 2013

When all the mailboxes are moved to Exchange 2013, it's time to move your other resources. Regular address lists reside in Active Directory, so when moving them to Exchange 2013, there's no need to pay extra attention; they will be used automatically by Exchange 2013.

Since the address lists were created in the previous version of Exchange Server, they should also be managed with the previous EMS or the Exchange Management Console. But to make them "ready" for Exchange 2013, just touch the address lists and store them without changing any values. To do this, use the Get-AddressList | Set-AddressList command in the 2013 Exchange Management Shell. The commands will show something like this on the console:

```
[PS] C:\Windows\system32>Get-AddressList | Set-AddressList
WARNING: The command completed successfully but no settings of '\All Contacts' have been modified.
WARNING: The command completed successfully but no settings of '\All Groups' have been modified.
WARNING: The command completed successfully but no settings of '\All Rooms' have been modified.
WARNING: The command completed successfully but no settings of '\All Users' have been modified.
WARNING: The command completed successfully but no settings of '\Public Folders' have been modified.
[PS] C:\Windows\system32>
```

Moving the Offline Address Book to Exchange 2013

A nice feature for Outlook clients is that they can work offline, also referred to as *cached mode*. When working in cached mode, clients need an address book, and so the offline address book (OAB) is used. This is a list of addresses aggregated in files that can be downloaded by the Outlook client for offline use. This way, clients can use the address lists at all times, even when they are not connected to the network.

Exchange 2010 uses an offline address book called *Default Offline Address Book*. Its format is version 3 or version 4, and it's distributed to clients using public folders (especially for Outlook 2003 clients) or web distribution—that is, it's a virtual directory on the Exchange 2010 CAS.

Exchange 2013 uses a new offline address book. It is based on version 4 and exclusively uses web distribution. The name of Exchange 2013's offline address book is *Default Offline Address Book (2013)*. You can use the 2013 Exchange Management Shell to view the available offline address books via the `Get-OfflineAddressBook` command:

```
[PS] C:\Windows\system32>Get-OfflineAddressBook

Name                                 Versions                AddressLists
----                                 --------                ------------
Default Offline Address Book         {Version3, Version4}    {\Default Global Address List}
Default Offline Address Book (Ex2013)  {Version4}            {\Default Global Address List}


[PS] C:\Windows\system32>
```

Outlook clients will automatically detect the new default offline address book, so there's no need to change anything here.

If you have custom offline address books in your organization, you cannot move them to Exchange Server 2013. Instead, you have to recreate them on Exchange Server 2013 using the `New-OfflineAddress` book command in the EMS. (This is covered in more detail in Chapter 4.)

When all the mailboxes are moved to Exchange 2013, the previous version's default offline address book is no longer needed and can be removed using the previous Exchange Server's Management Console. You will find the old default offline address book by opening the Management Console, expanding the Organization Configuration, and selecting the Mailbox option. In the Results pane, select the tab for the Offline Address Book and remove that address book by right-clicking it.

■ **Note**   Migrating public folders from a previous version of Exchange 2013 and migrating Unified Messaging (UM) from a previous version of Exchange 2013 to Exchange 2013 are also part of the transitioning process. (This is discussed in more detail in Chapters 4 and 8.)

Decommissioning the Previous Exchange Server

When all resources have been moved or removed, you can decommission the previous Exchange Server. This is not really a big deal at all, and it involves the following steps:

1. Make sure the old Hub Transport server is not responsible anymore for any mail traffic. This not only includes SMTP from and to the Internet but also third-party appliances or (custom) applications that might have been using the Hub Transport server for receiving or relaying messages. Caution: You don't want to remove the previous Exchange Server version and find out that your multifunctional devices cannot send out messages anymore. To achieve this, you have to enable SMTP logging on both the receive connector and the send connector, and check the corresponding log files. By default, you can find these log files at the following locations:

    -   SMTP receive: `C:\Program Files\Microsoft\Exchange Server\V14\TransportRoles\Logs\ProtocolLog\SMTPReceive`

    -   SMTP send: `C:\Program Files\Microsoft\Exchange Server\V14\TransportRoles\Logs\ProtocolLog\SMTPSend`

2. Remove the mailbox databases from the previous Exchange Server by using the Exchange Management Console or the Exchange Management Shell on the old Exchange Server.

3. Remove the previous Exchange Mailbox server role. This can be done by opening the control panel on the particular server and selecting "Uninstall Exchange Server." Uncheck the mailbox server roles and the Exchange management tools option in the setup application. This will remove the Mailbox server role for this particular server.

4. Remove the previous Exchange CAS and Hub Transport server roles. Again, this can be achieved by opening the control panel and uninstalling the Exchange Server. Uncheck the Client Access server role, the Hub Transport server role, and the Exchange management tools to completely remove these from the downlevel Exchange Server.

When all of these steps are successfully executed, the previous Exchange Server is now fully removed and only the Exchange 2013 servers remain in the Exchange organization.

■ **Important Note**   Decommissioning the previous version is not simply a matter of turning it off. Now this may sound silly, but it happens frequently in a virtualized server environment. It's tempting to turn off the virtual machines and just delete them, but this is absolutely *wrong*. When you do this, all information regarding previous versions of Exchange Server remains in Active Directory; from an Exchange 2013 point of view, "they" are still there (but not responding, of course). This can lead to erratic behavior. So, *fully uninstall* the previous Exchange Server!

Patch Management

Early in 2013, Microsoft announced a major change in the Exchange Server servicing model. Up until Exchange 2013, Microsoft had released a service pack every 12 to 18 months. A service pack is a collection of fixes and patches that were released during that period. The service pack can also contain new features and functions for the product. For Exchange Server, a service pack is a full install of the product, which means you can download, for example, Service Pack 3 for Exchange Server 2010, and install the full product for this version.

Between issuance of service packs, Microsoft released update rollups for Exchange Server on a regular basis—typically every three or four months. An update rollup also contains a collection of fixes and patches, but only rarely will one include new feature and functions. For example, Exchange Server 2010 Service Pack 2 Update Rollup 4 contained new options for calendar and task-retention policies.

Update rollups are version-specific, which means they are released for specific versions and service pack—for example, for Exchange Server 2010 Service Pack 1 or for Exchange Server 2010 Service Pack 2. Needless to say, these update rollups are not interchangeable. Also important to note is that an update rollup is not a full version of the product, just a collection of hotfixes. The size of these update rollups is typically between 60 and 70 GB.

To speed the deployment process and to react quickly to customer demand and market changes, Microsoft has changed its strategy for updates. Starting with Exchange Server 2013, Microsoft will release a cumulative update (CUs) on a quarterly basis. A cumulative update is a collection of fixes and patches from the past period, and can contain new features and functions, but the most important change is that it's a full product with a normal setup application. Because of this setup application, Microsoft can present major changes in a cumulative update—even schema updates can be included in a cumulative update. Using these cumulative updates, Microsoft can respond quickly to market demand, both on-premises and in Office 365 in Microsoft's data centers.

Cumulative updates are numbered sequentially. After Exchange 2013 RTM, there have been three CUs— CU1 to CU3. Also, CU4 is available, instead called SP1. The numbering continues, so after SP1, there is CU5 and later as available. Again, please note that these CUs are full versions of the product, so there's no need to install Exchange 2013 RTM or SP1 before installing the CU. You can install a CU directly.

Installing a Cumulative Update

As explained, a cumulative update is a full product. It is possible to install an Exchange 2013 server from scratch using a cumulative update or to upgrade a previous release to the latest software level. Installation of a new Exchange Server 2013 server from a cumulative update does not differ from what was explained earlier.

If you have language packs for Unified Messaging (UM) installed on your Exchange 2013 server, you need to uninstall these first before you can upgrade the server. To remove the additional language packs, open a command prompt, navigate to the installation media, and enter the following command:

```
setup.exe /RemoveUMLanguagePack: <UmLanguagePackName>
```

When the language pack is removed, you can continue upgrading the server. In the command prompt window, navigate to the installation media and enter the following commands:

```
Setup.exe /PrepareSchema /IAcceptExchangeServerLicenseTerms
Setup.exe /PrepareAD /IAcceptExchangeServerLicenseTerms
Setup.exe /PrepareDomain /IAcceptExchangeServerLicenseTerms
Setup.exe /Mode:Upgrade /IAcceptExchangeServerLicenseTerms
```

The first three command *might* not be required for each CU, but it's a best practice to make them part of your upgrade procedure because they *could* be required.

The last command is shown in Figure 2-34.

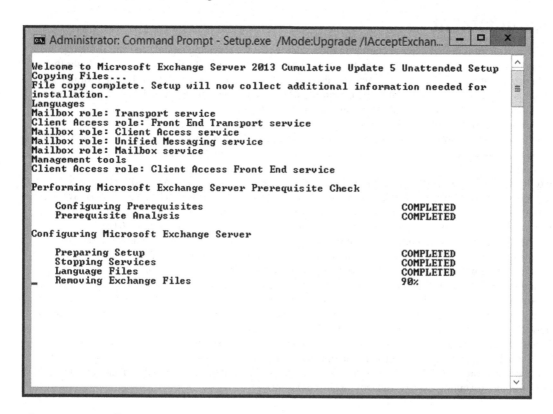

Figure 2-34. *Installing CU 5 on an existing Exchange 2013 server. Note the "Removing Exchange Files" message on the console*

Of course, it is also possible to upgrade a server to a newer cumulative update using the GUI setup; you just follow these steps:

1. To install a cumulative update, download it first from the Microsoft location and extract the download. Log on to the Exchange 2013 server as with an administrator account that's a member of the Enterprise Admins security group and the Schema Admins security group. Please note that it is possible that a cumulative update contains schema changes, but the setup will take care of that. When logged on, you navigate to the extracted cumulative update and start the graphic setup application `setup.exe`.

2. The setup application does have the option to automatically check for updates on the Microsoft site. If you want you can do this; otherwise select the Don't Check for Updates Right Now radio button.

3. The setup application is initialized and the appropriate installation files are copied to the right location on Exchange Server. After initializing, the upgrade window is shown; click Next to continue.

4. On the license agreement window, select the I Accept the Terms in the License Agreement radio button and click Next to continue. The prerequisite check will automatically be started.

5. When blocking issues are found, they are reported in the prerequisite analysis window, including the steps needed to fix them. If nothing is found, click Install to start the actual upgrade. Note: If you have the Unified Messaging configured for use with different (i.e., non-U.S.) language packs, the upgrade will fail. As noted above, the additional language packs need to be uninstalled before using the `setup.exe /RemoveUMLanguagePack:` `<UmLanguagePackName>` command.

6. The upgrade is multi-step process from changing the Active Directory to uninstalling the old binaries and installing the new binaries to reconfiguring the services (see Figure 2-35). Except for changes made, for example, in config files or customization to OWA, all old configuration settings should be preserved.

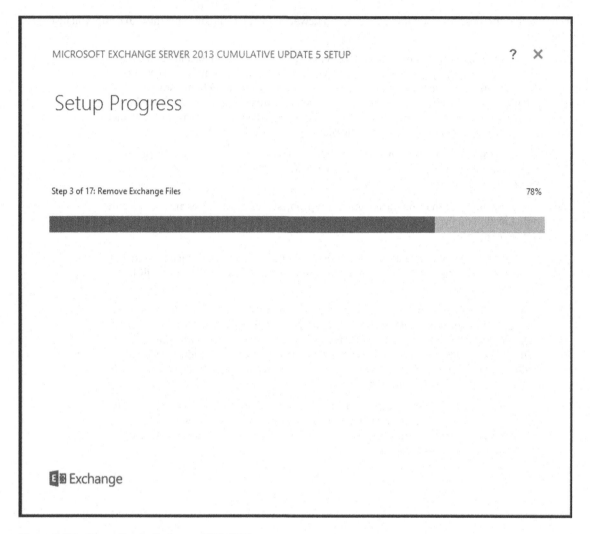

Figure 2-35. *Upgrading to Exchange 2013 CU 5*

7. After some time, the upgrade will be finished and a "Setup Completed" page will be shown. You reboot the server, and the Exchange 2013 server is up to date again. (If you've had to remove the UM language pack, you have to reinstall the new UM language pack for the new cumulative update.)

Summary

Installing Exchange 2013 is not that difficult, and the process does not differ much from previous versions of Exchange Server. Depending on the Exchange 2013 server role, you install the proper prerequisite software and install the new Exchange Server.

My personal preference is to use an *unattended setup*. This way there's no interaction via the console and you get a consistent deployment when installing multiple Exchange servers. Other than that, it's a great method for using installation scripts.

Before installing Exchange 2013, though, you need to make a proper design. To do this, you can use the Exchange 2013 Server Role Requirements Calculator, which can be downloaded from the Microsoft website. Based on the input requirements, the calculator determines the best configuration for your Exchange servers. This configuration might look like serious overkill, but when you assign fewer resources to your Exchange 2013 server, especially memory, you risk serious performance issues.

Not everybody is deploying a fresh, green-field Exchange 2013 environment, however. You can also build a coexistence scenario with Exchange 2007 or Exchange 2010, whereby Exchange 2013 is integrated into these versions. You have to take care about namespaces, especially with Exchange 2007, as well as with SSL certificates and proxy or redirection, before you can move resources from the previous Exchange version to Exchange 2013.

Once all your resources have been moved to Exchange 2013, you can decommission the previous version of Exchange Server. This means it has to be uninstalled properly, using the control panel in Windows. Just turning of the previous Exchange Server (which can easily happen when using virtual machines) is not a proper procedure; Exchange 2013 will think these servers are still around.

The next two chapters will cover the details of the Exchange 2013 Client Access server and the Exchange 2013 Mailbox server.

## CHAPTER 3

Exchange 2013 Client Access Server

The Client Access server role is the most important role in any Exchange deployment because it provides access for all mail clients to the mail data. Without a Client Access server you will have no access to your data. As someone from the Microsoft Exchange product group once said during a conference, "You can have the most beautiful and redundant Mailbox server environment with a DAG and everything, but without a Client Access server you cannot access it and it's useless."

And that's true. The Client Access server is used by all clients, whether they connect from the internal network or from the Internet. And whether they are Outlook clients or browser-based clients, or POP3 and IMAP4 clients, all clients connect to the Client Access server and then are routed to the correct Mailbox server.

So, whenever a Mailbox server is used, a Client Access server needs to be used as well. This can be on the same server as the Mailbox server, but it can also be a dedicated server.

The Client Access server consists of the following roles or services:

- Client Access Front End (CAFE), which is used to authenticate client requests and proxy connections to the correct Mailbox server.

- Front End Transport Server (FETS), which is used to accept inbound SMTP messages from other SMTP hosts. FETS can also be used to route outbound messages to other SMTP hosts, but this is optional.

- Unified Messaging Call Router (UMCR), which is used to redirect inbound voice calls (using the Session Initiated Protocol, or SIP) to the Unified Messaging service on the correct Mailbox server.

Because the Client Access server is nothing more than a proxy server, the Mailbox server also contains Client Access components. Both work together to offer one seamless service. Similarly, FETS is working together with the Transport service on the Exchange 2013 Mailbox server and together they form the "transport pipeline."

In this chapter we'll start with an overview of the Client Access technologies: client connectivity and the Client Access Front End role. Next will be a description of the Front End Transport server, and we'll close this chapter with some words about publishing the Exchange 2013 Client Access servers to the Internet. The Unified Messaging call router will be discussed in Chapter 8.

Overview of Client Access Technologies

Microsoft has made major infrastructural changes to the Client Access server role, ensuring it is possible to use it in a multiple data-center environment. In earlier versions of Exchange Server, this was possible to some extent, but it was far from optimal. Some parts of the technology haven't changed that much, like the virtual directories, the SSL certificates, and use of the single unified namespace. Other parts have changed significantly, though, like client behavior or Autodiscover. These Client Access technologies are a responsibility of both the Client Access server and the Mailbox server (for example, Autodiscover), so some technologies are covered in the following sections while others are covered in Chapter 4.

Introducing the Client Access Front End Service

In previous versions of Exchange Server (Exchange Server 2007 and 2010), the various server roles were "tightly coupled." The Client Access server and the Hub Transport server roles needed a high-bandwidth, low-latency network connection with the Mailbox server to facilitate the RPC traffic between them. This worked fine as long as all server roles were located on the same network in the same data center, but when someone was using multiple locations, that user faced some challenges.

One of the objectives in developing Exchange Server 2013 was to create a "loosely coupled" infrastructure whereby the server roles are less dependent on each other and on a good network connection. In Exchange 2013, the servers are no longer tied together using the RPC protocol; rather, they are now more independent and they communicate using the same protocol as the original client connection. But most important, all client protocols are Internet protocols and as such they are easy to route through the network, as well as not being 100 percent dependent on a high-speed, low-latency network connection, as were the previous versions of Exchange Server. Sometimes you hear the comment "Every server is an island," and that's a good description of this arrangement.

The Client Access server is a domain-joined server in the internal Active Directory forest. The Client Access server comprises three components:

- Client access protocols (HTTP, IMAP4, POP3)
- SMTP Front End Service
- UM call router

Compared to Exchange 2010, all business logic has been removed from the Client Access server and moved to the Mailbox server. At the same time, all the processing and rendering now takes place on the Mailbox server, whereas in Exchange 2010 this took place on the Client Access server.

The result is that the Exchange 2013 Client Access server is a thin and stateless server that handles all incoming connections in a load-balanced configuration. It is not truly stateless, though; the SSL connection is terminated at the Client Access, the client is authenticated, and the client is proxied to the correct Mailbox server or other down-level server. When a Client Access server is lost, all connected clients need to re-authenticate against another Client Access server. The fact that no data is stored on the Client Access server is the reason that Microsoft refers to the Client Access server as "stateless." Stateless, but not clueless, is a good description here. This service is referred to as the Client Access Front End (CAFE) service.

Since all processing is taking place on the Mailbox server and no longer on the Client Access server, session affinity or persistence is no longer needed on the Client Access server and therefore a layer-4 load balancer can be used in combination with the Exchange 2013 Client Access servers (see Figure 3-1).

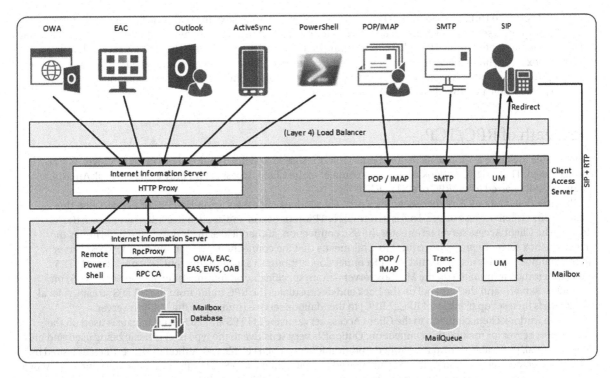

Figure 3-1. *Protocol flow through the Client Access server and Mailbox server*

■ **Note**   Since the Exchange 2013 Client Access server is a domain-joined server in the corporate forest, it is automatically located on the internal network. An Exchange 2013 Client Access server located in the perimeter network is not supported!

So, all clients on the internal and external networks connect to the load balancer and then to the Client Access server. Outlook Web App, Exchange Administration Console, Outlook Anywhere, Exchange ActiveSync, MapiHttp, and PowerShell all use HTTP as their underlying protocol. All requests are sent to the Internet Information server running on the Client Access server. After authentication, the Client Access server determines which Mailbox server hosts the active mailbox database copy, and the client request is proxied to this Mailbox server.

POP3 and IMAP4 have their own services running on both the Client Access server and the Mailbox server. Again, after authentication the POP3 or IMAP4 service determines the active copy of the mailbox database and proxies the request to this Mailbox server.

SMTP is a bit different. The SMTP connection request is sent to the Client Access server. The Front End Transport service running on the Client Access server proxies the request to a Mailbox server, based on the recipients of the message, which in turn accepts the actual SMTP message. The Client Access server does not accept the message and therefore it does not store any information regarding that message.

When it comes to Unified Messaging (UM), there's no proxying because of the real-time nature of SIP traffic. When a SIP request is sent to the Client Access server—for example, from a Lync Server 2010 or Lync Server 2013 Front End server—it is accepted by the UM call router running on the Client Access server. The UM call router determines which Mailbox server hosts the active copy of the mailbox database where the recipient is hosted, and it redirects the SIP request to the Unified Messaging service running on that particular Mailbox server. From that moment on, the Lync server communicates directly with the Mailbox server.

The Death of RPC/TCP

Clearly visible in Figure 3-1 is that all major clients are HTTP based and the traditional MAPI (or RPC over TCP) is no longer used. That's right, Outlook clients now connect to the Client Access server only using Outlook Anywhere, sometimes still referred to as "RPC over HTTP."

But how does Outlook Anywhere actually work? The Outlook client sets up an HTTPS connection with the Exchange 2013 Client Access server. This is a normal HTTPS connection and as such it is fully routable via the Internet. The Client Access server terminates the SSL connection, authenticates the request, and determines the correct Mailbox server to proxy the request to. This means that the connection between the Client Access server and the Mailbox server is also a normal HTTPS connection, although it's using a different TCP port. The HTTPS connection is then terminated on the Mailbox server—more specifically, on Internet Information Server (IIS) on the Mailbox server—and the AppPool on the back end decapsulates the RPC traffic from the HTTPS stream. A local connection is then set up using local RPC (LRPC) to the Mailbox service running on the Mailbox server.

So, the Outlook client connects to the Client Access server using HTTPS and an SSL certificate is used on the Client Access server for making this connection. Outlook is very sensitive to the type of certificate being used and only accepts normal, preferably third-party Unified Communications (UC) certificates, although UC certificates issued by an Active Directory Certification Authority can be used as well. When using SSL certificates issued by your local Active Directory CA, you have to be careful that all clients and servers trust this CA. If they don't, the server does not accept the SSL certificate and a certificate warning is shown.

Since the Outlook clients now connect to the correct Mailbox server, it is no longer necessary to use the RPC Client Access server array (also known as CAS array). This CAS array was introduced in Exchange 2010 and was used as the MAPI endpoint for Outlook clients. The FQDN of the CAS array was also the server name that was visible in the Outlook profile. But in Exchange 2013, the RPC CAS array is no longer needed. The FQDN being used in the Outlook profile has been replaced with the mailbox GUID, followed by the default accepted domain name (see Figure 3-2).

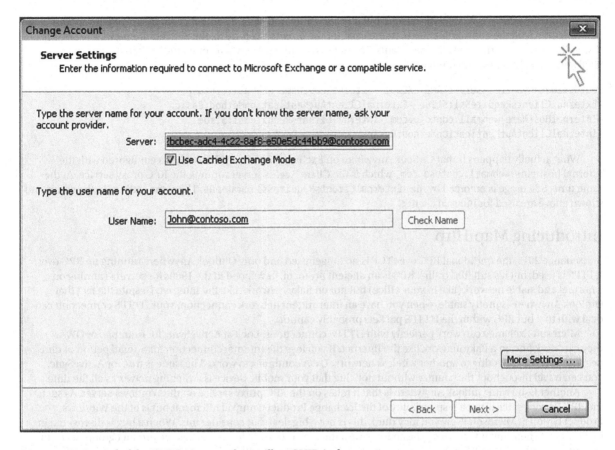

Figure 3-2. *Instead of the RPC CAS array, the mailbox GUID is shown*

The good thing is that this mailbox GUID is unique within the entire Exchange organization. If a mailbox is moved from one server to another, from one database availability group (DAG) to another, or from one data center to another, the mailbox GUID does not change. Therefore, the dreaded message "The Exchange administrator has made a change that requires you to quit and restart Outlook" no longer appears after whatever mailbox move you have performed.

In summary, the advantages of substituting the earlier MAPI client connectivity in Exchange 2013 are:

- There's a much more reliable connection between the Outlook client and the mailbox.

- The RPC CAS array is no longer needed.

- There's no more restarting Outlook after moving mailboxes.

- Data center redundancy is made easier.

So, the Client Access server is used to intercept connections from clients and to proxy these connections to the correct Mailbox server. But besides this traffic, there are a couple of other connections that are set up from the Outlook client to the Client Access server:

- Autodiscover

- Exchange Web Services (EWS)

- Offline Address Book downloads

Outlook Anywhere is enabled by default, but it is not configured at all. Therefore, Outlook Anywhere should be configured with the appropriate server name used for the proxy servers. Also, the SSL requirements must be set manually for both internal and external clients. To configure Outlook Anywhere, open the Exchange Management Shell and enter the following command:

```
Set-OutlookAnywhere -Server AMS-EXCH01 -ExternalHostname webmail.contoso.com
-ExternalClientsRequireSsl:$true -ExternalClientAuthenticationMethod:Basic
-InternalHostName webmail.contoso.com -InternalClientsRequireSsl:$true
-InternalClientAuthenticationMethod:Basic
```

What actually happens is that Outlook Anywhere on Exchange Server AMS-EXCH01 is configured with the external hostname webmail.contoso.com, which is the Client Access server running the RPC proxy service. At the same time, SSL usage is enforced by the -ExternalClientsRequireSsl parameter. The same settings in the command shown above are used for internal clients.

Introducing MapiHttp

In Exchange 2013, the traditional RPC over TCP is no longer used and only Outlook Anywhere running on RPC over HTTPS is used, but it's still RPC traffic. RPC is an ancient protocol, developed in the 1980s for servers running on a normal and stable network (like in your office) but not on flaky networks like the Internet. Despite the fact that Outlook Anywhere is pretty stable, when you have an intermittent network connection, your HTTPS connection can deal with that but RPC within the HTTPS packets probably cannot.

Microsoft Exchange can work perfectly with HTTPS connections. Look at ActiveSync, for example, or OWA; they can work fine on a flaky network like the Internet. If you lose the Internet connection for a small period of time because you're connecting to another wireless network, OWA continues to work. The same is true for ActiveSync. You can travel throughout the country without noticing that your mobile device is switching networks all the time.

Another issue with Outlook Anywhere is that it relies on the RPC proxy service on the Windows Server. As such, the RPC Proxy service is not a responsibility of the Exchange Product Group at Microsoft but is of the Windows Product Group at Microsoft. Now you may think this is not a big deal, but consider this. When a bug is discovered in Outlook Anywhere and it turns out to be an issue with the RPC Proxy service, the Exchange product group needs to submit an incident to the Windows product group and hope the latter will fix the problem. Needless to say, this is a less than desirable situation.

To overcome this problem, Microsoft has developed a new protocol called MapiHttp, which is basically native HTTPS traffic. The Outlook client is no longer using RPC for its MAPI communication but instead is using HTTPS directly. The same is true for the Exchange server, which also no longer uses RPC. The difference is shown in Figure 3-3.

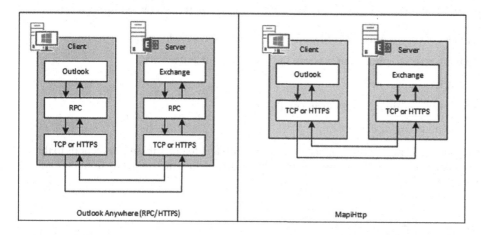

Figure 3-3. *The difference between Outlook Anywhere (RPC/HTTPS) and MapiHttp*

You can imagine that changing protocol usage like this has a tremendous impact from an engineering perspective, both on the Exchange server and on the Outlook client. That's the reason that right after the release of Exchange 2013 SP1, the only client supporting MapiHttp is Outlook 2013 SP1. At the moment of this writing it is unknown if Microsoft is going to release a (major) update for Outlook 2010 that could support MapiHttp. When it comes to Outlook 2007, I personally do not expect an update supporting MapiHttp. From a version perspective, this product is too old and not worth the investment at this point.

MapiHttp is enabled on a global level; you enable it in the entire organization at one moment. To enable MapiHttp, open the Exchange Management Shell and enter the following command:

```
Set-OrganizationConfig -MapiHttpEnabled $TRUE
```

Please note that it can take several hours for this change to take effect.

For the MapiHttp protocol, Microsoft introduced a new virtual directory on the Exchange 2013 SP1 Client Access server: the MAPI virtual directory. The MAPI virtual directory should be configured with the correct values for the InternalURL, ExternalURL, and IIS authentication properties. This can be achieved in EMS using the following command:

```
Get-MapiVirtualDirectory –Server AMS-EXCH01 | Set-MAPIVirtualDirectory -InternalURL
https://webmail.contoso.com/mapi -ExternalURL https://webmail.contoso.com/mapi
-IISAuthenticationMethods Basic
```

When all is configured, clients running Outlook 2013 SP1 will pick up this change using Autodiscover. The client will be reconfigured, basically the Outlook Anywhere settings will be removed from the Outlook Profile, and when finished the Outlook client will need to be restarted. The user will see a popup window as shown in Figure 3-4.

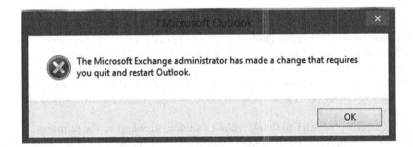

Figure 3-4. *The restart Outlook popup message*

Outlook 2013 SP1 will send an Autodiscover request to the Exchange 2013 SP1 Client Access server, and one of the additions in SP1 is that it adds a MapiHttp capability to this request. In return, the Client Access server sends the MapiHttp configuration back to the Outlook client. Since it can take some time before the Outlook client sends an Autodiscover request to the Client Access server, it can also take some time before Outlook "realizes" it has to reconfigure its profile and thus needs to be restarted.

For testing purposes, it is possible to temporarily change this behavior using the following registry key on the Outlook 2013 SP1 client:

```
[HKEY_CURRENT_USER\Software\Microsoft\Exchange]

"MapiHttpDisabled"=dword:00000001
```

To implement this registry key on your workstation, you can use the following PowerShell command:

```
New-ItemProperty -Path 'HKCU:\Software\Microsoft\Exchange' -Name MapiHttpDisabled -Value 1
-PropertyType DWORD
```

This will prevent Outlook from advertising its MAPI over HTTP capability in the Autodiscover requests, and Outlook will revert to using Outlook Anywhere. To allow Outlook 2013 SP1 to use the MapiHttp protocol again, simply delete the MapiHttpDisabled DWORD in the registry or set its value to "0."

For more information, you can check the "What's New in Outlook for Office 2013 SP1" article on the Microsoft website, `http://bit.ly/OL2013SP1`.

Client Connectivity

An Exchange 2013 Client Access server is interesting; in short, it's pretty useless without email clients. There are several email clients available that work with Exchange 2013; for example:

- Outlook clients

- Web-based clients

- Mobile clients

- POP3 and IMAP4 clients

These types of clients are treated in detail in the following sections.

Outlook Clients

One of the most important changes in Exchange Server 2013 is that Outlook no longer uses direct MAPI (RPC over TCP); Exchange Server 2013 is only accessible using Outlook Anywhere, using RPC over HTTPS. The reason for this change is the loose coupling of the Exchange 2013 server roles, as explained in Chapter 1. Direct MAPI is pretty rigid and requires a fast and reliable network connection. Also, routing issues when multiple data centers are used contributed to this decision for change. So, only RPC over HTTPS, also known as Outlook Anywhere, is always used by Outlook clients, both internally and externally.

A new protocol in Exchange 2013 SP1 is MapiHttp, which will slowly replace Outlook Anywhere as the primary protocol for Outlook. Initially, Outlook 2013 SP1 is supported, but over time MapiHttp will be supported by the latest version of Outlook 2010 as well. MapiHttp is discussed in the previous section of this chapter.

I already mentioned Outlook 2013, but Outlook 2010 SP1 (with April 2012 Cumulative Update) and Outlook 2007 SP3 (with July 2012 Cumulative Update) are also fully supported in combination with Exchange Server 2013; but again, they are supported only with Outlook Anywhere. Outlook 2007, 2010, and 2013 rely heavily on the Autodiscover functionality. Autodiscover is used not only for creating the Outlook profile during the initial startup of the Outlook client but also once an hour to request the latest configuration information from the Exchange 2013 server.

Outlook 2007, 2010, and 2013 also rely heavily on IIS. Using the Exchange Web Services (EWS), the Outlook client can request free/busy information or set an out-of-office message; the Offline Address Book is also downloaded via a normal IIS connection. The tricky part here is that when Autodiscover is not functioning correctly, the Outlook client will not get the appropriate information from the Exchange 2013 server, resulting in a non-working EWS environment, for example. Since HTTPS is playing such an important role in an Exchange 2013 environment, SSL certificates play an even more important role than in previous versions of Exchange Server. Not having a proper SSL certificate on the Exchange 2013 CAS will result in Outlook clients not connecting at all.

As mentioned in Chapter 1, Outlook 2003 clients are no longer supported. It's not only unsupported, it's also not working, so the oldest supported Outlook client working against an Exchange Server 2013 environment is Outlook 2007.

Outlook clients can run in cached mode, or in online mode where cached mode is the default (and preferred) mode. When run in cached mode, Outlook works with a copy of the mailbox on the local machine and all changes are made to this "cached" copy. Outlook automatically synchronizes this copy in the background with the mailbox on the Exchange Server. All processing takes place on the Outlook client's workstation, not on the Exchange Server, thereby reducing processor cycles and (expensive) disk I/O on the Exchange Server.

Please note that Outlook 2007 and Outlook 2010 will store a complete copy of the mailbox on the workstation's hard disk when running in cached mode. Outlook 2013 can be adjusted using the "slider bar" to prevent creating a full copy of the user's mailbox on the local hard disk.

When run in online mode, Outlook works directly against the Exchange Server and there's no copy of the mailbox on the local workstation. It's obvious that this will increase the load on the Exchange Server, plus the Outlook client will always need to be online. Offline working—for example, while traveling—is not possible in this scenario. Outlook running in online mode can be seen when used in a terminal server environment, although Outlook 2010 running in cached mode on a terminal server is fully supported nowadays.

Web-Based Clients

Web-based clients are becoming more and more important, and because of the increasing functionality and user friendliness, are easier to work with. The primary web-based client is Outlook Web App (OWA). This is driven by Office 365 because OWA was developed by the Microsoft Exchange product team, while Outlook was developed by the Microsoft Office product team. It's easier for the Microsoft Exchange product team to release updates for OWA than it is for the Office team to do likewise for Microsoft Outlook.

There are various web-based clients and protocols available in Exchange 2013:

- Outlook Web App (OWA)

- Exchange Admin Center (EAC)

- Exchange Web Services (EWS)

- Office Web Apps

- Mobile clients

- POP3 and IMAP4

These are discussed in more detail next.

Outlook Web App

Outlook Web App, or OWA, is the webmail client for Exchange Server 2013. A native part of Exchange 2013, it offers a rich client and a very similar look and feel as Outlook 2013. At the same time, OWA has a consistent view across different browsers on different operating systems. You can run OWA on IE11 and get the same user experience as when running OWA in a browser on an iPad or on Windows surface. The Microsoft Exchange Team blog contains an interesting posting about OWA running on different devices; see `http://bit.ly/OWARocks`.

New in Exchange Server 2013 is the option to use OWA offline, and integrated apps for OWA enrich the user interface and offer additional functionality.

Microsoft is offering cross-browser supportability, so besides Internet Explorer, also Mozilla Firefox 17 or later, Google Chrome 24 or later, and Apple Safari 5 or later are fully supported for use with Exchange Server 2013. Of course, the latest versions of these browsers support most features, but for an up-to-date overview of available functionality per browser version, please navigate to the Microsoft Technet site at `http://bit.ly/OWAWhatsNew`.

OWA Offline

In the past, a commonly heard feature request was the ability to use OWA offline. This is now possible with Exchange Server 2013. For this feature to work you need at least Internet Explorer 10, Safari 5.1(Mac only) or later, or Chrome 24 or later.

If your browser is capable of supporting offline OWA, it's just a matter of selecting "Offline settings" from the settings menu in OWA, as shown in Figure 3-5, and you're ready to go.

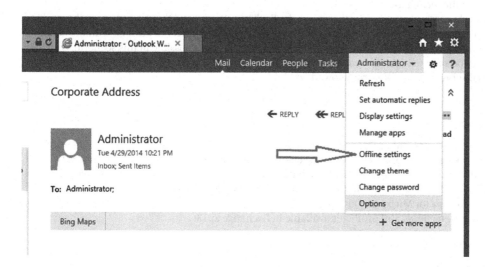

Figure 3-5. *To enable offline usage in OWA*

Not all information is available in OWA offline. It is comparable to, for example, the amount of information available in Windows Phone. Only three days of email (or 150 items, whichever is larger) will be available, as will the current and next month of calendar information; there are no archive folders, for example.

The browser determines where to store the offline information, and this poses a security risk. Anyone who has access to the PC where OWA offline is used also has access to this information, so it should not be used on a PC that is shared by multiple users.

Outlook Apps

New in Exchange Server 2013 is the concept of apps. Apps on the Exchange Server are integrated in OWA and Outlook 2013, and they give the user added functionality. For example, there is a default Bing Maps App (see Figure 3-6). If there's a street address in an email, the Bing Maps app can look it up and provide additional information regarding the address, such as the location on a map or directions to the site. At the time of this writing, only U.S. addresses are recognized, but Microsoft is actively working on world regional support.

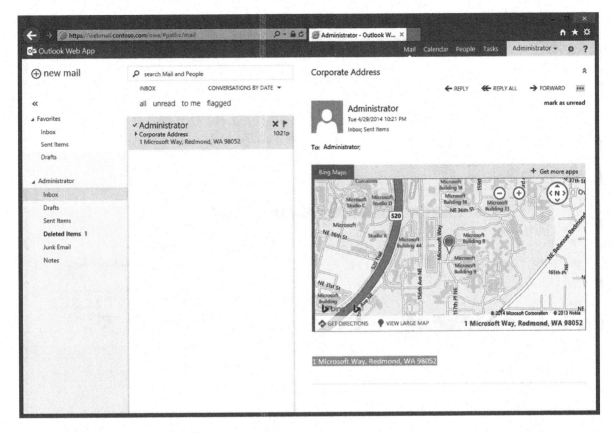

Figure 3-6. *Bing Maps shows the address in an email app*

By default, there are five apps available out of the box: Action Items, Bing Maps, My Templates, Suggested Meetings, and Unsubscribe. These are globally enabled by default.

The Exchange administrator has the option to add, remove, disable, or enable apps in the EAC as a global setting (see Figure 3-7), but the user can also install, enable, or disable apps in the EAC.

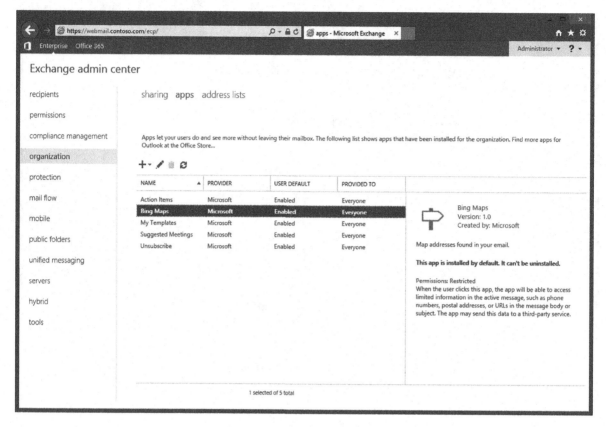

Figure 3-7. *The out-of-the-box apps are enabled by default*

Additional apps are available in the Office Store. Microsoft also encourages independent software vendors (ISV) to write additional apps and distribute them through the Office Store.

Exchange Admin Center

The Exchange Admin Center is the web-based management interface for Exchange 2013. You can access the EAC using your browser by navigating to a URL like https://webmail.contoso.com/ecp. The name of the EAC virtual directory is actually ECP, a leftover from the past when it was called Exchange Control Panel in Exchange 2010.

The EAC is accessible for everyone, both users and Exchange Administrators. Depending on the permissions granted to the account, you can have a variety of functions available. Normal users have very limited permissions; they can only manage their own user and mailbox properties. The Exchange Administrators can manage most of the functions available in EAC. That's most, but not all, because there are features not available by default, even not for Exchange Administrators like the Enterprise Search function, for example, and permissions are controlled via role-based access control (RBAC), which is discussed in Chapter 10.

It is possible to completely turn off the EAC. In an Exchange Management Shell window, enter the following command to turn off EAC for a particular server:

```
Set-ECPVirtualDirectory -Identity "AMS-EXCH01\ecp (default web site)" -AdminEnabled $false
```

■ **Note** You have to be very careful when changing this setting. When you do, it's no longer possible to manage the Exchange environment using the Graphical User Interface and the only management option you have then is the Exchange Management Shell.

Exchange Web Services

The Exchange Web Services is not a client but a protocol. Clients like Outlook 2007 and later use Exchange Web Services to retrieve additional information from the Exchange server, like free/busy. Also, the out-of-office settings on an Exchange server are controlled by an Outlook client via Exchange Web Services.

Another well-known client that relies heavily on the Exchange Web Services is Outlook for Mac, a version of Outlook that's actually completely built on top of Exchange Web Services. As such, it's not using MAPI or Outlook Anywhere. The Exchange Web Services is not a fast and efficient protocol for a mail client, and the downside of this is that Outlook for Mac isn't fast, either. Even worse, if you have a lot of Outlook for Mac clients communicating with your Exchange 2013 Client Access server, you'll see a dramatic increase in processor usage and disk I/O (in general, caused by writing to IIS log files).

Exchange Web Services can be leveraged for developing your own client applications, and these can also be PowerShell scripts. To achieve this, you have to install the Microsoft Exchange Web Services managed API, which can be downloaded from http://bit.ly/EWSAPIDownload. More information, including code samples, can be found on the MSDN Office | Dev Center—in particular, the "Explore the EWS Managed API" page at http://bit.ly/ExploreEWS.

Office Web Apps

In Exchange Server 2010, it was possible to use the attachment preview functionality in OWA. On the Exchange 2010 server, a technique called WebReady document viewing provided this function.

In Exchange Server 2013, the attachment preview function is still available, but instead a complete new server application, called Office Web Apps server 2013, may be used to render the actual document and send the HTML information to the OWA client. When an OWA client wants to preview an attachment, the request is forwarded to an Office Web Apps server. Exchange Online users in Office 365 have this function available by default; for an Exchange on-premises deployment, an additional dedicated Office Web Apps server is needed.

Installing and configuring the Office Web Apps server is beyond the scope of this book, but you can find more information on how to do this at http://bit.ly/WebApps2013 - Office Web Apps 2013.

When the Office Web Apps server is up and running, the Exchange 2013 environment can be configured. The first step is to enable it on an organizational level in Exchange 2013. You can use the following command in the Exchange Management Shell to achieve this:

```
Set-OrganizationConfig –WACDiscoveryEndpoint https://webapps.contoso.com/hosting/discovery
```

■ **Note** WAC is an acronym for Web Access Companion, a code name used when developing the Office Web Apps server.

When this is set on the organizational level, you can configure the OWA virtual directories for using the Office Web Apps server. You can configure the OWA virtual directories using the following commands in EMS:

```
Get-OWAVirtualDirectory –Server AMS-EXCH01 | Set-OWAVirtualDirectory
-WacViewingOnPublicComputersEnabled $true -WacViewingOnPrivateComputersEnabled $true
```

If you want to force users to the Office Web Apps, you can use the -ForceWacViewingFirstOnPublicComputers and -ForceWacViewingFirstOnPrivateComputers options:

```
Get-OWAVirtualDirectory –Server AMS-EXCH01 | Set-OWAVirtualDirectory
-WacViewingOnPublicComputersEnabled $true -ForceWacViewingFirstOnPublicComputers $true
-WacViewingOnPrivateComputersEnabled $true -ForceWacViewingFirstOnPrivateComputers $true
```

To check if the configuration change was applied successfully, you can enter the following commands:

```
Get-OrganizationConfig | select WACDiscoveryEndPoint
Get-OWAVirtualDirectory | Select Server,*WAC*
```

The output of these commands is shown in Figure 3-8.

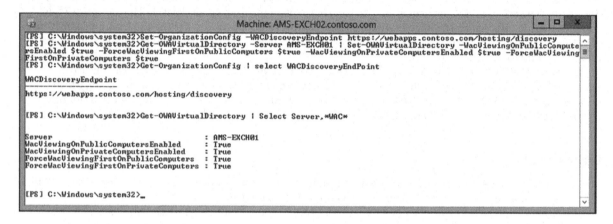

Figure 3-8. *Configuring the OWA virtual directory for use with Office Web Apps*

When you have configured this in your Exchange 2013 environment, and you receive an email message with Microsoft Office documents attached, you can open these in your browser without having a local installation of Microsoft Office on the workstation you're using. This can be valuable when reading email on a nontrusted workstation—for example, in an Internet café.

Mobile Clients

Exchange ActiveSync (EAS) is the protocol used by mobile clients connecting to the Exchange 2013 environment over the Internet. This includes Windows Phone clients, iOS clients like iPhone and iPad, and Android clients. Also, the Mail client on Windows 8 (i.e., Windows 8 running on a tablet) uses EAS to retrieve mail data from the Exchange 2013 server.

Microsoft is licensing the EAS protocol and its interfaces to third parties and independent software vendors. It is up to the vendor to write actual applications to use the EAS protocol. One of the problems with this is that Microsoft "forgot" to enforce standard implementations or quality control. Therefore, each vendor has its own interpretation of using the EAS protocol, resulting in some applications that run fine but others that are horrible to use. Additionally, there are applications that have a major performance impact on the Exchange 2013 server. For example, there are several known problems with iOS applications that result in poor performance or corrupt items in a user's mailbox, such as acceptance of recurring appointments, a common task users perform. Unfortunately, the (older) iOS client cannot handle this well.

Mobile clients are typically very sensitive when it comes to SSL certificates, and not all SSL certificates are accepted by mobile clients. To get EAS working properly, there needs to be a supported third-party SSL certificate.

Most mobile clients rely on the Autodiscover function of the Exchange 2013 server, as do Outlook clients, so again having a fully working Autodiscover environment is prerequisite for running EAS successfully.

A new development for mobile clients is the use of special mail apps—for example, those for the iPhone and iPad. These are apps built by Microsoft, but instead of using Exchange ActiveSync, they are running on top of OWA. Unfortunately these apps are available for use only with Office 365 at this point, and it is unknown if they will become available for the regular on-premises Exchange 2013 server. The reason for their not being available for Exchange 2013 on-premises is that these clients need a special subscription, a subscription that's not available in on-premises Exchange 2013 servers. More information can be found at http://bit.ly/OWAforIPhone.

POP3 and IMAP4

Although still widely used and still under active development, POP3 and IMAP4 are not commonly employed in a Microsoft environment. POP3 and IMAP4 are primarily used in (low-cost) hosting environments running some UNIX flavor, but they can also be configured for use on Exchange Server 2013. There are also business applications that can access a particular mailbox using the POP3 or IMAP protocol to retrieve messages.

POP3 and IMAP4 are installed on the Exchange 2013 server by default, but the relevant services are set to "manual start," so if they are needed, the POP3 or IMAP4 service has to be reset to "automatically start." Also, the authentication (encrypted login or plain text login) needs to be set. Exchange Server 2013 allows the basic POP3 and IMAP4 protocol, but also allows the encrypted version—that is, POP3S (POP3 over SSL) and IMAPS (IMAP4 over SSL).

■ **Note** The POP3 and IMAP4 protocols are only used for retrieving messages. The mail client should be configured for sending outbound mail via a SMTP mailhost. Of course, this can be the Exchange 2013 Client Access server running the Client Front End connector.

Namespaces

Namespaces play an increasingly important role in Exchange Server; this started with the introduction of Autodiscover and its namespace in Exchange 2007.

A namespace is a domain name used by clients to access the Client Access server to access the Exchange environment. An example of a namespace can be webmail.contoso.com, for example.

Browsers can use webmail.contoso.com/owa to access Outlook Web App, mobile devices can use webmail.contoso.com/Microsoft-Server-ActiveSync to retrieve content from the mailbox, and Outlook Anywhere can use webmail.contoso.com as the RPC proxy server.

An additional namespace being used in an Exchange server environment is autodiscover.contoso.com. This is used by Outlook clients to send the Autodiscover requests to the Client Access server.

The minimum number of namespaces in an Exchange environment is two: the protocol namespace and the Autodiscover namespace, as mentioned above. It is possible to add more protocol-specific namespaces. I have seen customers use smtp.contoso.com to set up an encrypted partner—send connector, for example. Another well-known namespace is pop.contoso.com for POP3 or IMAP4 clients.

■ **Note**   In Exchange 2010, there was another namespace used by the RPC Client Access service, something like `outlook.contoso.com`. This namespace was implemented by using the Client Access service array and was used by internal Outlook clients as the RPC endpoint. Since RCP/TCP is no longer used in Exchange 2013, the RPC CAS array is no longer used.

Namespaces are important to consider, especially when using multiple data centers. Another important factor is SSL certificate usage. More namespaces automatically means more domain names on your SSL certificate. In a typical environment the `webmail.contoso.com` and `autodiscover.contoso.com` namespaces are used, and therefore these are the only names that need to be configured on the SSL certificate.

From a load-balancing perspective as well, namespaces are an important factor to consider. In Exchange 2013, the only stateful connection that's used is between the Client Access server and the Mailbox server where the user's mailbox resides. All rendering now takes place on the Mailbox server and no longer on the Client Access server, as in Exchange 2010. Therefore a stateful connection between the client and the Client Access server is no longer required and thus a layer-4 load balancer can be used.

A layer-4 load balancer cannot do any content inspection and therefore cannot determine which protocol is used in a particular namespace. For example, a load balancer on layer-4 cannot determine whether a request is for Exchange Web Services, the MAPI Virtual Directory, or Active Sync; it only knows the namespace `webmail.contoso.com`. As a result, the load balancer cannot check the individual service's health.

It is possible to work around this by terminating the SSL connection at the load balancer, do the content inspection of the incoming traffic, and re-encrypt the traffic. In Exchange 2013 SP1, SSL offloading is fully supported by Microsoft, so this is no longer an important factor. Both SSL offloading and load balancing are discussed later in this chapter.

Another important namespace comes into play during a transition from Exchange 2007 to Exchange 2013 and you have to build a coexistence scenario, as explained in the previous chapter. Since Exchange 2013 cannot proxy client requests to the Exchange 2007 Client Access server, the request needs to be redirected to the Exchange 2007 Client Access server. Therefore, the Exchange 2007 Client Access server needs an additional unique namespace and in all Microsoft documentation the namespace `legacy.contoso.com` is used. Please note that this naming convention is not required; you can use any namespace to assign to the Exchange 2007 Client Access servers.

Split-DNS

In the previous section, namespaces were briefly discussed but these were external namespaces—that is, namespaces used by clients that do not reside on the internal network. Internal clients need to connect to the Exchange 2013 environment as well, so namespaces are also used on the internal network.

When an Exchange 2013 Client Access server is installed, it is typically accessed using its fully qualified domain name (FQDN), which can be something like:

- `Ams-exch01.contoso.com`
- `Ams-exch02.contoso.com`
- `Lon-exch01.contoso.com`

While these are all valid names and can be safely used, it makes life much easier if the same namespace is used on the internal as on the external network—that is, `webmail.contoso.com`. Using one namespace is not only clearer, there's also no need to use additional names on an SSL certificate.

When `webmail.contoso.com` is used from the Internet, the external IP address of the load-balanced array of Client Access server is resolved—for example, 176.62.196.244. When `webmail.contoso.com` is used on the internal network, the IP address of the internal load-balanced array of Client Access server is resolved, as in 10.38.96.244.

This configuration is called a *split-DNS,* or *split-brain DNS,* configuration and is the recommended approach for namespace planning.

Single Common Namespace

One of the advantages of the loosely coupled architecture of Exchange 2013 is its unified namespace. It is now possible to use only one or two namespaces for the entire Exchange organization. It is even possible to use only one namespace like `webmail.contoso.com` for all Exchange servers, even if there's worldwide deployment.

For example, a user called John logs on to `webmail.contoso.com` when he's in Amsterdam. This is where his mailbox is located. He is authenticated by the local Exchange 2013 Client Access server and his request is proxied to the appropriate Mailbox server, also in Amsterdam.

When John is traveling to New York, he still accesses `webmail.contoso.com`. The Geo-DNS solution resolves to a local Exchange 2013 Client Access server where his request is authenticated. The Client Access server detects that John's mailbox is located in Amsterdam, and thus proxies the request, over the internal network, to the Mailbox server in Amsterdam (see Figure 3-9).

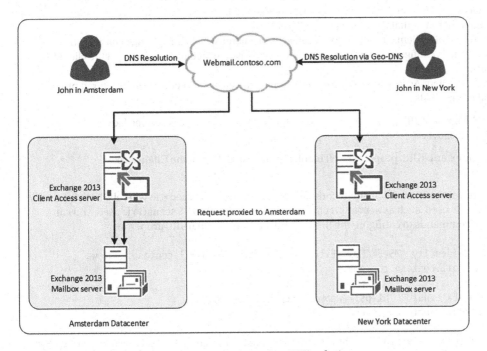

Figure 3-9. *A single, common namespace using a Geo-DNS solution*

Virtual Directories

By now it should be clear that Exchange 2013 uses the HTTP protocol extensively. The following Exchange 2013 services have their own virtual directories, which are also visible in the IIS Manager:

- Autodiscover (`/Autodiscover`)
- Outlook Web App (`/OWA`)
- Exchange Admin Console (`/ECP`)
- Exchange Web Services (`/EWS`)
- Exchange ActiveSync (`/Microsoft-Server-ActiveSync`)
- Offline Address Book (`/OAB`)

- Remote PowerShell (/Powershell)

- RPC Proxy (/RPC)

- MAPI (/Mapi)

For regular maintenance, the IIS Manager is not used at all; all Exchange 2013 maintenance is done using PowerShell (EMS) or EAC. When using EMS, you can configure every little detail of the Exchange 2013 virtual directories, but in EAC, only the most important parts of the virtual directories can be configured, so EMS is the preferred management interface.

Each virtual directory has a number of properties, and the internalURL and externalURL properties are the more important ones. These properties are stored in Active Directory, and they determine which URL the various clients use when accessing the services. This can be via the Internet (externalURL) or via the internal network (internalURL).

For OWA and EAC, it's not a big deal. You can use any URL to access OWA as long as the name is resolved to the IP address of the Client Access server. You'll see a certificate warning that the name in the request does not match the name on the certificate, but other than that, you can access the service.

For Outlook clients and mobile clients, it's different because these clients get their Exchange configuration via Autodiscover. And if something is configured incorrectly, the wrong data is returned to the client and the client in turn cannot connect to the various services.

When the Exchange 2013 Client Access server is installed, none of the virtual directories is configured properly with the internalURL and externalURL:

- The value of the internalURL property is set to the FQDN of the Client Access server, like ams-exch01.contoso.com.

- The value of the externalURL property is left blank during installation of the Client Access server.

As explained in the previous section, Microsoft recommends using a split DNS scenario whereby both internally and externally the same URL is used, such as webmail.contoso.com. When a split DNS scenario is used, you can provide the following EMS commands to configure the internalURL and the externalURL properties:

```
Set-OWAVirtualDirectory -Identity AMS-EXCH01 -ExternalURL https://webmail.contoso.com/owa
-InternalURL https://webmail.contoso.com/owa

Set-ECPVirtualDirectory -ExternalURL https://webmail.contoso.com/ecp
-InternalURL https://webmail.contoso.com/ecp

Set-ActiveSyncVirtualDirectory -ExternalURL https://webmail.contoso.com/Microsoft-Server-ActiveSync
-InternalURL https://webmail.contoso.com/Microsoft-Server-ActiveSync

Set-WebServicesVirtualDirectory -ExternalURL https://webmail.contoso.com/ews/Exchange.asmx
-InternalURL https://webmail.contoso.com/ews/Exchange.asmx

Set-OABVirtualDirectory -ExternalURL https://webmail.contoso.com/OAB
-InternalURL https://webmail.contoso.com/OAB

Set-PowershellVirtualDirectory -ExternalURL https://webmail.contoso.com/Powershell
-InternalURL https://webmail.contoso.com/Powershell

Set-MAPIVirtualDirectory -ExternalURL https://webmail.contoso.com/mapi
-InternalURL https://webmail.contoso.com/mapi
```

If there are multiple Client Access servers, be very careful when configuring the various options in the virtual directories; this is even more critical when using multiple Client Access servers in a load-balanced array. If one of the Client Access servers in the array is misconfigured, you'll see erratic results. This won't be consistent, though, because the remaining servers might be configured correctly. You'll see problems arise every now and then, and these problems are the toughest to troubleshoot.

Since all communication is going via virtual directories (in IIS) on the Exchange 2013 Client Access server, a lot of logging takes place on an IIS level. The default location of IIS log files is the directory `C:\inetpub\logs\LogFiles\W3SVC1`, and for an average Exchange 2013 Client Access server, it is not uncommon that hundreds of megabytes of data are stored on a daily basis. This amount of data can quickly fill up the system and boot disk of your Client Access server, so you need to act accordingly.

Fellow Exchange Server MVP Paul Cunningham has written a script that will compress the log files into monthly archives and store the archive files in a central archive location. You can find more information regarding this script and a download option on his `ExchangeServerPro.com` website at `http://bit.ly/IISLogsCleanup`.

SSL Certificates

Because Exchange 2013 extensively uses HTTP to communicate between the client and the Client Access server, the SSL certificates are very important. When a Client Access server is installed, a self-signed SSL certificate is created (see Figure 3-10). This self-signed certificate contains only the NetBIOS name of the server as its common name and the FQDN of the server in the "subject alternative name" field. Such a certificate can be used for encryption, but it cannot be used for server authentication, since its issuer (the Exchange server itself) is not trusted by any other machine.

Figure 3-10. *The self-signed certificate on a Client Access server*

■ **Note**   An exception to this is the "Default SMTP Certificate" in an Edge Subscription. When the Edge Subscription is created, the thumbprint of the certificate is copied to the Edge Transport server. This in turn is used for server authentication.

For the Client Access server, this self-signed certificate can be used for testing purposes to see if OWA and EAC are working correctly and to configure the server, but it is not meant for production purposes.

A normal SSL certificate has only one name on it; this is the certificate's common name (CN), and it will work perfectly when the server that's configured with this certificate is accessed by a URL that's equal to the common name. For example, a webshop can be accessed using a URL like `https://shop.contoso.com` and its certificate would have a common name of `CN=shop.contoso.com`. If this site is accessed with a URL like `https://webshop.contoso.com`, it will result in a certificate error such as the one shown in Figure 3-11, saying "The security certificate presented by this website was issued for a different website's address."

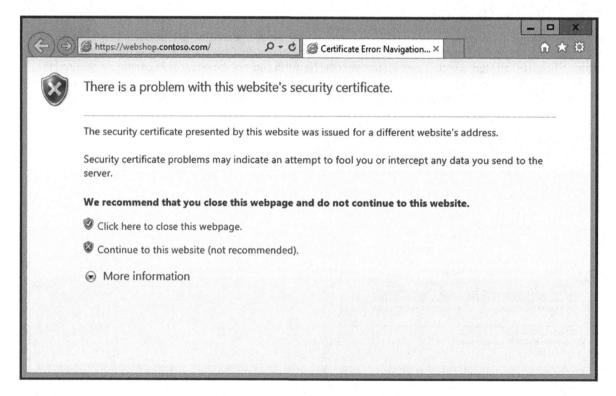

Figure 3-11. *Certificate warning when the URL does not match the certificate's common name*

If you select "Continue to this website (not recommended)," you can proceed with access, but you'll see a certificate warning in the navigation bar.

The "problem" with a Client Access server is that this server can be accessed using a normal URL like `webmail.contoso.com`, but external Outlook clients (that do not have access to Active Directory) automatically try to access the Client Access server using the URL `autodiscover.contoso.com`. If you have a normal SSL certificate, this attempt will fail because the `autodiscover.contoso.com` server name does not match the `CN=webmail.contoso.com` name.

To work around this problem, you can use a Unified Communications (UC) certificate. This UC certificate can hold multiple server names next to its normal common name. These additional server names are stored in an attribute called "subject alternative name." A typical UC certificate for contoso.com would have a CN=webmail. contoso.com and autodiscover.contoso.com entries. If a split-DNS configuration is used in your environment, these server names are sufficient and this is also according to Microsoft best practices. However, there are plenty of successful Exchange Server installations where the local hostname (for example, ams-exch01.contoso.com) is included in the subject alternative names attribute without any complications. Some organizations see this as a possible security issue and prefer not to include the local hostname in the UC certificate.

A UC SSL certificate can be issued by an Active Directory integrated certificate authority (CA), as shown in Figure 3-12, but this works fine only for other servers and workstations that are members of this particular Active Directory domain.

Figure 3-12. *The contoso Unified Communications certificate*

These domain members don't have to be connected to the Active Directory domain though, so domain-joined laptops should work fine when you are working at home or in a hotel and connecting via the Internet. Non-domain-joined computers will work fine as well, but you have to add the root certificate of the CA to the local certificate store of the client.

Doing the latter can become challenging when you're using mobile devices. You can add the root certificate of the CA to these devices, but it takes a considerable amount of work. You have to ask yourself if you want to spend your time on this additional labor or if it would be better to buy a third-party certificate.

The preferred way is to use a third-party certificate from a trusted CA. Both well-known and Microsoft-supported CAs include, for example, Verisign (now owned by Symantec), Entrust, Comodo, and Digicert.

> ■ **Note**   A list of all supported SSL certificates can be found in the Microsoft knowledge base article KB929395, "Unified Communications Certificate Partners," available at http://support.microsoft.com/kb/929395.

Of course, these certificates are not free, but the advantage is that almost all clients support the certificates and there's less certificate management to take care about.

Request a New SSL Certificate

To request a new SSL certificate, log on to the Exchange 2013 Client Access server (or multi-role server, for that matter) as an Exchange Administrator and enter a command in EMS similar to the following:

```
$Data = New-ExchangeCertificate -FriendlyName "Contoso SSL Certificate" -GenerateRequest
-SubjectName "c=US,o=Contoso,cn=webmail.contoso.com"
-DomainName webmail.contoso.com,autodiscover.contoso.com -PrivateKeyExportable $true

Set-Content -path "\\ams-fs01\management\SSLCertRequest.req" -Value $Data
```

> ■ **Note**   A management server with the Exchange Management Tools installed can also be used to request a new SSL certificate.

You have to use the UNC path when storing the SSL certificate request; EMS (and EAC) do not accept use of a local path like C:\Temp. You can use the contents of this file to request an SSL certificate from the Active Directory integrated CA or from your third-party CA, whichever you prefer. When the SSL certificate is returned from the CA, it is important that you finish the SSL certificate creation from the server you used for generating the initial request. In EMS, again use a command similar to the following to finalize the SSL certificate creation:

```
Import-ExchangeCertificate -Server AMS-EXCH01 -FileData ([Byte[]]$(Get-Content -Path "\\ams-fs01\
management\certnew.p7b" -Encoding byte -ReadCount 0)) | Enable-ExchangeCertificate
-Server AMS-EXCH01 -Services IIS
```

Export an SSL Certificate

When the SSL certificate is installed and configured correctly, you can use the Export-ExchangeCertificate command to create a backup file of the Exchange certificate. This backup file can be stored in a safe location, but it can also be used to import on additional Exchange 2013 Client Access servers.

To create an export file of the SSL certificate, you first have to find out the thumbprint of the SSL certificate. This thumbprint is a unique identifier of the SSL certificate within the Exchange environment. The thumbprint of the SSL certificates is shown when executing a Get-ExchangeCertificate command in EMS, as shown in Figure 3-13.

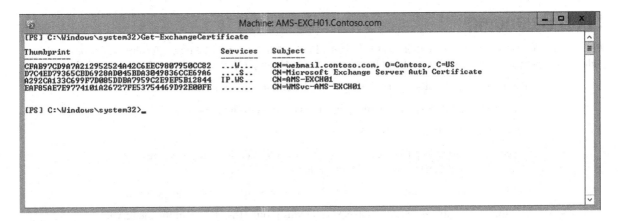

Figure 3-13. *Retrieving the thumbprint of the SSL certificate*

To request the properties of the webmail.contoso.com certificate, you can use the following command in EMS:

```
Get-ExchangeCertificate -Thumbprint 803AD1BD6E8CD3188E7493BFB4DAD679CE094D55 | fl
```

The following commands can be used to export the SSL certificate and store this export in an export file:

```
$ExportFile = Export-ExchangeCertificate -Thumbprint FAB97CD9A7A212952524A42C6EEC9807950CC82
-binaryencoded:$true -password (Get-Credential).password

Set-Content -Path \\ams-fs01\management\webmail-contoso-com.pfx -Value $ExportFile.FileData
-Encoding Byte
```

■ **Note** The Get-Credential command in the previous example shows a dialog box where credentials can be entered. For the Export-ExchangeCertificate command, only the password is used. Use of this password is a security matter when saving the exported certificate.

Import an SSL Certificate

When you have an exported SSL certificate, you can use PowerShell to import this SSL certificate on additional Exchange 2013 Client Access servers. To do this you can use commands similar to the following in EMS:

```
Import-ExchangeCertificate -FileData ([Byte[]]$(Get-Content
-Path \\ams-fs01\management\webmail-contoso-com.pfx -Encoding byte -ReadCount 0))
-Password:(Get-Credential).password | Enable-ExchangeCertificate –Services IIS
```

■ **Note** If you have a load-balanced array of Exchange 2013 Client Access servers, it is important that the SSL certificates used on these servers be identical.

Load Balancing

In the early days of Exchange Server, there was hardly any load balancing, and the Microsoft solution for load balancing was to use Windows Network Load Balancing (NLB). Although NLB works fine, it has some drawbacks:

- NLB is a service in Windows Server, and thus is dependant on the server.

- Scalability of an NLB cluster is not that great and is limited to eight nodes.

- The only option for affinity is source IP.

- When you are adding or removing nodes to or from an NLB cluster, all clients are automatically disconnected and have to reconnect.

- When NLB is used in unicast mode, it is possible that port- or switch-flooding occurs.

- NLB cannot be combined with a database availability group (DAG) on a multi-role server. A DAG is using fail-over clustering software that cannot be combined with NLB software.

- There's no service awareness, a possible "black hole"

Starting with Exchange Server 2010, Microsoft began recommending the use of hardware load balancers in front of Client Access servers, a recommendation that continues for Exchange 2013.

■ **Note**   A recommendation to use a hardware load balancer does not mean that use of NLB is no longer supported; this is absolutely not the case. In both Exchange Server 2010 and 2013, use of NLB is fully supported (when not used on servers that are also DAG nodes). It is just not the recommended approach.

In Exchange 2013, layer-4 load balancing is recommended, whereas in Exchange 2010 it was layer-7 load balancing that was recommended. Layer-4 load balancing is a relatively "dumb" load-balancing mechanism because it does not have access to the information within the requests.

Let's compare load-balancing layers to the OSI model. A layer-7 load balancer is a solution whereby the load balancing takes place on the application layer. The SSL session is terminated at the load balancer and the load balancer can do pretty smart things to the connection, like modifying the HTTP headers or using cookie information in the HTTP stream. This information is then employed to identify the session and make sure the session is always connected to the same Client Access server.

With a layer-4 load balancer, the load balancing takes place on the network layer. An incoming connection is accepted and distributed across multiple Exchange 2013 Client Access servers "as is"—no processing takes place at all. The Client Access server, in turn, accepts the connection and after authentication the connection is forwarded to the appropriate Mailbox server. Since the connections to the Client Access server are stateless, there's no need to worry about affinity. If a Client Access server fails the connection, it is rerouted to another Client Access server. There will be a minor performance penalty, owing to automatic re-authentication, but the connection on the Mailbox server is preserved.

The load balancer is configured with a virtual service, and this virtual service has an FQDN (like webmail. contoso.com) and an IP address. The IP address is referred to as the "virtual IP," or VIP. A client connects to this VIP and thus connects to the load balancer. The load balancer keeps track of the source IP of the connection request and forwards the request to one of the Exchange 2013 Client Access servers.

Keep in mind that, in a layer-4 load balancer, the SSL connection is terminated at the Client Access server and not at the load balancer. Therefore, the load balancer cannot inspect any of the traffic between the client and the Client Access server. If multiple services, such as OWA, EAC, Outlook Anywhere, PowerShell, and ActiveSync, all use the same VIP at the load balancer, the load balancer cannot inspect the traffic, nor can it inspect the destination virtual directory for health concerns.

Thus, if one service on the Exchange 2013 Client Access server fails, the load balancer only detects that the Client Access server in general has failed and it will initiate a fail-over to another Client Access server. To overcome this problem, there are two possible solutions:

- Use multiple VIPs for various services so that the individual VIPs can be checked for health (see Figure 3-14).

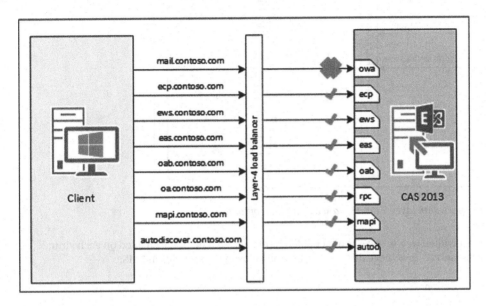

Figure 3-14. *Multiple VIPs on the load balancer for Exchange 2013*

- Use a layer-7 load balancer so that the load balancer can inspect the traffic for the individual services. This can be combined with SSL offloading.

In Figure 3-14, there are eight separate VIPs—one VIP for each server—and they are independent of each other. When the OWA AppPool on the Client Access server fails, only the OWA traffic is redirected to another Client Access server and other traffic continues to be serviced by this particular Client Access server.

SSL Offloading

New in Exchange 2013 SP1 is support for SSL offloading. When using SSL offloading, the SSL traffic is terminated at the load balancer; beyond the load balancer, the traffic can continue unencrypted. This was not supported in Exchange 2013 RTM, so re-encryption had to be used in Exchange 2013 versions prior to SP1.

With SSL offloading, it is possible to perform content inspection and thus evaluate the individual client request and then proxy these individual client requests to individual virtual directories on the Client Access server. In this scenario the individual services don't interact with each other, so when one service fails the other service continues working—like the example in the previous section with the multiple VIPs. A single namespace with SSL offloading is shown in Figure 3-15.

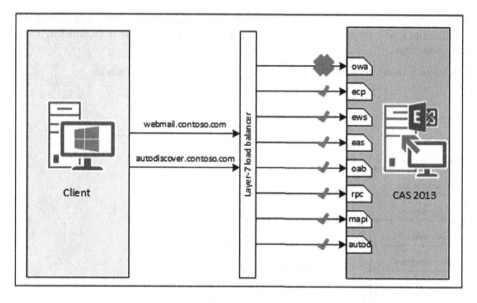

Figure 3-15. *A single namespace with layer-7 load balancing and SSL offloading*

SSL offloading for the individual web services is not enabled by default, so it has to be enabled on each virtual directory on the Client Access server. To achieve this you can use the following commands in EMS:

```
Import-Module WebAdministration

Set-WebConfigurationProperty -Filter //security/access -name sslflags -Value "None"
-PSPath IIS: -Location "Default Web Site/OWA"

Set-WebConfigurationProperty -Filter //security/access -name sslflags -Value "None"
-PSPath IIS: -Location "Default Web Site/ECP"

Set-WebConfigurationProperty -Filter //security/access -name sslflags -Value "None"
-PSPath IIS: -Location "Default Web Site/OAB"

Set-WebConfigurationProperty -Filter //security/access -name sslflags -Value "None"
-PSPath IIS: -Location "Default Web Site/EWS"

Set-WebConfigurationProperty -Filter //security/access -name sslflags -Value "None"
-PSPath IIS: -Location "Default Web Site/Microsoft-Server-ActiveSync"

Set-WebConfigurationProperty -Filter //security/access -name sslflags -Value "None"
-PSPath IIS: -Location "Default Web Site/Autodiscover"

Set-WebConfigurationProperty -Filter //security/access -name sslflags -Value "None"
-PSPath IIS: -Location "Default Web Site/MAPI"
```

■ **Note** These commands can be downloaded from the Apress website.

For Outlook Anywhere on Exchange 2013, SSL offloading is enabled by default. If for some reason the SSL offloading for Outlook Anywhere is not enabled, you can use the following commands in EMS to enable SSL offloading:

```
Get-OutlookAnywhere -Server AMS-EXCH01 | Set-OutlookAnywhere
-ExternalHostname webmail.contoso.com -ExternalClientsRequireSsl:$true
-ExternalClientAuthenticationMethod:Basic -InternalHostName webmail.contoso.com
-InternalClientsRequireSsl:$true -InternalClientAuthenticationMethod:Basic
```

SMTP Transport

In Exchange 2013, the complete set of services, components, connections, and queues that deal with item transport is called the "transport pipeline." This transport pipeline is made up of three different services:

- **Front End Transport service (FETS)** FETS is the part that is running on the Exchange 2013 Client Access server. It acts as a stateless SMTP protocol proxy for inbound and outbound SMTP traffic. FETS accepts connections from the Internet and routes them to the appropriate Mailbox server or down-level Hub Transport server. FETS does not store any information in a queue on the local disk, and therefore it cannot do any content inspection.

- **Transport service** The Transport service is comparable to the Hub Transport server role in Exchange Server 2010 and 2007, except that it is no longer a dedicated server role; instead, it is part of the Mailbox server. Because of this, the message routing, especially in multi-site database availability groups, is much more efficient. The Transport service performs message categorization and can perform message inspection. All internal routing between Exchange servers is always performed by the Transport service, but the Transport service never communicates with the Mailbox databases.

- **Mailbox Transport service** The Mailbox Transport service runs on all Mailbox servers and is made up of two different services:

  - The Mailbox Transport delivery service accept messages from the Transport service and delivers the message to the Mailbox database via a local RPC connection with the Mailbox database.

  - The Mailbox Transport submission service connects to the Mailbox database using local RPC, but retrieves messages from the Mailbox database that are in the user's outbox and delivers those messages, using SMTP to the Transport service for further processing.

■ **Note** The entire transport pipeline will be discussed in Chapter 4. That chapter is about the Exchange 2013 Mailbox server, and SMTP transport is a major component of this server role.

So, FETS running on the Client Access server accepts messages from the Internet and from the Transport service running on the Mailbox server. For receiving messages, "receive connectors" are used. For sending messages, a "send connector" is used. A send connector is used by the Transport service on the Mailbox server, but it can use the Client Access server as a local proxy that is controlled with the `FrontEndProxyEnabled` parameter when creating the send connector.

The Send Connector

To use the Front End proxy function in the Exchange 2013 Client Access server, you first have to create a send connector. You can create a new send connector by entering the following command in EMS:

```
New-SendConnector -Name "To_Internet" -Internet -AddressSpaces "*" -DNSRoutingEnabled:$TRUE
-SourceTransportServers "AMS-EXCH01","AMS-EXCH02" -FrontendProxyEnabled:$TRUE
```

This command will create a new send connector that's used to send messages to the Internet. It will use DNS to find the SMTP servers to deliver these messages to instead of using a smart host. The Transport servers in the Exchange 2013 environment are AMS-EXCH01 and AMS-EXCH02, and the last parameter will make sure the Exchange 2013 Client Access servers are used as an SMTP proxy.

New in Exchange 2013 SP1 is the (re)introduction of the Edge Transport server role. When an Exchange 2013 Edge Transport server is introduced in the Exchange 2013 environment, it sends messages to the Internet and receives messages from the Internet. The Edge Transport server is communicating directly with the Transport service on the Mailbox server, bypassing FETS on the Client Access server.

The Exchange 2013 Edge Transport server role will be discussed in more detail as part of message hygiene in Chapter 9.

The Receive Connectors

Receive connectors in Exchange 2013 are responsible for accepting SMTP messages from other messaging servers. These messaging servers can be internal Exchange servers or external SMTP servers.

By default, an Exchange 2013 Client Access server has three receive connectors:

- *Default front end <<server name>>* The default front-end receive connector is used to receive SMTP messages from external servers—that is, from the Internet. This receive connector is listening on port 25.

- *Client front end <<server name>>* The client front-end receive connector is used for sending SMTP messages by clients—that is, users needing an SMTP host to send messages. These users are authenticated before they are able to send messages. The client front-end receive connector uses port 587 to receive messages.

- *Outbound proxy front end <<server name>>* The outbound proxy front-end receive connector is used by the Client Access server to receive messages from the Mailbox server that are proxied to external hosts—for example, on the Internet. The outbound proxy front-end server uses port 717 to receive messages.

When the Exchange 2013 Client Access server is installed, all receive connectors are automatically created and configured properly, so with out-of-the-box installations there's no need to configure them manually.

Anti-Spam Features

In Exchange 2013, anti-spam features are configured on the Mailbox server and not on the Client Access server. Therefore, all SMTP messages including spam messages are accepted at the Client Access server and are proxied to the Mailbox server, where anti-spam processing takes place. The following anti-spam features are available:

- Sender filtering
- Recipient filtering
- Sender ID filtering
- Content filtering
- Sender reputation filtering

Unfortunately, connection filtering is not available on the Exchange 2013 Transport server. This is only available on the Exchange 2013 Edge Transport server.

■ **Note**   Since anti-spam features are running on the Mailbox server as part the Transport service, they will be discussed in more detail in Chapter 5. The anti-spam features of the Exchange 2013 Edge Transport server will be discussed in detail in Chapter 6.

Load-Balancing SMTP

It is obvious by now that a hardware load balancer is strongly recommended in front of the Exchange 2013 Client Access servers. This is true not only for handling client protocols like HTTPS, POP3, and IMAP4 but also for SMTP. Keep in mind that SMTP can also use multiple MX records for load-balancing purposes.

The load balancer can be used for inbound SMTP traffic from other SMTP hosts from the Internet on port 25, or for client SMTP submissions on port 587. The load balancer can be a simple layer-4 solution whereby the connections are directly sent to the Client Access server.

Publishing Exchange

An Exchange 2013 Client Access server needs to be connected to the Internet to have external clients connect to it. There are a few of possibilities:

- Direct connection
- Using TMG 2010 (and UAG 2010 to some extend)
- Using IIS/ARR
- Windows 2012 Web Proxy
- Load balancer reverse proxy

These options are explained in more detail next.

Direct Connection

A direct connection is one of my personal preferences. It is a configuration whereby the Exchange 2013 Client Access server has two network interfaces:

- NIC1 is connected to the internal network.

- NIC2 is connected to the external network.

The external network in this configuration can be the Internet, but of course in combination with a solid firewall solution where only the following ports are opened:

- Port 25 for SMTP

- Port 80 for HTTP

- Port 443 for HTTPS

- Port 587 for SMTP submission

- Ports 110 and 143 for POP3 and IMAP4

- Ports 993 and 995 for Secure POP3 and Secure IMAP4.

It depends on your own requirements which ports need to be opened.

Frequently, security officers in an organization have problems with a configuration like this. But remember that Windows Server is designed with the Internet threats in mind and is secure by default. Most issues still come from a bad configuration and sysadmin misinterpretation, and not from Windows. Also, Exchange 2013 is "hardened" by default.

Sure, you don't have pre-authentication in a configuration like this, and you don't have any deep content inspection of inbound traffic, although a decent firewall can do this when needed. But a direct connection is a fully supported scenario and there's nothing wrong with it.

TMG 2010

Microsoft ForeFront Threat Management Gateway (TMG) 2010 is used a lot by customers to publish Exchange servers to the Internet. It can do some load balancing, firewalling, content inspection, reverse proxy, or URL rewriting. And it doesn't cost too much, which is a big advantage for most customers.

The downside of TMG 2010 is that it's no longer available and support for TMG is being stopped by Microsoft. Mainstream support for TMG 2010 will end on April 14, 2015, and extended support will end on April 14, 2020.

The good thing is that although TMG 2010 is no longer available, it still works with Exchange 2013 and still is a fully supported scenario. The Microsoft Exchange product team has published an extensive blog on how to configure this, and you can find this blog post on `http://bit.ly/Ex2013TMG`.

But since TMG 2010 is no longer officially available, it's time to look for alternatives and the following are available:

- Application Request Routing (ARR), which is an add-on for Internet Information server.

- Web Application Proxy (WAP), which is part of Windows Server 2012 R2.

- Third- party solutions like Load Balancer Reverse Proxy.

These solutions offer very similar solutions, although they don't have as many options as TMG 2010 had. Of these three solutions, WAP is the strategic choice.

■ **Note** When Microsoft announced the end of life for TMG 2010, the official alternative was ForeFront Unified Application Gateway (UAG), but UAG's end of life has been officially announced as well.

IIS/ARR

Application Request Routing (ARR) is an IIS extension that allows IIS to act as a reverse proxy as well as a load balancer, free of charge! The only prerequisite for running IIS/ARR is that you have a Windows Server 2008 or later with IIS 7.0 (or later) on it. Furthermore, there's no need for this Windows server to be domain joined, so you can install it in your network's DMZ as well.

As shown in Figure 3-16, IIS/ARR consists of two parts. The URL rewrite module acts as the reverse proxy and the web farm. In the web farm properties, you can configure a load balancer when multiple Exchange 2013 Client Access servers are used.

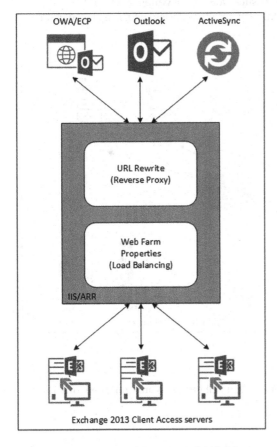

Figure 3-16. *Functional overview of IIS/ARR*

Besides load balancing, IIS/ARR can perform health checking, SSL offloading, and server affinity, and it can use both layer-4 and layer-7 routing. As explained earlier in this chapter, you can use IIS/ARR with a single namespace or with multiple namespaces, and you can use per-protocol health check. The only thing that IIS/ARR lacks is pre-authentication for clients.

■ **Note**   IIS/ARR also works with Exchange Server 2007 and Exchange Server 2010.

You can download the ARR module for IIS from the IIS.NET website at `http://bit.ly/ARRDownload`.

Windows 2012 R2 Web Application Proxy

The Microsoft strategic solution when it comes to a TMG 2010 replacement is the Web Application Proxy (WAP), which is part of the remote access role in Windows Server 2012 R2. As such, you need a Windows 2012 R2 ADFS installation in your environment. The WAP server itself acts as an ADFS proxy and is designed to be installed in the network's DMZ, as shown in Figure 3-17.

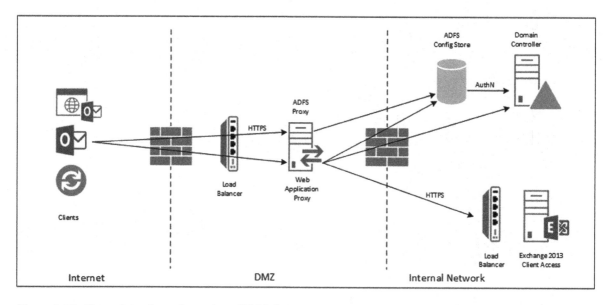

Figure 3-17. *Network topology when using a WAP infrastructure*

WAP is a fully supported solution for use with Exchange Server 2013, and all protocols are supported for proxying via the WAP server:

- OWA/ECP
- ActiveSync
- Outlook Anywhere
- MapiHttp

- Exchange Web Services

- Offline Address Book

- Autodiscover

WAP offers pre-authentication as well, but only for OWA and ECP, not for other protocols or clients. New in Exchange 2013 SP1 and WAP is support for ADFS authentication based on SAML 2.0 (claims-based authentication). One issue here is that it's not possible to mix different authentication mechanisms. Authentication is either ADFS or it's any other form of authentication, like Forms Based, NTLM, Basic, and so on. It also only works against a pure Exchange 2013 SP1 environment; any coexistence scenario, even with Exchange 2013 RTM, is not supported and will not work.

ADFS authentication is becoming more and more important (driven by Office 365) and developments in this area occur extremely fast. More information regarding the implementation of ADFS, including detailed installation steps, can be found in the article "Using AD FS Claims-based Authentication with Outlook Web App and EAC," at http://bit.ly/ADFS-Ex2013.

Load Balancer Reverse Proxy

Another solution for reverse proxy and pre-authentication is coming from load balancer vendors like Kemp Technologies or F5 Networks.

Load balancer vendors typically work closely with Microsoft on developing these kinds of solutions, so this should be fully supported as well. However, keep in mind that these are supported by the load balancer vendor, not Microsoft.

Kemp Technologies, and to a lesser degree F5 Networks, is working closely with the Exchange community to position its solutions. This means a lot of information can be found in Exchange user groups, webinars, articles, and blog posts. When you already have a (hardware) load balancer, this is certainly an area to examine.

Summary

The Exchange Server 2013's Client Access server role is an interesting and important one. It is a building block of Exchange 2013, as all clients always connect to the Client Access server. In Exchange 2013, there are no more clients connecting directly to the Mailbox server.

Changes with respect to previous versions of Exchange server include that the traditional MAPI (RPC over TCP) is no longer supported in Exchange 2013 and that all Outlook connectivity is via Outlook Anywhere (RPC over HTTP). New in Exchange 2013 SP1 is a protocol called MapiHttp, whereby Outlook is using native HTTP to communicate with the Exchange 2013 SP1 Client Access server, without the RPC encapsulation layer.

From an infrastructure point of view, the Exchange 2013 Client Access server is a "thin" one. It only accepts incoming requests, authenticates them, and proxies them to the Mailbox server where the mailbox is located. The only exception is SIP requests. These are authenticated and then redirected to the correct Mailbox server instead of proxying them to the correct Mailbox server. Connections between the clients and the Exchange 2013 Client Access server are stateless. The service that's responsible for this is the Client Access Front End service, or CAFE.

Important for an Exchange 2013 server is to configure your Client Access servers appropriately. Namespaces, virtual directories, SSL certificates, and Autodiscover need to be in good condition. If you fail to configure these properly, you will see strange things happen in client communications, ranging from an inability to set out-of-office messages to not being able to connect to the Client Access server at all.

All business logic in Exchange 2013 is removed from the Client Access server and transferred to the Mailbox server, and this includes Autodiscover.

The SMTP Front-End Transport service (FETS) is an SMTP proxy in the Exchange 2013 Client Access server. All inbound SMTP traffic is delivered on the Client Access server and proxied directly to the Exchange 2013 Mailbox server.

When it comes to publishing your Exchange 2013 Client Access server to the Internet, you should be aware that TMG 2010 is no longer available (but still supported). Viable alternatives are IIS/ARR and WAP (the latter being Microsoft's strategic alternative) or using a third-party hardware load balancer. WAP is emerging technology and difficult to understand, but this situation will change in the upcoming months, when more organizations start deploying WAP and more information is available.

From a management perspective, the Exchange 2013 Client Access server is not too challenging. Once you get it set up correctly, your management tasks may be monthly IIS log file archiving or yearly SSL certificate renewal. More configuration and management is required in the Exchange 2013 Mailbox server, which is the subject of the next chapter.

CHAPTER 4

■ ■ ■

Exchange 2013 Mailbox Server

The primary role of the Mailbox server is to host mailbox databases where the recipient mailboxes are hosted. But in Exchange Server 2013, there's more done besides hosting those mailboxes. The Hub Transport service is also running on the Mailbox server, and this service is responsible for all SMTP message routing in the Exchange organization. The Unified Messaging (UM)service is also part of the Mailbox server role, and there's a Client Access service (CAS) running on the Mailbox server as well. As explained in the previous chapter, the Client Access server is a stateless protocol proxy, proxying user requests to the Mailbox server; this is the server where all processing takes place. But in Exchange 2013, the business logic was moved from the Client Access server to the Mailbox server. This is the reason you'll find the Autodiscover section in this chapter instead of in Chapter 3.

An important part of the Mailbox server is hosting the mailbox databases where all the mailboxes are located. The database technology used in Exchange 2013 is the first part of this chapter, including the management tasks related to the mailbox database technologies. Also important are the various types of recipients, like mailboxes, distribution groups, or contacts; this is the third major section of this chapter.

The Transport service is the successor to the Hub Transport server role in down-level Exchange versions and is part of the Mailbox server role in Exchange 2013. A description of this is also included in this chapter. The Unified Messaging service is not covered in this chapter; it will be discussed in detail in Chapter 8.

The Mailbox Server Role

The Exchange 2013 Mailbox Server role is similar to the earlier Mailbox server role in Exchange Server 2010. It is responsible for processing all mail items, storing those items in the mailbox database, and showing them in the user's inbox.

All mail items are stored in a mailbox, and all mailboxes are stored in a mailbox database. This mailbox database is stored by default on the local hard disk of the Mailbox server, in the `C:\Program Files\Microsoft\Exchange Server\V15\Mailbox\<<database name>>` directory. Figure 4-1 shows this configuration for a mailbox database called `Mailbox Database 0833106092`.

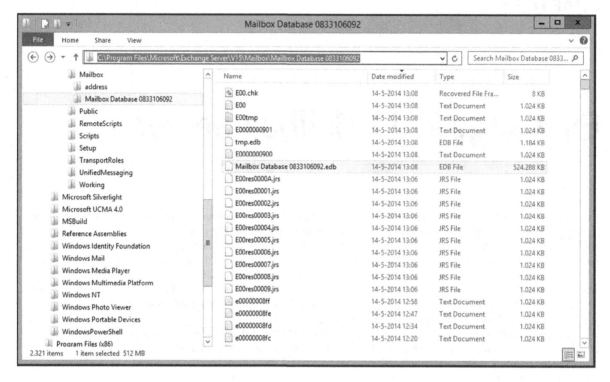

Figure 4-1. *Mailbox database files on disk*

The following files are available, as can be seen in Figure 4-1:

- The file Mailbox Database 0833106092.edb is the actual mailbox database where all the individual mail items are stored.

- Tmp.edb is a temporary file used by Exchange Server.

- E00 and subsequent log files are log files used for the transactional processing of information.

- E00.chk is a checkpoint file that keeps track of the transactions still in the log files, as well as those that are already written to the mailbox database. This file is not visible in Figure 4-1.

- E00res00001.jrs - E00res0000A.jrs are temporary log files reserved by Exchange Server in case of disk-full problems.

- E00tmp.log is a temporary log file used by Exchange Server.

All these files belong together, and they make up one mailbox database. One Exchange 2013 Enterprise Mailbox server can host up to 100 mailbox databases. Exchange 2013 now fully supports multiple mailbox databases on one physical disk if you have multiple copies of the mailbox databases in a database availability group (DAG).

■ **Note**   In Exchange 2013 Enterprise RTM and Enterprise CU1, the number of mailbox databases was limited to 50. In Exchange 2013 Enterprise CU2, this maximum was increased to 100. The maximum number of mailbox databases on an Exchange 2013 Standard, however, is limited to 5, independent of any cumulative update.

When you install a Mailbox server, a new mailbox database is automatically created on the system disk, as shown in Figure 4-1. When you create additional mailbox databases, they have a preference for this system disk as well. However, using this disk for those additional mailbox databases is not a good idea. It is best practice to move the initially created mailbox database and subsequently created mailbox databases to dedicated volumes that are capable of handling the load generated in processing the mailbox items.

The Mailbox Database

The mailbox database is the primary repository of the Exchange Mailbox server information; it's where all the Exchange data is stored. In theory, the mailbox database can be 16 TB, which is the NTFS size limit of a file, but it is normally limited to a size you can handle within the constraints of your service level agreement (SLA). The recommended maximum database size for a normal Exchange 2013 Mailbox server is 2 TB when you have multiple copies of the mailbox database in a database availability group. If this is not the case, the maximum recommended size is 200 GB—but in practice it is limited by your backup and restore solution and by the accompanying SLA.

The mailbox database in Exchange 2013 is an *extensible storage engine* (ESE) database. ESE is a low-level database technology, sometimes also referred to as a *JET database*. The ESE database has been used since Exchange Server 4.0. The Active Directory database, the WINS database, and the DHCP database also are ESE databases.

The ESE database processing follows the "acid" principle:

- **Atomic** – A transaction is all or nothing; there is no "unknown state" for a transaction.

- **Consistent** – The transaction preserves the consistency of the data being processed.

- **Isolated** – A single transaction is the only transaction on this data, even when multiple transactions occur at the same time.

- **Durable** – The committed transactions are preserved in the database.

Transactions are part of everyday life. Suppose you go to the bank to transfer money from your savings account to your checking account. The money is withdrawn from your savings account and then added to your checking account, and both actions are recorded and maybe even printed on paper. Yet this can be seen as one transaction. You don't want the transaction to end with the first step, in which the money is withdrawn from your savings account but it's not yet added to your checking account.

The same principle goes for Exchange Server. Suppose you move a message from your inbox to a folder named "Book Project" From a transaction point of view, it starts by adding the message to the Authoring folder, then it updates the message count for this folder, deletes the message from the inbox, and updates the message count for the inbox. All these actions can be seen as one transaction.

The data within a database is organized as a balanced tree, or B-tree. This binary arrangement can be easily envisioned as an upside-down tree where the leaves are at the bottom and the root at the top, as illustrated in Figure 4-2. The actual mail data is stored in the leaves. The mid-level pages contain the pointers. The upper level is the root. This B-tree design is an efficient way of storing data because it requires only two or three lookups to find a particular piece of data, and all the pointers can be kept in memory.

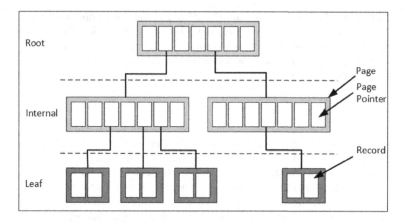

Figure 4-2. *A balanced tree setup*

Exchange actually uses an enhanced version of a B-tree, called the B+ tree. This B+ tree contains pointers between the pages, so every page in a leaf has a pointer to the next page and to the previous page, making it even more efficient. This arrangement is also referred to as an *indexed sequential access method* (ISAM) database.

One of the functions of ESE is to balance the tree. It's not hard to imagine that when lots of data is added to the database, the tree becomes unbalanced. When this happens, though, ESE reorganizes the tree by splitting and merging the pointer pages.

Similarly, when a page becomes full, ESE splits the page into two adjacent pages. If this happens, an additional key is put into the secondary key's parent page. The process continues until the parent page becomes full as well. Then, the parent page is split and the new secondary page's parent page is updated with a new key.

It can happen that the root level becomes full, and then the root level needs to be split also. If this happens, an additional layer of pages is inserted into the tree and the tree now has four layers instead of three. A balanced tree with four layers is shown in Figure 4-3. Obviously, a four-layer tree has many more leaves, containing more data.

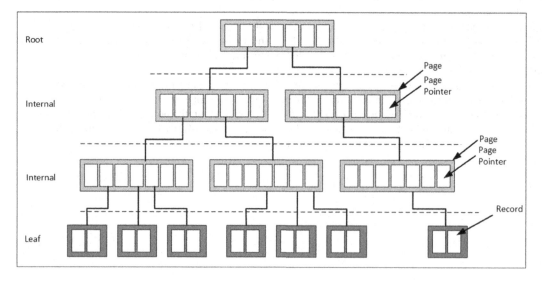

Figure 4-3. *A balanced tree after a tree split*

If data is removed from the mailbox database, the leaves are emptied and the parent pages become available again. When too many adjacent parent pages become available, ESE can merge those pages. Eventually, when lots and lots of merges happen, even up to the root level, ESE can remove an entire layer of pages, thereby shrinking the tree. Note that this happens *inside* the database. The tree can shrink, but the size of the database will never shrink! ESE pages are freed up and filled as a continuous process; once they are freed up, they are reorganized, as explained in a later section regarding online defragmentation.

To read data from a particular leaf, ESE starts at the root level and follows the tree down to the leaf. To reach the data, only three or four read actions are needed. Since most of the pages and pointers are stored in memory, this happens extremely fast—even in a 250 GB database, for example. ESE stores over 1,600 page pointers in a 32 KB page, making it possible to create a tree with a minimal number of parent/child levels.

One or more trees in a database make up a table. There are several kinds of tables in Exchange Server:

Mailbox table

Folders table

Message table

The tables hold the information that appears in the inbox. The tables consist of columns and records; the columns are identified as MAPI properties, and the records contain the actual information.

Database Pages

A *page* is the smallest unit of data in an Exchange environment. It consists of a header, pointers to other pages, checksum information to ensure that the page is not corrupted, and data from Exchange Server regarding messages, attachments, or folders. A database file can consist of millions of pages. For Exchange 2010 and 2013, the size of a page is 32 KB. The total number of pages can easily be calculated by dividing the total size of the database by this page size of 32 KB. If, for example, the size of a database is 250 GB, it consists of 250 GB times 32 KB, or approximately 8.2 million pages.

Each page is sequentially numbered. Whenever a new page is created, it gets a new, incremented number. When the pages are read from the database and altered, they also get new page numbers before being written to the log file and flushed to the database file. Needless to say, this sequential number must be very large. In fact, it's a 64-bit number, which means that 18 quintillion changes can be made to a database!

One question that's asked sometimes is if it's possible to read the actual pages to see if there's any content there, especially in a disaster recovery scenario when data seems to have been lost.

I'm afraid it's not that simple. It's true; there is content in all these pages, but it's not readable without sophisticated tools. It is possible to check the contents of individual pages inside a mailbox database using the ESEUTIL tool, but as shown in Figure 4-4, there's not much readable information there.

```
Machine: lies02.gelderen.local                                      _  □  X

[PS] F:\Mailbox Database 0833106092>eseutil /mh '.\Mailbox Database 0833106092.edb' /p32

Extensible Storage Engine Utilities for Microsoft(R) Exchange Server
Version 15.00
Copyright (C) Microsoft Corporation. All Rights Reserved.

Initiating FILE DUMP mode...
        Database: .\Mailbox Database 0833106092.edb
        Page: 32

HEADER checksum    = 0x2AB82AB87A396CCC:0x0000000000000020:0x0000000000000020:0x0255FDAA4C07481B
                     logged data checksum = 5ff178b26b350df2

                    checksum (0x000000AACCEA0000,  8):   3078257317120666828 (0x2AB82AB87A396CCC)
               dbtimeDirtied (0x000000AACCEA0008,  8):   3574632 (0x368B68)
                    pgnoPrev (0x000000AACCEA0010,  4):   0 (0x0)
                    pgnoNext (0x000000AACCEA0014,  4):   0 (0x0)
                     objidFDP (0x000000AACCEA0018,  4):   9 (0x9)
                      cbFree (0x000000AACCEA001C,  2):   31305 (0x7A49)
            cbUncommittedFree (0x000000AACCEA001E,  2):   0 (0x0)
                   ibMicFree (0x000000AACCEA0020,  2):   1315 (0x523)
                 itagMicFree (0x000000AACCEA0022,  2):   17 (0x11)
                      fFlags (0x000000AACCEA0024,  4):   10243 (0x2803)
                rgChecksum[0] (0x000000AACCEA0028,  8):   32 (0x20)
                rgChecksum[1] (0x000000AACCEA0030,  8):   32 (0x20)
                rgChecksum[2] (0x000000AACCEA0038,  8):   168319468958074907 (0x255FDAA4C07481B)
                        pgno (0x000000AACCEA0040,  4):   32 (0x20)
        Leaf page
        Root page
        FDP page
               Single Extent Space (ParentFDP: 1)
        Primary page
        New record format
        New checksum format
        PageFlushType = 2

TAG   0   cb:0x0010   ib:0x0000   offset:0x0050-0x0060   flags:0x0000 (    )
TAG   1   cb:0x003f   ib:0x0010   offset:0x0060-0x009f   flags:0x0000 (    )
TAG   2   cb:0x0038   ib:0x004f   offset:0x009f-0x00d7   flags:0x0000 (    )
TAG   3   cb:0x0049   ib:0x0087   offset:0x00d7-0x0120   flags:0x0000 (    )
TAG   4   cb:0x004d   ib:0x00d0   offset:0x0120-0x016d   flags:0x0000 (    )
TAG   5   cb:0x0047   ib:0x011d   offset:0x016d-0x01b4   flags:0x0000 (    )
TAG   6   cb:0x003b   ib:0x0164   offset:0x01b4-0x01ef   flags:0x0000 (    )
TAG   7   cb:0x007f   ib:0x019f   offset:0x01ef-0x026e   flags:0x0000 (    )
TAG   8   cb:0x004d   ib:0x021e   offset:0x026e-0x02bb   flags:0x0000 (    )
TAG   9   cb:0x0047   ib:0x026b   offset:0x02bb-0x0302   flags:0x0000 (    )
TAG  10   cb:0x007b   ib:0x02b2   offset:0x0302-0x037d   flags:0x0000 (    )
```

Figure 4-4. *The contents of a page inside a mailbox database are not readable*

■ **Note**   Special recovery tools like Kroll Ontrack PowerControls are able to open a mailbox database file (i.e., the actual Mailbox Database 033106092.edb file to retrieve content from the mailbox database without running an Exchange server. These tools have logic to read all the tables and convert them to actual mailbox content. This will be discussed in detail in Chapter 7.

Transaction Log Files

Mailbox items are processed by the Mailbox server in what are termed "transactions." A transaction can be:

- The creation of a new message or a new calendar item.
- The storage of a message received from SMTP in the mailbox.
- The creation of a new folder in the mailbox.
- The deletion of a message in the mailbox.
- The renaming of a folder in the mailbox.
- The creation of new mailbox database.

And so on.

All processing—that is, the creation of transactions—takes place in the server memory, in particular in the log buffers, the ESE cache (this is where the pages reside), and the version store. The *version store* is a small part in memory, tied to the ESE cache, that's used by ESE to keep track of all transactions while they are created. When something goes wrong with a transaction, ESE can create a new transaction and keep track of the various versions of those transactions, hence the name.

The log buffers, each 1 MB in size, contain the contents of a log file that's currently being created. When transactions are created, they are stored in a particular log buffer, and this log buffer represents a log file that belongs to a certain mailbox database.

When a log buffer is filled with transactions, the entire log buffer is flushed to disk (i.e., written to a log file), the log file is closed, and a new log buffer and accompanying transaction log file is created. If you look back at Figure 4-1, you'll see these transaction log files identified as E00.log, E00000008ff.log, E0000000900.log, and E0000000901.log. At this point no changes are made to the mailbox database and all pages are kept in memory. This mechanism is called *write ahead logging*, so the data in the log files is always ahead of the data in the mailbox database. A graphic representation of this techology can be seen in Figure 4-5.

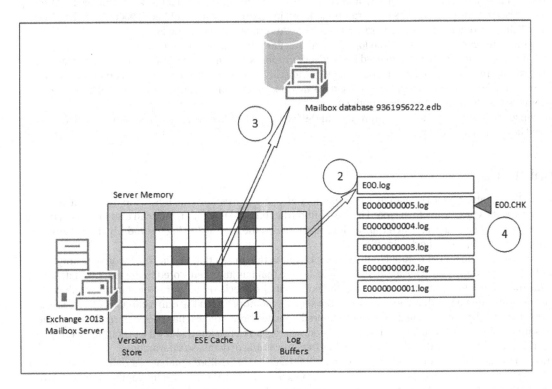

Figure 4-5. *The mailbox database, server memory, and log files*

Transactional logging is a sequential process, so subsequent transaction log files are numbered accordingly. Note that a *hexadecimal* notation is used, so after writing a transaction log file that ends with the number 9, the letter A is added. Only after writing a transaction log file ending with the letter F (the sixth letter of the alphabet) does Exchange Server start a new sequence.

The name of a log file can be split into two parts:

- **The prefix** This is the first three characters of the name—in this example, E00. Every mailbox database has its unique set of log files, and the prefix is what differentiates one from another. The first mailbox database has prefix E00, while mailbox database number 100 has prefix E99. In contrast to the sequential numbering of the transaction log files, the prefix is in *decimal* notation.

- **The number** This is an eight-character hexidecimal number that's generated sequentially, starting with 0x00000001 and theoretically ending with 0xffffffff. This hexidecimal number is not only used in the filename of the log file but also inside the log file as a sequence number. In ESE terms, it is called the *lGeneration number*.

The log file that's currently in use—that is, the log file where the contents of the log buffer will be flushed to—is a log file called E00.log (or any other prefix, of course). You might see a log file called E00TEMP.log occasionally; that's a log file that's pre-created by ESE. When the log buffers are flushed to the log file (i.e., E00.log), the log file is stored with a file name based on the prefix and its lGeneration number; in Figure 4-4, this would be E0000000006.log. The E00TEMP.log will then be renamed E00.log to save time during this processing of the log file.

By storing the transactions in a transaction log file, you safeguard the data against server failures, such as a power failure. In fact, the transaction log file can be used for recovery purposes. When a server fails, or a mailbox database fails, the information can be recovered and reconstructed because it has been stored in the transaction log files. For this reason it is not a good idea to manually delete the transaction log files from your server (unless you have no other option), as doing so will destroy your recovery options.

Transaction log files are automatically removed from the Exchange Mailbox server when you run a backup solution, as will be explained in Chapter 7.

Checkpoint File

As explained earlier, database pages remain in server memory after the transactions are flushed to the transaction log file. After some time, these pages are then stored in the mailbox database. At this point, they can also be removed from the server's memory. To keep track of which transactions are stored in the transaction log file and which are stored in the mailbox database, you need a checkpoint file.

The checkpoint file is an 8 KB file stored in the same location as the transaction log file, but it contains only a pointer. This pointer "points to" the page in the transaction log file that has just been stored in the mailbox database. All pages in the transaction log file that are older than the pointer in the checkpoint file are stored in the mailbox database; all pages that are newer, therefore, remain in the server's memory and in the transaction log file. In case of a problem—for example, when the Exchange server is rebooted unexpectedly—the Exchange Server reads the location in the checkpoint file and knows which information is stored where, and thus it knows how it can start recovering information. This is a simple and safe solution for trouble-free processing of database information.

The amount of data that's still in server memory and not flushed to the mailbox database, and thus the amount of data "above" the checkpoint, is called the *checkpoint depth*. In Exchange 2013, the checkpoint depth can be 100 MB; this means that 100 MB of data can be located in server memory but hasn't been flushed to the mailbox database, and so it is safely stored in the log files.

The checkpoint depth is per database; each database has its own set of log files, its own checkpoint file, and thus its own checkpoint depth. This means when you have, for example, 25 mailbox databases, you can have 25 × 100 log files, or 2.5 GB of mailbox data in server memory that's not been flushed to the mailbox database (but that is stored in the transaction log file, though!).

Why is this important to know? There are two reasons you want to know this:

1. Exchange Server uses this technique for recovery purposes when mounting a mailbox database, after restoring a mailbox database from a backup, or by using the ESEUTIL tool.

2. Mailbox data is dynamic, as data can be in server memory, in the mailbox database, or in the transaction log file. The backup application needs to be aware of this process so it can interact with the Exchange server while creating the backup. Needless to say, a regular file-level backup is not going to work when you are backing up mailbox databases.

How This All Fits Together

A mailbox database that is running (i.e., it is mounted) is always in an inconsistent state. That is, there's mailbox data spread across the Exchange server's memory, the transaction log file, and the mailbox database. This inconsistent state is also known as *dirty*.

A graphic representation can be seen in Figure 4-6. Clearly visible in this Figure is the part of the Mailbox databases that has been flushed to the transaction log files (and thus not yet to the mailbox database) and its relation to the checkpoint file.

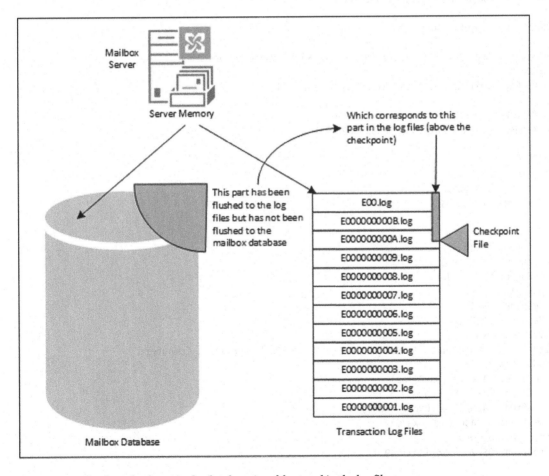

Figure 4-6. *The data that's not in the database is safely stored in the log files*

When you have a mailbox database on disk that's not mounted *and* is in a dirty shutdown state—for example, after a crash of the server—you need the corresponding transaction log file where the pages are stored that had not been previously written to the mailbox database. Only if you have these transaction log files is it possible to recover and bring the mailbox database to a consistent state. If you have a mailbox database in a dirty shutdown mode and you *do not* have the appropriate transaction log files, you're in trouble. The only thing that's left to do is to repair the mailbox database using the ESEUTIL tool, which will cause some data loss.

When a database is properly dismounted, it is brought into a consistent state. All data in server memory is flushed to the mailbox database, the checkpoint is moved to the last correct location, and all files are then closed. This is called a *clean shutdown* of the database.

Header Information

The transaction log files needed to get the database into a consistent state, and thus in a clean shutdown mode, are recorded in the header of the mailbox database. The header of the database is written into the first page of the database file, and it contains information regarding that mailbox database. The header information can be retrieved using the ESEUTIL tool. Just enter the following command in the directory where the database file resides:

ESEUTIL /MH " Mailbox Database 0833106092.edb "

This will result in an output such as:

```
Extensible Storage Engine Utilities for Microsoft(R) Exchange Server
Version 15.00
Copyright (C) Microsoft Corporation. All Rights Reserved.

Initiating FILE DUMP mode...
        Database: Mailbox Database 0833106092.edb

DATABASE HEADER:
Checksum Information:
Expected Checksum: 0x055ea355
  Actual Checksum: 0x055ea355

Fields:
        File Type: Database
         Checksum: 0x55ea355
   Format ulMagic: 0x89abcdef
   Engine ulMagic: 0x89abcdef
 Format ulVersion: 0x620,20
 Engine ulVersion: 0x620,20
Created ulVersion: 0x620,20
     DB Signature: Create time:04/23/2014 20:56:12.168 Rand:3896134121 Computer:
         cbDbPage: 32768
           dbtime: 3186602 (0x309faa)
            State: Dirty Shutdown
     Log Required: 3426-3439 (0xd62-0xd6f)
    Log Committed: 0-3440 (0x0-0xd70)
    Log Recovering: 0 (0x0)
   GenMax Creation: 05/23/2014 14:17:49.174
```

```
              Shadowed: Yes
            Last Objid: 12342
          Scrub Dbtime: 0 (0x0)
            Scrub Date: 00/00/1900 00:00:00
          Repair Count: 0
           Repair Date: 00/00/1900 00:00:00.000
      Old Repair Count: 0
       Last Consistent: (0xC45,AF,90)  05/21/2014 09:16:44.995
           Last Attach: (0xC46,2,268)  05/21/2014 09:30:06.635
           Last Detach: (0x0,0,0)  00/00/1900 00:00:00.000
         Last ReAttach: (0xC72,2,0)  05/21/2014 10:59:47.386
                  Dbid: 1
         Log Signature: Create time:04/23/2014 20:56:12.090 Rand:4000563479 Computer:
            OS Version: (6.2.9200 SP 0 NLS ffffffff.ffffffff)

Previous Full Backup:
         Log Gen: 0-0 (0x0-0x0)
            Mark: (0x0,0,0)
            Mark: 00/00/1900 00:00:00.000

Previous Incremental Backup:
         Log Gen: 0-0 (0x0-0x0)
            Mark: (0x0,0,0)
            Mark: 00/00/1900 00:00:00.000

Previous Copy Backup:
         Log Gen: 0-0 (0x0-0x0)
            Mark: (0x0,0,0)
            Mark: 00/00/1900 00:00:00.000

Previous Differential Backup:
         Log Gen: 0-0 (0x0-0x0)
            Mark: (0x0,0,0)
            Mark: 00/00/1900 00:00:00.000

Current Full Backup:
         Log Gen: 0-0 (0x0-0x0)
            Mark: (0x0,0,0)
            Mark: 00/00/1900 00:00:00.000

Current Shadow copy backup:
         Log Gen: 0-0 (0x0-0x0)
            Mark: (0x0,0,0)
            Mark: 00/00/1900 00:00:00.000


       cpgUpgrade55Format: 0
       cpgUpgradeFreePages: 0
cpgUpgradeSpaceMapPages: 0
```

```
            ECC Fix Success Count: none
        Old ECC Fix Success Count: none
              ECC Fix Error Count: none
          Old ECC Fix Error Count: none
        Bad Checksum Error Count: none
    Old bad Checksum Error Count: none

    Last checksum finish Date: 00/00/1900 00:00:00.000
  Current checksum start Date: 00/00/1900 00:00:00.000
          Current checksum page: 0

Operation completed successfully in 0.15 seconds.
```

There's quite a lot of information to retrieve from the mailbox database header:

- **DB Signature** A unique value of creation date and time, plus a random integer that identifies this particular database. This value is also recorded in the transaction log file and the checkpoint files, and this ties them together. In this example, the DB signature is "Create time:04/23/2014 20:56:12.168 Rand:3896134121," which means the mailbox database was created on April 23, 2014, at 8:56 P.M.

- **cbDbPage** The size of the pages used in this database; in Exchange 2013, the page size is 32 KB.

- **Dbtime** (Part of) the number of changes made to this database.

- **State** The state of the database—that is, whether it is in a consistent state or not. The database in this example is in a dirty shutdown. (I killed the Exchange Store Worker process using Task Manager to get in this state.) It needs a certain number of transaction log files to get to a clean shutdown state.

- **Log Required** If the database is not in a consistent state, these log files are needed to bring it into that consistent state. To make this database a consistent state again, the log files E0000000D62.log through E0000000D6F.log are needed. Exchange Server will perform the recovery process automatically when mounting a database, so under normal circumstances no administrator intervention is needed at this point, but it also possible to manually recover from a dirty shutdown using the ESEUTIL tool.

- **Last ObjID** The number of B+ trees in this particular database. In this example there are 12,342 B+ trees in the database.

- **Log Signature** A unique value of date, time, and an integer that uniquely identifies a series of log files. As with the database signature, this ties together the database file, the log files, and the checkpoint file.

- **Last Attach** The date and time when the database was last mounted. "Mounting" is actually attaching the mailbox database to a stream of log files, hence the entry label "Last Attach."

- **Last Detach** The date and time when the database was last dismounted, or detached from the stream of log files. In this example, the database was never dismounted; I only crashed it.

- **Backup information** Entries used by Exchange Server to keep track of the last full or incremental (VSS) backup that was made on this particular database.

The same kind of information is logged in the header of the transaction log file (ESEUTIL /ML E00.LOG) and in the header of the checkpoint file (ESEUTIL /MK E00.CHK). As these files are grouped together, you can match the files using the header information; for example:

```
ESEUTIL /ML E00.log
```

The output is something like the following:

```
Extensible Storage Engine Utilities for Microsoft(R) Exchange Server
Version 15.00
Copyright (C) Microsoft Corporation. All Rights Reserved.

Initiating FILE DUMP mode...

      Base name: e00
      Log file: e00.log
      lGeneration: 3440 (0xD70)
      Checkpoint: (0xD62,30,0)
      creation time: 05/23/2014 14:17:49.174
      prev gen time: 05/23/2014 14:17:49.111
      Format LGVersion: (8.4000.4.5)
      Engine LGVersion: (8.4000.4.5)
      Signature: Create time:04/23/2014 20:56:12.090 Rand:4000563479 Computer:
      Env SystemPath: F:\Mailbox Database 0833106092\LogFiles\
      Env LogFilePath: F:\Mailbox Database 0833106092\LogFiles\
      Env Log Sec size: 4096 (legacy, unknown actual)
      Env (CircLog,Session,Opentbl,VerPage,Cursors,LogBufs,LogFile,Buffers)
         (    off,    1000,  100000,   16384,  100000,    2048,     256,   16383)
      Using Reserved Log File: false
      Circular Logging Flag (current file): off
      Circular Logging Flag (past files): off
      Checkpoint at log creation time: (0xD62,1,0)
      1 F:\Mailbox Database 0833106092\Mailbox Database 0833106092.edb
                  dbtime: 3437800 (0-3437800)
                  objidLast: 13613
                  Signature: Create time:04/23/2014 20:56:12.168 Rand:3896134121 Computer:
                  MaxDbSize: 0 pages
                  Last Attach: (0xC46,2,268)
                  Last Consistent: (0xC45,AF,90)

      Last Lgpos: (0xd70,93,0)

Number of database page references: 246

Integrity check passed for log file: e00.log

Operation completed successfully in 0.172 seconds.
```

When you look at this output and compare it to the output of the mailbox database header, you'll notice that the mailbox database signature mentioned in the transaction log file is identical to the mailbox database signature in the mailbox database header. This means these files are tied together. Of course, the transaction log file was created recently, but in this header information you'll also find information regarding the location of the checkpoint file on disk as stored in the Env SystemPath property. Also, the location of the transaction log files is recorded in the Env LogFilePath property.

The last part to have a closer look at is the checkpoint file. As we now know, it references a page in one transaction log file. To look at the header information of the checkpoint file, this command is used:

```
ESEUTIL /MK E00.CHK
```

This generates output like the following:

```
Extensible Storage Engine Utilities for Microsoft(R) Exchange Server
Version 15.00
Copyright (C) Microsoft Corporation. All Rights Reserved.

Initiating FILE DUMP mode...
      Checkpoint file: e00.chk

      LastFullBackupCheckpoint: (0x0,0,0)
      Checkpoint: (0xD62,30,0)
      FullBackup: (0x0,0,0)
      FullBackup time: 00/00/1900 00:00:00.000
      IncBackup: (0x0,0,0)
      IncBackup time: 00/00/1900 00:00:00.000
      Signature: Create time:04/23/2014 20:56:12.090 Rand:4000563479 Computer:
      Env (CircLog,Session,Opentbl,VerPage,Cursors,LogBufs,LogFile,Buffers)
          (    off,   1000, 100000,  16384, 100000,   2048,    256,  16383)
       1 F:\Mailbox Database 0833106092\Mailbox Database 0833106092.edb LogOff VerOn RW
         dbtime: 3437801 (0-3437801)
         objidLast: 13613
         Signature: Create time:04/23/2014 20:56:12.168 Rand:3896134121 Computer:
         MaxDbSize: 0 pages
         Last Attach: (0xC46,2,268)
         Last Consistent: (0xC45,AF,90)

Operation completed successfully in 0.47 seconds.
```

This checkpoint file was created during creation of the mailbox database, as can be derived from the signature of the mailbox database. If you examine these examples closely, you'll find that the three files are closely related.

Single-Instance Storage

Up until the 2007 version, Exchange Server had a feature called *single instance storage* (SIS). Using SIS, Exchange Server stored items in the mailbox database only one time per mailbox database. When an item had to be delivered to multiple mailboxes, it was stored only once and the other mailboxes contained a pointer to this particular item. In the early days, when expensive 9 GB SCSI disks were used, this method could save valuable disk space and would increase performance dramatically. It made sense, since writing a large item takes much more time than writing a pointer.

Microsoft started to move away from SIS beginning with Exchange Server 2007, and Exchange Server 2010 and 2013 do not use SIS at all. Newer disk technology and improved ESE technology make it possible to use large 3 TB SATA disks (or larger) without impacting disk performance—that is, of course, if the disk subsystem is not overcommitted. Microsoft's getting rid of SIS made it possible for the Exchange developers to create a less complex mailbox database structure, which in turn lowered the IOPS requirements.

Is this a bad development? No, it hasn't led to "exploding" mailbox databases, as a lot of people feared. Over the years, Microsoft has improved its compression techniques in the mailbox database, which balances the loss of SIS.

Microsoft Exchange Information Store

While ESE is just the database engine, it stores the transactions in the transaction log file and in the mailbox database, as explained in the previous sections. If you open this database file with some sort of binary editor, however, there's absolutely no readable information. The same is true for the transaction log file—no readable information.

The *Information Store* is the process running on the Mailbox server that's responsible for the logical part of the database processing. It transforms the information read from the mailbox database into something readable, like your inbox, the folders in the inbox, or the individual message items. In essence, this process hasn't changed since the original release of Exchange Server 4.0 in 1997. Of course, there have been improvements, such as the introduction of the 64-bit version of Exchange 2007, increasing the number of mailbox databases or expanding the page size to 8 KB in 2007 and to 32 KB in 2010, but the overall concept hasn't changed.

In Exchange 2013, however, the Information Store process has been completely rewritten in managed code—in other words, it is now a .NET application. More interesting, for every mailbox database that is mounted on an Exchange 2013 Mailbox server, a new Information Store worker process is spawned and responsible for this particular database (see Figure 4-7). The huge advantage of this system is that all mailbox databases and the accompanying processes are fully independent of each other. That is, if you have an Exchange 2013 Mailbox server with 25 mailbox databases mounted, and one of those databases crashes, including the Information Store, the other 24 mailbox databases are not affected. (This is in contrast to earlier versions of Exchange Server, where all mailbox databases were dismounted if such a scenario took place.) Besides a new Information Store worker process, an additional search instance is started, minimizing the risk of affecting other mailbox databases in the event of a problem.

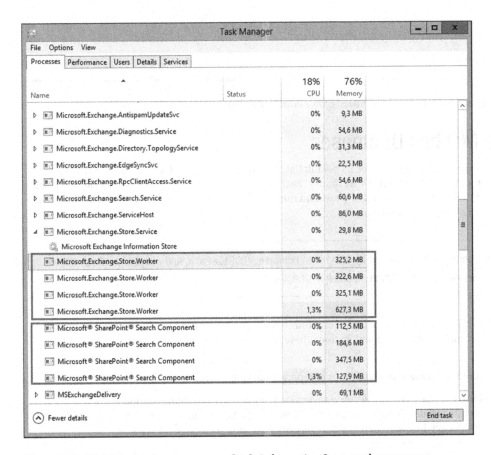

Figure 4-7. *Multiple databases means multiple Information Store worker processes*

Database Caching

For optimal performance, the Information Store wants to do only one thing: cache as much information as possible. Reading and writing in memory is much faster than reading and writing on disk. The more information that is kept in the server's memory, the better the server's performance will be.

The amount of memory assigned to a particular mailbox database is determined at the start time of the Information Store process. This also means that when additional mailbox databases are added, the server's memory used for database caching needs to be redistributed. This is the reason a warning message such as "Please restart the Microsoft Exchange Information Store service on server <<name>> after adding new Mailbox databases" appears (see Figure 4-8).

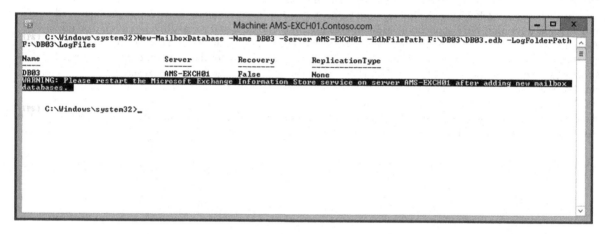

Figure 4-8. *The Information Store needs to be restarted after adding a mailbox database*

Managing the Mailbox Databases

When you install an Exchange 2013 Mailbox server, its default behavior is to create a mailbox database on the system disk, typically in the directory C:\Program Files\Microsoft\Exchange Server\V15\Mailbox\. The name of the new mailbox database is "Mailbox database," followed by a random number, so we get something like "Mailbox Database 0833106092," as we've seen in the previous section.

■ **Note** This random numbering can be avoided by using the /MdbName, /DbFilePath, and /LogFolderPath options during unattended setup. This was explained more in detail in Chapter 2.

Although this mailbox can be used in a production environment, most likely it does not fit into your company's naming convention and it is not stored in a proper location. Therefore, things you might want to do after the initial installation are:

1.   Rename the mailbox database to match your company's naming convention.

2.   Move the mailbox database and the accompanying log files to a more suitable location— for example, an external disk, whether it be direct attached storage (DAS) or some sort of SAN storage solution. Be aware that you can only do this *before* you create a DAG with additional mailbox database copies!

3. Enable circular logging when you are using a DAG.

4. Change quotas for the mailbox database or change the retention times for deleted items.

5. Assign an Offline Address Book (OAB) to a mailbox database.

To Rename a Mailbox Database

Renaming a mailbox database in Exchange 2013 is not a big deal; it's just a matter of one PowerShell command. To change a mailbox database name from Mailbox database 0833106092 to AMS-DB01, enter the following command in EMS:

```
Get-MailboxDatabase -Identity "Mailbox database 0833106092" |
Set-MailboxDatabase -Name "AMS-DB01"
```

■ **Note**   In the previous example, the logical name of the mailbox database is renamed as they show up in EMS or in EAC. The actual EDB file or the directory on disk is not renamed. To rename these, you need to move the EDB file to another directory.

To Move a Mailbox Database

It is strongly recommended that you move mailbox databases to a separate location, preferably a dedicated disk. In Exchange 2013, you can have up to four mailbox databases per disk. To move a mailbox database named AMS-DB01 and its log files to a different location, just enter the following command in EMS:

```
Move-DatabasePath -Identity AMS-DB01 -EdbFilePath F:\AMS-DB01\MD01.edb
-LogFolderPath F:\AMS-DB01\LogFiles
```

An interesting option is the -ConfigurationOnly parameter. Normally when you use the Move-DatabasePath cmdlet, the mailbox database settings in Active Directory are changed and the mailbox database and its log files are moved to the assigned location. When the -ConfigurationOnly parameter is used, though, the settings are changed in Active Directory, but the actual file move does not occur. This can be useful in a disaster-recovery scenario, where a particular mailbox database is recovered in another location and the Mailbox server needs to use this particular mailbox database. This will be explained in more detail in Chapter 7.

To Enable Circular Logging

As explained earlier in the chapter, circular logging is a technique whereby only a very limited number of transaction log files are kept on the server. Normally, transaction log files are kept until a backup has successfully run, but when circular logging is enabled, the transaction log files are removed from the server once all the transactions have been successfully committed to the mailbox database and shipped to the passive copies of that mailbox database when using a DAG.

In a single-server scenario, circular logging is not recommended because of its lack of recovery options, but in a DAG environment circular logging poses less risk of data loss. Recovery options are provided by the DAG itself, so if a mailbox database is lost, another server in the DAG takes over.

To enable circular logging on a mailbox database named AMS-DB01, enter the following command in EMS:

```
Set-MailboxDatabase -Identity AMS-DB01 -CircularLoggingEnabled:$TRUE
```

If you enable circular logging on a server that's not a DAG member, you'll get a warning message that the circular logging will become active only when the mailbox database is dismounted and mounted again. When the Mailbox server is a DAG member, the circular logging option is applied immediately and there's no need for remounting the mailbox database.

To disable the circular logging, the -CircularLoggingEnabled option should be set to $FALSE.

To Change Quota Settings

When a new mailbox database is installed, the default quotas are set on the mailbox database. Quotas are limits set on a mailbox; if they are not explicitly set on the mailbox itself, the mailbox database quotas are enforced on the mailboxes.

The following quota settings are set by default:

- **Issue Warning at 1.9 GB** This value determines when Exchange starts sending warning messages to the user about the fact that he's reaching his mailbox limit. By default this limit is 100 MB lower than the next limit, whereby the user cannot send email anymore.

- **Prohibit Send at 2.0 GB** This value determines when the user cannot send email anymore.

- **Prohibit Send and Receive at 2.1 GB** This value determines when the user cannot send email but at the same time cannot receive email either. By default this value is 100 MB higher than the previous limit—the Prohibit Send quota. Some customers prefer to leave this quota setting open, especially on mailboxes that receive email from customers, so as to prevent bouncing back email to the customers.

While these settings are sufficient for the majority of users, they can be extended to a very large level. In Exchange 2013, a mailbox of 100 GB is not a problem at all on a server level; the only thing you have to be aware of is that the storage sizing must be able to accommodate these large mailboxes.

To change the default quota settings on a mailbox databases called AMS-DB01 to 20 GB, you can use the following command in EMS:

```
Set-MailboxDatabase -Identity AMS-DB01 -IssueWarningQuota 19GB -ProhibitSendQuota 20GB
-ProhibitSendReceiveQuota 22GB
```

■ **Note**   Having a 20 GB mailbox on an Exchange server is not a problem, but complications may arise when using Outlook 2010 and when running Outlook in cached mode. If so, Outlook will create an OST file that matches the size of the mailbox, so 20 GB of mail data will be downloaded to the client and stored on the local hard disk. When running a laptop with a 5400 rpm hard drive, this for sure will give problems. A solution is to use an SSD disk in the laptop, or use Outlook 2013 where the size of the OST file can be controlled by the end user.

Exchange periodically sends warning messages to users who have almost hit their quota (the Issue Warning), or who have hit their quota and cannot send (the Prohibit Send), or have hit their quota and cannot send and receive (the Prohibit Send and Receive limit). The frequency of these warning messages is set using the QuotaNotificationSchedule property on a mailbox database, which you can check using EMS:

```
Get-MailboxDatabase -Identity AMS-DB01 | fl Name,QuotaNotificationSchedule
```

Besides the name of mailbox database, it will also show the quota notification schedule, which by default is set to this:

```
QuotaNotificationSchedule : {Sun.1:00 AM-Sun.1:15 AM, Mon.1:00 AM-Mon.1:15 AM, Tue.1:00 AM-Tue.1:15 AM,
Wed.1:00 AM-Wed.1:15 AM, Thu.1:00 AM-Thu.1:15 AM, Fri.1:00 AM-Fri.1:15 AM, Sat.1:00 AM-Sat.1:15 AM}
```

Mailboxes inherit their quotas from the mailbox database where they reside. It is possible to override these limits by setting the quotas directly on the mailbox. The quota can be higher or lower than the mailbox database setting.

To Assign an Offline Address Book

When a mailbox database is created, an Offline Address Book (OAB) is not assigned to it. In a typical environment this is not needed, but there are situations where you can put one set of mailboxes in one mailbox database and another set of mailboxes in another mailbox database, and then you can assign a specific OAB to a specific mailbox database, and thus to the mailboxes in these databases.

You can use the following command to assign an Offline Address Book called Custom Department OAB to a mailbox Database called AMS-MDB01:

```
Set-MailboxDatabase -Identity AMS-MDB01 -OfflineAddressBook "Custom Department OAB"
```

To Create a New Mailbox Database

If you have a larger environment, then it's likely that you will need some additional mailbox databases besides the default mailbox database. When you have multiple mailbox databases, you can spread your mailboxes across these mailbox databases. Even better, when provisioning the mailboxes, you do not assign a mailbox database; Exchange Server will look for a mailbox database to host this new mailbox.

Creating a new mailbox database using PowerShell is fairly easy; just enter a command similar to the following:

```
New-MailboxDatabase -Name AMS-MDB03 -Server AMS-EXCH02
-EdbFilePath F:\AMS-MDB03\AMS-MDB03.edb -LogFolderPath F:\AMS-MDB03\LogFiles
```

This command creates a new mailbox database called AMS-MDB03, which is hosted on Mailbox server AMS-EXCH02. The mailbox database file and the accompanying transaction log files are located in the F:\AMS-MDB03 directory. After creation of the mailbox database, you can mount it using the following command:

```
Mount-Database -Identity MDB03
```

▪ **Note** When you create a new mailbox database, this information is stored in Active Directory. The information needs to be replicated across all domain controllers. It can happen that, when creating a new mailbox database using the EMS, this information is not replicated across all domain controllers when you enter the Mount-Database command. If that happens, the Mount-Database command will fail and an error will be shown on the console. Nothing to worry about; just wait a couple of minutes and retry the Mount-Database command. However, this can be prevented by using the -DomainController option when using the Mount-Database command.

To Delete a Mailbox Database

For some reason, you may want to delete a mailbox database. Before a mailbox database can be deleted, however, all the mailboxes in it need to be either deleted or moved to another mailbox database. When the mailbox database is empty (and you've made a backup, just in case), you can remove it. You can use the following PowerShell command to remove a mailbox database:

```
Remove-MailboxDatabase -Identity AMS-MDB01 -Confirm:$false
```

When the mailbox database is deleted, it is only deleted from Active Directory. The files themselves still exist on the Mailbox server and have to be manually deleted.

But one day you'll run into the following snag. Suppose you've moved all the mailboxes to another mailbox database and you want to delete the mailbox database. An error message says:"This mailbox database contains one or more mailboxes, mailbox plans, archive mailboxes, public folder mailboxes, or arbitration mailboxes."

When you check again, the mailbox database looks empty because nothing shows up in EAC and nothing is shown when you enter a `Get-Mailbox -Database AMS-MDB01` command in ESM. This situation is caused by system mailboxes in this particular mailbox database, and these system mailboxes are not shown by default. They can only be shown in the ESM by using the `Get-Mailbox -Database MDB01 -Arbitration` command. To move these mailboxes to another mailbox database called MDB02, you can use the following command in ESM:

```
Get-Mailbox -Database AMS-MDB01 -Arbitration | New-MoveRequest
-TargetDatabase AMS-MDB02
```

When these system mailboxes are moved and the mailbox database is *really* empty, it is possible to remove the mailbox database.

Online Mailbox Database Maintenance

Maintenance is a broad term and describes several tasks. Discussed here are (1) the Deleted Items retention settings; and (2) Online mailbox maintenance in the Exchange environment.

Deleted Items Retention Settings

When items are removed from the mailbox database (messages, folders, mailboxes), they are not immediately deleted from the mailbox or the mailbox database; they are kept in the background for a particular amount of time called the *retention time,* and it is set by default to 14 days for individual mailbox items and 30 days for mailboxes.

The Deleted Items retention time and the Mailbox retention time are properties of a mailbox database and can be retrieved using the following command:

```
Get-MailboxDatabase -Identity AMS-DB01 | select MailboxRetention,DeletedItemRetention
```

The retention time is shown as a time span: dd.hh:mm:ss, where d=days, h=hours, m=minutes, and s=seconds. Figure 4-9 shows the default retention time settings.

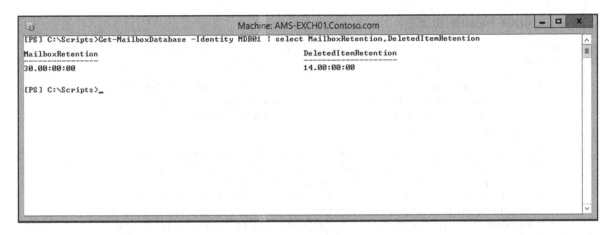

Figure 4-9. The default retention time settings of a mailbox database

Changing the retention times of a mailbox database is similar to retrieving these settings, but instead of using "Get," you use "Set" in the PowerShell command.

To change the Deleted Items retention time to 90 days, for example, you use the following command:

```
Set-MailboxDatabase -Identity AMS-DB01 -DeletedItemsRetention 90.00:00:00
```

When deleted items are past their retention time they are permanently deleted from the mailbox database. When this happens there's no way to get these items back.

There's an option in Exchange that only deletes these items permanently after they have been backed up. This option called `RetainDeletedItemsUntilBackup` and is set to FALSE by default, so you have to set it explicitly. To set this in combination with the 90 days Deleted Items retention time we set in the previous example, you can use the following PowerShell command:

```
Set-MailboxDatabase -Identity AMS-DB01 -DeletedItemsRetention 90.00:00:00
-RetainDeletedItemsUntilBackup $TRUE
```

So what actually happens? When a user deletes a message and purges it from the Deleted Items folder in his mailbox, or when an administrator deletes a mailbox, it is actually moved to the Recoverable Items folder. This is a special location in the mailbox database, not visible for users, where items are stored for as long as stipulated by the retention time.

Online Mailbox Maintenance

Online mailbox maintenance is a process in Exchange Server that maintains the internal structure of the mailbox database and it consists of two parts:

1. **Content maintenance** Responsible for purging deleted items, purging indexes, purging deleted mailboxes, and checking for orphaned messages. This part focuses on content maintenance—that is, it is responsible for purging old content and keeping the mailbox database as accurate as possible.

2. **ESE maintenance** Keeps track of all database pages and indexes inside the mailbox database and performs checksum checks of all individual pages inside the database. It reads all pages in the database and performs a checksum check on each page to see if the page is valid. Single-bit errors can be fixed on the fly by ESE maintenance. ESE maintenance also performs online defragmentation (also known as OLD) to optimize the internal structure of the mailbox database. Online defragmentation reads all pages and indexes in the database and reorganizes these pages. The idea is to free up pages inside the database so new items can be written in the free space inside the database, preventing unnecessary growth of the database.

Content maintenance can finish in a couple of hours, even on the largest mailbox databases. By default, content maintenance runs from 1 A.M. until 5 A.M. on the Mailbox server. This maintenance schedule is also a property of a mailbox database and can be retrieved using the following PowerShell command:

```
Get-MailboxDatabase | Select MaintenanceSchedule
```

This is shown in Figure 4-10.

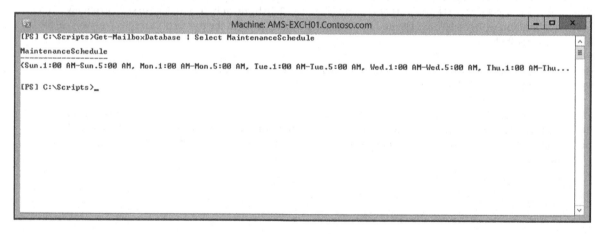

Figure 4-10. *The online maintenance schedule of a mailbox database*

If you want to change this time span, you have to use all different times as input for the `Set-MailboxDatabase` command using the `–MaintenanceSchedule` parameter; for example:

```
Set-MailboxDatabase -Identity AMS-DB01 -MaintenanceSchedule "Sun.00:00 AM-Sun.04:00 AM",
"Mon.00:00-Mon.04:00","Tue.00:00-Tue.04:00","Wed.00:00-Wed.04:00","Thu.00:00-Thu.04:00",
"Fri.00:00-Fri.04:00","Sat.00:00-Sat.04:00"
```

If you run this command, the time spans are set, but you are also presented a warning message that this parameter is being deprecated. For now this works, but it is unknown if the next version of Exchange Server still supports the –MaintenanceSchedule parameter.

The second part of online maintenance is the ESE maintenance. This is a 24/7 background process. By default, it is enabled and it is recommended that you leave this enabled. If for some reason you want to disable ESE maintenance, you can set the –BackgroundDatabaseMaintenance parameter to FALSE; for example:

```
Set-MailboxDatabase -Identity AMS-DB01 -BackgroundDatabaseMaintenance $FALSE
```

■ **Note**   To prevent overwhelming the Mailbox server with checksum requests, and therefore possibly influencing client requests, ESE maintenance is a throttled process.

Managing the Mailboxes

There are multiple types of mailboxes available in Exchange 2013:

- **User Mailboxes** Regular mailboxes used by individuals to send and receive email messages.

- **Resource Mailboxes** Mailboxes that are not assigned to human beings but to resources, like a conference room or a beamer in an office; as such they can be scheduled for meeting purposes.

- **Linked Mailboxes** Regular mailboxes, tied to user accounts in another Active Directory forest and not to user accounts in the same Active Directory forest as the Exchange 2013 servers.

- **Public Folder Mailboxes** Replacements for the traditional public folders in down-level versions of Exchange Server. Since there are so many changes in public folders, there's a complete section on these later in the chapter, called "Modern Public Folders."

Although they are all mailboxes, there are differences between them, as outlined next.

To Create a User Mailbox

There are a few ways to create new user mailboxes in Exchange 2013:

- Create a new mailbox and corresponding user account in Active Directory.

- Mailbox-enable an existing user account.

- Use bulk management—for example, import user accounts from a CSV file or an Excel spreadsheet.

Let's look at these more closely.

New Mailbox/New User Account

It is possible to create a new user account and corresponding mailbox with the New-Mailbox command; for example:

```
New-Mailbox -Name "John Brown" -FirstName John -LastName Brown -Alias JBrown -DisplayName "John
Brown IV" -OrganizationalUnit "FourthCoffee" -Database MDB01 -UserPrincipalName jbrown@contoso.com
```

This command is shown in Figure 4-11.

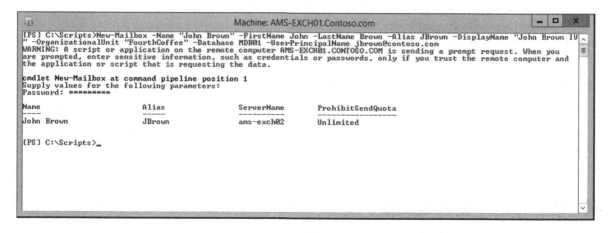

Figure 4-11. *Creating a new mailbox with PowerShell*

This command will create a new user account called "John Brown" in the OU=Accounts Organizational Unit in the contoso.com Active Directory. His user principal name will be set to jbrown@contoso.com and his mailbox will be created in the AMS-MDB01 mailbox database.

It is not possible to enter a password on the command line because passwords are only accepted as a secure string in Active Directory; therefore, you are prompted for a new password for this user account.

To work around this, you can use the ConvertTo-SecureString function in PowerShell. This will convert a clear text string like P@$$w0rd1 into a secure string that will be accepted by PowerShell when creating a new user. The command for creating a new user with a mailbox and for setting the password will be something like this:

```
New-Mailbox -Name "Marina Baggus" -OrganizationalUnit FourthCoffee -Password (ConvertTo-SecureString
-String 'P@$$w0rd1' -AsPlainText -Force) -Database MDB01 -FirstName Marina -LastName Baggus
-DisplayName "Marina Baggus" -UserPrincipalName "Marina@baggus.nl"
```

In the example above, a mailbox database is explicitly set. It is also possible to omit the –Database option when creating a new mailbox. If you do this, the Mailbox server automatically determines the best location for the new mailbox.

The algorithm used here first determines which mailbox databases are available in Active Directory and are not excluded for provisioning. Then it looks at the number of mailboxes in each mailbox database and picks the mailbox database with the lowest number of mailboxes.

Mailbox-Enabling an Existing User

It is possible that an account in Active Directory already exists; it could have been created by the Active Directory team, for example. If so, you can mailbox-enable this user account—that is, add a mailbox to it.

If you have an existing user account in Active Directory called "Samuel Smith" and you want to assign a mailbox to him located in the Mailbox Database 0833106092 database, you can enter the following PowerShell command:

```
Get-User -Identity samuel | Enable-Mailbox -Alias Samuel -Database "Mailbox Database 0833106092
```

Personally, I'd like to use a Get-User cmdlet first to see if it retrieves the correct user account from Active Directory. If it does, I repeat the command and pipe it into the Enable-Mailbox cmdlet.

Bulk Managing the User Accounts

If you have a lot of mailboxes that need to be created, you can use a PowerShell script to do this. This PowerShell script can read the accounts from a CSV or XLSX file and import it into Active Directory and create the mailboxes. Especially when you have a lot of mailboxes to create, this is a convenient way to use PowerShell.

Suppose you have a number of Mailboxes to create in your environment; a CSV that is supplied to you can be formatted as follows:

```
FirstName,LastName,DisplayName,Alias,Password,OU
Michael,McDonald,"M. McDonald",MichaelM,Pass1word,"Contoso.com/Accounts/Contoso/Users"
John,Doe,"J. Doe",JohnD,Pass1word,"Contoso.com/Accounts/Contoso/Users"
Kim,Akers,"K. Akers",KimA,Pass1word,"Contoso.com/Accounts/Contoso/Users"
Liesbeth,Gelderen,"L. van Gelderen",Liesbeth,Pass1word,"Contoso.com/Accounts/Contoso/Users"
```

In contrast to the earlier command where a new Mailbox was created a user password is supplied in clear text in this CSV file. The New-Mailbox cmdlet cannot work with a clear text password but using a script we can convert this clear text to a secure string.

A PowerShell script that reads this CSV file can be like this:

```
$Database="Mailbox Database 0833106092"
$UPNsuffix="contoso.com"
Param{
  [string]$Users
}

ForEach ($user in $users)
{
  $sp = $NULL
  $upn = $NULL
  $sp = ConvertTo-SecureString -String $user.password -AsPlainText -Force $user.password
  $upn = $user.FirstName + "@"+ $upnSuffix
  New-Mailbox -Password $sp -Database $Database -UserPrincipalName $UPN -Alias $User.alias -Name
$User.DisplayName -FirstName $User.FirstName -LastName $User.LastName -OrganizationalUnit $user.OU
}
```

The first three commands are obvious. The variables are created where the mailbox database is defined, the user principal name is created, and an array is created containing all the accounts.

The second step is a function that converts the clear text password into a secure string that is accepted by the New-Mailbox cmdlet.

The last step is a loop where a new user account and mailbox are created for every user in the array. Script execution is shown in Figure 4-12.

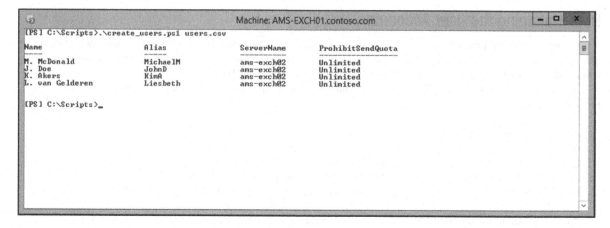

Figure 4-12. *Creating new users using a PowerShell script can be very efficient*

To Set Additional Mailbox Properties

When the new mailbox is created, you can set additional properties for the mailbox; for example:

- Set properties like Company or Department

- Set quota setting on a mailbox

- Set regional configuration properties

- Assign a policy to the mailbox

- Add additional email address

- Create an archive mailbox

- Implement cmdlet extension agents

Setting Properties

Properties like Company or Department are not Exchange-specific and therefore you cannot use the Set-Mailbox cmdlet to set these. Instead, you can use the Set-User cmdlet to set them; for example:

```
Set-User –Identity JBrown –Company "Fourth Coffee" –Department "Sales"
```

Setting Quotas

In a previous section I explained that quota settings are put on a mailbox database. It is also possible to put quota settings on a mailbox, and these quota settings will override the mailbox database quotas. To change the quota settings for all users in, say, the FourthCoffee Organizational Unit, you can use the following command:

```
Get-Mailbox -OrganizationalUnit "FourthCoffee" | Set-Mailbox -IssueWarningQuota 10GB
-ProhibitSendQuota 11GB -ProhibitSendReceiveQuota 15GB -UseDatabaseQuotaDefaults $false
```

It is important to set the UseDatabaseQuotaDefaults property to $false. If you don't do this, the mailbox database quota settings are not overridden.

Setting Regional Configurations

The first time you log on to OWA, you are requested to set the time zone and to select a language. In a typical environment, these will be identical across all mailboxes. An exception could be if you are living in a dual-language country like Belgium. You would set the default Time zone to "W. Europe Standard Time" and set the language to French or Dutch, depending on the location of the user. For example, Brussels based users you would set it to:

```
Set-MailboxRegionalConfiguration -Identity Pascal -Language fr-FR -LocalizeDefaultFolderName
$TRUE -Timezone "W. Europe Standard Time"
```

And for Antwerp based users you would set it to:

```
Set-MailboxRegionalConfiguration -Identity Johan -Language nl-NL -LocalizeDefaultFolderName
$TRUE -Timezone "W. Europe Standard Time"
```

■ **Tip**   If you want to get the time zone you're currently in, you can use the TZUTIL utility. Run this in a command prompt and it will show you the current time zone of the Windows machine you're logged on to.

Assigning an Address Book Policy

An Exchange-specific address book policy can be assigned to a mailbox using the Set-Mailbox cmdlet. If you have an address book policy called "Fourth Coffee ABP" and you want to assign it to the JBrown mailbox, you can use the following command:

```
Set-Mailbox -Identity JBrown -AddressBookPolicy "Fourth Coffee ABP"
```

■ **Note**   Address book policies are discussed in more detail later in this chapter.

Adding Email Addresses

Adding email addresses to a mailbox is a little more difficult because the EmailAddress property of a mailbox is a multivalued property; that is, this particular property can have more than one value.

If you add a value to a property, the original value is overwritten, which is something to be avoided when using multivalued properties. To change a multivalued property, add an Add or Remove option to the value. For example, to add two additional email addresses to John's mailbox, you can use the following command:

```
Set-Mailbox -Identity JBrooks -EmailAddresses @{Add="John.Brooks@contoso.com", "John.A.Brooks@
contoso.com"}
```

Removing a value from a multivalued property is similar; you would use:

```
Set-Mailbox -Identity JBrooks -EmailAddresses @{Remove=John.A.Brooks@contoso.com}
```

Creating an Archive Mailbox

An archive mailbox is a secondary mailbox connected to a user's primary mailbox. To create an archive mailbox, you can use the Enable-Mailbox cmdlet with the –Archive option. For example, to enable the archive mailbox to John Brook's mailbox, you can use the following command:

```
Enable-Mailbox -Identity JBrooks -Archive
```

Exchange Server will automatically provision the archive mailbox in one of the available mailbox databases; it uses the same algorithm when creating a normal mailbox. If you want to set the mailbox database manually, you can use the –ArchiveDatabase option; for example:

```
Enable-Mailbox -Identity JBrooks -Archive -ArchiveDatabase AMS-DB10
```

Using Cmdlet Extension Agents

Not directly related to the creation of new mailboxes but interesting enough to discuss here are the *cmdlet extension agents*. Using cmdlet extensions, it is possible to expand the functionality of PowerShell cmdlets and tailor them to your organizational needs.

An example of such an extension could be the automatic creation of an archive mailbox whenever a normal user mailbox is created. The scripting agent configuration is stored in the file called ScriptingAgentConfig.xml, which is stored in a directory C:\Program Files\Microsoft\Exchange Server\V15\Bin\CmdletExtensionAgents on the Exchange 2013 Mailbox server.

■ **Note**   There's a ScriptingAgentConfig.xml.sample file located in this directory that you can use as a reference.

To create a cmdlet extention that's executed when the new-mailbox cmdlet has finished ("onComplete"), and create a new archive mailbox in the same mailbox database as the original user mailbox, you create a ScriptingAgentconfig.xml that contains the following code and store this file in the directory, as mentioned above:

```
<?xml version="1.0" encoding="utf-8" ?>
<Configuration version="1.0">
  <Feature Name="MailboxProvisioning" Cmdlets="New-Mailbox">
    <ApiCall Name="OnComplete">
    If($succeeded) {
      $Name= $provisioningHandler.UserSpecifiedParameters["Name"]
      If ((Get-Mailbox $Name).ArchiveDatabase -eq $null) {
        $ArchiveDatabase= (Get-Mailbox $Name).Database
        Enable-Mailbox $Name -Archive -ArchiveDatabase $ArchiveDatabase
        }
      }
    </ApiCall>
  </Feature>
</Configuration>
```

To enable the cmdlet extension agent, you run the following PowerShell command on each Mailbox server:

```
Enable-CmdletExtensionAgent "Scripting Agent"
```

The actual provisioning of the mailbox and the archive mailbox takes place on the Mailbox server, so you have to copy the XML files to all Exchange 2013 Mailbox servers in your Exchange environment because you never know where a specific command is executed.

When you run the new-mailbox command, an archive mailbox is automatically created. It is now shown when the mailbox is created, but when you request the properties after creating it, they are shown as displayed in Figure 4-13.

Figure 4-13. *With the cmdlet extention, an archive mailbox is automatically created*

To Use Mailbox Delegation

Another important item to be aware of is the *mailbox delegation,* a feature that's widely used in a manager and assistant scenario where the manager needs to grant his assistant access to his mailbox. There are three types of mailbox delegation in the EAC:

- **Send As permission** The assistant can send a message from the manager's mailbox. The recipient will see only the manager as the sender of the email message.

- **Send on Behalf permission** The assistant can send email on behalf of the manager. The recipient of the message will see that the message was sent on behalf of the manager, and the sender of the message will be shown as "Assistant on behalf of manager."

- **Full Access permission** The assistant has full access (read, write, edit, and delete) to all items in the manager's entire mailbox.

For example, if Cindy McDowell is a manager at Contoso and John Doe is her assistant, you can follow these commands to set the different permissions:

- To grant the Send As permission to user John on Cindy's mailbox using the EMS, you can use the following command:

```
Add-ADPermission -Identity Cindy -User John -ExtendedRights "Send As"
```

- To grant the Send on Behalf permission to user John on Cindy's mailbox using the EMS, you can use the following command:

```
Set-Mailbox -Identity Cindy -GrantSendOnBehalfTo John
```

- To grant Full Access permissions to user John on Cindy McDowell's mailbox using the EMS, you can use the following command:

```
Add-MailboxPermission -Identity Cindy -User John -AccessRights FullAccess
-InheritanceType all
```

Now John can use his own mailbox, but when he sends a message he can select his manager (i.e., Cindy McDowell) in the From field. When he does, and he sends a message to Michael McDonald, Michael sees in his mailbox the sender information as shown in Figure 4-14.

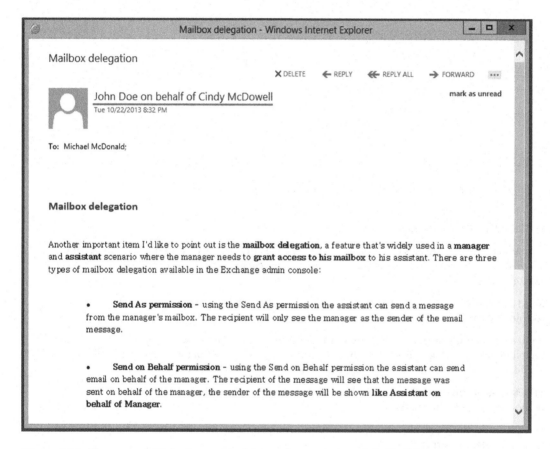

Figure 4-14. *The message Michael sees when John sends a message on behalf of his manager*

■ **Note** When a user is granted Full Access permission to a mailbox, this user cannot send email messages from the mailbox he's been granted permission to. To achieve this, the user also needs the Send As or Send on Behalf permission.

To Create a Resource Mailbox

A resource mailbox is a normal mailbox with the exception that it does not belong to a normal user; instead, it belongs to a resource. In Exchange 2013, there are two types of resource mailboxes:

- **Room Mailbox** Represents a (conference) room in your office.

- **Equipment Mailbox** Represents some sort of equipment, like a beamer, that's not tied to a conference room.

A resource mailbox represents something that can be booked by regular users when scheduling meetings. Since these resources cannot log on to the mailbox, the accompanying user account in Active Directory is disabled. They also do not require any user licences.

However, they are quite useful. It is possible to use a resource mailbox to schedule meetings, such as a conference room, thereby indicating when this resource is available. Like a regular email, this meeting request is sent to the resource mailbox, but in contrast, the request is automatically accepted when the resource is available. The response, whether the meeting is accepted or not, is sent back to the sender to confirm that availability. To create this type of room mailbox—say, with a capacity of 20 persons—you use the following command:

```
New-Mailbox -Room -UserPrincipalName ConfRoom2ndFloor@contoso.com -Alias ConfRoom2ndFloor
-Name "Conference Room 2nd Floor" -ResourceCapacity 20 -Database "MDB01" -OrganizationalUnit
FourthCoffee -ResetPasswordOnNextLogon $true -Password (ConvertTo-SecureString -String 'P@$$wOrd1'
-AsPlainText -Force)
```

Creating an equipment mailbox is similar; the only difference is that there is less to configure. There's no location, no phone number, and no capacity to enter, but otherwise the process is the same. To create an equipment mailbox for a Sony Beamer, you can use the following command:

```
New-Mailbox -Equipment -UserPrincipalName SonyBeamer@contoso.com -Alias SonyBeamer -Name "Sony
Beamer" -Database "MDB01" -OrganizationalUnit FourthCoffee -ResetPasswordOnNextLogon $true -Password
(ConvertTo-SecureString -String 'P@$$wOrd1' -AsPlainText -Force)
```

To Create a Shared Mailbox

A shared mailbox is a mailbox that has a user account, but the user account is disabled. As such, a user cannot log on to a shared mailbox directly. To access a shared mailbox, a user must have appropriate permission (Send As or Full Access) to use this mailbox. Once the user has Full Access, he or she can log on to his or her own mailbox and open the shared mailbox as a secondary mailbox.

A shared mailbox for the Contoso Sales Department could be created using the following command:

```
New-Mailbox -Shared -UserPrincipalName Sales@contoso.com -Alias Sales -Name "Sales" -DisplayName
"Contoso Sales Department" -Database "MDB01" -OrganizationalUnit contoso -ResetPasswordOnNextLogon
$true -Password (ConvertTo-SecureString -String 'P@$$wOrd1' -AsPlainText -Force)
```

To grant all users in the Contoso Organizational Unit Full Access permission for this shared mailbox, you could use the following command:

```
Get-Mailbox –OrganizationalUnit Contoso | ForEach { Add-MailboxPermission -Identity Sales -User
$_.Identity -AccessRights FullAccess -InheritanceType all }
```

To grant all users in the Contoso Organizational Unit Send As permission for this shared mailbox, you could use the following command:

```
Get-Mailbox -OrganizationalUnit Contoso | ForEach { Add-ADPermission -Identity Sales -User $_.Identity -ExtendedRights "Send As" }
```

To check if this command was successful, you can use the following command:

```
Get-Mailbox -Identity Sales | Get-MailboxPermission | Select Identity, User, AccessRights
```

This command will show a list of all users who have permission on this particular mailbox, as shown in Figure 4-15.

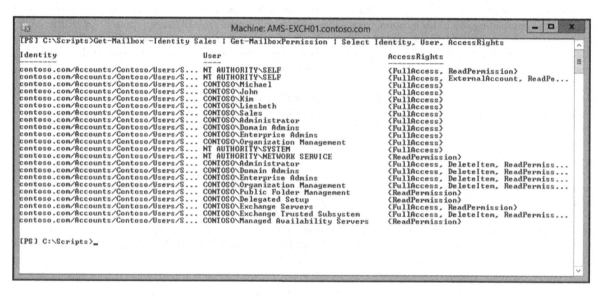

Figure 4-15. *All users who have permissions on the sales mailbox*

To Create a Linked Mailbox

A *linked mailbox* differs from a regular mailbox in that it does not have an active user account in Active Directory. Instead, it is used by a normal user, and that user is created in another Active Directory forest. There's a forest "trust" between the forest holding the user account and the forest holding the mailboxes. Thus, the user account is linked to the mailbox. The forest that holds the Exchange servers, and thus the mailboxes, is sometimes also referred to as a *resource forest*.

A regular mailbox always has an accompanying user account, but when a linked mailbox is used, this accompanying user account is disabled. For this scenario, you need some sort of provisioning process. This is the means by which the user account in forest A and the mailbox in forest B are linked, as can be seen in Figure 4-16. Note that the Active Directory forest A does not have any Exchange servers installed, and thus the user accounts do not have any Exchange-related properties. Since there's a trust relationship, users in forest A can log on and seamlessly access their mailboxes in forest B.

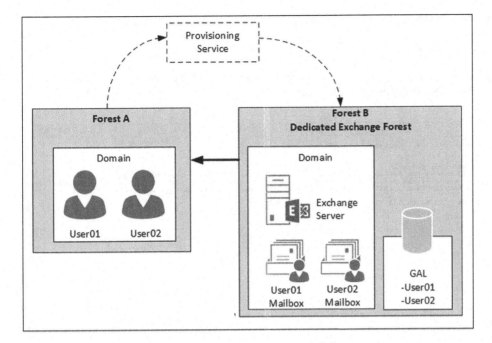

Figure 4-16. *A linked mailbox scenario consists of an account forest A and an Exchange forest B*

The advantage of this arrangement is that it makes it possible to have multiple, fully separated Active Directory forests where the user accounts reside, but have only one Exchange forest with all the mailboxes of all the (trusted) Active Directory accounts.

You may want to implement linked mailboxes if you have multiple Active Directory forests holding user accounts governed by strict security policies that do not allow multiple departments in one Active Directory forest. Using linked mailboxes makes it possible to create one Exchange environment for multiple, fully separated departments. While this might seem strange from an Active Directory point of view, when viewed from an Exchange perspective it is a fully supported scenario.

To Remove a Mailbox

Mailboxes need to be created and at some point mailboxes need to be removed as well. When it comes to removing mailboxes, there are two options:

1. **The mailbox is disabled** In this case, the mailbox is deleted and the values of the Exchange-related properties are removed from the user account. Important to note here is that the user account in Active Directory continues to exist, so the user can still log on to Windows and Active Directory and can continue to access other resources on the network. A resource mailbox has a disabled user account associated with it, and as such a resource mailbox cannot be disabled.

2. **The mailbox is removed** In this case, the mailbox is deleted, including the user account, from Active Directory. An archive mailbox cannot be deleted; it can only be disabled.

When a mailbox is deleted, it remains in the mailbox database until the retention time for the deleted mailbox expires. Up until this point, this mailbox is referred to as a *disconnected mailbox*.

To disable a mailbox, the following command can be used:

```
Disable-Mailbox -Identity "J. Doe"
```

When you perform this command, a confirmation is requested, as can be seen in Figure 4-17. You can avoid this question by adding the –Confirm:$false option to the Disable-Mailbox cmdlet.

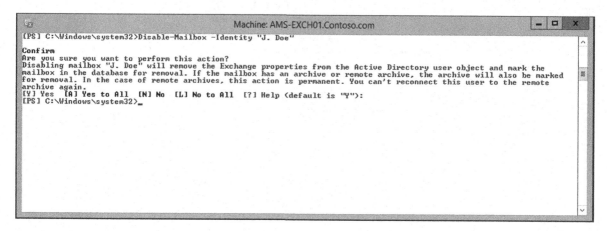

Figure 4-17. *Disabling a mailbox-enabled user*

Removing a mailbox is similar to disabling a mailbox. To remove a mailbox and its accompanying user account, you enter the following command:

```
Remove-Mailbox -Identity "John Brown" -Confirm:$false
```

To check if the mailbox has been deleted (or actually disconnected), you can run the following commands:

```
Get-MailboxDatabase | Get-MailboxStatistics | Where { $_.DisplayName -eq "J. Doe" } | fl
DisconnectReason,DisconnectDate
```

```
Get-MailboxDatabase | Get-MailboxStatistics | Where { $_.DisplayName -eq "John Brown" } | fl
DisconnectReason,DisconnectDate
```

When a mailbox is properly deleted, the DisconnectReason property will show "Disabled." Another value for the DisconnectReason is "SoftDeleted." A mailbox is soft deleted when it is moved from one mailbox database to another mailbox database. Just as when removing a mailbox, the source mailbox is deleted in the source mailbox database, and it remains there until the retention period expires.

Modern Public Folders

Public folders have been around since the first version of Exchange Server, back in 1996. These are another repository of information where messages, appointments, or contacts can be stored and shared among recipients. Starting with Exchange Server 2007, Microsoft decommissioned the public folders, a decision that was not popular with Exchange customers; after endless debate, Microsoft decided to restore and completely redesign the public folders for Exchange Server 2013. This has resulted in the *modern public folders.*

Some Background on Public Folders

From their start, public folders were a repository for information; it was even possible to store office documents in these public folders, although the negative side effect of this capability was the problem of ever-growing public folders.

These public folders used to have their own databases, called *public folder databases*. The databases were the same as mailbox databases, using the same ESE database technology and managed by the same Information Store. Only the database schema and the information inside the database were different. The public folder databases also had their own replication mechanism, making it possible to create multiple databases with the same information and thus offering database redundancy. And to make these folders even more compelling, they used a multi-master replication technology, so that it was possible to make changes to documents on different servers, with the two copies in sync.

The public folders consisted of two parts:

- **The hierarchy** This is the structure of the items kept in the public folder database, or how and where the individual items are stored in the folders. The hierarchy is similar to a directory structure on a local hard disk, with all its folders and subfolders. In public folders, you can set permissions on the folders, making it possible to create a departmental information solution—for example, where only employees of the accompanying department can view the information contained in the designated folder.

- **The content** This is the actual information that is stored in the public folders.

The hierarchy is an entity in itself, and the entire folder structure is stored in the hierarchy. The hierarchy is then replicated across all public folder databases, including all public folders and their permissions. When a new public folder database is created, the hierarchy needs to be replicated to this new database before the database can be used.

There are two types of folders in a traditional public folder database:

- **System folders** These are system-generated folders that contain free/busy information and the Offline Address Book. The system folders are used by older Outlook clients—Outlook 2003 and earlier. Without the system folders, these older Outlook clients would not even be able to get started! When using Outlook 2003 or earlier, the calendaring information is stored locally and published every 15 minutes to the free/busy folder on the Exchange server. The Offline Address Book is generated once a day, typically in the middle of the night, and stored in the Offline Address Book folder. Outlook clients then download a copy of the Offline Address Book during business hours.

- **Public folders** These are the normal public folders where recipients can store information, where permissions are set, and whose contents can be replicated across multiple public folder databases.

Public folder replication is set on a per-folder basis; this means that data from one server—say, Public Folder A—can be replicated to a second Exchange server, while data from another server—say, Public Folder B—can be replicated to a third Exchange server, making it possible to create a flexible, distributed, and powerful information solution.

For accessing public folder information, Outlook would connect directly to the Exchange 2010 Mailbox server hosting the public folder database, whereas the same Outlook client would connect to the RPC Client Access service running on the Exchange 2010 CAS to retrieve information from the inbox. So one Outlook client connects in two different ways. Using the RPC Client Access service running on multiple Exchange 2010 CAS servers created a redundant connection mechanism, something that was not possible for the public folders. There can be multiple copies of a particular public folder on multiple public folder databases, but there is no automatic failover mechanism built into the "old" public folder solution. However, this situation was corrected in Exchange Server 2010 SP2 RU2, when an alternative server tag was introduced. This alternative server tag introduced a public folder failover function.

The bad thing is that there wasn't much development involving public folders after the early 2000s. As mentioned earlier, by Exchange Server 2007, Microsoft had started to decommission the public folders. However, in the development phase of Exchange 2013, Microsoft decided to reinstate the public folders. At that point, they decided to completely rewrite the public folder architecture and bring it back to life.

Public Folders in Exchange Server 2013

The basic idea behind the public folders has not changed. There still is a hierarchy containing the public folder structure, and there still is the actual content that is stored in the public folders. However, the completely redesigned public folders no longer use a separate public folder database; the public folders are now stored in mailbox databases. This makes it possible to do the following:

- Use the Client Access server to access the public folder information, offering redundancy on the way clients connect to public folders.

- Use the database availability group (DAG) for redundancy on the public folder and mailbox database level, as discussed in the next part of this chapter.

The hierarchy in Exchange Server 2013 public folders is now stored in a new type of mailbox: the *public folder mailbox*. If new public folders are created, they are stored in the hierarchy in this public folder mailbox. It is possible to create multiple hierarchies in an Exchange 2013 environment, but there's only one primary or master public folder mailbox (also referred to as the *primary hierarchy mailbox*). The public folder mailbox is stored in a normal mailbox database, which can be identified during creation of the public folder database. For redundancy, this mailbox database can be located in a database availability group, but it is important to note that there's only one writeable copy of the public folder mailbox.

Once the hierarchy mailbox is created, the public folders can be created and permissions can be assigned to these new public folders.

To Create Public Folders

Initially, nothing is configured regarding public folders so the first step is to establish the public folder settings on the organizational level in Exchange 2013, and then create a new hierarchy located in a public folder mailbox. By default, the sizing quotas for public folders are set to unlimited, and the deleted items retention and moved item retention are set to 14 days. Organizational settings can be set only using the EMS, so to change these settings and reflect your company's standards, open the EMS and enter a command similar to this:

```
Set-OrganizationConfig -DefaultPublicFolderIssueWarningQuota 1.9GB
-DefaultPublicFolderProhibitPostQuota 2.3GB -DefaultPublicFolderMaxItemSize 200MB
-DefaultPublicFolderDeletedItemRetention 30.00:00:00 -DefaultPublicFolderMovedItemRetention
30.00:00:00
```

The first step to create a public folder infrastructure is to create a primary hierarchy mailbox:

```
New-Mailbox -PublicFolder -Name MasterHierarchy -OrganizationalUnit
"contoso.com/accounts/service accounts" -Database MDB01
```

When the public folder mailbox is created, you can create content public folders. To create a new top-level public folder called "Contoso" you can use the following command:

```
New-PublicFolder -Name Contoso -Path \ -Mailbox MasterHierarchy
```

To create a new public folder called "Marketing"and mail-enable this public folder, you can use the following commands:

```
New-PublicFolder -Name Marketing -Path \Contoso
Enable-MailPublicFolder -Identity \Contoso\Marketing
```

By default, users do not have permissions on public folders, so to grant user MichaelM full access to the Marketing public folder, you can use the following command:

```
Add-PublicFolderClientPermission -Identity \Contoso\Marketing -User MichaelM -AccessRights
PublishingEditor
```

Public folders appear in Outlook as did the legacy public folders. There's a stub on the Exchange 2013 Mailbox server so that the new public folders are fully transparent for users.

Distribution Groups

In Active Directory, there are two types of groups:

- **Security Group** – Used for granting permissions to users or other groups that are members of this group.

- **Distribution Group** – Used for distributing email to users or other groups that are members of this group.

Before Exchange 2013 can use these groups, the groups have to be mail-enabled. When a group is mail-enabled, all Exchange-related properties are set and you can start using the group for distributing email messages.

■ **Note**   Both a Security Group and a Distribution Group can be mail-enabled. As such, you can use a Security Group for mail-related purposes. On the other hand, a Distribution Group cannot be used for granting permission to resources, as you can with a Security Group. If you want to grant permission to a Distribution Group, you have to first convert it to a Security Group using the Active Directory Users and Computers (ADUC) MMC snap-in.

In Exchange, it is possible to create a new Distribution Group, as well as to mail-enable a Distribution Group or Security Group that exists in Active Directory.

In Active Directory, there are three types of groups:

- Domain local groups

- Global groups

- Universal groups

When it comes to Exchange 2013, only universal groups are used. The primary subject of this section is the Universal Distribution Group.

To Create a New Distribution Group

To create a new Distribution Group in Active Directory and automatically mail-enable it, you can use the following command:

```
New-DistributionGroup -Name "Management" -OrganizationalUnit FourthCoffee
```

To create a new Security Group in Active Directory and automically mail-enable it, you can add the –Type Security option to the previous command:

```
New-DistributionGroup -Name "Management" -OrganizationalUnit FourthCoffee -Type Security
```

To Mail-Enable an Existing Group

An existing group in Active Directory (either Distribution Group or Security Group) can be mail-enabled as well. To do this, you can use the following command:

```
Enable-DistributionGroup -Identity AllEmployees -Alias AllEmployees
```

If the existing group in Active Directory has a non-universal group scope, an error message is displayed saying "You can't mail-enable this group because it isn't a universal group. Only a universal group can be mail-enabled." So, before an existing group can be mail-enabled, its group scope needs to be converted to universal. This can be achieved using the following command:

```
Set-ADGroup -Identity AllEmployees -GroupScope Universal
```

Once converted, the group can be mail-enabled, as shown in Figure 4-18.

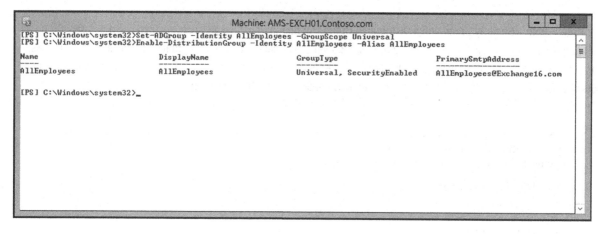

Figure 4-18. *An existing group can be mail-enabled when its group scope is converted to universal*

To Manage Distribution Group Membership

Adding or removing a member to a Distribution Group is pretty straightforward. To add a member to a Distribution Group, just enter the following command:

```
Add-DistributionGroupMember -Identity AllEmployees -Member "John Doe"
```

Removing a member from a Distribution Group is similar:

```
Remove-DistributionGroupMember -Identity AllEmployees -Member "John Doe"
```

Instead of adding mailboxes as members of a Distribution Group, it is possible to add other Distribution Groups as a member, a process called *nesting*. The commands are identical. To add a Distribution Group called HR to the AllEmployees Distribution Group, you can use the following command:

```
Add-DistributionGroupMember -Identity AllEmployees -Member "HR"
```

To Set Membership Approval

Users can decide whether or not they are members of a Distribution Group. This can be useful for special-interest groups, but not for company-wide Distribution Groups. You don't want users to leave a Distribution Group like "All Employees" or to join certain Distribution Groups like "HR," for example.

Distribution Group membership approval has the following options:

- **Open** – Anyone can join or leave the Distribution Group without approval of the group manager.

- **Closed** – No one can leave or join the group. All requests will automatically be rejected.

- **Owner Approval** – The group manager has to approve a request to joint the group. This option is for joining only.

■ **Note**   Mail-enabled Security Groups are closed.

The New-DistributionGroup cmdlet has the -MemberJoinRestriction and the -MemberDepartRestriction options to control group membership behavior. To create a new Distribution Group called "All Employees" where no users can automatically join or leave, you can use the following command:

```
New-DistributionGroup -Name "All Employees" -OrganizationalUnit FourthCoffee
-MemberDepartRestriction Closed -MemberJoinRestriction Closed
```

An interesting option is the ApprovalRequired. When this is used and a user wants to join the Distribution Group, a request message is sent to the manager or owner of the Distribution Group. For example, suppose we create a Distribution Group called "Exchange Authoring," with the ApprovalRequired set for the join restriction:

```
New-DistributionGroup -Name "Exchange Authoring" -OrganizationalUnit FourthCoffee
-MemberDepartRestriction Closed -MemberJoinRestriction ApprovalRequired -ManagedBy Contoso\Jaap
```

Now, when user John Lee wants to join this Distribution Group, a message is sent to the manager of the group, as shown in Figure 4-19.

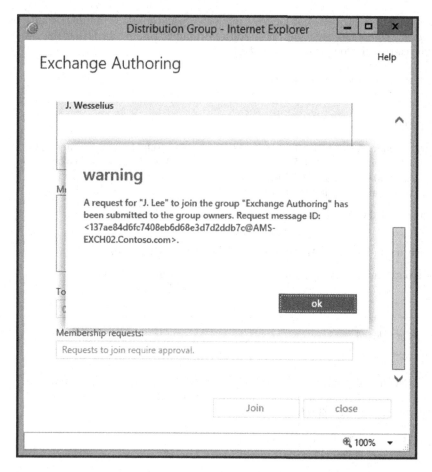

Figure 4-19. A membership request is sent to the Distribution Group's manager

The manager of this group receives the message and can either approve or reject the request, as shown in Figure 4-20.

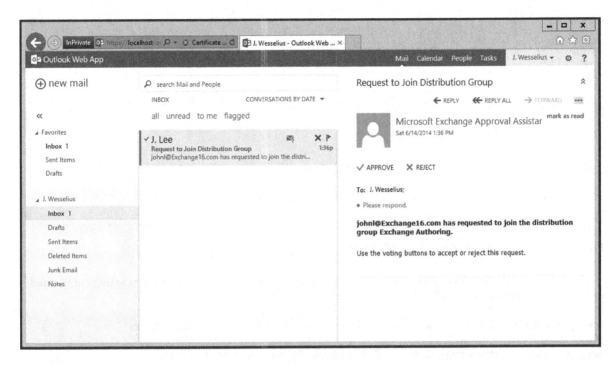

Figure 4-20. *The manager of the group can either approve or reject the request*

Group membership for a regular Distribution Group is static: you have to manually add or remove members. For large organizations, this can be quite some administrative work. Instead of using regular Distribution Groups, you can use Dynamic Distribution Groups.

Dynamic Distribution Groups

A Dynamic Distribution Group is similar to a regular Distribution Group, but group membership is dynamically determined, based on certain properties of the mailboxes.

For example, you can create a Dynamic Distribution Group called "All Employees" that contain all recipients (i.e., mailboxes, public folders, contacts, and other distribution groups) that have the value "Contoso" in their company attribute:

```
New-DynamicDistributionGroup -Name "All Employees" -IncludedRecipients AllRecipients
-ConditionalCompany "Contoso"
Set-DynamicDistributionGroup -Identity "All Employees" -ManagedBy Contoso\Jaap
```

When the New-DynamicDistributionGroup is used, you cannot set the –ManagedBy option, although this option is shown on the console when the group is created. You have to use the Set-DynamicDistributionGroup cmdlet to set this option, as shown in Figure 4-21.

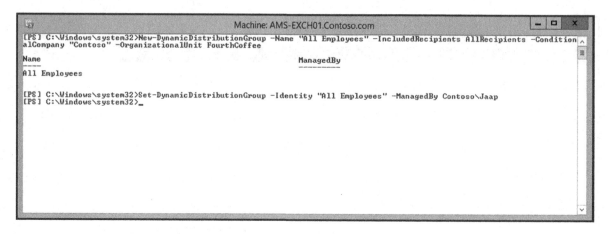

Figure 4-21. *Creating a new Dynamic Distribution Group*

It is possible to include fewer recipients by using only the mailbox users in the -IncludedRecipients option and using the department filter instead of the companyfilter; for example:

```
New-DynamicDistributionGroup -Name "HR Employees" -IncludedRecipients MailboxUsers
-ConditionalDepartment "HR"
Set-DynamicDistributionGroup -Identity "HR Employees" -ManagedBy Contoso\Jaap
```

More granularity can be achieved by filtering on the custom attributes. In a migration scenario, you can stamp CustomAttribute1 with a value "Migrated_To_2013" after a successful mailbox migration to Exchange 2013. To create a Dynamic Distribution Group that contains only mailboxes that are migrated to Exchange 2013, you can use something like this:

```
New-DynamicDistributionGroup -Name "Migrated Mailboxes" -IncludedRecipients MailboxUsers -
ConditionalCustomAttribute1 "Migrated_To_2013"
Set-DynamicDistributionGroup -Identity "Migrated Mailboxes" -ManagedBy Administrator
```

To check which mailboxes are members of a Dynamic Distribution Group, you have to use the recipient filter functionality. Load the group into a variable and retrieve the recipients by using the filter, like this:

```
$HREmp = Get-DynamicDistributionGroup "HR Employees"
Get-Recipient -RecipientPreviewFilter $HREmp.RecipientFilter
```

This will provide a list of all recipients who are members of this Dynamic Distribution Group, as shown in Figure 4-22.

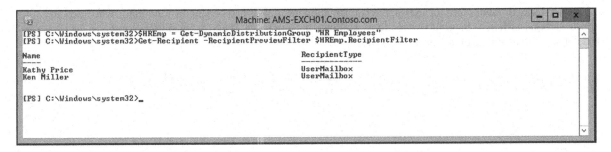

Figure 4-22. Check the mailboxes that are members of a Dynamic Distribution Group

Moderated Distribution Groups

A Moderated Distribution Group is a Distribution Group where messages that are intended for this group are first sent to a moderator, and the moderator approves or rejects the message. After approval, the message is sent to all members of the Distribution Group.

To use the moderation function, the Distribution Group has to be enabled for moderation by employing the –ModerationEnabled option and using the –ModeratedBy option to set the moderator. These options are available on the New-DistributionGroup and the Set-DistributionGroup.

To enable moderation on a Distribution Group called "Finance" and set user Steve Johnson as the moderator, for example, you can use the following command:

```
Set-DistributionGroup -Identity Finance –ModerationEnabled:$TRUE -ModeratedBy "Steve Johnson"
```

When a user named Jacky Graham, who is a member of the Finance Distribution Group, tries to send a message to members of this Distribution Group, a mail tip appears indicating the moderation of this Distribution Group, as shown in Figure 4-23.

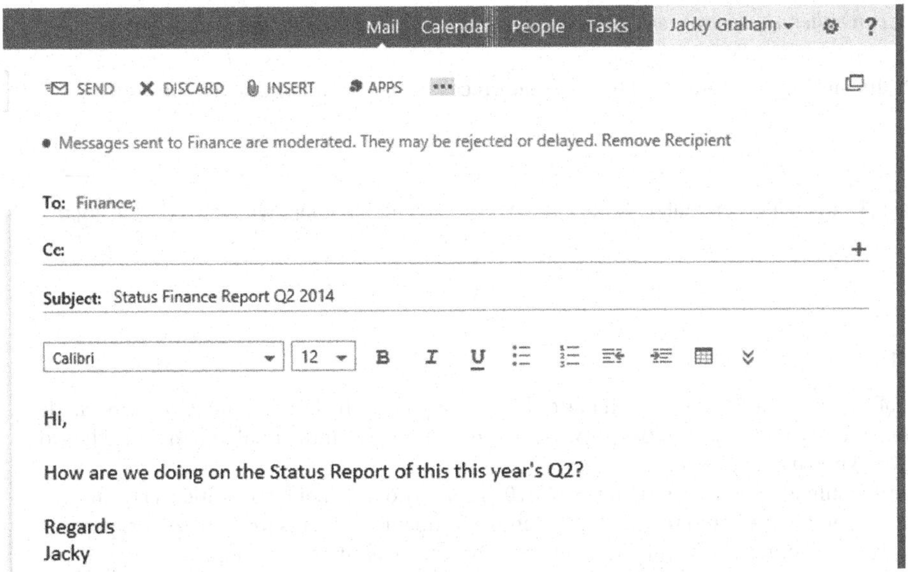

Figure 4-23. A mail tip is shown, indicating moderation of the message

When Jacky Graham sends the message, a confirmation message is first sent to the moderator, who finds an approval request when he logs onto his mailbox, as shown in Figure 4-24. When Steve Johnson approves the message, it is delivered to members of this Distribution Group.

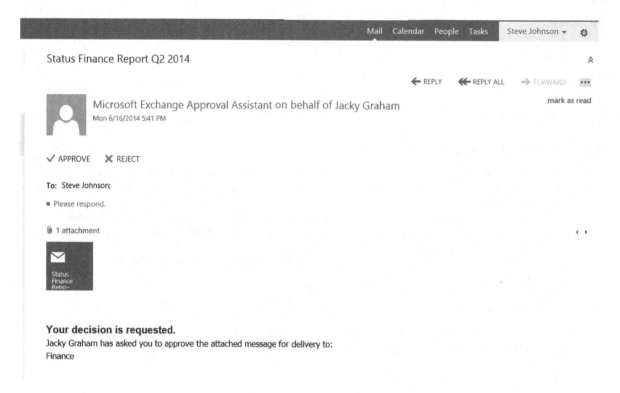

Figure 4-24. *The moderator can either approve or reject the message sent to the Finance Distribution Group*

If the moderator rejects the message, the sender of that message receives confirmation that the message was rejected.

■ **Note** A moderator can also be an entire Distribution Group. In that case, the first member who reponds will approve or reject the message.

The Expansion Server

When a message is sent initially to a Distribution Group, it has only one recipient—the Distribution Group itself. The Transport service running on an Exchange 2013 Mailbox server has to determine the individual that message has to be forwarded to. This process is known as *expansion*.

Distribution Group membership is static, based on the memberOf property of the mailboxes. Since a Dynamic Distribution Group has no membership the way a regular Distribution Group has, and thus there are no properties set, an Active Directory query is used for retrieving the members of a Dynamic Distribution Group.

An *Expansion server* is an Exchange 2013 Mailbox server that's responsible for expanding the Distribution Groups when it is processing messages. By default, no Expansion server is set for a Distribution Group, so any Mailbox server to which an email is delivered can perform the expansion.

Setting a dedicated Expansion server on a Distribution Group can be useful in a multi-site environment. Suppose Contoso.com has a Distribution Group in the UK with lots of members; it would make sense to use a Mailbox server at the local site for expansion purposes. This way, a message sent to this Distribution Group is dispatched to the UK before being expanded.

It the Expansion server is set, the Mailbox server accepting the message doesn't do any processing; it just routes the message to the Expansion server. If this server is, for some reason, not available, the message will not be delivered until the Expansion server again becomes available.

You can set the ExpansionServer property on a Distribution Group by using the following command:

```
Set-DistributionGroup -Identity "All Employees" -ExpansionServer AMS-EXCH02
```

▪ **Note**   This command can be used for both Distribution Groups and Dynamic Distribution Groups.

To Remove a Distribution Group

A Distribution Group can be removed as well as disabled. As with disabling mailboxes, disabling a Distribution Group retains the group in Active Directory but removes all Exchange properties, whereas removing a Distribution Group deletes the group from Active Directory as well.

To disable a Distribution Group, you can use the following command:

```
Disable-DistributionGroup -Identity "All Employees" -Confirm:$FALSE
```

To remove a Distribution Group, you can use the following command:

```
Remove-DistributionGroup -Identity "All Employees" -Confirm:$FALSE
```

Contacts

A *contact* in Active Directory is not a security principal, as is a user account. It cannot be used to log on to the network and access network resources, as you can with a normal user account. Instead, a contact in Active Directory can be compared to a business card in a Rolodex: you can use it to store contact information.

In Exchange 2013, a contact can also be mail-enabled, and as such it becomes a recipient. However, a mail-enabled contact in Exchange 2013 does not have a mailbox; it does have an external email address. For internal purposes, it might also have a local address, but when message are sent to this local address, theyare routed to the contact's external address.

A mail-enabled contact also appears in the Exchange 2013 address lists, and thus it can be selected as a recipient by clients.

To create a mail-enabled contact, you can use the following command:

```
New-MailContact -ExternalEmailAddress Beau@hotmail.com -Name "Beau Terham" -OrganizationalUnit
FourthCoffee -FirstName Beau -LastName Terham
```

When a contact already exists in Active Directory, it can be mail-enabled using the following command:

```
Enable-MailContact -Identity "Greg McGain" -ExternalEmailAddress Greg@TailSpinToys.com
```

When a user checks the All Contacts address list, all mail-enabled contacts show up, as indicated in Figure 4-25. The contact can be selected for receiving an email message or for scheduling a meeting with the person, depending on the icon selected.

Figure 4-25. *The mail-enabled contacts are listed in the All Contacts address list*

Mail-enabled contacts can be removed or disabled. When removed, the accompanying contact in Active Directory is deleted as well; when just disabled, the accompanying contact in Active Directory is preserved.

To disable a mail-enabled contact, you can use the following command:

```
Disable-MailContact –Identity "Beau Terham" –Confirm:$FALSE
```

To remove a mail-enabled contact, and remove the accompanying contact from Active Directory as well, you can use the following command:

```
Remove-MailContact –Identity "Greg McGain" –Confirm:$FALSE
```

Address Lists

In Exchange 2013, an address list is a collection of recipients. There are several types of default address lists created during installation of the first Exchange 2013 servers, and there are custom address lists that can contain specific recipients in your Exchange 2013 environment. To create a segregated address list in your Exchange environment, you can use *address book policies*. All three types of address lists are discussed next.

Default Address Lists

There are multiple types of default address lists:

- **All Users** – An address list that contains all mailbox-enabled users in the Exchange environment.

- **All Rooms** – An address list that contains all resource mailboxes of the type "Room" in the Exchange environment.

- **All Distribution Lists** – An address list that contains all mail-enabled Distribution Groups in the Exchange environment. This includes both Distribution Groups and Security Groups.

- **All Contacts** – An address list that contains all mail-enabled contacts in the Exchange environment.

- **Default Global Address List** (GAL) – An address list that contains all recipients in the Exchange environment.

- **Public Folders** – An address list that contains all public polders in the Exchange environment.

Address lists are dynamically generated, so clients need to be online with the Exchange server to view the various address lists. To overcome this obstacle, especially for Outlook clients, there's an Offline Address Book (OAB) that contains the information in the Default Global Address List. Outlook clients can download this OAB to use when they are not connected to the network and thus are not connected to the Exchange server.

Custom Address Lists

It is possible to create custom address lists, tailored to the needs of your organization. Very large organizations with large departments can especially benefit from having custom address lists. One example that comes to mind is a large university, where custom address lists exist for every department's faculty. Similarly, large corporations use multiple customer address lists.

For example, suppose **Contoso.com** has three large departments: FourthCoffee, TailSpinToys, and Fabrikam. A manager might want to create an address list for each department. Custom address lists can be based on organizational units in Active Directory, but it is recommended that you use an Active Directory attribute to differentiate the address lists. To create address lists based on department attribute, you can use the following commands:

```
New-AddressList -Name "FourthCoffee All Users Address List" -ConditionalDepartment FourthCoffee
-IncludedRecipients MailboxUsers
New-AddressList -Name "Fabrikam All Users Address List" -ConditionalDepartment Fabrikam
-IncludedRecipients MailboxUsers
New-AddressList -Name "TailSpinToys All Users Address List" -ConditionalDepartment TailSpinToys
-IncludedRecipients MailboxUsers
```

The –ConditionalDepartment and -IncludedRecipients options are automatically converted to a recipient filter, as shown in Figure 4-26.

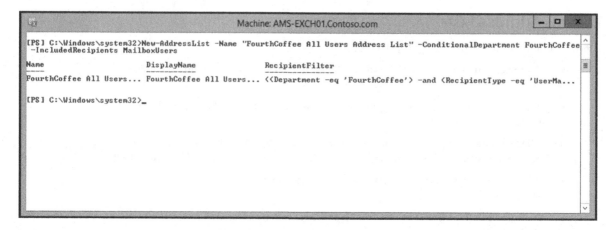

Figure 4-26. *Creating an address list for the FourthCoffee Department*

Checking the membership of an address list is similar to checking the membership of a Dynamic Distribution Group. You read the address list and filter out the recipients:

```
$AL = Get-AddressList "FourthCoffee All Users Address List"
Get-Recipient -RecipientPreviewFilter $AL.RecipientFilter
```

All members in the address list are shown on the console, as can be seen in Figure 4-27.

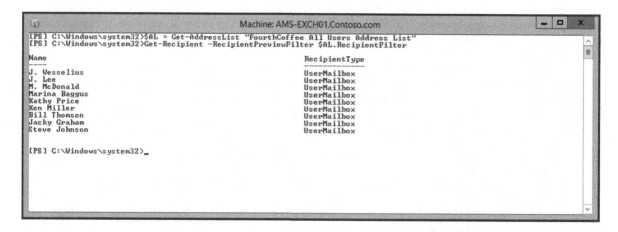

Figure 4-27. *Members of a custom address list*

The newly created custom address lists haven't been applied or updated yet; this means they exist in Active Directory, are shown in a client like OWA, but they do not return any mailboxes yet. To apply these new address lists, you enter the following commands:

```
Update-AddressList -Identity "FourthCoffee All Users Address List"
Update-AddressList -Identity "Fabrikam All Users Address List"
Update-AddressList -Identity "TailSpinToys All Users Address List"
```

Now, when a user in the FourthCoffee Department checks the FourthCoffee address list, he will see all users with this department property correctly displayed, as shown in Figure 4-28.

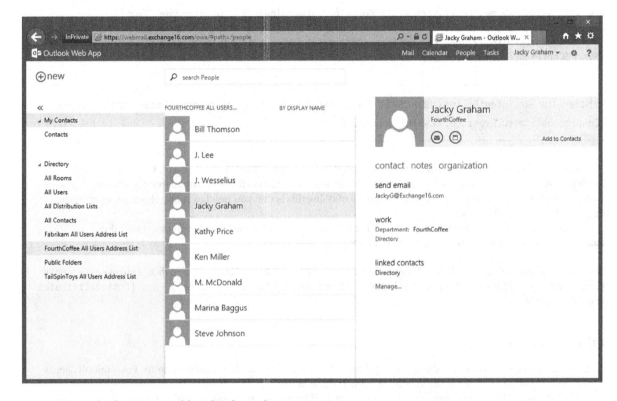

Figure 4-28. *The department address list shows the correct recipients*

It is possible to create address lists that contain other recipients than mailboxes; you can do this using the –IncludedRecipients option. The following values are available for the –IncludedRecipients option:

- None
- MailboxUsers
- MailUsers
- Resources
- MailGroups
- MailContacts
- AllRecipients

Instead of using the –IncludedRecipients option, you can use the –RecipientFilter option. Using the –RecipientFilter option gives you more flexibility because you can also build powerful filters.

For example, to create an address list that contains all "room" mailboxes in your organization that have an alias and for which the department attribute is set to "FourthCoffee," you can use the following command:

```
New-AddressList -Name "FourthCoffee All Rooms AL" -Container "\" -DisplayName "FourthCoffee
All Rooms AL" -RecipientFilter "((Alias -ne '`$NULL') -and (Department -eq 'FourthCoffee')
-and ((RecipientDisplayType -eq 'ConferenceRoomMailbox') -or (RecipientDisplayType -eq
'SyncedConferenceRoomMailbox')))"
```

■ **Note** The -RecipientFilter option cannot be used with the -ConditionalCompany, -ConditionalDepartment, -ConditionalStateOrProvince, or -IncludedRecipients options.

If you need to create address lists that span multiple departments, the standard -ConditinalDepartment (or department property) won't work. However, you can use a custom attribute for the search filter in an address list, which gives you even more flexibility. The downside of doing this is that you need to stamp this custom attribute during provisioning, of course.

To create an address list that's targeted to all employees across all departments, you can stamp the CustomAttribute1 with "Finance" and create the following address list:

```
New-AddressList –Name "Contoso Finance Employees" –DisplayName "Contoso Finance Employees Address
List" -RecipientFilter "((Alias -ne '`$NULL') -and (objectClass -eq 'user') -and (CustomAttribute1
-eq 'Finance'))"
```

Offline Address Book

As mentioned in the beginning of this section, address lists are only available for online clients. For Outlook clients who can work offline, the Offline Address Book (OAB) is available.

The OAB is a collection of address lists that is generated typically once a day, available for download on the Exchange server. For this download, there's a virtual directory called "OAB" available on the Client Access server.

To create a dedicated Offline Address Book for the FourthCoffee Department, and that includes the "FourthCoffee All Users Address List" and the "FourthCoffee All Rooms AL" address lists (created in the previous section), you can use the following command:

```
New-OfflineAddressBook –Name "FourthCoffee OAB" -AddressLists "\FourthCoffee All Users Address
List","FourthCoffee All Rooms AL" -VirtualDirectories "AMS-EXCHO1\OAB (Default Web Site)"
–GeneratingMailbox "CN=SystemMailbox{bb558c35-97f1-4cb9-8ff7-d53741dc928c},CN=Users,DC=Contoso,
DC=com"
```

The arbitration mailbox, as defined in the –GeneratingMailbox option, is the mailbox responsible for generating the OAB. If you omit the –GeneratingMailbox option, the OAB is created but it is never generated and thus is not available for download.

Address Book Policies

In the previous section, we created multiple address lists based on all kinds of filtering techniques and properties. While this works fine, it has one drawback: all address lists are visible for everybody in the organization. As long as someone has a mailbox and can log on to it, he is able to view all the address lists.

There are large companies that want to segregate their address lists so that every department or division has its own address lists and only users included in those address lists can view their own address lists and cannot view the address lists of other departments.

In Exchange 2003 and Exchange 2007, this was possible by explicitly granting or denying permissions on objects in Active Directory. While this worked great in these versions of Exchange, it is not feasible in Exchange 2010 and Exchange 2013. To achieve such segregation of adddress lists, Microsoft introduced the *address book policy* (ABP). The ABP is applied to a mailbox and represents a view on the address lists. That is, via the ABP you define which address lists are available for particular mailboxes.

Suppose that FourthCoffee Department has the following address lists:

- FourthCoffee Global Address List

- FourthCoffee All Rooms

- FourthCoffee All Users

- FourthCoffee All Contacts

- FourthCoffee All Groups

- FourthCoffee OAB

To create an ABP that includes all these address lists, you can use the following command:

```
New-AddressBookPolicy -Name "FourthCoffee ABP" -GlobalAddressList "\FourthCoffee Global Address
List" -OfflineAddressBook "\FourthCoffee OAB" -RoomList "\FourthCoffee All Rooms" -AddressLists
"\FourthCoffee All Users","\FourthCoffee All Groups","\FourthCoffee All Contacts"
```

When the ABP is created, it can applied to a particular mailbox:

```
Set-Mailbox -Identity JackyG -AddressBookPolicy "FourthCoffee ABP"
```

Now, when user Jacky Graham logs in to her mailbox and checks the address lists, she will see only the FourthCoffee Department address lists, as shown in Figure 4-29.

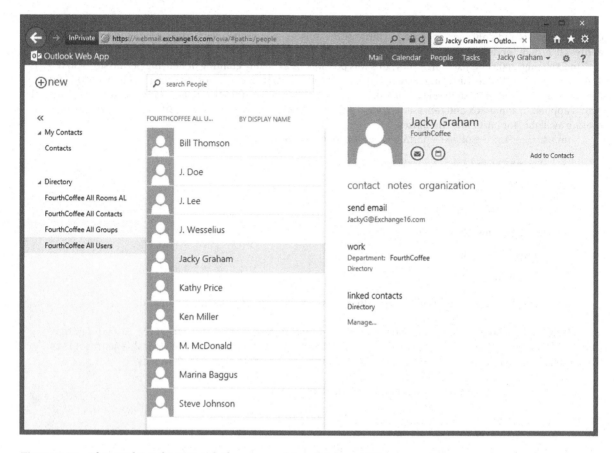

Figure 4-29. *After applying the ABP, only the proper address lists are visible*

■ **Note**   Using address book policies is the only supported and properly functioning way to achieve segregation of address lists.

The Transport Service

One of the major changes introduced in Exchange 2013 is that the Hub Transport service no longer exists as a separate server role, as it had in Exchange Servers 2007 and 2010. It is now integrated into the Exchange 2013 Mailbox server role. Thus, the Hub Transport service on the Mailbox server is responsible for routing messages, both on the internal network and to the Internet. Outbound messages to the Internet can be routed through the Front End Transport service (FETS) running on the Exchange 2013 Client Access server, or through an Exchange Edge Transport server.

In Exchange 2013 SP1, the Edge Transport server is reintroduced, but Exchange 2007 or Exchange 2010 Edge Transport servers can be used as well, in combination with Exchange 2013. Edge Transport servers are discussed in detailed in Chapter 6.

Inbound messages are routed via the Exchange 2013 Client Access server and from the Client Access server proxied to a Mailbox server. Exchange 2013 does have some anti-spam features, but they are pretty limited. Exchange 2013 also comes with a default anti-malware engine, but this is limited as well.

The Transport Pipeline

The complete, end-to-end mail delivery process, from accepting external SMTP messages on the Exchange 2013 Client Access server to delivering the actual message to the mailbox, is called the *transport pipeline* (see Figure 4-30 for a graphic view of the pipeline). The transport pipeline consists of several individual components:

- **Front End Transport service** (FETS) FETS is running on the Exchange 2013 Client Access server and is responsible for accepting SMTP messages from external SMTP hosts. FETS can also be configured as a front-end proxy on send connectors to proxy all messages through the Exchange 2013 Client Access servers.

- **Transport Service** The Transport service runs on the Exchange 2013 Mailbox server and is responsible for processing all inbound and outbound SMTP messages. It receives messages on the receive connector from the FETS, from the Transport server running on other Exchange 2013 Mailbox servers, or from any down-level Hub Transport servers. When the messages are received, they are queued in the submission queue.

  - The submission queue also receives messages from the pickup directory and from the replay directory. When messages are properly formatted (in an .EML format), you can drop them into the pickup directory and they will be automatically processed.

  - From the submission queue, the messages are sent to the categorizer. This is the process whereby the Transport server determines whether the message has to be delivered locally or remotely, whether it is on an internal Exchange server or an external one on the Internet. When categorized, the messages are delivered to a send connector. It is important to note that the Transport server never communicates directly with the mailbox databases.

- **Mailbox Transport Service** The Mailbox Transport service is also running on the Exchange 2013 Mailbox server and consists of two parts:

  - *Mailbox Transport Submission Service.* This is responsible for picking up messages from a user's drafts or outbox folder. Remote procedure calls (RPC) are used to communicate with the Information Store to pick up messages and then the SMTP is used to deliver messages to the local Transport server or to the Transport server running on other Exchange 2013 Mailbox servers in the organization.

  - *Mailbox Transport Delivery Service.* This is responsible for receiving messages from the Transport server and delivering those messages to the user's inbox or underlying folder. Messages are accepted from the local Transport server or from the Transport server running on other Exchange 2013 Mailbox servers in the organization. Next, RPC is used to communicate with the Information Store to deliver the messages to the inbox and the SMTP is used to communicate with the Exchange 2013 Transport server.

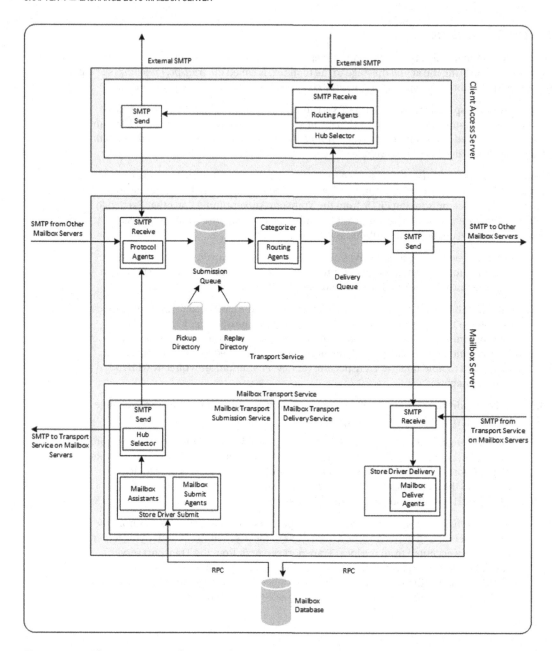

Figure 4-30. *The transport pipeline in Exchange 2013*

The Transport service running on an Exchange 2013 Mailbox server can work with other Exchange 2010 Mailbox servers (naturally), but also with any down-level Hub Transport servers. The Mailbox Transport server only works with the Transport server running on the Exchange 2013 Mailbox server in the same Active Directory site.

The transport pipeline is the *complete* Transport service, on both the Exchange 2013 Mailbox server and the Client Access server. In regard to the transport pipeline, there are topics to address here, such as the routing destinations, delivery groups, queues and how to manage them, and some redundancy features, like shadow redundancy and safety net.

Routing Destinations

When a message arrives at the Hub Transport service on an Exchange 2013 Mailbox server, it has to be categorized—that is, the recipient or recipients need to be determined. Once Exchange 2013 knows the list of recipients, the server knows where to route the message.

The destination for a message is called the *routing destination*. Routing destinations can be:

- A mailbox database containing a mailbox or a public folder.

- A connector responsible for sending a message to another Active Directory site with an Exchange server or to an external SMTP server.

- A Distribution Group Expansion server, or an Exchange server that's responsible for extracting recipients from a Distribution Group if the message is destined for a Distribution Group.

Delivery Groups

The concept of delivery groups was created in Exchange 2013. A *delivery group* is a collection of Exchange 2013 Mailbox servers (holding the Hub Transport service) or a collection of Exchange 2010 Hub Transport servers. These servers are responsible for delivering SMTP messages within this group of servers. The following delivery groups can be identified in Exchange 2013:

- **Routable DAG.** These are all the Exchange 2013 Mailbox servers that are members of a DAG. The mailbox databases in this DAG are the routing destinations of the delivery group. A message can be delivered to one particular Exchange 2013 Mailbox server in a DAG, and this Mailbox server is responsible for routing the message to the Exchange 2013 Mailbox server that holds the active copy of the mailbox database in the DAG. Since the DAG can span multiple Active Directory sites, the routing boundary for the routable DAG is the DAG itself, not the Active Directory site.

- **Mailbox Delivery Group.** This is a collection of Exchange 2010 or Exchange 2013 Mailbox servers in one Active Directory site that is *not* a member of a DAG. In a mailbox delivery group, the routing boundary is the Active Directory site itself. Mailboxes located on Exchange 2013 Mailbox databases are processed by the Hub Transport service running on the Exchange 2013 Mailbox servers in that Active Directory site. Mailboxes located on Exchange 2010 Mailbox databases are processed by the Hub Transport servers in that Active Directory site.

- **Connector Source Server.** This is a collection of Exchange 2010 Hub Transport or Exchange 2013 Mailbox servers that act as the source server for a particular send connector. These are only the source servers of a particular send connector; Exchange servers that are not defined as source servers of the send connector, but that are in the same Active Directory site, are *not* part of this delivery group.

- **Active Directory Site.** This is an Active Directory site that's not the final Active Directory site—that is, the message is in transit through this particular Active Directory site. For example, it can be a hub site or a connecting Active Directory site for an Exchange 2007 or 2010 Edge Transport server. An Exchange 2013 Mailbox server cannot contact an Exchange 2010 Edge Transport server that has an Edge subscription to an Exchange 2013 Mailbox server in another site, so the message has to pass through this Active Directory site in order to be relayed via the Exchange 2010 Edge Transport server.

- **Server List.** This is one or more Exchange 2013 Mailbox servers or Exchange 2010 Hub Transport servers that are configured as Distribution Group Expansion servers.

Queues

Generally speaking, in Exchange Server, a queue is a destination for a message, as well as a temporary storage location on the Exchange server. For every destination there's a queue, so there are queues for other submissions, for message delivery to the mailbox, for routing to other Exchange servers in the organization, or for routing to an external destination.

■ **Note**   Queues are a Transport service feature and thus they exist on Exchange 2013 Mailbox server, but also on Exchange 2007 and 2010 Hub Transport service, as well as on Exchange 2007 and 2010 Edge Transport service.

When messages arrive at the Transport service, they are immediately stored on the local disk of the Exchange server. The storage technology used is the *extensible storage engine* (ESE), which is the same engine as used for the mailbox databases. The mailqueue database and its accompanying log files and checkpoint file can be found on C:\Program Files\Microsoft\Exchange Server\V15\TransportRoles\data\Queue (see Figure 4-31). The ESE database has circular logging enabled. This means that log files no longer needed are automatically deleted and, as such, there's no recovery method, such as replay of log files.

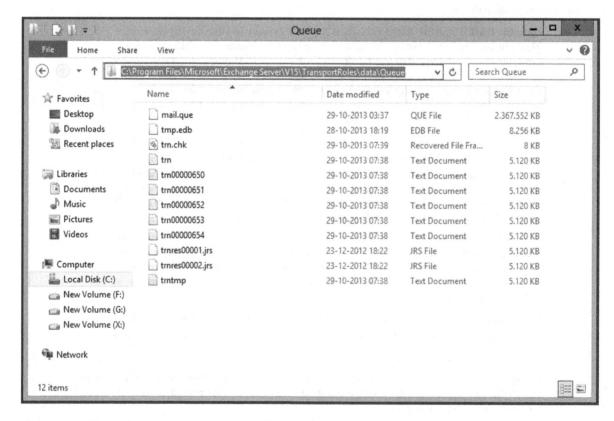

Figure 4-31. *The mailqueue database is a normal ESE database*

It is possible to change some of the configuration options of the mailqueue database. When Exchange Server 2013 is installed in the default location, all configuration settings are stored in the EdgeTransport.exe.config file, which can be found in C:\Program Files\Microsoft\Exchange Server\V15\bin. Most settings in this file can be left at their default values, but it is possible to change the location of all mailqueue-related files and directories to another disk. The advantage of doing this is that, if there's unexpected growth in these files, that won't affect the normal system and boot drives. If these fill up, there's always the possibility that the services running on this particular server will gradually stop working; worse, the entire server might stop working. Needless to say, this is an undesirable situation for Exchange Server.

If you open the EdgeTransport.Config.Exe file and browse through the file, you'll see the following keys:

- QueueDatabasePath
- QueueDatabaseLoggingPath
- IPFilterDatabasePath
- IPFilterDatabaseLoggingPath
- TemporaryStoragePath

By default, these keys point to the location %ExchangeInstallPath%TransportRoles\data\, but by changing the values to, for example, D:\TransportRoles\data\<variable>, another disk can be used.

To automate this process, Microsoft has created a script called Move-TransportDatabase.ps1, which is located in the $ExScripts directory. To use this script to move the mailqueue database to another location, use the following commands:

```
CD \$ExScripts
.\Move-TransportDatabase.ps1 -queueDatabasePath 'D:\TransportRoles\data\Queue'
-queueDatabaseLoggingPath 'D:\TransportRoles\data\Queue'
-iPFilterDatabasePath 'D:\TransportRoles\data\IpFilter'
-iPFilterDatabaseLoggingPath 'D:\TransportRoles\data\IpFilter'
-temporaryStoragePath 'D:\TransportRoles\data\Temp'
```

Shadow Redundancy

There's one type of queue that always raises questions. At first look, there are always messages in this queue, and they don't seem to disappear that quickly. *Shadow queues*, also referred to as *shadow redundancy*, are there for message redundancy: messages are stored in shadow queues until the next hop in the message path that moves toward delivering the message reports a successful delivery. Only then is the message deleted from the shadow queue.

Imagine an Exchange 2013 Mailbox server in New York that's sending messages to the Internet, but has no Internet connection of its own. There are also two Exchange 2013 Mailbox servers in Amsterdam, and Amsterdam has its own Internet connection. A network connection exists between the two locations.

1. The Exchange 2013 Mailbox server in New York sends an SMTP message to Exchange 2013 Mailbox server (A) in Amsterdam, AMS-EXCH02. As soon as the message is delivered in Amsterdam, it is stored in the shadow queue on the server in New York.

2. Exchange 2013 Mailbox server (A) in Amsterdam sends the message to server (B) in Amsterdam, AMS-EXCH01. As soon as the message is accepted, it is stored in the shadow queue on server (A).

3. Server (A) knows the message was successfully delivered and reports back to the server in New York. At this moment the message can safely be deleted from the New York shadow queue because there still is a backup message, but now it's on server (A).

4. Server (B) sends the message to the Edge Transport server in the perimeter network, and when delivered, server (B) reports back to server (A), who can now delete the message from its shadow queue.

Sending a message from the Exchange server to the Internet is difficult, of course, because not all SMTP servers on the Internet support shadow queues. If not supported, the messages are automatically deleted from the sender's shadow queue after a period of time.

Shadow queue redundancy is built into Exchange 2013 when messages are in transit. If one server fails, for whatever reason, and the server is no longer available, the previous Exchange server in the message path can retry delivering the message via a different available path.

■ **Note**   The shadow queue function was available in Exchange Server 2010 as well.

Don't confuse the shadow queues with Exchange 2010's Transport Dumpster. While the Transport Dumpster also offers redundancy for SMTP messages, its primary purpose is to offer redundancy for messages that are delivered to Mailboxes in a DAG. The Transport Dumpster evolved into Safety Net, which is explained a little later in this chapter.

Managing Queues

Most of Exchange 2013 Mailbox server queues exist for only a limited time. When the Transport server cannot deliver a message, the message stays in the queue until the server can successfully deliver the message (it keeps trying) or until the message expires; the default message expiration time is two days.

These queues can be managed by using the Queue Viewer, which is a graphic tool, or by using the EMS. The Queue Viewer can be found in the toolbox, an MMC snap-in that's automatically installed during the installation of Exchange Server. Caution: The toolbox in Exchange 2013 has the same icon as the EMC in Exchange Server 2010, so don't let this fool you. Open the Exchange toolbox and select "Queue Viewer" under mail flow tools. The Queue Viewer shows the queues on the server currently operating, but if you select "Connect to Server" in the actions pane, you can use it to view information on other Exchange 2013 Mailbox servers as well (see Figure 4-32).

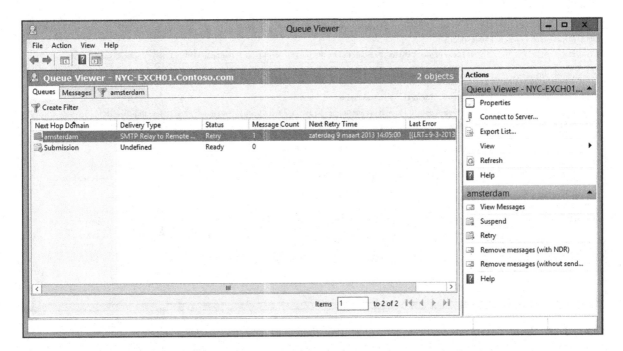

Figure 4-32. *A message is stuck in the queue on the New York server, destined for the Amsterdam server*

The Queue Viewer is an incredibly valuable tool for troubleshooting purposes. It shows messages that are in a queue, of course, but if you open the message, it also shows the reason why the messages cannot be delivered. The tool also gives you the option of suspending a queue or removing messages from a queue, either with or without generating a nondelivery report (NDR).

It is also possible to manage the queues using the EMS. This method is more complex, but it offers many more granular options. The basic command to get queue information is the Get-Queue cmdlet. The Get-Queue cmdlet will show the queues on the server where the cmdlet is executed (see Figure 4-33). Using the identity of the queue, you can obtain more information by using the Get-Queue -Identity NYC-EXCH01\6 cmdlet, for example. The actual error is not shown when using this cmdlet, but you can use the Get-Queue -Identity NYC-EXCH01\6 | FL cmdlet for all information regarding the queue, or the Get-Queue -Identity NYC-EXCH01\6 | select Identity,DeliveryType, Status,MessageCount,NexthopDomain,LastError to show the actual error message the transport service is experiencing.

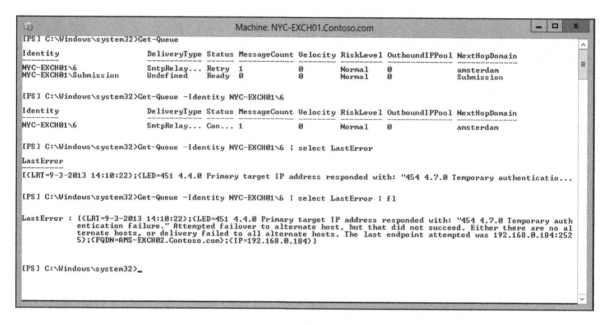

Figure 4-33. *Use the Get-Queue cmdlet to get information about messages stuck in the queue*

The Get-Queue cmdlet will only show results from the Exchange server where the cmdlet is executed. You can also use the Get-TransportService cmdlet to get a list of all Transport services running on all Exchange 2013 Mailbox servers, and pipe this output into the Get-Queue cmdlet: Get-TransportService | Get-Queue. This will show all queues on all Transport services in the organization.

■ **Note** In the example in Figure 4-33, the message is not delivered owing to authentication problems. All servers are running in a Hyper-V environment, and you have to be careful with time synchronization complications. In the example, it turned out that some servers had major time differences because they were synchronizing against their Hyper-V host instead of against the PDC emulator. This situation sometimes also results in problems with the EMS (WinRM won't function correctly) or with the Server Manager.

When a message cannot be delivered, it will stay in the queue and it can stay here for up to two days, which is the default wait time. When this happens, there's no need for any concern; Exchange will keep trying to deliver the message. Also, the number of messages in a queue can vary over time; for example, you could have 20 to 30 messages in a queue for an Internet send connector. But the messages have to be delivered after some time, of course. If there's a steady increase in the number of messages in a queue, or if many queues are created and the messages get stuck in there, then it's time to dig deeper into the cause of the excessive queuing. (Chapter 6 will cover this more in detail.)

Safety Net

Safety Net is a new redundancy feature in Exchange 2013 for the Transport service and is the successor of the Transport Dumpster in Exchange Server 2007 and 2010. The Transport Dumpster was developed to provide message redundancy when these messages were delivered to the mailbox. The messages were kept on the Hub Transport server, and when a database in a DAG failed for some reason and a message was not replicated to the passive copy, the missing message was retransmitted to the passive copy. This would result in minimum data loss.

Safety Net provides the same function for Exchange 2013. As such, Safety Net stores in a queue the messages that were successfully delivered to the mailboxes. Safety Net is still associated with the Transport service, but now it stores information on the Mailbox server. The difference between Safety Net and the Transport Dumpster is that Safety Net does not require a DAG. It also stores copies of messages for Mailbox servers that are not DAG members.

Another major change is that Safety Net is redundant by itself; there's a primary Safety Net and a shadow Safety Net. The primary Safety Net exists on the Mailbox server where the message originates, while the shadow Safety Net exists on the Mailbox server where the message is delivered. As soon as the message is delivered, it is stored in the Safety Net queue. Messages are kept in the Safety Net queue for 48 hours, which is the default time.

Safety Net and shadow redundancy are complementary. That is, shadow redundancy is responsible for messages in transit, while Safety Net is responsible for messages that have been delivered to mailboxes. The cool thing is that Safety Net is a fully automated feature; there's no need for any manual action. All coordination is done by the Active Manager, who is also responsible for failover scenarios in the DAG.

When something untoward happens, the Active Manager requests a resubmission from Safety Net. For large organizations, these messages most likely exist on multiple Mailbox servers so (a lot of) duplicate messages can occur. Exchange 2013, however, has a mechanism that detects duplicate messages; it finds and eliminates those duplicate message, preventing the recipient from receiving multiple copies. Unfortunately, resubmitted messages from Safety Net are also delivered to mail servers outside the Exchange organization. Since these servers don't have the duplicate-message detection mechanism, external users can receive multiple identical messages.

When the primary Safety Net is not available, Active Manager tries requesting a resubmit for 12 hours. If unsuccessful after this time, Active Manager then contacts the other Mailbox servers and requests a resubmit of messages for the particular mailbox database. Either way, no messages should be lost during a failover, whether the failover is planned or not.

Autodiscover

Autodiscover was introduced in Exchange 2007 to support Outlook 2007, and it has been developed into one of the most important parts of the Exchange environment. If you don't have a proper Autodiscover implementation, you will experience all kinds of nasty problems, ranging from not being able to check free/busy information when scheduling a meeting, to not being able to download an Offline Address Book, to not being able to set the out-of-office message using the Outlook client, to not being able to connect at all.

Autodiscover is most visible for end users when they set up their Outlook client. Users have only to enter their names, their email addresses, and their Active Directory passwords, and the Outlook client will configure itself automatically. It actually discovers all the information regarding the Exchange Server implementation and uses this information to configure the Outlook profile. But not only does it do this on the initial setup, it also performs this action on a regular basis to check for any changes in the Exchange environment.

Autodiscover works by an XML request sent from the Outlook client to the Client Access server. The Client Access server checks Active Directory for the location of the user's mailbox. If the mailbox is on an Exchange 2013 Mailbox server, the request is proxied to this Mailbox server and the Mailbox server retrieves the user's mailbox settings using the Autodiscover server.

If the mailbox is still on a down-level Exchange server, the request is proxied to a down-level Client Access server, where the request is processed. Handling on the down-level Client Access server is similar to handling on the Exchange 2013 Mailbox server, shown in Figure 4-34.

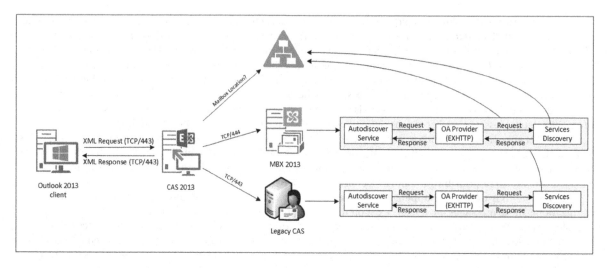

Figure 4-34. *Autodiscover information flow*

Important to note is that, in a coexistence scenario, the Autodiscover request is always sent to the Exchange 2013 Client Access server. After the user's mailbox location is checked, the request is proxied to the appropriate server. How does the Outlook client discover which Client Access server to send its request to? The answer is twofold:

- Domain-joined Outlook clients who are actually logged on to the Active Directory domain retrieve this information directly from Active Directory.

- Non-domain-joined Outlook clients, or domain-joined Outlook clients who cannot access Active Directory (when working at home, for example), build the Autodiscover URL based on the user's SMTP address.

Both scenarios are covered next.

Domain-Joined Clients

When a Client Access server is installed, a computer object is created in Active Directory. Besides this computer object, a *service connection point* (SCP) is also created in Active Directory. For every Client Access server that's installed, a corresponding SCP is created. So, if you have six Client Access servers, you also have six SCPs.

An SCP has a well-known GUID (Global Unique Identifier) that's unique for the type of application that's using the SCP. In the case of Exchange Server, this application is Outlook. All service connection points created by installing Client Access servers have the same well-known GUID, and Outlook clients query Active Directory for this GUID. This GUID is stored in the keywords attribute together with the Active Directory site name where the Client Access server is installed, as shown in Figure 4-35.

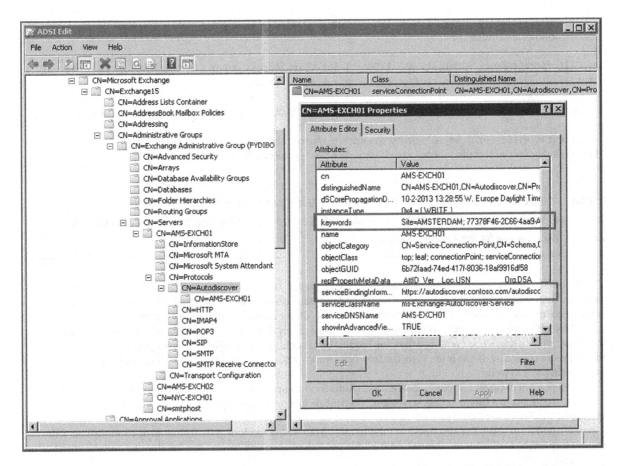

Figure 4-35. *The service connection point in Active Directory, with keywords and* ServiceBindingInformation *properties*

Once found, the serviceBindingInformation attribute is retrieved and, by default, this value contains the FQDN of the Client Access server—for example, ams-exch01.contoso.com. If there are multiple Client Access servers in the Exchange environment, a virtual IP (VIP) on the load balancer should be created. This VIP should be the IP address of a load-balanced FQDN (for example, autodiscover.contoso.com), and it should contain all Client Access servers. Clients connect to this VIP instead of to an individual Client Access server, and all client requests are distributed across all Client Access servers.

The Outlook client retrieves the Autodiscover FQDN from Active Directory and sends an HTTP post command to this URL. The Client Access server then accepts the request and proxies it to the Mailbox server. The Mailbox server gathers all the required information and returns this as an XML package to the Outlook client. The Outlook client then can use the XML package to configure its profile (when it's a new setup) or reconfigure its profile (when changes are detected in the Exchange environment).

This process happens always, not only during the initial setup of the Outlook client; the request is sent once an hour to determine if there are any changes in the Exchange configuration. Since it is an HTTP request that's secured on the server, the SSL certificates come into play. The autodiscover.contoso.com needs to be in the certificate as well, next to the webmail.contoso.com name.

The Autodiscover URL is configurable only by using the Exchange Management Shell. You open the shell and enter the following command:

```
Get-ClientAccessServer -Identity AMS-EXCH01 | Set-ClientAccessServer -AutoDiscoverServiceInternalUri
https://autodiscover.contoso.com/autodiscover/autodiscover.xml
```

If all the Client Access servers need to be configured with this URL, the following command can be used:

```
Get-ClientAccessServer | Set-ClientAccessServer -AutoDiscoverServiceInternalUri
https://autodiscover.contoso.com/autodiscover/autodiscover.xml
```

■ **Note**   If there are no Outlook clients connecting via the Internet, or there are only domain-joined clients, or if you want to use service records (SRV records) in the public DNS, it is possible to configure the Client Access server with webmail.contoso.com for the Autodiscover URL.

Autodiscover will retrieve all information from the Exchange environment, as well as other information such as virtual directories for OWA, EAC, MAPI, Offline Address Book downloads, or Exchange web services. These web services are used for retrieving free/busy information or for setting the out-of-office information.

Therefore, if there are problems with Autodiscover, most likely these will result in not being able to check for free/busy information when creating a meeting request or in setting the out-of-office message in Outlook. And to make it more confusing, if this is the case, the free/busy information is visible in OWA and you can set the out-of-office message in OWA as well.

In 99 percent of cases, any complications with Autodiscover are caused by SSL certificate errors. When using a browser to connect to a Client Access server and a certificate error arises, it is possible to continue despite the error message.

It is possible to verify the Autodiscover functionality from within Outlook. When Outlook is running, check the system tray for the Outlook icon. Control-right-click this Outlook icon and select "Test Email AutoConfiguration" (see Figure 4-36).

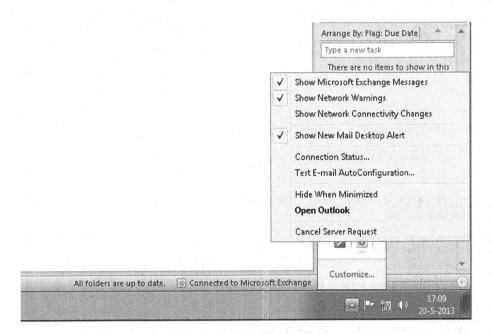

Figure 4-36. *Testing Autodiscover from within the Outlook client*

You then enter the email address and password, clear both the "Use Guessmart" and the "Secure Guessmart Authentication" check boxes, and click the Test button. The Outlook client will perform an Autodiscover check against the Exchange Server and display the information as shown in Figure 4-37.

```
┌─────────────────────────────────────────────────────────────────────────────┐
│ Test E-mail AutoConfiguration                                          [✕]    │
│                                                                               │
│  E-mail Address   John@contoso.com                                            │
│  Password         •••••••••|                                                  │
│  ☐ Legacy DN                                                                  │
│                                                                               │
│         ☑ Use AutoDiscover  ☐ Use Guessmart  ☐ Secure Guessmart Authentication │
│                                                          [  Test  ]  [ Cancel ]│
│  ═══════════════════════════════════════════════════════════════════════════ │
│  ┌────────┬─────┬─────┐                                                        │
│  │ Results│ Log │ XML │                                                        │
│  ┌──────────────────────────────────────────────────────────────────────┐▲   │
│  │Autoconfiguration has started, this may take up to a minute            │    │
│  │Autoconfiguration found the following settings:                        │    │
│  │Display Name: John Doe                                                  │    │
│  │Internal OWA URL: https://webmail.contoso.com/owa/                      │≡   │
│  │External OWA URL: https://webmail.contoso.com/owa/                      │    │
│  │                                                                        │    │
│  │Protocol: Exchange RPC                                                  │    │
│  │Server: 5e2bcbec-adc4-4c22-8af8-e50e5dc44bb9@contoso.com                │    │
│  │Login Name: John                                                        │    │
│  │Availability Service URL: https://webmail.contoso.com/ews/exchange.asmx │    │
│  │OOF URL: https://webmail.contoso.com/ews/exchange.asmx                  │    │
│  │OAB URL: https://webmail.contoso.com/OAB/db93c05a-ac23-423a-b2f7-00b4bdf20f66/│
│  │Unified Message Service URL: https://webmail.contoso.com/ews/UM2007Legacy.asmx│
│  │Auth Package: Unspecified                                               │    │
│  │Exchange Control Panel URL: https://webmail.contoso.com/ecp/            │    │
│  │ECP Sub URL: ?rfr=olk&p=customize/voicemail.aspx&exsvurl=1&realm=contoso.com│ │
│  │ECP Sub URL: ?rfr=olk&p=personalsettings/EmailSubscriptions.slab&exsvurl=1&realm=contoso.com│
│  │ECP Sub URL: ?rfr=olk&p=sms/textmessaging.slab&exsvurl=1&realm=contoso.com│  │
│  │ECP Sub URL: Personal Settings/Delivery Reports... ...                  │▼   │
│  └──────────────────────────────────────────────────────────────────────┘    │
└─────────────────────────────────────────────────────────────────────────────┘
```

Figure 4-37. *Autodiscover information returned from the Autodiscover check*

There are three tabs visible:

- Results: The returned information is shown in a readable format.

- Log: The various options are shown for how the Outlook client tried to retrieve the information.

- XML: The raw XML data that is returned from the Exchange server is shown.

This utility is extremely useful when troubleshooting the Exchange environment.

Non-Domain-Joined Clients

Non-domain-joined clients, or domain-joined clients who do not have access to Active Directory, use a different approach for getting Autodiscover information.

Initially, Outlook will construct an FQDN based on the right-hand part of the email address. So if the user's email address is john@contoso.com, Outlook will start looking at https://contoso.com/autodiscover/autodiscover.xml to try to get to the Client Access server.

Once the URL is constructed, Outlook will automatically send an HTTP XML post request to the Autodiscover URL and will get all the necessary information as it does for an internal Outlook client. If this doesn't work, Outlook will fall back to the same URL, but with an Autodiscover prefix, like https://autodiscover.contoso.com/autodiscover/autodiscover.xml.

For external clients, it is crucial to have the SSL certificate correctly set up with an FQDN `webmail.contoso.com` and an `autodiscover.contoso.com` domain name in the certificate. There's no easy way to get around this unless you implement a solution based on SRV records in public DNS. Any Outlook client who has no access to Active Directory will automatically try to connect to the Client Access server using a self-constructed URL `autodiscover.contoso.com`. This is hard-coded in the Outlook application!

The built-in Outlook test utility, as shown in Figure 3-12, also works when Outlook is operating via the Internet; but Microsoft alternatively offers a remote test tool called *remote connectivity analyzer* (RCA), which can be reached via `https://www.testexchangeconnectivity.com/` (see Figure 4-38). This tool will automatically check the Exchange configuration via the Internet using the normal Autodiscover options.

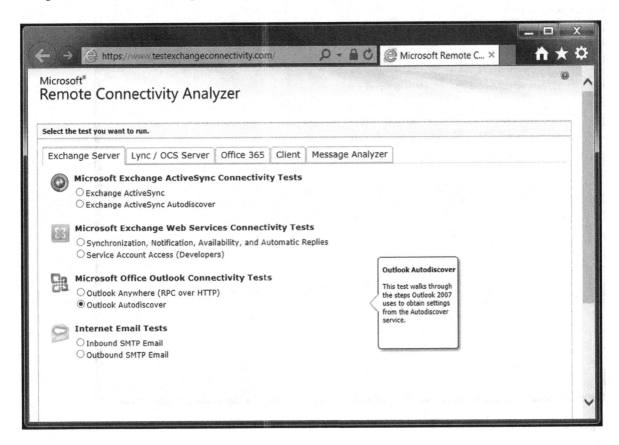

Figure 4-38. *The remote connectivity analyzer*

To use this tool, select Outlook Autodiscover on the Exchange Server tab and click Next (not visible in Figure 4-38). Enter the email address, user name, and password; select the "I Understand that I Must Use the Credentials of a Working..." check box and enter the verification string. Click "Perform Test" and the RCA will start testing the Exchange environment using the various Autodiscover methods; the results are shown in seconds.

There are multiple methods for retrieving Autodiscover information, and these are shown as a red circle with a white cross in it, or a green circle with a white checkbox in it. When one method fails, Outlook (and RCA) will automatically continue with the next available option. There's no need to panic when you see the red circle; only when you only see red circles and no green ones is it time to start worrying. One failed and one successful test can be seen in Figure 4-39.

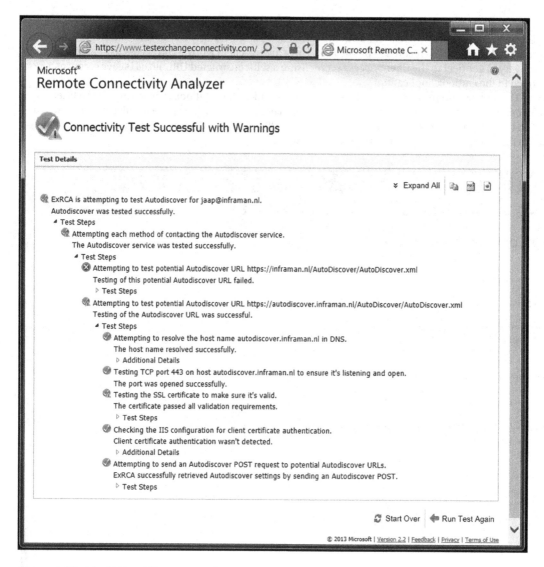

Figure 4-39. *The RCA results*

■ **Note** The remote connectivity analyzer is a publicly available tool to test your Exchange environment. Since it has to access your Exchange environment from the Internet, your Client Access server needs to be accessible from the Internet. It also needs a valid and trusted third-party UC certificate on the Client Access server. Important: it *does not work* with the default self-signed certificate.

Remember that the Exchange 2013 Autodiscover process works for Outlook 2007 clients (with Service Pack 3 and the November 2012 Public Update or later; earlier versions of Outlook are not supported at all by Exchange 2013) connecting from an internal network, as well as those connecting from the external network.

If you check the IIS log files, which can be found by default on `%SystemDrive%\inetpub\logs\LogFiles\W3SVC1`, you'll see numerous entries like:

```
2012-12-29 09:05:31 192.168.0.55 POST /autodiscover/autodiscover.xml - 443 CONTOSO\jaap 80.101.27.11
Microsoft+Office/14.0+(Windows+NT+6.1;+Microsoft+Outlook+14.0.6129;+Pro) - 200 0 64 156
```

Using the IIS log files, it is possible to troubleshoot your Autodiscover process. Shown here are, for example, the URI that's used, the port number, the account, the source IP address, the client (okay, I'm still running Windows 7 and Office 2010 on my laptop), and that the request returned a "200" response, which is okay.

Autodiscover Redirect

As we've seen in the previous section, Outlook automatically constructs an Autodiscover FQDN based on the user's primary SMTP address, and this FQDN needs to be on the Exchange 2013 Client Access server's SSL certificate. While this works fine if you have only one or two primary SMTP domains in your Exchange organization, things become challenging when you have more SMTP domains.

One of my clients is a worldwide publisher, and over the years it has acquired several hundred small publishing companies all over the globe, each with its own identity. It's not hard to imagine that an SSL certificate with so many domains is difficult to work with. Most third-party SSL certificate vendors support up to 20 or 25 domain names on an SSL certificate. This is a practical limitation set by these vendors. When you have a lot of domain names in your SSL certificate, it takes a lot of time to validate all those domain names—plus, the cost of such an SSL certificate skyrockets. It's not possible to predict the maximum number of domain names on an SSL certificate, but Digicert, for example, will support up to approximately 100 domain names.

Suppose in the `contoso.com` Exchange 2013 environment there are two other SMTP domains hosted, `Fabrikam.com` and `FourthCoffee.com`, and the Exchange 2013 Client Access server has only the `webmail.contoso.com` and the `autodiscover.contoso.com` domain names on the SSL certificate.

For this scenario, Microsoft has developed the `Autodiscover Redirect` option. What happens is that the Exchange 2013 Client Access server has an additional website (listening on port 80) with an FQDN called `autodiscoverredirect.contoso.com`. Internally, in IIS, requests for this site are automatically redirected to `autodiscover.contoso.com`. The additional domains (`Fabrikam.com` and `FourthCoffee.com`) do have an Autodiscover record in public DNS, but it does not contain a regular A record; instead, it contains a CNAME record pointing to the `autodiscoverredirect.contoso.com` site on the Exchange 2013 Client Access server.

When a user with a primary SMTP address Todd@Fabrikam.com opens his Outlook, Outlook wants to connect automatically to `autodiscover.fabrikam.com`. This attempt will fail because the Client Access server will not respond on port 443 to this request. The next step is that Outlook will try the redirect option. `Autodiscover.fabrikam.com` is resolved to `autodiscoverredirect.contoso.com` and Outlook will try to connect on port 80 (regular HTTP) to the Exchange 2013 Client Access server. The request is accepted, and a 302/Redirect is returned and the client request is redirected to `https://autodiscover.contoso.com/autodiscover/autodiscover.xml`. This is a valid name, has a valid IP address, and has a valid domain name on the SSL certificate. As a result, the Autodiscover request succeeds and a valid XML package is returned from the Exchange 2013 Client Access server to the Outlook client.

This can be seen in Figure 4-40, but since `Contoso.com` and `Fabrikam.com` are not publicly available domain names, the `exchange16.com` and `inframan.nl` domain names are used instead.

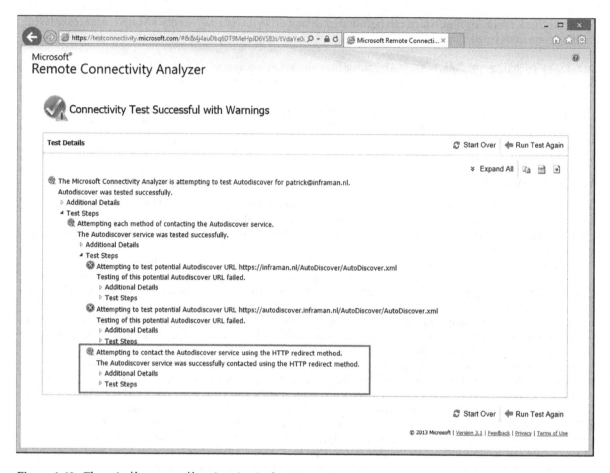

Figure 4-40. *The autodiscoverredirect option in the RCA*

Clearly visible in Figure 4-40 is that the tests for `https://inframan.nl/Autodiscover/Autodiscover.xml` and `https://autodiscover.inframan.nl/Autodiscover/Autodiscover.xml` fail but succeed on the HTTP redirect method. Just as in the earlier examples, there's no need to panic because of the red circles with the white crosses; as long as there's one green circle, you're fine.

■ **Note**   In my lab environment I will be using the domain `Exchange16.com` as the base domain, so I'll have `autodiscover.exchange16.com` and `autodiscoverredirect.exchange16.com`. The additional domain I'm hosting on this environment is `inframan.nl`; our user there is `patrick@inframan.nl`.

To implement the Autodiscover redirect method, you have to:

1.   Add an additional IP address to the Client Access server.

2.   Create an additional website on the Client Access server.

3.   Set the bindings and the IP addresses correctly.

4.   Set the redirection on the additional website to the original (Autodiscover) site.

The following commands can be used in the Exchange Management Shell:

```
Remove-WebBinding -Name 'default web site' -BindingInformation "*:443:"
New-WebBinding -Name "Default Web Site" -IPAddress "176.62.196.244" -Port 443 -Protocol https

New-Item -ItemType Directory -Path $env:systemdrive\Inetpub\AutodiscoverRedirect
New-Item -ItemType Directory -Path $env:systemdrive\Inetpub\AutodiscoverRedirect\Autodiscover

New-WebSite -Name AutodiscoverRedirect -Port 80
-PhysicalPath "$env:systemdrive\inetpub\AutodiscoverRedirect" -IPAddress "176.62.196.243"

New-WebVirtualDirectory -Name Autodiscover -Site AutodiscoverRedirect
-PhysicalPath "$env:systemdrive\inetpub\AutodiscoverRedirect\Autodiscover"

Set-WebConfiguration system.webServer/httpRedirect "IIS:\sites\autodiscoverredirect\autodiscover"
-Value @{enabled="true";destination="https://autodiscover.exchange16.com/autodiscover/autodiscover.xml";
exactDestination="false";httpResponseStatus="Found"}
```

■ **Note**   This script can also be downloaded from the Apress website.

I can imagine you want to use the GUI when making this kind of infrastructural change to you Exchange environment. If so, you can use the following steps to implement the Autodiscover redirect method:

1. Configure an additional IP address on the Client Access server.

2. In IIS Manager, bind the default website to the original IP address of the Client Access server for port 443, as shown in Figure 4-41. Before you continue, make sure the Client Access server keeps working with this new binding.

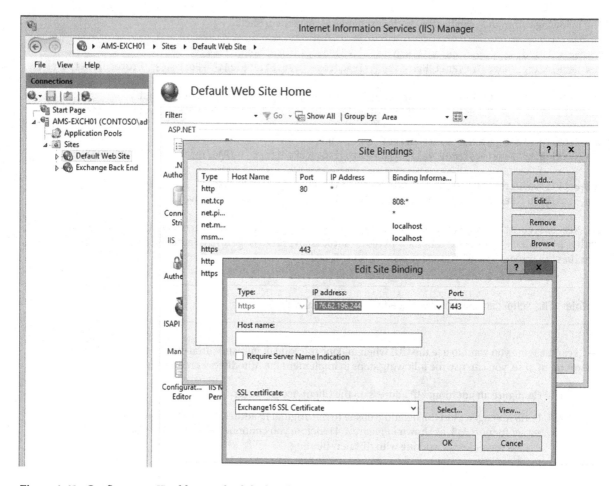

Figure 4-41. *Configure one IP address to the default website*

3. In Windows Explorer, create two additional directories C:\Inetpub\
   AutodiscoverRedirect and C:\Inetpub\AutodiscoverRedirect\Autodiscover.

4. In IIS Manager, create a new website, name it AutodiscoverRedirect and use the
   C:\Inetpub\Autodiscover as its physical path. Make sure the binding of this website is set
   to the additional IP address we configured earlier, as shown in Figure 4-42.

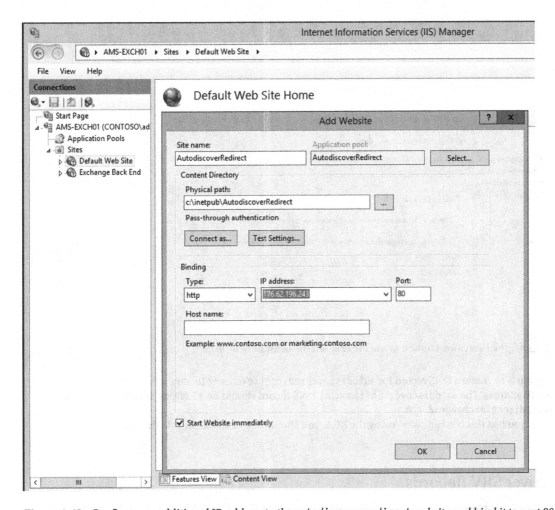

Figure 4-42. *Configure an additional IP address to the autodiscoverredirect website and bind it to port 80*

5. In the AutodiscoverRedirect website in IIS Manager, you'll see an Autodiscover virtual directory show up. Select this Autodiscover virtual directory, and in the details pane, double-click "HTTP Redirect."

6. In the HTTP Redirect window, check the "Redirect" request to this destination and enter the normal Autodiscover URL, like https://autodiscover.exchange16.com/autodiscover/autodiscover.xml, as shown in Figure 4-43.

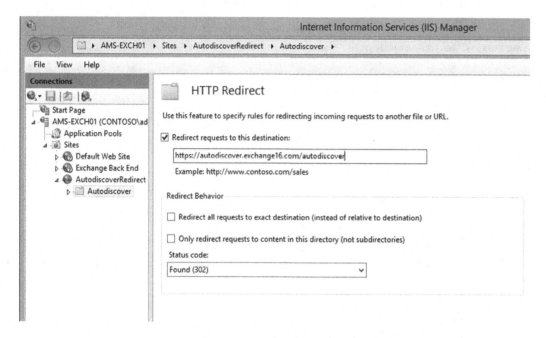

Figure 4-43. *Configure the redirect option to use the original **Autodiscover** website*

The only thing left is to create a DNS record for autodiscoverredirect.exchange16.com, which should point to the additional IP address. The autodiscover.inframan.nl DNS record should be a CNAME record and point to autodiscoverredirect.exchange16.com.

Now, when you test this configuration using the RCA, you should see similar results to those as shown in Figure 4-40.

Autodiscover SRV Records

If you don't want to configure the additional website on your Exchange 2013 Client Access server—for example, because you don't have enough public IP addresses—you can always use service records (SRV) in public DNS to access the Exchange 2013 Client Access server.

For the domain names used in the previous section, you would create an SRV record for the inframan.nl domain, pointing to the Autodiscover FQDN in the original domain exchange16.com. This service record will be _autodiscover._tcp.inframan.nl and it will point to autodiscover.exchange16.com on port 443.

Depending on your hosting provider, entering a SRV record in public DNS can be challenging, but in my environment it would look like that shown in Figure 4-44.

Figure 4-44. *Entering the Autodiscover SRV record in public DNS*

When using NSLOOKUP (on the client) to check the SRV entry, you'll see something similar to that shown in Figure 4-45.

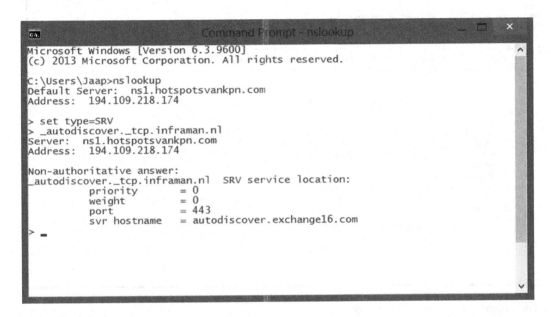

Figure 4-45. *Resolving the Autodiscover SRV record in DNS*

Now, when checking with the RCA, you'll see that the Autodiscover redirect options fail, but that the SRV option succeeds, as shown in Figure 4-46.

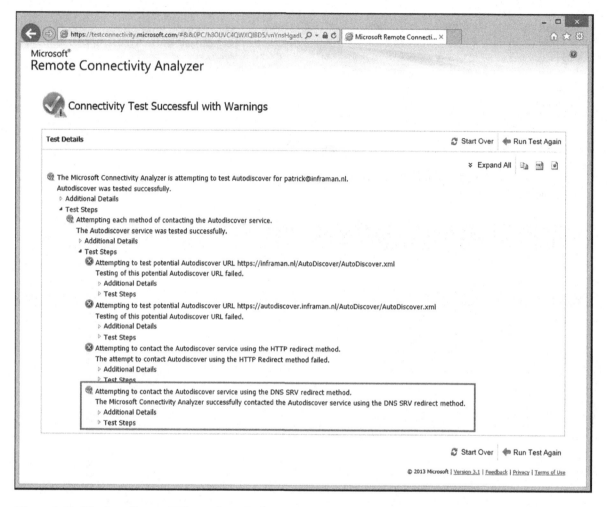

Figure 4-46. *The Autodiscover SRV records test in the RCA*

It is even more interesting that, instead of using the `autodiscover.exchange16.com,` it is now possible to use the `webmail.exchange16.com` FQDN in the SRV record. This way, Autodiscover no longer uses the `autodiscover.exchange16.com` entry and it is now possible to use a standard SSL certificate and *not* a UC certificate. This standard certificate only contains the name `webmail.exchange16.com`. If configured this way, the RCA reveals the following information, as shown in Figure 4-47.

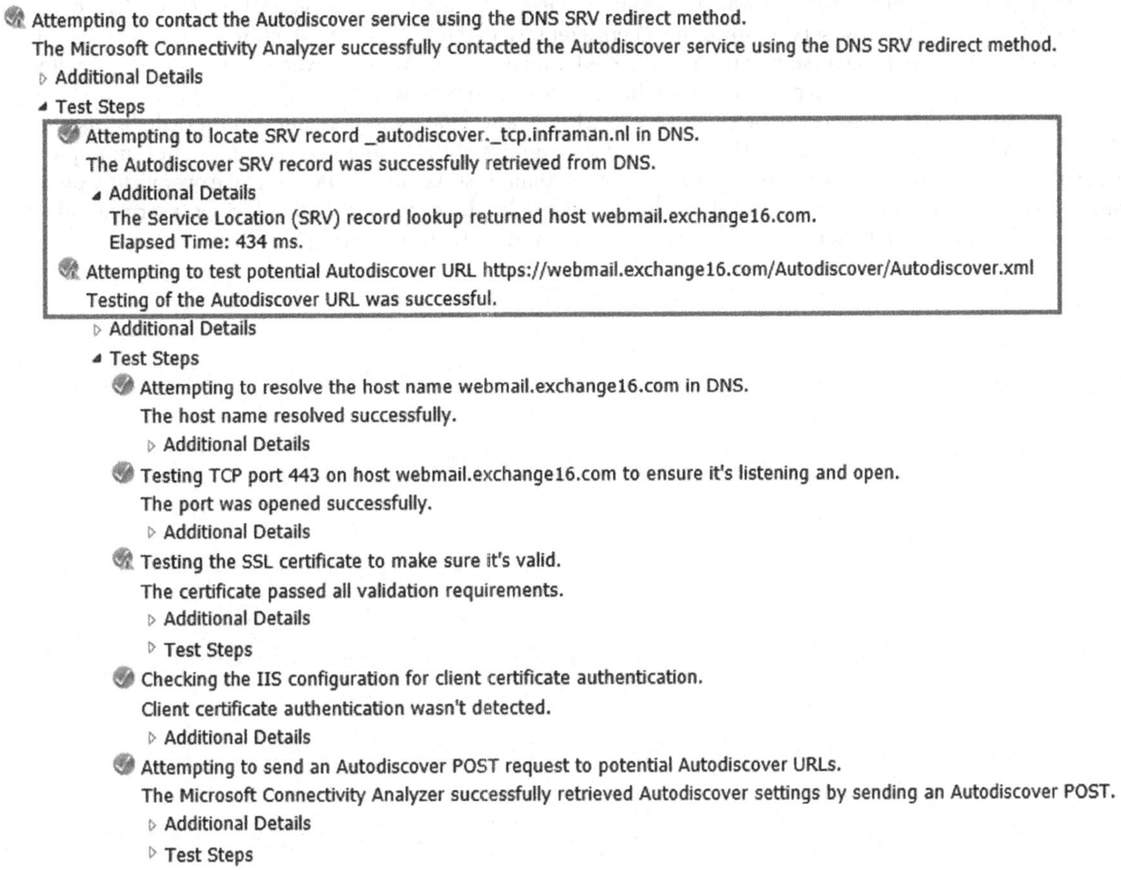

🔍 Attempting to contact the Autodiscover service using the DNS SRV redirect method.

The Microsoft Connectivity Analyzer successfully contacted the Autodiscover service using the DNS SRV redirect method.

▷ Additional Details

◢ Test Steps

> ✅ Attempting to locate SRV record _autodiscover._tcp.inframan.nl in DNS.
>
> The Autodiscover SRV record was successfully retrieved from DNS.
>
> ◢ Additional Details
>
> The Service Location (SRV) record lookup returned host webmail.exchange16.com.
>
> Elapsed Time: 434 ms.
>
> 🔍 Attempting to test potential Autodiscover URL https://webmail.exchange16.com/Autodiscover/Autodiscover.xml
>
> Testing of the Autodiscover URL was successful.

    ▷ Additional Details

    ◢ Test Steps

      ✅ Attempting to resolve the host name webmail.exchange16.com in DNS.

      The host name resolved successfully.

        ▷ Additional Details

      ✅ Testing TCP port 443 on host webmail.exchange16.com to ensure it's listening and open.

      The port was opened successfully.

        ▷ Additional Details

      🔍 Testing the SSL certificate to make sure it's valid.

      The certificate passed all validation requirements.

        ▷ Additional Details

        ▷ Test Steps

      ✅ Checking the IIS configuration for client certificate authentication.

      Client certificate authentication wasn't detected.

        ▷ Additional Details

      ✅ Attempting to send an Autodiscover POST request to potential Autodiscover URLs.

      The Microsoft Connectivity Analyzer successfully retrieved Autodiscover settings by sending an Autodiscover POST.

        ▷ Additional Details

        ▷ Test Steps

Figure 4-47. *Autodiscover SRV records configured with only one FQDN*

■ **Note** The SRV records solution only works with a client that supports these kinds of records. Mobile clients, for example, do not support this.

Summary

The Exchange 2013 Mailbox server hosts almost all functions in an Exchange environment:

- **Mailbox Service** Responsible for storing all mail data in mailbox databases. This can be in mailboxes or in public folders stored in mailbox databases.

- **Transport Service** Responsible for routing SMTP messages, not only to and from the Internet but also within the Exchange 2013 Mailbox server or between various Exchange 2013 Mailbox servers.

- **Unified Messaging Service** Responsible for offering voicemail functions with mailboxes. This feature will be covered in detail in Chapter 8.

The Exchange 2013 Mailbox server always needs an Exchange 2013 Client Access server. Clients connect to this server, and then the Client Access server proxies the client's request to the appropriate Mailbox server. An exception is SIP traffic originating from the Lync server; this is redirected from the Client Access server to the appropriate Mailbox server; however, all processing takes place on the Exchange 2013 Mailbox server.

Exchange 2013 Mailbox servers can be single servers without any database redundancy, or they can be installed in a database availability group (DAG). A DAG consists of a maximum of 16 Mailbox servers and can host multiple copies of mailbox databases. If one Mailbox server fails, other Mailbox server in the DAG can take over its functions, offering a seamless experience for users. Combine this with the redundancy features in the Transport service—like shadow redundancy and Safety Net—and you get a serious, high-availability messaging infrastructure.

## CHAPTER 5

High Availability

When you have a single Exchange server, whether it be a single multi-role server or two separate servers each hosting one server role, you have a single point of failure, or SPOF. When this server fails, it is not available anymore and your users are without their messaging service.

To overcome this problem you have to implement a high availability solution; in short, that means implementing more servers offering the same service. In the case of Exchange 2013, there are three distinct servers affected.

In Exchange 2013, high availability is implemented by means of a database availability group, or DAG. A DAG is a collection of up to 16 Mailbox servers that can host a set of mailbox databases and can provide recovery from mailbox database failures or Mailbox server failures.

To achieve high availability on the Exchange 2013 Client Access servers, you have to implement an array of Client Access servers that can service client requests. Besides an array of Client Access servers, though, you also need some form of load balancing in front of the array of Client Access servers to distribute the client requests and provide connection failover when one Client Access server fails.

To achieve high availability on the transport layer, you can implement multiple Exchange 2013 SP1 Edge Transport servers—next to multiple Exchange 2013 Mailbox servers, of course.

In this chapter, we discuss high availability on all three Exchange 2013 server roles.

Mailbox Server High Availability

In Exchange Server 2003 and earlier, it was possible to use Windows clustering to create some sort of high availability in Exchange Server. On the underlying Windows operating system, a failover cluster was created that consisted of two or more physical servers called *cluster nodes*. These nodes used shared storage—that is, storage that could be used by only one of the nodes at a time. Exchange Server was installed as a *virtual server* on this cluster. When one cluster node failed, another cluster node in the cluster could take over the Exchange virtual server. While this concept works fine for server redundancy, there's still a single point of failure: the mailbox database.

For Exchange Server 2007, Microsoft improved the cluster technology, which led to the concept of *cluster continuous replication* (CCR). In a CCR cluster, two Exchange Mailbox servers are combined whereby each server hosts one copy of the mailbox database. If one server fails, the other cluster node takes over the Exchange virtual server and activates the other copy of the mailbox database.

To lower the complexity, and to minimize the downtime in case of a server failure, the CCR technology evolved into the database availability group (DAG) in Exchange Server 2010, a technology that's also available in Exchange 2013. A DAG is a logical grouping of a set of Exchange 2013 Mailbox servers that can hold copies of each other's mailbox databases. So, when there are six Mailbox servers in a DAG, mailbox database MBX01 can be active on the first server in the DAG, but it can have a copy on the fourth and sixth servers in the DAG. When the first server in the DAG fails, the mailbox database copy on the fourth server becomes active and continues servicing the user requests with minimal downtime for the user.

Under the hood, a DAG is using components of Windows failover clustering, and as such we have to discuss some of these components in more detail.

Cluster Nodes and the File Share Witness

A DAG usually consists of at least two Exchange 2013 Mailbox servers. It is possible to have a DAG with only one Exchange 2013 Mailbox server, but in this case there's no redundancy. Another server is involved in a DAG as well, and this is the Witness server.

By way of explanation, the DAG uses Windows failover clustering software, and in Windows 2012 R2, there are some major changes that Exchange 2013 SP1 can take advantage of. In particular, there are two new options to discuss here:

- **Dynamic Quorum** In Windows 2012 and Windows 2012 R2, the quorum majority is determined by the nodes that are active members of the cluster at a given time, whereas in Windows 2008 R2, the quorum majority is fixed and determined at the moment of cluster creation. This modification means that a cluster can dynamically change from an eight-node cluster to a seven- or six-node cluster, and in case of issues the majority changes accordingly. In theory it is possible to dynamically bring down a cluster to only one (1) cluster node, also referred to as the "last man standing." Besides changing automatically, an administrator can also change a member manually by setting the cluster's NodeWeight property to 0. The official Exchange product team's best practice is to leave the dynamic quorum enabled, but not to take it into account when designing an Exchange environment.

- **Dynamic Witness** Prior to Windows Server 2012 R2, when the file share witness (FSW) was not available, the cluster service would try to start the FSW resource once. If it failed, the cluster might become unavailable and all mailbox databases would be dismounted.

  In Windows Server 2012 R2, though, when a cluster is configured with dynamic quorum, a new feature called *dynamic witness* becomes available. The witness vote with a dynamic witness is automatically adjusted, based on the status of the FSW. If it's offline and not available, its witness vote is automatically set to 0, thereby eliminating the chances of an unexpected shutdown of the cluster. Just as with dynamic quorum, the recommendation is to leave the dynamic witness enabled (by default). Exchange 2013 SP1 is not aware of the dynamic witness, but it can take advantage of this cluster behavior.

From an Exchange Server point of view, the failover clustering software and its new features are fully transparent, so there's no need to start worrying about clusters, and there's no need to start managing the DAG with the failover cluster manager. All management of the DAG is performed using the Exchange Management Shell or the Exchange Admin Center. In fact, I strongly recommend *not* using the Windows failover cluster management tool in that case.

The witness server and the file share witness (the latter which is a shared directory on the witness server) are used only when there is an even number of Mailbox servers in the DAG, but as explained before, it is automatically adjusted. Furthermore, the witness server stores no mailbox information; it has only a cluster quorum role.

The following are the prerequisites for the witness server:

- The witness server cannot be a member of the DAG.

- The witness server must be in the same Active Directory forest as the DAG.

- The witness server must be running Windows Server 2003 or later.

- A single server can serve as a witness for multiple DAGs, but each DAG has its own witness directory.

The witness server plays an important role when problems arise in the DAG—for example, when an Exchange 2013 Mailbox server is not available anymore. The underlying principle is based on an *N/2+1* number of servers in the DAG. This means that for a DAG to stay alive when disaster strikes, at least half the number of Mailbox servers plus one need to be up and running.

So, if you have a six-node DAG, the DAG can survive the loss of two Exchange 2013 Mailbox servers (6/2 +1). The file share witness, however, is an additional server or vote in this process. So, if there are six Exchange 2013 Mailbox servers in the DAG and three servers fail, the file share witness is the +1 server or vote, and the DAG will survive with four members: three Mailbox servers plus the additional file share witness.

■ **Note** Following the Microsoft recommendation, the dynamic quorum and dynamic witness are not involved in this example.

Microsoft recommends you use an Exchange server as a file share witness, which of course cannot be a Mailbox server that is part of the DAG. The reason for this is that an Exchange server is always managed by the Exchange administrators in the organization, and the Exchange Trusted Subsystem Universal Security Group has control over all Exchange servers in Active Directory.

When you're using a multi-role setup, which is the Exchange 2013 Client Access server and Mailbox server on the same box, and these servers are DAG members, there's no additional Exchange server that can hold the file share witness role. In this case, it is also possible to use another Windows server as the file share witness. The only prerequisite is that the Exchange Trusted Subsystem have full control over the Windows server, so the Exchange Trusted Subsystem needs to be a member of the local Administrators Security Group of the Windows server. As domain controllers do not have local groups, it would be necessary to add the Exchange Trusted Subsystem to the Domain Administrators Security Group. However, this imposes a security risk and it is therefore not recommended.

There's no reason to configure the file share witness in a high-availability configuration such as on a file cluster. Exchange Server periodically checks for the file share witness—by default, every four hours—to see if the file share witness is still alive. If it's not available at that moment, the DAG continues to run without any issues. The only time the file share witness needs to be available is during DAG changes, when an Exchange 2013 Mailbox server fails, or when Exchange 2013 Mailbox servers are added to or deleted from the DAG.

A question that pops up on a regular basis is whether or not to store the file share witness on a DFS share, especially when the company is using a server with multiple locations. This is not a good idea. Imagine this: There are two locations, A and B, and the Exchange location has three Exchange 2013 Mailbox servers configured in one DAG. The file share witness is located on a DFS share, and thus potentially available in both locations. Now, suppose the network connection between locations A and B fails for some reason. The DAG will notice the connection loss, and in both locations, Exchange will try to determine the number of available Mailbox servers and attempt to contact the file share witness. In location A, this will succeed and the DAG will continue to run with four nodes (three Exchange 2013 Mailbox servers plus the file share witness). In location B, the same will happen, so Exchange will try to contact the file share witness as well. Since the file share witness is available via the DFS share in location B also, the DAG will claim the file share witness in location B and continue to run as well. And Exchange 2013 in each location will assume that the DAG members in the other location have been shut down—which of course is not the case. This is called a *split-brain scenario*, a highly undesirable situation that will lead to unpredictable results, and it is a situation that is not supported at all.

■ **Note** Using a DFS share for the file share witness is not supported and can lead to undesirable results, and should therefore never be done.

Cluster Administrative Access Point

When a Windows failover cluster is created, an access point for the cluster is created as well. An access point is a combination of a name and an IP address. This IP address can be IPv4 or IPv6; it can be statically assigned or dynamically assigned using DHCP.

The first access point that gets created is the cluster administrative access point, sometimes also referred to as the cluster name and cluster IP address.

In Exchange 2013, this cluster administrative access point is the name of the DAG and its IP address. As the name implies, this is only used for management purposes. Important to note is that clients connect to the Exchange 2013 Client Access server and the Client Access server connects to a particular mailbox database where a mailbox resides. The Client Access server does nothing whatsoever with the cluster administrative access point.

New in Windows Server 2012 R2 is the concept of failover clusters without a cluster administrative access point. In Exchange Server, this means that you create a DAG with a name and without an IP address. Is this bad? No, not at all, since nothing connects to the cluster administrative access point, except for the failover cluster manager. But since all cluster management is performed using the Exchange Management Shell, this is not needed for Exchange 2013. In the section about the DAG creation process, we will show how to create a DAG without an administrative access point.

Replication

A database availability group consists of a number of Exchange 2013 Mailbox servers, and these Mailbox servers have multiple mailbox databases (see Figure 5-1). There's only one copy of a given mailbox database on a given Mailbox server in a DAG, so the total number of copies of a specific mailbox database can never exceed the number of Mailbox servers in the DAG.

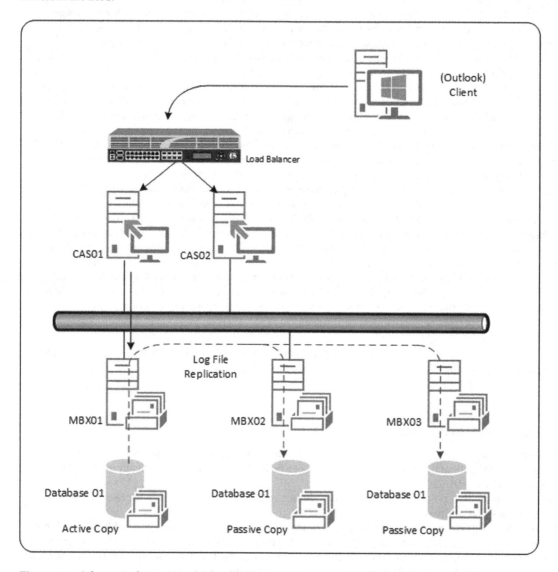

Figure 5-1. *Schematical overview of a database availability group (DAG)*

The mailbox databases can be either active or passive copies. The *active* copy is where all the mailbox data processing takes place, and it's no different from a normal Exchange 2013 Mailbox server that's not part of a DAG. Now, another Exchange 2013 Mailbox server in the DAG can host another copy of this same database; this is called a *passive* copy. A regular passive copy should be close to 100 percent identical to the active copy, and it is kept up to date by a technology called *log shipping* or *log file replication*.

There are two ways of replicating data from one Mailbox server to another:

- File mode replication
- Block mode replication

File Mode Replication

As explained in the previous chapter, all transactions are logged in the transaction log files. When the Mailbox server has stored all the transactions in one log file, a new log file is generated and the "old" log file is written to disk. At this moment, the log file is also copied to the second Mailbox server, where it is stored on disk. The log file is then inspected; if it's okay, the contents of the log file are replayed into the passive copy of the mailbox database. Since the log file on the passive copy is identical to the log file on the active copy, all contents are the same in both the active and the passive copies.

The process of copying transaction log files is called *file mode replication*, since all log files are copied to the other Mailbox server.

Block Mode Replication

Another mode, which was actually introduced in Exchange 2010 SP1, is *block mode replication*. In this process the transactions are written into the active server's log buffer (before they are flushed into the active log file), and at the same time the transactions are copied to the passive server and written into that server's log buffer. When the log buffers are full, the information is flushed to the current log file and a new log file is used. Both servers do this at the same time. When the Mailbox server is running block mode replication, the replication of individual log files is suspended; only individual transactions are copied between the Mailbox servers. The advantage of block mode replication is that the server holding the passive copy of the mailbox database is always 100 percent up to date and therefore failover times are greatly reduced.

The default process is block mode replication, but the server falls back to file mode replication when that server is too busy to cope with replicating individual transactions. If this happens, the Exchange server can replicate the individual transaction log files at its own pace, and even queue some log files when there are not enough resources.

An active mailbox database copy can have multiple passive copies on multiple Mailbox servers (remember that one server can hold only one copy of a specific mailbox database, active or passive). The active copy of a mailbox database is where all the processing takes place and all the replication, whether it is file mode or block mode, takes place from this active copy to all passive copies of the mailbox database. There's absolutely no possibility that one passive copy will replicate log files to another passive copy. The only exception to this is when a new copy of a mailbox database is created from another passive copy, but that's only the initial creation, which is seeding.

Seeding

Creating the passive copy of an active mailbox database is called *seeding*. In this process, the mailbox database is copied from one Mailbox server to another Mailbox server. When seeding, the complete mailbox database (the actual mailbox database.edb) is copied from the first Mailbox server hosting the active copy of this mailbox database to the second Mailbox server. This is not a simple NTFS file copy, though; the information store *streams* the file from one location to another. In this process, the Information Store is reading the individual pages of a mailbox database—a process that's very similar to the streaming backup process that was used in Exchange server 2003 and earlier.

233

Here's how it works: The Information Store reads the contents of the mailbox database page by page, automatically checking them. If there's an error on a particular page (i.e., a corrupt page), the process stops and the error is logged. This way, Exchange prevents copying a mailbox database to another location that has corrupted pages. Since the pages of the mailbox database are copied from one Mailbox server to another Mailbox server, the passive copy is identical to the active copy. When the entire mailbox database is copied to the other Mailbox server, the remaining log files are copied to the other Mailbox server as well.

When a new mailbox database is seeded, the process takes only a couple of minutes because there's not too much data to copy. But imagine a mailbox database of 1 TB in a normal production environment. When that has to be seeded, it can take a considerable amount of time. And not only is the timing an important factor but also the process puts additional load on the servers. The 1 TB of data needs to be read and checked, copied via the network, and written to disk on the other Mailbox server.

AutoReseed

A new feature in Exchange 2013 is automatic reseed, or *AutoReseed*. When a disk in an Exchange server fails, it is replaced and an Exchange administrator creates a new copy of a mailbox database on the new disk. AutoReseed is basically the same process, but automated; the idea behind AutoReseed is to get a mailbox database up and running again immediately after a disk failure. To achieve this, Exchange 2013 can use the Windows 2012 feature of multiple mount points per volume.

When AutoReseed is configured, the Exchange 2013 Mailbox server has one or more spare disks in its disk cabinet. When a disk containing a mailbox database fails, the Microsoft Exchange Replication service automatically allocates a spare disk and automatically creates a new copy of this particular mailbox database.

The DAG has three properties that are used for the AutoReseed feature:

- **AutoDagVolumesRootFolderPath** This is a link to the mount point that contains all available volumes—for example, `C:\ExchVols`. Volumes that host mailbox databases, as well as spare volumes, are located here.

- **AutoDagDatabasesRoolFolderPath** This is a link to the mount point that contain all mailbox databases—for example, `C:\ExchDBs`.

- **AutoDagDatabaseCopiesPerVolume** This property contains the number of mailbox database copies per volume.

Important to note is that although there's one mailbox database on a particular location, it can be located through two possible ways. The first is via the `C:\ExchVols` mount point; the second is via the `C:\ExchDBs` mount point.

AutoReseed is regularly monitoring to come into action by using the following steps:

1. The Microsoft Exchange Replication service constantly scans for mailbox database copies that have failed—that is, that have a copy status of "FailedAndSuspended."

2. If a mailbox database is in a "FailedAndSuspended" status, the Microsoft Exchange Replication services does some prerequisite checks to see if AutoReseed can be performed.

3. If the checks are passed successfully, the Replication service automically allocates a spare disk and configures it into the production disk system.

4. When the disk is configured, a new seeding operation is started, thus creating a new copy of the mailbox database.

5. When seeding is done, the Replication service checks if the new copy is healthy and resumes operation.

There is one manual step left at this point: the Exchange administrator has to replace the faulty disk with a new one and format the new disk appropriately.

■ **Note**   For the AutoReseed to function correctly the disks need to be configured in a mount point configuration. You cannot use dedicated drive letters in combination with AutoReseed.

In the section about the DAG creation process, implementing and configuring the AutoReseed is explained in detail.

Replication (Copy) Queue and Replay Queue

In an ideal situation, transaction log files are replicated to other Exchange 2013 Mailbox server directly after the log files are written to disk, and they are processed immediately after being received by the other Exchange 2013 Mailbox server. Unfortunately, we don't live in an ideal world, so there might be some delay somewhere in the system.

When the Exchange 2013 Mailbox servers are extremely busy, it can happen that more transaction log files are generated than the replication process can handle and transmit. If this is the case, the log files will queue on the Mailbox server holding the active copy of the mailbox database. This queue is called the *replication queue*. Queuing always happens, and it is normally not reason for concern as long as the number of log files in the queue is low and the log files don't stay there too long. However, if there are thousands of messages waiting in line, it's time to do some further investigation.

When the transaction log files are received by the Exchange 2013 Mailbox server holding the passive copy of the mailbox database, those transaction log files are stored in the *replay queue*. Queuing up in the replay queue happens as well, and is generally speaking also not reason for concern when the number of transaction log files is low. There can be small spikes in the number of transaction log files in the replay queue, but when the number of transaction log files is constantly increasing, there's something wrong. It can happen that the disk holding the mailbox database is generating too many read-and-write operations. Or, there may not be enough resources to flush the queue, and so the queue will grow. As long as the system is able to flush the queue in a reasonable time, and there aren't thousands of messages in the queue, you should be fine.

Lagged Copies

Regarding the replay queue, there's one exception to note: lagged copies. If you have implemented lagged copies in your DAG, and you experience a large number of log files in the replay queue, then there's nothing to worry about. Lagged copies are passive copies of a mailbox database that aren't kept up to date. This means that log files are replicated to the Exchange 2013 Mailbox server holding the lagged copy, but the log files themselves are kept in the replay queue. This lag time between replication and writing to the server can be as little as 0 second (the log file is replayed immediately) or up to 14 days. A very long lag time will have a serious impact on scalability, of course. A full 14 days' worth of log files can mean a tremendous amount of data being stored in the replay queue; also, replaying the transaction log files of a lagged copy can take quite some time when longer time frames are used.

Lagged copies are not a high-availability solution; rather, they are a disaster recovery solution. (Lagged copies and disaster recovery are explained in detail in Chapter 7.)

Active Manager

The active manager is a component of Exchange 2013, and it runs inside the Microsoft Exchange Replication services on all Exchange 2013 Mailbox servers. The Active Manager is the component that's responsible for the high availability inside the database availability group.

There are several types of active managers:

- **Primary Active Manager** (PAM) The PAM is the role that decides which copy of a mailbox database is the active copy and which ones are the passive copies; as such, PAM reacts to changes in the DAG, such as DAG member failures. The DAG member that holds the PAM role is always the server that also holds the quorum resource or the default cluster group.

- **Standby Active Manager** (SAM) The SAM is responsible for providing DAG information—for example, which mailbox database is an active copy and which copies are passive copies—to other Exchange components like the Client Access service or the Hub Transport service. If the SAM detects a failure of a mailbox database, it requests a failover to the PAM. The PAM then decides which copy to activate.

- **Standalone Active Manager** The Standalone Active Manager is responsible for mounting and dismounting databases on that particular server. This active manager is available only on Exchange 2013 Mailbox servers that are not members of a DAG.

DAG Across (Active Directory) Sites

In the previous examples, the DAG has always been installed in one Active Directory site. However, there's no such boundary in the DAG, so it is possible to create a DAG that spans multiple Active Directory sites, even in different physical locations. For instance, it is possible to extend the DAG for anticipating two potential scenarios:

- **Database Disaster Recovery** In this scenario, mailbox databases are replicated to another location exclusively for offsite storage. These databases are safe there should disaster, like a fire or flood, strike at the primary location.

- **Site Resiliency** In this scenario, the DAG is (most likely) evenly distributed across two locations (see Figure 5-2). The second location, however, also has (multiple) Exchange 2013 Client Access servers with a full-blown Internet connection. When disaster strikes and the primary site is no longer available, the second site can take over all functions.

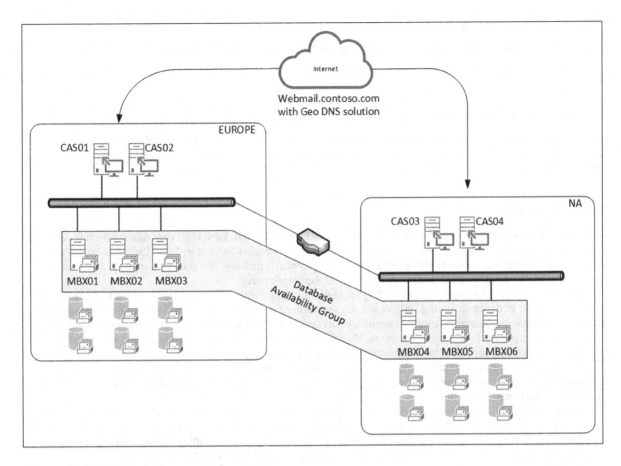

Figure 5-2. *A DAG stretched across two locations*

When using a Geo DNS solution, only one FQDN (i.e., webmail.contoso.com) can be used. For example, in Figure 5-2, there are two Active Directory sites, one location in Europe and another in North America (NA). When a user tries to contact webmail.contoso.com when traveling in Europe, he's automatically connected to the Europe site. When he tries to access webmail.contoso.com in the United States, he's connected to the NA site. In either case, after authentication the client is automatically proxied to the correct Mailbox server to get the mailbox information.

By default, a site failover is not an automated process. If a data-center failover *needs* to happen, especially when the site holding the file share witness is involved, administrative action is required. However, with Exchange 2013, it is possible to work around this limitation by placing the file share witness in a third Active Directory site.

It is possible to create an active/active scenario whereby both data centers are active, servicing users and processing mail data. In this case, two DAGs have to be created; each DAG is active in one data center and its passive copies are located in the other data center. Note, however, that an Exchange Mailbox server can be a member of only one DAG at a time. This could mean that you need more servers in an active/active scenario, a downside of having two DAGs.

Creating a site-resilient configuration with multiple DAGs requires careful planning, plus asking yourself a lot of questions, both technical and organizational. Typical questions are:

- What level of service is required?

- What level of service is required when one data center fails?

- What are the objectives for recovery point and recovery time?

- How many users are on the system and which data centers are these users connecting to?

- Is the system designed to service all users when one data center fails?

- How are services moved back to the original data center?

- Are there any resources available (like IT Staff) for these scenarios?

These are just basic planning questions to be answered before you even think about implementing a site-resilient configuration. And remember: the more requirements there are and the stricter they are, the more expensive the solution will be!

DAG Networks

A DAG uses one or more networks for client connectivity and for replication. Each DAG contains at least one network for client connectivity, which is created by default, and zero or more replication networks. In Exchange 2010, this default DAG network was called *MAPI network*. The MAPI protocol is no longer used in Exchange 2013 as a native client protocol, but the default DAG network is still called MapiDagNetwork.

For years Microsoft has been recommending the use of multiple networks to separate the client traffic from the replication traffic. With the upcoming 10Gb networks, separating client traffic from replication traffic is no longer an issue. Also, the use of a Serverblade infrastructure with its 10Gb backbone separation of traffic was more a logication separation then a physical separation. Therefore, Microsoft moves away from the recommendation of separating network traffic, thereby simplifying the Mailbox server network configuration.

When you still want to separate client traffic from replication traffic, you can do so in a supported manner. In Exchange 2013, the network is automatically configured by the system. If additional networks need to be configured, you set the DAG to manual configuration, then create the additional DAG networks.

When using multiple networks, it is possible to designate a network for client connectivity and the other networks for replication traffic. When multiple networks are used for replication, Exchange automatically determines which network to use for replication traffic. When all the replication networks are offline or not available, Exchange automatically switches back to the MAPI network for the replication traffic (as was the case in Exchange 2010).

Default gateways need to be considered when you are configuring multiple network interfaces in Windows Server. The only network that needs this configuring with a default gateway is the client connectivity network; all other networks should not be configured with a default gateway.

Other recommendations important for replication networks are the following:

- Disabling the DNS registration on the TCP/IP properties of the respective network interface.

- Disabling the protocol bindings, such as client for Microsoft networks and file and printer sharing for Microsoft networks, on the properties of the network interface.

- Rearranging the binding order of the network interfaces so that the client connectivity network is at the top of the connection order.

When using an iSCSI storage solution, make sure that the iSCSI network is *not used at all* for replication purposes. Remove any iSCSI network connection from the replication networks list.

DAG Creation Process

Creating a database availability group consists of several steps. The first step in the process is to create the cluster name object in Active Directory, followed by creation of the DAG itself, adding the Mailbox servers to the DAG, configuring the DAG networks when needed, and adding the mailbox database copies. But let's take each step in order.

Creating the Cluster Name Object

As explained earlier, under the hood, a DAG is using Windows failover clustering binaries. From a failover clustering perspective, the DAG is nothing more than a failover cluster, and this cluster is using a cluster name, formally known as the *cluster name object,* or CNO. When creating a DAG in Exchange 2013 that's running on Windows Server 2008 R2, the CNO is created automatically. In Windows Server 2012 or later, this is no longer the case because of tightened security, and thus the CNO needs to be created manually.

The CNO is established as a new, disabled computer object in Active Directory and is assigned the appropriate permissions. To create the CNO, follow these steps.

```
Import-Module ActiveDirectory
New-ADComputer -Name "AMS-DAG01" -Path "OU=Accounts,DC=Contoso,DC=com" -Enabled $false
Add-AdPermission -Identity "AMS-DAG01" -User "Exchange Trusted Subsystem" -AccessRights GenericAll
```

Coauthor Michel de Rooij has written a complete PowerShell script around the creation of this CNO, including all prerequisite checks. You can find more information regarding this script at http://bit.ly/CNOPreStage.

Creating the DAG

Now that the computer account needed for the DAG is in Active Directory, you continue with creating the DAG itself. To create the DAG using EMS, you can use the following commands:

```
New-DatabaseAvailabilityGroup -Name AMS-DAG01 -WitnessServer AMS-FS01.contoso.com -WitnessDirectory
C:\DAG01\DAG01_FSW -DatabaseAvailabilityGroupIPAddresses 192.168.0.187
```

Creating the DAG is simple—it's only an entry written in the configuration partition of Active Directory. If you want to check it, you can use ADSIEdit and navigate to

```
CN=AMS-DAG01, CN=Database Availability Groups, CN=Exchange Administrative Group (FYDIBOHF23SPDLT),
CN=Administrative Groups, CN=Contoso,CN=Microsoft Exchange, CN=Services, CN=Configuration,
DC=Contoso, DC=com.
```

This is shown in Figure 5-3.

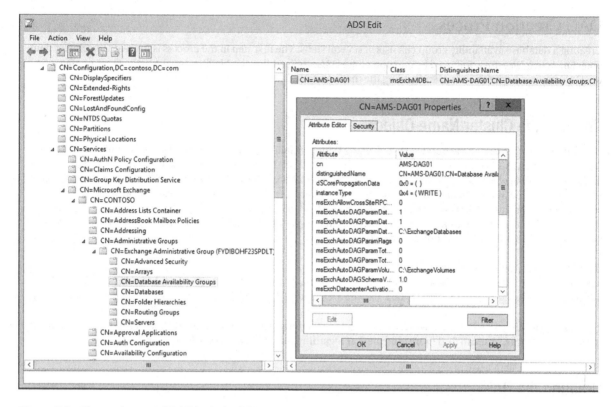

Figure 5-3. *The newly created DAG in Active Directory*

The information that's returned when running a `Get-DatabaseAvailabilityGroup` command is just a representation of this object in Active Directory, combined with information taken from the local registry (when using the -status parameter).

■ **Note** Microsoft recommends that the file share witness best be another Exchange server. This Exchange server cannot be a DAG member; however, this is not always possible and another server must be used as a file share witness. In this example, a file server called AMS-FS01 is used. Since Exchange Server cannot control a non-Exchange Server, the Active Directory's security group Exchange-trusted subsystem should be added to the local administrator's security group on the file share witness server.

Adding the Mailbox Servers

Once the DAG exists, the Mailbox servers can be added to it, which is a straightforward process; just run the following commands to add the servers AMS-EXCH01 and AMS-EXCH02 to the DAG created in the previous step:

```
Add-DatabaseAvailabilityGroupServer -Identity AMS-DAG01 -MailboxServer AMS-EXCH01
Add-DatabaseAvailabilityGroupServer -Identity AMS-DAG01 -MailboxServer AMS-EXCH02
```

When the Windows failover clustering components are not installed on the Mailbox server, the Add-DatabaseAvailabilityGroupServer cmdlet will install these automatically, as shown in Figure 5-4.

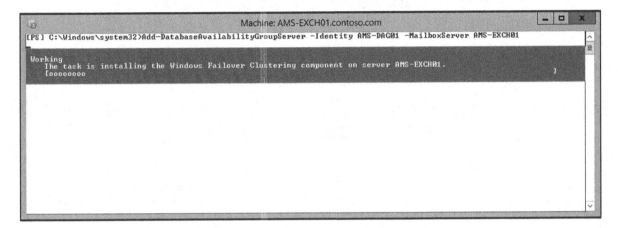

Figure 5-4. *The failover clustering components will be installed automatically*

At this point, a DAG is created with two members using a file server as a witness server.

Adding the Mailbox Database Copies

Now that the DAG is fully up and running, it's time for the last step: making additional copies of the mailbox databases. Initially there's only one copy of the mailbox database, but you can create redundancy when you add multiple copies on other Mailbox servers in the DAG.

It is important to note that the location of the mailbox database is identical on all Mailbox servers holding a copy of a particular mailbox database. So if you have a mailbox database F:\MDB01\MDB01.edb of server EXCH01, the copy of the mailbox database on server EXCH02 is on F:\MDB01\MDB01.edb as well. This might sound obvious, but every now and then I talk to people who are not aware of this.

The same is true for mount points, of course. If you have a mailbox C:\ExchDbs\MDB01\MDB01.edb on server EXCH01, the mailbox database copy on server EXCH02 will be at the same location, C:\ExchDbs\MDB01.

To create additional copies of a mailbox database in a DAG, you can use the Add-MailboxDatabaseCopy cmdlet. To add copies of mailbox databases called MDB01 and MDB02 on Exchange 2013 Mailbox server AMS-EXCH02, you can use the following commands:

```
Add-MailboxDatabaseCopy -Identity AMS-MDB01 -MailboxServer AMS-EXCH02 -ActivationPreference 2
Add-MailboxDatabaseCopy -Identity AMS-MDB02 -MailboxServer AMS-EXCH01 -ActivationPreference 2
```

The activation preference is meant for administrative purposes and for planned switchovers. It is not used by an automatic failover. In case of an automatic failover, a process called the *best copy selection* on the Mailbox server is used to determine the optimal passive copy for activation.

Configuring the DAG Networks

In our example, the DAG is now configured with two Mailbox servers; by default, only one DAG network is configured, the default MapiDagNetwork. You can quickly see this in the EAC, in the lower right part of the DAG view, as shown in Figure 5-5.

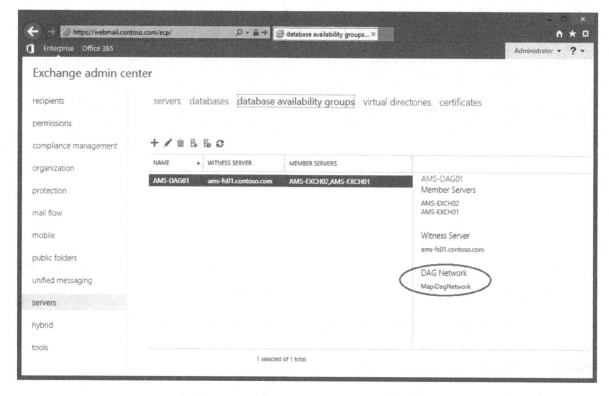

Figure 5-5. *Only one network is configured by default in a DAG*

To add an additional DAG network (assuming that the servers have multiple network interfaces, of course), the DAG itself should be set to manual configuration, as mentioned earlier. This can only be done using the EMS with the following command:

```
Set-DatabaseAvailabilityGroup -Identity AMS-DAG01 -ManualDagNetworkConfiguration $true
```

To create a new additional network for replication purposes you can use the following command:

```
New-DatabaseAvailabilityGroupNetwork -DatabaseAvailabilityGroup AMS-DAG01
-Name "Contoso Replication Network" -Subnets 192.168.0.0/24 -ReplicationEnabled:$true
```

To designate this new network as a dedicated replication network, you have to disable the replication feature of the regular MapiDagNetwork in the DAG. To disable this, you can use the following command:

```
Set-DatabaseAvailabilityGroupNetwork -Identity AMS-DAG01\MapiDagNetwork -ReplicationEnabled:$false
```

After running these commands, you have created a separate network in the DAG specifically for replication traffic.

AutoReseed Configuration

As explained earlier in this chapter, you can use AutoReseed to have Exchange 2013 automatically reseed a mailbox database when one mailbox database or a disk containing mailbox databases in a DAG fails, assuming you have configured multiple copies, of course.

Configuring AutoReseed involves several steps:

- Configure the database availability group.

- Install and configure database disks.

- Create the mailbox databases.

- Create mailbox database copies.

These steps are explained in the next sections.

Configuring the Database Availability Group

The AutoReseed feature uses a number of properties on the database availability group that need to be populated:

- AutoDagDatabasesRootFolderPath

- AutoDagVolumesRootFolderPath

- AutoDagDatabaseCopiesPerVolume

You can use the following command to set these:

```
Set-DatabaseAvailabilityGroup AMS-DAG01 -AutoDagDatabasesRootFolderPath "C:\ExchDbs"
-AutoDagVolumesRootFolderPath "C:\ExchVols" -AutoDagDatabaseCopiesPerVolume 2
```

Installing and Configuring the Database Disks

To implement AutoReseed you have to create multiple disks on your Exchange 2013 Mailbox server where the disks are configured using mount points. In this example we have two Exchange 2013 Mailbox servers, each configured with three disks, Vol1, Vol2 and Vol3. Vol1 has two mailbox databases called AMS-MDB01 and AMS-DB02, and Vol2 has two mailbox databases called AMS-MDB03 and AMS-MDB04. Vol3 is a spare disk that will be used if either Vol1 or Vol2 fails.

These three disks will be mounted in a directory C:\ExVols, but they will also be mounted in a directory C:\ExDBS, as shown in Figure 5-6

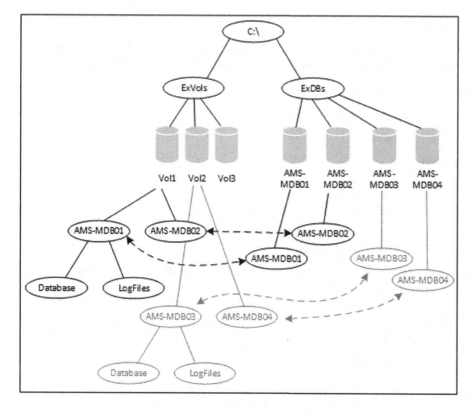

Figure 5-6. *Schematical overview of an AutoReseed configuration*

When the disks are installed, you can create the root directories for the volumes and mailbox database mount points:

```
MD C:\ExchVols
MD C:\ExchDBs
```

You format the disks and mount them into the appropriate volume folders:

- C:\ExchVols\Vol1

- C:\ExchVols\Vol2

- C:\ExchVOls\Vol3

Then you create the mailbox database folders in the appropriate location:

```
MD C:\ExchDBs\AMS-MDB01
MD C:\ExchDBs\AMS-MDB02
MD C:\ExchDBs\AMS-MDB03
MD C:\ExchDBs\AMS-MDB04
```

Creating the mount points for the mailbox databases is a bit trickier. You can use the Disk Management MMC snap-in, or you can use the command-line tool Mountvol.exe to achieve this.

When using the the Disk Management MMC snap-in, you have to select a disk that was created in the previous step—for example, C:\ExchVols\Vol1. To add an additional mount point, right-click the disk and select "Change Drive Letter and Path." Use the Add button to select a mailbox database directory—for example, C:\ExchDBs\AMS-MDB01. Repeat this step for the second mailbox database directory as well, as shown in Figure 5-7:

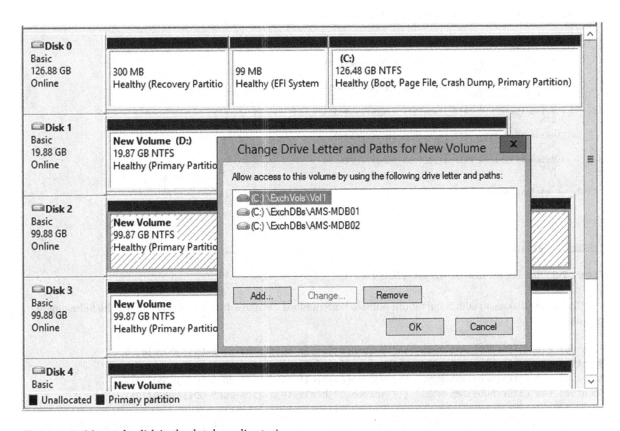

Figure 5-7. *Mount the disk in the database directories*

The steps as shown in Figure 5-7 need to be repeated for the remaining two directories for mailbox databases AMS-MDB03 and AMS-MDB04. The second volume should be mounted in these two directories.

Instead of using the Computer Management MMC snap-in, it is possible to use the Mountvol.exe command-line utility. The Mountvol.exe utility is used as follows:

```
Mountvol.exe c:\ExchDbs\AMS-MDB01 \\?\Volume (GUID)
Mountvol.exe c:\ExchDbs\AMS-MDB02 \\?\Volume (GUID)
```

You can retrieve the GUIDs of the individual volumes using Mountvol.exe as well; just use a command similar to Mountvol.exe C:\ExchVols\ and you'll see something like what's shown in Figure 5-8.

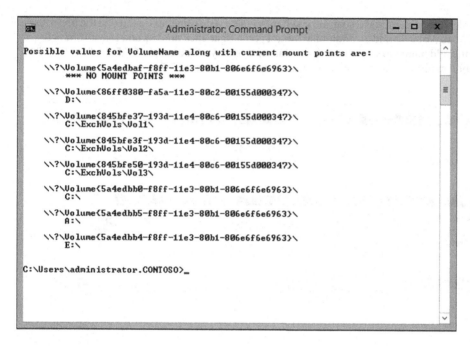

Figure 5-8. *Retrieve the disk GUIDs using* Mountvol.exe

To add the disk as an additional mount point to both mailbox database directories, you can use the following commands:

```
Mountvol.exe C:\ExchDbs\AMS-MDB01 \\?\Volume{845bfe37-193d-11e4-80c6-00155d000347}\
Mountvol.exe C:\ExchDbs\AMS-MDB02 \\?\Volume{845bfe37-193d-11e4-80c6-00155d000347}\
Mountvol.exe C:\ExchDbs\AMS-MDB03 \\?\Volume{845bfe3f-193d-11e4-80c6-00155d000347}\
Mountvol.exe C:\ExchDbs\AMS-MDB04 \\?\Volume{845bfe3f-193d-11e4-80c6-00155d000347}\
```

You can check the results by running the Mountvol.exe utility without any parameters. The output is shown in Figure 5-9.

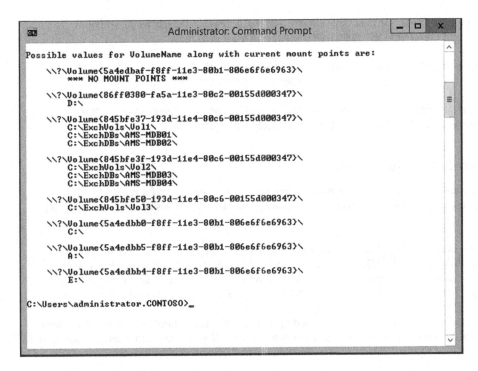

Figure 5-9. *The disk is mounted in three different locations*

Creating the Mailbox Databases

The next step is to create the directory structure on both Mailbox servers where the mailbox database files will be stored. This depends on your own naming convention, of course, but it could look something like this:

```
md c:\ExchDBs\AMS-MDB01\AMS-MDB01.db
md c:\ExchDBs\AMS-MDB01\AMS-MDB01.log

md c:\ExchDBs\AMS-MDB02\AMS-MDB02.db
md c:\ExchDBs\AMS-MDB02\AMS-MDB02.log

md c:\ExchDBs\AMS-MDB03\AMS-MDB03.db
md c:\ExchDBs\AMS-MDB03\AMS-MDB03.log

md c:\ExchDBs\AMS-MDB04\AMS-MDB04.db
md c:\ExchDBs\AMS-MDB04\AMS-MDB04.log
```

The mailbox database file itself will be stored in the AMS-MDB01.DB subdirectory while the accompanying transaction log files will be stored in the AMS-MDB01.log subdirectory.

New mailbox databases will be created in the directories you just created; just use the following commands in the Exchange Management Shell:

```
New-MailboxDatabase -Name AMS-MDB01 -Server AMS-EXCH01 -LogFolderPath C:\ExchDbs\AMS-MDB01\
AMS-MDB01.log -EdbFilePath C:\ExchDbs\AMS-MDB01\AMS-MDB01.db\AMS-MDB01.edb
```

```
New-MailboxDatabase -Name AMS-MDB02 -Server AMS-EXCH01 -LogFolderPath C:\ExchDbs\AMS-MDB02\
AMS-MDB02.log -EdbFilePath C:\ExchDbs\AMS-MDB02\AMS-MDB02.db\AMS-MDB02.edb

New-MailboxDatabase -Name AMS-MDB03 -Server AMS-EXCH02 -LogFolderPath C:\ExchDbs\AMS-MDB03\
AMS-MDB03.log -EdbFilePath C:\ExchDbs\AMS-MDB03\AMS-MDB03.db\AMS-MDB03.edb

New-MailboxDatabase -Name AMS-MDB04 -Server AMS-EXCH02 -LogFolderPath C:\ExchDbs\AMS-MDB04\
AMS-MDB04.log -EdbFilePath C:\ExchDbs\AMS-MDB04\AMS-MDB04.db\AMS-MDB04.edb
```

Creating the Mailbox Database Copies

Of course, you need to create an additional copy of the mailbox database on the second Exchange 2013 Mailbox server. As explained in the previous section, you can create copies of the mailbox databases by using the following commands:

```
Add-MailboxDatabaseCopy –Identity AMS-MDB01 –MailboxServer AMS-EXCH02 –ActivationPreference 2
Add-MailboxDatabaseCopy –Identity AMS-MDB02 –MailboxServer AMS-EXCH02 –ActivationPreference 2
Add-MailboxDatabaseCopy –Identity AMS-MDB03 –MailboxServer AMS-EXCH01 –ActivationPreference 2
Add-MailboxDatabaseCopy –Identity AMS-MDB04 –MailboxServer AMS-EXCH01 –ActivationPreference 2
```

At this point you have created a DAG with the AutoReseed option. If Vol1 fails, it should automatically reseed the mailbox databases to another disk. The best way to test this is to set Vol1 offline in the Computer Management MMC snap-in.

The AutoReseed Process

When a disk fails and goes offline, Exchange will notice almost immediately and activate the copy of the mailbox databases on the second Exchange server as expected. This is clearly visible when we execute a Get-MailboxDatabaseCopyStatus command, as shown in Figure 5-10. The mailbox databases on AMS-EXCH01 are in a FailedAndSuspended state while they are mounted on server AMS-EXCH02.

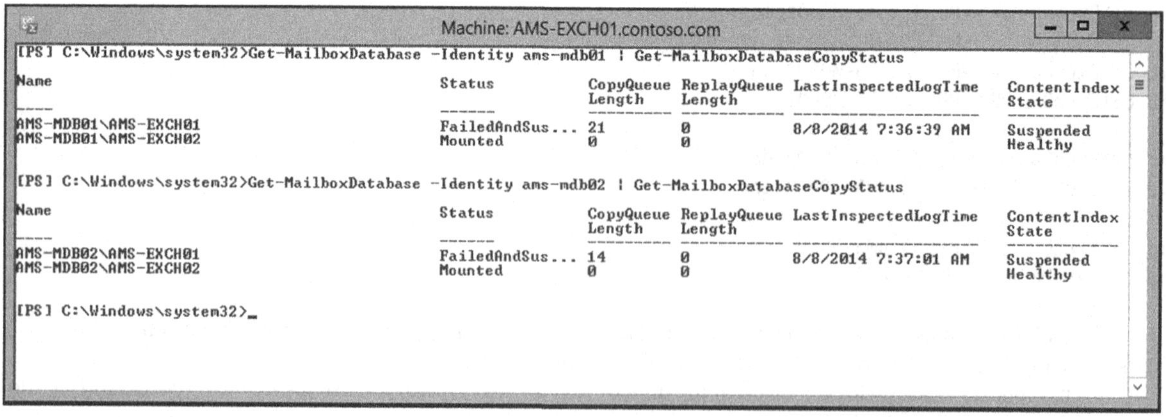

Figure 5-10. *The mailbox databases on the first Mailbox server are FailedAndSuspended*

What happens next is that a repair workflow is started. The workflow will try to resume the failed mailbox database copy, and if this fails the workflow will assign the spare volume to the failed disk. This is the exact workflow:

1. The workflow will detect a mailbox database copy that is in Failed and Suspended state for 15 minutes.

2. Exchange will try to resume the failed mailbox database copy three times with a 5-minute interval.

3. If Exchange cannot resume the failed copy, Exchange will try to assign a spare volume five times with a 1-hour interval.

4. Exchange will try an `InPlaceSeed` with the `SafeDeleteExistingFiles` option five times with a 1-hour interval.

5. If all retries are completed with no success, the workflow will stop. If it is successful, Exchange will finish the reseeding.

6. When everything fails, Exchange will wait three days and see if the mailbox database copy is still in Failed and Suspended state, then it will restart the workflow from step 1.

All events are logged in the event log. There's a special crimson channel for this, which you can find in `Applications and Services Logs | Microsoft | Exchange | HighAvailability | Seeding`.

The first event that's logged is EventID 1109 from the AutoReseed manager, indicating that something is wrong and that no data can be written to location `C:\ExDbs\AMS-MDB01\AMS-MDB01.log`. This makes sense because the disk has actually "failed" and is no longer available. This event is shown in Figure 5-11.

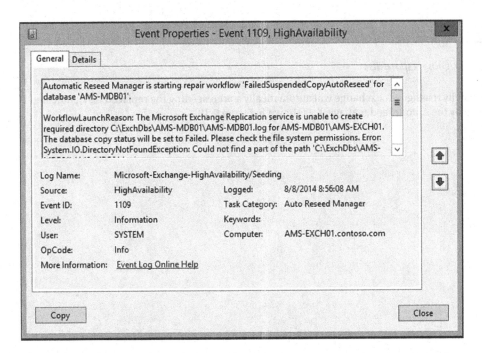

Figure 5-11. *The first AutoReseed event indicating something is wrong with the disk containing the mailbox database*

Subsequent events in the event log will indicate the AutoReseed manager attempting to resume the copy of the mailbox database. As outlined earlier, it will try this three times, followed by an attempt to reassign a spare disk. This event is shown in Figure 5-12. Please note that it takes almost an hour before Exchange moves to this step.

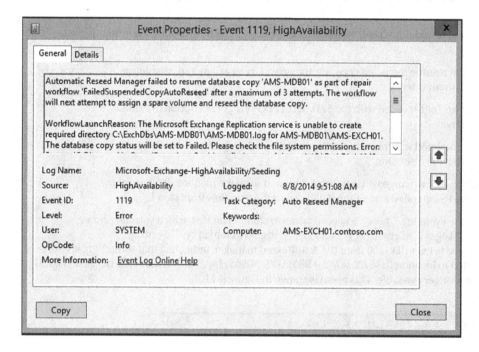

Figure 5-12. *Exchange is reassigning a spare disk*

When the disk is succesfully reassigned, Exchange will automatically start reseeding the replaced disk, indicated by EventID 1127 (still logged by the AutoReseed manager), as shown in Figure 5-13.

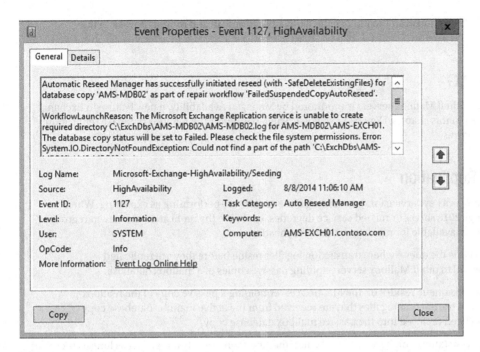

Figure 5-13. *Exchange automatically reseeds the new disk*

Depending of the size of your mailbox databases, it can take quite long time for this step to finish.

You can use the Mountvol utility again to check the new configuration. If all went well, you'll see the mailbox databases now on volume 3, as shown in Figure 5-14.

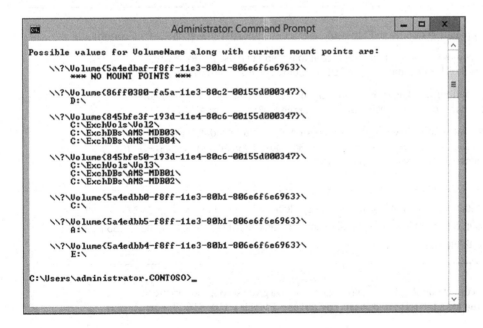

Figure 5-14. *After AutoReseed has kicked in, volume 3 is active*

At this point it is up to the administrator to replace the faulty disk, format it, and mount the disk in the C:\ExchVols directory.

Monitoring the DAG

The DAG including the individual Mailbox servers is monitored by Managed Availability, a new feature in Exchange 2013. (This is discussed later in this chapter.) You can use PowerShell to monitor the mailbox database replication, which is a very powerful feature.

Mailbox Database Replication

Mailbox database replication is a key service for determining if the servers are performing as expecting. When the performance of an Exchange 2013 server or related service degrades, you'll see the replication queues start growing. There are two types of queues available for mailbox database replication:

- **Copy queue** This is the queue where transaction log files reside before they are replicated (over the network) to other Mailbox servers holding passive copies of a mailbox database.

- **Replay queue** This queue resides on the Mailbox server holding a passive copy of the mailbox database. It holds transaction log files that are received from the active mailbox database copy but haven't yet been replayed into the passive mailbox database copy.

Both queues fluctuate constantly, and it's no big deal when they are momentarily increasing as long as they start decreasing in minutes.

■ **Note** When you have lagged copies in your DAG, especially when the lag time is long, you can expect a large number of items in the replay queues. If so, there's no need to worry since this is expected behavior.

You can monitor the replication queues in EMS using the Get-MailboxDatabaseCopyStatus command:

1. To monitor all copies of a particular mailbox database, you can use the following command: Get-MailboxDatabaseCopyStatus -Identity DB1 | Format-List

2. To monitor all mailbox database copies on a given server, you can use the following command: Get-MailboxDatabaseCopyStatus -Server MBX1 | Format-List

3. To monitor the status and network information for a given mailbox database on a given server, you can use the following command: Get-MailboxDatabaseCopyStatus -Identity DB3\MBX3 -ConnectionStatus | Format-List

---

■ **Note** The syntax of the identity of the mailbox database copy looks a bit odd, but it is the name of the mailbox database located on the Mailbox server holding the passive copy. In this case, it is mailbox database DB3 located on Mailbox server MBX3, thus DB3\MBX3.

---

4. To monitor the copy status of a given mailbox database on a given server, you can use the following command: Get-MailboxDatabaseCopyStatus -Identity DB1\MBX2 | Format-List

I often combine the Get-MailboxDatabaseCopyStatus command with the Get-MailboxDatabase command to get a quick overview of all mailbox databases, their passive copies, and the status of the replication queues (see Figure 5-15). To do this, use the following command: Get-MailboxDatabase | Get-MailboxDatabaseCopyStatus.

```
Machine: MBX04                                                                    _  □  ×

C:\windows\system32>Get-MailboxDatabase | Get-MailboxDatabaseCopyStatus

Name                            Status       CopyQueue ReplayQueue LastInspectedLogTime   ContentIndex
                                             Length    Length                             State
----                            ------       --------- ----------- --------------------   ------------
MDB01\MBX02                     Mounted      0         0                                  Healthy
MDB01\MBX04                     Healthy      0         0           16-10-2013 09:50:07    Healthy
MDB02\MBX02                     Mounted      0         0                                  Healthy
MDB02\MBX04                     Healthy      0         0           16-10-2013 09:53:51    Healthy
MDB03\MBX02                     Mounted      0         0                                  Healthy
MDB03\MBX04                     Healthy      0         0           16-10-2013 09:50:27    Healthy
MDB04\MBX02                     Mounted      0         0                                  Healthy
MDB04\MBX04                     Healthy      0         0           16-10-2013 09:53:04    Healthy
MDB05\MBX02                     Mounted      0         0                                  Healthy
MDB05\MBX04                     Healthy      0         0           16-10-2013 09:52:37    Healthy
MDB06\MBX04                     Healthy      0         0           16-10-2013 09:51:34    Healthy
MDB06\MBX02                     Mounted      0         0                                  Healthy
MDB07\MBX04                     Healthy      0         0           16-10-2013 09:54:02    Healthy
MDB07\MBX02                     Mounted      0         0                                  Healthy
MDB08\MBX04                     Healthy      0         0           16-10-2013 09:52:36    Healthy
MDB08\MBX02                     Mounted      0         0                                  Healthy
MDB09\MBX04                     Healthy      0         0           16-10-2013 09:53:04    Healthy
MDB09\MBX02                     Mounted      0         0                                  Healthy
MDB10\MBX04                     Healthy      0         0           16-10-2013 09:51:01    Healthy
MDB10\MBX02                     Mounted      0         0                                  Healthy

C:\windows\system32>_
```

Figure 5-15. *Monitoring the status of mailbox database copies*

■ **Note** When you are moving mailboxes from one Mailbox server to another Mailbox server, a lot of transaction log files are generated. It is quite common that, under these circumstances, replication cannot keep up with demand, and you will see a dramatic increase in the replication queues. Things can get even worse when you are using circular logging in a DAG, since the log files will be purged only when the transaction log files are replayed into the mailbox database and all the DAG members agree on purging the log files. When there are too many log files, replication will slow down, the disk holding the log files will fill up, and the mailbox database can potentially dismount. The only way to avoid this situation is to throttle down the mailbox moves so that replication can keep up with demand.

Health Check Commands

Another way in EMS to check for mailbox replication is to use the Test-ReplicationHealth command. This command tests the continuous replication, the availability of the Active Manager, the status of the underlying failover cluster components, the cluster quorum, and the underlying network infrastructure. To use this command against server AMS-EXCH01, you can enter the following command:

Test-ReplicationHealth -Identity AMS-EXCH01

The output of this command is shown in Figure 5-16.

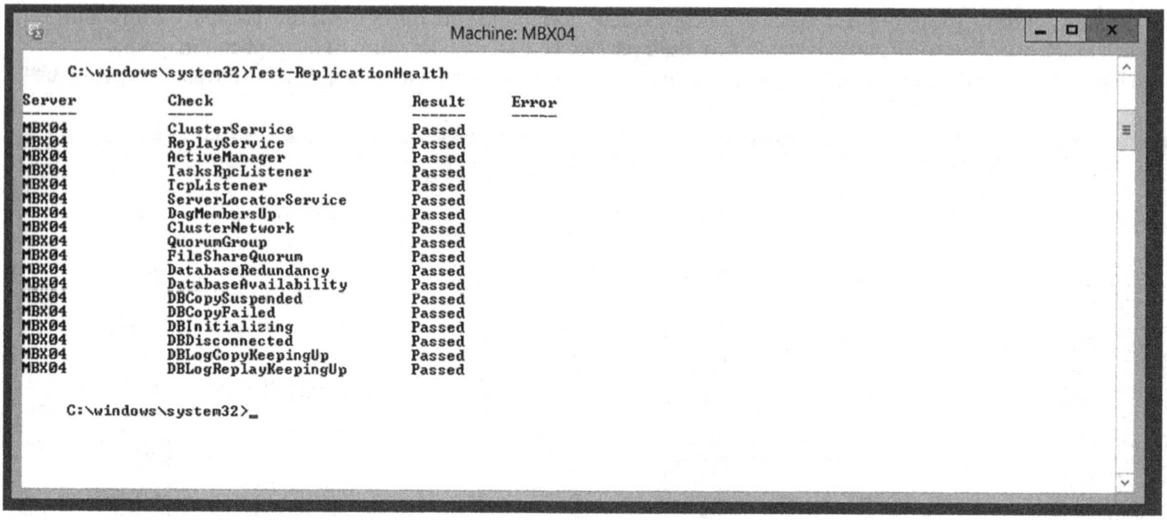

Figure 5-16. *The Test-ReplicationHealth command checks the entire replication stack*

Microsoft has written two health metric scripts, which are located in the C:\Program Files\Microsoft\Exchange Server\v15\Scripts directory that gathers information about mailbox databases in a DAG. These scripts are:

1.   CollectOverMetrics.ps1

2.   CollectReplicationMetrics.ps1

The CollectOverMetrics.ps1 script reads DAG member event logs to gather information regarding mailbox database operations for a specific time period. Database operations can be mounting, dismounting, database moves (switchovers), or failovers. The script can generate an HTML file and a CSV file for later processing in Microsoft Excel, for example.

To show information in a DAG called DAG01, as well as all mailbox databases in this DAG, you can navigate to the scripts directory and use a command similar to the following:

```
.\CollectOverMetrics.ps1 -DatabaseAvailabilityGroup DAG01 -Database:"DB*" -GenerateHTMLReport
-ShowHTMLReport
```

The CollectReplicationMetric.ps1 is a more advanced script, since it gathers information in real time while the script is running. Also, it gathers information from performance monitor counters related to mailbox database replication. The script can be run to:

1.   Collect data and generate a report (CollectAndReport, the default setting)

2.   Collect data and store it (CollectOnly)

3.   Generate a report from earlier stored data (ProcessOnly)

The scripts start PowerShell jobs that gather all information and, as such, it is a time- and resource-consuming task. The final stage of the script, when all data is processed to generate a report, can also be time- and resource-intensive. To gather one hour of performance data from a DAG using a one-minute interval and generate a report, the following command can be used:

```
.\CollectReplicationMetrics.ps1 -DagName DAG1 -Duration "01:00:00" -Frequency "00:01:00"
-ReportPath
```

To read data from all files called `CounterData*` and generate a report, the following command can be used:

```
.\CollectReplicationMetrics.ps1 -SummariseFiles (dir CounterData*) -Mode ProcessOnly -ReportPath
```

■ **Note**   Do not forget to navigate to the scripts directory before entering this command. This can be easily done by entering `cd $exscripts` in EMS.

Not directly related to monitoring an Exchange server is the `RedistributeActiveDatabases.ps1` script. It can happen, especially after a failover, that the mailbox databases are not properly distributed among the Mailbox servers. For example, in such a scenario, one Mailbox server may be hosting only active copies of mailbox databases while another Mailbox server is hosting only passive copies. To redistribute the mailbox database copies over the available Mailbox servers, you can use the following command:

```
.\RedistributeActiveDatabases.ps1 -DagName DAG1 -BalanceDbsByActivationPreference
-ShowFinalDatabaseDistribution
```

This command will distribute all mailbox databases by their activation preference, which was set during creation of the mailbox database copies. If you have a multi-site DAG, you can use the `-BalanceDbsBySiteAndActivationPreference` parameter. This will balance the mailbox databases to their most preferred copy, but also try to balance mailbox databases within each Active Directory site.

Client Access Server High Availability

In a high-availability environment, not only do the mailboxes databases need to be highly available but also the Client Access servers need to be highly available.

This is done by implementing multiple Client Access servers where a load balancer is distributing the client connections across these Client Access servers. When one Exchange 2013 Client Access server fails, another Client Access server takes over the service, the load balancer will take of this and the failed Client Access server will automatically be disabled in the list of servers in the load balancer configuration.

■ **Note**   Load balancing is discussed in detail in Chapter 4.

Managed Availability

In the past, you could use a separate monitoring solution like System Center Operations Manager or some less-sophisticated solution based on SNMP to monitor your Exchange environment. While these are certainly good solutions, their only task is to monitor the Exchange environment. Imagine that you're running an environment with thousands of servers in a high-availability environment. This will result in millions and millions of events being generated, and so you are having to take action on a continuous basis. That's no fun when you need a good night's sleep, but there are tools to help you avoid this situation.

This is where Managed Availability comes into play. Managed Availability is a new service in Exchange 2013 that constantly monitors the Exchange servers and takes appropriate action when needed, without any system administrator intervention. Managed Availability not only monitors the various services within an Exchange server for their availability but also does end-to-end monitoring from a user's perspective.

So, Managed Availability monitors if the Information Store is running and if the mailbox database is mounted; at the same time, it monitors if the mailbox itself is available. Similarly, Managed Availability not only checks if the Internet Information Server (IIS) is running and is offering the Outlook Web App (OWA) function, but it also tries to log in to a mailbox to see if the OWA service is actually available.

This service represents a huge difference from past versions of Exchange Server and their earlier monitoring solutions, where the only monitoring was to determine if the web server was up and running. If a logon page was shown, then OWA was supposed to be running fine. Likewise, SMTP monitoring in the past was a matter of setting up a Telnet session on port 25 so you would get a banner showing the service as up and running; however, there was no monitoring to determine if a messages could actually be delivered.

According to Microsoft, Managed Availability is cloud trained, user focused, and recovery oriented.

Cloud Trained

Microsoft developed Managed Availability in Exchange Online, sometimes referred to as "the service," and brought it back to the on-premises Exchange installations. Multiple years of running the services allowed for the incorporation of experience and best practices from operations in a large environment and with a diverse, worldwide client base running operations 24/7.

In Exchange Online, developers were responsible for building, maintaining, and improving Managed Availability. Those developers also handled escalations in Exchange Online that allowed them to take feedback, not only for the software they were coding but also for improvements in the monitoring process itself. The developers were paged in the middle of the night when problems escalated, so they had to focus on improving Managed Availability.

This service is included in the Exchange 2013 product and is installed out of the box by default; no additional configuration is needed. At the same time, Microsoft has the ability to make changes and improvements to Managed Availability every time a cumulative update is released.

User Focused

Managed Availability is based on end-user experience. Listening on port 443 for OWA or on port 25 for SMTP does not guarantee successful message delivery. Managed Availability, however, performs monitoring checks for the following:

- Availability: Is the service being monitored actually accessible and available?

- Latency: Is the service working with an acceptable degree of latency?

- Error: When accessing the service, are there any errors logged?

These items result in a *customer touch point*—a test that ensures the availability of the service; it responds at or below an acceptable latency and returns no error when performing these operations.

Recovery Oriented

Managed Availability protects the user experience through a series of recovery actions. It's basically the recognition that problems may arise, but the user experience should not be impacted. An example of Managed Availability's monitoring of OWA is as follows:

1. The monitor attempts to submit a message via OWA and an error is returned.

2. The responder is notified and tries to restart the OWA application pool.

3. The monitor attempts to verify OWA and checks if it's healty. When healthy, the monitor again attempts to submit a message and again an error is returned.

4. The responder now moves the active mailbox database to another Mailbox server.

5. The monitor attempts to verify OWA and checks for health status. When healthy, the monitor attempts to submit a message and now receives a success.

Managed Availability is implemented through the new Microsoft Exchange Health Manager service running on the Exchange 2013 server. How does the Health Manager service gets its information? Through a series of new crimson channels. As described earlier, a *crimson channel* is a channel where applications can store certain events, and these events can be consumed by other applications or services. In this case, various Exchange components write the events to a crimson channel and the Health Manager service consumes those events to monitor the service and take appropriate actions.

The configuration files that are used by Managed Availability are XML files supplied by Microsoft and stored on the local hard drive on C:\Program Files\Microsoft\Exchange Server\V15\Bin\Monitoring\Config (see Figure 5-17).

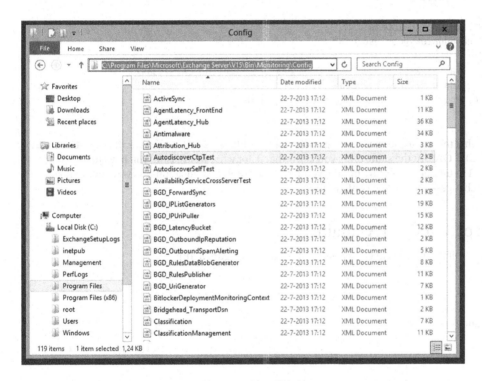

Figure 5-17. The XML config files for Managed Availability

■ **Note** While it is interesting to check out these XML files, it's not a good idea to modify them—not even when you know 120 percent of what you're doing. You will most likely see unexpected results and Managed Availability will do things you don't want, like rebooting servers that have no problems, only because you incorrectly changed some configuration file.

You have to be careful. When you look at the SmtpProbes_Frontend.xml, for example, you'll see the following in the WorkContext:

```
<WorkContext>
  <SmtpServer>127.0.0.1</SmtpServer>
  <Port>25</Port>
  <HeloDomain>InboundProxyProbe</HeloDomain>
  <MailFrom Username="inboundproxy@contoso.com" />
  <MailTo Select="All" />
  <Data AddAttributions="false">X-Exchange-Probe-Drop-Message:FrontEnd-CAT-250&#x
000D;&#x000A;Subject:Inbound proxy probe</Data>
  <ExpectedConnectionLostPoint>None</ExpectedConnectionLostPoint>
</WorkContext>
```

Above all, this tells us that the Health service is using port 25 on IP address 127.0.0.1 to check the front-end proxy function on the Exchange 2013 C AS. At the same time, you know that if, for whatever reason, you have to unbind LOCALHOST from 127.0.0.1 in the server's configuration, you'll get unwanted complications. So you have to take special care when making changes to the server configuration!

The Architecture of Managed Availability

Managed Availability consists of three different components (illustrated in Figure 5-18):

- Probe engine
- Monitor
- Responder engine

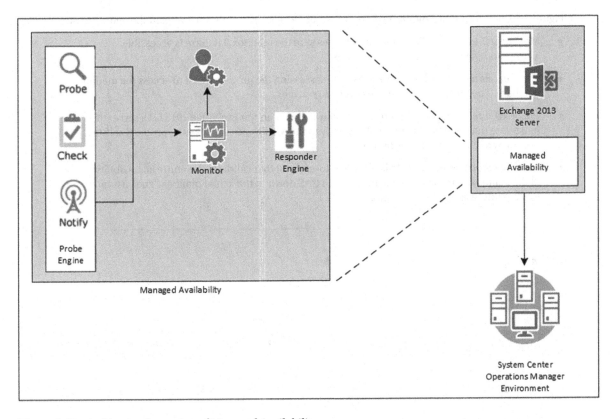

Figure 5-18. *Architectural overview of Managed Availability*

The probe engine consists of three different components:

- **Probe** Determines the success of a particular service or component from an end-user perspective. A probe performs an end-to-end test, also known as a synthetic transaction. One probe may perform a portion of a stack, such as checking if a web service is actually running, while another probe tests the full stack—that is, it sees if any successful data is returned. Each component team in the Exchange Product Group is responsible for building its own probe.

- **Check** Monitors end-user activity and looks for trends within the Exchange server that might indicate (known) issues. A check is implemented against performance counters where thresholds can be monitored. A check is a passive monitoring mechanism.

- **Notify** Processes notifications from the system that are known to be issues in an Exchange 2013 server. These are general notifications and they do not automatically mean they have originated from a probe. The notifier makes it possible to take immediate action when needed, instead of waiting for a probe to signal that something is wrong.

The monitor receives data from one or more probes. The feedback from a probe determines if a monitor is healthy or not. If a monitor is using multiple probes, but one probe returns unhealthy feedback, the entire monitor is considered unhealthy. Based on the frequency of the probe feedback, the monitor decides whether a responder should be triggered.

In Figure 5-19, it is clear that a monitor works at different levels. The levels illustrated in the figure include:

- *Mailbox self-test (MST)* This first check makes sure the mailbox database is accessible. The mailbox self-test runs every 5 minutes.

- *Protocol self-test (PST)* This second test is for assessing the protocol used to access the mailbox database. The protocol self-test runs every 20 seconds.

- *Proxy self-test (PrST)* This third test is actually running on the Exchange 2013 CAS server to make sure that requests are proxied correctly to the Mailbox server. Like the protocol self-test, this proxy self-test runs every 20 seconds.

- *Customer touch point (CTP)* This is an end-to-end test that validates the entire accessibility of the mailbox, starting at the Exchange 2013 CAS down to the actual mailbox. The customer touch point runs every 20 minutes.

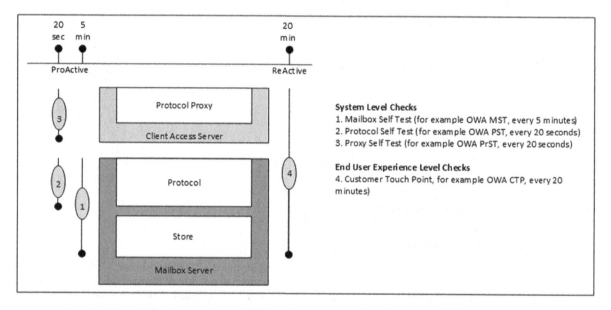

Figure 5-19. *Monitoring occurs at different layers*

The advantage of this multi-layer approach is that it is possible to check various components using different probes, and to respond in different ways using the responder. Thus, a responder is a component that responds with a predefined account when a monitor turns unhealthy. The following responders are available:

- *Restart responder:* This responder terminates and recycles a particular service.

- *Reset AppPool responder:* This responder can recycle the IIS application pool.

- *Failover responder:* This responder can take an Exchange 2013 Mailbox server out of service by failing all the mailbox databases on this Mailbox server over to other Mailbox servers.

- *Bugcheck responder:* This responder can bug-check a particular server—that is, it will restart with a "blue screen."

- *Offline responder:* This responder can take a protocol running on an Exchange 2013 server out of service. Especially when if you're using a load balancer, this is important. When the Offline responder kicks in and a protocol component is shut down, the load balancer will notice and disable the Exchange 2013 CAS (or this particular protocol), so it stops servicing client requests.

- *Escalate responder:* This responder can escalate an issue to another application, like System Center 2012 Operations Manager. It is an indication that human intervention is required.

The responder sequence is stopped when the associated monitor becomes healthy again. Responders can also be throttled. Imagine that you have three Exchange 2013 Mailbox servers in a DAG. You don't want two different responders (each on a Mailbox server) to bug-check this particular Mailbox server, since it will result in a complete outage of the DAG. When two Mailbox servers are bug-checked, then the remaining Mailbox server loses quorum and shuts down the DAG, which of course will result in downtime for all users.

Exchange 2013 CAS and Managed Availability

In theory, this monitoring is nice, but how does it work in a production environment? When looking at the Exchange 2013 CAS protocols, Managed Availability dynamically generates a file called healthcheck.htm. Since this file is dynamically generated to test a particular protocol, you will not find it anywhere on the Exchange 2013 CAS's hard disk.

This is a basic HTM file; the only thing it does is to return a 200 OK code plus the name of the server. You can easily open the file using a browser. It doesn't reveal much information, but when it returns the information as shown in Figure 5-20, you know your server is fine from an OWA protocol perspective.

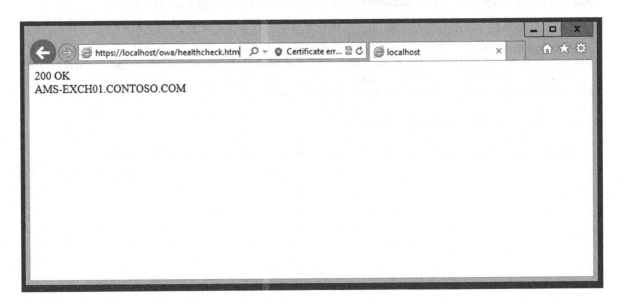

Figure 5-20. *A dynamically generated file for health checking by a probe*

All other protocols, like ECP, EWS, Autodiscover, and Outlook Anywhere, have their own healthcheck.htm files when the server is running fine. A hardware load balancer as shown in Figure 5-21 can use this information as well. When the load balancer checks for this file, and a 200 OK is returned, the load balancer knows that the respective protocol is doing fine. If an error is returned, the load balancer knows there's something wrong and it should take this protocol out of service.

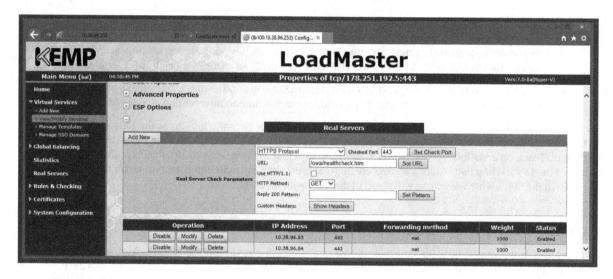

***Figure 5-21.** The load balancer is using the healthcheck.htm file for checking availability*

■ **Note** This is only a protocol check and doesn't say anything if a user can actually log in or not.

What can you do with this information? The offline responder, for example, can be invoked to place a node in maintenance mode—say, when you're patching your servers or updating to the latest cumulative update. To accomplish this, you have to change the server component state of an Exchange server. The server component state of an Exchange server can be requested using the Get-ServerComponentState command in EMS like this:

Get-ServerComponentState -Identity AMS-EXCH01

This command will show the state of all server components on the console, as displayed in Figure 5-22.

```
Machine: AMS-EXCH01.Contoso.com                                   _  □  x

C:\Windows\system32>Get-ServerComponentState -Identity AMS-EXCH01

Server                       Component                    State
------                       ---------                    -----
AMS-EXCH01.Contoso.com       ServerWideOffline            Active
AMS-EXCH01.Contoso.com       HubTransport                 Active
AMS-EXCH01.Contoso.com       FrontendTransport            Active
AMS-EXCH01.Contoso.com       Monitoring                   Active
AMS-EXCH01.Contoso.com       RecoveryActionsEnabled       Active
AMS-EXCH01.Contoso.com       AutoDiscoverProxy            Active
AMS-EXCH01.Contoso.com       ActiveSyncProxy              Active
AMS-EXCH01.Contoso.com       EcpProxy                     Active
AMS-EXCH01.Contoso.com       EwsProxy                     Active
AMS-EXCH01.Contoso.com       ImapProxy                    Active
AMS-EXCH01.Contoso.com       OabProxy                     Active
AMS-EXCH01.Contoso.com       OwaProxy                     Active
AMS-EXCH01.Contoso.com       PopProxy                     Active
AMS-EXCH01.Contoso.com       PushNotificationsProxy       Active
AMS-EXCH01.Contoso.com       RpsProxy                     Active
AMS-EXCH01.Contoso.com       RwsProxy                     Active
AMS-EXCH01.Contoso.com       RpcProxy                     Active
AMS-EXCH01.Contoso.com       UMCallRouter                 Inactive
AMS-EXCH01.Contoso.com       XropProxy                    Active
AMS-EXCH01.Contoso.com       HttpProxyAvailabilityGroup   Active
AMS-EXCH01.Contoso.com       ForwardSyncDeamon            Active
AMS-EXCH01.Contoso.com       ProvisioningRps              Active
AMS-EXCH01.Contoso.com       MapiProxy                    Active


C:\Windows\system32>_
```

Figure 5-22. Requesting the component state of an Exchange 2013 server

The items listed in Figure 5-22 are all components on the Exchange 2013 server AMS-EXCH01, which is a multi-role server—that is, with both the CAS and a Mailbox server installed on it. The components are not the individual services running on the Exchange server, but they are an abstraction layer that mimics the individual services. For example, in Figure 8-15 you can see the Hub Transport component. In this case, the Hub Transport component represents all services running on the Mailbox server, as explained in Chapter 4.

The components that reside on an Exchange 2013 CAS are the ones with "proxy" in their name, with UMCallRouter and FrontEndTransport as exceptions (also components of the Exchange 2013 CAS). The Hub Transport is a component that belongs to the Mailbox server role, while the Monitoring and RecoveryActionsEnabled component belong to both roles.

When a component is shut down, the requester acts as a label on the actual shutdown. There are five types of requesters defined:

1. HealthAPI

2. Maintenance

3. Sidelined

4. Functional

5. Deployment

Since these act as labels, you can use them when you want to shut down a component manually. To do this, you can use the Set-ServerComponentState command in EMS:

```
Set-ServerComponentState -Identity AMS-EXCH01 -Component OWAProxy -State Inactive -Requester
Maintenance
```

When this command is run, and you check the state of the components using the `Get-ServerComponentState -Identity AMS-EXCH01 -Component OWAProxy` command in EMS, you'll see on the console that the OWA component is actually inactive:

```
Server                          Component       State
------                          ---------       -----
AMS-EXCH01.Contoso.com          OwaProxy        Inactive
```

When you open a browser and navigate to `https://localhost/owa/healthcheck.htm`, you'll observe that an error message is generated. The load balancer will determine that the OWA component is no longer available and will automatically disable this server. You can see this in the load balancer configuration, since the inactive server is marked in red (the top Real Servers IP Address in Figure 5-23, which appears as a different shade of gray in the printed book).

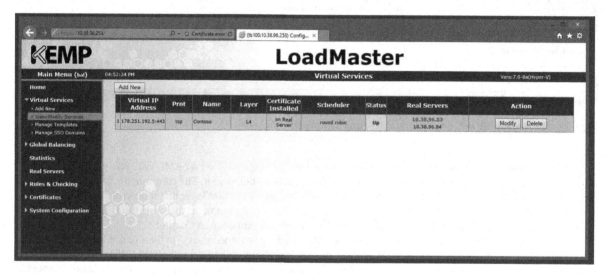

Figure 5-23. *The load balancer detects that OWA is not available on the Exchange 2013 CAS*

■ **Note** All server components change their status immediately, with the exception of the Hub Transport and the Front End Transport components. When these components are disabled in EMS, they continue to run until the service is restarted. This can be confusing when you are not aware of this situation; you will think you disabled the component (actually you did!), but it continues working. However, Managed Availability will notice this inconsistency and force a restart of the service after some time.

The component state is stored in two places:

1. **Active Directory** In Active Directory, it is stored in a property of the Exchange server object in the configuration partition. You can find this server object in:

   ```
   CN=Servers, CN=Exchange Administrative Group (FYDIBOHF23SPDLT), CN=Administrative Groups,
   CN=Contoso, CN=Microsoft Exchange, CN=Services, CN=Configuration, DC=Contoso, DC=COM.
   ```

The value in Active Directory is used when performing `Set-ServerComponentState` commands against a remote server.

2. **Local Registry** When checking the registry, you have to check:

   `HKEY_LOCAL_MACHINE\Software\Microsoft\ExchangeServer\v15\ServerComponentStates`

and then the component you want to check. This can be seen in Figure 5-24.

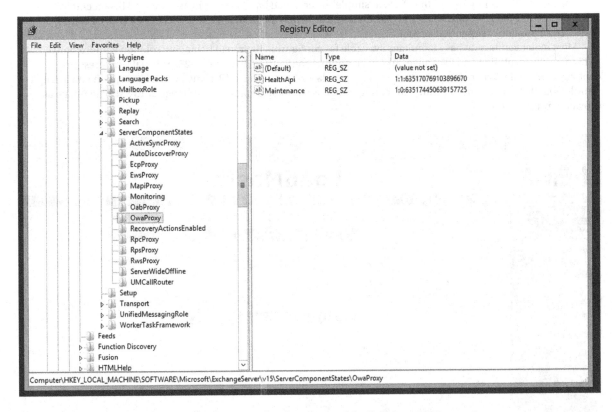

Figure 5-24. *The Server Component state is stored in the registry of the Exchange 2013 server*

When the work on the Exchange 2013 server is finished, the components can be activated again in EMS, using the following command:

```
Set-ServerComponentState -Identity AMS-EXCH01 -Component OWAProxy -State Active -Requester
Maintenance
```

If you check the server component state using the `Get-ServerComponentState` command in EMS, you'll see that it is active again:

```
Server                         Component        State
------                         ---------        -----
AMS-EXCH01.Contoso.com         OwaProxy         Active
```

When you check the load balancer, you'll see that the Exchange 2013 server is back online again.

Front End Transport Server High Availability

The Front End Transport server (FETS) running on the Client Access server is the primary point of entry for SMTP messages from external messaging servers. These can be regular SMTP server, but also multi-functional devices that use SMTP to send incoming faxes or send scanned documents to mailboxes.

To implement high availability for FETS on the Client Access servers—that is, the "Default Frontend <<servername>>" receive connector—you need to use a load balancer to distribute the incoming request across the available Client Access servers and to react on a failing Client Access server.

For a load balancer in front of the FETS, a "simple" layer-4 load balancer can be used: a load balancer that accepts incoming SMTP connections and distributes these across the available Client Access servers. Of course, a layer-7 configuration is supported as well.

Most major vendors do have templates available for configuring their load balancing solution with Exchange 2013 to use their solution and Exchange 2013 in an optimal configuring. In Figure 5-25, a virtual IP address configuration on the load balancer is shown running on layer-7 with source IP as the persistence option and a simple round-robin distribution mechanism. This configuration is based on a standard Exchange 2013 SMTP template as provided by the vendor.

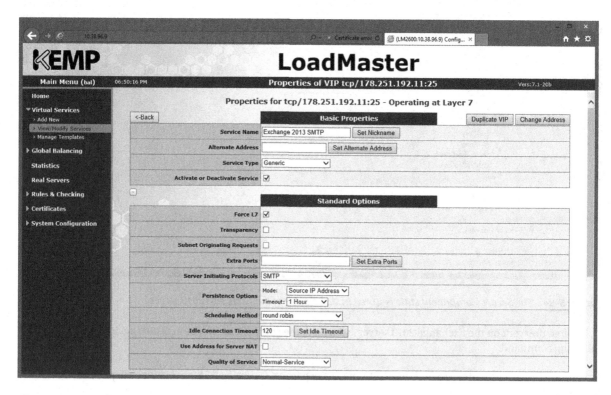

Figure 5-25. *Configuring the load balancer for SMTP use in front of the Client Access servers*

The load balancer will check each Client Access server on port 25 to see if the SMTP service is still healthy. If not, the load balancer will automatically disable this Client Access server in its configuration.

Transport High Availability

When it comes to transport high availability in Exchange 2013, there are two server roles we have to focus on:

- Exchange 2013 Mailbox Transport server role
- Exchange 2013 Edge Transport server role

Transport in the Exchange Mailbox server role has been discussed in more detail in Chapter 4; transport in the Edge Transport server role will be discussed in more detail in Chapter 6.

In this section, I discuss the high-availability options in both server roles.

Mailbox Server Transport High Availability

When it comes to transport in Exchange 2013, things are relatively easy. The Transport service is part of the Mailbox server role in Exchange 2013, so when multiple Mailbox servers are added to achieve higher availability, the transport availability increases at the same time.

If a Mailbox server fails or when mailbox databases are failed over to another Mailbox server, the processing of SMTP messages is automatically moved to another Mailbox server as well.

Is a load balancer needed to distribute SMTP messages across multiple Exchange 2013 Mailbox servers? Well, it depends on the workload—that is, the type of SMTP messages.

SMTP messages routed between a Exchange 2013 Mailbox server or any down-level Hub Transport service do not need a load balancer because Exchange 2013 automatically determines the most effective path to deliver its messages. Things are different, though, when you have created receive connectors on Exchange 2013 that are used by multifunctional devices (fax, scanner, and printer) that use these connectors to route messages to other recipients. These connectors can also be used by third-party applications on your network to route messages to various recipients.

Receive connectors don't have any knowledge about high availability, so you need to create a virtual service on a load balancer. Then, the load balancer will distribute the submitted SMTP messages across available Exchange 2013 Mailbox servers. The application or the multifunctional device needs to submit its messages to the virtual service on the load balancer.

Edge Transport High Availability

Edge Transport servers are located in the perimeter network and are not domain joined. To achieve high availability on the Edge Transport servers, you need to implement multiple Edge Transport servers in the perimeter network, as shown in Figure 5-26.

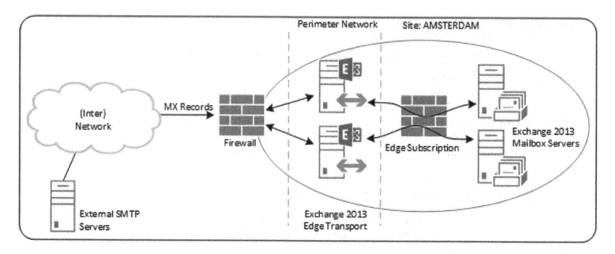

Figure 5-26. *Multiple Edge Transport servers in the perimeter network*

Edge Transport servers are connected to the Exchange 2013 Mailbox servers using Edge subscriptions, and each Edge Transport server has its own subscription.

Multiple subscriptions provide a means of achieving high availability for communications between the Exchange 2013 Mailbox servers and the Edge Transport servers. Both the Mailbox servers and the Edge Transport servers automatically distribute their SMTP messages across the Edge subscriptions. The load is therefore automatically distributed; if one server fails, other servers automatically take over.

For inbound messages from the Internet to the Edge Transport servers, there are two mechanisms for achieving high availability:

1. When multiple Edge Transport servers are used, it is possible to have multiple MX records. Each MX record points to one Edge Transport server, so the messages will automatically be distributed. The down side of this is that if that Edge Transport server is not available, the sending SMTP host has no notion of this and keeps trying on this particular Edge Transport server.

2. You can use a load balancer in front of the Edge Transport servers and create a virtual service on this load balancer. The MX records in public DNS point to this virtual service and external SMTP hosts deliver their messages to this virtual service. The load balancer distributes the inbound SMTP messages across the available Edge Transport servers. If one Edge Transport server fails, the load balancer automatically redistributes inbound message across the remaining Edge Transport servers.

Summary

High availability in Exchange 2013 can be implemented on Mailbox databases, Client Access, and Transport servers. When it comes to Client Access servers, it is just a matter of implementing multiple Exchange servers and using a load balancer to distribute the load across multiple servers. If one server fails, the load balancer automatically redistributes the load across the remaining servers.

Multiple Mailbox servers automatically mean multiple Transport servers in your Exchange organization. Exchange Server automatically distributes the processing of SMTP messages, so that if one server fails in a DAG configuration, the processing of SMTP messages is automatically moved to other Mailbox servers. When Edge Transport servers are used, high availability is achieved with multiple Edge Transport servers and multiple Edge subscriptions, with the Mailbox servers on the internal network.

High availability for mailboxes is achieved by implementing multiple Mailbox servers configured in a database availability group, or DAG. Multiple copies of a mailbox database are configured in a DAG, so if one mailbox database fails, or if one Mailbox server fails, another copy of the mailbox database on another Mailbox server automatically takes over.

Using a DAG is pretty complex, but doing so well will dramatically increase the availability of your Exchange environment.

■ ■ ■

## CHAPTER 6

Message Hygiene

About 95 percent of all messages sent across the Internet are some kind of spam—commercial messages from malicious organizations or infected computers. Well-known spam messages are for illegal Viagra pills, penis enlargement, and imitation Rolex watches, or are solicitations from Nigerian banks or people in Hong Kong who want to offer you millions of dollars if only you'd give them your bank account password.

But not all messages are spam. There's a second category of bulk mail, which are advertisements whose sponsors have drawn your email address from a distribution list that you might once have subscribed to but have forgotten about.

Message hygiene is the term for dealing with all these unsolicited email messages. They have to be filtered out, so that only your expected and customary messages are delivered to your inbox.

There are two basic ways of performing message hygiene:

1. **Using an on-premises message hygiene solution.** The Exchange 2013 Edge Transport server is a common example of this. You install, configure, and maintain the server, and it takes care of all those unsolicited email messages.

2. **Using an online message hygiene solution.** The Exchange Online Protection (EOP) is such a solution. All messages destined for your organization are delivered to the Microsoft data center; Microsoft cleans out the unsolicited email and delivers only your regular email to your internal Exchange organization.

In this chapter we discuss the on-premises message hygiene solution utilizing the Exchange 2013 Edge Transport server. The online message hygiene solution using Exchange Online Protection is discussed in Chapter 11.

The Exchange 2013 Edge Transport Server

Microsoft introduced the Edge Transport server in Exchange Server 2007, continued it in Exchange Server 2010, and unfortunately made it unavailable in Exchange 2013 RTM. However, it was reinstituted in Exchange 2013 SP1.

The Edge Transport server is a first line of defense, so it is located in the perimeter network and is not, therefore, a member of the internal Active Directory domain. In fact, you can have, and probably do have, multiple Edge Transport servers on your perimeter network. The positive side of this is that when the Edge Transport server gets compromised, the internal Active Directory is untouched. The downside, however, is that there's no shared configuration and so you have to configure all the Edge Transport servers manually, although there's an export and import utility to keep all the Edge Transport servers identical; the mechanism it uses is called *cloning*(more about this later in chapter).

The Edge Transport servers need to have some knowledge of the Exchange configuration on the internal network, however; otherwise, it would be hard to route messages to the correct Mailbox server on that internal network or to perform recipient filtering. Therefore, there exists a synchronization mechanism between the Mailbox servers on the internal network and the Edge Transport server on the perimeter network. This mechanism is called *edge synchronization*. Using edge synchronization, the Mailbox servers push (limited) information to the Edge Transport servers on a regular basis.

So, the Edge Transport servers act as your primary defense when it comes to Simple Mail Transfer Protocol (SMTP) traffic, and all inbound messages are routed via your Edge Transport servers. The MX records in the public Domain Name Service (DNS) point to your Edge Transport servers. You can have multiple MX records whereby each MX record points to a particular Edge Transport server.

A simple representation of a network of two Edge Transport servers and two Mailbox servers is shown in Figure 6-1.

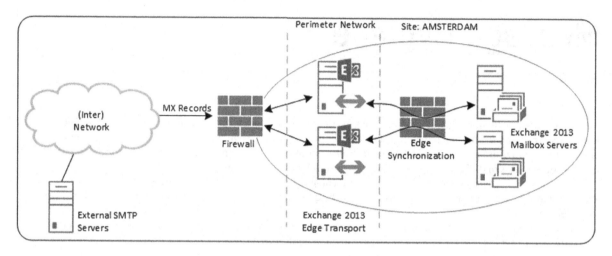

Figure 6-1. *The Edge Transport servers are typically located in the perimeter network*

The Edge Transport servers are not bound to a particular site, but edge synchronization is bound to a particular site in Active Directory. So, if you have two Edge Transport servers at a site called Amsterdam, as shown in Figure 6-1, the two Edge Transport servers are synchronized with the two Mailbox servers at this site. If you have an additional site in London, the Edge Transport servers will not send information directly to the Mailbox servers in Amsterdam. If you want to implement two Edge Transport servers at a site called London, then, you have to create an edge synchronization there as well, and then this edge synchronization is bound to the Mailbox servers at that London site. There have to be separate MX records pointing to these Edge Transport servers as well. When building a configuration like this, you automatically get site redundancy.

The Edge Transport servers are not only used for inbound SMTP traffic; they are also used for outbound SMTP traffic. The Exchange 2013 Mailbox servers use the Edge Transport servers to route SMTP messages to the Internet. So, besides performing message hygiene, the Edge Transport servers process inbound and outbound messages, following transport rules. Such rules may include adding a disclaimer to a message, putting a tag or header on a message, or maybe even blocking an inbound or outbound message based on certain criteria.

Installation of an Exchange 2013 Edge Transport Server

Installing an Exchange 2013 Edge Transport server involves four main steps: preparing the server, installing the actual Exchange software, creating the edge subscription, and starting the edge synchronization.

Preparing the Server

The latest version of Windows is my preferred operating system for installing Exchange 2013. Exchange 2013 SP1 and higher is supporting Windows Server 2012 R2. Windows Server 2012 R2 has mainstream support until 2018, and extended support until 2023. Of course, it is also possible to install Exchange 2013 on Windows Server 2008 R2, but mainstream support ends in January 2015. Remember that it is not possible to upgrade the operating system once Exchange 2013 is installed, so if you want to upgrade your operating system on the Exchange 2013 server, you have to fully reinstall the Edge Transport server.

As just mentioned, the Edge Transport servers are installed in the perimeter network and are not members of the internal Active Directory domain. The Edge Transport servers do, however, need a *fully qualified domain name* (FQDN). To set a FQDN like `AMS-EDGE01.CONTOSO.COM`, you have to change the name of the computer and click the More button, as shown in Figure 6-2. Here, you can change the primary DNS suffix of this server: you enter the domain name, click OK twice, and reboot the server.

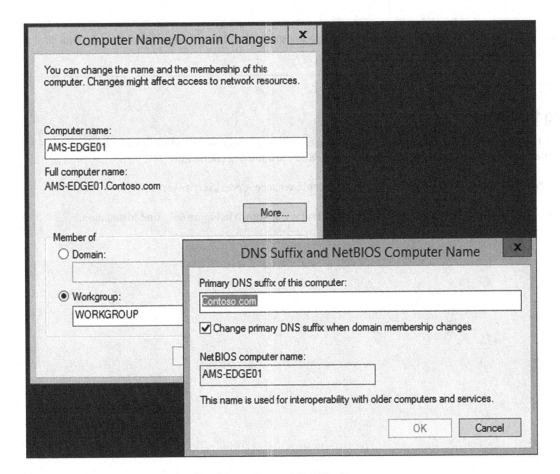

Figure 6-2. Changing the DNS suffix of the Exchange 2013 Edge Transport server

---

■ **Note**   You can only change the FQDN of the server *before* the Edge Transport server role is installed. Changing the FQDN when the Edge Transport server is installed will break everything, and the Edge Transport server will need to be reinstalled.

When the server is configured and the latest fixes from Windows Update (or any other updating mechanism you use) are installed, the prerequisite software can be installed. For the Edge Transport server, only the .NET framework (part of Window Server 2012 R2) and the Active Directory lightweight directory service (AD LDS) need to be installed. You can install this prerequisite software by entering the following command in a PowerShell window with elevated privileges:

```
Install-WindowsFeature NET-Framework, ADLDS, Telnet-Client
```

■ **Note**   The Telnet Client is not officially needed for the Edge Transport server to work properly, but I find it useful for troubleshooting purposes.

Installing the Server

To install the Exchange 2013 Edge Transport server, you open a Windows command prompt with elevated privileges, navigate to the Exchange 2013 SP1 installation media, and enter the following command:

```
Setup.exe /Mode:Install /Roles:EdgeTransport /IAcceptExchangeServerLicenseTerms
```

This will install the Exchange 2013 SP1 Edge Transport server, as shown in Figure 6-3. After installation, the server needs to be rebooted.

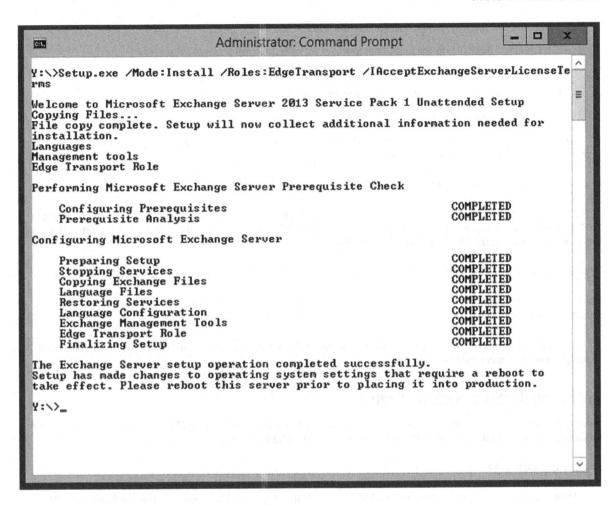

Figure 6-3. *Installing the Exchange 2013 Edge Transport server*

■ **Note** Make sure that the Edge Transport server can resolve the Exchange 2013 Mailbox servers on the internal network. This can be achieved by using DNS on the internal network (depending on your preferred server configuration, of course) or by using a HOSTS file where the FQDN and the IP addresses of the internal Exchange 2013 Mailbox servers are entered.

Creating an Edge Subscription

When the Edge Transport server is installed, you can create the edge subscription. When the edge subscription is created, you can start the edge synchronization, which will push all needed information from the Mailbox server to the Edge Transport server.

Creating the edge subscription consists of the following steps:

1. Create an XML file on the Edge Transport server with the configuration information.

2. Copy the XML file to the Exchange 2013 Mailbox server.

3. Import the XML file into the Exchange 2013 Mailbox server.

4. Start the edge synchronization.

To create the configuration XML file on the Edge server, you open an Exchange Management Shell with elevated privileges and enter the following command:

```
New-EdgeSubscription -FileName C:\Temp\Edge01.xml
```

This will create an XML file with all information from the Edge Transport server that's needed by the Exchange 2013 Mailbox server. You copy the XML file to the Exchange 2013 Mailbox server, and on this server you enter the following command in the Exchange Management Shell:

```
[byte[]]$FileData = Get-Content -Path C:\Temp\edge01.xml -Encoding Byte -ReadCount 0

New-EdgeSubscription -FileData $FileData -Encoding Byte -Site Amsterdam -CreateInternetSendConnector $true -CreateInboundSendConnector $true
```

This will begin the edge subscription. Please note the –Site parameter that defines which Active Directory site the Edge Transport server will be bound to.

Beginning the Edge Synchronization

To start the synchronization between the Exchange 2013 Mailbox server and the Edge Transport server, you enter the following command in the Exchange Management Shell on the Mailbox server:

```
Start-EdgeSynchronization
```

As mentioned before, for this synchronization to work properly you have to make sure that the Exchange 2013 Mailbox server can resolve the Edge Transport server using the DNS; this typically involves adding the Edge Transport server to the DNS on your internal network.

An informational message is shown on the console when the edge subscription is created. This is one of the most common signs when the edge synchronization will not start. Another pitfall is the firewall between the Exchange 2013 Mailbox server and the Edge Transport server. The edge synchronization is using port 50636 to push information to the Edge Transport server, so you have to make sure that this port is open on the firewall to the perimeter network.

When name resolution and the firewall are properly configured, the edge synchronization should start immediately, as shown in Figure 6-4.

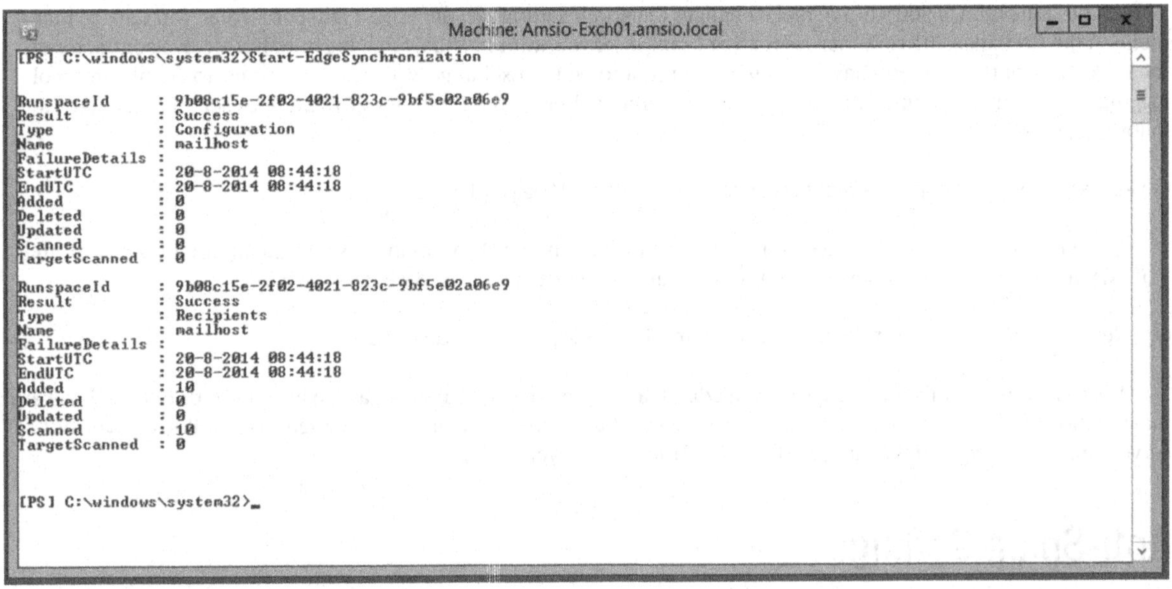

Figure 6-4. Proper start of the edge synchronization

That is all it takes to install the Exchange 2013 Edge Transport server, create the edge subscription, and start the edge synchronization. All relevant settings configured on the internal Exchange 2013 organization for proper functioning of the mail flow are synchronized at this point, including the accepted domains on the internal organization and the send connectors between the Edge Transport server and the internal Exchange 2013 Mailbox servers. You can open the Exchange Management Shell on the Edge Transport server and execute the Get-AcceptedDomain command. This will reveal the accepted domains as they are configured on the internal Exchange organization, as shown in Figure 6-5.

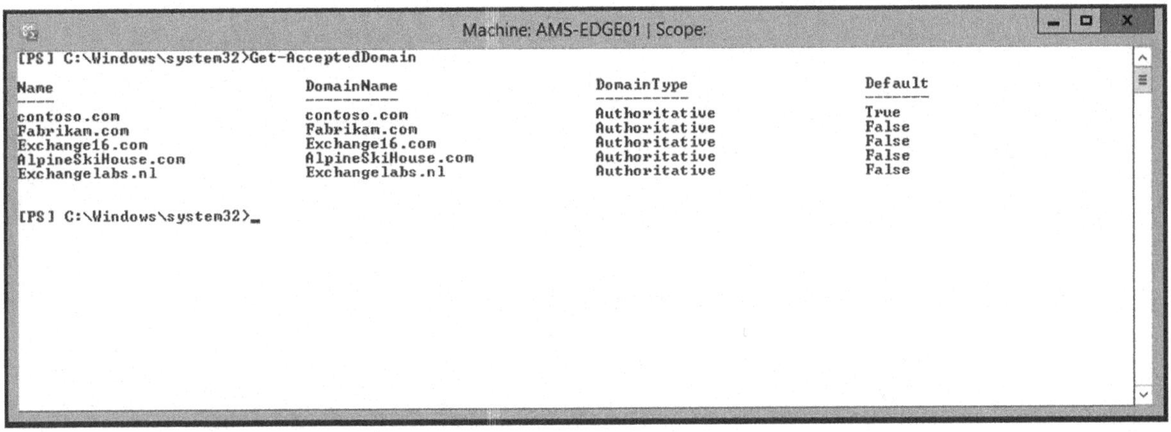

Figure 6-5. The accepted domains now available on the Edge Transport server

At the same time, if you want to make changes to certain settings on the Edge Transport server, you have to make them on the Exchange 2013 Mailbox server. For example, if you want to enable logging onto the receive connector of the Edge Transport server, you have to issue the command on the Exchange 2013 Mailbox server. To enable protocol logging, for example, you open the Exchange Management Shell on the Exchange 2013 Mailbox server and enter the following command:

```
Get-ReceiveConnector | Set-ReceiveConnector -ProtocolLoggingLevel Verbose
```

To change the FQDN of the Edge Transport server when an EHLO command is sent from another host to another FQDN, you can execute the following command, again on the Exchange 2013 Mailbox server:

```
Get-ReceiveConnector | Set-ReceiveConnector -Fqdn smtphost.contoso.nl
```

When it comes to making changes to the Edge Transport server, you always have to be conscious of where you are making those changes. Changes related to message flow have to be made on the Exchange 2013 Mailbox server, but server-specific settings can be made on the Edge Transport server itself.

Anti-Spam Settings

Inbound SMTP messages from the Internet are delivered to the Edge Transport server and are processed there for message hygiene in a certain order, as shown in Figure 6-6.

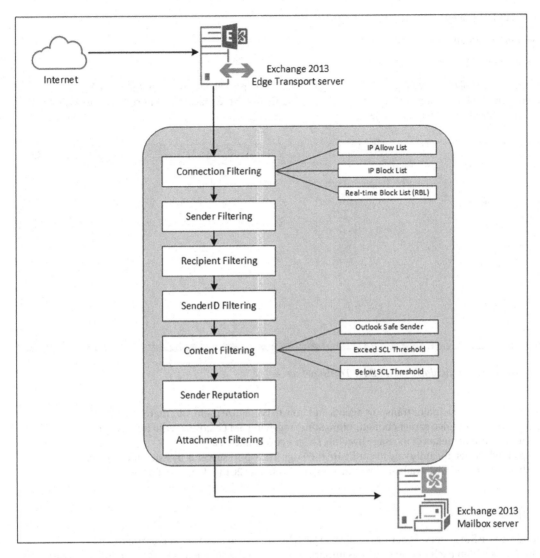

Figure 6-6. *The order of message processing on an Exchange 2013 Edge Transport server*

As can be seen in Figure 6-6, the first and most important step in message hygiene is *connection filtering*. This is where messages that come from IP addresses or ranges that are on block lists are filtered out. In fact, this constitutes the majority of all email entering the Edge Transport server.

The Edge Transport server works with *transport agents*. The following transport agents are available on the Edge Transport server:

- Connection filtering agents

- Sender Filter agent

- Recipient Filter agent

- Sender ID agent

- Content Filter agent

- Sender Reputation agent

- Attachment Filter agent

You can retrieve a list of transport agents by running the Get-TransportAgent cmdlet in the Exchange Management Shell on the Edge Transport server, as shown in Figure 6-7. Note that all transport agents are enabled by default and are configured with default settings.

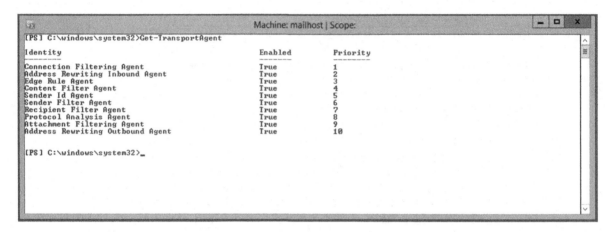

Figure 6-7. *Transport agents available on an Edge Transport server*

In this section I explain the major transport agents and how to configure them, but there's one thing to note here that's *not* a default Transport Edge server configuration. Some receiving SMTP hosts on the Internet perform a reverse DNS lookup as an additional means of message hygiene, so let's cover that first.

Also, as explained earlier, the only way to configure the Edge Transport server is by using the Exchange Management Shell. There's no GUI available for managing the Exchange 2013 Edge Transport server.

Reverse DNS

As just mentioned, some SMTP servers perform a reverse DNS lookup when an SMTP server tries to deliver a message. Although it's not an Exchange feature, it is important. When doing so, the receiving server tries to determine whether the source IP address really matches the FQDN being used. For example, suppose the Edge Transport server is using 176.62.196.249; when a reverse DNS lookup is performed, it should return ams-edge02.exchange16.com, as shown in Figure 6-8 (https://www.misk.com/tools/#dns).

Figure 6-8. *Testing the DNS reverse lookup by using* `misk.com`

■ **Note**   There are mail servers that graylist or even block messages when the PTR message doesn't match or isn't available, so it's important to pay attention to the reverse DNS lookup!

Connection Filtering Agents

Connection filtering is the first default layer of defense when SMTP messages access the Exchange 2013 Edge Transport server. When a sending SMTP server on the Internet sets up a connection on port 25 to the Edge Transport server, the server checks this sending SMTP server. If there's something wrong, the connection is closed, even before any mail data is sent to the Edge Transport server.

There are four ways to configure the connection filtering:

- IP Allow list
- IP Allow list providers
- IP Block list
- IP Block list providers

IP Allow List

When a remote SMTP server sets up a connection with the Edge Transport server to send a message, the Edge Transport server checks to see if the IP address this remote SMTP server is using is white-listed. In general, a white-list is a list of server names or IP addresses of SMTP servers that are trusted. If it is, this remote SMTP server is assumed to be safe and the connection is allowed; the message is accepted.

To add an IP address to the IP Allow list, you can use the Add-IPAllowListEntry, followed by the IP address of the remote SMTP server; for example,

```
Add-IPAllowListEntry -IPAddress 194.165.34.254
```

The output is shown in Figure 6-9.

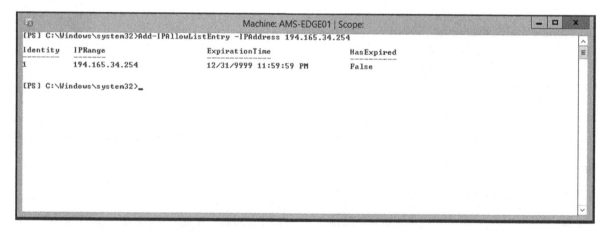

Figure 6-9. *Adding an IP address to the IP Allow list*

When a remote SMTP server is white-listed by the Edge Transport server, a special rating of -1 is stamped on the message; more specifically, an X-header is added to the message. This way Exchange knows the message is safe and treats it as such—that is, this message is not processed by any other anti-spam agent on the Edge Transport server.

When checking the header of a message originating from this host, you will see something like this:

```
Return-Path: administrator@contoso.com
X-MS-Exchange-Organization-Antispam-Report: IPOnAllowList
X-MS-Exchange-Organization-SCL: -1
X-MS-Exchange-Organization-AuthSource: SMTPHOST.exchangelabs.nl
```

IP Allow List Providers

Instead of adding IP addresses manually to the IP Allow list, it is possible to use IP Allow list providers. These providers have lists of trusted SMTP servers—that is, servers that are definitely not associated with any spam activity.

You have to be careful when implementing these providers. As explained in the previous section, messages sent by allowed SMTP hosts are automatically tagged an SCL of -1, which means these messages flow through the Exchange organization without being inspected by any other anti-spam agent; therefore, the provider needs to be completely trustworthy.

There are a number of providers, sometimes referred to as white-list providers, available on the Internet; for example, there is Spamhaus Whitelist (http://www.spamhauswhitelist.com) or the DNS White Label organization (http://www.dnswl.org).

Be aware that this is a matter of getting what you pay for; there are no reliable and free IP Allow list providers. Therefore, I suggest *not* using an IP Allow list provider and instead relying on the IP Block lists and IP Block list providers.

IP Block List

An IP Block list is the exact opposite of an IP Allow list. When an external SMTP server sets up a connection with the Exchange 2013 Edge Transport server, and this SMTP server is on the Edge Transport server's Block list, the connection is automatically voided.

To add an IP address to the Edge Transport server's Block list, you can use the `Add-IPBlockLIstEntry` command followed by the IP address of the SMTP server you want to block; for example,

```
Add-IPBlockListEntry -IPAddress 192.168.10.100
```

It is also possible to add a range of IP addresses to the Block list; for example,

```
Add-IPBlockListEntry -IPRange 192.168.10.0/24
```

To add an IP address to the Block list temporarily, you use the `-ExpirationTime` parameter. To add the SMTP server to the Block list but have it automatically removed on September 1, 2014, you would use the following command:

```
Add-IPBlockListEntry -IPAddress 192.168.10.100 -ExpirationTime "9/1/2014 00:00"
```

To get an overview of all IP addresses that are on the Edge Transport server's Block list, you can use the `Get-IPBlockLIstEntry` command, without any parameters.

To review the IP Block list configuration of the Edge Transport server, you can use the `Get-IPBlockListConfig` command.

■ **Note** The IP Block list is configured on a per server basis. If you have multiple Edge Transport servers, you have to configure them individually, but this is prone to error. When deploying the Edge Transport servers, you can also configure one Edge Transport server and export the configuration to subsequent Edge Transport servers. However, remember that changes also need to be made to lists on all Edge Transport servers.

Configuring and maintaining the IP Block lists is quite some work, so it's better to automate this task by using an IP Block list provider.

IP Block List Providers

To automate maintenance of the IP Block list, you can use an IP Block list provider. The process is identical to a regular IP Block list as discussed in the previous section, but instead of your maintaining the IP Block list entries manually, the entries are maintained by a provider.

One well-known provider is SpamHaus (www.spamhaus.org), in particular their Zen Combined Block List. To configure this provider, you open the Exchange Management Shell on the Edge Transport server and enter the following command:

```
Add-IPBlockListProvider -Name SpamHaus -LookupDomain zen.spamhaus.org -Enabled $true -BitmaskMatch
$null -Priority 1 -AnyMatch $true -RejectionResponse 'Message blocked due to black listing'
```

This is shown in Figure 6-10.

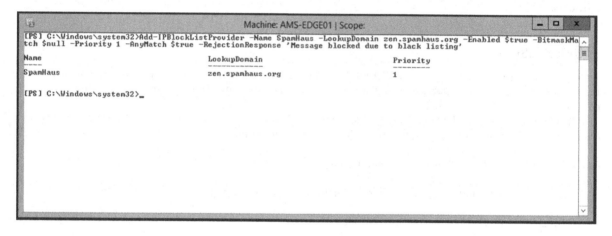

Figure 6-10. *Adding SpamHaus as a Block list provider*

You can use the -RejectionResponse parameter of the Add-IPBlockLIstProvider command to add a customer message that's returned to the sender of the message, but the message cannot exceed 240 characters.

It is possible to disable the IP Block list function on a per-user basis. This way, it is always possible for particular recipients to receive email messages, regardless of any IP Block list provider. To set this, you can use the Set-IPBlockListProvidersConfig command with the -ByPassedRecipients parameter. For example, to bypass the IP Block list filtering for a user named jaap@contoso.com, you can use the following command:

```
Set-IPBlockListProvidersConfig -ByPassedRecipients "jaap@contoso.com"
```

To add or remove multiple recipients at the same time as when the IP Block list provider is configured, you can use the @{Add="recipient"} syntax:

```
Set-IPBlockListProvidersConfig -ByPassedRecipients @{Add="jaap@contoso.com","michel@contoso.com";
Remove="marina@contoso.com"}
```

The IP Block list typically works for connections coming from the Internet—that is, external connections. It is also possible to configure the IP Block list for internal use; you use the -InternalMailEnabled parameter. By default this function is turned off, but you can enable it using the following command:

```
Set-IPBlockListProvidersConfig -InternalMailEnabled $true
```

Sender Filtering

Sender filtering is a default feature in the Edge Transport server that enables you to filter messages based on the sender. This agent does the blocking based on the SMTP header Mail From in the message. If the agent reads a name that's also in the Sender Filter list, the messages is blocked.

You can use the Get-SenderFilterConfig command to check the current configuration of the Sender Filter configuration, as shown in Figure 6-11.

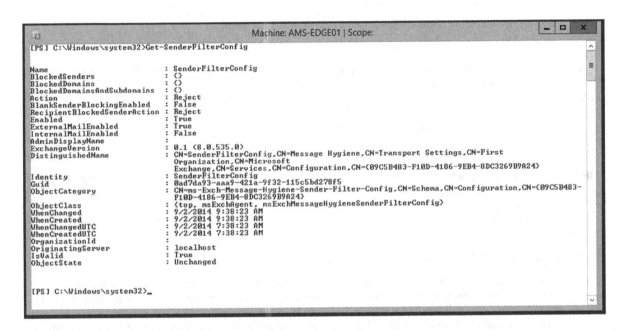

Figure 6-11. *The configuration of the Sender Filter*

To add a particular sender to the Sender Filter configuration, you can use the Set-SenderFilterConfig command. This command takes the –BlockedSenders parameter to add specific senders, but you can also use the –BlockedDomains and –BlockedDomainsAnsSubdomains parameters to add complete domains to the Sender Filter configuration. For example, to add a user called john@alpineskihouse.com to the blocked senders list, and to add the cheapwatches.com domain to the list of blocked senders, you can use the following command:

```
Set-SenderFilterConfig -BlockedSenders "John@alpineskihouse.com" -BlockedDomains "cheapwatches.com"
```

If you want to block senders from the northwindtraders.com and all its subdomains, you can use the following command:

```
Set-SenderFilterConfig -BlockedDomainsAndSubdomains northwindtraders.com
```

These properties are multi-value, which means they can contain more than one value. If you want to add multiple senders to the Sender Filter configuration later on, you have to use the @{Add="sender"} syntax. If you want to remove senders from the Sender Filter configuration, you have to use the @{Remove="sender"} syntax. For example,

```
Set-SenderFilterConfig -BlockedSenders @{Add="onlinecasino@gmail.com","enlargement@hotmail.com";
Remove="john@alpineskihouse.com"}
```

You have to use the same syntax if you want to add or remove domains from the BlockedDomains and BlockedDomainsAndSubDomains properties.

To get an overview of all blocked senders and domains on your Edge Transport server, you can use the Get-SenderFilterConfig again; for example,

```
Get-SenderFilterConfig | Format-List BlockedSenders,BlockedDomains,BlockedDomainsAndSubdomains
```

■ **Note** Only anonymous connections are processed by the Sender Filter agent.

It is possible to configure the Sender Filter agent to filter out messages that don't have anything listed in the Mail From header of a message. This safeguards your organization from NDR attacks from the Internet. To configure this, you use:

```
Set-SenderFilterConfig -BlankSenderBlockingenabled $true
```

■ **Note** It is relatively easy to spoof the Mail From header in an email message. Therefore, it is not recommended you rely exclusively on the Sender Filter agent.

Recipient Filtering

Recipient filtering on the Edge Transport server gives you the opportunity to accept messages only for existing recipients in your Exchange environment. As its name implies, the Recipient Filter agent on the Edge Transport server only accepts messages with a valid recipient in your Exchange 2013 organization.

The accepted domains configured in an Exchange 2013 environment have a property called *AddressBookEnabled*. This property enables or disables recipient filtering for an accepted domain. By default, the Recipient Filter agent is enabled for authoritative accepted domains and is disabled for accepted domains that are configured as internal relay domains or as external relay domains.

To check the value of the AddressBookEnabled property, and thus the status of the Recipient Filter agent, you can use the following command:

```
Get-AcceptedDomain | Format-List Name,AddressBookEnabled
```

If you want to disable the Recipient Filter agent, you can use the following command:

```
Set-RecipientFilterConfig -Enabled $false
```

You can use recipient filtering not only to block messages to unknown recipients but also to block individual recipients in your Exchange 2013 organization; you do this by adding them individually, using the following command:

```
Set-RecipientFilterConfig -BlockedRecipients joe@contoso.com
```

Just as described for sender filtering, you can use the @{Add="<recipient>" syntax to add other recipients to the blocked recipients list. This adds john@contoso.com and blake@contoso.com, and removes joe@contoso.com at the same time.

```
Set-RecipientFilterConfig -BlockedRecipients @{Add="john@contoso.com","blake@contoso.com";
Remove="joe@contoso.com"}
```

You can use the –RecipientValidationEnabled parameter to enable recipient validation, which blocks messages to recipients in your Exchange 2013 organization who do not exist. To enable recipient validation, you can use the following command:

```
Set-RecipientFilterConfig -RecipientValidationEnabled $true
```

When you enable the recipient validation, the Recipient Filter agent does a recipient lookup. Since the Edge Transport server does not have access to the internal Active Directory, it performs this lookup in the local Active Directory Lightweight Directory Service (AD LDS), which contain a list of internal users. To prevent any information from being exposed when the Edge Transport server is compromised, the user information is stored directly in AD LDS but only a one-way hash is used with a secure hash algorithm (SHA)-256.

Sender ID Filtering

Sender ID filtering is a DNS-based technique whereby the receiving SMTP server (in our case, this is the Exchange 2013 Edge Transport server) checks for certain DNS records (called SPF records) of the sending organization.

This SPF record in DNS, which is the responsibility of the sending organization, defines which SMTP servers are actually allowed to send SMTP messages on behalf of this SMTP domain. When properly configured, the IP address of the sending SMTP record matches the SPF record in the public DNS. When this does not match, it might signal spoofing of the SMTP domain, and thus be a spamming technique.

When the Edge Transport server performs the Sender ID check, there are two potential results:

- **Pass** The IP address of the remote SMTP server matches the information in the SPF record and a header indicating the successful test is added to the message. This also contributes to the sender's reputation data. (Sender reputation is explained later in this chapter.)

- **Fail** The IP address of the remote SMTP server does not match the information in the SPF record, or an SPF record was not found. The first can indicate a malicious message or SMTP server. It is also possible that the SPF is not configured or is misconfigured owing to some changes in the sender's messaging infrastructure. A failed Sender ID test contributes to the sender's reputation data, but in a negative way, of course.

The reputation data contributes to the spam confidence level (SCL) of an email message; in turn, this determines what happens to a message, as shown in Figure 6-12.

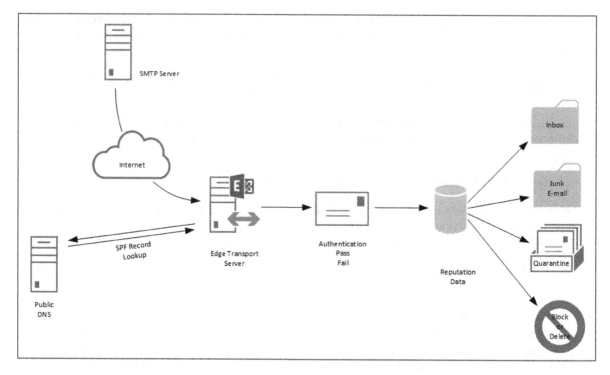

Figure 6-12. *Overview of the Sender ID framework*

The SPF record (a TXT record can be used as well) is registered in the public DNS of the sending organization, and this is checked by the receiving Mail server—that is, your Edge Transport server.

When you open the EMS and enter the `Get-SenderIDConfig` cmdlet, you'll see the default settings for the Sender ID agent. You might want to change the SpoofedDomainAction setting; this setting determines what the agent needs to do when the Sender ID check returns an error (wrong IP on sending SMTP server and possibly a spoofed domain). There are multiple options:

- **StampStatus** This is the default setting. It stamps an additional header on the message and the server continues processing.

- **Reject** This option returns an NDR to the sender, notifying her that something is wrong.

- **Delete** This option deletes the message without returning an NDR to the sender. In this case when it is a legitimate sender, he never knows the message got lost.

It is also possible to bypass certain sending SMTP domains using the `BypassedSenderDomains` parameter. To change the Sender ID setting to Reject and add the `Microsoft.com` SMTP domain to the bypassed sender domains, you can use the following command:

```
Set-SenderIDConfig –SpoofedDomainAction Reject –BypassedSenderDomains Microsoft.com
```

If you want external recipients to perform a Sender ID check on the email messages sent by your organization, and thus contribute to a higher success rate for your messages, you have to implement an SPF record in your public DNS domain as well.

To create an SPF record, Microsoft has a wizard available on their website that you can find at http://bit.ly/SenderIDWizard.

This wizard consists of four steps:

1. Identify the SMTP domain—that is, exchange16.com.

2. The wizard determines that there's no SPF record and retrieves the IP address for the domain (contoso.com) and its MX record, as shown in Figure 6-13:

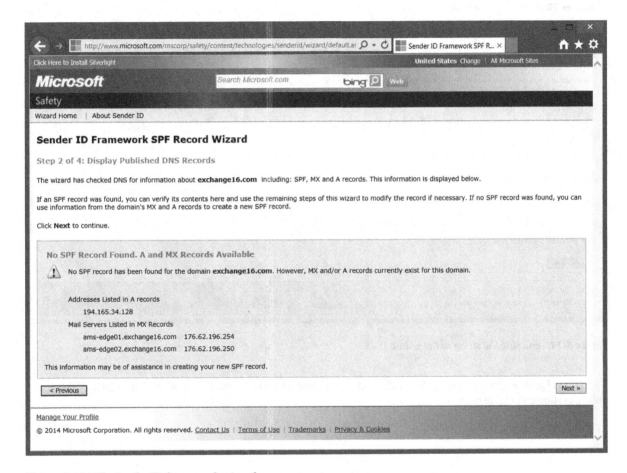

Figure 6-13. *The Sender ID framework wizard*

3. You enter details about the sending SMTP server that the wizard then uses to create the actual SPF record. If you also have a valid PTR record for the Edge Transport server, you can check the All PTR Records Resolve to Outbound Email Servers option under "Reverse DNS Lookup."

4. The value for the SPF record is indicated, as shown in Figure 6-14.

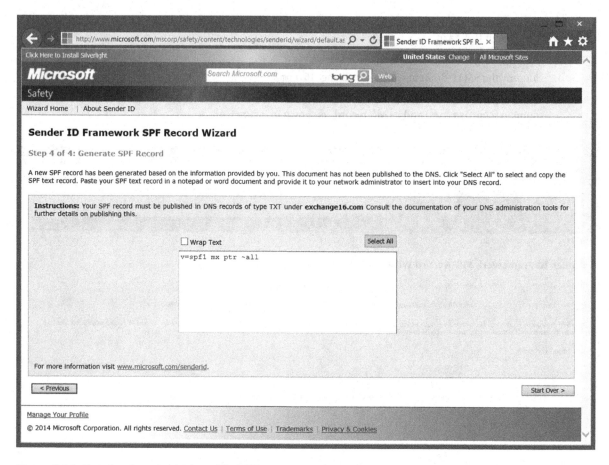

Figure 6-14. *Entering the string in the public DNS*

This value should be entered in the public DNS. Once entered, you can check its availability using the NSLookup utility, as shown in Figure 6-15.

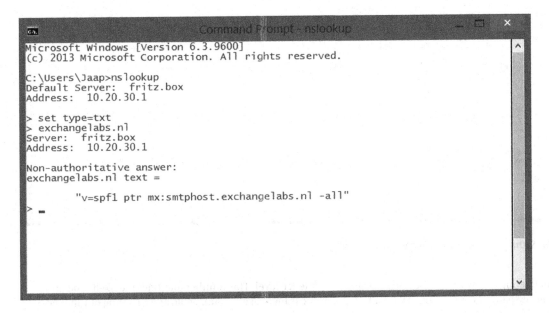

Figure 6-15. *Checking your SPF record using NSLookup utility*

When you've configured this and send a new email message—for example, to your Hotmail mailbox—you can check the message header. You'll find something like this:

```
Authentication-Results: hotmail.com; spf=pass (sender IP is 176.62.196.254) smtp.mailfrom=john@
exchange16.com; dkim=none header.d=exchange16.com; x-hmca=pass header.id=john@exchange16.com
```

Content Filtering

Content filtering is another important feature of the Edge Transport server. Using content filtering, it's possible to filter and delete incoming messages based on certain keywords like "online casino," "cheap watches," "Viagra," or whatever other words you want to target. You can use the Add-ContentFilterPhrase cmdlet to add specific words to the Content Filter agent, as done here and shown in Figure 6-16:

```
$Phrases = 'Online Casino','V I A G R A','Nigeria Bank'
$Phrases | ForEach-Object {Add-ContentFilterPhrase -Phrase $_ -Influence BadWord}
```

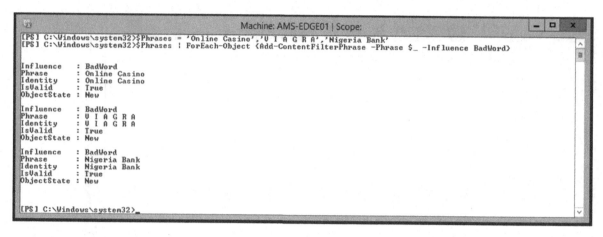

Figure 6-16. *Setting specific words for content filtering*

Content filtering also works with an SCL, or spam confidence level. This number identifies the likelihood an email message is spam. An SCL rating of 9 means the message is most likely spam, while an SCL rating of 1 indicates the message is likely legitimate.

Based on the SCL rating, you can block messages, reject messages (and NDR is returned to the sender), or send the messages to a quarantine mailbox. My personal preference is to block no. 9 messages, reject no. 8 messages, and forward no. 7 messages to a quarantine mailbox.

These settings are set using the `Set-ContentFilterConfig` cmdlet on the Edge Transport server, as shown in Figure 6-17:

```
Set-ContentFilterConfig -QuarantineMailbox quarantaine@exchange16.com -SCLQuarantineEnabled $true
-SCLQuarantineThreshold 7
Set-ContentFilterConfig -SCLDeleteEnabled $true -SCLDeleteThreshold 9
Set-ContentFilterConfig -SCLRejectEnabled $true -SCLRejectThreshold 8
```

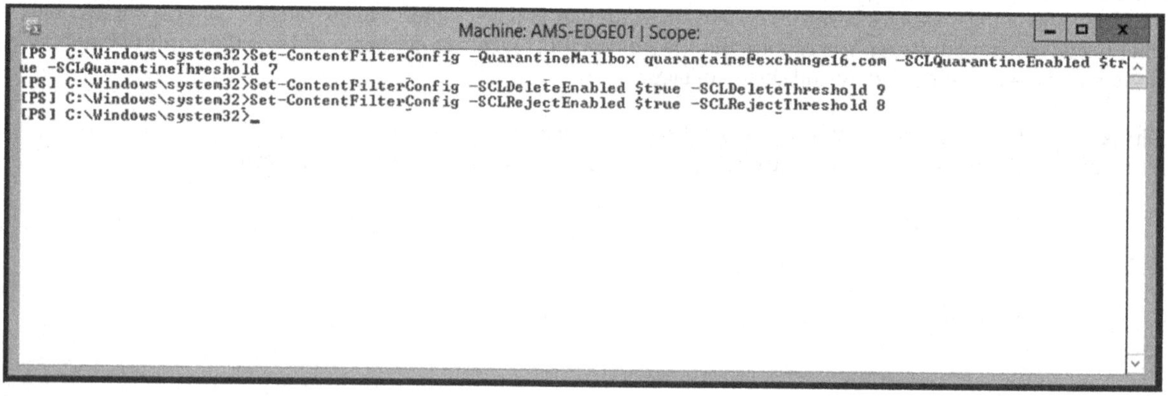

Figure 6-17. *Using the spam confidence level ratings*

It is also possible to bypass certain recipients from content filtering. A common candidate for this is the email address postmaster@contoso.com or abuse@contoso.com. These settings are also made using the Set-ContentFilterConfig cmdlet:

Set-ContentFilterConfig -BypassedRecipients postmaster@exchangelabs.nl, abuse@exchangelabs.nl

There are a couple of best practices you can take into consideration:

1. Use a dedicated mailbox and user account for the quarantine mailbox, and remove the quota limits from this mailbox. If there's a quota on the mailbox and the contents exceed this limit, the mail will get lost.

2. Use a dedicated mailbox database for the quarantine mailbox.

3. Configure Outlook so that the original sender, recipient, and BCC fields are shown in the Message view.

To get an overview of all Content Filter agent settings, you can use the Get-ContentFilterConfig command, as shown in Figure 6-18:

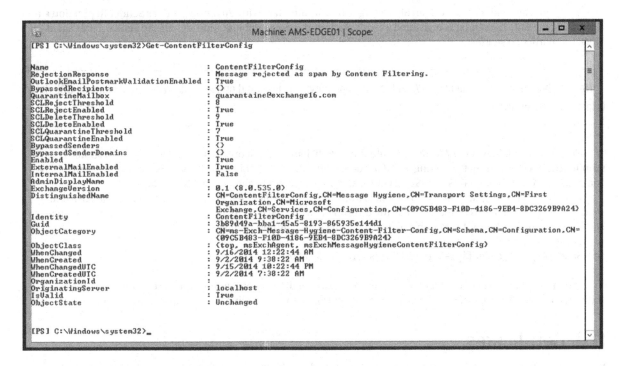

Figure 6-18. *Retrieving all content filtering settings*

Sender Reputation

On the Edge Transport server, a Protocol Analysis agent is running which analyses statistics from SMTP senders. The Protocol Analysis agent is a non-configurable agent and Sender Reputation relies on persistent data that's received from this Protocol Analysis agent.

A sender reputation level (SRL) is calculated based on the following characteristics:

- EHLO/HELO analysis of the sending SMTP server

- Reverse DNS lookup

- SCL ratings of a particular sender

- Open proxy test on the sending SMTP server

Based on the outcome of these tests, an SRL is calculated, and this SRL is an indication of the likelihood of a spammer; it's somewhat like the SCL ratings for individual messages. An SRL rating of 0 indicates that the sending SMTP server most likely is a spam-sending server, while a rating of 9 indicates that the sending SMTP server is a normal SMTP server.

Based on the SRL rating, actions can be taken on the messages as follows:

- Rejected

- Deleted and archived

- Accepted and marked as a blocked sender

By default, all senders start with an SRL rating of 0. Only after receiving 20 messages does Sender Reputation start calculating the SRL. If a sender is registered as a blocked sender, Sender Reputation signals the Sender Filter agent to block this particular sender.

■ **Note**   The SRL is kept in memory. When the Transport service is restarted on the Edge Transport servers, all SRL data is lost and Sender Reputation restarts with 0.

The SRL threshold is set to 7 by default, and this is sufficient for most organizations. However, you should monitor the effectiveness of this setting and if needed, adjust the threshold using the Set-SenderReputationConfig command. This command takes the -SrlBlockThreshold parameter to change the SRL setting.

Another interesting parameter is the -SenderBlockinPeriod, which defines the number of hours a particular sender is blocked when this sender exceeds the threshold. To change the SRL threshold to a value of 6 and set the blocking period to 36 hours, for example, you can use the following command:

```
Set-SenderReputationConfig -SrlBlockThreshold 6 -SenderBlockingPeriod 36
```

When the Transport Edge server's anti-spam configuration is fully configured, you can continue with the other settings, such as the SSL certificates (which is optionally) and can start testing the Transport Edge server.

SSL Certificates

When the Exchange 2013 Edge Transport server is installed, a self-signed certificate is created. This certificate can be used for encryption by the opportunistic TLS feature. Using opportunistic TLS, the Edge Transport servers secure the communication when the receiving SMTP host also supports TLS.

It is not really necesssary to replace the self-signed certificate, but every now and then I see customers who want to install a third-party SSL certificate on the Edge Transport server.

> **Note**   The SSL certificate is also used for encrypting the edge synchronization. If the (self-signed) certificate is replaced by a third-party certificate, the edge subscription needs to be re-created.

The only way to create a new SSL certificate on the Edge Transport server is by using PowerShell. The first step is to generate a request file for the new SSL certificate. This request file is created using the following command:

```
$data = New-ExchangeCertificate -GenerateRequest -SubjectName "c=NL, o=Contoso Enterprise, cn=edge.
contoso.com" -PrivateKeyExportable $true
Set-Content -Path "c:\temp\mailhost.req" -Value $Data
```

The request file is stored in a variable called $data, and the contents of this request are flushed to disk using the Set-Content command.

This request file can be used to request the actual SSL certificate at the certificate authority (CA) of your preference. When the certificate is issued, you receive the actual certificate from your CA. Store this file on the local disk of your Edge Transport server and execute the following command:

```
Import-ExchangeCertificate -FileData ([Byte[]]$(Get-Content -Path c:\temp\edge_contoso_com.cer
-Encoding Byte -ReadCount 0))
```

This will import the certificate on your Edge Transport server.

Important to note here is that you need to execute this step on the server you used to create the certificate request file. If you do this on a different server, you'll end up with an SSL certificate that lacks the corresponding private key, making the certificate useless.

For backup purposes, you want to export the SSL certificate to a local disk and store it in a safe location. The first step is to retrieve the thumbprint of the newly created SSL certificate using the Get-ExchangeCertificate command. You copy and paste the thumbprint to the clipboard of the computer, and execute the following command:

```
$file = Export-ExchangeCertificate -Thumbprint 18A5F6909F8E2668D7E884FBD31D0F87FDCB20E2
-BinaryEncoded $true -Password (Get-Credential).Password
Set-Content -Path c:\temp\edge_contoso_com.pfx -Value $file.FileData -Encoding Byte
```

> **Note**   The Get-Credential command shows a credential windows. Only the password entered in this dialog box is used for exporting the SSL certificate.

Test of the Edge Transport Server

The easiest way to test the installation of your Edge Transport server is to start sending email. You can also use the remote connectivity analyzer (RCA) (www.testexchangeconnectivity.com) to test the environment. To use the analyzer, you open the RCA in your browser and under Internet Email Tests, you select the Outbound SMTP Email option. Then, you enter the IP address of the outbound SMTP server, select the options you want to check, and enter your email address, as shown in Figure 6-19.

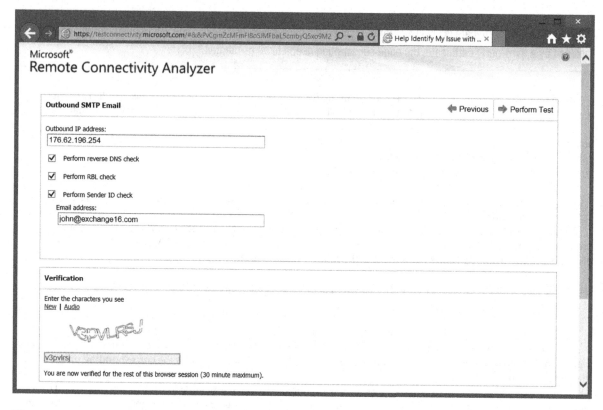

Figure 6-19. *Testing the Outbound SMTP email configuration*

When all is well, you will see the results in seconds; all options should show the green balls with the white checkmark, as shown in Figure 6-20.

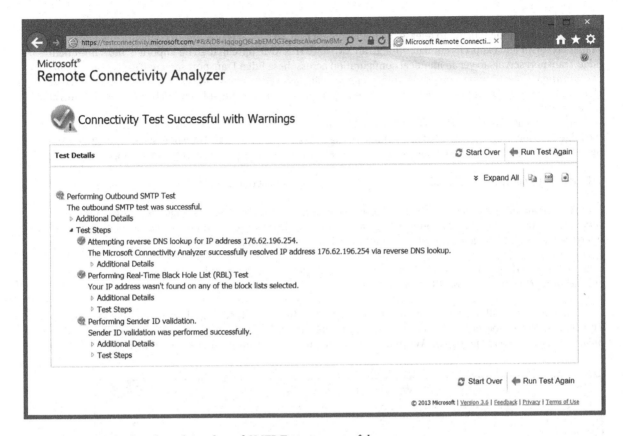

Figure 6-20. *Results that show the outbound SMTP Test was successful*

For a complete and up-to-date overview of all anti-spam and anti-malware cmdlets available in Exchange 2013, visit the Microsoft documentation at `http://bit.ly/AntiSpamCmdlets`.

Export and Import Edge Configuration

Regular Exchange 2013 servers are domain-joined and almost all configuration is stored in Active Directory. This means that configuration information can be shared among multiple Exchange 2013 servers.

For example, information regarding transport rules on Exchange 2013 Mailbox servers is stored in Active Directory, and it is used by all Exchange 2013 Mailbox servers in the organization. The Exchange 2013 Edge Transport server, however, is not a member of the Active Directory domain and therefore configuration information cannot be shared among multiple Edge Transport servers.

■ **Note**   Joining the Edge Transport servers to an Active Directory domain is supported. For example, some customers have an Active Directory domain in their perimeter network for management purposes; it aids deployment of GPOs or System Center clients to domain members. This does not mean the Edge Transport server can use this Active Directory domain, however. Even though they are domain-joined from an Exchange point of view, they are still standalone servers.

As mentioned earlier in the chapter, if you have multiple Exchange 2013 Edge Transport servers, you have to configure them individually. To release the management burden a bit, it is possible to configure one Edge Transport server and export its configuration to an XML file. This XML file can then be imported into subsequent Edge Transport servers to get an identical configuration across these Edge Transport servers. This is called a *cloned configuration*. Note: Cloning works only when you're installing the Edge Transport servers. When making regular changes to the Edge Transport server during normal operation, these changes still have to be made to the individual Edge Transport servers.

Microsoft has written a script that can be used for multiple installations, located in the $ExScripts directory on the Edge Transport server and called ExportEdgeConfig.ps1. To export the Edge Transport server configuration, you open the Exchange Management Shell, navigate to the $ExScripts directory, and enter the following command:

```
.\ExportEdgeConfig.ps1 -CloneConfigData:"C:\Temp\EdgeClonedConfig.xml"
```

This command will generate a configuration file that contains the individual settings of the Edge Transport server. You copy this XML file to another Edge Transport server. To do so, on the other Edge Transport server, you open the Exchange Management Shell and enter the following command:

```
.\ImportEdgeConfig.ps1 -CloneConfigData:"C:\Temp\EdgeClonedConfig.xml" -IsImport $false
-CloneConfigAnswer:"C:\Temp\CloneAnswerFile.xml"
```

This command will run a trial import of the configuration file, and any settings that are not valid for this Edge Transport server are logged into the answer file. Any errors that are logged in the answer file can be edited in the clone answer file, as shown in Figure 6-21. When no changes are needed, the answer file will be empty!

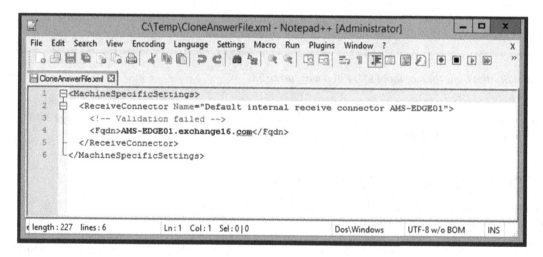

Figure 6-21. *The answer files show any problems that need to be fixed when cloning*

To run a full import to the subsequent Edge Transport server, you can run the same command but change the value of the -IsImport parameter to $true; for example:

```
.\ImportEdgeConfig.ps1 -CloneConfigData:"C:\Temp\EdgeClonedConfig.xml" -IsImport $true
-CloneConfigAnswer:"C:\Temp\CloneAnswerFile.xml"
```

■ **Note** You cannot run the ImportEdgeConfig.ps1 script on an Edge Transport server that's subscribed to the internal Exchange 2013 servers; therefore, you have to do this in advance of creating the edge subscription.

Load-Balancing the Edge Transport Servers

When you have multiple Exchange 2013 Edge Transport servers, most likely you want to load-balance the SMTP traffic. The good thing is that you only have to worry about load-balancing the incoming SMTP traffic; traffic between the Edge Transport servers and the internal Exchange 2013 Mailbox servers is automatically load balanced.

One Edge Transport server is bound to an Active Directory site through the edge subscription. This means that all Exchange 2013 Mailbox servers will use this Edge Transport server. Going the other way, this one Edge Transport server will use all the Exchange 2013 Mailbox servers so that SMTP traffic will be load-balanced across those Mailbox servers using a round robin mechanism.

If you have multiple Edge Transport servers in your perimeter network, then each Edge Transport server will have its own edge subscription. Of course, each Edge Transport server will automatically load-balance the inbound SMTP traffic across all available Exchange 2013 Mailbox servers. The Mailbox servers in turn automatically use all the edge subscriptions and therefore automatically load-balance their outbound SMTP traffic across the multiple Edge Transport servers.

Inbound SMTP traffic originating from external hosts (i.e., from the Internet) is a different story, though. If you have multiple Edge Transport servers, you will have multiple external IP addresses and multiple FQDNs, so you have to distribute that inbound SMTP traffic across these servers. The easiest way to do this is to use multiple MX records in the public DNS. These MX records are used by sending SMTP hosts and by using multiple MX records the inbound connections are automatically distributed.

Another option is to use a (hardware) load balancer for inbound SMTP traffic. In the load balancer, you create a virtual IP (VIP), and this IP address is used in an MX record. This way, only one MX record is used and this MX record points to the load balancer.

In the load balancer, then, you can use layer-4 (L4) load balancing to distribute the incoming requests across all available Edge Transport servers. If for some reason one server fails, the load balancer will automatically disable this server so it is no longer used by the VIP in the load balancer.

So, balancing the load to the Edge Transport servers is not a big deal and is relatively easy to implement.

■ **Note** If you have multiple Edge Transport servers, you can also use Windows Network Load Balancing (NLB) as a load-balancing solution. However, the official Microsoft recommendation is to use a (hardware) load balancer for load-balancing your Exchange traffic.

Exchange 2013 Anti-Malware

The Edge Transport server is all about anti-spam and filtering out messages received from malicious senders. it can do content inspection, but only on certain keywords as a way to filter out unsolicited email. It does not do content inspection to filter out viruses, for example. A legitimate email message coming from a reliable source could still contain a virus and be passed successfully through the Edge Transport server without any problem.

■ **Note**   Message hygiene services in the cloud—for example, from Microsoft Exchange Online Protection—do scan the messages for viruses. If viruses are found, these messages can be cleaned-up or deleted. This is in sharp contrast with the Edge Transport server, which cannot offer this protection.

Besides the anti-spam features of the Edge Transport server, the Exchange 2013 Mailbox server comes with a default anti-malware engine. This anti-malware engine can perform content scanning for viruses. Th Exchange 2013 anti-malware service is a single engine (whereas the old Forefront Protection for Exchange consisted of four separate engines) and it scans all inbound and outbound messages in transit. There's no option to scan messages that are already in the Mailbox database, however; it's only scanning messages in transit.

Malware definition files are downloaded once per hour from the Microsoft download site. This means that the Exchange 2013 Mailbox servers need to be able to access the Internet on port 80. The URL of this download location is http://forefrontdl.microsoft.com/server/scanengineupdate.

It is possible to manually update these definition files. Microsoft has written a script that can be found in the $ExScripts directory, which you can use with the following command, as shown in Figure 6-22:

```
Set-Location $ExScripts
.\Update-MalwareFilteringServer.ps1 -Identity ams-exch02.contoso.com
```

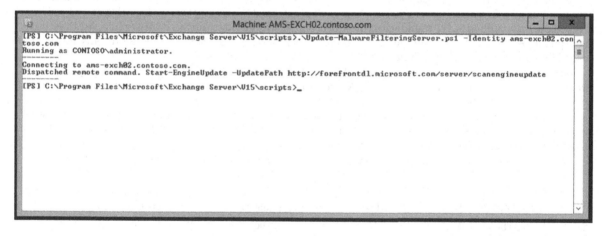

Figure 6-22. *Updating the anti-malware engine using the script*

Another option is to manually download the definition files and store them on a file share. To update the Mailbox server with the definition files stored on a file share, you use the following command:

```
CD $ExScripts
.\Update-MalwareFilteringServer.ps1 -Identity ams-exch01.contoso.com -EngineUpdatePath \\ams-fs01\
UpdateShare
```

> ▉ **Note** In this command, CD is used to change to the proper directory, whereas in the previous command, Set-Location was used. CD is a common command for an IT Pro, as it has been used for years, but it is an alias for the Set-Location command.

When the definition files are updated, events are logged in the event log from source FIPFS. EventID 6033 shows detailed information when the update is downloaded and what version it is, as follows:

```
Log Name:      Application
Source:        Microsoft-Filtering-FIPFS
Date:          9/16/2014 4:34:11 PM
Event ID:      6033
Task Category: None
Level:         Information
Keywords:
User:          NETWORK SERVICE
Computer:      AMS-EXCH02.contoso.com
Description:
MS Filtering Engine Update process performed a successful scan engine update.
 Scan Engine: Microsoft
 Update Path: http://forefrontdl.microsoft.com/server/scanengineupdate
 Last Update time:2014-09-16T14:34:11.000Z
 Engine Version:1.1.11005.0
 Signature Version: 1.185.109.0
```

To disable malware scanning on an Exchange 2013 Mailbox server, you can use the PowerShell script that's located in the $ExScripts Directory, with this command:

```
CD $ExScripts
.\ Disable-Antimalwarescanning.ps1
```

If you want to temporarily stop the malware scanning, you can bypass it instead of disabling it. This can be achieved using the Set-MalwareFilteringServer command:

```
Set-MalwareFilteringServer -Identity ams-exch01 -BypassFiltering $true
```

To stop bypassing the malware filter, you can use the same command with a $false value.

The malware filtering in Exchange 2013 is using default anti-malware policies. The default anti-malware policies can be edited, but not deleted. It is also possible to create custom anti-malware policies that are targeted toward groups of mailboxes.

You can view the default malware filtering policy using the Get-MalwareFilterPolicy command, as shown in Figure 6-23.

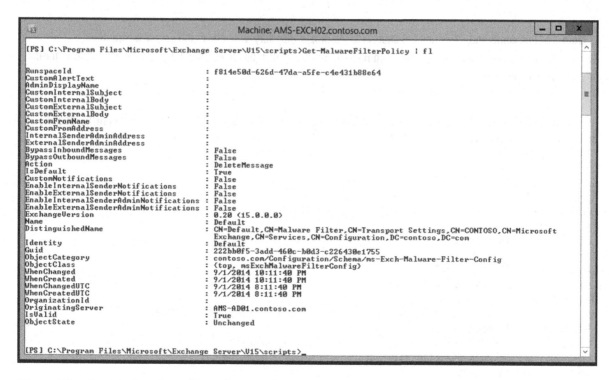

Figure 6-23. *The default malware filter policy in Exchange 2013*

You can also create custom alert messages for both internal and external alerts, as well as what should happen when an infected message is found. New malware filter policies can be created using the `New-MalwareFilterPolicy` command. The following example creates a new malware filter policy named "Contoso Malware Filter Policy" that enables notifications to the administrator mailbox. Messages that contain malware are blocked, and the sender of the message is not notified.

```
New-MalwareFilterPolicy -Name "Contoso Malware Filter Policy"
-EnableInternalSenderAdminNotifications $true -InternalSenderAdminAddress administrator@contoso.com
```

If you want to use a custom notification, you have to use the `–CustomNotifications` parameter and set it to $true. At the same time, you have to configure the following options:

- `CustomFromAddress`

- `CustomFromName`

- `CustomExternalSubject`

- `CustomExternalBody`

- `CustomInternalSubject`

- `CustomInternalBody`

A malware filter rule contains one or more malware filter policies; a malware filter rule can be assigned to a mailbox. For example, to create a new malware filter rule that contains the Contoso malware filter policy created in the previous example, you can use the `New-MalwareFilterRule` command as follows:

```
New-MalwareFilterRule -Name "Contoso Recipients Rule" -MalwareFilterPolicy "Contoso Malware Filter
Policy" -RecipientDomainIs contoso.com
```

You can use the −SentTo parameter to select the recipients to whom the malware filter rule is applied. For a broader scope, you can use the −SentToMemberOf parameter to define the members of a distribution group where the malware filter rule will be applied.

You can test the anti-malware settings using the EICAR test virus. This is a small text file that contains a test virus pattern, and is used by anti-virus and anti-malware vendors for testing purposes. To do so, you create a new text file and copy this exact line into the text file:

```
X5O!P%@AP[4\PZX54(P^)7CC)7}$EICAR-STANDARD-ANTIVIRUS-TEST-FILE!$H+H*
```

Make sure that this is the only string in the file. When done, you will have a 68-byte file that can be stored as EICAR.TXT. Be careful with local virus scanners on your workstation, as these scanners will pick up the EICAR pattern as well. Send a new message to yourself, attach the EICAR.TXT file, and see what happens.

Summary

Exchange Server 2013 SP1 has a new server role called the Edge Transport server. This server is typically located in the perimeter network and is used for anti-spam purposes. It can perform the most standard types of anti-spam actions, like connection filtering, sender filtering, recipient filtering, and content filtering.

The only management interface of the Exchange 2013 Edge Transport server is the Exchange Management Shell. The Edge Transport server is not a member of the internal Active Directory domain, and as such it cannot use this method to share configuration information as can regular Exchange 2013 servers. If you have multiple Edge Transport servers, you can configure the first Edge Transport server and clone the configuration to the remaining Edge Transport servers.

The Exchange 2013 Mailbox server comes with a built-in anti-malware solution. It's not as efficient as the former Forefront Protection for Exchange, but it can perform the most basic anti-malware functions. This anti-malware solution only scans messages in transit, however; it does not scan messages that are stored in the mailbox database.

As you have seen in this chapter configuration of the Edge Transport server is quite some work and is prone to error. A viable alternative to using the Edge Transport server for hygiene purposes is to employ an online anti-spam (and anti-virus) solution like Microsoft Exchange Online Protection. Of course, this comes with a monthly fee per mailbox, but it saves an IT administrator a lot of hassle (plus servers, licenses, and maintenance!).

CHAPTER 7

■ ■ ■

Backup, Restore, and Disaster Recovery in Exchange Server 2013

One of the things a typical Exchange Server administrator doesn't want to talk about is restoring information or disaster recovery, because those can be so very difficult to do in Exchange 2013. The first matter, backing up data, is not that difficult; you just install a backup application and have it run on a regular basis. So far, no need to worry.

But what happens if a Mailbox database crashes and you've got users complaining they can't work? What do you do then? What's a good time to start looking at tools like ESEUTIL? Or, when do you decide to restore a mailbox database from your backup?

Even worse, what happens when an entire Exchange 2013 server crashes and is completely lost? Do you rebuild the server? Do you restore it from backup? Or, maybe you rely on snapshot technology, which you've been told is a good thing?

In this chapter we're going to explore backup technologies in Exchange 2013. In particular, we'll cover:

- **VSS backups,** or Volume Shadowcopy service, sometimes also referred to as "snapshot backup." We'll explore the default Windows Server Backup (WSB) and a low-level tool called DiskShadow, which shows you what's happening when you're creating a VSS backup.

- **Restoring techniques,** to both a standard location and an alternative location.

- **Recovery techniques,** using ESEUTIL.

- **Disaster recovery techniques,** to rebuild an entire server.

- **Exchange Native Data Protection,** sometimes also referred to as "backupless environment."

When your Exchange 2013 server crashes dramatically, it's time to recover your Exchange Server 2013, and we're going to explore your options there as well. In short, we're going to rebuild and recover the entire Exchange 2013 server, but we'll also have a look at rebuilding and recovering a mailbox database.

The last topic that's explored in this chapter is a new technology introduced in Exchange 2010 (so it's not so new), called *Exchange Native Data Protection.* This is also sometimes referred to as a "backupless" Exchange environment. This backupless thing scares a lot of IT administrators, but in fact it is possible to recover from all major outages without having a backup. The only thing you have to do is evaluate the requirements for implementing this Exchange Native Data Protection solution to determine if it fits your needs.

Let's get started.

Backing up Exchange 2013

Backing up Exchange 2013 is a process of storing your Exchange server data, like the mailbox databases, on another medium. This medium, in turn, can be stored on another location as a safeguard if you face the loss of an entire location.

But not only mailbox databases need to be backed up; you can also back up information like your transport log files or protocol log files, SSL certificates, or maybe even the entire Exchange 2013 Server.

Before we dive into backing up Exchange 2013, especially the mailbox databases, though, we have to take a closer look at the mailbox databases themselves and the database internals. Only this way can you fully understand what's happening when a backup of a mailbox database is created; this knowledge is necessary to successfully recover a mailbox database after a failure.

A Refresher on Mailbox Database Technologies

In Chapter 4, I explained the basic principles of the Exchange Server mailbox database and its database engine. The database engine in Exchange 2013 is based on ESE, or *extensible storage engine*. This is a database engine that's highly optimized for use with Exchange Server.

A mailbox database consists of several parts:

- The mailbox database, where the actual data is stored in transactions.

- The transaction log files, where the transactions are stored as soon as processing of a transaction is finished in memory.

- The checkpoint file, which keeps track of which transactions are stored in the transaction log files but have not yet been flushed to the mailbox database.

- Reserved transaction log files, which are stored as reserved transaction log files in case a disk where these transaction log files are stored becomes full.

Transactions are processed in memory, and as soon as the processing of a transaction has finished, the transaction is stored immediately in a transaction log file. At this time the transaction is not committed to the mailbox database file but is kept in memory; since the transaction is stored safely in a transaction log file, data that suffers a server crash is fully recoverable.

Later on these transactions are flushed into the mailbox database. To keep track of which transactions are flushed into the mailbox database, ESE uses a checkpoint file. This checkpoint file points to the location in the transaction log files of the latest transaction that has been flushed into the mailbox database. Newer transactions than are located in this checkpoint file are not in the mailbox databases, while older transactions are.

It's important to remember is that all transactions are always stored in the transaction log files before they are flushed into the mailbox database. More detailed information regarding the mailbox database and its database engine can be found in Chapter 4. You need to know the workings of the mailbox database and its database technologies so as to understand the backup and restore technologies used in Exchange 2013, but also as might be useful for recovery purposes.

The Backup Technologies

The Exchange 2013 mailbox databases are backed up using snapshots. Microsoft utilizes a framework for this called the *Volume Shadowcopy service* (VSS). Let's look at what VSS is and how it works with Exchange 2013.

VSS Backup

Windows Server 2003 was the first Microsoft operating system capable of creating snapshot backups using the Volume Shadowcopy service (VSS) framework. Unfortunately, in those days it was not possible to create VSS backups of Exchange Server itself. Exchange Server 2007 running on Windows Server 2008 was the first version of Exchange Server capable of using the VSS technology, and VSS backups have been in use in Exchange Server ever since.

There are two kinds of snapshot backups:

- **Clone** This is a full copy or split mirror. In this scenario, a complete copy, or mirror image, is maintained until an application or administrator effectively "breaks" the mirror. From this point on, the original and the clone are fully independent of each other. The mirror copy is effectively frozen in time.

- **Copy on Write** This is a differential copy. A shadow copy is created that is different from a full copy of the original data, made before the original data has been overwritten. Effectively, the backup copy consists of the data in the shadow copy combined with the data in the original location. Both copies need to be available to reconstruct the original data.

The VSS consists of the VSS service itself, as well as requestors, writers, and providers. The central part is the VSS running on the computer. It is responsible for coordinating all activities concerning backups and restores.

The *requestor* typically is the backup application. This can be the default out-of-the-box Windows Server Backup, or it can be any third-party backup solution or a Windows tool like DiskShadow.

The *writer* is the application-specific part of VSS. Writers exist for Microsoft Exchange, Active Directory, IIS, NTFS, SQL Server, and so on. The Exchange writer is responsible for coordinating all Exchange-related activities, such as flushing data to the mailbox database, freezing the mailbox database during the VSS snapshot, and so on.

In Exchange Server 2010, the writer had two parts: one writer inside the Microsoft Information Store (`store.exe`) and one inside the Microsoft Exchange Replication service (`MSExchangeRepl.exe`). In Exchange 2013, the functions of the Information Store writer have been moved to the Microsoft Exchange Replication service, thereby forming one new writer, called *Exchange writer*. This new writer is used by Exchange-aware backup applications, which include the out-of-the-box Windows Server Backup, to create snapshot backups of both the active copy and the passive copies of a mailbox database.

The *provider* works with storage. It can be the Windows provider, which can create copy-on-write snapshots of a disk, or it can be a vendor-specific hardware provider.

Thus, the VSS is at the core, as can be seen in Figure 7-1. The arrows show the communication paths within the VSS function.

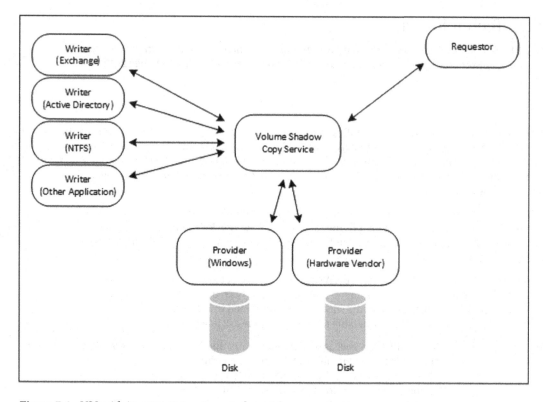

Figure 7-1. *VSS with its requestor, writers, and providers*

For a VSS backup to be created, the following steps occur sequentially:

1. The backup application or requestor sends a command to the VSS to make a shadow copy of the mailbox database.

2. The VSS sends a command to the Exchange writer to prepare for a snapshot backup.

3. The VSS sends a command to the appropriate provider to create a shadow copy of the mailbox database. (The storage provider can be a hardware storage provider provided by the hardware vendor or the default Windows storage provider.)

4. The Exchange writer temporarily stops or pauses the mailbox database and puts it into read-only mode; all data in the server memory is then flushed to the mailbox database. Also, a log file rollover is performed to make sure that all data will be in the backup set. This holds for a couple of seconds while the snapshot is taken. All write IOs are queued at this point.

5. The shadow copy is created.

6. The VSS releases the Exchange server to resume ordinary operations, and all queued write IOs are completed.

7. The VSS queries the Exchange writer to confirm that the write IOs were successfully held while the snapshot was taken. If the write operations were not successfully held, there could potentially be an inconsistent shadow copy. If this is the case, the shadow copy is deleted and the requestor is notified of the failed snapshot.

8. If the snapshot was successful, the requestor verifies the integrity of the backup set (the clone). If the clone integrity is good, the requestor informs Exchange Server that the snapshot was successful. The snapshot can now be transferred to a backup device.

9. When all data is successfully moved to the backup device, the requestor informs VSS that the backup was successful and that the log files can be purged.

In contrast to the streaming backup, where consistency is checked by ESE, the Exchange writer itself does not perform this consistency check.

Steps 1 through 6 usually take between 10 and 15 seconds. Note that this is the time it takes to take the actual snapshot; it does not include the time needed to write all the data to the backup device which is step 9 in the above list. Depending on the size of the mailbox database, this step can take up to several hours to complete.

If you're already working with Exchange Server, you might be familiar with a VSS administrative tool called VSSADMIN. You can use VSSADMIN to quickly check the various components in the VSS infrastructure. For example, to list all the VSS writers on a server, simply use the VSSADMIN List Writers command in a command prompt window. For Exchange Server 2013, the output will be something like that shown in Figure 7-2.

Figure 7-2. *A list of VSS writers on an Exchange 2013 server*

Similarly, you can list the VSS providers, existing shadow copies, or volumes eligible for creating shadow copies. VSSADMIN, however, was replaced in Windows 2008 by a new administrative tool called DiskShadow, which is more powerful than VSSADMIN and as such will return more detailed information about the VSS infrastructure. It is even possible to create backups using DiskShadow (discussed later in this chapter).

Backing up a Mailbox Database

For backing up your mailbox databases, there are various applications available. Which one you use is a matter of personal experience (or maybe your company has a license for some applications), but the most important factor in making your choice is that the application be "Exchange aware." Windows Server 2008 R2 and later versions were shipped with Windows Server Backup (WSB), which is also capable of backing up Exchange 2013 mailbox databases. It's a pretty simple and limited backup application, but it is used quite often. DiskShadow is a low-level tool you can use for backing up your Exchange 2010 mailbox databases, but I don't recommend it for daily use because it is quite complex. Let's discuss both applications.

Using WSB in PowerShell

Exchange 2013 contains a VSS plug-in that can be used with WSB. Although WSB has limited functionality, it can create backups and restore them if needed. Another advantage of WSB is that it's free and comes with Windows Server 2008 R2 and Windows Server 2012.

To install Windows Server Backup, you open PowerShell and enter the following command:

```
Add-WindowsFeature -Name Windows-Server-Backup
```

■ **Note** PowerShell 3.0, included in Windows 2012, has a new feature called *module auto-loading*. When you're adding features that are dependent on other modules, these modules are automatically loaded. If you want to add the Windows Server Backup feature in Windows 2008 R2, you have to use the Import-Module ServerManager command before using the Add-WindowsFeature command.

When WSB is installed, you then load the WSB PowerShell snap-in each time you run Windows PowerShell. You can do this by entering the following command in PowerShell:

```
Import-Module WindowsServerBackup
```

■ **Note** To get an overview of all available WSB cmdlets, you can use the following URL: http://bit.ly/WSBCommands. You can also use the Get-Command -Module WindowsServerBackup command on the Exchange Server.

WSB uses a backup policy that needs to be created at the outset. You can use the New-WBPolicy command to create a new policy; to store it in a variable, you then use the following command: $WBPolicy = New-WBPolicy. This will create an empty policy that can be shown on the console by calling the variable, as displayed in Figure 7-3.

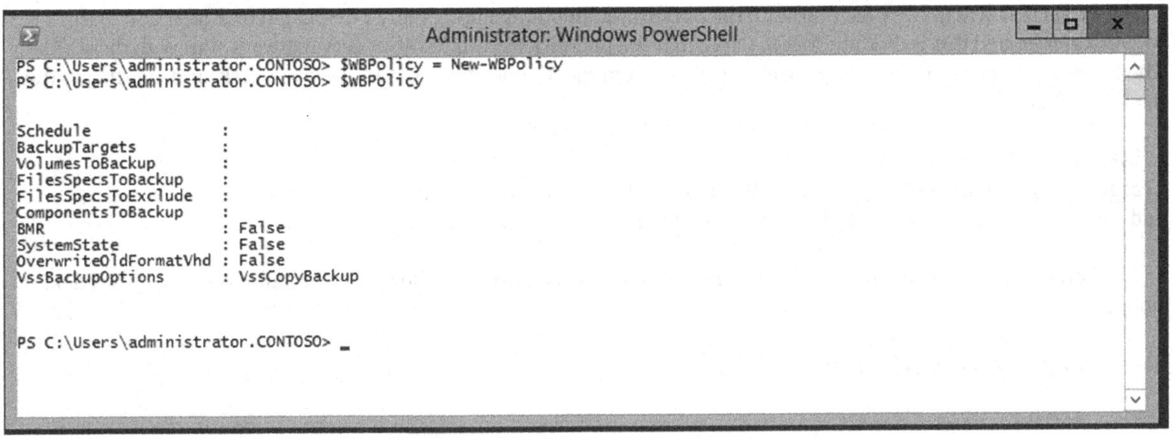

Figure 7-3. *Newly created, and empty, WSB policy*

This policy now needs to be populated with the following configuration options:

- Schedule: when the backup will be running.

- VSS options: whether a full backup or a copy backup will be created.

- Volumes to backups: the volumes containing the mailbox databases.

- Target disk: a disk where the backup will be stored.

To set the schedule and add it to the backup policy, you can use the following commands:

```
$Schedule = Set-Date "10/29/2014 01:30:00"
Set-WBSchedule -Policy $WBPolicy -Schedule $Schedule
```

This will set the next backup to be run at October 15, 2014, at 01:30 A.M., and it will run every 24 hours.

The VSS options are set to establish what kinds of backups will be created. For example, a full backup will create a complete backup of the mailbox database (or databases) on the stated volume and purge the accompanying transaction log files when the backup has been completed successfully. You can set the VSS full backup option by using the –VssFullBackup switch parameter. The other option is to create a VSS copy backup, which is a full backup, but the transaction log files aren't purged when the backup is created successfully. To set this latter option, you can use the following command:

```
Set-WBVssBackupOptions -Policy $WBPolicy –VssFullBackup
```

In our example, there are three disks attached to the Mailbox server, and these disks are mounted in a directory called C:\ExchVols. You can use the following commands to create an array that contains all the volumes in the C:\ExchVols directory, and add it to the backup policy, as follows:

```
$Volumes = Get-WBVolume -AllVolumes | Where-Object {$_.MountPath -like "C:\ExchVols\*"}
Add-WBVolume -Policy $WBPolicy -Volume $Volumes
```

A target disk will then be used to store the backup set. In our example, there's dedicated disk attached to the Mailbox server, and this is disk number 5. (Note that the first disk in your Mailbox server always start with disk 0.) The following three commands will retrieve all disks from the Mailbox server, create a target disk, and add this to the backup policy:

```
$Disks = Get-WBDisk
$Target = New-WBBackupTarget -Disk $Disks[5] -Label "Backup Disks"
Add-WBBackupTarget -Policy $WBPolicy -Target $Target
```

When everything in the backup policy is configured, you can use the following command to activate the backup policy:

```
Set-WBPolicy -Policy $WBPolicy -Force
```

■ **Note**   The -Force option is used to bypass a confirmation when running the Set-WBPolicy command.

The backup will start automatically during the next cycle that's been configured with the schedule option, but to start the backup before then, you can use the following command:

```
Get-WBPolicy | Start-WBBackup
```

When this command is executed, a full VSS backup of the volumes containing the mailbox databases will be created. It will start with a VSS snapshot of these volumes, followed by a consistency check of the mailbox databases to ensure the mailbox database's integrity.

When the consistency check is finished successfully, the data is backed up to the backup location; the backup can take a couple of hours if you have a large mailbox database.

If you check the application log in the event viewer, you'll see the following entries:

- *Event ID 2021 (MSExchangeRepl)* Successfully collected metadata document in preparation for backup.

- *Event ID 2110 (MSExchangeRepl)* Successfully prepared for a full or a copy backup of database MDB01.

- *Event ID 2023 (MSExchangeRepl)* VSS writer successfully prepared for backup.

- *Event ID 2005 (ESE)* Shadow copy instance started.

- *Event ID 2025 (MSExchangeRepl)* VSS successfully prepared for a snapshot.

- *Event ID 2001 (ESE)* MDB01 shadow copy freeze started.

- *Event ID 2027 (MSExchangeRepl)* VSS writer instance has successfully frozen the databases.

- *Event ID 2003 (ESE)* MDB01 shadow copy freeze ended.

- *Event ID 2029 (MSExchangeRepl)* VSS writer instance has successfully thawed the databases.

- *Event ID 2035 (MSExchangeRepl)* VSS writer has successfully processed the post-snapshot event.

- *Event ID 2021 (MSExchangeRepl)* VSS writer has successfully collected the metadata document in preparation for backup.

- *Event ID 224 (ESE)* MDB01 deleting log files C:\ExchVols\MDB01\Log Files\E0000000001.log to C:\ExchVols\MDB01\Log Files\E000000002B.log.

- *Event ID 225 (ESE)* MDB01—no log files can be truncated; will be logged instead of Event ID 224 when circular logging is used.

- *Event ID 2046 (MSExchangeRepl)* VSS writer has successfully completed the backup of database MDB01.

- *Event ID 2006 (ESE)* MDB01 shadow copy completed successfully.

- *Event ID 2033 (MSExchangeRepl)* VSS writer has successfully processed the backup completion event.

- *Event ID 2037 (MSExchangeRepl)* VSS writer backup has been successfully shut down.

When you check the location of the log files using Windows Explorer, you'll notice that most of the log files have indeed been purged. The information in the mailbox database itself has also been updated with backup information. You can use the following command to retrieve backup information from the mailbox database in EMS, and see information similar to that shown in Figure 7-4:

```
Get-MailboxDatabase -Identity MDB01 -Status | Select Name,*backup*
```

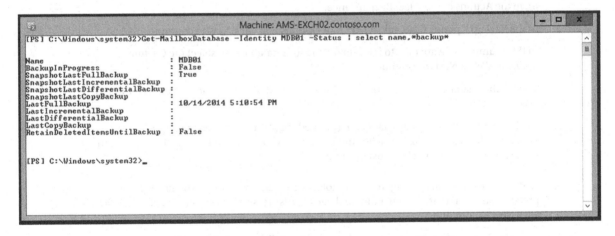

Figure 7-4. *Checking the backup status using the EMS*

You can also use the `ESEUTIL /MH MDB01.edb` command to check the header for backup information; if so, you'll see something like this:

```
Previous Full Backup:
        Log Gen: 4636-4637 (0x121c-0x121d) - OSSnapshot
          Mark: (0x121E,1,0)
          Mark: 10/14/2014 17:10:54.015

Current Full Backup:
        Log Gen: 0-0 (0x0-0x0)
          Mark: (0x0,0,0)
          Mark: 00/00/1900 00:00:00.000
```

> ■ **Note**   It is only possible to check the header information of a mailbox database when the database is dismounted. If the database is mounted, an error saying "The file is in use" is shown.

You might ask yourself why this information is written under Previous Full Backup, while the entry under Current Full Backup is empty. This is because when you create a backup, the entry Current Full Backup is written with information regarding the backup as it runs. When the backup is finished, the entries are moved from the Current Full Backup section to the Previous Full Backup section, and the Current Full Backup is emptied. When a backup is restored to disk, and you check the header information after a restore, you can always identify the database as a backup that's been restored instead of a "normal" mailbox database because it will show as Previous Full Backup.

Using the Windows Server Backup GUI

I can imagine that, for backup purposes, you don't want to use PowerShell; although it's interesting, it can also become complex; let's look at the Graphical User Interface (GUI) as well.

To create a backup of your Exchange 2013 databases, you use the following steps:

1. In the administrative tools section, select Windows Server Backup. This is an MMC snap-in. In the Actions pane, select Backup Once.

2. In the Backup Options page, select Different Options and click Next to continue.

3. In this example we want only to back up the mailbox database, so select the Custom option and click Next to continue.

4. The mailbox database is located on disk C:\ExchVols\MDB01; use the Add Items button to select this disk.

5. To change the type of backup that's being created, click the Advanced Settings button, select the VSS Settings tab, and select the VSS Full Backup radio button. Click OK to return to the previous page and click Next to continue.

6. WSB has the option of backing up to a remote share or to a local disk, whichever you prefer. On our server there's an additional backup disk (disk X), so select Local Drives and click Next to continue.

7. In the Backup Destination drop-down box, select the disk where the backup needs to be stored; on our server this would be disk X. Click Next to continue.

8. The selection is now complete. Click Backup to start the actual backup process.

> ■ **Note**   By default, WSB will create a copy backup instead of a full backup. This is understandable, as it will not interfere with a normal backup cycle when you're using another backup solution and you want to test using WSB. If you want to make a regular backup using WSB, make sure you change this setting. This is a common pitfall with WSB.

The backup will now start with the creation of the VSS snapshot, and it will perform a consistency check of the mailbox data, as shown in Figure 7-5. Be aware that this information can be visible for a small amount of time, especially when the mailbox database is not that large and the consistency check takes only a few seconds. This backup status check is the only visual indication you have that an Exchange-aware backup is running.

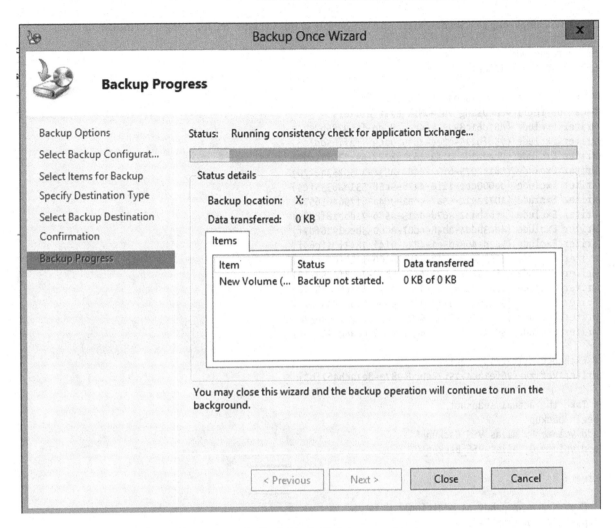

Figure 7-5. *Windows Server Backup automatically checks for database consistency*

When the consistency check is finished successfully, the data is backed up to the backup location, and after a while (which can take a couple of hours if you have a large mailbox database), the backup is completed.

Using DiskShadow to Create Backups

As mentioned earlier, DiskShadow is a VSS management tool you can use to manage your VSS infrastructure at a low level. DiskShadow lets you check your writers, providers, shadow copies, and so on much as with VSSADMIN, but you'll get more detail. You can also use DiskShadow to create VSS snapshots on a low level, which is a great way to demonstrate what exactly happens during VSS backup creation.

DiskShadow can be used in interactive mode, but it can also be used in scripting mode, where it accepts input from a text file. For example, in our earlier Contoso environment, there were two Exchange 2013 multi-role servers at the Amsterdam site, and these were configured in a DAG. Each server has one active mailbox database and one passive mailbox database. The mailbox databases are located on drive F: (DB01) and driver G: (DB02).

When employing DiskShadow to create a VSS backup in this scenario, the following input file can be used:

```
SET verbose on
SET context persistent

# Exclude other writers on Exchange Server
# Can be retrieved using VSSADMIN List Writers
Writer Exclude {d61d61c8-d73a-4eee-8cdd-f6f9786b7124}
Writer Exclude {75dfb225-e2e4-4d39-9ac9-ffaff65ddf06}
Writer Exclude {0bada1de-01a9-4625-8278-69e735f39dd2}
Writer Exclude {e8132975-6f93-4464-a53e-1050253ae220}
Writer Exclude {be000cbe-11fe-4426-9c58-531aa6355fc4}
Writer Exclude {1072ae1c-e5a7-4ea1-9e4a-6f7964656570}
Writer Exclude {afbab4a2-367d-4d15-a586-71dbb18f8485}
Writer Exclude {4dc3bdd4-ab48-4d07-adb0-3bee2926fd7f}
Writer Exclude {542da469-d3e1-473c-9f4f-7847f01fc64f}
Writer Exclude {4969d978-be47-48b0-b100-f328f07ac1e0}
Writer Exclude {a6ad56c2-b509-4e6c-bb19-49d8f43532f0}
Writer Exclude {2a40fd15-dfca-4aa8-a654-1f8c654603f6}
Writer Exclude {7e47b561-971a-46e6-96b9-696eeaa53b2a}
Writer Exclude {41e12264-35d8-479b-8e5c-9b23d1dad37e}
Writer Exclude {59b1f0cf-90ef-465f-9609-6ca8b2938366}

# Exchange writer is required
Writer Verify {76fe1ac4-15f7-4bcd-987e-8e1acb462fb7}

# Take the actual snapshot
begin backup
add volume F: alias VSS_Backup_F
add volume G: alias VSS_Backup_G

create

# Expose the snapshot as additional drive S:
expose %VSS_Backup_F% S:
expose %VSS_Backup_G% T:

End backup
```

The first two entries are to turn on verbose logging and set the context to persistent so the information won't be lost. Then, all VSS writers on the Exchange servers are disabled except the VSS Exchange writer. The GUIDs of the VSS writers can be retrieved by using the VSSADMIN List Writers command.

Volumes F: and G: are used for creating the VSS snapshots, and an alias VSS_Backup_F and VSS_Backup_G is assigned. (You could use any readable name you like.)

At this point, the actual snapshot is created using the CREATE command. In Windows, this is a copy-on-write snapshot whereby the snapshot information is written on the same disk and on the mailbox database (i.e., drive F: and drive G:), but it's not visible for a regular user or administrator. (All the steps as explained in the previous section are performed here, and all the events are recorded in the event log as well.) This step usually takes between 15 and 30 seconds, depending on the hardware that's used.

When the snapshot is created, it is exposed using the EXPOSE command. This way it is visible as a regular disk to the operating system, and thus accessible, as shown in Figure 7-6.

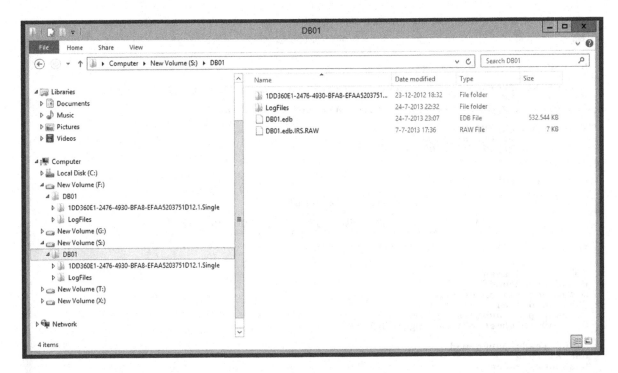

Figure 7-6. *The VSS snapshots are published as additional drives in Windows*

When the backup in DiskShadow is ended using the End Backup command, a request is sent to ESE to purge any log files that are no longer needed for recovery purposes. If the VSS snapshot was created on a single Exchange server, or a DAG member with active copies of the mailbox database, then the request is processed locally. If the snapshot was created using a passive copy of a mailbox database, the request is automatically sent to the Mailbox server that is hosting the active copy of the mailbox database. The log files are purged on that particular Mailbox server, and the truncation itself is replicated to the Mailbox servers hosting the passive copies of the mailbox database. This means that you no longer need to know which mailbox database in a DAG you back up; the appropriate log files are automatically purged.

This is the pure VSS snapshot function: a snapshot of the mailbox database is created, and its log files are purged (when successful, of course). But remember that the mailbox database has not been checked for consistency, nor has it been backed up to a safe location. To check the consistency of a mailbox database, you use the ESEUTIL tool again, but now with the /k switch:

```
ESEUTIL /K db01.edb
```

This command will read all the pages in the database and check the consistency of all those pages, as shown in Figure 7-7.

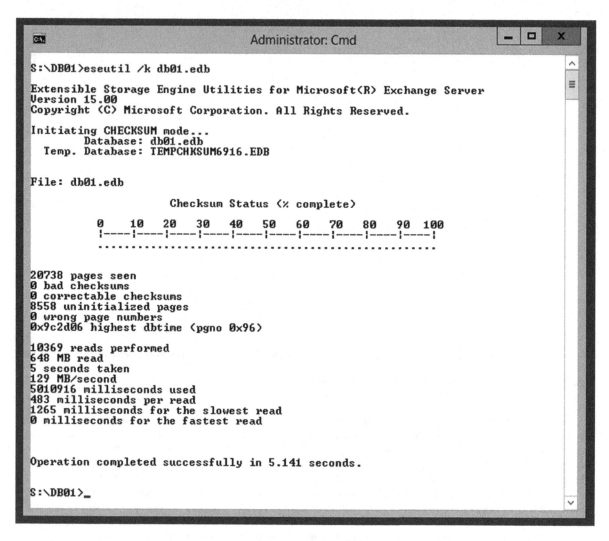

Figure 7-7. Checking the database consistency using the ESEUTIL tool

The final step in a backup, then, is to copy the mailbox database snapshots from the published locations (drive S: and drive T:) to another safe location using, for example, Explorer. Once this is done, you have been successful in manually creating a full backup.

■ **Note**   Don't forget to remove the exposed VSS snapshots using the UNEXPOSE command in DiskShadow, and remove the actual VSS shadow copies using the DELETE SHADOWS command.

Backup of Other Configuration Information

The previous section discussed how to back up mailbox databases in Exchange 2013, since this is the most important aspect of an Exchange server's role. There are a couple more things that need to be backed up, however, either in a regular backup sequence or maybe after there have been configuration changes. For example:

- **Log files** (not transaction log files), as Exchange 2013 logs quite a lot of information in log files—for instance, in IIS log files located `C:\inetpub\logs\logfiles,` which contain logging from all HTTPS-based clients like Outlook WebApp, Exchange Web Services, Autodiscover, Outlook Anywhere, and ActiveSync.

- **SMTP Transport Protocol logs**, located in `C:\Program Files\Microsoft\Exchange Server\V15\TransportRoles\Logs\ Hub\ProtocolLog`. These are disabled by default, but when enabled these might be included in a daily backup routine.

- **Message tracking information**, located in `C:\Program Files\Microsoft\Exchange Server\V15\TransportRoles\ Logs\MessageTracking`.

- **Entire directory**, depending on the (legal) backup requirements of your company; it might be necessary to back up the entire logging directory in `C:\Program Files\Microsoft\Exchange Server\V15\Logging`.

- **CONFIG files,** such as transport configuration files located in `C:\Program Files\Microsoft\ Exchange Server\V15\Bin`. This file is used to relocate the SMTP message database and log files to another location. No need to include this in a daily backup sequence, but it is necessary to back up after configuration changes.

- **SSL certificate**, especially on the Exchange 2013 Client Access server. No need to back up this on a daily basis, but you should back up after the initial installation of the certificate. It is needed when rebuilding a Client Access server, or maybe when adding an additional Client Access server. Make sure that when you create a backup of your SSL certificate you also include the private key in the certificate backup. If not, it's still useless when rebuilding your Client Access server.

- **System State or entire server,** depending on your disaster recovery plan. You might want to back up the server's system state, or maybe the entire server, for rebuilding purposes. (We'll get back to this later in this chapter.)

When using server virtualization, it is an option to back up the entire virtual machine using a backup solution. Veeam, for example, is a third-party vendor that offers backup solutions in a virtual environment. Veeam can back up the VMs, and using the Hyper-V Integration Components, the VSS backup information is sent to the operating system inside the VM. This way the virtual machine is also aware that a snapshot is being made.

Restoring Exchange Server 2013

Backing up your Exchange 2013 environment does make sense, but restoring the backup is even more important. In all my years as an Exchange consultant I have regularly met customers who thought that their backup solutions were fine, but they did not have any idea how to restore them if needed. The worst way to find out is during a disaster, when you must restore information rapidly, as there likely are hundreds of users and managers complaining. Most often, the restoration will fail at this moment if there's lack of experience.

■ **Note**   Restoring your Exchange backups is not a daily management routine. Therefore, it is not feasible to create an entire restore process in PowerShell. Doing so is a complex task and very labor-intensive. This section only covers the Windows Server Backup GUI.

Here, I focus on restoring the mailbox databases, since these are where all the data is. In the next part, I explain how to restore the Exchange servers as part of a disaster recovery operation.

There are two options for restoring mailbox databases:

- **Restore the mailbox database to its original location** In this scenario, the original mailbox database is taken offline and is overwritten by the mailbox database in the backup set. Since all the information is also stored in the log files, the information processed by the Mailbox server since the last backup was created will automatically be replayed by the Mailbox server. If all goes well, no information, or almost no information, will be lost and the mailbox database will be in the same state as before.

- **Restore the mailbox database to another location** In this scenario, the mailbox database from the backup set is restored to another location, most likely a dedicated restore disk on your Mailbox server. When the mailbox database is restored to another location, the original mailbox database can continue running and thus continue servicing client requests. A recovery mailbox database can be used as well. This is a special mailbox database, not visible for regular clients (only for the Exchange administrator), that can be used to restore a particular mailbox; you can move this mailbox into the production mailbox database or export it to a PST file.

Restoring a Mailbox Database to Its Original Location

A lot of interesting technologies are used to make the mailbox database backup process as smooth as possible without interrupting any users. Restoring a mailbox database to its original location is straightforward work.

The mailbox database has to be taken offline, and thus users will face some downtime because Exchange Server is not available anymore. The mailbox database is then restored from the backup set, additional log files are replayed automatically, and the mailbox database can then be mounted again. There's nothing fancy to do when restoring a mailbox database.

In the previous section, WSB was used to back up the mailbox database, so you have to use WSB again to restore the mailbox database. For testing purposes, you can log on to the mailbox before the restore action and send some messages around to see if these are actually replayed after the backup is restored. To restore a previous backup using WSB, you can use these steps:

1.   Log on to the Exchange 2013 Mailbox server and dismount the mailbox database.

2.   Log in to the EAC as an administrator. In the Feature pane, select Servers and then select the Databases tab.

3.   Select the Mailbox database you want to restore (and you dismounted in step 1), and open its properties. In the navigation menu, select Maintenance and check the "This database can be overwritten by a restore" checkbox, as shown in Figure 7-8.

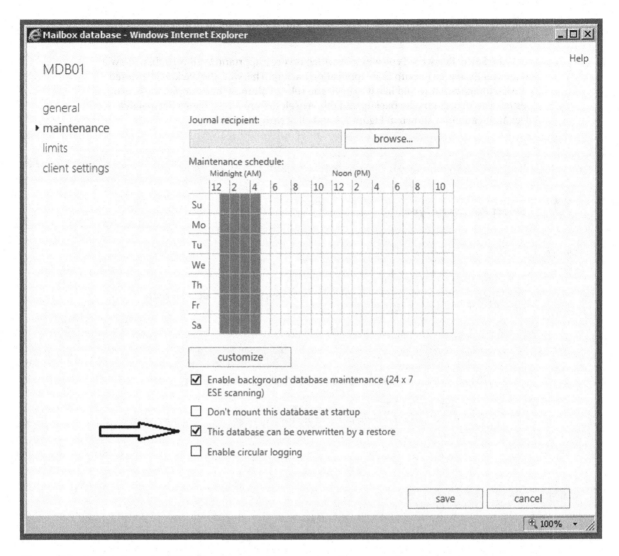

Figure 7-8. *Setting the option "This database can be overwritten by a restore"*

■ **Note** This option can be set in PowerShell by using the command Set-MailboxDatabase –Identity MDB01 –AllowFileRestore $true.

---

4. Open WSB, and in the Actions pane, select Recover.

5. In the Recovery wizard that starts, select where the backup is located. This can be on a disk attached to the server itself or it can be a remote location. Select the appropriate option and click Next to continue.

6. In the Select Backup Date window, select the backup set you want to restore to this server. Once selected, click Next to continue.

7. Next is the Select Recovery Type window, which is very important. WSB is Exchange-aware and thus an Exchange backup is an application backup. This way, the backup is restored as the Exchange writer would like it to be. If you select Volumes, for example, the backup is restored as an ordinary file backup and this is useless from an Exchange perspective. Select Applications as shown in Figure 7-9 and click Next to continue.

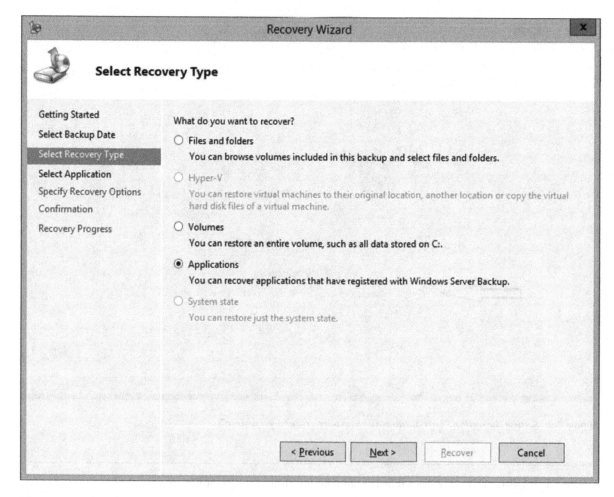

Figure 7-9. *Select the Applications radio button when restoring a mailbox database*

8. In the Select Application window, make sure Exchange is selected and click Next to continue.

■ **Note**   This option is only available when the mailbox database is not located on the system drive and boot drive, typically drive C:\. That is, it's only available when the mailbox database is on a separate drive.

---

9. Since the backup will be restored to its original location, select the Recover to Original Location option and click Next to continue.

10. In the Confirmation window, WSB will show the backup set that was selected. If this is correct, click Recover to start the restore process.

11. The restore operation will run in the background so it is safe to close WSB at this point.

During the restore process, the mailbox database and the log files that are in the backup set are restored to the original location. After the initial restore of the individual files, the mailbox database is still in an inconsistent (i.e., dirty shutdown) state. Exchange will try to start a recovery process with the log files that are also restored from the backup set.

When finished, any additional log files that are written to disk after the previous backup was taken are replayed into the mailbox database as well, so no mail data will be lost when restoring a mailbox database from a backup.

■ **Note**   Exchange Server has always been very sensitive when it comes to transaction log files and with replaying these into the mailbox database. In the "A Refresher on Mailbox Database Technologies" section earlier in this chapter, I explained the ESE internals and so it should be clear that Exchange Server is 100 percent dependent on all transaction log files. If only one log file is missing, the replay of the log files will fail. Therefore, you should never delete any of the log files manually; or do so only if you're 150 percent sure of what you're doing, or if Microsoft support instructs you to do so!

During the restore process, several events are written to the event log, indicating the progress of the restore operation or if any problems have arisen during the process. For example:

- *Event ID 4347 (MSExchangeRepl)* Exchange Replication Service VSS writer will restore a backup set to database MDB01\EXCH01, which is the same database from which the backup was originally taken.

- *Event ID 4367 (MSExchangeRepl)* Exchange Replication Service VSS writer successfully restored the backup set. In order to bring the restored databases to a clean shutdown state, database recovery will be performed using the information in the restore environment document MDB01\EXCH01.

- *Event ID 4370 (MSExchangeRepl)* Exchange Replication Service VSS writer will perform database recovery on database MDB01.edb as part of the restore process for MDB01\EXCH01, followed by a number of events from ESE, indicating the recovery steps for the restored Mailbox database.

- *Event ID 40008 (MSExchangeIS)* Mount completed successfully for database <<GUID>>.

- *Event ID 3156 (MSExchangeRepl)* Active Manager successfully mounted database MDB01 on server EXCH01.contoso.com.

- *Event ID 737 (Backup)* The operation to recover component(s) d7f01671-c9c7-46d6-abac-00fd27e1ebf2 has completed successfully at 2013-07-25T14:52:38.059000000Z.

If you log on to your mailbox and check any messages that were sent after the last backup was taken, you'll see that these are still available in the mailbox and thus successfully recovered.

Restoring a Mailbox Database to Another Location

Restoring a mailbox database to its original location is only useful when the original mailbox database is lost, for whatever reason. Restoring to its original location means you have to dismount the mailbox database, resulting in an outage for users. So, in a normal production situation you don't want to dismount your mailbox database for restoring purposes unless there's no other option.

Restoring a backup to another location has the advantage of leaving the original mailbox mounted, allowing users to continue working. Also, when using this method, there's no risk in accidentally overwriting the mailbox database with a database that's restored, since the original database is still mounted and thus reports as "file in use." The procedure for restoring the mailbox database to another location does not differ that much from restoring the mailbox to its original location.

The Restore Process

If you want to restore to another location, you follow these steps:

1. Log on to the Exchange 2013 Mailbox server, open WSB, and in the Actions pane, select Recover.

2. In the Recovery wizard that starts, select where the backup is located. This can be on a disk attached to the server itself or it can be a remote location. Select the appropriate option here and click Next to continue.

3. In the Select Backup Date window, select the backup set you want to restore to this server. Once selected, click Next to continue.

4. Next, the Select Recovery Type window is very important. WSB is Exchange-aware and thus an Exchange backup is an application backup. This way, the backup is restored as the Exchange writer would like it to be. If you select Volumes, for example, the backup will be restored as an ordinary file backup and this is useless from an Exchange perspective. Select Applications and click Next to continue.

5. In the Select Application window, make sure Exchange is selected and click Next to continue.

6. Since the backup will be restored to another location, select the Recover to Another Location option, and use the Browse button to select a disk and directory where you want to restore the mailbox database. Typically a dedicated restore LUN is used for this purpose. In our example, we use G:\RestoreDB to restore the mailbox database from backup. This is shown in Figure 7-10.

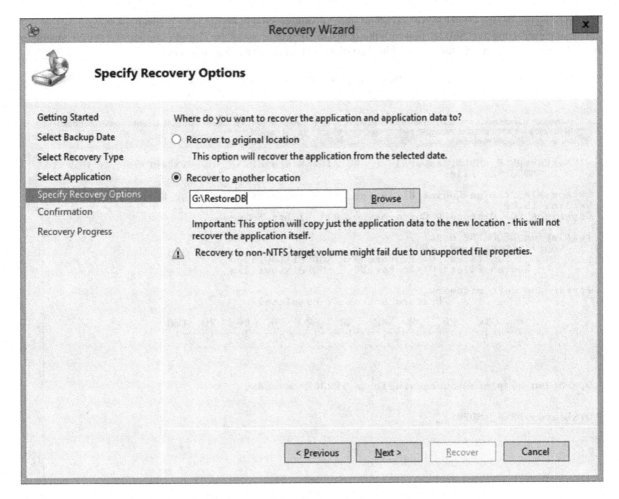

Figure 7-10. Restoring a mailbox database to an alternative location

7. The selection is shown in the confirmation window. If all is okay, then click the Restore button to start the recover process.

8. Since only the mailbox database and its log files are restored from backup, the process finishes much faster than when restoring to its original location. In this process, no additional recovery steps are performed so you have to do this manually.

The mailbox database and the accompanying log files are now restored from the backup set. The file location is also restored, so now there's a mailbox database DB01 located in G:\RestoreDB\F_\MDB01 and the log files are stored in G:\RestoreDB\F_\MDB01\LogFiles. This file is taken from a running copy of the mailbox database and thus the mailbox database is in a dirty shutdown state. You can check this using the ESEUTIL /MH command, which would produce something like this:

```
State      : Dirty Shutdown
Log Required: 82-84 (0x52-0x54)
```

To bring this database back into a consistent state, the mailbox database has to be recovered—something that can be achieved using the ESEUTIL tool with the /R option for recovery and the /l and /s options for the file locations of the log files and the system file (i.e., the checkpoint file). This is shown in Figure 7-11.

```
ESEUTIL /R E00 /lG:\RestoreDB\F_\MDB01\Logfiles /sG:\RestoreDB\F_\MDB01\Logfiles
```

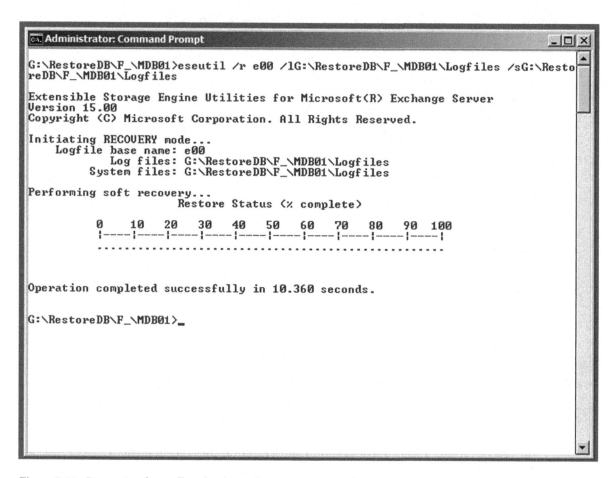

Figure 7-11. *Recovering the mailbox database after a restore to an alternative location*

Now when you check the database again using the ESEUTIL /MH command, the database will be in a clean shutdown state and ready to use.

Recovery Database

A *recovery database* in Exchange 2013 is a special mailbox database, invisible to normal users, where you can mount a normal database restored from backup. This means that you will have one normal mailbox database MDB01 running in its original location and one recovery mailbox MDB01 running in recovery mode.

Creating a recovery mailbox database is not very different from creating a regular mailbox database, but it can be managed only by using EMS. When creating the recovery mailbox database, you have to use the -Recovery switch to tell Exchange that a recovery mailbox database is created.

To create a recovery mailbox database using the database we've restored in the previous section, you would use an EMS command like this:

```
New-MailboxDatabase -Name "MDB01 Recovery" -Recovery -Server EXCH01 -EdbFilePath
G:\RestoreDB\F_\MDB01\MDB01.edb -LogFolderPath G:\RestoreDB\F_\MDB01\LogFiles
```

When the recovery mailbox database is created, it can be mounted, again only using the EMS since the recovery mailbox database is not visible in EAC.

Now that the recovery mailbox database is up and running, you can view what's inside this database. An ordinary Get-Mailbox command is not going work, since this is targeted to the normal mailbox database, but the Get-MailboxStatistics command does work to get a recovery mailbox database. Just use the following command to retrieve the mailbox data from the recovery mailbox database. Figure 7-12 shows the output from this command.

```
Get-MailboxStatistics -Database "MDB01 Recovery" | Select-Object DisplayName,ItemCount |
-Format-Table -AutoSize
```

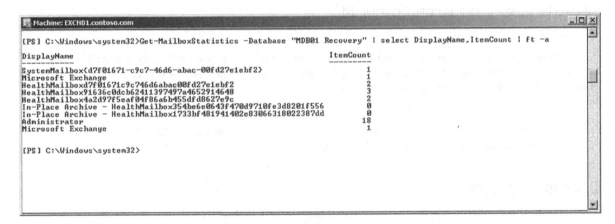

Figure 7-12. *Using the Get-MailboxStatistics command to view what's inside the recovery mailbox database*

This information can be used to restore mailbox content from the recovery mailbox database into the normal production mailbox database by using the New-MailboxRestoreRequest command in the EMS.

To retrieve mailbox content from the administrator mailbox inside the recovery mailbox database into the normal administrator mailbox, you can use the following command:

```
New-MailboxRestoreRequest -SourceDatabase "MDB01 Recovery" -SourceStoreMailbox Administrator
-TargetMailbox administrator
```

The content will be imported into the normal mailbox, but content will not be overwritten. If items already exist in the target mailbox, an additional copy of the item is created so that no information gets lost.

■ **Note** If you're uncertain what will happen during a command like the New-MailboxRestoreRequest, you can always use the -WhatIf switch parameter. The command will be the same, but it won't be executed. The results, however, will be shown on the console. If you're satisfied with the results, you can then rerun the command but without the -WhatIf parameter.

The example above will restore the entire mailbox from the recovery mailbox database, but it is possible to use a more granular approach. For instance, you can use the -IncludeFolders parameter to specify the folder in the mailbox that needs to be restored. To include the contents from the inbox, the option -IncludeFolders "Inbox/*" can be used; or in case of restoring only the Deleted Items folder, the option -IncludeFolders "DeletedItems/*" can be used. For example,

```
New-MailboxRestoreRequest -SourceDatabase "MDB01 Recovery" -SourceStoreMailbox Administrator
-TargetMailbox administrator -IncludeFolders "DeletedItems/*"
```

■ **Note** There's a dependency here on the regional settings of the mailbox. In English, you have an "inbox" while in Dutch the same folder is called "Postvak in"; in Spanish, it is "bandeja de entrada." You have to be aware of the regional setting of the mailbox when performing this command.

For certain purposes, it is possible to restore mailbox content from the mailbox in the recovery mailbox database to another mailbox that's not the original mailbox—for example, a legal mailbox. Suppose there's a mailbox called "Legal" and this mailbox is used to gather information from a mailbox from a backup. A command similar to this can be used:

```
New-MailboxRestoreRequest -SourceDatabase "MDB01 Recovery" -SourceStoreMailbox Administrator
-TargetMailbox legal -TargetRootFolder "Recovery Items"
```

Dial-tone Recovery

A recovery database is also used in a process called *dial-tone recovery*. In this recovery scenario, you get the users back online as quickly as possible after a mailbox database crash, and you work on mailbox database recovery in the background.

Suppose a mailbox database has crashed beyond repair, but you need to get users back online immediately. In this case you can remove all corrupted files from the disk and mount the mailbox database again. Since Exchange does not find any mailbox database files, it creates a new mailbox database and new log files (after showing a warning message).

Users who had their mailboxes in the crashed mailbox database can now start their mail client, and new mailboxes will automatically be created in the new mailbox database. Of course, that database is empty, but users are online again. They can send mail, but more important, they can receive mail again. The last thing you want to have happen is for external customers to send email to your organization and they receive error messages like "Mailbox info@contoso.com is not available."

Since users are online, they can continue to function and you can work in the background on restoring the last mailbox database backup to a recovery mailbox database. When the mailbox database is restored and all remaining log files are replayed into the recovered mailbox database, you can swap the two mailbox databases. The recovered mailbox database is then moved to the production location while the newly created mailbox database, which now also has items in it, is moved to the recovery mailbox database location.

The trick you perform at this point is to mount the newly created mailbox database as a recovery mailbox database and move the new content, using the New-MailboxRestoreRequest command as explained in the previous section, into the restored mailbox database. Once finished, you will have the mailbox database up and running again, without having lost any data.

The good part here is that you can restore the mailbox database from a backup, but your users are able to log on again and continue sending and receiving email. Yes, at that moment they won't have their "old" mailbox content available (not only email items but also the temporary mailbox don't contain any information or additional permissions), but at least they are online during the restore procedures.

■ **Note**   Some third-party backup applications use a granular restore technology, whereby it is possible to restore individual items directly from the VSS backup. What happens is that the VSS backup is completely indexed after the backup, indexing all individual email messages. These messages can then be restored directly from the backup, where the MAPI CDO is used for storing directly into the mailbox. While this works very well, it is not an official Microsoft-supported solution.

Disaster Recovery with Exchange Server 2013

The previous section discussed mailbox database technologies: how they work, how to back them up, and how to restore them. It showed how it is possible to restore a mailbox database to its original location or to an alternative location. In the last scenario, you created a recovery mailbox database, restored data from this recovery mailbox database, or used it in a dial-tone scenario.

But what happens if an entire server is lost and it is beyond repair? Then you need to rely on your disaster recovery skills.

Rebuilding the Exchange Server

When the Exchange 2013 Mailbox server is lost, it needs to be rebuilt, and the services, configuration, and data need to be restored. Earlier in this chapter I described where all the information is stored that's needed to rebuild an Exchange 2013 server; for example,

- Mailbox data is stored in the mailbox database, which should be on additional disks. If you're in luck, these are still safe after losing your Exchange server.

- Configuration data is sometimes stored in config files, located somewhere in the C:\Program Files\Microsoft\Exchange Server directory.

- All kinds of log files are also stored in the C:\Program Files\Microsoft\Exchange Server directory.

- SSL certificates are stored somewhere safe.

- Server configuration is stored in Active Directory.

Now, assuming that you've take care of the first four items listed above, the last one about Active Directory is interesting. All configuration data that's not in the config files is stored in Active Directory, and that can be used when rebuilding the Exchange 2013 Mailbox server. But instead of entering all the details manually during setup, this information is retrieved from Active Directory during installation.

Rule number 1 in a crisis situation is: Don't panic and don't destroy any data—not from disks and not from Active Directory. Otherwise, this action will backfire on you at some point!

To successfully rebuild an Exchange 2013 server, you can use the following steps:

1. Reset the computer account. When the server has crashed beyond repair and you have to rebuild your server, *do not remove* the Computer object from Active Directory. Instead, reset the Computer object in Active Directory, as follows:

   a. Log on to a domain controller, or any other member server that has the Active Directory tools installed, and open the Active Directory and Computers MMC snap-in.

   b. Locate the Computer object, right-click it, and select Reset Account (see Figure 7-13). This will reset the Computer object so you can join a new Windows Server (using the same name) to Active Directory.

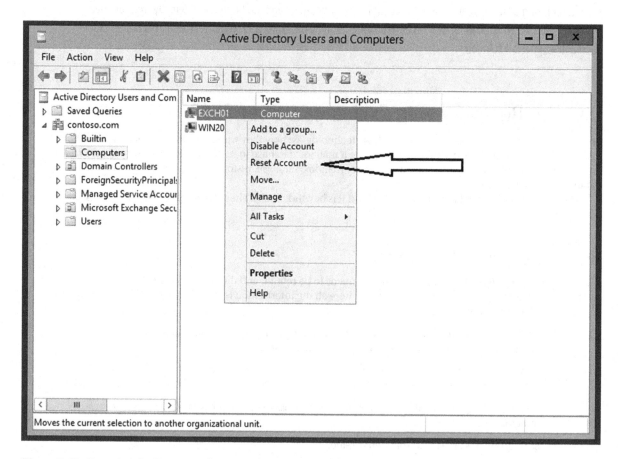

***Figure 7-13.** Resetting the Computer object in a disaster recovery scenario*

2. Install a new Windows server with the same specifications as the "old" Mailbox server. Use the same operating system and bring it up to date with the same hot fixes and service packs as were applied to the old Exchange 2013 server. Very important: *use the same server name* as was for the old Exchange 2013 server. That is, when the old server name was EXCH01, the new server name needs to be EXCH01 as well.

3. Join the new server, using the original name, to the Active Directory domain. When joined, reboot the server and log on to the new server as a domain administrator.

4. When logged on as a domain administrator, install the prerequisite software. This is explained in Chapter 2, but as a friendly reminder this is the prerequisite software when using a Windows Server 2012 server:

```
Import-Module ServerManager
Install-WindowsFeature AS-HTTP-Activation, Desktop-Experience, NET-Framework-45-Features,
RPC-over-HTTP-proxy, RSAT-Clustering, RSAT-Clustering-CmdInterface, Web-Mgmt-Console,
WAS-Process-Model, Web-Asp-Net45, Web-Basic-Auth, Web-Client-Auth, Web-Digest-Auth, Web-
Dir-Browsing, Web-Dyn-Compression, Web-Http-Errors, Web-Http-Logging, Web-Http-Redirect,
Web-Http-Tracing, Web-ISAPI-Ext, Web-ISAPI-Filter, Web-Lgcy-Mgmt-Console, Web-Metabase,
Web-Mgmt-Console, Web-Mgmt-Service, Web-Net-Ext45, Web-Request-Monitor, Web-Server,
Web-Stat-Compression, Web-Static-Content, Web-Windows-Auth, Web-WMI, Windows-Identity-
Foundation
```

The following prerequisite software need to be installed as well:

- Microsoft Unified Communications Managed API 4.0, Core Runtime 64-bit - http://go.microsoft.com/fwlink/p/?linkId=258269

- Microsoft Office 2010 Filter Pack 64 bit - http://go.microsoft.com/fwlink/p/?linkID=191548

- Microsoft Office 2010 Filter Pack SP1 64 bit - http://go.microsoft.com/fwlink/p/?LinkId=254043

■ **Note**   It looks strange, but the filter pack components used here are really version 2010.

---

5. When the server is fully up to date, the (external) disks containing the "old" mailbox databases must be accessible to the new Exchange 2013 server. The setup application will look for these disks; this is one kind of information that is stored in Active Directory as part of the Exchange 2013 server object. If you omit this step, the setup application will halt and will generate error messages on the console.

6. When the disks are connected and configured with the previous drive letters, the Exchange 2013 server can be recovered. To do this, open a command prompt, navigate to the installation media, and enter the following command:

```
Setup.exe /mode:RecoverServer /IAcceptExchangeServerLicenseTerms
```

This will install Exchange 2013, and all the configuration information that's normally entered in the setup application is now retrieved from Active Directory.

7. When the setup application is finished and the server is reinstalled, shown in Figure 7-14, reboot the server.

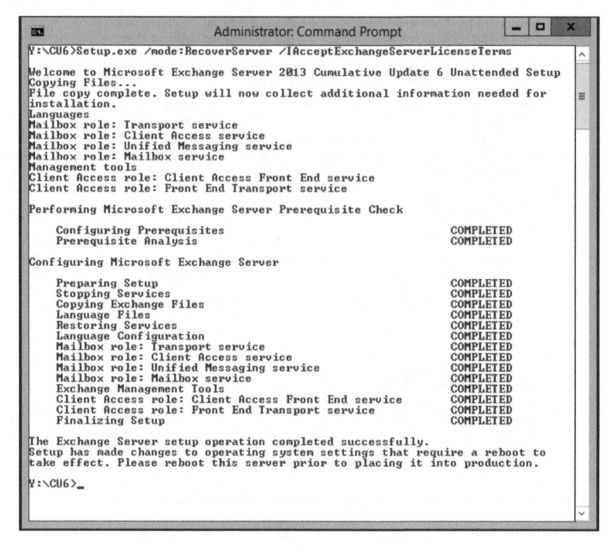

Figure 7-14. Recovering an Exchange 2013 server with information from Active Directory

After rebooting, you can check the mailbox databases that were on the (external) disk drives; they should be good, although dismounted. When you mount the mailbox databases on the recovered server, you're good to log in to your mailbox using OWA. The last steps are to restore or reconfigure additional items like the SSL certificate, virtual directories, additional config files, or other log files, as explained earlier in this chapter (see "Backup of Other Configuration Information").

When done, though your server has been unavailable for some time, it is now restored to its original location. If you're unhappy with the downtime, you should refer to the "Database Availability Group" section in Chapter 5, which explains how to avoid or minimize downtime.

ESEUTIL and Corrupted Databases

Although rare these days, it can happen that you end up with a corrupted mailbox database and no backup of your mailbox database. In this case, you have to rely on tools that can repair your mailbox database. ESEUTIL is such a tool and it comes with Exchange Server; you can use ESEUTIL to repair a corrupted mailbox database.

When a mailbox database is corrupted, that means it has corrupted pages in it and most likely it will not mount. When you perform an integrity check on the mailbox database using ESEUTIL /G, it will report that the mailbox database is corrupted (see Figure 7-15).

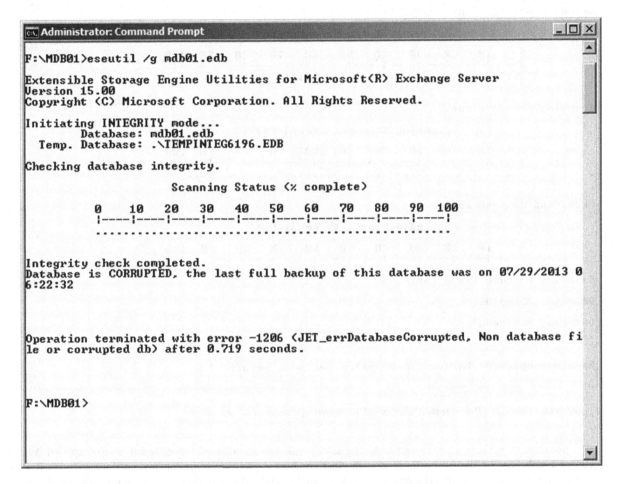

Figure 7-15. *ESEUTIL report of mailbox database as corrupted*

ESEUTIL also has an option to repair a mailbox database, but it is a very destructive way of repairing. What it does is open the mailbox database and check all the pages in the database. When a page is found to contain corrupted pointers (i.e., pointers to other pages containing data), it will remove these pointers from the page. The result is that no pages contain invalid pointers anymore, but the data that was referenced using those pages is automatically lost. It is not possible to predict which pages and pointers are corrupted, and thus it's not possible to anticipate what data you will be missing. Unfortunately, your users will find this out in the end.

You can start a repair with ESEUTIL /P MDB01.edb. A warning message is shown saying that you should only run Repair on damaged or corrupted databases. The caution is that Repair will not apply information in the transaction log files to the database and may cause information to be lost. And it will ask you if you want to continue.

If you do, click the OK button to continue. ESEUTIL will perform a consistency check first, then scan the database and repair any damaged information that it found (see Figure 7-16).

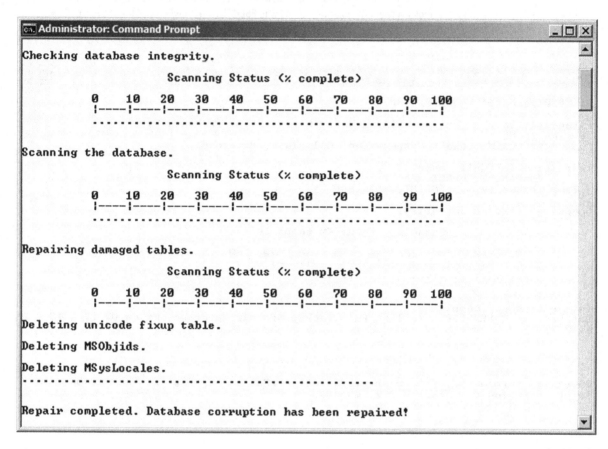

Figure 7-16. *ESEUTIL /P does several checks before repairing damaged information*

One question that always pops up is how long it actually takes for a mailbox database repair to be completed. As a rule of thumb, I use 10 GB per hour for processing. So, if you have a 250 GB mailbox database you have to repair, it will take approximately 25 hours to complete. There's no need to panic when you don't see any dots moving on the console; ESEUTIL just needs time to do its work.

This is the reason Microsoft recommends not using large mailbox databases (i.e., larger than 200 GB) when a DAG is not used. If you're using a 500 GB mailbox database in a single Mailbox server environment, and you run into a situation like this, you will have a hard time ensuring service delivery (which should be documented in the SLA).

■ **Note**　It is my personal experience that it's best not to use a large mailbox database when using a single Mailbox server. Although Microsoft recommends a maximum size of 200 GB for a mailbox database in such a scenario, I think it's still too large. When you run into problems and have to start repairing your mailbox database, it will take too much time to do so. Stay on the safe side and keep your mailbox database between 50 and 75 GB. When more space is needed, just create additional mailbox databases.

It is recommended that you create a new mailbox database after a corrupted mailbox database has been repaired. This can be done in two ways:

- Create a new mailbox database on the Exchange server and move all the mailboxes from the old and repaired mailbox database to the new mailbox database. Once they are moved, the old mailbox database can be removed. Do not forget to create a new backup of the new mailbox database when done.

- Use ESEUTIL /D to perform an offline defragmentation. The net effect of this is that a new mailbox database is created with the old name. When you use ESEUTIL /D to perform an offline defragmentation, it will create a new mailbox database file next to the old mailbox database file. Then it will read all information from the old file and merge it into the new file. This way not only is a new file created but also new indices, new tables, new pointers, and so on—so basically you end up with a new mailbox database. When the copy process is complete, the old (and previously corrupted) mailbox database will be deleted.

In the Exchange Server 5.5 days, it was a best practice to run ESEUTIL /D on a biweekly or monthly basis to maintain relatively fresh mailbox databases. Considering the quality and stability of ESE in those days, this made perfect sense. But Exchange Server and ESE have come a long way, and now it doesn't make much sense to run this on a regular basis.

The only time you should run ESE is when you have moved a large number of mailboxes (and thus a lot of data) from one mailbox database to another mailbox database. This will result in large amounts of white space inside the mailbox database, which won't be reclaimed by online defragmentation (OLD) as part of online maintenance. Yes, this will restructure the data inside the mailbox database, but it won't shrink the mailbox database.

If you are in a situation like this and you do not have a DAG, you can use ESEUTIL /D to offline defragment the mailbox database and reclaim this white space.

■ **Note**　Offline defragmentation is what its name implies—an offline process. During this, the mailbox database is not available for users. It is hard to predict how long it will take for an offline defrag to finish. A good rule of thumb is 10 GB per hour, depending on the amount of database inside the mailbox database that needs to be moved. If you have a 200 GB mailbox database with 150 GB of white space, you have to move 50 GB of data, which can take up to five hours to complete.

File Recovery Tools

This is not really a native Exchange Server topic, but it is interesting enough to mention when viewed from a disaster recovery perspective.

There are situations when you do have a mailbox database file and you are in urgent need of data inside this mailbox database file, but you don't have an Exchange server available to perform these kinds of recovery services. In this case, a file recovery tool can be helpful. Several tools are available, but the most well known is called PowerControls, from Kroll Ontrack.

Tools such as these let you open the mailbox database file (the EDB file), regardless of whether they are in a clean shutdown state or are taken from a backup and thus in a dirty shutdown state. Either way, you don't need an Exchange server for opening the EDB file.

You can connect to a source, which in Figure 7-17 is a mailbox database taken from a backup. This is shown in the top pane. You can also connect to a target, which can be a PST file or a live Exchange 2013 server. It is possible to connect to all the folders in a mailbox; even the Recoverable Items folder is available.

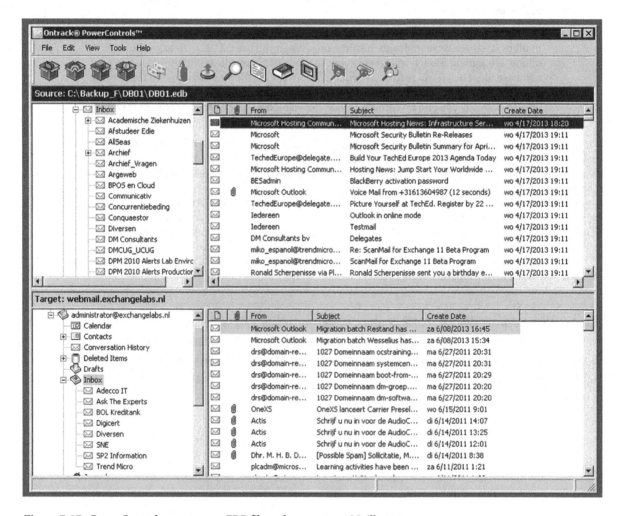

Figure 7-17. *PowerControls can open an EDB file and connect to a Mailbox*

Messages can be exported to MSG, TXT, or EML files, but can also be exported to a PST file. Besides being able to export to one of these files, you can move these items from the source mailbox database files to a live mailbox when the tool is connected to an Exchange 2013 server.

The tool uses MAPI under the hood, so Outlook needs to be installed on the server and there must be a working Outlook profile on the recover server to make sure that the tool can connect to the Exchange 2013 server.

A recovery tool like Kroll Ontrack PowerControl can be an interesting addition to your toolbox of restore or disaster recovery solutions.

■ **Note** Opening a mailbox database directly by a recovery tool is not supported by Microsoft, nor is a direct restore by this tool using the MAPI interfaces.

Exchange Native Data Protection

Exchange Native Data Protection is a solution that was introduced in Exchange Server 2010, sometimes also referred to as a "backupless environment." This is an Exchange server environment where a traditional backup solution is not used, and where native Exchange functions are the replacement—when possible, of course.

■ **Note** In some market segments, such as legal, finance, or health care, there are (legal) requirements that dictate how to create regular backups, keep them for a certain amount of time, and/or store them on a separate location. For these, Exchange Native Data Protection is not a solution.

Exchange Native Data Protection should be able to help you in scenarios where:

- Users have unintentionally deleted items from their mailboxes and need them urgently.

- You need to restore items from a user's mailbox for legal purposes.

- A mailbox was deleted unintentionally.

- Hardware failures caused loss of a mailbox database or maybe loss of an entire server.

- There has been failure or loss of an entire datacenter.

Exchange 2013 has a lot of built-in features that can take care of some of these items; for example, there are deleted items retention, in-place hold, single item recovery, archive mailboxes, retention policies, and a database availability group (DAG).

Using these features, it is possible to create an environment where a traditional backup is not used, but where the disasters mentioned earlier would be fully covered. The advantage of this arrangement is that the total cost of ownership of a full-fledged Exchange 2013 environment is most likely lower than that of a regular Exchange 2013 environment with a traditional backup solution.

Microsoft recommends evaluating your various requirements and the available options before deciding whether this is a viable solution for your organization. For more information, visit the Microsoft Exchange team site at http://bit.ly/BackupLess.

Deleted Items Retention

When users delete items from their mailboxes, the items are not visible to the users anymore, but they are still in the users' mailboxes. They are stored in hidden folders in their mailboxes, which is part of the "dumpster."

Deleted items are kept in the Recoverable Items folder for a time called the *deleted item retention period*. By default, the retention time for deleted items is 14 days, while for a deleted mailbox it is 30 days. This means that after these times, the items are deleted from the server. *Deleted item retention* is a property of the mailbox database and can be set using the Set-MailboxDatabase command with the –DeletedItemRetention parameter, and is specified as a time span: dd.hh:mm:ss. To set the deleted item retention time to 60 days, for example, you can use the following command:

```
Set-MailboxDatabase -Identity MDB01 -DeletedItemRetention 60.00:00:00
```

To set the deleted item retention time for mailboxes, the same command is used but with the MailboxRetention option. For example, to change the deleted mailbox retention time to seven days, you can use the following command:

```
Set-MailboxDatabase -Identity MDB01 -MailboxRetention 7.00:00:00
```

Within this deleted items retention time, users can recover deleted items themselves in Outlook. In Outlook 2013, you select the Folders tab and then click the Recover Deleted Items button. A new window will pop up showing all messages that are not in the Deleted Items folder but can still be recovered from the Recoverable Items folder (see Figure 7-18).

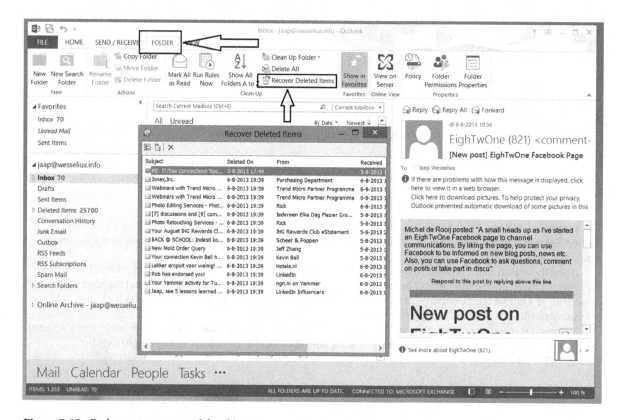

Figure 7-18. End users can recover deleted items

In Outlook WebApp, the deleted items can be recovered as well. In the OWA navigation pane, right-click the Deleted Items folder and select the Recover Deleted Items option.

When the user permanently deletes a message (i.e., purges the Deleted Items folder), the message can no longer be recovered—not even by administrators—unless the Single Item Recovery option is enabled. (This is covered later in this section.)

In-Place Hold

Although you now know it is possible to stretch the deleted item retention period, it is not really a good idea to stretch this time to a couple of years; doing so would have a disastrous effect on the size of the mailbox database. So Exchange 2010 came up with a new feature called *litigation hold*, which was then replaced by *in-place hold* in Exchange 2013. With in-place hold, you have the possibility of:

- Placing user mailboxes on hold and preserving mailbox content from any possible alteration.

- Preserving delete items; that is, items that can be deleted manually by the user or by an automated process like messaging records management (MRM).

- Searching for and retaining items matching specified criteria.

- Preserving items indefinitely or for a specific duration.

- Keeping in-place hold transparent from the user by not having to suspend MRM.

- Enabling in-place eDiscovery searches of items placed on hold.

In short, items can be on hold in a user's mailbox without the user knowing it.

Litigation hold allowed putting all items on hold for an indefinite amount of time. In-place hold is more granular, with the following possible parameters:

- **What to hold** It is possible to specify which items to put on hold by using parameters such as keywords, recipients, senders, start and end dates, and type of items, such as messages, calendar items, and so forth.

- **How long to hold** It's possible to specify how long these items should be on hold.

■ **Note**   With in-place hold, the previous indefinite hold is still possible.

To place a mailbox on in-place hold, you need to have specific permissions. These permissions are granted to users who are members of the Discovery Management RBAC group or users who are assigned the Legal Hold and Mailbox Search management roles.

■ **Note**   In-place hold is a premium feature that requires an Enterprise Client Access License (CAL). You only need the Enterprise CAL for mailboxes that use this feature.

To create a new in-place hold using PowerShell, you can use the following command:

```
New-MailboxSearch -Name "In-place hold Joe Jackson Mailbox" -SourceMailboxes "joe@contoso.com"
-InPlaceHoldEnabled $true
```

When a new mailbox search is begun, an informational warning message is shown saying that the new Mailbox server won't be effective immediately and that it can take up to 60 minutes before becoming active (see Figure 7-19).

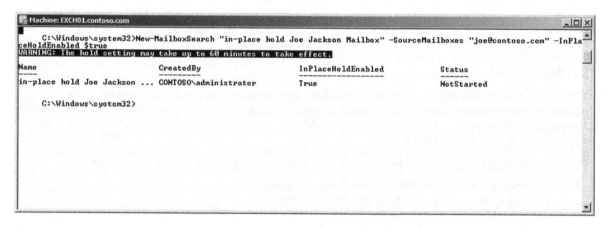

Figure 7-19. Creating a new mailbox search using the EMS. Note the warning message

For example, all items in Joe's mailbox will now be on hold for an indefinite period. When Joe deletes items and purges his deleted items manually, they will be stored. If Joe receives a message and deliberately makes changes to this message, the original and the changed messages will both be kept. It is good practice to monitor the deleted items quota in the mailboxes for which you have enabled in-place hold.

■ **Note**   This will work only for mailboxes on Exchange 2013. For mailboxes stored on an Exchange 2010 Mailbox server, the corresponding cmdlet has to be used on an Exchange 2010 server.

Single Item Recovery

Single item recovery was introduced in Exchange 2010 and is still available in Exchange 2013.

When a message is deleted from a mailbox, it is stored in the Recoverable Items folder of that mailbox. Items stay in this folder until the deleted items retention period expires. Only then are they fully removed from the Exchange server by the server's online maintenance. When a user permanently deletes a message, it is removed immediately from the Recoverable Items folder and the user is no longer able to recover that message—not even the administrator is able to recover it. One exception, however, is when the mailbox is on in-place hold. Then, deleted items are retained until the in-place hold is removed.

To be able to recover these deleted items when they have been permanently deleted by the user, you can enable single item recovery on the mailbox. When this is enabled, permanently deleted messages are retained in the Recoverable Items folder until the deleted item retention period is passed and then the message is fully removed from the Recoverable Items folder.

Single item recovery can be enabled only with PowerShell and by using the following command:

```
Set-Mailbox -Identity "April Summers" -SingleItemRecoveryEnabled $true
```

For mailboxes that have single item recovery enabled, it is also possible to set a different deleted items retention time using the -RetainDeletedItemsFor option, as follows:

```
Set-Mailbox -Identity "Kim Akers" -SingleItemRecoveryEnabled $true -RetainDeletedItemsFor 30
```

Recovering items when single item recovery is enabled consists of two steps:

1. Searching for the missing items and recovering them.

2. Restoring the recovered items.

Searching for deleted items in mailboxes that have single item recovery enabled or mailboxes that are on in-place hold is part of in-place eDiscovery. As such, you need special permissions to search for these deleted items or to search in these mailboxes. This makes sense, since you're looking into somebody else's potentially private information. With the permission stipulation in place, it is impossible to "accidentally" search others' mailboxes. Permission is granted to members of the Discovery Management RBAC role group. To perform a search, you follow these steps:

1. Select Compliance Management in the Feature pane and select the In-Place eDiscovery and Hold tab. In the toolbar, click the New icon.

2. In the New In-Place eDiscovery and Hold wizard, enter a name and a description for the new hold you're creating. Click Next to continue.

3. The next window lets you choose if you want to search all mailboxes or only specific mailboxes. Assuming the latter, select the Specify Mailboxes to Search radio button and use the Add button to select a mailbox that needs to be added to the new search. Select the mailbox, use the Add button, and click OK to return to the previous window. This mailbox should now be listed in the Results pane. Click Next to continue.

4. In the Search Query window, you can define the query that needs to be used. Enter the keywords, start and end dates, recipient and sender, and the item type, like email, meeting, notes, and so forth. Select the options you need and click Next to continue.

5. If needed, you can opt to place the content matching the search query on hold. It can be on hold indefinitely or for a certain number of days. Click Finish to continue.

The search is not executed immediately, but an estimate of the search results is shown in the Details pane, including the number of items returned by the search and its size (see Figure 7-20).

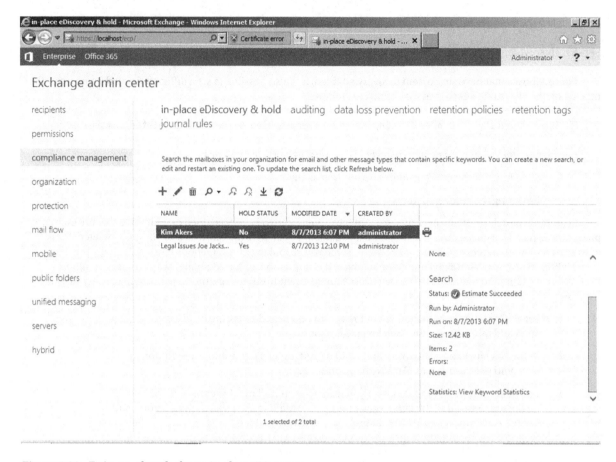

Figure 7-20. *Estimate of results for an in-place eDiscovery*

6. When the results are satisfactory, the search can be executed. Click the Down arrow next to the search icon and select the Copy Search Results option. You can select which options can be enabled, such as:

- Include unsearchable items

- Enable de-duplication

- Enable full logging

- Send me mail when the copy is completed

7. The last action is to select where the search will store its results; typically this is the Discovery Search mailbox. Click Copy to start copying the search results to the Discovery Search mailbox.

Members of the Discovery Search RBAC role group are automatically assigned full access permission to the Discovery Search mailbox. When you open the Discovery Search mailbox, either in Outlook or in OWA, you should see a folder with the name you specified in the eDiscovery wizard. This is where the search results are stored (see Figure 7-21).

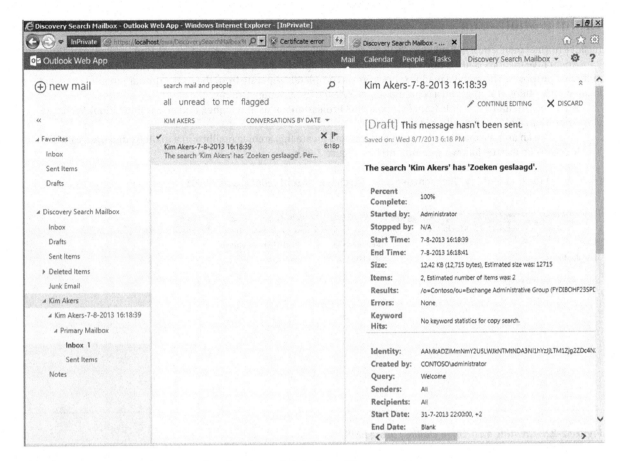

Figure 7-21. *Search results are stored in the Discovery Search mailbox*

When the results are stored in the Discovery Search mailbox, it is possible to export those results to the user's mailbox using the `Search-Mailbox` command:

```
Search-Mailbox "Discovery Search Mailbox" -SearchQuery "Welcome" -TargetMailbox "Kim Akers"
-TargetFolder "Recovered Messages" -LogLevel Full -DeleteContent
```

For example, this command moves the items from the search results into Kim Akers's mailbox in a folder called Recovered Messages. When this is done, the items in the Discovery Search mailbox are deleted.

Using `New-MailboxExportRequest`, it is also possible to export the search results to a PST file. The same prerequisites apply as when using a normal export request. The MRS processes the request, so the PST file needs to be stored to a fileshare where the Exchange Trusted Subsystem USG has permission for full access.

For example, the following command will start a new export request of the folder called Kim Akers in the Discovery Search mailbox, where the subject of the items is "Welcome," and will store the PST file on a fileshare called HelpDeskPst on a server called AMS-FS01:

```
New-MailboxExportRequest -Mailbox "Discovery Search Mailbox" -SourceRootFolder "Kim Akers"
-ContentFilter {Subject -eq "Welcome"} -FilePath \\AMS-FS01\HelpDeskPst\KimAkersRecovery.pst
```

Archive Mailboxes

Besides normal mailboxes, in Exchange 2013 there are archive mailboxes, a concept introduced in Exchange 2010.

An archive mailbox is just a normal mailbox, but it's connected to a user as a secondary mailbox and is used for archiving purposes. The archive mailbox, however, is completely separate from the user's primary mailbox and can be located on additional storage, on a separate server, or even in Exchange Online.

An archive mailbox is visible from Outlook 2007 Professional Plus and higher, and also from Outlook WebApp; it appears as an additional mailbox in the client.

To create an archive mailbox for a user call Joe, and locate this archive mailbox in a mailbox database called MDB01, you can use the following command (see Figure 7-22):

```
Enable-Mailbox -Identity Joe@contoso.com -Archive -ArchiveDatabase MDB01
```

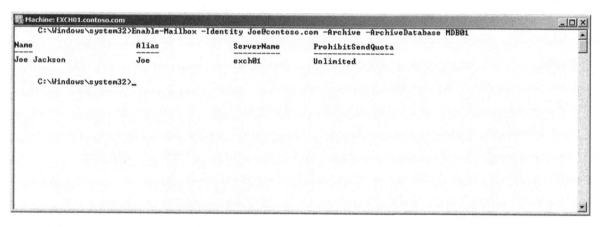

Figure 7-22. *Creating an archive Mailbox using EMS*

■ **Note**   In-place archiving is a premium feature and requires an Exchange Enterprise Client Access License (CAL).

By default, an archive mailbox has an archive quota of 100 GB and an archive quota warning at 90 GB. This means that a warning message will be sent to the user when the archive reaches 90 GB, but this is sufficient to store tons of information.

■ **Note**   Archive mailboxes are a perfect "PST killer." By nature, PST files are stored on the user's workstation or laptop, where they are not backed up and are prone to getting lost when the laptop is stored. Storing PST files on a network share is not supported and can give erratic results in Outlook. Also, a backup application can skip these files when they are still open in Outlook. But when they are moved to archive mailboxes, they are stored safely, available for the user and backed up frequently. It's a perfect solution for getting rid of your PST files.

The user can manually move data to the archive mailbox, but an administrator can also import data into that archive mailbox. The `New-MailboxImportRequest` command can be used to import PST files from a fileshare directly into an archive mailbox. To achieve this in EMS, use a command similar to this example:

```
New-MailboxImportRequest -Mailbox Joe@contoso.com -FilePath \\AMS-FS01\PSTFiles\Archive2011.pst
-IsArchive
```

Another way to automatically move data from the user's mailbox into the archive mailbox is by using retention policies.

Retention Policies

Over the years, the amount of information stored in mailboxes has kept growing and growing. To deal with this, Microsoft introduced messaging records management (MRM) in Exchange 2007. The implementation of MRM was by means of managed folders, which are folders created by an Exchange administrator. On top of these managed folders, the Exchange administrator had to create rules that govern certain actions performed on items in the folders, such as marking them as past retention or to permanently delete. Users were able to store information in these managed folders, and after a retention time set by the administrator, the information would be processed.

In addition to using MRM to manage amounts of information, and thus meet larger storage requirements, MRM can be used to:

- **Meet business requirements** Depending on your organization's messaging policies, you may need to retain important email messages for a certain period. It is not uncommon that HR information with resumes of non-hired people are kept for only six months, or information regarding business strategies or transactions is kept for only a certain amount of time. When items are stored for a limited time in Exchange 2013, the items are not set to read-only, so that users are able to delete these items if they want to.

- **Meet legal and regulatory requirements** Many organizations have a legal or regulatory requirement to store messages for a designated period and to remove messages older than that time. Storing messages longer than necessary may increase your organization's legal or financial risks.

- **Increase user productivity** The amount of information, or the ever-increasing amount of information, has a negative impact on productivity. For example, consider those newsletters that are kept for ages but never read. Using MRM, it is possible to remove these after a certain amount of time, thereby reducing the clutter in a user's mailbox and increasing the productivity.

MRM version 2 was introduced in Exchange 2010 and included the personal archive and retention tags and retention policies, a concept further developed in Exchange 2013.

As an Exchange administrator, you can choose the tags that can be assigned to items in a mailbox. There are various types of tags available:

- A default policy tag (DPT)

- Personal tags applied to folders or individual items by the user

- Retention policy tags (RPT) assigned to specific folders to expire items in those folders

Retention policy tags can be created for the folders listed in Table 7-1.

Table 7-1. *Folder in a Mailbox that Can Have RPTs Applied*

Folder Name	Details
Calendar	Default folder used to store meeting dates and appointments.
Conversation History	Created by Microsoft Lync (when implemented); although not treated as a default folder by Outlook, it's regarded as a special folder by Exchange and can have RPTs applied.
Delete Items	Default folder used to store items deleted from other folders in the mailbox. Outlook and Outlook WebApp users can manually empty this folder. Users can also configure Outlook to empty the folder upon closing Outlook.
Drafts	Default folder used to store draft messages that haven't been sent by the user. Outlook WebApp also uses this folder to save messages that were sent by the user but not submitted to the Hub Transport server.
Inbox	Default folder used to store messages delivered to a mailbox.
Journal	Default folder for actions selected by the user. These actions are automatically recorded by Outlook and placed in a timeline view.
Junk Email	Default folder used to save messages marked as junk email by the content filter on an Exchange server or by the anti-spam filter in Outlook.
Notes	Contains notes created by users in Outlook.
Outbox	Default folder used to temporarily store sent messages until processed by a Hub Transport server. Messages usually remain in this folder for a brief period so it isn't necessary to create an RPT for this folder.
RSS Feeds	Default folder containing RSS feeds.
Recoverable Items	Hidden folder in the non-IPM sub-tree. It contains the Deletions, Versions, Purges, and Audits sub-folders. Retention tags for this folder move items from the Recoverable Items folder in the user's primary mailbox to the Recoverable Items folder in the user's archive mailbox. You can assign only the Move To Archive retention action to tags for this folder.
Sent Items	Default folder used to store messages that have been sent.
Sync Issues	Contains synchronization logs.
Tasks	Default folder used to store tasks.

You can create a DPT that will move all items in a mailbox to the personal archive in 180 days, but create personal tags that will keep items in the mailbox for one or two years. These personal tags can be assigned by the user to items and will override the DPT.

Additionally, it is possible to create RPTs that will mark messages as past retention after a certain number of years or when legal or company requirements dictate, then permanently remove those items. Another RPT can be applied to the junk email folder in the mailbox that will permanently remove items after, for example, seven days.

When creating an RPT, you can specify the following actions to be taken when the retention time expires:

- **Move to Archive** Items are moved to the archive mailbox. Naming in the archive mailbox will be identical, so when a folder named "Finance" exists in the primary mailbox, it will automatically be created as such in the archive mailbox.

- **Delete and Allow Recovery** Items are deleted, but kept in the Recoverable Items folder.

- **Permanently Delete** Items are permanently deleted (and not stored in the Recoverable Items folder) and cannot be recovered. When the in-place hold is set on a mailbox, the item is kept in the Recoverable Items folder. If single item recovery is enabled for a mailbox, the item will be kept in the Recoverable Items folder until the deleted item retention time for this mailbox database or the single item recovery setting is reached.

- **Mark as Past Retention** Messages are marked as past retention. Outlook and OWA will show this message with a notification string "This item has expired."

To apply the retention tags to a mailbox, you must add them to a retention policy, and this retention policy is applied to the mailbox. A mailbox can have only one retention policy applied, but a retention policy can have multiple retention tags.

By default, 11 retention policy tags are created and two retention policies are created. One retention policy is for the arbitration mailboxes; the other retention policy is applied to mailboxes that have an archive mailbox.

■ **Note** The EMS shows 11 retention policy tags (Get-RetentionPolicyTag) and two retention policies (Get-RetentionPolicy). For some reason, EAC only shows 10 retention policy tags and one retention policy.

Table 7-2 shows the default retention policy tags that are used in the default retention policy.

Table 7-2. *The Default Retention Policy and its Retention Policy Tags*

Name	Type	Retention Time	Retention Action
Default 2 years move to archive	DPT	730	Move to archive
Personal 1 year move to archive	Personal Tag	365	Move to archive
Personal 5 year move to archive	Personal Tag	1,825	Move to archive
Personal never move to archive	Personal Tag	N/A	N/A
Recoverable items 14 days move to archive	Recoverable Items folder	14	Move to archive
1 week delete	Personal Tag	7	Delete and allow recovery
1 month delete	Personal Tag	30	Delete and allow recovery
6 months delete	Personal Tag	180	Delete and allow recovery
1 year delete	Personal Tag	365	Delete and allow recovery
5 years delete	Personal Tag	1,825	Delete and allow recovery
Never delete	Personal Tag	N/A	N/A

The managed folder assistant is a service running on the Mailbox server that's responsible for processing the mailboxes with retention policies indicated. It applies the retention policy by inspecting items in the mailbox and determines whether they are subject to retention. It then stamps the items subject to retention with the appropriate retention tags and takes the specified retention action when items are past their retention age.

The managed folder assistant is a throttled service. This means that it is running 24 hours a day, but it does not have full control over system resources to prevent depletion of resources.

■ **Note** The managed folder assistant doesn't take any action on messages that aren't subject to retention.

When items are moved from one folder in the inbox to another folder in the inbox, the items inherit the retention policy tag that has been applied to the target folder.

The default 11 retention policy tags are most likely sufficient for 99 percent of all Exchange 2013 implementations, but if you want to create additional RPTs, it's easily done. To create a new RPT that deletes an item after 14 days, but allows recovery for the item, for example, you can use the following PowerShell command:

```
New-RetentionPolicyTag -Name "Delete after 14 days" -Type Personal -RetentionAction
DeleteAndAllowRecovery -AgeLimitForRetention 14 -Comment "Items with this tag will be deleted after
14 days"
```

RPTs are grouped together in retention policies. Suppose you want to create a new policy called "My Exchange 2013 Policy" and assign the default policy tag "Default 2 years move to archive" and the RPT you just created; you would use the following PowerShell command:

```
New-RetentionPolicy "My Exchange 2013 Policy" -RetentionPolicyTagLinks "Default 2 years move to
archive","Delete after 14 days"
```

To assign this retention policy to a mailbox in PowerShell, you use the following command:

```
Set-Mailbox -Identity joe@contoso.com -RetentionPolicy "My Exchange 2013 Policy"
```

■ **Note** Personal tags are a premium feature. Mailboxes with retention policies require an Enterprise Client Access License.

Database Availability Groups

Chapter 5 talked about the database availability groups, or DAGs, and how a DAG can be used to improve the uptime of an Exchange 2013 environment. Here, we revisit the DAG, but now it's to see what it can do for a backupless environment.

A DAG is a logical grouping of Exchange 2013 Mailbox servers that are used to host multiple copies of mailbox databases. One Mailbox server in a DAG holds an active copy of a mailbox database; this is the mailbox database that's used by clients. One or more Mailbox servers in a DAG hold a passive copy of a mailbox database, and these passive copies are not used by any clients; they are only for redundancy purposes. One exception can be a backup application that uses a passive copy to create backups.

Figure 7-23 illustrates how redundancy works with a DAG. Clients like Outlook use a load balancer to connect to an Exchange 2013 Client Access server, where they are authenticated. After authentication, the request is proxied to the Mailbox server holding the active copy of the mailbox database. On this Mailbox server, the data is retrieved from the mailbox and returned to the client. The most important part of this process to remember is that all mail processing is taking place on the Mailbox server holding the *active* copy of the mailbox database.

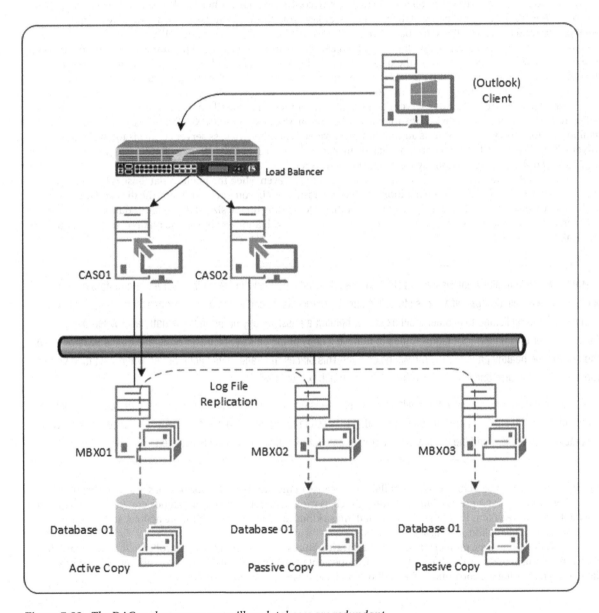

Figure 7-23. *The DAG makes sure your mailbox databases are redundant*

As shown earlier in this chapter, mailbox data is in the Mailbox server's memory, the transaction log file, or the mailbox database. During processing, new transaction files are created; once they are stored on the server's hard disk, they are sent to the Mailbox server holding a passive copy of that mailbox database. At minimum, there's one passive copy of the mailbox database, but more passive copies can be used as well.

In a DAG, there's always one active copy of the mailbox database and replication always takes place from this active copy to all the passive copies. So how do the passive copies get on the other Mailbox servers? This is a process called *seeding*. It's the actual copying of the mailbox database from the server holding the active copy to another Mailbox server. Seeding a mailbox database is not an NTFS copy; instead, a technique called *streaming* is used—very similar to the streaming backup technology explained earlier in this chapter. When streaming, the active mailbox copy is read (database) page by page. When the page is read, its checksum is checked; when it's okay, the page is sent to the other Mailbox server, where it is stored. This way the new passive copy is always identical to the active copy of the mailbox database and it's 100 percent consistent.

What happens when a Mailbox server fails? Clients are connected to the Client Access server. Referring back to Figure 7-21, you can see that when the mailbox database on Mailbox server MBX01 fails, the passive copy of the mailbox database on server MBX02 is automatically activated. The Client Access server connects to this Mailbox server within seconds. Clients do notice a small disturbance; in the taskbar, a balloon will pop up saying "Connection lost," followed shortly by a balloon saying "Connection restored."

So, if a mailbox database is lost, the service continues to run even when the mailbox database is beyond repair. When a disk containing one or more mailbox databases is lost, though, you have to replace the disk and manually perform a reseed of the mailbox database to the new disk. Depending on the size of the mailbox database, this can take considerable time, but since the users can continue to work with another copy of the mailbox database, this is no big deal.

■ **Note** Multiple mailbox databases in a DAG have another advantage. When a Mailbox server encounters a corrupted page, a process called *page patching* is started. A special marker is placed in the current transaction log file, which is then closed and replicated to another Mailbox server holding a passive copy of the mailbox database. When this Mailbox server encounters the marker, it tries to retrieve a copy of the patch (which should be fine on the passive copy) and returns the healthy page to the first Mailbox server. This places the page in its cache buffer, where it is then written into one of the log files and eventually written into the mailbox database.

When this happens, the header of the mailbox database file is updated as well. There's a special entry called "patch count" for this with the number of patches applied. It is possible to check this using the ESEUTIL /MH command. When the patches are applied and the database header is updated, the mailbox database is repaired.

By using a DAG, you achieve higher availability because of the multiple mailbox databases and replication technology, but it doesn't prevent human failures, such as the accidental deletion of mailbox content or even deletion of a mailbox itself. As far as Exchange is concerned, these kinds of deletions are legitimate actions and thus are replicated across all mailbox databases.

A DAG does, however, protect you against hardware failures, like server failure, controller failure, or a hard disk failure, resulting in physical database corruption. It does not protect you against logical corruption of a mailbox database. Though logical corruption of a mailbox database is rare, it can lead to data loss.

There are two types of logical corruption:

- **Database logical corruption** In this case, the checksum of a page in the mailbox database is correct but the data inside the page is wrong. This can happen when ESE tries to write a page to disk (and ESE gets a success message back from disk), but the page isn't actually written to disk or is written to the wrong location. This is also referred to as a "lost flush." A common cause is that an NFS volume is used instead of block-level storage.

- **Store logical corruption** Data inside a page is added, modified, deleted, and so on in an unexpected way, usually caused by a third-party application. From an Exchange Server point of view, this is not really corruption, as the database pages contain valid operations, but the user still experiences this as message corruption in his or her mailbox.

Among other solutions like in-place hold, which was explained earlier, a means to help guard against logical corruption is to use a lagged copy in the DAG.

Lagged Copies

A *lagged copy* is a passive mailbox database copy, but one that has a lag time in replaying the log files into the mailbox database. This lag time can be anywhere between one second and 14 days. The lagged copy of a mailbox database can be in the same (Active Directory) site as the active copy of the mailbox database, but it can also be located in another, remote (Active Directory) site for offsite storage.

■ **Note**   Lagged copies are not a high-availability solution, as outlined in Chapter 5, but they are a disaster-recovery solution. Manual intervention is needed to activate a lagged copy, and when you're using a 14-day lag time, that means you need a substantial amount of time to replay the log files and activate the lagged mailbox copy.

In a DAG, the log files are replicated from the Mailbox server holding the active copy of the mailbox database to the Mailbox servers holding the passive copies of the mailbox database. This is no different for lagged copies. Normal passive copies of the mailbox database inspect the log file that was received, and at some point the log file is read and the information is replayed into the passive copy of the mailbox database. Just like the active copy of the mailbox database, there can be some delay in replaying—in other words, there is a certain checkpoint depth.

For lagged copies, however, the log files are not replayed into the passive copy of the mailbox database during the time, as specified in the lag time. When the lag time is two hours, this is not a big deal; but when the lag time is seven days, it means that seven days of log files will be stored on the Mailbox server holding the passive copy. Consequently, you have to take this into account when it comes to your storage design, since seven days of log files can consume a considerable amount of storage space. The Exchange 2013 Server role requirements calculator can do this math for you.

As stated, a lagged copy is not part of a high-availability solution but is part of a disaster-recovery solution. The lagged copy is activated manually, not automatically. When a lagged copy is activated, the log files that are stored during the lag time need to be replayed into the passive copy first. When the lag time is set to seven days, this can take quite some time to finish.

When creating a lagged copy, there are two choices:

- There are already copies of a mailbox database running and the only thing you have to do is add the lag time.

- You want to create an additional copy of a mailbox database and include the lag time during creation of that additional copy.

To create an additional copy of a mailbox database and add the lag time during creation, you can use the following command to create an additional copy and set the replay lag time to four days, seven hours, and 36 minutes:

```
Add-MailboxDatabaseCopy -Identity MDB01 -MailboxServer AMS-EXCH02 -ReplayLagTime 00:10:00
-TruncationLagTime 4.7:36:00 -ActivationPreference 2
```

When you already have a copy of a mailbox database and want to add a replay lag time to this copy, you can use the following example:

```
Set-MailboxDatabaseCopy -Identity MDB01\AMS-EXCH01 -ReplayLagTime 7.0:0:0
```

■ **Note**   For redundancy purposes in transport, the SafetyNet feature is used. To prevent unwanted data loss, the SafetyNet hold time should be higher than the replay lag time of the mailbox database copy. The `Set-TransportConfig` cmdlet can be used to set this using the `-SafetyNetHoldTime` option.

When you have a lagged copy of a mailbox database, the log files from the active copy of the mailbox database are continuously sent to the passive copies, including the lagged copy. On the Mailbox server holding the lagged copy of the mailbox database, the log files are kept in a queue until the lag time expires. If a lag time of seven days is used, this can become a tremendous amount of data. You can check the number of log files in the replay queue using the `Get-MailboxDatabase | Get-MailboxDatabaseCopyStatus` command in EMS. This will show the mailbox database, its status, the copy queue length, and the replay queue length. The copy queue length should be close to zero (although it can increase occasionally), but the replay queue will show the number of log files waiting for the lag time to expire. So don't be alarmed when you see a high number of log files in this queue!

Another option that's only settable using EMS is the `TruncationLagTime` option. This is the lag time that the Microsoft Exchange Replication service should wait after replaying the information into the passive copy of the mailbox database before the log file is actually deleted. The minimum value of the truncation lag time is 0 seconds, the maximum value is 14 days.

Having lagged copies is only one part of the story; recovering from a lagged copy is another part. This is covered in the "Point in Time (PIT) Recovery" section a bit later in this chapter.

Circular Logging

As explained in Chapter 5 about the Mailbox server, using circular logging on a production Mailbox server is, generally speaking, not a good idea since this will block log file replay during recovery. You can restore from a backup without the proper log files, but you cannot recover to a newer point in time, since this information is missing.

When a DAG is configured in your Exchange 2013 environment, things are a bit different. Since there are multiple copies of a mailbox database, there's no need to restore from a backup. In case of a failure, another copy of the mailbox database takes over and continues servicing the user requests.

If there are no legal requirements to create backups, it is possible to use only the Mailbox servers running in a DAG. When one mailbox database fails, another one takes over without the need for an Exchange administrator to restore a mailbox database from backup.

But one of the functions of a backup is to purge log files that are not needed anymore after a backup was taken. To overcome this, circular logging can be enabled within the DAG. Circular logging in a DAG isn't a function of ESE as in a normal scenario, but it is performed by the Microsoft Exchange eplication service.

Circular logging in a DAG is called *continuous replication circular logging* (CRCL). There's a major difference with the default circular logging as used by ESE. In a normal circular logging scenario, log files are deleted once the data in the files is stored in the mailbox database. When using CRCL, however, the log files are deleted only when they have been replicated to the passive copies of the mailbox database. The Microsoft Exchange Replication service communicates using RPC with each other to determine the status of the replication and which log files can be safely deleted.

The following must be true for log files to be deleted:

- CRCL must be enabled.

- The log file is below the checkpoint.

- Other copies of the mailbox database agree with the deletion.

- The log file has been inspected by all lagged copies of the mailbox database.

Log files are also deleted on Mailbox servers holding a lagged copy of the mailbox database. For this to happen, the following must be true:

- The log file is below the checkpoint.

- The log file is older than the combined value of the replay lag time and the truncation lag time.

- The log file is already deleted on the active copy of the mailbox database.

So when using CRCL, you should always be safe, able to recover from a mailbox database failure with minimum loss of data.

Point-in-Time Recovery

When using a lagged copy of a mailbox database, it is possible to return to a specific point in time between the active copy of the mailbox database and the replay lag time of the lagged copy of a mailbox database. This means that it is possible to recover to an exact point in time between 0 seconds and a maximum of 14 days ago.

The technology behind *point-in-time* (PIT) recovery is that all information stored in log files is replayed into the lagged copy of the mailbox database—up to the exact moment you want to recover to.

■ **Note**   Although a very rare occasion, this technique can be used to recover from a logical mailbox database corruption.

The steps to recover to a certain PIT are as follows:

1. Suspend the replication to the lagged copy of the mailbox database.

2. Determine the last log file you want to replay into the mailbox database. This is the PIT you want to recover to.

3. Use ESEUTIL to replay the log files into the lagged copy of the mailbox database.

4. Use this copy of the mailbox database for recovery purposes.

A PIT recovery cannot be performed by the EAC, so the EMS is the only option you have here. To suspend the replication of the lagged copy of the mailbox database, use an EMS command similar to this:

```
Suspend-MailboxDatabaseCopy DB01\AMS-EXCH02 -SuspendComment "Activate lagged copy of DB01 on Server
AMS-EXCH02" -Confirm:$false
```

Determine which log file you want to use for recovery purposes. All log files that are more recent than the chosen one should be moved to a different location to prevent accidental replay of information.

Before replaying the log files, you need to remove the checkpoint file. Replaying the log files starts at the location of the checkpoint file; by removing the checkpoint file, replay starts automatically at the oldest available log file. If information found in these log files is already in the mailbox database, then that's no problem; it will just be skipped. At one point, though, information inside the log files that's not in the mailbox database will be replayed into the mailbox database until the last available log file is replayed. Then, the replaying stops and the mailbox database is closed, as in a clean shutdown state. The mailbox database is available for any recovery purpose you have in mind—for example, a recovery database.

When the checkpoint file is deleted, you open a command prompt, navigate to the location where the lagged copy is stored, and enter a command similar to this:

```
ESEUTIL /R E00 /LF:\DB01\Logfiles /D /I
```

The E00 prefix is the prefix used by this lagged copy, the /L option is used to point to the location of the log files, and the /S option is used to point to the location of the system file. The /D option is used to point to the location of the mailbox database, but in this example it is the current directory. The /I option is used to ignore any missing attachments into the log files that need to go into the mailbox database. All options should have values that correspond to your environment, of course.

Summary

This chapter explained about backup, restore, and disaster recovery, and especially how the three work together. The last part of the chapter described the Microsoft Exchange Native Data Protection, sometimes referred to as a "backupless environment."

Exchange 2013 uses snapshot technology provided by the Virtual Shadowcopy Services (VSS). The out-of-the-box tool Windows Server Backup is able to create VSS backups of the mailbox database. New to Exchange 2013 is the fact that Windows Server Backup can back up passive copies of a mailbox database—something that was not possible to do before.

Mailbox databases can be restored from a backup on the original location, but a recovery mailbox database can be used as well, where the mailbox is restored to a different location, after which all kinds of recovery actions can be taken.

The ultimate disaster recovery is needed when an entire server is lost. It is possible to rebuild a new but identical Exchange 2013 server using the setup application with the /Mode:RecoverServer option. This will retrieve all information from Active Directory.

The Exchange Native Data Protection is a set of technologies that can be used to overcome all kinds of disasters, ranging from messages that are accidentally deleted to additional copies of a mailbox database stored in another location. When things are designed properly, there are situations where a traditional backup is not needed anymore but, of course, this fully depends on your organizational needs and requirements.

The next chapter is about monitoring Exchange 2013—something that's needed as well, and quite a lot of times is forgotten because the typical administrator is too busy. But when monitoring is not performed properly, there's always a risk encountering disaster and having to perform the subsequent recovery.

CHAPTER 8

■ ■ ■

Unified Messaging

With the rise of varied forms of electronic communications has come the need to converge these communication streams into integrated forms known as *unified communications*. Presently, this involves the integration of primarily real-time services, such as instant messaging, telephony (voice over IP, or VOIP), and video conferencing. Unified communications allows messages to be sent through one medium and received on a different medium. Though VOIP was well adopted by enterprises at the time of its inception, there remained a clear desire to extend the functionality to other forms of communication—for example, being able to leave voice-mail messages in mailboxes instead of on proprietary voice-mail systems.

Unified messaging, according to the International Engineering Consortium, is the integration of different electronic messaging and communications media technologies into a single interface that's accessible from a variety of devices and that's applicable to email, SMS, fax, voice mail, and video messaging. This description of the term embraces the concept's multi-disciplinary aspects and its complexity, reflecting the extensive technical knowledge required of the involved components.

In what seems decades ago, vendors like Cisco, Avaya, and Mitel offered products to integrate their telephony solutions with messaging—for example, through dedicated voice-mail systems. Starting with Exchange Server 2007, Microsoft attempted to bridge the gap between PBX solutions and messaging by natively offering integration with supported IP-PBX systems. Most prominent, its unified messaging feature provided a universal inbox for email, inbound faxes, and voice-mail messages, as well as voice-controlled mailbox access using Outlook Voice Access (OVA).

In Exchange 2010, the Unified Messaging (UM) server role was enhanced with an MP3 codec, which allowed Exchange to encode or decode audio streams. Another unified messaging feature that was introduced with Exchange 2010 was *voice-mail preview*, at that time an innovative function that attempted to insert a transcript of the recorded voice-mail message into the body of the accompanying email message. With Exchange 2010, inbound FAX integration was dropped, as Microsoft deemed it not popular. Customers looking to integrate FAX-over-IP solutions as part of their unified messaging strategy, therefore, needed to incorporate third-party solutions.

Exchange 2013 provides solid, cost-effective UC features that can replace third-party solutions such as voice-mail services. In conjunction with supported IP telephony solutions such as Lync Server, Exchange can offer a rich end-user experience that tightly integrates voice communications with an email solution via a single, unified user interface. This chapter explores these features, with the next section presenting an overview and the following sections explaining them in more detail.

Features of Unified Messaging

The unified messaging services provided by Exchange 2013 include the following features:

- *Voice mail*, a complete built-in voice-mail system, tightly integrated with the user's mailbox, that offers access to the voice mails on every device and at any time.

- *Voice-mail preview*, a speech-to-text transcription of recorded voice-mail messages, whereby the text is added to the message body. This voice-mail preview is created only when there are enough resources available on the UM server, a UM language pack is installed for the language used, and the language pack supports voice-mail preview. (There's more information on language packs later.)

- *Outlook voice access*, for using a normal phone to access the Exchange mailbox (email, calendar). You can, for example, have your messages read by the system or you can change meeting requests when you are running late.

- *Play on phone*, such that after a voice mail is delivered, it can generate a phone call to the dialed number and play the message.

- *Call answering*, for answering incoming calls and playing or recording messages. Users can create rules to control the answering of phone calls, with methods that are similar to those for setting up inbox rules; for example, here are some possibilities:

  - Leaving a voice-mail message

  - Transferring the call to another recipient

  - Transferring the call to another recipient's voice mail

  - Transferring the call to an external phone number

- *Message waiting indicator*, a popular notification option whereby a signal is shown when a new voice-mail message has arrived.

- *Missed call and voice-mail notifications using SMS*, for notifying users on configured cell phones of missed calls or new voice-mail messages.

- *Protected voice mail*, allowing users to utilize Rights Management Services (AD RMS) to protect their voice-mail messages or disallowing the forwarding of voice-mail messages.

- *Group addressing*, allowing users to send email and voice messages to a group that is defined in their Contacts folder.

- *Caller ID*, as enhanced in Exchange Server 2013, tries to resolve the caller's telephone number and display it in a voice-mail notification message. It consults Active Directory and the user's Personal Contacts folder.

When you combine Exchange 2013's unified messaging with a Microsoft Lync Server 2013 environment, especially when the Lync Server 2013 is configured for Enterprise Voice, you can build a consolidated, powerful voice-mail system.

■ **Note**　The examples in this chapter assume you have a fully functional IP telephony infrastructure set up, like Lync Server 2013 with Enterprise Voice enabled.

The Role of Unified Messaging

In Exchange Server 2007 and Exchange Server 2010, the unified messaging functionality was offered through the UM server role. This was a separate server role that could be installed on a dedicated server. The architectural changes in Exchange 2013 reduced the UM server role to those of the Client Access servers and Mailbox servers, and this had consequences for the UM server role. Whereas previously the unified messaging function was a separate Exchange server role, in Exchange 2013 it is separated into two functions:

- *Unified messaging call router* runs on the Exchange 2013 Client Access server and is responsible for receiving initial requests from Session Initiation Protocol (SIP) messages from the IP-PBX and redirecting those requests to the appropriate Mailbox server where the designated mailbox is active.

- *The Unified messaging service* runs on Exchange 2013 Mailbox servers, and is responsible for recording the messages and sending them to the corresponding user's mailbox through the Transport service.

SIP is the protocol to create or manage sessions; by default, it uses port 5060 for unsecured SIP traffic, whereas secure SIP uses port 5061 (see Figure 8-1). Media, or the audio stream, is transported directly between the IP-PBX or VoIP gateway and the Mailbox server using the Real-time Transport Protocol (RTP) or secure Real-time Transport Protocol (SRTP) protocol.

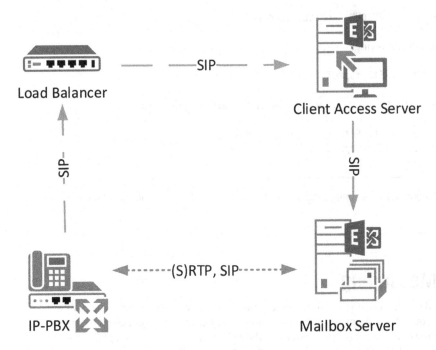

Figure 8-1. *Exchange 2013 unified messaging traffic*

> ■ **Note** The SIP is the de facto signaling protocol for controlling audio or video sessions over IP networks. Discussing SIP would produce a book in itself. If you're looking for more informaiton on SIP, you'll find information from the Internet Engineering Task Force in RFC 3261, available at `https://www.ietf.org/rfc/rfc3261.txt`.

The UM call router running on Exchange 2013 CAS servers will, by default, listen for unsecured (TCP/5060) and secured (TLS/5061) SIP traffic. If you want to change this, you can adjust the UM startup mode by using the `Set-UMCallRouterSettings` cmdlet with the `UMStartupMode` parameter. For example, to configure all Client Access servers to use only unsecured mode, you use:

```
Get-ClientAccessServer | Set-UMCallRouterSettings -UMStartupMode TCP
```

The UM service running on the Exchange 2013 Mailbox servers will listen for unsecured (TCP/5062) and secured (TLS/5063) SIP traffic as well, but on different ports. To adjust this, you can change the UM startup mode by using the `Set-UMService` cmdlet. For example, to configure all Mailbox servers to use only unsecured mode, you use:

```
Get-MailboxServer | Set-UMService -UMStartupMode TCP
```

Note that you can change behavior for a single server by specifying its identity; for example,

```
Set-UMCallRouterSettings -Identity EX2010UM1 -UMStartupMode TLS
```

Or, for Mailbox servers, you use the following:

```
Set-UMService -Identity EX2010UM2 -UMStartupMode TLS
```

To restore UM services to listen to both ports, you specify Dual as the startup mode, as follows:

```
Get-ClientAccessServer | Set-UMCallRouterSettings -UMStartupMode Dual
Get-MailboxServer | Set-UMService -UMStartupMode Dual
```

> ■ **Note** Using TLS or TLS in dual mode requires configuring a valid TLS certificate. There's more on configuring TLS certificates later in this chapter.

Objects of Unified Messaging

To integrating the Exchange unified messaging function into your existing telephony infrastructure, you define several components that make up your IP telephony infrastructure and set your connection options. Successful implementation of unified messaging depends on proper definition of these components: UM dial plans, UM IP gateways, and UM hunt groups. Let's look at each of these objects and see how to configure them.

> ■ **Note** To perform management tasks on UM-related objects, you need to be assigned the UM Management or Organization Management role.

UM Dial Plans

An important piece of information in telephony is a dial plan, or in this case, a UM dial plan. This dial plan defines the groups of telephone extension numbers, similar to subnets in IPv4 addressing. Using the same analogy, the number of digits in an UM dial plan can be viewed as the opposite of a subnet mask. Whereas the subnet mask defines the number of bits used to separate subnet information from host address information, the number of digits in a UM dial plan defines the number of digits used in digit sequence as part of a group of extensions. A UM dial plan contains a single range of numbers; it cannot contain multiple ranges.

For Exchange UM to answer incoming calls, you need to create at least one UM dial plan. Creating a dial plan requires the following pieces of information:

- *Name.* This name is used to identify the dial plan and is also used to create a similarly named default policy that's related to the dial plan.

- *Number.* The number of digits used to specify the extension in `NumberOfDigits`.

- *UriType.* Used to define how to link phone numbers to mailboxes; depends on the IP PBX used in your organization. You can specify one of the following types:

  - `TeleExtn` for IP PBXs supporting the telephone extension URI; for example, Tel:1234 or 1234@172.16.10.123.

  - `SIPname` for IP PBXs supporting the email address-like SIP URIs; for example, sip:<user>@<domain>. To integrate Exchange 2013 with Lync, you use UriType SIPname.

  - `E.164` for IP PBXs supporting E.164 routing; for example, Tel:+31101234567890.

  - *VoIPSecurity* to specify if you want Exchange to communicate with IP-PBXs and other Exchange servers in unsecured, SIP secured, or secured mode.

■ **Note** In VoIP unsecured security mode, all traffic is unencrypted. In secured mode, all traffic is encrypted, including signaling (SIP) and media (RTP). In SIP secured mode, only SIP signaling traffic is encrypted; RTP media remains unencrypted.

- *Country code.* Optionally, you specify `CountryOrRegionCode` to configure the associated language of the pre-recorded prompts, automatic speech recognition (ASR) of spoken audio, and pronunciation and rules for text-to-speech synthesis and the related name recognition.

- *Telephone numbers.* You specify the telephone numbers to be used for Outlook Voice Access. On UM dial plans, greetings and informational announcements are played when calling an Outlook Voice Access number.

■ **Caution** Before a configured `CountryOrRegionCode` is used by Exchange, the language pack supporting the specified language should be present on the Exchange Mailbox server.

To create a UM dial plan, you can use the Exchange Admin Center, via Unified Messaging ➤ UM dial plans section (see Figure 8-2). Click the + sign to add a new dial plan, and enter the required information, such as the name of the dial plan and the extension length.

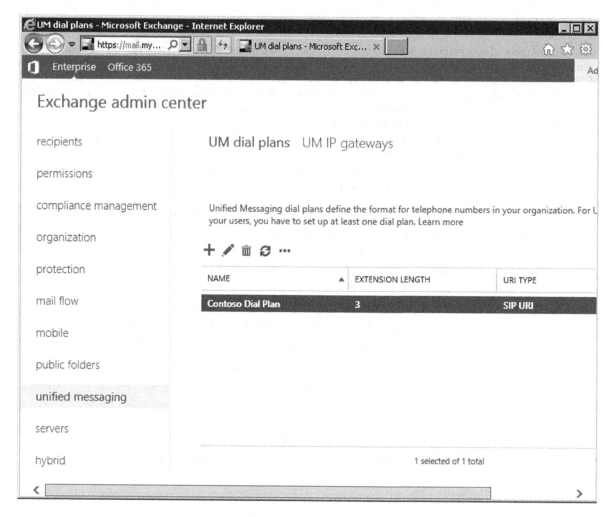

Figure 8-2. UM dial plan choices in Exchange Admin Center

Some UM dial plan configuration options are only configurable after you've created a new UM dial plan, done by editing its properties. You select the just created UM dial plan, and choose the Edit option. You will notice that there are a lot more options available now than when you were creating the UM dial plan. To access the UM dial plan settings, you click the Configure button. You can now configure all available UM dial plan options (see Figure 8-3).

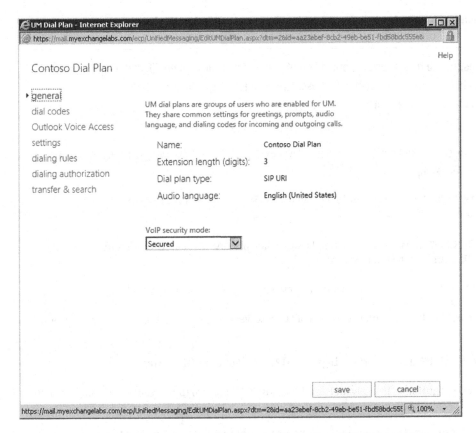

Figure 8-3. Configuring the UM dial plan settings using Exchange Admin Center

■ **Note** When testing, you may need to configure the UM dial plan's dialing rules and dialing authorization to allow unrestricted calling. Following the examples used in this chapter, you use the following to configure the UM dial plan to allow unrestricted calls:

```
Set-UMDialPlan 'Contoso Dial Plan' -ConfiguredInCountryOrRegionGroups 'Anywhere,*,*,*'
```

`-AllowedInCountryOrRegionGroups "Anywhere"`. You may also need to set unrestricted authorization on UM mailbox policies—for example, `Set-UMMailboxPolicy -Identity 'Contoso Dial Plan Default Policy'` `-AllowedInCountryOrRegionGroups 'Anywhere'`. Be sure to remove or reconfigure these settings before going live.

The cmdlet to create a dial plan is `New-UMDialPlan`. For example, to create a dial plan for Lync, using three digits, unsecured mode, using US (code 1) as the associated language, and using 900 as the subscriber number for Outlook Voice Access, you employ something like this:

```
New-UMDialPlan -Name 'Contoso Dial Plan' -Uritype SIPName -NumberofDigits 3 -VoIPSecurity Secured
-CountryOrRegionCode 1 -AccessTelephoneNumbers 900
```

Next, you associate a unified messaging IP gateway and Mailbox server with the UM dial plan.

■ **Note**   Should your infrastructure require use of ports different from 5060 for unsecured SIP and 5061 for secured SIP, you can use Set-UMCallRouterSettings to reconfigure those ports using the SipTcpListeningPort and SipTlsListeningPort parameters—for example,

Set-UMCallRouterSettings -SipTcpListeningPort 5560 -SipTlsListeningPort 5561.

Should you need to change those required ports for any down-level Exchange 2010 UM server, you use Set-UMService with the same parameters—for example,

Set-UMService -Identity EX2010UM1 - SipTcpListeningPort 5560 - SipTlsListeningPort 5561.

When using Lync or OCS 2007 R2 as IP-PBX, you need to associate the CAS servers (UM call routers) with a UM dial plan using Set-UMCallRouterSettings; for example,

```
Set-UMCallRouterSettings -Server ams-exch01.contoso.com -DialPlans 'Contoso Dial Plan'
```

If you want to reconfigure the UM call router service on all CAS servers at once so that they use only the Contoso dial plan, you enter:

```
Get-ClientAccessServer | Set-UMCallRouterSettings -DialPlans 'Contoso Dial Plan'
```

DialPlans is a multi-valued attribute. If you want to add 'Contoso Dial Plan' to the current set of configured dial plans, you use:

```
Get-ClientAccessServer | Set-UMCallRouterSettings -DialPlans @{Add='Contoso Dial Plan'}
```

Should you need to remove 'Contoso Dial Plan' from all CAS servers, you can use:

```
Get-ClientAccessServer | Set-UMCallRouterSettings -DialPlans @{Remove='Contoso Dial Plan'}
```

And should you need to remove a CAS server from servicing any UM dial plan, you set DialPlans to $null; for example,

```
Set-UMCallRouterSettings -Server lon-exch01.contoso.com -DialPlans $null
```

If you want to configure Outlook Voice Access, you can do so by editing the related UM dial plan from the Exchange Admin Center, assigning it at least one E.164 telephone number, also known as the subscriber access number, on which Outlook Voice Access should be reachable.

To configure an Outlook voice access number for an UM dial plan, you can also use Set-UMDialPlan providing the E.164 numbers to be used, with the AccessTelephoneNumbers parameter; for example,

```
Set-UMDialPlan -Identity 'Contoso Dial Plan' -AccessTelephoneNumbers @('+3112345601')
```

When integrating Exchange UM with OCS or Lync Server, you can use a tool OcsUmUtil.exe, which performs the following tasks:

- Creates contact objects for each UM auto attendant.

- Creates contact objects for each subscriber access number.

- Verifies the Lync Enterprise voice location profile information against the UM dial plans.

The OcsUmUtil.exe tool is by default located in the %CommonProgramFiles%\Microsoft Lync Server 2013\ Support folder on a Lync 2013 server. When run without parameters, the tool starts in GUI mode. You can also provide the forest to scan for Exchange UM objects and the SIP domain for which to configure contact objects using the /forest and /domain parameters, after which the tool will create the required objects (see Figure 8-4). If you have relocated the UM auto attendant objects from their default location, which is the RTC Special Accounts OU in the root of your Active Directory tree, you may need to specify /ou as well together with correct location.

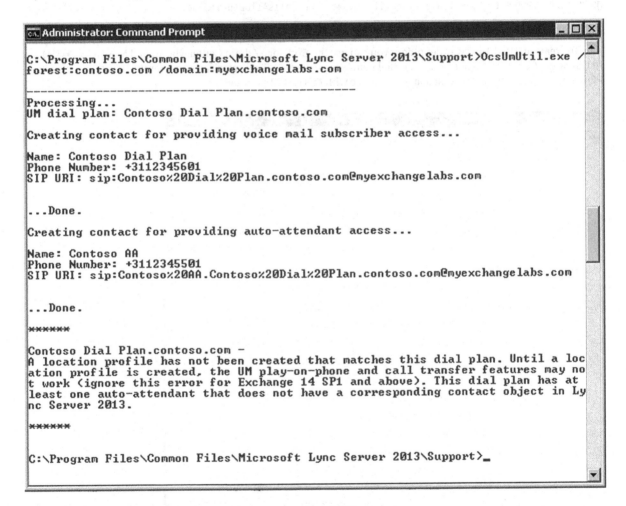

Figure 8-4. Creating Exchange UM contact objects using OcsUmUtil.exe

UM IP Gateway

To configure where Exchange can receive and send calls to, you need to configure an UM IP gateway, which represents your IP telephony endpoint that could be an IP-PBX or voice gateway. New in Exchange 2013 is that unified messaging now fully supports IPv6. Thus, unlike earlier versions of unified messaging in Exchange, it is no longer necessary to have IPv4 next to IPv6 so that unified messaging will work on IPv6 networks.

■ **Caution**   If you are running OCS or Lync Server, you can skip manually creating the UM IP gateway and instead run the script `ExchUcUtil.ps1`, which is located in the $exscripts folder. Run this script from a Mailbox server. This script will create an UM IP gateway for each existing Lync pool and it will give Lync groups the necessary permissions on Exchange UM objects in Active Directory. If you have any existing UM IP gateway definitions, disable outgoing calls on those UM IP gateways by using `Set-UMIPGateway -Identity <Name> -OutCallsAllowed $false`.

To create an UM IP gateway definition, you can use the Exchange Admin Center, via Unified Messaging ➤ UM IP Gateways. Click the + sign to add a new dial plan (see Figure 8-5). Then specify a name for the IP gateway, give its FQDN or address, and select a dial plan to associate with this UM IP gateway.

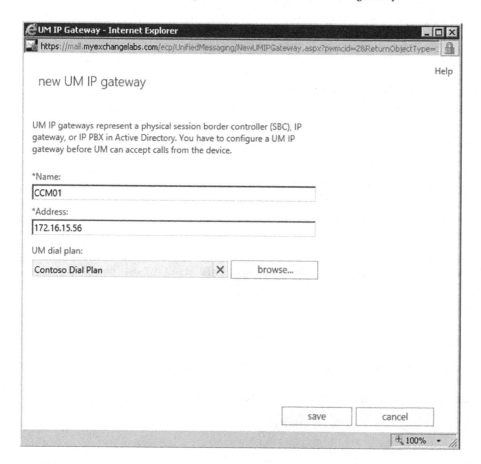

Figure 8-5. *Creating a UM IP gateway using Exchange Admin Center*

■ **Note** You can have up to 200 UM IP gateways configured per dial plan.

To create an UM IP gateway object using Exchange Management Shell, employ the `New-UMIPGateway` cmdlet, specifying a name, give its FQDN or address, and select the UM dial plan to associate it with this UM IP gateway; for example,

```
New-UMIPGateway -Name 'CCMO1' -Address 172.16.15.51 -UMDialPlan 'Contoso Dial Plan'
```

The output of this cmdlet is shown in Figure 8-6.

```
Machine: AMS-EXCH02.contoso.com                                                          _□×
     C:\>New-UMIPGateway -Name 'CCMO1' -Address 172.16.15.52 -UMDialPlan 'Contoso Dial Plan'

Name              Address                HuntGroups           OutCallsAllowed  Status
----              -------                ----------           ---------------  ------
CCMO1             172.16.15.52           <:Contoso Dial Plan>  True             Enabled


     C:\>_
```

Figure 8-6. *Creating a UM IP gateway definition using* `New-UMIPGateway`

If you want to specify an IPv6 address, you need to use the `IPAddressFamily` parameter as well, as by default it will be set to use `IPv4Only`, which means IPv4 is used. To enable use of the IPv6 address, set `IPAddressFamily` to `IPv6Only`. Alternatively, you can configure `IPAddressFamily` as Any, in which case Exchange will try connecting by using IPv6 and only fall back to IPv4 if it can't connect using IPv6.

So, to reconfigure the previously created UM IP gateway to use a FQDN of `lync.contoso.com`, and to use protocols IPv6 with fallback to IPv4, you use:

```
Set-UMIPGateway -Identity 'CCMO1' -Address 'lync.contoso.com' -IPAddressFamily Any
```

■ **Note** If your IP-PBX is listening on a port other than 5060, you can use `Set-UMIPGateway` with the `Port` parameter to use a different port—for example, `Set-UMIPGateway -Identity 'CCMO1' Port 5061`.

When required, you can disable and (re)enable a UM IP gateway object. When disabled, calls will not be routed to the host or address configured with the disabled UM IP gateway definition. To disable a UM IP gateway, you use `Disable-UMIPGateway`; for example,

```
Disable-UMIPGateway -Identity 'CCMO1'
```

Note that this will gracefully disable the UM IP gateway by finishing the current sessions but disallow new calls. When required, you can forcefully terminate current calls as well by setting the `Immediate` parameter to `$true`; for example,

```
Disable-UMIPGateway -Identity 'CCMO1' -Immediate $true
```

To enable the UM IP gateway again, you use `Enable-UMIPGateway`, as follows:

```
Enable-UMIPGateway -Identity 'CCMO1'
```

UM Hunt Groups

A *hunt group* is a single telephone number that can be associated with sets of extensions to distribute incoming calls. For example, a support desk can have 10 extension numbers all of which are associated with a single hunt group telephone number.

In Exchange UM, an extension number associated with a hunt group is also called a *pilot number*. This number is contained in the SIP INVITE message from the IP-PBX, allowing an Exchange server to match it against the hunt group to which it belongs. If there is a match, the call is answered.

A UM hunt group definition consists of the following elements:

- *Name* of the Hunt Group.

- *UMDialPlan* to specify the name of the UM dial plan to associate with the UM hunt group.

- Optionally, *PilotIdentifier* to specify one or more pilot numbers attached to the hunt group in use.

- *UMIPGateway* to specify the name of the UM IP gateway object to associate with the hunt group.

So, to create a new hunt group named ContosoIT, using a pilot identifier of 123, and associating it with UM dial plan 'Contoso Dial Plan' and UM IP Gateway 'LyncHQ,' you use:

```
New-UMHuntGroup -Name 'ContosoIT' -PilotIdentifier 123
 -UMDialPlan 'Contoso Dial Plan' -UMIPGateway 'LyncHQ'
```

The output of this cmdlet is shown in Figure 8-7.

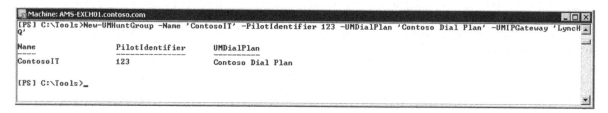

Figure 8-7. *Creating a UM hunt group using New-UMHuntGroup*

■ **Note**   Previous versions of Exchange unified messaging required hunt groups to be associated with a pilot number. This is optional in Exchange 2013. When not specified, calls can be routed from a UM call routing server to any Exchange 2013 Mailbox server.

UM Mailbox Policies

Much like regular mailbox policies, UM mailbox policies determine the UM-related settings that apply to UM-enabled users, done by creating UM mailbox policy objects and assigning them to UM-enabled users. UM mailbox policies allow organizations to configure the following settings:

- UM features

- PIN policies

- UM message-customization options

- Call authorization options

- Voice-mail security options

To create a UM mailbox policy from the Exchange Admin Center, navigate to unified messaging ➤ UM dial plans. Select a UM dial plan and click the Edit icon. You will notice that there are now additional settings available compared to when you were creating a UM dial plan. Notice also that there is a default UM mailbox policies section, which shows the UM mailbox policy that was created when the UM dial plan was established. This default UM mailbox policy is named <UM Dial Plan> Default Policy, as shown in Figure 8-8.

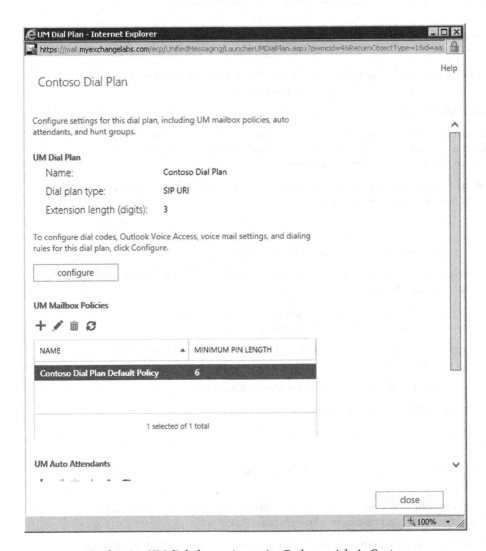

Figure 8-8. *Configuring UM dial plan options using Exchange Admin Center*

Now you can edit the properties of the existing UM mailbox policy or click the New icon to create a new UM mailbox policy and have it associated with the active UM dial plan. To configure some of the most common UM mailbox policy settings, you specify one or more of the following parameters when using `New-UMMailboxPolicy`, or use them together with the `Set-UMMailboxPolicy` cmdlet:

- `AllowAutomaticSpeechRecognition` specifies if users can use automatic speech recognition (ASR).

- `AllowCallAnsweringRules` specifies if users are allowed to configure *call answering rules*. (There's more on call answering rules later in this chapter.)

- `AllowCommonPatterns` specifies if users are allowed obvious PIN codes, such as 11111 or 12345.

- `AllowFax` specifies if the user is allowed to receive inbound faxes. Make sure to configure `FaxServerURI` as well.

- `AllowMessageWaitingIndicator` specifies if the user is allowed to receive message waiting indicator (MWI) notifications when a new voice mail is received.

- `AllowMissedCallsNotifications` specifies if the user will receive missed call notifications.

- `AllowPinlessVoicemailAccess` specifies if the user can access voice mail without being required to enter a PIN code. Note that a PIN is still required to access the user's regular mailbox—for example, email and calendar information.

- `AllowPlayOnPhone` specifies if the user can play back voice-mail messages on her phone. (There's more on play on phone later in this chapter.)

- `AllowSMSNotification` specifies if the user is allowed to receive text messages. Note that in order to receive these messages, the `UMSMSNotification` option needs to be configured as `VoiceMail` or `VoiceMailAndMissedCalls,` using `Set-UMMailbox`.

- `AllowSubscriberAccess` specifies if the user is allowed subscriber access to his mailbox to receive voice-mail messages, for instance.

- `AllowVoiceMailPreview` specifies if the user is enabled to receive voice-mail previews for call-answer-rule answered messages, or voice-mail messages the user sent to other users.

- `AllowVoiceResponseToOtherMessageTypes` specifies if users can attach voice-mail messages to email messages or calendar items.

- `FaxMessageText` specifies the text to include in the body of fax messages.

- `FaxServerURI` specifies the SIP URI of the fax solution.

- `LogonFailuresBeforePINReset` specifies the number of failed PIN logins before the PIN is automatically reset. To disable this behavior, set `LogonFailuresBeforePINReset` to Unlimited.

- `MaxGreetingDuration` limits the time of the greeting, ranging from 1 to 10 minutes. Default is 5 minutes.

- `MaxLogonAttempts` specifies the maximum number of failed logons after which to lock an UM-enabled mailbox. Value can range from 1 to 999. Default value is 15.

- `MinPINLength` specifies the minimum required PIN length, ranging from 4 to 24 digits. Default value is 6.

- PINHistoryCount specifies the number of previous PINs to remember, disallowing their usage. This setting can range from 1 to 20. Default is set to 5.

- PINLifetime specifies the number of days until a new PIN is required, ranging from 1 to 999. The default value is 60. Set this value to Unlimited to have a non-expiring PIN.

- ResetPINText specifies the text to include in PIN reset email messages.

- UMDialPlan specifies the name of the associated UM dial plan.

- UMEnabledText specifies the text to include in the email message sent when a user gets UM-enabled.

- VoiceMailText specifies the text to include in voice-mail notification email messages.

So, to reconfigure an existing UM mailbox policy named 'Contoso Dial Plan Default Policy,' you use:

```
Set-UMMailboxPolicy -Identity 'Contoso Dial Plan Default Policy'
 -LogonFailuresBeforePINReset Unlimited -MinPINLength 4 -PINLifetime 30
```

■ **Note** The "Message Waiting" indicator feature leverages Exchange's Search folder functionality. A separate Voice Mail Search folder is created for UM-enabled users, to which the mailbox assistant subscribes and sends SIP NOTIFY messages when new messages are found. "Message Waiting" indicator messages are not available to users with a mailbox hosted on Exchange 2010 or Exchange 2007.

■ **Caution** When a new voice mail has been detected by the mailbox assistant, it triggers the UM server to send a SIP NOTIFY message to the IP-PBX, which should notify the user or endpoint. This kind of unsolicited notification needs to be supported by your IP-PBX or the user will not receive MWI notifications.

UM Auto Attendant

Exchange unified messaging allows you to create UM auto attendants. These are optional configuration objects per UM dial plan. They allow callers to receive corporate or information messages, locate users, or automatically answer and route incoming calls through a voice-menu system. Some of these settings can be made dependent on the current date and time, allowing for use during business and non-business hours.

An UM auto attendent can also be configured for a language other than the default U.S. English, or even for multiple languages. This requires installation of the UM language pack for the desired language. (There's more on UM language packs later in this chapter.) Enabling a different language for an UM auto attendant will result in different default prompts and will not translate any custom prompts.

You can configure only one language per UM auto attendant. Should your organization require support for multiple languages, you can create a UM auto attendant for each language, with each attached to its extension, and then create a main UM auto attendent to provide a language selection menu. From the language selection, the caller is transferred to the UM auto attendent of the requested language.

■ **Caution** If you have created an UM auto attendant and are using OCS or Lync Server, you may need to rerun `OcsUmUtil.exe` tool to provision a contact object in Active Directory before you can access the UM auto attendant. See the "UM Dial Plan" section earlier in this chapter for more information.

Configuring UM Auto Attendent with Exchange Admin Center

To configure an UM auto attendent using the Exchange Admin Center, you navigate to unified messaging ➤ UM dial plans. Select the UM dial plan for which you want to create an UM auto attendant, and click the Edit icon. At the bottom of the dial plan configuration screen, there is a section "UM Auto Attendants." Here you can manage the UM auto attendants associated with this UM dial plan. Click the + sign to create a new UM auto attendant and enter details such as the name of the UM auto attendant, or voice command settings. It is recommended you leave unchecked the option "Create This Auto Attendant as Enabled," as you first may want to configure details before the UM auto attendant becomes active.

As with the UM Dial Plan, creating and configuring an UM auto attendant from the Exchange Admin Center is a two-stage process. After creation of the initial object, you need to edit it in order to configure the details (see Figure 8-9), such as:

- General settings, like the access numbers, the language to use for the default prompts, and if the UM auto attendent is to support voice commands.

- Greetings and informational message, the first optionally for business and non-business hours. The default greeting in English is "Welcome, you are connected to Microsoft Exchange." You can customize this to, for example, "Welcome to Contoso."

- The designation of business hours on a weekly calendar, with the option to configure holidays.

- A custom menu, optionally voice controlled, to manage call flow and transfer. It is possible to configure a separate menu for business and non-business hours. The menu options will only be synthesized by the UM text-to-speech engine when a default greeting is configured.

- Access to the address book and if the caller is allowed to search the address book based on the current dial plan, the GAL, or by using a specific address list. You can also configure the operator extension number, which is to support the option of escaping the voice-controlled menu and getting a person on the phone, or when the caller does not select an option for a certain period.

- Authorizations for rerouting the caller by the UM auto attendant.

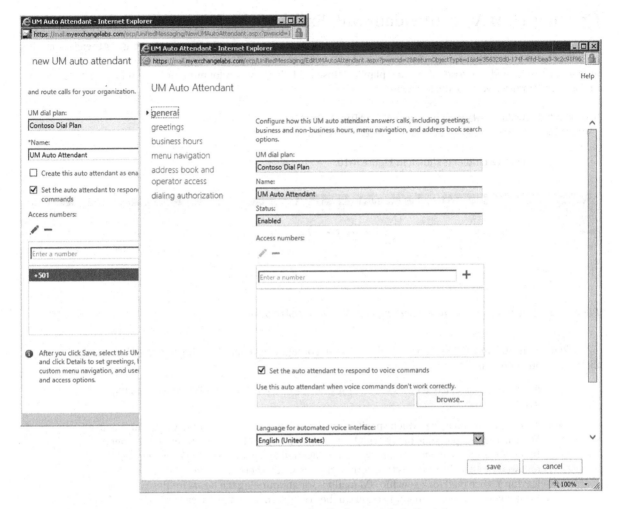

Figure 8-9. *Creating and editing an UM auto attendant using Exchange Admin Center*

On UM auto attendants, the greetings, informational announcements, and menu options are played when an UM auto attendant is called. When you are happy with the results, you enable the UM auto attendant by clicking the Enable icon from the UM dial plan details screen.

■ **Tip**   Depending on your requirements, the call flow between UM auto attendants can become quite complex. It is recommended you plan the call flow and determine the requirements before implementing the UM auto attendants structure.

Creating a UM Auto Attendant with Exchange Management Shell

To create an UM auto attendant using the Exchange Management Shell, you employ the New-UMAutoAttendant cmdlet or Set-UMAutoAttendant to reconfigure any existing UM auto attendant. For example, to create a speech-enabled UM auto attendant named 'Contoso AA' for dial plan 'Contoso Dial Plan,' using pilot number 501 but leaving it disabled for further configuration, you use the following:

```
New-UMAutoAttendant -Name 'Contoso AA' -UMDialPlan 'Contoso Dial Plan'
 -PilotIdentifierList 501 -Status Disabled -SpeechEnabled $true
```

The output of this cmdlet is shown in Figure 8-10.

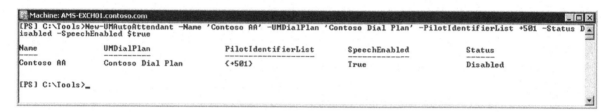

Figure 8-10. *Creating an UM auto attendant using New-UMAutoAttendant*

After creating the initial UM auto attendant, you can configure its details by using Set-UMAutoAttendant. Some of the most popular options are:

- AfterHoursKeyMappingEnabled, which specifies if the non-business-hour key mappings are active.

- AfterHoursKeyMapping, which specifies an array of non-business-hour key mappings to use. You can define up to nine items, which are assigned to keys 1-9, as 0 is reserved for operator. Items consist of the menu option, which is converted using the text-to-speech engine, followed by an action such as transferring the call to another extension or UM auto attendant, leaving a voice mail for a specific UM mailbox, or announcing the hours for the business location or business. A timeout action can be configured for when the caller does not select an option, using key '-'.

- AfterHoursMainMenuCustomPromptEnabled, which specifies if the non-business-hours custom prompt is enabled.

- AfterHoursMainMenuCustomPromptFilename, which specifies the custom audio file to use as non-business-hours custom prompt, when AfterHoursMainMenuCustomPromptEnabled is $true.

- AfterHoursTransferToOperatorEnabled, which specifies if transfer to the operator is allowed during non-business hours.

- AfterHoursWelcomeGreetingEnabled, which specifies if the greeting is played during non-business hours.

- AfterHoursWelcomeGreetingFilename, which specifies the custom audio file to play as greeting message when AfterHoursWelcomeGreetingEnabled is $true.

- `BusinessHoursKeyMappingEnabled`, `BusinessHoursKeyMapping`, `BusinessHoursMainMenuCustomPromptEnabled`, `BusinessHoursMainMenuCustomPromptFilename`, `BusinessHoursTransferToOperatorEnabled`, `BusinessHoursWelcomeGreetingEnabled`, and `BusinessHoursWelcomeGreetingFilename`, which configure the equivalent of their AfterHours* counterparts, except that they apply during business hours.

- `AllowDialPlanSubscribers`, which specifies if subcribers of the associated dial plan are allowed to dial numbers in the same dial plan.

- `DTMFFallbackAutoAttendant`, which specifies the dual-tone multi-frequency (DTMF) UM auto attendant to use when `SpeechEnabled` is `$true` and UM fails three times to recognize the voice input.

- `BusinessHoursSchedule`, which specifies the business hours. The value is an array of values formatted as <Day>.<Hours>:<Minutes>, where Sunday is day 0. So, 1.13:15 is Monday 13:15.

- `HolidaySchedule`, which specifies the holiday schedule. On those days, non-business hours are in effect. The schedule is an array of values formatted as 'Description,<file name for prompt>,<date>[,<end date>]', where the filename is the name of an imported UM prompt (more on that later). So, 'Christmas,GreetingChristmas.wav,12/25/2015,12/26/2015' will result in non-business-hours behavior on December 25, 2015, until December 26, 2015, playing the stored UM prompt `GreetingChristmas.wav` as greeting message.

- `BusinessLocation`, which specifies the location to be announced by the UM auto attendant when the business location option has been selected.

- `BusinessName`, which specifies the name of the business to announce as part of the default *greeting.

- `CallSomeoneEnabled`, which specifies if the Call Someone feature is enabled, in which case the caller can call someone from directory search.

- `ContactRecipientContainer`, which specifies the organizational unit to use for directory searches.

- `ContactScope`, which specifies the scope of directory searches when callers indicate the name of a user to call. Possible values are `GlobalAddressList`, `AddressList`, or `DialPlan`. When set to `AddressList`, the `ContactAddressList` needs to be set to the address list used for directory searches.

- `ForwardCallsToDefaultMailbox`, which when set to `$true`, forwards all inbound calls headed to the UM auto attendant to the UM-enabled mailbox specified by `DefaultMailbox`.

- `InfoAnnouncementEnabled`, which specifies if the informational announcement, indicated by `InfoAnnouncementFilename`, should be played.

- `Language`, which specifies the language used by the UM auto attendant.

- `MatchedNameSelectionMethod`, which specifies the method to differentiate between similar user names. Options are `Department`, `Title`, `Location`, `PromptForAlias` to prompt for an alias, `InheritedFromUMDialPlan` to use the UM dial plan setting, or `None`.

- `NameLookupEnabled`, which specifies if the caller is allowed to perform directory searches by dialing or saying the name.

- `OperatorExtension`, which specifies the extension of the operator. When not specified, the operator extension configured on the UM dial plan will be used.

- PilotIdentifierList, which specifies one or more pilot numbers to be used by the UM auto attendant. The pilot numbers should be in E.164 format.

- SendVoiceMsgEnabled, which specifies if the Send Message feature is enabled. in which case the caller is allowed to send voice-mail messages to other UM-enabled users.

- SpeechEnabled, which specifies if the UM auto attendant is speech-enabled.

- Timezone, which specifies the time zone to be used with the UM auto attendant. When not specified, the time zone configured on the Mailbox server is used. TimeZoneName specifies the name to partially match against the built-in list of time-zone specifications.

- WeekStartDay, which specifies the day to be treated as the first day of the week.

Additional Configurations

Assume you want to reconfigure the previously created UM auto attendant 'Contoso AA.' First, let's define the business hours from Monday (day 1, as you do not reconfigure WeekStartDay) to Friday, 8:00 to 18:00, as follows:

```
Set-UMAutoAttendant -Identity 'Contoso AA' -BusinessHoursSchedule 1.08:00-18:00, 2.08:00-18:00,
3.08:00-18:00, 4.08:00-18:00, 5.08:00-18:00
```

Now, assume you want to configure Christmas as the holiday schedule, using a custom greeting. You have created a PCM/8 kHz/mono .wav file containing a custom greeting. Before you can use this file in an UM auto attendant, you need to read the file as a byte array and import it using Import-UMPrompt. This will store the audio file under a given name in the SystemMailbox{e0dc1c29-89c3-4034-b678-e6c29d823ed9}arbitration mailbox.

■ **Tip** Unlike previous versions of Exchange, where the greeting and informational messages had to be present on all Unified Messaging servers, the custom prompts in Exchange 2013 are imported in the SystemMailbox{e0dc1c29-89c3-4034-b678-e6c29d823ed9}. The prompts can be in one of the following formats: WMA 9.2 (96 kbps/44 kHz/stereo/1pass CBR, WMA9 8 kbps/8 kHz/Mono), or Linear PCM (16 bit/8 kHz). You can import custom prompts using Import-UMPrompt or you can export them using Export-UMPrompt. These custom prompts can be referred to by specifying the filename of the audio prompt in the HolidaySchedule parameter value when using Set-UMAutoAttendant, for example.

```
[byte[]]$CG = Get-content -Path "c:\UMPrompts\GreetingChristmas.wav'
 -Encoding Byte -ReadCount 0
Import-UMPrompt -UMAutoAttendant 'Contoso AA' -PromptFileName 'GreetingChristmas.wav'
 -PromptFileData $CG
```

■ **Tip** Importing custom prompts for use as greetings in a UM dial plan is identical to importing them for UM auto attendants. In order to configure UM dial plan greetings, you need to specify the filename—for example, as WelcomeGreetingFilename. For example, if you have imported a greeting using the prompt filename 'welcome.wav,' you can configure it as a welcome greeting using Set-UMDialPlan -Identity 'Contoso Dial Plan' -WelcomeGreetingEnabled $true -WelcomeGreetingFileName 'welcome.wav'.

The audio file is now stored under the name specified with `PromptFileName`, `'GreetingChristmas.wav'` and can be referenced to from the 'Contoso AA' UM auto attendant using this name. So, to configure a holiday schedule for December 25 and 26, employing the previously imported custom UM prompt, you use:

```
Set-UMAutoAttendant -Identity 'Contoso AA'
 -HolidaySchedule 'Christmas,GreetingChristmas.wav,12/25/2015,12/26/2015'
```

▓ Tip `HolidaySchedule` supports adding and removing values using the Add/Remove hash table. So, to add, for example, New Year's Day with a figurative `NY.wav` prompt, you can use:

```
Set-UMAutoAttendant -Identity 'Contoso AA'
 -HolidaySchedule @{Add='New Year,NY.wav,01/01/2015'}.
```

Creating a Custom Navigation Menu

Suppose you want to create a custom navigation menu for the UM auto attendant that must be active during business hours. You have the options listed in Table 8-1 to choose from.

Table 8-1. *UM Auto Attendant Navigation Menu Options*

Action	Example	Comment
Transfer to extension	'1, Transfer,123'	2nd field is extension.
Transfer to UM auto attendant	'2,Transfer UMAA,,Contoso AA'	3rd field is name of the UM auto attendant.
Leave voice-mail message	'3,Leave VM,,,,,727011cb-a607-4c1c-a46d-6c0adf9a65e7'	7nd field is Mailbox GUID of the UM mailbox to receive the voice mail.
Announce business location	'4,Location,,,,,,,,1,'	9th field is set to 1.
Announce business hours	'5,Hours,,,,,,,,,1'	10nd field is set to 1.

Optionally, you can play an audio file. Import the UM prompt using Import-UMPrompt, associating it to the UM auto attendant, and specify its name as the 5th field—for example, '1,Transfer,,,TransferHelp.wav.' Use menu option '-' to specify the timeout action that will be selected when the called does not select an option in a timely fashion.

So, suppose you want 1 to transfer the call to sales on extension 201, 2 to transfer the caller to the service desk on 999. When no menu option is selected, the UM auto attend should drop back to extension 001 after playing the UM prompt named Timeout.wav:

```
Set-UMAutoAttendant -Identity 'Contoso AA' -BusinessHoursKeyMappingEnabled $true
 -BusinessHoursKeyMapping @('1,Sales,201', '2,Service Desk,999',
 '-,Timeout,001,,GreetingChristmas.wav')
```

When ready, you can inspect the UM auto attendant configuration using `Get-UMAutoAttendant`:

```
Get-UMAutoAttendant -Identity 'Contoso AA' | Format-List:
```

The output of this cmdlet should be similar to the output shown in Figure 8-11.

```
Machine: AMS-EXCH01.contoso.com                                                                    _ □ ×

[PS] C:\>Get-UMAutoAttendant -Identity 'Contoso AA'  | fl

RunspaceId                                 : f1d02e15-cbec-47b4-8006-ca1ea795fd4d
SpeechEnabled                              : True
AllowDialPlanSubscribers                   : True
AllowExtensions                            : True
AllowedInCountryOrRegionGroups             : {}
AllowedInternationalGroups                 : {}
CallSomeoneEnabled                         : True
ContactScope                               : DialPlan
ContactAddressList                         :
SendVoiceMsgEnabled                        : False
BusinessHoursSchedule                      : {Mon.8:00 AM-Mon.6:00 PM, Tue.8:00 AM-Tue.6:00 PM, Wed.8:00 AM-Wed.6:00
                                             PM, Thu.8:00 AM-Thu.6:00 PM, Fri.8:00 AM-Fri.6:00 PM}
PilotIdentifierList                        : {+501}
UMDialPlan                                 : Contoso Dial Plan
DTMFFallbackAutoAttendant                  :
HolidaySchedule                            : {Christmas,GreetingChristmas.wav,12/25/2015,12/26/2015}
TimeZone                                   : W. Europe Standard Time
TimeZoneName                               : (UTC+01:00) Amsterdam, Berlin, Bern, Rome, Stockholm, Vienna
MatchedNameSelectionMethod                 : InheritFromDialPlan
BusinessLocation                           :
WeekStartDay                               : Monday
Status                                     : Disabled
Language                                   : en-US
OperatorExtension                          :
InfoAnnouncementFilename                   :
InfoAnnouncementEnabled                    : False
NameLookupEnabled                          : True
StarOutToDialPlanEnabled                   : False
ForwardCallsToDefaultMailbox               : False
DefaultMailbox                             :
BusinessName                               :
BusinessHoursWelcomeGreetingFilename       :
BusinessHoursWelcomeGreetingEnabled        : False
BusinessHoursMainMenuCustomPromptFilename  :
BusinessHoursMainMenuCustomPromptEnabled   : False
BusinessHoursTransferToOperatorEnabled     : False
BusinessHoursKeyMapping                    : {1,Sales,201,,,,,,,,, 2,Service Desk,999,,,,,,,,,
                                             -,Timeout,001,,GreetingChristmas.wav,,,,,}
BusinessHoursKeyMappingEnabled             :
AfterHoursWelcomeGreetingFilename          :
AfterHoursWelcomeGreetingEnabled           : False
AfterHoursMainMenuCustomPromptFilename     :
AfterHoursMainMenuCustomPromptEnabled      : False
AfterHoursTransferToOperatorEnabled        : False
AfterHoursKeyMapping                       : {}
AfterHoursKeyMappingEnabled                : False
AdminDisplayName                           :
ExchangeVersion                            : 0.10 (14.0.100.0)
Name                                       : Contoso AA
DistinguishedName                          : CN=Contoso AA,CN=UM AutoAttendant Container,CN=Litware,CN=Microsoft
                                             Exchange,CN=Services,CN=Configuration,DC=contoso,DC=com
Identity                                   : Contoso AA
Guid                                       : 90188e13-d2af-4cd0-94c6-966533456d3f
ObjectCategory                             : contoso.com/Configuration/Schema/ms-Exch-UM-Auto-Attendant
ObjectClass                                : {top, msExchUMAutoAttendant}
WhenChanged                                : 10/13/2014 11:58:02 PM
WhenCreated                                : 10/13/2014 8:57:59 PM
WhenChangedUTC                             : 10/13/2014 9:58:02 PM
WhenCreatedUTC                             : 10/13/2014 6:57:59 PM
OrganizationId                             :
OriginatingServer                          : AMS-DC01.contoso.com
IsValid                                    : True
ObjectState                                : Unchanged

[PS] C:\>_
```

Figure 8-11. *Viewing UM auto attendant configuration using Get-UMAutoAttendant*

When configuration is finished, you can enable the UM auto attendant from the Exchange Admin Center or use Enable-UMAutoAttendant; for example,

```
Enable-UMAutoAttendant -Identity 'Contoso AA'
```

UM Language Packs

A UM language pack is a set of installable files that enable using particular languages in UM dial plans or UM auto attendants. An UM language pack contains the following:

- Pre-recorded prompts, such as "After the tone, please record your message. When you've finished recording, hang up or press the # key for more options" in the language of the UM language pack.

- Grammar files are used by Mailbox servers to search the directory for given users in the language of the UM language pack. Grammar files are processed by the Mailbox server hosting the arbitration mailbox, and are downloaded by other Mailbox servers. The mailbox assistant, responsible for generation of the grammar files, runs every per day.

- Text-to-speech (TTS) translation, allowing UM to dictate the contents of email, calendar, contact information, and so on to callers in the language of the UM language pack.

- Automatic speech recognition (ASR) support, allowing callers to interact with UM using voice commands in the language of the UM language pack.

- Voice-mail preview support, allowing users to read a transcript of voice-mail messages in a specific language.

UM language packs should be installed as an add-in to Microsoft Exchange Server 2013 and are version-specific. This means you should not install Exchange 2013 RTM language packs on an Exchange 2013 Cumulative Update SP1 installation.

■ **Tip**   An overview of the available Exchange UM language packs, including links to download these packages, can be found at `http://bit.ly/Ex2013UMLP`.

There are two methods for installing a UM language pack:

1. Run the downloaded UM language pack executable—for example,

   `UMLanguagePack.nl-NL.exe /IAcceptExchangeServerLicenseTerms`

2. Run setup, specifying /AddUmLanguagePack followed by the language codes of the UM language pack to install, using /s to specify the location of the UM language packs. For example,

   `setup.exe /AddUmLanguagePack:nl-NL /s:c:\UMLanguagePacks /`
   `IAcceptExchangeServerLicenseTerms`

   You can specify multiple language packs to install; for example,

   `setup.exe /AddUmLanguagePack:nl-NL,de-DE /s:c:\UMLanguagePacks /`
   `IAcceptExchangeServerLicenseTerms`

■ **Caution**   UM language pack files are installed in:

$exinstall\Unified Messaging\Prompts\<Language Code>

These system prompt files should not be customized.

Be advised that when upgrading Exchange 2013 by installing a new cumulative update, you first need to remove any installed UM language pack. After that, you can upgrade your Exchange Server and consecutively install the UM language pack released for the new version. You can remove a UM language pack by using the Control Panel or Exhange setup, as follows:

```
setup.exe /RemoveUMLanguagePack: <UmLanguagePackName>
```

Certificates

If you want the UM components to support the TLS protocol, you need to install and assign a valid certificate for Exchange 2013 servers performing the UM call routing (CAS servers) and the UM server function (Mailbox servers). The earlier discussion of the UM server role showed how to alter the startup mode of the UM call routing and UM Server using `Set-UMCallRouterSettings` and `Set-UMService,` respectively. When you configure those services to utilize TLS, either by configuring `StartupMode` as TLS or dual mode, you need to assign a valid certificate. Since this certificate will be used by Exchange as well as the IP-PBX—for example, Lync Server 2013—a certificate generated by the internal PKI infrastructure may suffice.

Assume you want to configure startup to TLS mode, supporting TLS connections instead of unencrypted TCP sessions. You try to configure UM startup mode of the UM call router components to TLS; for example,

```
Get-ClientAccessServer | Set-UMCallRouterSettings -UMStartupMode TLS
```

You will be presented with a warning notification containing follow-up instructions:

> *WARNING: Changes to UMStartupMode will only take effect after the Microsoft Exchange Unified Messaging Call Router service is restarted on server <SERVER NAME>. The Microsoft Unified Messaging Call Router service won't start unless there is a valid TLS certificate.*

> *WARNING: To complete TLS setup, do all of the following: (1) Create a new certificate using the New-ExchangeCertificate cmdlet. (2) Associate this certificate with the server using the Enable-ExchangeCertificate cmdlet. (3) For self-signed certificates, copy this certificate to the UM IP gateway and correctly import it. For CA-signed certificates, correctly import the CA certificate to the UM IP gateway.*

Next, you configure the UM server to use TLS as well, as follows:

```
Get-UMService | Set-UMService -UMStartupMode TLS
```

You then are presented with the same notification.

Next, you create a certificate request, install it on the the designated UM servers—both UM call router and UM server—and enable the certificate for UM services.

To request a certificate for a server named `AMS-EXCH01.contoso.com` (the internal FQDN), you can use the Exchange Admin Center, via server > certificates, selecting the server you wish to request the UM certificate for at Select server, followed by clicking the New icon to request the certificate from an internal CA or to create a certificate request for an offline request (see Figure 8-12).

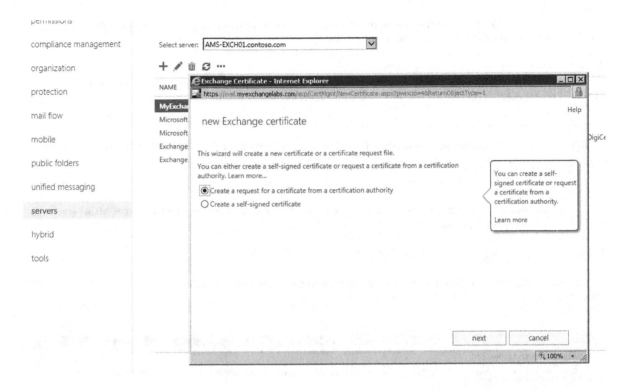

Figure 8-12. *Creating a UM certificate request using Exchange Admin Center*

■ **Caution** Exchange UM doesn't support wildcard certificates with Microsoft Lync Server. Use the server FQDN as the subject name. Alternatively, you can use a valid third-party certificate and import that one on all servers running the UM call router or UM Server components, IP-PBXs, and when Lync is used, other Lync servers as well. When you use a self-signed certificate, you also need to import it on the IP-PBX.

You can use New-ExchangeCertificate from the Exchange Management Shell to create a certificate request—for example, to generate a request for UM on the AMS-EXCH01:

```
$CR = New-ExchangeCertificate -GenerateRequest -SubjectName "c=NL,o=MyExchangeLabs,cn=ams-exch01.
contoso.com" -FriendlyName "AMS-EXCH01 UM"
Set-Content -path "C:\AMS-EXCH01UM.req" -Value $CR
```

On the Exchange server, you use the command line utility certutil.exe to submit the certificate request to a local certificate authority. You will be asked to pick the certificate authority server to process the certificate request:

```
certreq.exe -submit -attrib "CertificateTemplate: WebServer"
  "c:\AMS-EXCH01UM.req" "c:\AMS-EXCH01UM.cer"
```

When the certificate request is processed by the certificate authority, and the certificate is stored in a local .cer file, you can import it and enable it for UM in one go, using:

```
Import-ExchangeCertificate -Server AMS-EXCH01
 -FileData ([Byte[]]$(Get-Content -Path "c:\AMS-EXCH01UM.cer" -Encoding byte -ReadCount 0)) |
Enable-ExchangeCertificate -Server AMS-EXCH01 -Services UM,UMCallRouter
```

■ **Caution**   Be sure to enable the certificate for the UM services as well as the UM call routing services where applicable. Enabling the certificate for UM does not enable it for UM call routing services.

When succesful, you restart the UM service (MSExchangeUM) or UM call router (MSExchangeUMCR) service to make the changes effective, as follows:

```
Get-Service MSExchangeUM* | Restart-Service
```

The output of these cmdlets to create a certificate request, processing the certificate and assigning them to UM should be similar to the output shown in Figure 8-13.

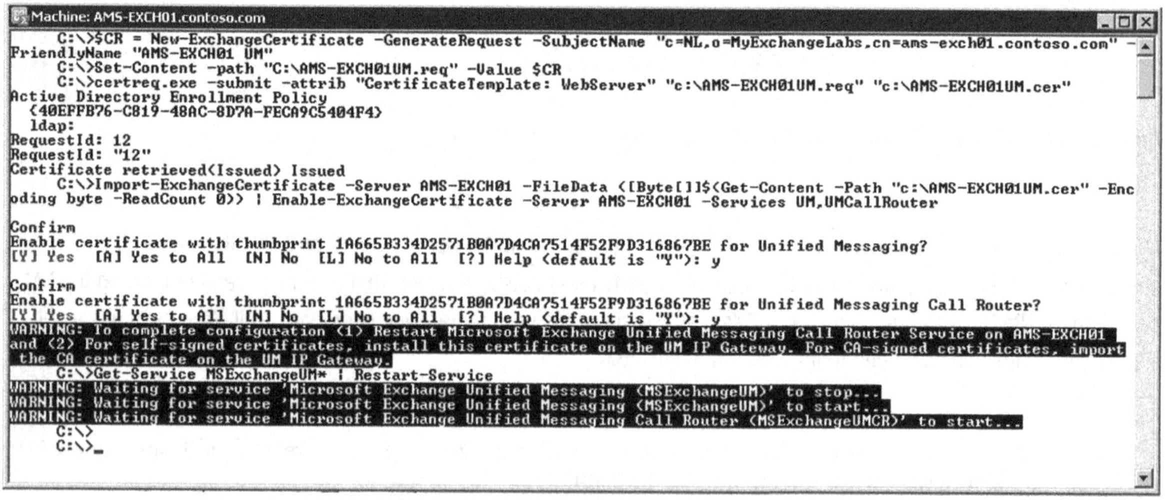

Figure 8-13. *Generating, issuing, and installing a UM certificate*

UM Mailbox Management

With UM configured, you can start enabling mailboxes for voice mail and other UM-related features. You can UM-enable a mailbox from the Exchange Admin Center via recipients > mailboxes. Select the user you want to enable for UM, and click Enable in the right pane, where it says "Phone and Voice Features", as shown in Figure 8-14. If you use the Exchange Admin Center, then enabling mailboxes for UM features is a per-mailbox process.

| Olrik | User (Archive) | olrik@myexchangelabs.com |
| Philip Mortimer | User (Archive) | philip@myexchangelabs.com |

Phone and Voice Features

Unified Messaging: Disabled

Enable

Figure 8-14. *Enabling a mailbox for UM features*

The output of this cmdlet should be similar to the output as shown in Figure 8-15.

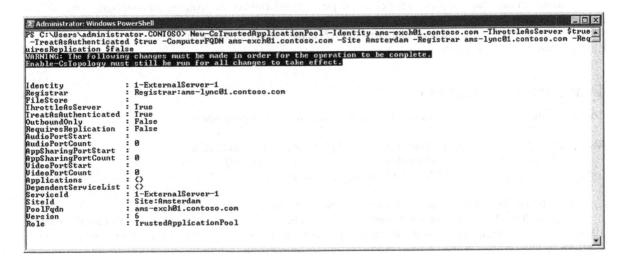

Figure 8-15. *Creating Exchange as a trusted application in Lync*

When you UM-enable a mailbox, you need to provide the following information:

- *UM Mailbox policy* to assign to the mailbox.

- *SIP address* to assign to the mailbox. This address will also be configured as an additional proxy addres of the type EUM (Exchange Unified Messaging) with the address corresponding to the SIP address configured here.

- *Extension number* to assign to the mailbox, which depends on the UM dial plan.

- *PIN* to assign for accessing the mailbox. You can also let Exchange generate a PIN. Optionally, the user can be required to reset the PIN after signing in. When finished, Exchange will send an email containing the extension number, the Outlook voice access number, and the configured PIN to the mailbox for reference.

■ **Note** Unified messaging requires an Enterprise Client Access License (CAL) for the mailbox.

Lync Server 2013 Integration

Integration of Exchange unified messaging and IP-PBX solutions produces the unified communications experience, something best achieved with Exchange UM in combination with Lync Server. Tight integration makes these products complementary rather than their being connected, individual-point solutions.

In the sections on the UM dial plan and UM IP gateway, it was shown how to connect Exchange UM and OCS or Lync Server via automatic provisioning of Exchange UM configuration objects in Active Directory, using Lync Server configuration information such as the UM IP gateway for Lync creation and using the ExchUcUtil.ps1 script, or the creation of UM contact objects using OcsUmUtil.exe.

Some other integration features are the display of presence information in OWA, instant messaging from OWA, archiving Lync instant messaging messages in your mailbox, and the Unified Contact Store. These require that you define the Exchange servers as trusted application servers in the Lync Front-End pool and configure Exchange to enable Lync-related functionality.

Lync Server Configuration

For each Exchange UM server, you run the following in the Lync Management Shell:

```
New-CsTrustedApplicationPool -Identity <Exchange UM Server> -ThrottleAsServer $true
 -TreatAsAuthenticated $true -ComputerFQDN <Exchange UM Server FQDN> -Site <Site>
 -Registrar <Lync FE Pool FQDN> -RequiresReplication $false
```

The output of this cmdlet should be similar to the output as shown in Figure 8-15.

Next, you define Exchange UM as a trusted application in this pool. This requires a vacant IP port per Exchange UM server; make sure it is free and that traffic on this port between this server and the Lync Front End servers is not blocked:

```
New-CsTrustedApplication -ApplicationId <Exchange Server Name>
 -TrustedApplicationPoolFqdn <Server FQDN> -Port 5170
```

The output of this cmdlet should be similar to the output as shown in Figure 8-16.

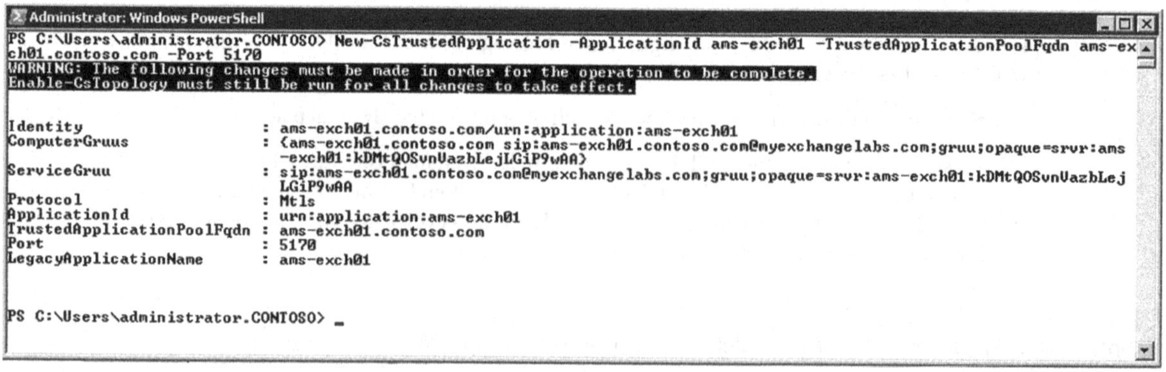

Figure 8-16. *Adding Exchange Server as a trusted application to the Trusted Application pool*

Next, you configure Exchange as a trusted partner. Note that the URL used is the external Autodiscover URL:

```
New-CsPartnerApplication -Identity Exchange -ApplicationTrustLevel Full
 -MetadataUrl https://autodiscover.contoso.com/autodiscover/metadata/json/1
Set-CsOAuthConfiguration -Identity global
 -ExchangeAutodiscoverUrl https://autodiscover.contoso.com/autodiscover/autodiscover.svc
```

Then, you run Enable-CsTopology to enable these topology changes.

Configuring Exchange Server

First, you run the following scripts from the $exscripts folder on one of the trusted Exchange UM servers, using the Lync Front End pool FQDN; for example,

```
Configure-EnterprisePartnerApplication.ps1
 -AuthMetaDataUrl 'https://ams-lync01.contoso.com/metadata/json/1' -ApplicationType Lync
```

Next, you reconfigure the Outlook WebApp virtual directories, enabling them for Lync functionality, such as presence indicators and instant messaging from Outlook WebApp. To accomplish this, you need to get the thumbprint of the certificate that is used for UM service. Then, you enable OCS functionality for each OWA virtual directory, providing the thumbprint used by that UM server and the FQDN of the Lync enterprise pool:

```
$UMThumb= (Get-ExchangeCertificate -server ams-exch01 | Where { $_.Services
 -like '*UM*'}).ThumbPrint
Get-OwaVirtualDirectory -server ams-exch01 | Set-OwaVirtualDirectory
 -InstantMessagingEnabled $true -InstantMessagingType OCS
 -InstantMessagingCertificateThumbprint $UMThumb
 -InstantMessagingServerName ams-lync01.contoso.com
```

With these UM features enabled on OWA, you then enable the related features through the mailbox policy. To enable instant messaging for all defined mailbox policies, for example, you use:

```
Get-OwaMailboxPolicy | Set-OwaMailboxPolicy -InstantMessagingEnabled $true
 -InstantMessagingType OCS
```

You run the following cmdlets on each Mailbox server to complete the OWA integration, using the Lync Front End pool FQDN. Better yet is to add these cmdlets to a file such as AddOWAIM.ps1, which allows you to run the configuration steps on multiple Mailbox servers by just running the script:

```
$UMThumb= (Get-ExchangeCertificate | Where { $_.Services -like '*UMCR*'}).ThumbPrint | Select -
First 1
$WebConfigFile= join-path $exinstall "ClientAccess\Owa\web.config"
$wc= [XML](Get-Content $WebConfigFile)
$el= $wc.CreateElement("add")
$key= $wc.CreateAttribute( 'key')
$key.psbase.value = 'IMCertificateThumbprint'
$val= $wc.CreateAttribute('value')
$val.psbase.value= $UMThumb
$el.SetAttributeNode($key)
$el.SetAttributeNode($val)
$wc.configuration.appSettings.Appendchild( $el)
```

```
$el= $wc.CreateElement("add")
$key= $wc.CreateAttribute( 'key')
$key.psbase.value = 'IMServerName'
$val= $wc.CreateAttribute('value')
$val.psbase.value= 'ams-lync01.contoso.com'
$el.SetAttributeNode($key)
$el.SetAttributeNode($val)
$wc.configuration.appSettings.Appendchild( $el)
$wc.Save( $WebConfigFile)
```

When running this as a script, the output you receive should be similar to the following:

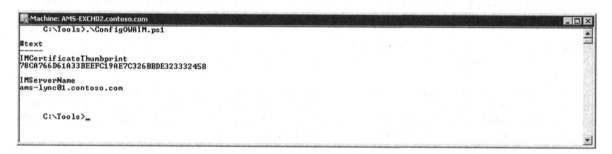

Figure 8-17. *Adding IM integration to OWA* `web.config`

After running this, the web.config file in <Exchange Install Path>\ClientAccess\OWA should have two new entries in the app settings element, as shown in Figure 8-18. If preferred, you can insert these elements manually, using the thumbprint of the certificate assigned to the UM services.

```
<add key="AccountTerminationEnabled" value="false" />
<add key="IMCertificateThumbprint" value="1A665B334D2571B0A7D4CA7514F52F9D316867BE" />
<add key="IMServerName" value="ams-lync01.contoso.com" />
</appSettings>
<!-- The following entries allow fusion to load our dependent assemblies from locations ou
```

Figure 8-18. *Changes in web.config for IM integration*

When you are finished configuring, you recycle the OWA app pool and restart the UM services:

```
Import-Module Web-Administration
Restart-WebAppPool -Name 'MSExchangeOWAWebAppPool'
Get-Service MSExchangeUM* | Restart-Service
```

■ **Caution**   Installing Exchange 2013 cumulative updates will overwrite these web.config files, requiring you to redo the edits on web.config, as stated above.

After configuring the OWA integration for Lync, you will notice in Outlook WebApp that presence information is displayed with the contacts, and you have the ability to send those contacts an instant message or you can check or update your Lync status information, as displayed in Figure 8-19.

Figure 8-19. Outlook WebApp and Lync integration

Unified Contact Store

The Unified Contact Store allows users to maintain a single Contacts folder and have this information shared among the Outlook client, Outlook WebApp, and the Lync client. When a user is UCS enabled, his Lync contacts are stored in his Exchange mailbox, in a folder named Lync Contacts (see Figure 8-20). This information is retrieved by the Lync client using Exchange Web Services.

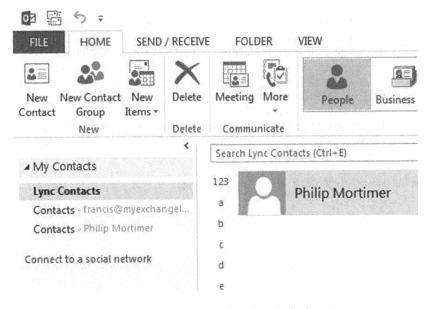

Figure 8-20. Unified Contact Store as manifested in Outlook 2013

To enable the Unified Contact Store from the Lync Management Shell, you run the following cmdlets. First, if you want to enable UCS for the default global user policy, you use:

```
Set-CsUserServicesPolicy -Identity global -UcsAllowed $True
```

Alternatively, you can create a new policy and enable the UCS setting:

```
New-CsUserServicesPolicy -Identity "AllowUnifiedContactStore" -UcsAllowed $True
```

If you created a new policy, you then need to assign users to this new policy for them to enable UCS. For example, to enable UCS for a user named Philip, using the AllowUnifiedContactStore policy, you run the following cmdlet:

```
Grant-CsUserServicesPolicy -Identity "Ken Myer" -PolicyName "AllowUnifiedContactStore"
```

To enable UCS for all Lync-enabled users, you run this cmdlet:

```
Get-CsUser | Grant-CsUserServicesPolicy -PolicyName "AllowUnifiedContactStore"
```

Exchange Archiving

Lync Server 2013 can be configured to store Lync conversations and conferencing transcripts in Exchange, rather than in the Lync SQL database. When Lync is configured to trust Exchange and vice-versa, you can enable the Exchange archiving by running the following cmdlet from the Lync Management Shell:

```
Set-CsArchivingConfiguration -Identity 'global' -EnableArchiving ImOnly
 -EnableExchangeArchiving $True
```

Instead of archiving only instant messages using the default ImOnly setting, you can choose not to archive by setting EnableArchiving to None, or to archive instant messages and web conference transcripts by setting it to ImAndWebConf.

Next, you also need to configure what kind of communications to archive, whether internal or external, as archiving for these two types of communications is disabled by default. This status is based in user policy. To configure Lync to archive instant messages exchanged with internal and external partners, you can reconfigure the default global policy by using:

```
Set-CsArchivingPolicy -Identity 'global' -ArchiveInternal $True -ArchiveExternal $True
```

When Exchange archiving is enabled, the Exchange archiving policies prevail over the Lync Server archiving policies. However, if Lync and Exchange are hosted in different forests, you must set the Exchange archiving policy on each Lync user object to ArchivingToExchange; for example,

```
Set-CsUser -Identity philip -ExchangeArchivingPolicy ArchivingToExchange
```

Call Answering Rules

Rules for call answering enable users to control how inbound calls headed for their voice mail are handled, much in the way inbox rules are established. The settings are per-user and they stored in their mailbox.

Users can manage call answer rules from Outlook or Outlook WebApp. From Outlook WebApp, the call answering rules are accessible through OWA ➤ Options ➤ phone ➤ voice-mail (see Figure 8-21). However, when you are selecting File ➤ Account Information ➤ Voice Mail in Outlook, you will be taken to the same page, as there is no native Outlook interface for managing call answering rules.

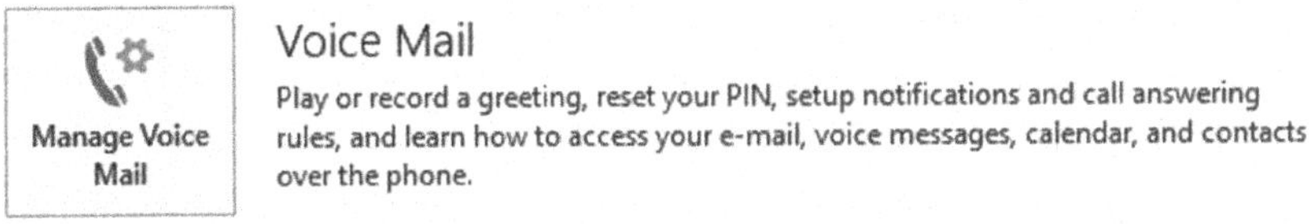

Voice Mail

Play or record a greeting, reset your PIN, setup notifications and call answering rules, and learn how to access your e-mail, voice messages, calendar, and contacts over the phone.

Figure 8-21. *Accessing call answer rules from Outlook 2013*

Besides having a name, each call answering rule consists of conditions and actions. Possible conditions are as follows:

- *If (automatic replies are on)*: when you have activated your out of office (OOF) response.

- *My schedule shows that I am. . .*: when your current calendar status shows you are free, tentative, busy, or out of office.

- *The caller calls me at. . .*: allows you to create different rules for each extension you may have configured—that is, different rules when someone calls your public or your private number.

- *It's during this period. . .*: lets you create a rule that matches a certain time frame, including working or non-working hours, as defined by Outlook ➤ Options ➤ Calendar ➤ Work Hours.

- *The caller is. . .*: allows you to create rules for when a specific person, telephone number, or someone from your Contacts folder calls you. The latter allows you to create different rules for people who are in your Contacts folder or those who are not.

- *None*: applies the rule to all incoming calls.

The caller can be presented with a user-definable menu (see Figure 8-22) whereby caller has the following options:

- Leave a voice-mail message

- Find me

- Transfer the call to a different number

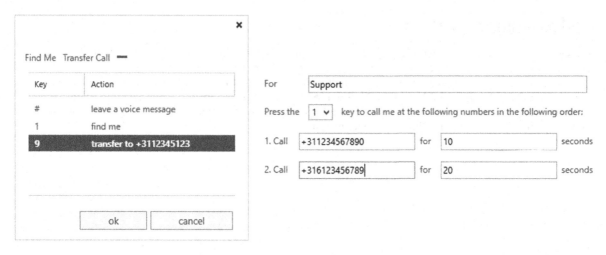

Figure 8-22. Configuring the call answering rules and find me details

---

■ **Caution**   Menu entries cannot be edited. If you want to make changes, you need to remove the entry and re-add it with the changed options.

Rules are processed in order; the first condition matching a rule fires. If no action is defined, the call is disconnected after the greeting is played.

■ **Tip**   Not every organization fancies the idea of its end users building all sorts of call flows from their mailbox. To disable the call answering rules, administrators can use

`Set-UMMailbox <UserID> -CallAnsweringRulesEnabled $false`, or reconfigure it for groups of users through their mailbox policy; for example,

`Set-UMMailboxPolicy -Identity 'NoCAR Policy' -AllowCallAnsweringRules $false`.

To manage the call answering rules remotely, Exchange administrators can use `New-UMCallAnswerRule` to create new call answering rules using the following parameters:

- `Mailbox` specifies the UM-enabled mailbox to configure the call answering rule on. If not specified, the mailbox of the currently logged on user is used.

- `Name` specifies the name of the call answering rule.

- `Priority` specifies the priority of the rule; lower priority rules are matched first.

- `CallersCanInterruptGreeting` specifies if callers can interrupt the greeting.

These parameters specify the following conditions:

- CallerIds notes a "If the caller is. . ." condition, and can be a telephone number, contact, or Personal Contacts folder. You can specify up to 50 comma-separated entries.

- CheckAutomaticReplies specifies an "If automatic replies are enabled" condition.

- ExtensionsDialed specifies an "If the caller dials. . ." condition.

- ScheduleStatus specifies a "My schedule shows. . ." condition. This is a bit-masked value, allowing you to mix multiple statuses (anding the values). Possible values are:

  - None: 0x0

  - Free: 0x1

  - Tentative: 0x2

  - Busy: 0x4

  - Away: 0x8

- TimeOfDay specifies an "It's during this period" condition.

The parameters specifying actions are:

- KeyMappings specifies one or more key mapping entries offered to callers. Format is <Order>, <Key>,<Name>,,,,,<Number>, so "2,2,Support,,,,,123," will offer the option to dial support at 123 as a second option by keying in "2."

These conditions and how the key mappings can be used are best explained by an example. In this call answering rule, you are matching against the following conditions:

- The caller is +311234567890.

- My schedule shows I am busy or away.

- The caller calls me at francis@myexchangelabs.com.

- The caller calls me during working hours.

If all these are true, you provide the caller with the option to:

- Press # to leave a voice message.

To implement this call answering rule on an UM-enabled mailbox named 'Francis,' you use the following cmdlet:

```
New-UMCallAnsweringRule -Mailbox Francis -Name 'My CAR Rue 1'
 -CallerIds '1,+311234567890,,,' -ExtensionsDialed 'francis@myexcangelabs.com'
 -ScheduleStatus 0x12 -TimeOfDay '1,0,,' -KeyMappings '4,10,,,0,,0,,'
```

As you can see, with KeyMappings and CallerIds containing values with multiple, comma-separated fields, this is a less friendly way to manage the settings. Therefore, it is recommended instead that you create the rules using the Exchange Control Panel and get the values you need with Get-UMCallAnsweringRules, providing you with information you could use in a script to provision other mailboxes as well.

Voice-Mail Preview

Exchange uses speech-to-text to transcribe the voice-mail message. This transcription is inserted in the body of the voice-mail message. The easiest way to test how voice-mail preview sends voice mail is by using a Lync client, selecting a contact, and selecting Call ➤ Voice Mail (see Figure 8-23).

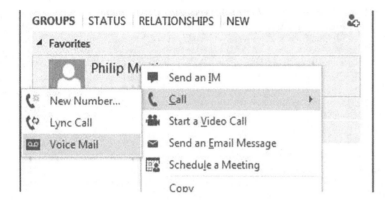

Figure 8-23. *Leaving a voice-mail message*

After you leave a voice mail, the recipient will find a voice-mail item in her inbox, which offers some options on top of the regular email choices, such as:

- Play the recorded voice-mail message.

- Play on phone, allowing the user to play her voice-mail message on a phone rather than through her computer's speakers.

- Add notes to the voice-mail message.

As you can see in Figure 8-24, voice-mail preview contains a transcript of the message. While it's not guaranteed 100 percent correct, it may help recipients quickly triage unprocessed voice-mail messages in their inbox.

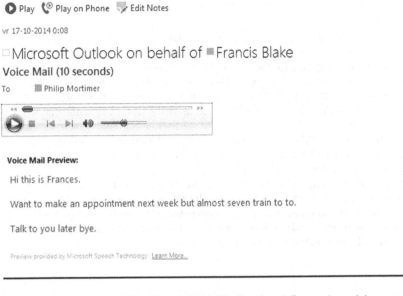

● Play ℂ Play on Phone ✏ Edit Notes

vr 17-10-2014 0:08

☐Microsoft Outlook on behalf of ■Francis Blake

Voice Mail (10 seconds)

To   ■ Philip Mortimer

Voice Mail Preview:

Hi this is Frances.

Want to make an appointment next week but almost seven train to to.

Talk to you later bye.

Preview provided by Microsoft Speech Technology. Learn More...

You received a voice mail from Francis Blake (Work) at francis@myexchangelabs.com.

Work: francis@myexchangelabs.com
Email: francis@myexchangelabs.com

Figure 8-24. *Voice-mail message*

■ **Note**   Unlike previous versions of Exchange UM, transcription of voice-mail messages now happens to all messages, even if they are over 75 seconds long. If a message is over 75 seconds, it is transcribed, but the text for the message isn't included.

Outlook Voice Access

Outlook Voice Access (OVA) allows users to call their UM-enabled mailbox to access their voice mail, email, calendar, and contacts information, all using text-to-speech and voice-controlled communications. To access Outlook Voice Access, you call the pilot number configured for OVA, pick the OVA entry from the global address list, or dial your own extension.

When users use OVA, they first need to set up OVA and in doing so, they are given the option of customizing the pronunciation of their names, as well as to record a personal greeting message that is played when the users are busy. Details on which commands OVA understands and instructions for using them can be found at
http://bit.ly/OVA2013.

Summary

In this chapter, the UM feature set of Exchange 2013 was explored, describing the UM functionality as divided between the Client Access server and the Mailbox server roles.

Then, the chapter introduced how to create and configure the UM configuration objects that are required to integrate Exchange UM with supported IP telephony solutions such as UM dial plans, UM IP gateway objects, and UM hunt groups. We also showed how to use the OcsUMUtil.exe tool to create the initial configuration objects for Exchange UM and Lync integration. Then, we explained how to create and configure the UM mailbox policies, which define the UM features that are available to end users.

We also showed how to create and configure the UM auto attendants to assist end users or inbound callers, offering voice-controlled text-to-speech options for call routing, dialing into user voice mail, or checking mailbox information like the inbox or calendar by using Outlook Voice Access.

Finally, we demonstrated how to integrate Exchange UM with Lync, offering UM features through supported clients, like instant messaging and presence information through Outlook WebApp or presence information through Outlook. Also, specific features of the Exchange UM and Lync combination were discussed, such as the Unified Contact Store, how call answering rules can be used by end users to manage call flow during absence, and how voice-mail preview can help users assess the critical nature of their voice-mail messages.

■ ■ ■

## CHAPTER 9

Compliance

In today's world of complex electronic communications, many organizations utilize email for communicating both internally and with other organizations. Because everybody has become used to sending and receiving email on all sorts of devices, and because some of the underlying complexities and potential adverse consequences are unknown to end-users, many companies want their communications to conform to certain rules—whether those rules are company policies for sending email containing sensitive information to external organizations or are operations to comply with external laws and regulations, such as the Sarbanes-Oxley Act in the United States or the European Union's Data Protection Directive.

Exchange Server 2010 brought certain features that address some of those concerns. Exchange Server 2013 introduced new ones while extending existing features, albeit using different names for some of them.

In this chapter we discuss the following compliance-related features:

- In-place archiving
- In-place eDiscovery
- In-place dold
- Messaging records management (MRM)
- Data loss prevention (DLP)
- Transport rules
- Auditing
- Information rights management (IRM)

In-Place Archiving

An in-place archive is an extension of a regular, primary mailbox, and it is hosted on an Exchange server or online (e.g., Exchange Online Archive). This feature was introduced with Exchange Server 2010 as *personal archive* or *archive mailbox*; as of Exchange Server 2013, this feature is known as *in-place archiving*.

An in-place archive can be used to offload contents from the primary mailbox, keeping the primary mailbox small and tidy; it also helps organizations manage the space occupied by a large offline cache, or .OST files. However, OST size management has become less of an issue with Outlook 2013, which contains an option. This option in the form of a slider limits the information that can be stored in the offline cache to a certain age, and then Outlook is capable of retrieving the non-cached mailbox information from the online mailbox as required; this slider is shown in Figure 9-1.

Figure 9-1. Outlook 2013 offline cached Exchange mode slider

■ **Note** In-place archives are always accessed in online mode. Keep this in mind when considering use of Exchange Online Archives.

Second, and perhaps more important, is that the in-place archives serve as a much better alternative for the infamous personal folders, or .PST files. This is because in-place archives are stored in Exchange (or the cloud when using Exchange Online Archives), and this has several advantages over .PST files:

- The information is stored in Exchange and does not require inventory and collection of end-user .PST files for discovery, which might be inaccessible and can be tampered with.

- Information stored in Exchange is not prone to theft or loss as are .PST files, which are often hosted on laptops or are transported using USB sticks.

- In-place archives are treated just like mailboxes, and thus can be incorporated into your Exchange backup solution, or you can replicate the information using a database availability group.

- Information stored in in-place archives can be discovered from a compliance perspective, just like regular mailboxes.

Offloading your mailbox contents to an in-place archive can be done manually or retention policies can be used to move the items from the primary mailbox to the in-place archive, depending on criteria such as the age of the item. In-place archives also come with certain limitations you should be aware of:

- They are not supported by all clients. For example, mobile devices or Outlook for Mac will not allow you to access your in-place archives.

- They and their related primary mailboxes are tightly coupled; you can't simply detach an in-place archive and attach it to a different primary mailbox. This is because both the primary mailbox and the in-place archive have the same legacyExchangeDN. A possible workaround for this limitation would be to export the contents of the in-place archive and import it elsewhere. Be advised, though, that if the primary mailbox is deleted, the in-place archive will be deleted also.

■ **Note** In-place archiving is a premium feature and requires an Enterprise CAL when used on premises; as such, it has specific Outlook licensing requirements. For more information, see http://office.microsoft.com/en-us/outlook-help/license-requirements-for-personal-archive-and-retention-policies-HA102576659.aspx. To quickly check how many mailboxes are configured with in-place archives, use (Get-Mailbox -Archive).Count.

Enabling In-Place Archives

■ **Note**   When you consider using in-place archives, check if the clients used in your organization support in-place archives.

To create an in-place archive for a mailbox using the Exchange Admin Center, you do the following:

1.   Open up the Exchange Admin Center.

2.   Navigate to Recipients ➤ Mailboxes.

3.   In the in-place archive section, select Enable.

4.   In the Create In-Place Archive Wizard, select Browse. . . and then select the mailbox database (see Figure 9-2). If you do not select a database, the database used to store the mailbox will be selected.

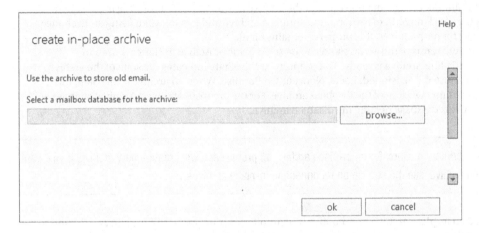

Figure 9-2.   *Dialog for creating in-place archive*

5.   Confirm the creation of the in-place archive by selecting OK.

To create an in-place archive from the Exchange Management Shell, use the Enable-Mailbox cmdlet in conjunction with the Archive parameter. For example, to create an in-place archive for a user with the identity Philip, you would use:

```
Enable-Mailbox -Identity Philip -Archive
```

The target database for the in-place archive will automatically be picked by the mailbox resources management agent. You can also create an in-place archive on a specific mailbox database by specifying the archive database, as follows:

```
Enable-Mailbox -Identity Philip -Archive -ArchiveDatabase MDB2
```

After an in-place archive is enabled, additional mailbox properties will get populated. For example, when you are retrieving the mailbox properties using Get-Mailbox, you will see the following archive-related attributes:

```
ArchiveDatabase             : MDB1
ArchiveGuid                 : d972ef60-8eca-4b0b-a36d-cb9d0903883c
ArchiveName                 : {In-Place Archive - Philip Mortimer}
JournalArchiveAddress       :
ArchiveQuota                : 100 GB (107,374,182,400 bytes)
ArchiveWarningQuota         : 90 GB (96,636,764,160 bytes)
ArchiveDomain               :
ArchiveStatus               : None
ArchiveState                : Local
DisabledArchiveDatabase     :
DisabledArchiveGuid         : 00000000-0000-0000-0000-000000000000
ArchiveRelease              :
```

The property ArchiveDatabase contains the name of the database where the archive is stored. ArchiveGuid identifies the in-place archive mailbox. The quota settings are inherited from the default values of the hosting database and they limit the amount of information stored in the archive as well as when a warning is generated. ArchiveDomain contains the SMTP domain of the tenant hosting the archive and it is set when using an Exchange Online Archive, for example; for on-premises, this property remains blank.

ArchiveStatus indicates the status of the archive and can be set to None or Active; the latter is used to indicate when the Exchange Online Archive is ready. The property ArchiveState indicates the state of the archive and can be Hosted Pending, Hosted Provisioned, Local, None, or On Premise. When an archive is disabled, the DisabledArchiveGuid will contain the value of the disabled archive. For on-premises archives, ArchiveDatabase will contain the name of the mailbox database hosting the disabled archive.

■ **Caution** If you enable a primary mailbox for an in-place archive on premises, it will create a new archive. If you want to reuse a formerly disabled archive, see the section on reconnecting in-place archives.

When you have added an in-place archive to a mailbox, the Autodiscover response will contain an additional alternative mailbox section that provides information to the client, such as that there is an in-place archive configured for this mailbox. The client can leverage Autodiscover to connect to the in-place archive. Because the information is contained in the initial Autodiscover response, no additional configuration is required on the client, and the archive will automatically be configured and added onto the supported clients, as shown in Figure 9-3.

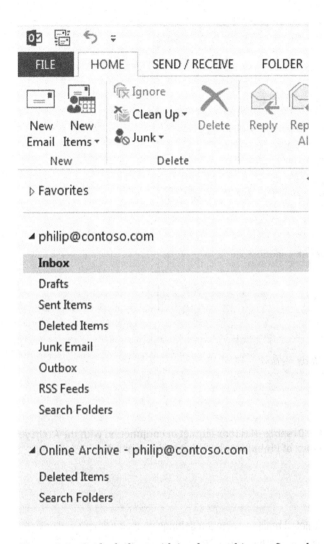

Figure 9-3. *Outlook client with in-place archive configured*

For example, in the excerpt of the Autodiscover response shown in Figure 9-4, you can see that there is an additional mailbox of type Archive configured, which has the identity shown at the LegacyDN attribute and is accessible through the provided Server attribute.

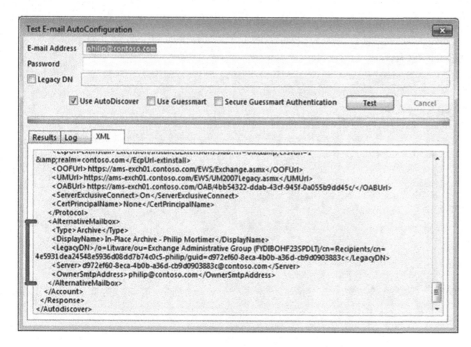

Figure 9-4. Autodiscover in-place archive alternative mailbox section

Disabling In-Place Archives

To disconnect an archive from the primary mailbox, use the `Disable-Mailbox` cmdlet in conjunction with the `Archive` parameter. For example, to disable the archive for the mailbox of Philip, use the following command:

```
Disable-Mailbox –Identity Philip –Archive
```

■ **Note** Disconnected in-place archives follow the same deleted mailbox retention settings as their primary mailboxes. By default this means that they will be removed from the mailbox database after 30 days.

Reconnecting In-Place Archives

Just as when you disable a mailbox, the mailbox doesn't get deleted but it does get disconnected. This means the user object is stripped of its in-place archive–related properties and the in-place archive is retained in the mailbox database until the mailbox retention expires; after that, it is physically removed from the database.

■ **Note** If you want to reconnect a disabled Exchange Online Archive, just enable the Exchange Online Archive for the primary mailbox.

As with mailboxes, you can reconnect a disabled on-premises archive to a mailbox-enabled user, and this will be the original primary mailbox. To get a list of all disconnected in-place archives, use the following command:

```
Get-MailboxDatabase | Get-MailboxStatistics | Where {$_.DisconnectDate -and $_.IsArchiveMailbox}
```

To connect an on-premises archive to its original primary mailbox, use the Connect-Mailbox cmdlet in conjunction with the Archive parameter; for example:

```
Connect-Mailbox -Identity d972ef60-8eca-4b0b-a36d-cb9d0903883c -Archive -User Philip -Database MDB2
```

Checking and Modifying in-Place Archive Quotas

Primary mailboxes and their related in-place archives can have different quota settings. You can query the in-place archive quota settings for all mailboxes by using the following command, receiving results as shown in Figure 9-5:

```
Get-Mailbox -Archive | fl Name, Archive*Quota
```

```
[PS] C:\>get-mailbox -Archive | select Name, Archive*Quota

Name                          ArchiveQuota                          ArchiveWarningQuota
----                          ------------                          -------------------
francis                       100 GB (107,374,182,400 bytes)        90 GB (96,636,764,160 bytes)
philip                        100 GB (107,374,182,400 bytes)        90 GB (96,636,764,160 bytes)
```

Figure 9-5. *In-place archive quota settings*

You can modify the in-place archive quota settings using Set-Mailbox; for example,

```
Set-Mailbox -Identity Philip -ArchiveQuota 200GB -ArchiveWarningQuota 190GB
```

Relocating the in-Place Archives

Since Exchange Server 2010 SP1, the primary mailbox and the archive don't need to be hosted in the same mailbox database. This means you can have dedicated mailbox servers for hosting primary mailboxes and for hosting archives.

When you want to relocate only the in-place archives to a different database, you can utilize the New-MoveRequest cmdlet in conjunction with the ArchiveOnly parameter. In addition, you can use the ArchiveTargetDatabase parameter to specify the target database for the in-place archives. For example, to relocate all the in-place archives to a database called MDB2, you use the following command:

```
Get-Mailbox -Archive | New-MoveRequest -ArchiveOnly -ArchiveTargetDatabase MDB2
```

Don't forget to clean up your move requests when the archives have been moved successfully; you do this by using this command:

```
Get-MoveRequest | Where {$_.Status -eq 'Completed'} | Remove-MoveRequest
```

Exporting and Exporting in-Place Archives

Should you need to physically move the contents of an in-place archive to a different mailbox, you can opt to export and import the information. To export or import mailbox contents, you first need to have the mailbox import/export management role. You can use the Exchange Admin Center to assign this role or you can use the following command:

```
New-ManagementRoleAssignment –Role 'Mailbox Import Export' –User Administrator
```

Next, you create a network share for hosting the .PST files. (Exporting and importing require a network share because it is undetermined which Exchange server will ultimately handle the import or export request in a multi-Exchange server environment.) You make sure the Exchange Trusted Subsystem has read/write permissions.

Then, to export the contents in an in-place archive, you use New-MailboxExportRequest in conjunction with the –IsArchive parameter, and use –FilePath to specify the full UNC filename of the .PST file; for example,

```
New-MailboxExportRequest –Mailbox Philip –FilePath '\\AMS-FS01\PST\Philip_Archive.pst' -IsArchive
```

To import the contents in a subfolder, you use TargetRootFolder; for example,

```
New-MailboxImportRequest –Mailbox Philip –FilePath '\\AMS-FS01\PST\Philip_Archive.pst' -IsArchive
-TargetRootFolder 'Imported Archive'
```

When you're finished, you can remove the import and export requests using Remove-MailboxExportRequest and Remove-MailboxImportRequest.

In-Place eDiscovery

Electronic discovery, or eDiscovery, refers to the discovery or the ability to discover exchange of information. Exchange Server 2010 introduced *multi-mailbox search* and *legal hold*, which were features to discover organization-wide contents of mailboxes or to freeze mailbox contents and record changes for legal purposes. Both features are renamed in Exchange Server 2013: multi-mailbox search has become *in-place eDiscovery,* and legal hold is now known as *in-place hold* (there's more on in-place hold later in this chapter).

Early versions of Exchange did not contain such features and had no options to retain deleted information, let alone retain changed information. If Exchange administrators were requested to provide mailbox information for a certain period, that would most certainly result in having to restore mailbox backups and to extract the requested information.

■ **Caution**   When you are in a co-existence scenario of Exchange Server 2013 with Exchange Server 2010, you need to move the system mailbox to Exchange Server 2013. If you do not, you will not be able to perform eDiscovery searches, as eDiscovery also stores configuration information in the system mailbox.

Management of In-Place eDiscovery

In-place eDiscovery of information stored in Exchange and management of in-place hold on mailboxes are secure processes dealing with potentially confidential information, and thus they are subject to privacy legislation. To be able to create eDiscovery searches, the user needs to be a member of the RBAC role group Discovery Management. This group is empty by default.

■ **Note** To be able to create in-place eDiscovery searches, the user needs to be member of the Discovery Management role group.

To manage the Discovery Management role group using the Exchange Admin Center, you follow these steps, as shown in Figure 9-6:

1. Open up the Exchange Admin Center.

2. Navigate to Permissions ➤ Admin Roles.

3. Select Discovery Management.

4. Select the Edit icon to add or remove members to the role group.

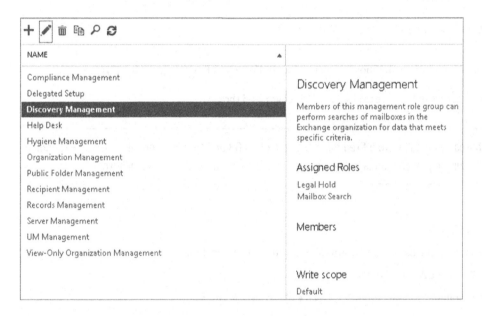

Figure 9-6. Manage the Discovery Management role group using EAC

To use the Exchange Management Shell to add users to the Discover Management group, so as to perform eDiscovery searches or put mailboxes on in-place hold, you use the following command (where Philip is the identity of the user you want to be able to create eDiscovery searches):

```
Add-RoleGroupMember -Identity 'Discovery Management' -Member Philip
```

To list the current members of the Discovery Management role group, you use:

```
Get-RoleGroupMember -Identity 'Discovery Management'
```

When the investigation is over, do not forget to remove the user from the role group, as follows:

```
Remove-RoleGroupMember -Identity 'Discovery Management' -Member Philip
```

Discovery Mailbox

A discovery mailbox is a mailbox that can be used for storing contents retrieved as part of an in-place eDiscovery search. During setup, Exchange Server 2013 creates a default discovery mailbox whose name starts with DiscoverySearchMailbox followed by a GUID. You can create additional discovery mailboxes when you need them— for example, to support multiple searches. Because they are like ordinary mailboxes, you can remove a discovery mailbox when it no longer serves a purpose.

To create a discovery mailbox, you use New-Mailbox in conjunction with the discovery switch; for example,

```
New-Mailbox DiscoveryBox1 -Discovery -UserPrincipalName discoverybox1@contoso.com
```

```
[PS] C:\Tools>New-Mailbox DiscoveryBox1 -Discovery -UserPrincipalName discoverybox1@contoso.com

Name                    Alias             ServerName       ProhibitSendQuota
----                    -----             ----------       -----------------
DiscoveryBox1           discoverybox1     ams-exch02       50 GB (53,687,091,200 bytes)
```

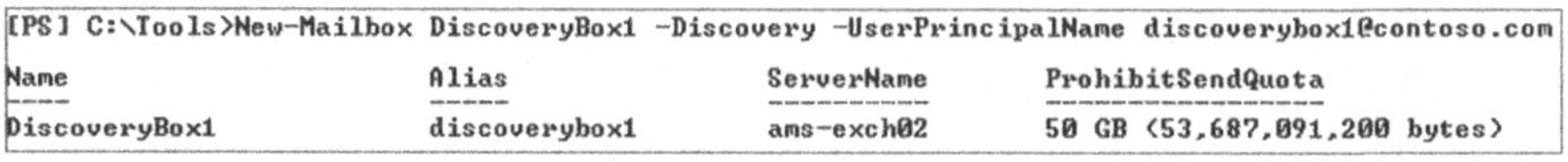

Figure 9-7. *Creating a discovery mailbox*

To list the currently known discovery mailboxes, you use Get-Mailbox and filter on RecipientTypeDetails:

```
Get-Mailbox | Where {$_.RecipientTypeDetails -eq 'DiscoveryMailbox'}
```

■ **Note**   Discovery mailboxes by default have a fixed mailbox quota of 50 GB and so they might fill up easily, depending on the underlying query. Be sure to properly manage the storage used by these large discovery mailboxes.

Searching Mailboxes

To define a discovery search from the Exchange Admin Center, you do the following:

1. Open up the Exchange Admin Center.

2. Navigate to Compliance Management ➤ In-Place eDiscovery & Hold.

3. Select New.

4. Enter a name and optionally a description, and select Next.

5. Select Search All Mailboxes to perform an organization-wide discovery on all mailboxes or specify the mailboxes to search and select Next.

6. Choose whether you want to search all content or enter search criteria, such as keywords or a specific date range. When you're finished entering the criteria, select Next.

7. Select Finish to save the discovery search.

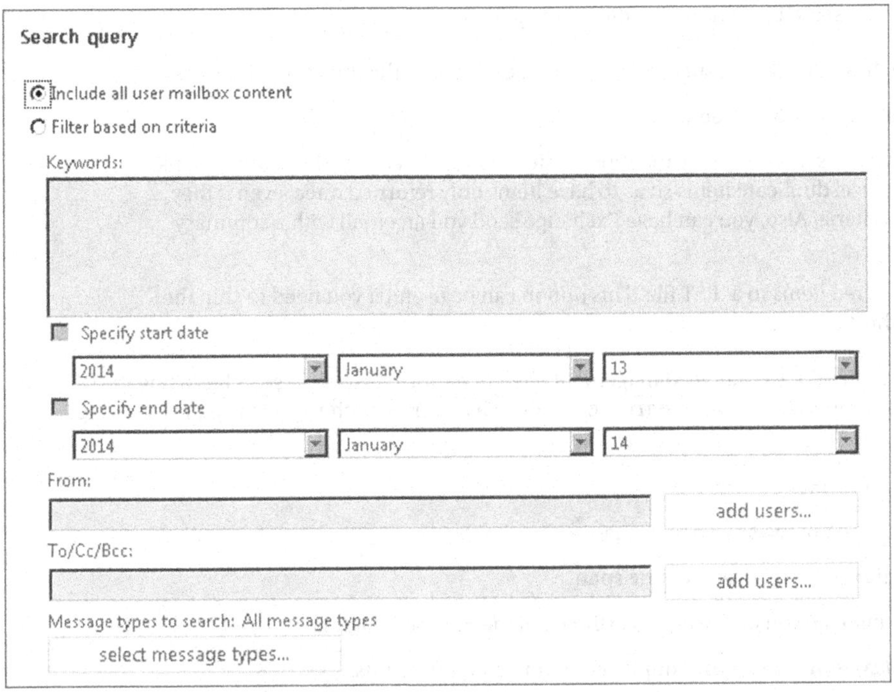

Figure 9-8. *Search query for new in-place discovery and in-place hold*

■ **Tip** When specifying search query keywords, you can use "and" or "or" Boolean operators to construct queries using multiple keywords. For example, to search for *fabrikam* and *options*, enter FABRIKAM AND OPTIONS. To influence the evaluation order, you can use parentheses—that is, X AND Y OR Z is not the same as X AND (Y OR Z). To include spaces in a search string, put the string in quotes—for example, "WINGTIP TOYS." To look for words in each other's vicinity, you can use the NEAR(N), where N is the number of words before or after to take into account—for example, FABRIKAM NEAR(5) OPTIONS. Finally, you can use asterisk (*) for wildcard matching—for example, CON* matches words starting with CON (e.g., *consultant, connection, construction*).

After defining the discovery search criteria, the results will be shown in the in-place discovery and hold section. Exchange will then start to estimate the amount of data and number of unsearchable items. Note that the query will only be activated when you view or export the results, meaning the query will also return items added after the discovery search was created.

■ **Note** Unsearchable items are items that can't be or are not indexed because of unrecognized, nonindexed file types or encryption. IRM protected messages can be indexed.

After defining the discovery search, you have the following options:

1. Update the search results figures, such as the amount of data and the number of items.

2. Preview the search results on-screen.

3. Copy the search results to a discovery mailbox. Besides the option to exclude unsearchable items, you can cancel duplicate items so as to have items only returned once, even if they match multiple criteria. Also, you can have Exchange send you an email with a summary of the results.

4. Export the discovered items to a .PST file. This option can be useful if you need to ship the information to third parties.

Of course, you can also utilize the Exchange Management Shell to perform discovery searches using the New-MailboxSearch cmdlet. When using New-MailboxSearch to perform discovery searches, you have the following parameter options:

- *Name* to set the name of the search.

- *EndDate* to set the end of the search time span.

- *StartDate* to set the start of the search time span.

- *EstimateOnly* to indicate you only want an estimate of the number of items.

- *ExcludeDuplicateMessages* to remove duplicates items from the results.

- *IncludeUnsearchableItems* to include include items not indexed by Exchange Search.

- *LogLevel* to set the level of logging; options are Supress, Basic, or Full.

- *MessageTypes* to limit the search to a specific message type. Valid options are Email, Meetings, Tasks, Notes, Docs, Journals, Contacts, and IM. When omitted, all items are searched.

- *Recipients* to limit the search to certain recipients (examines TO, CC, and BCC fields).

- *SearchQuery* to specify terms to search for.

- *Senders* to limit the search to certain senders (FROM).

- *SourceMailboxes* to specify the mailboxes to be searched.

- *StatusMailRecipients* to specify users who should receive status reports.

- *TargetMailbox* to set the mailbox that should receive a copy of the search results.

■ **Note**   When a start date or end date is specified, it is matched against the receive date or creation date (depending on the item type) of discovered items.

For example, to create a discovery search titled DiscoverySearch1 for all mailboxes on items received or created between January 1, 2013, and December 31, 2013, of type Email, with the keyword *fabrikam* and the destination set to DiscoveryBox1, you use the following command:

```
New-MailboxSearch DiscoverySearch1 -StartDate 1/1/2013 -EndDate 12/31/2013 -TargetMailbox
'DiscoveryBox1' -SearchQuery 'FABRIKAM' -MessageTypes Email
```

```
[PS] C:\>New-MailboxSearch DiscoverySearch1 -StartDate 1/1/2013 -EndDate 12/31/2
013 -TargetMailbox "DiscoveryBox1" -SearchQuery '"FABRIKAM"' -MessageTypes Email

Name                 CreatedBy            InPlaceHoldEnabled  Status
----                 ---------            ------------------  ------
DiscoverySearch1     CONTOSO\administ...  False               NotStarted
```

Figure 9-9. *Creating a new discovery search using New-MailboxSearch*

To get a list of your current discovery search entries, you use the Get-MailboxSearch cmdlet. To run a discovery search, use Start-MailboxSearch. When you have selected to copy the discovered data to a discovery mailbox, you start the mailbox search, which clears any existing results for that specific mailbox search from that discovery mailbox, as follows:

```
Start-MailboxSearch -Identity DiscoverySearch1
```

■ **Note**   You cannot change the properties of a running discovery search; to do that, you need to restart the search by using Stop/Resume in EAC or by using the cmdlets Stop-MailboxSearch and Start-MailboxSearch.

To modify a discovery search, you use Set-MailboxSearch; for example,

```
Set-MailboxSearch -Identity DiscoverySearch1 -StatusMailRecipients philip@contoso.com
```

When the search is finished, the configured StatusMailRecipients will receive a status report, which will look similar to what is shown in Figure 9-10.

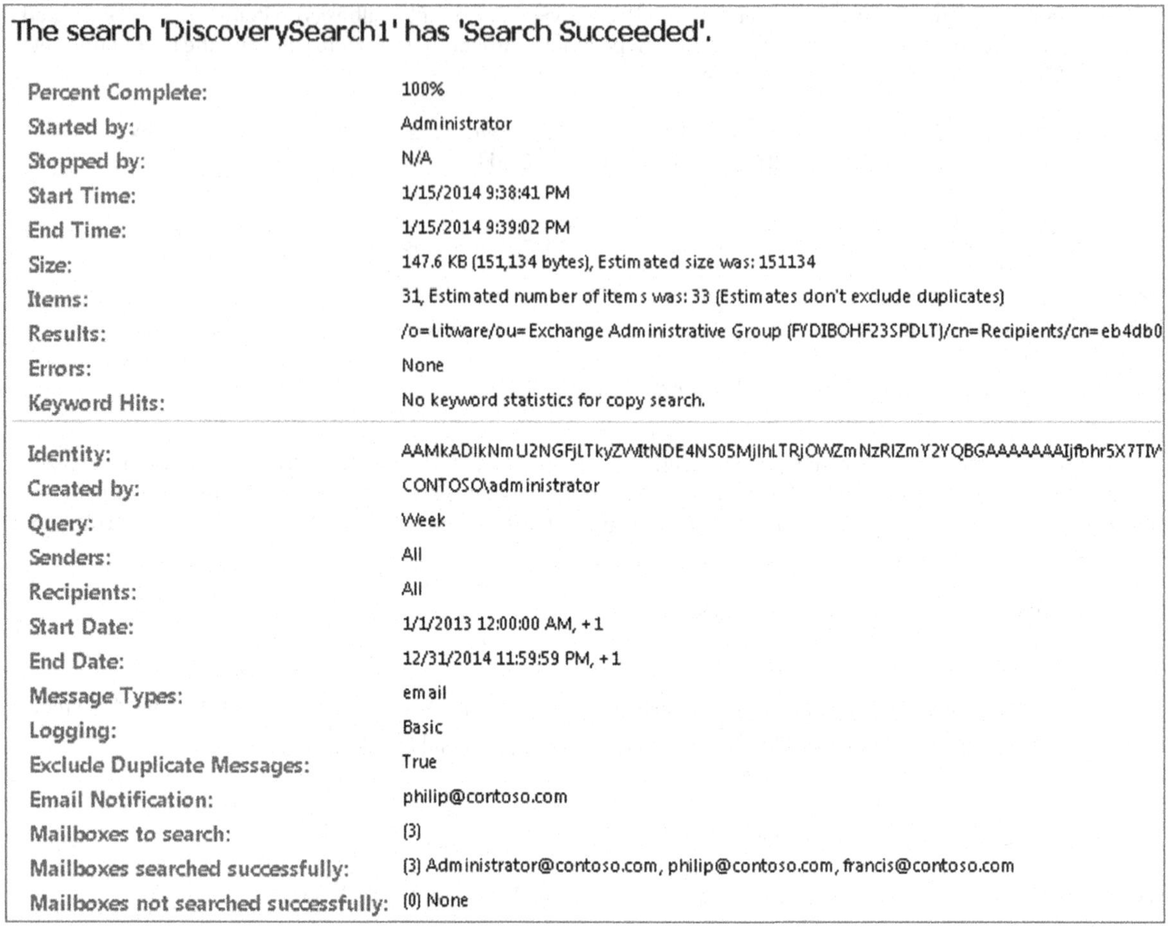

The search 'DiscoverySearch1' has 'Search Succeeded'.

Percent Complete:	100%
Started by:	Administrator
Stopped by:	N/A
Start Time:	1/15/2014 9:38:41 PM
End Time:	1/15/2014 9:39:02 PM
Size:	147.6 KB (151,134 bytes), Estimated size was: 151134
Items:	31, Estimated number of items was: 33 (Estimates don't exclude duplicates)
Results:	/o=Litware/ou=Exchange Administrative Group (FYDIBOHF23SPDLT)/cn=Recipients/cn=eb4db0
Errors:	None
Keyword Hits:	No keyword statistics for copy search.
Identity:	AAMkADIkNmU2NGFjLTkyZWItNDE4NS05MjIhLTRjOWZmNzRlZmY2YQBGAAAAAAAIjfbhr5X7TIV
Created by:	CONTOSO\administrator
Query:	Week
Senders:	All
Recipients:	All
Start Date:	1/1/2013 12:00:00 AM, +1
End Date:	12/31/2014 11:59:59 PM, +1
Message Types:	email
Logging:	Basic
Exclude Duplicate Messages:	True
Email Notification:	philip@contoso.com
Mailboxes to search:	(3)
Mailboxes searched successfully:	(3) Administrator@contoso.com, philip@contoso.com, francis@contoso.com
Mailboxes not searched successfully:	(0) None

Figure 9-10. In-place eDiscovery search report

When you explore a discovery mailbox, you'll notice the discovered data is stored in a folder named after the discovery search.

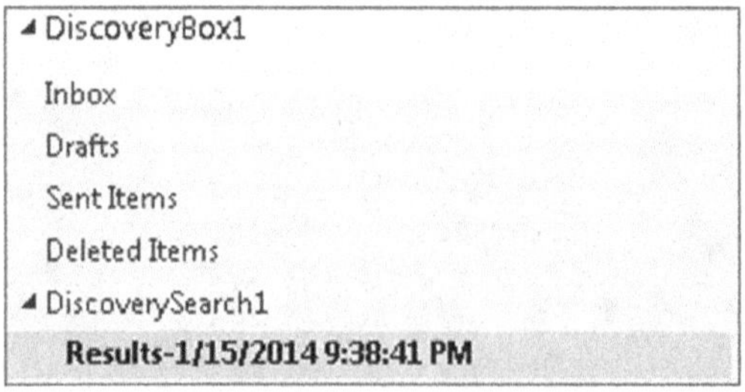

▲ DiscoveryBox1
  Inbox
  Drafts
  Sent Items
  Deleted Items
▲ DiscoverySearch1
  Results-1/15/2014 9:38:41 PM

Figure 9-11. Contents of in-place eDiscovery folder

While the search is running, you will notice a folder named <SEARCH NAME>.Working. This folder is used to temporarily store the search results and will be renamed after the search is finished.

Finally, you have the option to delete the contents from mailboxes using discovery search. For this purpose, you can use Search-Mailbox with the DeleteContent parameter; for example,

```
Search-Mailbox -Identity DiscoverySearch1 -DeleteContent
```

To preview the information that would potentially be deleted, you can first use Search-Mailbox with the LogOnly parameter. Be advised that the in-place eDiscovery search process is throttled, and by default is subject to the following limitations:

- The maximum number of concurrent searches per user is two (DiscoveryMaxConcurrency).

- The maximum number of mailboxes searches per discovery is 5,000 (DiscoveryMaxMailboxes).

- The maximum number of keywords per search is 500 (DiscoveryMaxKeywords).

- The maximum number of items displayed per page in preview is 200 (DiscoveryMaxSearchResultsPageSize).

- The maximum running time of a search before it times out is 10 minutes (DiscoverySearchTimeoutPeriod).

Should you need to adjust these limitations, you can create a new throttling policy with the ThrottlingPolicyScope set to Organization so it applies to all users in the organization. For example, to create a custom throttling policy named OrgInPlaceDiscoveryPolicy using different limits, use the following:

```
New-ThrottlingPolicy -Name OrgInPlaceDiscoveryPolicy -DiscoveryMaxConcurrency 10
-DiscoveryMaxMailboxes 1000 -ThrottlingPolicyScope organization
```

To verify the current settings, use Get-ThrottlingPolicy; for example,

```
Get-ThrottlingPolicy OrgInPlaceDiscoveryPolicy | fl Discovery*
```

In-Place Hold

There could be circumstances when an organization needs to preserve its email records, such as for a legal investigation. It may also be necessary to freeze the contents of a mailbox, preventing it from being processed by the managed folder assistant (MFA) as part of the messaging records management (MRM) process. A possible task of the managed folder assistant is, for example, the automatic removal of items after a certain period.

To support requests to preserve mailbox information, Exchange Server 2013 contains a feature called *in-place hold*. (This feature was introduced with Exchange Server 2010 as *litigation hold*.) In-place hold allows organizations to freeze mailbox contents, prevent manual or automatic updating, and/or not remove expired items that have passed the retention period.

In-place hold integrates with in-place eDiscovery, allowing you to limit the hold items by using criteria such as keywords or senders. It is also possible to specify a time span or to search for specific item types, such as email or calendar items.

■ **Note** When the managed folder assistant processes a mailbox, and it finds five or more query-based holds applying to the same mailbox, it will put the whole mailbox on in-place hold. If the number of matching queries drops below five, the MFA will revert to query-based in-place hold again.

Normally, when a mailbox is not on in-place hold, deleted messages are moved to the deleted items folder. When items get deleted from the deleted items folder or when the user shift-deletes the messages, those messages get moved to the recoverable items\deletions folder. This is the folder in which contents are displayed when, for example, you use the Recover Deleted Items option in Outlook. When the managed folder assistant processes the mailbox, the deleted items that had passed the retention period are purged.

When a mailbox is put on in-place hold, though, items that would normally be purged from the recoverable items\deletions folder are instead moved to the recoverable items\discoveryholds folder. These items remain there until the in-place hold is lifted.

▪ **Note**   To use query-based in-place hold, such as queries based on sender or start time, the user requires both the Mailbox Search and the Litigation Hold management roles. Without the Mailbox Search management role, the user cannot specify the criteria and can only put whole mailboxes on in-place hold. The Discovery Management role group is assigned both these management roles.

When a mailbox is put on in-place hold, *copy-on-write* is used when updating or removing messages from the mailbox. This is to preserve original copies of modified messages and to prevent tampering. Copies of original messages are stored in the recoverable items\versions folder.

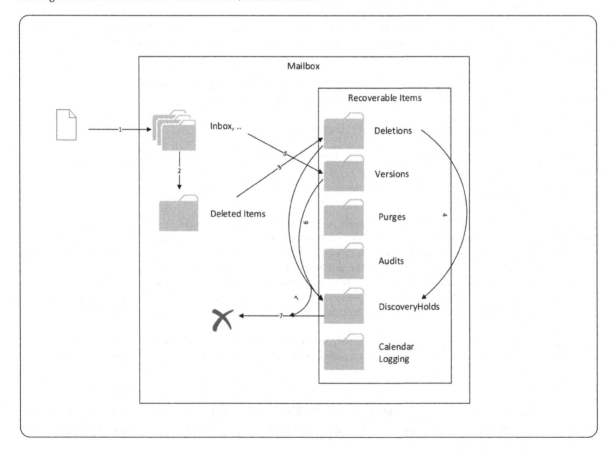

Figure 9-12. How in-place hold and copy-on-write works

Here 's how in-place hold and copy-on-write works is as follows:

1. A message is delivered to the mailbox. The message can be stored in the inbox or any of the other folders.

2. When the user deletes a message, it is moved to the deleted items folder.

3. When the deleted items folder is emptied, the messages are removed from the deleted items folder, or the user hard-deletes a message (shift-delete), and those messages are moved to the recoverable items\deletions folder. The contents of this folder are displayed when the user selects Recover Deleted Items from Outlook or the Outlook WebApp.

4. Messages from the recoverable items\deletions folder are purged when the user removes those messages from the recoverable items folder in Outlook or Outlook Web Access. When the mailbox is on in-place hold, messages are moved to the recoverable items\discoveryholds folder instead of getting purged.

5. When the user edits a message, a copy of the original message is stored in the versions folder using copy-on-write.

6. When the mailbox is on in-place hold, expired messages from the recoverable items\deletions folder and recoverable items\versions folder are moved to the recoverable items\discoveryholds folder if they are touched by any current in-place hold query. The managed folder assistant is responsible for keeping track of messages in relation to any in-place hold queries.

7. Expired messages will be purged from the recoverable items\deletions and recoverable items\versions folders when the mailbox is no longer on in-place hold. Messages not touched by any current in-place hold query are also purged from the recoverable items\ discoveryholds folder when they expire.

Not listed above is that when a user shift-deletes an item, it will go straight to the recoverable items\deletions folder.

To get a sense of how this looks under the hood, you can use tools like MFCMAPI, available from `http://mfcmapi.codeplex.com`. Note that to be able to view the recoverable items in MFCMAPI, you need to go to Tools ➤ Options and check the following options:

- Use the `MDB_ONLINE` flag when calling `OpenMsgStore`
- Use the `MAPI_NO_CACHE` flag when calling `OpenEntry`

▨ **Warning**   Low-level utilities like MFCMAPI can be powerful tools providing lots of insight, but they can also operate on the low-level structures and contents of your Exchange data and create inconsistencies or corruption. Tools like these offer great power to administrator, and consequently using them comes with great responsibility.

From MFCMAPI, you can open up the mailbox via Session Logon (selecting an Outlook profile), double-click the Mailbox store entry, and expand the root container.

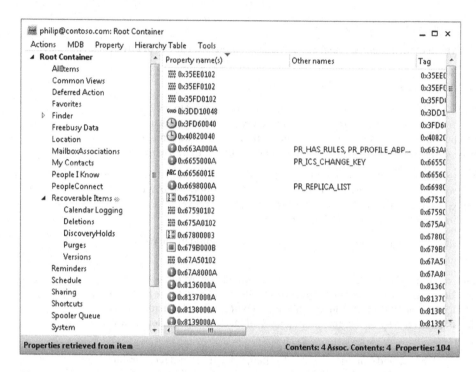

Figure 9-13. *Recoverable items folder in mailbox on in-place hold*

Within the recoverable items folder, you will find the actual aforementioned deletions, versions, and discoveryholds folders, among others, and you can inspect their contents.

■ **Note**   You can't change messages in the versions folder; when you try to save an edited item, the save attempt will fail. You can remove messages from the versions or discoveryholds folders, but these will end up in the purges folder. Messages can't be removed from the purges folder, thereby preventing (malicious) removal or alteration of original Imessages.

Enabling in-Place Hold

To define an in-place hold from the Exchange Admin Center, you perform the following steps:

1.   Open up the Exchange Admin Center.

2.   Navigate to Compliance Management ➤ In-Place eDiscovery & Hold.

3.   Select New.

4.   Enter a name and optionally a description, and select Next.

5. Select Specify to indicate which mailboxes to search. Use the + sign to add mailboxes to put on hold. When done, select Next.

6. Choose whether you want to search all content or enter some search criteria, like keywords or a specific date range. When finished entering the criteria, select Next.

7. Check Place for putting on hold the content matching the search query into the selected mailboxes. You can specify if you want to keep the records indefinitely or only for a certain number of days following message receipt or creation. Select Finish to save the query definition and activate the in-place hold.

■ **Note** If an in-place archive is configured for the primary mailbox and the mailbox is put on in-place hold, the in-place hold will be applied to the in-place archive as well.

To put a mailbox on in-place hold using the Exchange Management Shell, you use the same cmdlet as you would use for in-place discovery, new-mailboxsearch, additionally specifying the parameter inplaceholdenabled while setting it to $true. Since in-place hold leverages in-place eDiscovery, you have all the query options of new-mailboxsearch at your disposal.

The simplest form of in-place hold is a mailbox hold, for which you need only specify the mailboxes to be put on hold. For example, to put the mailbox of a user named Philip on hold, use the following:

```
New-MailboxSearch -Name HoldQuery1 -SourceMailboxes Philip -InPlaceHoldEnabled $true
```

■ **Note** Use of switches and Boolean parameters is not always consequent, despite serving the same purpose. For example, when you want to enable creation of an in-place archive, you specify New-Mailbox .. -Archive; but when you want to put a mailbox on hold, you need to set InPlaceHoldEnabled to $true.

The fact that a mailbox is put on hold doesn't manifest itself in any way for the end user. If it's required and deemed acceptable, you could send the user a notification or utilize the RetentionComment and RetentionURL mailbox settings to put a notice on the account settings section in Outlook; for example,

```
Set-Mailbox -Identity Philip -RetentionComment 'Your mailbox is put on In-Place Hold' -RetentionUrl
'http://intranet.contoso.com/faq/mailboxhold'
```

This message and its clickable URL will be displayed on the Outlook account page, as shown in Figure 9-14.

Account Information

Figure 9-14. *Outlook notification of in-place hold*

You can clear the message by setting these properties to $null:

```
Set-Mailbox -Identity Philip -RetentionComment $null -RetentionUrl $null
```

Disabling in-Place Hold

To disable in-place hold, you set the InPlaceHoldEnabled attribute of the related in-place discovery search to $true, as follows:

```
Set-MailboxSearch –Name HoldQuery1 –InPlaceHoldEnabled $false
```

When an in-place hold is lifted, the mailbox and its messages will again fall under the applicable retention policy regime. Any messages stored in the recoverable items\versions folders as part of the in-place hold will get removed by the managed folder assistant.

■ **Caution**　When an in-place hold is removed, it may release messages from being placed on hold, thus possibly expiring and removing those messages if they no longer match any other current in-place hold query. After an in-place hold is lifted, the managed folder assistant purges all messages from the discoveryhold, versions, and purges folders.

Note that this doesn't remove the underlying search; to remove the discovery search definition, use Remove-MailboxSearch, for example,

```
Remove-MailboxSearch –Name HoldQuery1
```

Messaging Records Management

In the world of ever-growing mailbox sizes, organizations require controls to manage the volume of email stored within their corporate environments. When these mailboxes are left unmanaged and unrestricted, there could be disruption of email services and higher storage costs. Additionally, organizations may have a legal obligation to store certain electronic communications for a given period of time. This makes email management crucial in many organizations.

Messaging records management (MRM) is the feature of Exchange Server 2013 that deals with the organization and management of email by using an established set of rules. Messaging records management was introduced with Exchange Server 2010, based on its managed folders and is now known as MRM 1.0. The MRM version introduced in Exchange Server 2010 SP1 and later, and also in Exchange Server 2013, is MRM 2.0. In MRM 2.0, mailboxes are managed by definition of the retention policies that have been assigned to those mailboxes. Those retention policies consist of retention policy tags that identify the rules that could be applied to the mailbox or elements of the mailbox. A retention policy tag can be part of one or more retention policies. The retention policies are enforced by the managed folder assistant. Let's discuss these elements next.

Retention Policy Tags

A *retention policy tag* defines what retention setting is to be used for a message or folder to which that tag is assigned. There are three types of retention tags:

- **Default Policy Tag** (DPT). This is assigned to items that do not otherwise have a tag assigned. A retention policy can have only one DPT.

- **Retention Policy Tag** (RPT). This tag is assigned to default well-known folders, such as inbox, deleted items, calendar, and so on.

- **Personal Tag**. This tag can be assigned by users using Outlook or Outlook Web Access to apply retention settings to specific items or folders.

■ **Note**   Personal tags are a premium feature and require an Enterprise CAL or Exchange Online Archiving License.

To create a retention policy tag using the EAC, you do the following:

1. Open the Exchange Admin Center.

2. Navigate to Compliance Management ➤ Retention Tags.

3. Click the + sign and select one of the following options:

    - *Applied automatically to entire mailbox* (default) to create a default policy tag.

    - *Applied automatically to a default folder* to create a retention policy tag.

    - *Applied by users to items and folders* (personal) to create a personal tag.

4. Depending on type of tag you choose, you are now asked to complete the creation of the retention policy tag by providing details such as name, retention period, and action to take.

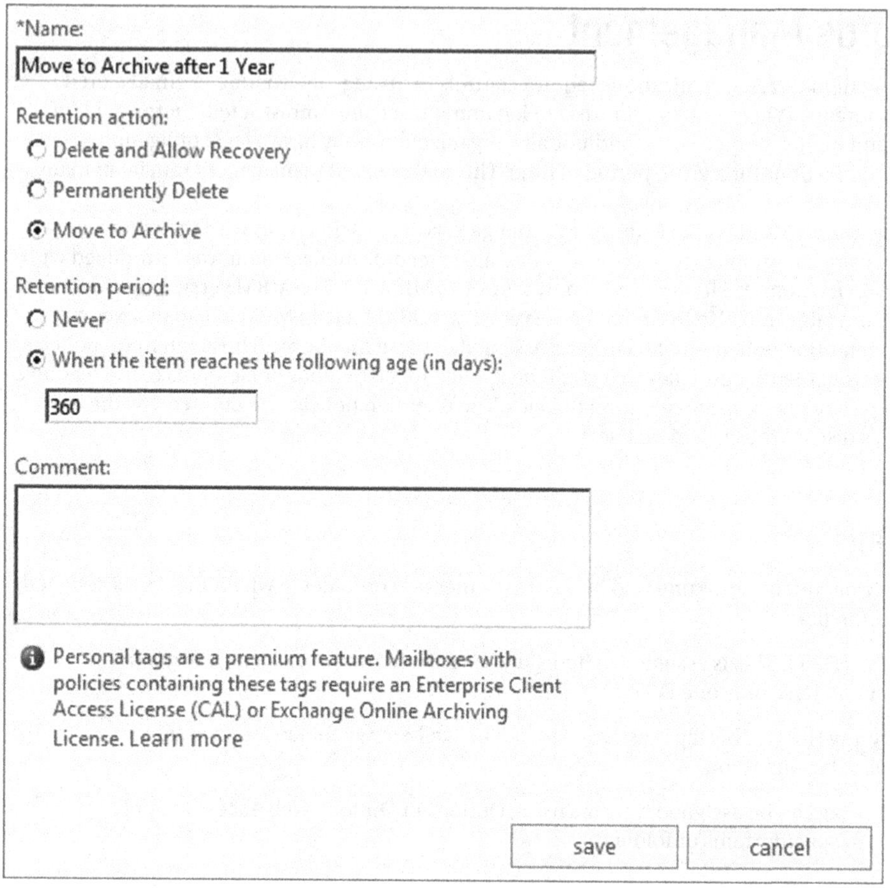

*Name:

Move to Archive after 1 Year

Retention action:
- ○ Delete and Allow Recovery
- ○ Permanently Delete
- ◉ Move to Archive

Retention period:
- ○ Never
- ◉ When the item reaches the following age (in days):

360

Comment:

ⓘ Personal tags are a premium feature. Mailboxes with
policies containing these tags require an Enterprise Client
Access License (CAL) or Exchange Online Archiving
License. Learn more

save   cancel

Figure 9-15. *Creating a retention policy tag using EAC*

To apply a retention policy to a folder or an item, you select the object in Outlook or Outlook Web Access, and right-click to select one of the Assign Policy options in the popup menu.

Figure 9-16. *Applying a retention policy tag using Outlook*

■ **Tip** You also have the option to configure localized names and comments on a tag. These are picked up and displayed in Outlook when the user has matching language settings. OWA does not support localized tags or comments.

A retention tag is defined by the following:

1. **Name** Identifies the tag; LocalizedRetentionPolicyTagName can be used to specify localized tag names. Use the format <LANGUAGECODE>:"Localized Name" to configure, for example, LocalizedRetentionPolicyTagName nl-NL:'Archiveren na 1 jaar'.

2. **Type** Defines to which items the tag applies. Valid options are:

   - *Well-known folders*: calendar, contacts, deleted items, drafts, inbox, junk mail, journal, notes, outbox, sent items, tasks, recoverable items. Items with this tag apply to items in the corresponding mailbox folder.

   - *All*. This tag is considered a default policy tag and items with this tag apply to all items.

   - *RssSubscriptions*. Items with this tag apply to the mailbox folder for RSS feeds.

   - *SyncIssues*. Items with this tag apply to the mailbox folder where synchronization issues are stored.

- *ConversationHistory.* Items with this tag apply to the mailbox folder where Lync IM conversations are stored.

- *Personal.* Items with this tag are personal tags.

3. **AgeLimitForRetention** Specifies the age limit after which the action defined by retention action should be performed.

4. **RetentionEnabled** Set to $true if the tag is enabled.

5. **RetentionAction** Defines the action to take when retention limit has been reached. Possible actions are:

   - *MarkAsPastRetentionLimit.* Items with this tag are marked as passed the retention limit. This will only result in a visual clue in Outlook—that is, a notice that the item has expired will be shown and it will appear in strikethrough font.

   - *DeleteAndAllowRecovery.* Items with this tag will be soft-deleted and moved to the deleted items folder.

   - *PermanentlyDelete.* Items with this tag will be hard-deleted and cannot be recovered. When the mailbox is on hold, those items can be found using in-place discovery.

   - *MoveToArchive.* Items with this tag will be move to the archive (when configured). You can use this tag only for all, personal, and recoverable item types.

6. **Comment** Used to specify a comment for the tag; `LocalizedComment` can be used to specify localized comments. Use the same format as with `LocalizedRetentionPolicyTagName` to create localized information.

7. **MessageClass** Used to limit the tag to certain items. Currently only one message class is supported: UM voice mail messages. To select these, specify `MessageClass IPM.Note.Microsoft.Voicemail*` as the message class. The default message class value is `*`, which means the tag applies to all items.

A default policy tag is created by establishing a policy tag with the All type. For example, to create a default policy tag that moves items to the archive after a year, you use the following command:

```
New-RetentionPolicyTag -Name 'Default 1 year move to archive' -Type All -AgeLimitForRetention 365
-RetentionAction MoveToArchive
```

To create a retention policy tag for a well-known folder, you specify the type. For example, to create a policy to soft-delete calendar items after two years, you use the following command:

```
New-RetentionPolicyTag –Name 'Delete Calendar Items after 2 year' –Type Calendar
-AgeLimitForRetention 730 -RetentionAction DeleteAndAllowRecovery
```

To create a personal tag, you use the Personal type. For example, to create a personal tag that can be used to tag items that should never be processed for retention, you use the following command:

```
New-RetentionPolicyTag –Name 'Never Move to Archive' -Type Personal -RetentionEnabled $false
-RetentionAction MoveToArchive
```

To configure a localized string for an existing policy tag, you can use `Set-RetentionPolicyTag -Name '1 Week Delete' LocalizedRetentionPolicyTagName nl-NL:'Na 1 Week verwijderen'`.

Assigning Personal Tags

Personal tags can be assigned by end users using Outlook 2010 or later, Outlook Web Access, or programmatically (Exchange Web Services). To assign a personal tag, you follow these steps:

1. Open up Outlook or Outlook Web Access.

2. Right-click the folder or item you want to assign a personal tag to and select Assign Policy.

3. Pick a personal tag from the list. You may also see the following options:

    - *Use Folder Policy*, which is to revert to the folder retention policy.

    - *Set Folder Policy*, to set the parent folder retention policy.

    - *View Items Expiring Soon*, to show items that will expire within the next 30 days.

■ **Tip** You can adjust the window of expiring items to return using a registry key. Assuming N is the number of days, for Outlook 2010, you set `HKCU\Software\Policies\Microsoft\Office\14.0\Outlook\ExpiringSoon=N` (DWORD); for Outlook 2013, you set `HKCU\Software\Policies\Microsoft\Office\15.0\Outlook\ExpiringSoon=N` (DWORD).

You can automatically apply personal tags to items using inbox rules. For example, you can create a rule to automatically apply the "1 Year Delete" tag to electronic newsletters to have them automatically removed from your mailbox by the managed folder assistant after a year.

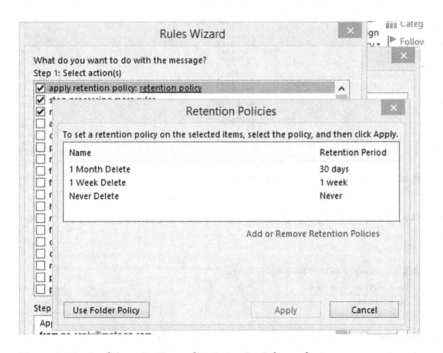

Figure 9-17. *Applying retention policy tags using inbox rules*

By default, the following retention tags are available:

- Default: 2 year move to archive

- Personal: 1 year move to archive, five-year move to archive, or never move to archive

  - 1 Week Delete

  - 1 Month Delete

  - 6 Month Delete

  - 1 Year Delete

  - 5 Year Delete

  - Never Delete

  - Recoverable Items: 14 days move to archive

Understanding System Tags

The tags mentioned earlier are in fact non-system tags, which implies that there also is something called "system tags." Indeed, system tags are used by Exchange internally for automatic management of, for example, arbitration mailboxes.

You can retrieve a list of retention tags, including system tags, by using the Get-RetentionPolicyTag including the -IncludeSystemTags parameter, as shown in Figure 9-18.

```
[PS] C:\>Get-RetentionPolicyTag -IncludeSystemTags | Select Name,Type,SystemTag

Name                                      Type              SystemTag
----                                      ----              ---------
AutoGroup                                 Personal               True
ModeratedRecipients                       Personal               True
AsyncOperationNotification                Personal               True
Personal 1 year move to archive           Personal              False
Default 2 year move to archive            All                   False
Personal 5 year move to archive           Personal              False
Personal never move to archive            Personal              False
1 Week Delete                             Personal              False
1 Month Delete                            Personal              False
6 Month Delete                            Personal              False
1 Year Delete                             Personal              False
5 Year Delete                             Personal              False
Never Delete                              Personal              False
Recoverable Items 14 days move to ar...   RecoverableItems      False
Never Move to Archive                     Personal              False
Delete Calendar Items after 2 years       Calendar              False
```

Figure 9-18. *Retrieval results showing retention policy tags including system tags*

System tags can be queried just like regular retention tags, as shown in Figure 9-19. It is generally recommended you leave these retention tags as is.

```
[PS] C:\>Get-RetentionPolicyTag -Identity AutoGroup | Select Name,Age*,*Action

Name                AgeLimitForRetention                        RetentionAction
----                --------------------                        ---------------
AutoGroup           30.00:00:00                                 DeleteAndAllowRecovery
```

Figure 9-19. *Retrieval of system tag properties*

Retention Policies

A retention policy is a collection of retention tags assigned to a mailbox. A default policy tag is applied to the assigned mailbox overall, and a retention policy can only contain one default policy tag. Retention policies can also contain retention policy tags that are applied to the related folder in the assigned mailbox. Finally, the user of the mailbox can select those personal tags made available by assigning a retention policy containing those personal tags to that mailbox, thus explicitly overriding any existing retention settings.

In an Exchange Server 2013 deployment, by default there are two retention policies available:

- **Default MRM Policy**. This is the default retention policy assigned to mailboxes. Note that it contains the default two-year move to archive retention policy tag, which configures the mailbox to automatically move its contents to the in-place archive when such an archive is configured for the mailbox.

- **ArbitrationMailbox**. This policy is by default assigned to system mailboxes and contains, for example, the retention policy tag autogroup, which deletes items after 30 days.

To see which retention policy tags are part of a retention policy, inspect the RetentionPolicyTagLinks attribute:

```
Get-RetentionPolicy -Name 'Default MRM Policy' | Select RetentionPolicyTagLinks
```

To create a retention policy using EAC, you do the following steps:

1. Open the Exchange Admin Center.

2. Navigate to Compliance Management ➤ Retention Policies.

3. Select the + sign.

4. In the new retention policy dialog, enter the name of the policy to create. In the retention tags section, use the + and – signs to add or remove retention tags.

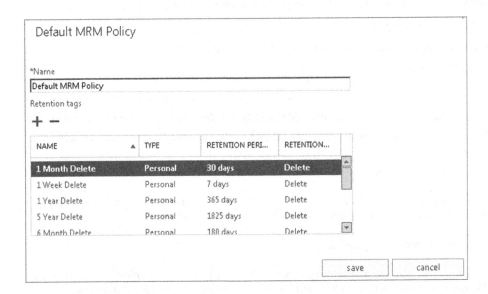

Figure 9-20. *Creating a retention policy*

To create a new retention policy using the Exchange Management Shell, use New-RetentionPolicy and provide retention policy tags as a parameter, separating tags using a comma (thus, providing the tags as an array), as follows:

```
New-RetentionPolicy -Name 'Contoso MRM Policy' -RetentionPolicyTagLinks 'Default 1 year move to
archive','Never Delete'
```

To add a retention policy tag to a retention policy, you need to add it as an element:

```
Set-RetentionPolicy -Name 'Contoso MRM Policy' -RetentionPolicyTagLinks @{Add='1 Week Delete'}
```

Should you need to remove a retention policy tag from a retention policy, you can remove the element:

```
Set-RetentionPolicy -Name 'Contoso MRM Policy' -RetentionPolicyTagLinks @{Remove='1 Week Delete'}
```

■ **Warning** Don't use Set-RetentionPolicy "Contoso MRM Policy"–RetentionPolicyTagLinks "1 Week Delete," as this would overwrite any current retention policy tags entries with the value specified.

Assigning a Retention Policy

For a retention policy and its tags to become effective or available in case of personal tags, it needs to be assigned to a mailbox. To assign a retention policy to a mailbox using EAC, you do the following steps:

1. Open the Exchange Admin Center.
2. Navigate to Recipients ➤ Mailboxes.
3. Select the mailbox you want to assign a retention policy to and click the Edit icon.
4. Select the Mailbox Features section.
5. Select the desired retention policy in the dropdown listbox of the same name.
6. Click Save to save the new setting.

■ **Tip** If you select multiple mailboxes, you can use the Bulk Edit option. Select More Options. . . and click Update below the Retention Policy heading. You will then see a dialog where you can pick a retention policy that you want to apply to the mailboxes you have selected.

When using the Exchange Management Shell, the Set-Mailbox cmdlet is used to configure a retention policy. For example, to apply the Contoso MRM Policy retention policy to Philip's mailbox, you enter:

```
Set-Mailbox -Identity Philip -RetentionPolicy 'Contoso MRM Policy'
```

If you want to assign the retention policy to a certain group of people, you can utilize PowerShell's ability to pipe objects to Set-Mailbox. For example, if you want to clear retention policy on smailboxes starting with P, you assign each onethe retention policy value $null, as follows:

```
Get-Mailbox -Identity P* | Set-Mailbox-RetentionPolicy $null
```

Managed Folder Assistant

The managed folder assistant (MFA) is responsible for enforcing retention policies on items in mailboxes. It is a background process that checks items in each mailbox it processes against the policy that has been configured on the mailbox (dpt), folder (rpt), and personal tags level. The process is throttled to limit the number of resources and cycles consumed.

You can monitor MFA activity by looking in the application event log for Event ID 9018, generated by the MSExchange mailbox assistants. It will mention what database was processed by the MFA, how many mailboxes were processed, and how long it took. If the MFA couldn't complete a work cycle, it will also mention how many mailboxes couldn't be processed.

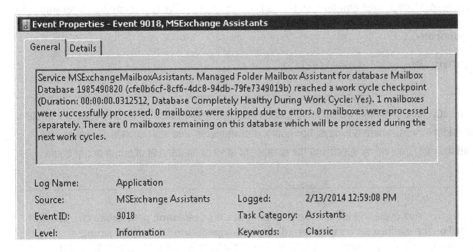

Figure 9-21. Managed folder mailbox assistant work cycle log

■ **Note** The managed folder assistant will resume processing where it left off, so there's no problem if the MFA can't complete a work cycle at a particular time. However, retention policy application and executing retention policy actions might be delayed for unprocessed mailboxes.

By default, the MFA is configured to process mailboxes continuously. This behavior can be overridden by setting the ManagedFolderAssistantSchedule parameter using the Set-MailboxServer cmdlet. If you want to limit the running time of MFA during which it applies retention policies to folders, you configure ManagedFolderAssistantSchedule. You can use the following values when configuring those start and stopping times:

- Full or abbreviated name of the day.

- Integer representing day number, where 0=Sunday and 6=Saturday.

- Format is DD.HH:MM-DD.HH:MM, where DD=day, HH=hours, MM=minutes.

- Specify multiple entries separated by a comma.

There must be a minimum of 15 minutes between the stop and start times.

You can also customize the interval after which the MFA should check for new mailboxes to process. The default is one day, but there might be circumstances when you would like to change this interval. You can do so by means of adjusting the ManagedFolderWorkCycleCheckpoint setting.

For example, to configure the MFA to run each work day from 2 AM until 6 AM and check for new mailboxes every other day, you would use the following command:

```
Set-MailboxServer -ManagedFolderAssistantSchedule 'Mon.2:00 AM-Mon.6:00 AM', 'Tue.2:00 AM-
Tue.6:00 AM','Wed.2:00 AM-Wed.6:00 AM', 'Thu.2:00 AM-Thu.6:00 AM', 'Fri.2:00 AM-Fri.6:00 AM'
-ManagedFolderWorkCycleCheckpoint 2.00:00:00
```

In addition, you can configure the MFA to use a different schedule for processing mailboxes. This is configured on a per-server basis using the Set-MailboxServer cmdlet with the ManagedFolderWorkCycle parameter. For example, to configure the MFA on server AMS-EXCH01 to process mailboxes every seven days, use Set-MailboxServer with the ManagedFolderWorkCycle parameter:

```
Set-MailboxServer AMS-EXCH01 -ManagedFolderWorkCycle 7
```

■ **Note** ManagedFolderWorkcCycle and ManagedFolderWorkCycleCheckpoint are specified as time span parameters that should be in the format dd.hh:mm:ss, where dd=days, hh=hours, mm=minutes, and ss=seconds. However, input is flexible so you can also set the daily interval by specifying the number of days or an interval of a number of hours, <hours>:00:00.

Needless to say, adjusting the work cycle will impact the frequency of which retention policies are checked and enforced on mailboxes hosted on the mailbox server with the adjusted ManagedFolderWorkCycle setting.

You can also manually start the MFA to perform a work cycle. To manually trigger the MFA, use the Start-ManagedFolderAssistant and specify the mailbox you want the MFA to run against. For example, to run the MFA for Philip's mailbox, you would use the following command:

```
Start-ManagedFolderAssistant -Identity Philip
```

Transport Rules

One of the critical components in an Exchange infrastructure is the transport service, which is responsible for processing messages traveling within or entering or leaving an Exchange organization. In Exchange Server 2007, the Hub Transport server role was introduced to transport messages, accompanied by the optional Edge Transport server for handling messages entering or leaving the organization. In Exchange Server 2013, the Hub Transport functionality is split between the Front End Transport service, hosted on the Client Access server, and the Transport service, which is hosted on the Mailbox Server.

Part of an organization's compliance and security requirements could be that messages transported within the organization or messages entering or leaving the Exchange infrastructure must comply with certain rules. Here is where the Exchange transport rules can come into play. An example of such a restriction is an *ethical wall*, also known as a Chinese wall, whose purpose is to prevent conflict of interest and disclosure of valuable information.

■ **Note** Transport rules can be used to accomplish lots of other goals as well, such as adding disclaimers. They are building blocks for features like data loss prevention and information rights management. If you're interested in these areas, consider employing the transport rules to achieve your ends.

Basically, transport rules are rules that define operations for messages that satisfy certain conditions. Examples of such rules are dropping or redirecting messages or applying information rights management templates. To manage transport rules you need to be assigned an Organization Management or Records Management role. Transport rules are organization-wide unless their specific conditions narrow the scope, and they are processed by the transport rule agent.

Creating a Transport Rule

Let's assume you're working for a law firm where lawyers representing client A (distribution list RepCaseAClientA) may not exchange messages with lawyers representing client B (distribution list RepCaseAClientB). So, you want to create an ethical wall between the users in those groups via a transport rule. To create a transport rule using EAC, you do the following:

1. Open the Exchange Admin Center.

2. Navigate to Mail Flow ➤ Rules

3. Select the + sign and select Create a New Rule from the popup menu to create a transport rule from scratch.

4. Enter a name—for example, EW_CaseAClientAClientB.

5. Configure the predicate: "Apply this rule if. . ." as "The sender and the recipient . . . the message is between members of these groups," selecting RepCaseAClientA and RepCaseAClientB.

6. Configure: "Do the following" as "Block the message. . ." as "Reject the message with an explanation and enter a message to return to the sender." Note that the message will be returned in a delivery service notification (DSN) message using a default return code of 5.7.1, a common code for access-denied types of DSN messages.

7. Optionally, configure: "Audit this rule with severity level" if you want to generate audit log entries when the rule is triggered.

8. Click Save to save and activate the rule.

To create a transport rule using the Exchange Management Shell, use the New-TransportRule cmdlet. For example, to institute the same transport rule, use the following command:

```
New-TransportRule -Name 'EW_ EW_CaseAClientAClientB' -BetweenMemberOf1 RepCaseAClientA
-BetweenMemberOf2 RepCaseAClientB –RejectMessageReasonText 'Communications between reps of ClientA
and ClientB restricted' -Mode Enforce
```

By using the RejectMessageEnhancedStatusCode parameter, you can override the default DSN status code of 5.7.1 for rejected messages.

> ■ **Caution** Transport rules are stored in Active Directory. Therefore, you may experience delays when implementing changes and you should consider replication latency before those changes will be propagated to Mailbox servers throughout organization.

When a user in one group tries to send a message to a member in the other group, he will receive a 5.7.1 delivery service notification message indicating failure. The explanation will be shown and the diagnostic information will indicate that a transport rule has governed rejection of the message, as shown in Figure 9-22.

Figure 9-22. *Notification message of ethical wall delivery service*

Another example of using transport rules for compliance is with regard to a corporate disclaimer. For such disclaimers, you can select to have the disclaimer applied only to messages sent outside of the organization. To accomplish this, you use the scope NotInOrganization (displayed in EAC as Outside the organization. Possible scope options for sender (FromUserScope) or receiver (SendToScope) are:

- **InTheOrganization**. The sender or receiver is located in Active Directory or the domain name is an accepted, non-external relay domain name using an authenticated connection.

- **NotInTheOrganization**. The domain name of the sender or receiver isn't an accepted domain or is an external relay accepted domain.

- **ExternalPartner** (ToUserScope only). The domain name of the receiver is configured to use a domain secure security setting.

- **ExternalNonPartner** (ToUserScope only). The domain name of the receiver is not using a domain secure security setting.

A complication with disclaimers is that inserting text in the body of a message may invalidate any signed or encrypted messages. Because only a signed or encrypted message can be excluded (not both), you can leverage the Exchange message classification to tag the message, using transport rules to tag that encrypted or signed message. In the disclaimer transport rule, you can then select to not apply the rule to tagged messages.

■ **Note**   If your company policy is to disallow sending signed or encrypted messages externally, you can replace the action of adding the disclaimer by an action that will drop the message, quarantine it, or forward it for moderation.

Message classifications can only be created from the Exchange Management Shell, using the New-MessageClassification. In this example, you would use the label SignedOrEncrypted, as follows:

```
New-MessageClassification 'SignedOrEncrypted' -DisplayName 'Signed or Encrypted Message'
-SenderDescription 'Signed or Encrypted Message' -PermissionMenuVisible:$false
```

■ **Note**   PermissionMenuVisible determines if the message classification can be assigned to messages in Outlook or Outlook Web App. Setting this parameter to $false disables this option.

You create the transport rules that will tag messages using this message classification. First, you create a transport rule that applies the message classification SignedOrEncrypted (ApplyClassification) to encrypted messages (MessageTypeMatches "Encrypted"), as follows:

```
New-TransportRule -Name 'Tag Encrypted Messages' -Enabled $true -MessageTypeMatches 'Encrypted'
-ApplyClassification 'SignedOrEncrypted'
```

Next, you create a transport rule that applies the message classification SignedOrEncrypted to signed messages (MessageTypeMatches "Signed"), as follows:

```
New-TransportRule -Name 'Tag Signed Messages' -Enabled $true -MessageTypeMatches 'Signed'
-ApplyClassification 'SignedOrEncrypted'
```

Finally, you create the transport rule that applies the disclaimer to outgoing messages:

```
New-TransportRule -Name 'Disclaimer' -Enabled $true -SentToScope 'NotInOrganization'
-ExceptIfHasClassification 'SignedOrEncrypted' -ApplyHtmlDisclaimerLocation 'Append'
-ApplyHtmlDisclaimerFallbackAction 'Wrap' -ApplyHtmlDisclaimerText '<P>This email and any files
transmitted with it are confidential and intended solely for the use of the individual or entity to
whom they are addressed.</P>'
```

The ApplyHtmlDisclaimerFallbackAction parameter specifies where to put the disclaimer text. In the example, it is appended to the message. By setting ApplyHtmlDisclaimerFallbackAction to Wrap, the message will be wrapped in a new message containing the disclaimer. The parameter ApplyHtmlDisclaimerText specifies the text to use for the disclaimer. Note that the disclaimer text can be HTML, allowing you to use HTML IMG tags, which reference externally hosted images for embedding, or to use a link to point to an online disclaimer.

If you want to use disclaimers for internal communications as well, you will face an additional challenge. As the message passes each Transport service, a disclaimer is added, thereby potentially resulting in multiple disclaimers. Of course, you can add an additional exception that will check the body of the message for disclaimer text fragments. A different and perhaps more elegant approach, though, is to insert a sentinel in the message header after a disclaimer has been appended, and add the condition to exclude messages containing the sentinel.

To implement such a condition and transform the disclaimer created earlier in a global disclaimer, you use the following command, where you set the SentToScope to $null to make it apply to all messages:

```
Set-TransportRule -Identity 'Disclaimer' -SetHeaderName 'X-Disclaimer' -SetHeaderValue '1'
-ExceptIfHeaderContainsMessageHeader 'X-Disclaimer' -ExceptIfHeaderContainsWords '1'
```

Now, when you receive a message with a disclaimer, you can see "proof" in the header, which will contain an entry X-Disclaimer: 1, as shown in Figure 9-23. That is, the header will contain an additional header entry, X-Disclaimer, which will be set to 1 for messages subject to the rule you just created.

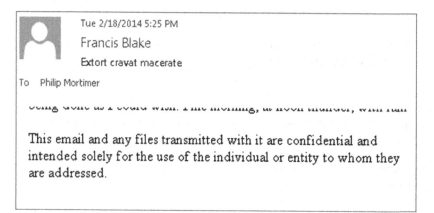

Figure 9-23. Disclaimer added to message using transport rules

As a result, the message will now contain only a single disclaimer, as shown in Figure 9-24.

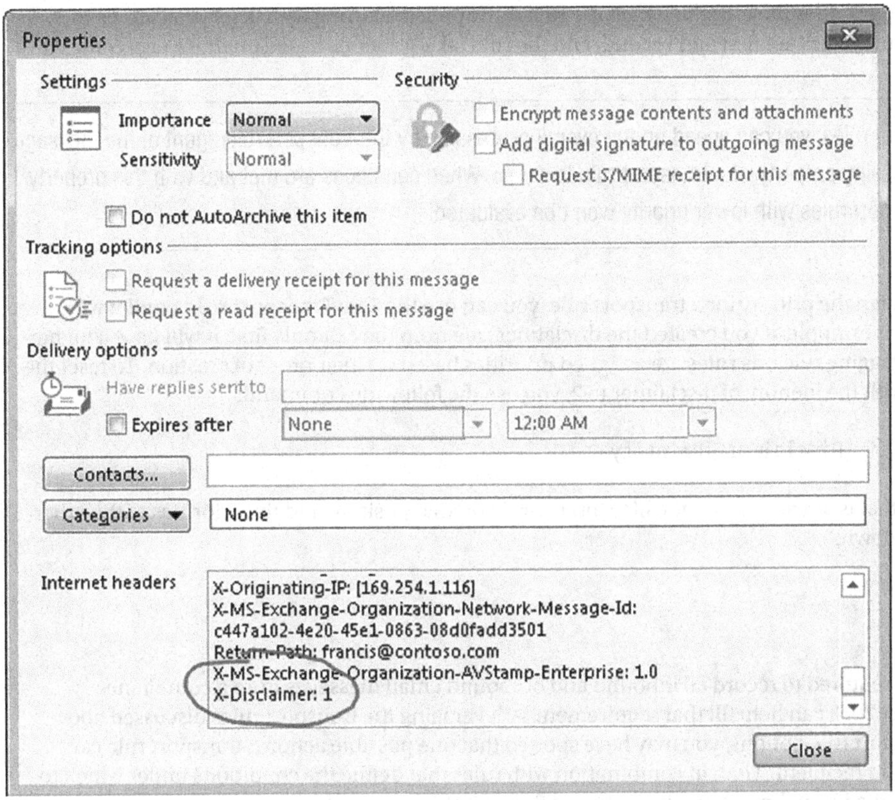

Figure 9-24. *Message header sentinel*

Priority Rankings for Transport Rules

When you have multiple transport rules configured, the way they are ordered becomes important. For instance, if you have configured one transport rule to tag messages and another transport rule to process the tagged messages, the tagging needs to take place first.

To query the current list of transport rules and their assigned priority, use the Get-TransportRule cmdlet, with results as shown in Figure 9-25.

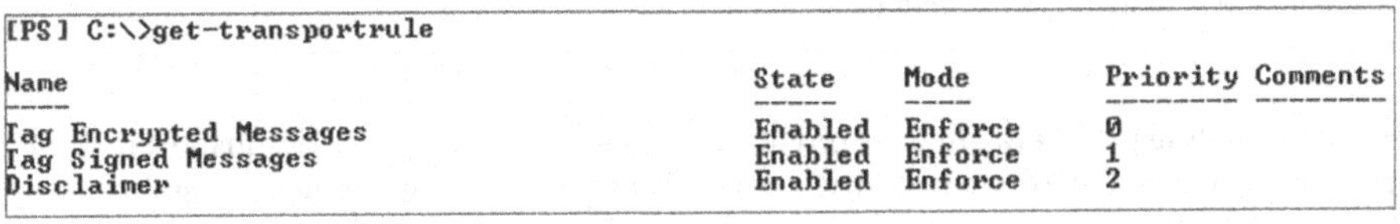

```
[PS] C:\>get-transportrule

Name                      State    Mode      Priority Comments
----                      -----    ----      -------- --------
Tag Encrypted Messages    Enabled  Enforce   0
Tag Signed Messages       Enabled  Enforce   1
Disclaimer                Enabled  Enforce   2
```

Figure 9-25. *Retrieving a list of transport rules*

The priority property determines the order in which the rules are applied, starting with 0. As you can see in Figure 9-25, the rules to tag messages are first and second, and the rule taking actions based on those tags comes next.

▪ **Tip** When you have lots of rules, you can speed up the overall processing by the transport rule agent of the message by setting the StopRuleProcessing property of a transport rule to $true. When conditions are met and with this property set to $true, additional transport rules with lower priority won't be evaluated.

When you want to reassign the priority for a transport rule, you can use the Set-TransportRule cmdlet with the -Priority parameter. For example, if you created the disclaimer rule from the example first, it will have a higher execution priority than the tagging rules, as rules are assigned priorities based on their order of creation. To reset the priority of a transport rule with the identity of disclaimer to 2, you use the following command:

```
Set-TransportRule –Identity Disclaimer –Priority 2
```

If you assign a priority that is already in use, it will insert the rule on that position and the priorities of the other rules will shift one position down.

Journaling

Some organizations may be required to record all inbound and outbound email messages from a compliance perspective. Exchange Server 2013 can help fill that requirement by leveraging the transport rules discussed above. When considering the transport rule options, you may have spotted that one possible action a transport rule can perform is copying to a certain recipient. That, in combination with rules that define the conditions under which to journal messages, makes up the journaling option in Exchange Server 2013.

In Exchange Server 2013, all email is handled by Mailbox servers, or by the Transport service to be exact. The journaling agent is a transport agent that processes messages on Mailbox servers, either when they are submitted or when they are routed. Exchange provides the following journaling options:

- **Standard journaling** Configured on the mailbox database and can be used to journal all messages that are either received by or sent through mailboxes hosted on that mailbox database.

- **Premium journaling** Can utilize rules, allowing you to journal based on criteria such as the recipient, distribution group, or internal vs. external messages.

▪ **Note** Premium journaling requires an Enterprise CAL license.

So far, a journal rule, or even journaling in general, may sound like just an implementation of a transport rule, but there is a difference. While transport rules can be used to forward messages, journaling generates integral copies of the original messages in the form of journal reports, including the original messages as an attachment with the original header information. This makes journal reports suitable as evidence, as contrasted with forwarded messages retrieved by means of a transport rule. See Figure 9-26 for a sample journal report.

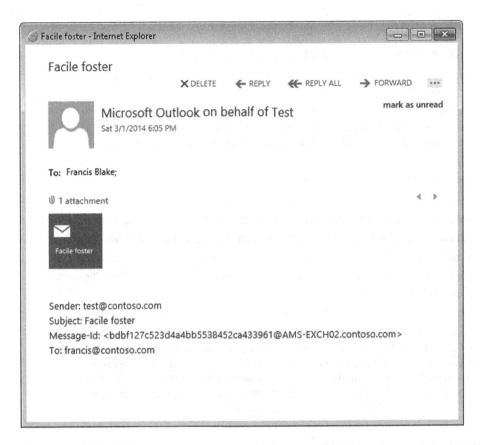

Figure 9-26. Journal report

A journal report for an externally sent message may differ from that for an internal message. This is because internal messages contain more information in the header regarding source and destination. The information provided in journal reports contains:

- **Sender** This is the SMTP address of the sender of the message.

- **Subject** This is the subject of the journaled message.

- **Message-ID** This is the internal message ID generated by Exchange when the message is submitted in the organization by the Transport service.

- **To** These are the SMTP addresses of the message recipients. This list includes recipients indicated as TO, CC, or BCC addresses. If groups are expanded, it will also be mentioned at this line.

Options for Journaling Rules

When you're defining a journal rule, there are three parameters you need to consider:

1. The scope of the messages to be journaled. Possible scope options are internal messages only, external messages only, or all messages.

2. The recipients you want to journal. These can be an Exchange mailbox, distribution group, mail user, or contact. By being specific in whose messages to journal, you can minimize the required storage but still comply with legal and regulatory requirements for evidence collection.

3. The mailbox where the journal reports should be sent.

■ **Tip** To reduce the amount of storage needed to maintain journal reports, you can omit voice mail and missed-call notifications from UM-enabled users. This is an organization-wide setting and can be enabled using `Set-Transport Config -VoicemailJournalingEnabled $false`. Or, you can enable journaling of voice mail and missed-call notification messages using `Set-TransportConfig -VoicemailJournalingEnabled $true`. To retrieve the current setting, use `Get-TransportConfig | Select VoiceMailJournalingEnabled`.

The journaling mailbox is a configured mailbox where the journal reports are collected. The configuration of this journaling mailbox itself depends on the policies that have been set by the organization or by regulatory or legal requirements. For example, you can define a retention policy on the mailbox so there will be some form of automatic housekeeping on the mailbox itself. Also, you can make sure the quota setting doesn't prevent the journal mailbox from receiving journal reports, as the size of that journal mailbox can grow quiet big depending on the number of journal reports generated. So, make sure your journal mailboxes are properly managed.

■ **Note** You can utilize multiple journal mailboxes for different journal rules. On a side note, you cannot utilize a mailbox hosted in Office 365 for journaling.

In addition, the journal mailbox needs to be treated as a special, secured mailbox, as it may contain sensitive information. It is recommended that you configure your journal mailboxes as follows, where Journal Box 1 is the name of the journal mailbox in this example:

```
$ExRcpt= (Get-OrganizationConfig).MicrosoftExchangeRecipientEmailAddresses | select -ExpandProperty
SmtpAddress
Set-Mailbox -Identity 'JournalBox1' --RequireSenderAuthenticationEnabled $true
-HiddenFromAddressListsEnabled $true -AcceptMessagesOnlyFromSendersOrMembers $ExRcpt
```

Doing this will lock the mailbox and not allow external senders to send messages to it, will hide it from the address books so users won't see it, and will only allow Exchange to send messages to that mailbox.

■ **Note** `(Get-OrganizationConfig).MicrosoftExchangeRecipientEmailAddresses` will return the SMTP addresses of the named Microsoft Exchange recipients. It will contain an entry in the format `MicrosoftExchange329e71e-c88ae4615bbc36ab6ce41109e@domain` for each configured accepted domain. Note that the primary address is used as sender for internal DSN messages.

■ **Warning**   If you ever decide to change the primary SMTP address of a Microsoft Exchange recipient by configuring it directly or indirectly through email address policies, make sure you adjust the `AcceptMessagesOnlyFromSendersOrMembers` setting accordingly.

Besides establishing the journaling mailbox, you can also define an alternative journal recipient, often used in cases when Exchange encounters problems delivering the journal report to the configured journal recipient. The alternative journal recipient will receive NDRs with the journal report attached, allowing you to resend the original message if the journaling mailbox becomes available again. If there is no alternative journaling recipient configured, Exchange will just requeue the journal report.

Journal reports do not generate NDR reports unless an alternate recipient is configured. If an alternate journal recipient is configured, it will receive an NDR with the original journal report. If no alternative journal recipient is configured, Exchange will re-queue the journal report indefinitely and those messages will never expire.

The alternative journal recipient is an organization-wide setting, collecting journal reports for all unavailable journal recipients. Because it collects journal reports for all failing journal recipients, it might grow very fast when an outage hits multiple original journal recipients. Also, because it possibly collects NDRs of journal reports for all journal recipients, be sure to check with your legal department to see if sending all those journal reports to an alternative journal recipient is allowed under existing regulations and applicable laws.

■ **Note**   Multiple journaling reports could be generated if the number of recipients exceeds the `ExpansionSizeLimit` setting in `%ExchangeInstallPath%\EdgeTransport.exe.config`, which could happen after group expansion. The default value is set to 1,000 recipients. Multiple journal reports are also generated when a message is bifurcated—that is, the message is split as it gets routed to different destinations.

Creating a Standard Journal Rule

To create a standard journal rule using EAC, you do the following, as shown in Figure 9-27:

1. Open the Exchange Admin Center.

2. Navigate to Servers ➤ Databases.

3. Select the database you want to enable journaling on and click the Edit icon.

4. Select Maintenance.

5. For selecting the journal recipient, click Browse and select the journal mailbox you want to use for collecting journal reports generated for mailboxes hosted on this database.

6. Click Save to confirm.

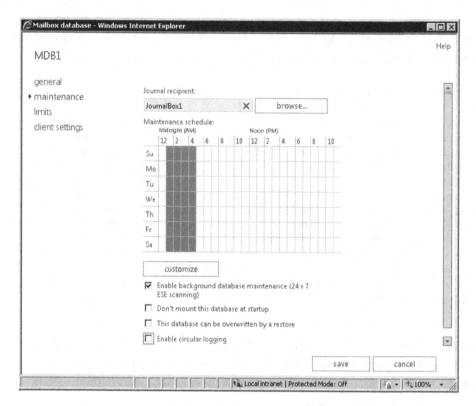

Figure 9-27. *Configuring standard journaling*

To accomplish this using the Exchange Management Shell, use the Set-MailboxDatabase cmdlet. For example, to enable standard journaling to database MDB1 using journaling mailbox Journal Box 1, use the following command:

```
Set-MailboxDatabase -Identity MDB1 -JournalRecipient JournalBox1
```

To check which mailbox database has been configured for standard journaling, use the following command:

```
Get-MailboxDatabase | Where { $_.JournalRecipient } | Select Identity,JournalRecipient
```

To disable standard journaling, set the JournalRecipient to $null; for example,

```
Set-MailboxDatabase -Identity MDB1 -JournalRecipient $null
```

Creating a Premium Journal Rule

To create a premium journal rule using EAC, you do the following, as shown in Figure 9-28:

1. Open the Exchange Admin Center.

2. Navigate to Compliance Management ➤ Journal Rules.

3. Select the + sign to add a journal rule.

4. Configure "Send journal reports to. . ." with the SMTP address of the journal report recipient.

5. Enter a name for the journal rule at Name.

6. At "If the message is sent to or received from. . .," configure the recipient, which can be a user or distribution group for which you want to generate journal reports. You can also generate journal messages for all recipients by selecting "Apply to all messages."

7. Finally, at "Journal the following messages. . ." you can specify the scope of the journal rule. This can be global (all messages), messages generated within the Exchange organization (internal messages only), or messages with an external recipient or sender SMTP address (external messages only).

8. Click Save to save the rule.

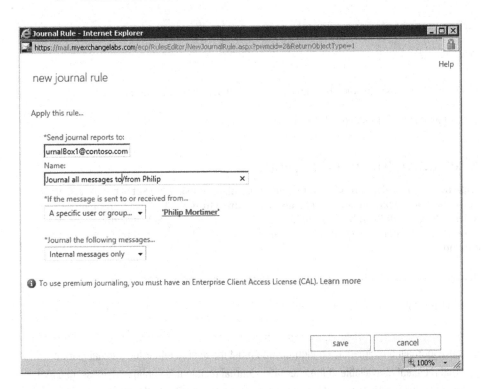

Figure 9-28. *Journal rule creation*

The cmdlet to create a journal rule is New-JournalRule. To create the journal rule in the example above, you would use the following command:

```
New-JournalRule –Name 'Journal all messages to/from Philip' –JournalEmailAddress JournalBox1@
contoso.com –Recipient philip@contoso.com -Scope Internal –Enabled $true
```

Possible options for the scope are global, internal, or external.

If you want to see which journal rules are in configured, use Get-JournalRule, as shown in Figure 9-29.

Figure 9-29. *Get-JournalRule output*

If you want to remove a journal rule, use the Remove-JournalRule cmdlet, as in this command:

```
Remove-JournalRule –Name 'Journal all messages by Philip'
```

Configuring an Alternative Journal Recipient

The alternative journal recipient is an organization-wide setting and is configured using the Set-TransportConfig cmdlet using the JournalingReportNdrTo parameter. You can also configure it from the EAC via Compliance Management ➤ Journal Rules ➤ Send Undeliverable Journal Reports To... option, using Select Address to pick a recipient. For example, to configure the alternative journaling recipient to AlternativeJournalingBox@contoso.com, you use the following command:

```
Set-TransportConfig –JournalingReportNdrTo AlternativeJournalingBox@contoso.com
```

To remove the alternative journaling recipient, set it to $null.

■ **Warning**   When an alternative journaling recipient is configured, you must make sure either the original journal recipient or the alternative journal recipient is available. If the alternative journal recipient is configured, messages that cannot be delivered to the original journal recipient are not requeued and the related NDR, which Exchange will try to deliver to the alternative journal recipient, will be lost.

Data Loss Prevention (DLP)

Part of compliance is not only having the instruments to verify that an organization or its employees are operating within applicable regulations and laws, but also providing the controls to manage sensitive data and prevent data leakage, such as credit card information. With email being used to send business reports as well as those invitations for dinner to family, users could be unaware of the sensitivity of the information they are sending or ignorant of the potential business impact of sending certain information over the public network which is the Internet.

An Exchange feature that focuses on managing or preventing the exposure of sensitive information is *data loss prevention* (DLP). For this purpose, DLP policies can be seen as a package of transport rules that prevent users from sending sensitive information by filtering those messages. Alternatively, you can use policy tips to notify users that they might be sending sensitive information. Policy tips are similar to mail tips, and they are shown as a notification in Outlook.

■ **Caution**   Policy tips require Office 2013 Professional Plus. Policy tips do not work when you install Outlook 2013 separately. Also, policy tips are not supported on Office 2010 or earlier versions of Office. Exchange Server 2013 Service Pack 1 adds support for policy tips to Outlook WebApp and OWA for Devices.

Exchange Server 2013 Service Pack 1 introduced document fingerprinting, which can be used to identify sensitive material in your organization. By uploading sensitive text-based forms used by your organization, you can create DLP policies to match those forms. For example, you can add HR documents and create a DLP policy to prevent messages containing those HR documents from leaving the Exchange organization.

■ **Note**   Data loss prevention is a premium feature that requires an Enterprise CAL when used with on-premises Exchange Server 2013.

Creating the DLP Policies

There are two ways to create a DLP policy in Exchange Server 2013. The first method is to use a template. This template can be an Exchange-supplied one or one provided by a third-party or yourself. After creating a DLP policy using a template, you can then customize the transport rules.

■ **Note**   To be able to create DLP policies, the user needs to be a member of the Compliance Management group.

You can see which templates are available by using the Get-DlpTemplate cmdlet, as shown in Figure 9-30.

```
Select Machine: AMS-EXCH01.contoso.com                                                    _ □ ✕
[PS] C:\>Get-DlpPolicyTemplate

Name                                    Publisher            Version
----                                    ---------            -------
Australia Financial Data                Microsoft            15.0.3.0
Australia Health Records Act (HRIP Act) Microsoft            15.0.3.0
Australia Personally Identifiable In... Microsoft            15.0.3.0
Australia Privacy Act                   Microsoft            15.0.3.0
Canada Financial Data                   Microsoft            15.0.3.0
Canada Health Information Act (HIA)      Microsoft            15.0.3.0
Canada Personal Health Act (PHIPA) -... Microsoft            15.0.3.0
Canada Personal Health Information A... Microsoft            15.0.3.0
Canada Personal Information Protecti... Microsoft            15.0.3.0
Canada Personal Information Protecti... Microsoft            15.0.3.0
Canada Personally Identifiable Infor... Microsoft            15.0.3.0
France Data Protection Act              Microsoft            15.0.3.0
France Financial Data                   Microsoft            15.0.3.0
France Personally Identifiable Infor... Microsoft            15.0.3.0
Germany Financial Data                  Microsoft            15.0.3.0
Germany Personally Identifiable Info... Microsoft            15.0.3.0
Israel Financial Data                   Microsoft            15.0.3.0
Israel Personally Identifiable Infor... Microsoft            15.0.3.0
Israel Protection of Privacy            Microsoft            15.0.3.0
Japan Financial Data                    Microsoft            15.0.3.0
Japan Personally Identifiable Inform... Microsoft            15.0.3.0
Japan Protection of Personal Informa... Microsoft            15.0.3.0
PCI Data Security Standard (PCI DSS)    Microsoft            15.0.3.0
Saudi Arabia - Anti-Cyber Crime Law     Microsoft            15.0.3.0
Saudi Arabia Financial Data             Microsoft            15.0.3.0
Saudi Arabia Personally Identifiable... Microsoft            15.0.3.0
U.K. Access to Medical Reports Act      Microsoft            15.0.3.0
U.K. Data Protection Act                Microsoft            15.0.3.0
U.K. Financial Data                     Microsoft            15.0.3.0
U.K. Personal Information Online Cod... Microsoft            15.0.3.0
U.K. Personally Identifiable Informa... Microsoft            15.0.3.0
U.K. Privacy and Electronic Communic... Microsoft            15.0.3.0
U.S. Federal Trade Commission (FTC) ... Microsoft            15.0.3.0
U.S. Financial Data                     Microsoft            15.0.3.0
U.S. Gramm-Leach-Bliley Act (GLBA)      Microsoft            15.0.3.0
U.S. Health Insurance Act (HIPAA)       Microsoft            15.0.3.0
U.S. Patriot Act                        Microsoft            15.0.3.0
U.S. Personally Identifiable Informa... Microsoft            15.0.3.0
U.S. State Breach Notification Laws     Microsoft            15.0.3.0
U.S. State Social Security Number Co... Microsoft            15.0.3.0

[PS] C:\>_
```

Figure 9-30. *Retrieving available DLP policy templates*

To create a template-based DLP policy using EAC, you do the following:

1. Open the Exchange Admin Center.

2. Navigate to Compliance Management ➤ Data Loss Prevention.

3. Select the + sign and select New DLP policy from the list of templates.

4. Enter a name for the DLP policy, optionally a description. Then, in "Choose a template," you pick the template to use as a basis for your DLP policy.

5. When expanding "More options," you can choose to test the DLP policy first by selecting "Test DLP policy with Policy Tips" or "Test DLP policy without Policy Tips." This is especially helpful when customizing DLP policies, as an improperly configured DLP policy could result in unwanted behavior, like blocking the mail flow of valid messages. You can also initially disable the DLP policy, which is recommended if you need to customize it, as the DLP policy becomes effective after saving it, potentially affecting mail flow.

6. Click Save to create the policy.

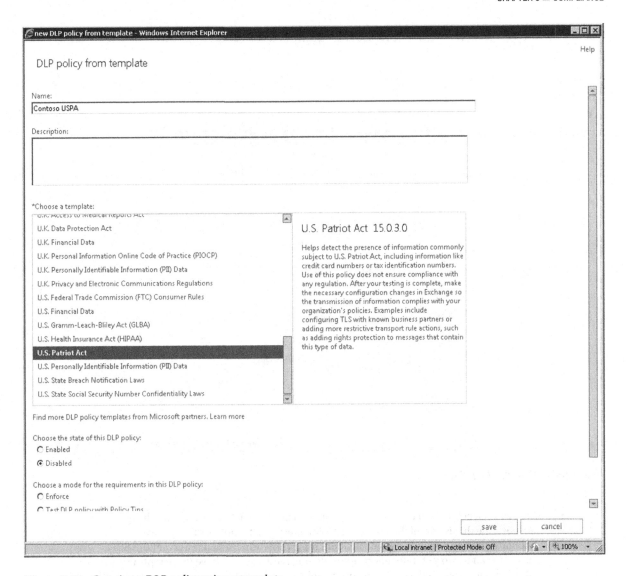

Figure 9-31. *Creating a DLP policy using a template*

If you are happy with the template, you can leave the DLP policy as is. When you want to inspect or customize the DLP policy, in EAC you do the following:

1. In Compliance Management ➤ Data Loss Prevention, select the DLP policy.

2. Click the Edit button.

3. Select Rules.

4. You will now be presented a list of rules contained in the DLP policy. You can turn them on or off individually or edit them to customize each rule.

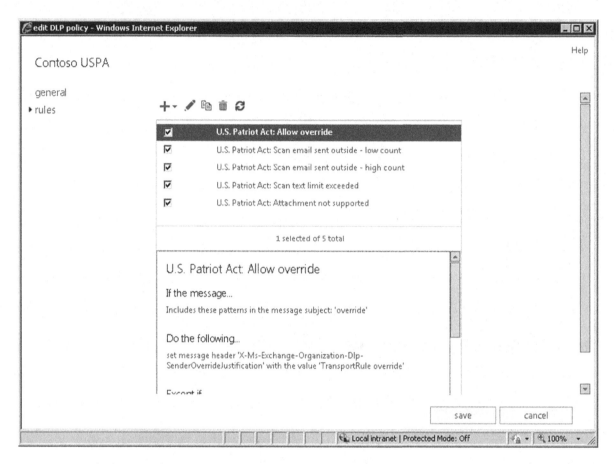

Figure 9-32. Editing DLP policy

5. When you select Edit, you will have the option to inspect or customize the underlying transport rule that is part of the DLP policy. When testing DLP policy rules, you can temporarily add an action "Generate incident report" (new in Exchange Server 2013 SP1), which you can use to generate reports for matching messages and have those reports sent to the recipients specified. Depending on the selected information to report, these reports can contain information like sender, recipients, detected classifications, and matching rules. When specified, the reports will also contain the justification provided by the sender when overriding the policy. This is helpful information when debugging your DLP policy rules or when collecting statistics on justifications to see if the policy perhaps requires adjustment.

6. When you have finished, click Save to store your customized transport rule.

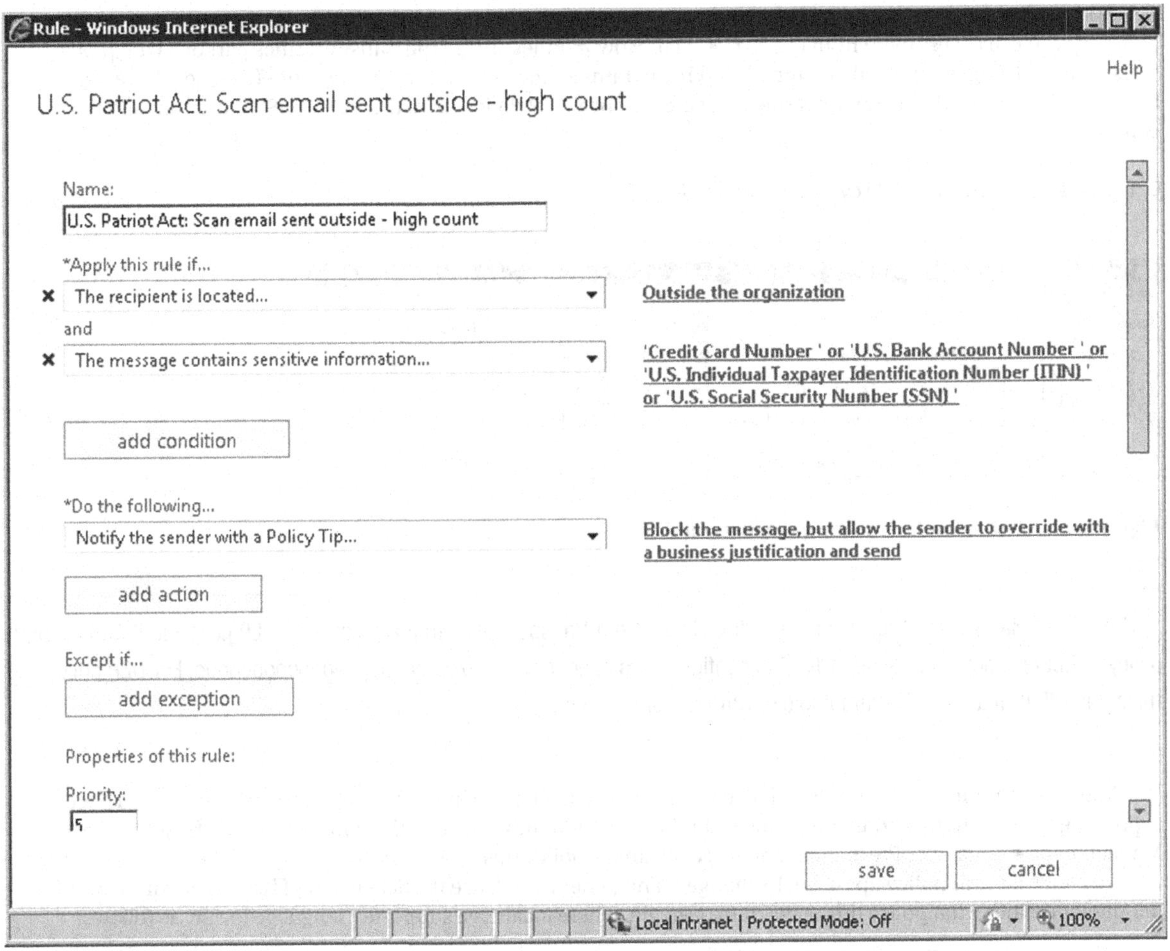

Figure 9-33. *Editing DLP policy rule*

If you want to create a DLP policy using the Exchange Management Shell, use the `New-DlpPolicy` cmdlet, specifying a name and the template to use as a basis for your DLP policy. You can also specify mode (audit, audit and notify, or enforce—the latter will block sending messages with detected possible sensitive information without notification) and the initial state (enabled or disabled) of the transport rule. For example, to create a new DLP policy named Contoso USPA based on the U.S. Patriot Act template, you use the following command:

```
New-DlpPolicy –Name 'Contoso USPA' –Template 'U.S. Patriot Act' –Mode AuditAndNotify –State Enabled
```

You can view the list of current DLP policies using `Get-DlpPolicy`, as shown in Figure 9-34.

```
[PS ] C:\>Get-DlpPolicy

Name                        Publisher                 State           Mode
----                        ---------                 -----           ----
Contoso USPA                Microsoft                 Enabled         AuditAndNotify
```

Figure 9-34. *Viewing the configured DLP policies*

You can use the Get-TransportRule cmdlet to retrieve the collection of transport rules that belong to a DLP policy, or you can access them from the EAC ➤ Mail Flow ➤ Rules. To get the transport rules part of a DLP policy in Exchange Management Shell, use the DlpPolicy parameter in conjunction with the Get-TransportRule cmdlet. For example, to retrieve the transport rules that are part of a DLP Policy named Contoso USPA, use the following command:

```
Get-TransportRule -DlpPolicy 'Contoso USPA'
```

```
Machine: AMS-EXCH01.contoso.com
[PS] C:\>Get-TransportRule -DlpPolicy 'Contoso USPA'

Name                                            State     Mode       Priority Comments
----                                            -----     ----       -------- --------
U.S. Patriot Act: Allow override                Enabled   AuditAnd... 3
U.S. Patriot Act: Scan email sent outside...    Enabled   AuditAnd... 4
U.S. Patriot Act: Scan email sent outside...    Enabled   AuditAnd... 5
U.S. Patriot Act: Scan text limit exceeded      Enabled   AuditAnd... 6
U.S. Patriot Act: Attachment not supported      Enabled   AuditAnd... 7
```

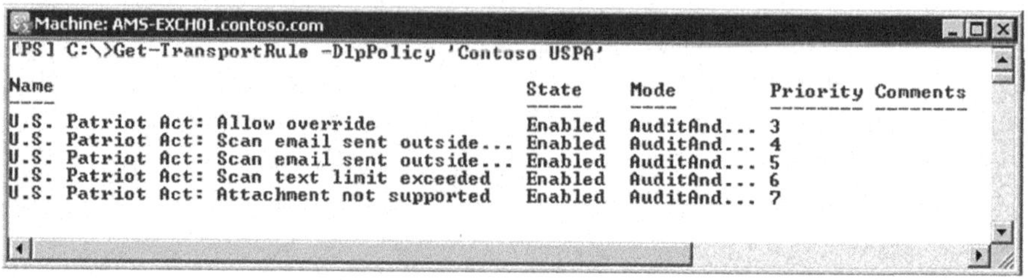

Figure 9-35. Retrieving DLP policy transport rules

■ **Note**   Regular transport rules can be distinguished from transport rules that are part of a DLP policy, in that their DLP policy attribute is not set and their DIP ID is configured as 00000000-0000-0000-0000-000000000000. For DLP policy rules, the DIP ID matches the Immutable ID attribute of the DLP policy.

You can customize policy tips with localized messages or a URL, which you can use to direct users to a page explaining the communications compliance standards. To add these custom elements, go to EAC ➤ Compliance Management ➤ Data Loss Prevention, and select "Manage policy tips."

To create custom policy tips using Exchange Management Shell, use the New-PolicyTip cmdlet. The Name parameter defines what policy tip you want to override, where locale is a supported language locale, as follows:

- **<Locale>\NotifyOnly** To customize the message used for notifications in <Locale>.

- **<Locale>\RejectOverride** To customize the message used for notifications in <Locale> when the user is still allowed to send the message.

- **<Locale>\Reject** To customize the message used when used for notifications in <Locale> and when the sending of the message is prevented.

- **Url** To add a link to a URL for policy tips. There can be only one URL policy tip. The URL will be accessed when the sender clicks the link in "Learn more about your organization's rule," which will be shown in the policy tip.

For example, to customize the Dutch locale notification when users are notified of possibly sending a message with sensitive information, you could use:

```
New-PolicyTipConfig -Name 'nl\RejectOverride' -Value 'Uw bericht bevat mogelijk gevoelige informatie'.
```

▦ **Note**   If the transport rule is configured to only notify users and you configure a custom policy tip for "en\RejectOverride," your custom notification message will not be displayed. You will need to configure a notification message for all three possible modes.

To configure a compliance URL to show with the policy tip, you use:

```
New-PolicyTipConfig -Name 'Url' -Value 'http://compliance.contoso.com'
```

Figure 9-36.   *Customizing the policy tips*

To retrieve the current set of customized policy tips, use `Get-PolicyTipConfig`.

Optionally, you can use the locale parameter to only return the custom policy tips for a given locale; for example, `Get-PolicyTipConfigLocale -Locale nl`.

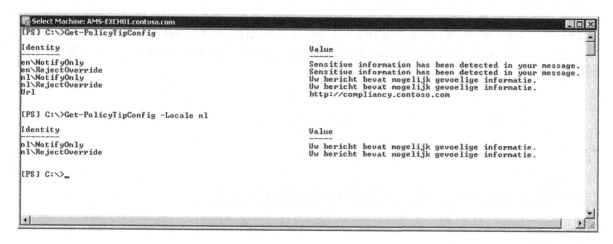

Figure 9-37. *Using* Get-PolicyTag *to list customized policy tips*

The way DLP policy tips manifest themselves to users is similar to how mail tips operate. A small notification bar is shown when sensitive information is detected and the DLP policy and related DLP policy rules are configured to generate a notification, as shown in Figure 9-38.

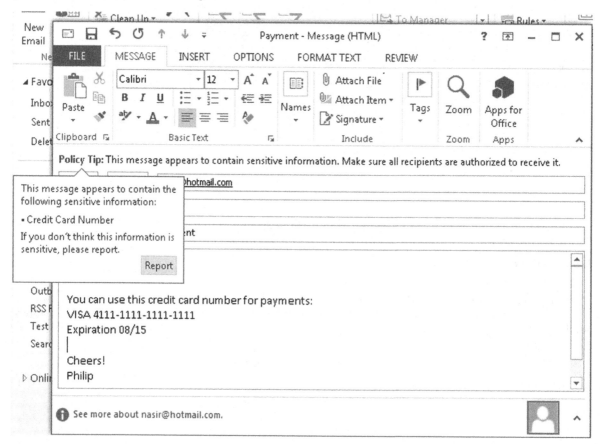

Figure 9-38. *DLP policy tip shown in Outlook 2013*

When such a message is sent—when allowed by the DLP Policy—and you have configured to generate incident reports for DLP policy rules, the configured recipients will receive a report as well as a copy of the message attached. The information in the report depends on the selected fields and may include such items as matching rules and data classifications that were detected, including the number of occurrences.

> ■ **Note** Currently, policys tips in OWA will not be shown unless the DLP policy mode is set to Enforced. When the mode is set to one of the test options, policy tips will not be displayed in OWA. This bug will be fixed in a future release.

All rules that are evaluated and have resulted in a hit are mentioned in the report. The report shown in Figure 9-39 also mentions that a disclaimer was added by a rule called "Disclaimer using ApplyHtmlDisclaimer and SetHeader actions."

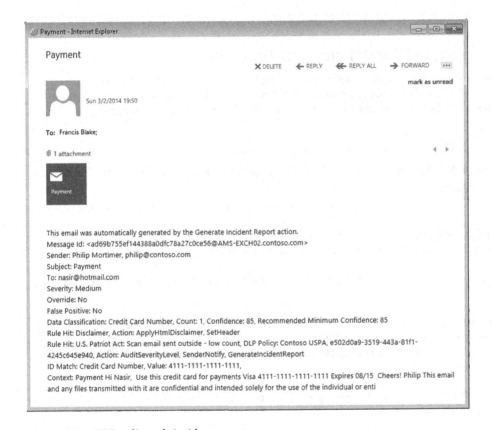

Figure 9-39. DLP policy rule incident report

If you want to adjust a DLP Policy, use the Set-DlpPolicy cmdlet; for example,

```
Set-DlpPolicy -Identity 'Contoso USPA' -Mode Enforce -State Enabled
```

When you want to remove a DLP policy, you use Remove-DlpPolicy; for example,

```
Remove-DlpPolicy -Identity 'Contoso USPA'
```

■ **Note**   Unfortunately, Exchange Server 2013 does not contain built-in reports for DLP-related incidents. Office 365 does, though, and you can find them at Exchange admin center ➤ Compliance Management ➤ Data Loss Prevention ➤ Reports. You can generate information on DLP policy matches for sent mail, received mail, and DLP rule matches for sent or received mail.

Importing and Exporting DLP Policies and Templates

As mentioned earlier, you can import DLP policy templates or you can import or export a DLP policy collection from XML files. Either way, you can quickly implement a customized DLP policy in an Exchange environment. You can duplicate the DLP policies from a test environment to your production environment. The DLP policy settings are stored in an XML file.

■ **Warning**   When you import a DLP policy collection, that collection of policies will overwrite any existing DLP policies defined in your Exchange organization.

To import a DLP policy template file, you use the Import-DlpPolicyTemplate cmdlet. For example, to import a DLP policy from a file named C:\ContosoTemplate.xml, you would use the following command:

```
Import-DlpPolicyTemplate -FileData ([Byte[]]$(Get-Content -Path 'C:\ContosoTemplate.xml' -Encoding
Byte -ReadCount 0))
```

You can also import a DLP policy template from the EAC, via Compliance Management ➤ Data Loss Prevention, and clicking the arrow next to the + sign and selecting the import policy option.

Alternatively, you can create a new DLP policy directly from a file-based template using New-DlpPolicy with the TemplateData parameter; for example,

```
New-DlpPolicy -Name 'DLPPolicy' -TemplateData ([Byte[]]$(Get-Content -Path 'C:\ContosoTemplate.xml'
-Encoding Byte -ReadCount 0))
```

■ **Tip**   Besides importing DLP policy template files from third parties, you can develop your own template file. For more information on developing your own DLP policy template files, see http://bit.ly/ExchangeDevDLPTemplate.

You can also import or export the complete collection of DLP policies. To export the current DLP policy collection, use `Export-DlpCollection`. For example, to export the DLP policy collection to a file named C:\ContosoDLP.xml, you would use the following command:

```
Set-Content -Path 'c:\ContosoDLP.xml' -Value (Export-DlpPolicyCollection).FileData -Encoding Byte
```

The XML file will contain all DLP policies, all DLP policy settings, and the related transport rules.

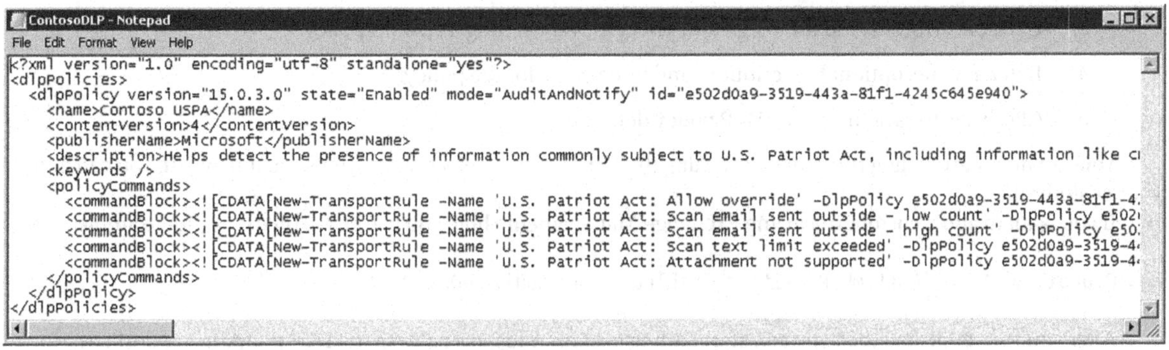

Figure 9-40. *DLP policy collection XML file*

To import a file containing a DLP policy, you use the `Import-DlpPolicyCollection` cmdlet. For example, to import the DLP policy collection settings stored in C:\ContosoDLP.xml, you would use the following command:

```
Import-DlpPolicyCollection -FileData ([Byte[]]$(Get-Content -Path 'C:\ContosoDLP.xml' -Encoding Byte -ReadCount 0))
```

■ **Caution** `Export-DlpPolicyCollection` seems to contain a bug, as it exports the `New-TransportRule` cmdlets to create the related DLP policy rules, but it forgets to state some mandatory values. For example, it does not save the `AttachmentProcessingLimitExceeded` value in the XML file, after which `Import-DlpPolicyCollection` will complain because no value is specified for the `AttachmentProcessingLimitExceeded` parameter. Try correcting the cmdlets in the XML file and then retry the importing when you encounter this obstacle.

Customizing Your DLP Policy

An alternative to using a template to create a DLP policy is to create a custom DLP policy when you have specific requirements. That DLP policy will be empty after creation, so you need to add your own transport rules to it.

To create a custom DLP policy using EAC, you do the following:

1. Open the Exchange Admin Center.

2. Navigate to Compliance Management ➤ Data Loss Prevention.

3. Click the arrow next to the + sign and select New for setting a custom policy.

4. Enter a name, optional description, and initial state for the policy.

5. Click Save to save the empty DLP policy definition.

You can now start adding rules to it by clicking the Edit icon and selecting the rules section, where you can add your custom rules.

If you want to add a custom rule using Exchange Management Shell, you use `New-DlpPolicy`; for example,

```
New-DlpPolicy -Name 'CustomDLP' -State Enabled -Mode AuditAndNotify
```

After you've established that, you can start adding custom transport rules to the DLP policy using the `New-TransportRule` cmdlet with the `DlpPolicy` parameter to attach the transport rules to the DLP policy.

In addition, you can use the mode to determine how the rule operates. Choices for mode are Audit (rule is evaluated but actions are skipped), AuditAndNotify (audit with policy tips), or Enforce (audit and notify plus actions are performed). For example, to create a transport rule to generate policy tips for all messages in which a credit card number is detected, and further attach it to a DLP policy named 'CustomDLP,' you would use the following command:

```
New-TransportRule –Name 'CustomDLP : All Messages with Credit Card Number' –DlpPolicy 'CustomDLP'
–Mode AuditAndNotify –MessageContainsDataClassifications @{'Name'='Credit Card Number'}
-SetAuditSeverity Medium –NotifySender NotifyOnly
```

Here's a short explanation of the DLP-specific parameter used in this example:

- `DlpPolicy` is used to specify the DLP policy to attach the rule to.

- `NotifySender` is a DLP-specific parameter that determines how a user is notified when entering DLP policy-violating information. It needs to be specified together with the `MessageContainsDataClassifications` parameter. The Options for NotifySender are:

  - *NotifyOnly* notifies the sender that message is sent.

  - *RejectMessage* notifies the sender that message is rejected.

  - *RejectUnlessFalsePositiveOverride* notifies the sender; sender can send message marking it as a false positive.

  - *RejectUnlessSilentOverride* message is rejected unless sender overrides policy restriction.

  - *RejectUnlessExplicitOverride* message is rejected unless sender overrides, allowing sender to specify justification.

- If any of the reject options are selected for NotifySender, you can specify a rejection status code and reason using the `RejectMessageEnhancedStatusCode` and `RejectMessageReasonText` parameters.

- The parameter `MessageContainsDataClassifications` is a new predicate in Exchange Server 2013 SP1 and can be is used to specify rules for searching for sensitive information. In the example, it was used to filter messages for the classification "Credit Card Number."

  You can also define thresholds for the minimum and maximum numbers of occurrences, as well as for the confidence level, which is a percentage indicating how sure the DLP engine is that the information is a match. For example, something that looks like a credit card number near something else that looks like an expiration date is more likely to be credit card information than something that looks like a series of numbers. Note that when the parameter is omitted, as in the example, a default minimum of 1 occurrence and 100 percent maximum confidence level is set.

- Not shown in the example but other DLP-specific predicates are `ExceptIfHasClassification` (to exclude one specific data classification), `ExceptIfHasNoClassification` (to apply the rule to messages without a classification). Predicates `HasSenderOverride` and `ExceptIfHasSenderOverride` can be used to control rule evaluation whether or not the sender has selected to override DLP policy for the message.

You can verify the creation of the DLP policy rule using `Get-TransportRule` with the `DlpPolicy` parameter.

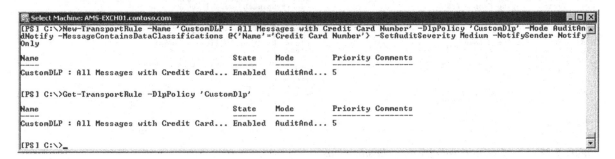

Figure 9-41. *Creating a custom DLP policy rule using New-TransportRule*

■ **Note** For more information on creating your own sensitive information, or even your own template containing these definitions, see `http://bit.ly/ExchangeSensitiveInformation`. To get a list of currently defined types of sensitive information, use `Get-DataClassification|Sort Name`.

The list of default-available data classifications in Exchange Server 2013 SP1 is shown in Figure 9-42.

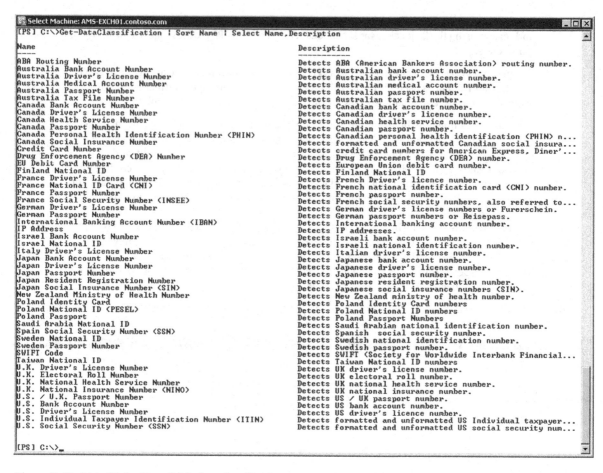

Figure 9-42. *List of default available data classifications*

DLP Document Fingerprinting

A new feature in Exchange Server 2013 SP1 is DLP document fingerprinting. This fingerprinting allows you to enhance DLP by customizing your sensitive information types by uploading particular documents. These documents should represent the information you are trying to protect—for example, HR documents or tax forms. You can then create DLP policy rules to detect these types of documents and take appropriate action.

■ **Note** Documents uploaded for document fingerprinting are not stored in Exchange Information Store. Instead, a hash is generated using the contents of the document used by the DLP engine for detecting matching information. The hashes are stored with the data classification object in Active Directory. There could be one or more document fingerprints per data classification.

To create document fingerprints using EAC, you do the following:

1. Open the Exchange Admin Center.

2. Navigate to Compliance Management ➤ Data Loss Prevention.

3. Select Manage Document Fingerprints.

4. In the document fingerprints window, select the + sign to create a new document fingerprint.

5. In the new document fingerprint window, enter a name for the kind of document fingerprint you are creating and a mandatory description.

6. In the document list section, select the + sign to add a new document for which you want to create a fingerprint. The document fingerprinting supports the same file types as transport rules. For a list of supported file types, see `http://bit.ly/ ExchangeTransportRulesFileTypes`.

7. When you are done uploading the documents to fingerprint, click Save.

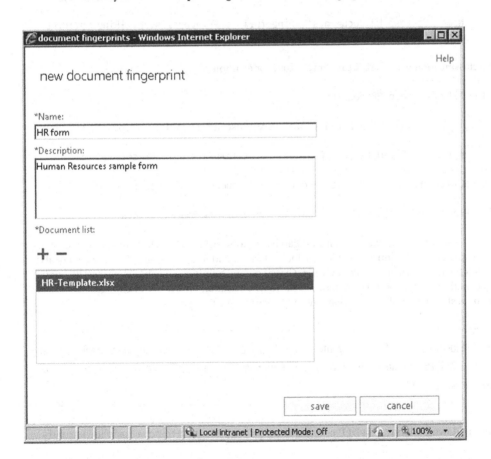

Figure 9-43. *Creating a document fingerprint*

■ **Tip** You can add multiple documents to a single document fingerprint. This allows you to create a single fingerprint for the same type of information in various formats—for example, .docx and .pdf—or different versions of the document. You can also configure a localized name to display in supported clients for the fingerprint via Edit document fingerprints ➤ Language settings—for example, EN/'HR Documents' and DE/'HR Documents'

If you want to create a new document fingerprint using Exchange Management Shell, use New-FingerPrint to create the document fingerprint after which you can provide that information to New-DataClassification to create the data classification holding one or more document fingerprints.

For example, to create a new data classification "HR Form" using the document fingerprints of the files c:\HR-Template-EN.doc and c:\HR-Template-NL.doc, you use the following commands:

```
$Fingerprint1= New-Fingerprint –FileData (Get-Content 'C:\HR-Template-v1.doc' -Encoding Byte)
-Description 'HR document v1'
$Fingerprint2= New-Fingerprint –FileData (Get-Content 'C:\HR-Template-v2.doc' -Encoding Byte)
-Description 'HR document v2'
New-DataClassification –Name 'Contoso HR documents' -Fingerprints $FingerprintEN, $FingerprintNL
-Description 'Message contains HR documents'
```

You can validate the classification using Get-Classification; for example,

```
Get-Classification -Identity 'Contoso HR documents'
```

If you want to add a fingerprint to an existing data classification, you use Set-DataClassification, as follows:

```
$FingerprintPDF= New-Fingerprint –FileData (Get-Content 'C:\HR-Template.pdf' -Encoding Byte)
-Description 'HR document PDF'
$Fingerprints= (Get-DataClassification -Identity 'Contoso HR documents').Fingerprints +
$FingerprintPDF
Set-DataClassification -Identity 'Contoso HR documents' -Fingerprints $Fingerprints
```

Changes made to a DLP policy may not take effect immediately. Outlook 2013 caches DLP policies in two local XML files that are refreshed every 24 hours. The files are located in the folder %UserProfile%\AppData\Local\Microsoft\Outlook and their file names start with PolicyNudgeClassificationDefinitions (cached data classifications) and PolicyNudgeRules (cached rule information). Keep this in mind when implementing policy changes in production or when you are testing DLP policies. Luckily, there is a workaround.

■ **Note** Outlook will use the locally cached DLP policy information to evaluate the message and attachments against document fingerprints or other DLP Policy rules, using the same DLP engine as Exchange. This means attachments are not send over the network for evaluation.

To force Outlook 2013 to download the latest DLP policies, close Outlook 2013 and remove the following entry from the registry:

```
HKEY_CURRENT_USER\SOFTWARE\Microsoft\Office\15.0\Outlook\
PolicyNudges\LastDownloadTimesPerAccount
```

After removal, start Outlook 2013. When you create a message, the updated DLP policies will be downloaded.

■ **Caution**   Document fingerprinting doesn't work for password-protected files or files containing solely images. Also, documents won't be detected if they do not contain all the text used in the document employed to create the document fingerprint. Use documents or forms with blank fields, for example, to create the fingerprints.

Now, you need to create a DLP policy rule in which you specify this data classification data to match your sensitive information contents. In EAC, this is a matter of editing the DLP policy, selecting the rules, clicking the + sign to create each new rule, and in the rule options window, selecting "The message contains sensitive information as. . . Apply this rule if. . ." using the data classification holding the document fingerprints.

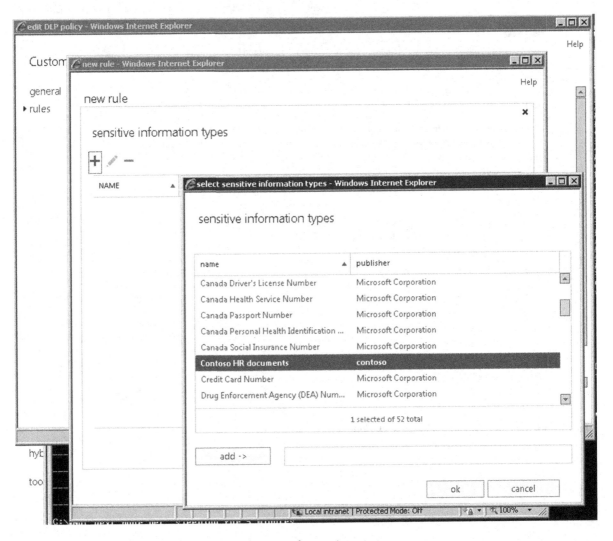

Figure 9-44. *Creating a DLP policy rule using document fingerprints*

To create such a DLP policy in the Exchange Management Shell, use the New-TransportRule you would also use to create a custom DLP policy rule; for example,

```
New-TransportRule –Name 'CustomDLP: HR docs'  -MessageContainsDataClassifications @
{'Name'='Contoso HR documents'} -NotifySender 'RejectUnlessExplicitOverride'
-RejectMessageReasonText 'Delivery not authorized, message refused'  -SetAuditSeverity 'Medium'
-Mode 'AuditAndNotify' -DlpPolicy 'CustomDLP'
```

Now, when a user tries to send a message using a document with an attachment that matches the document fingerprint, the sender will get a policy tip, as shown in Figures 9-45 and 9-46.

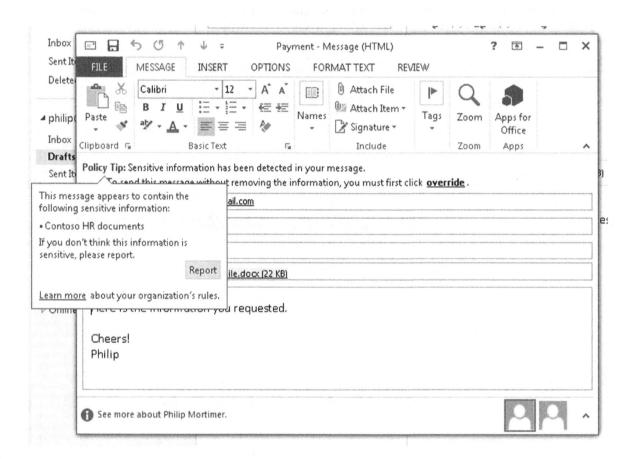

Figure 9-45. *DLP pingerprint policy tip in Outlook*

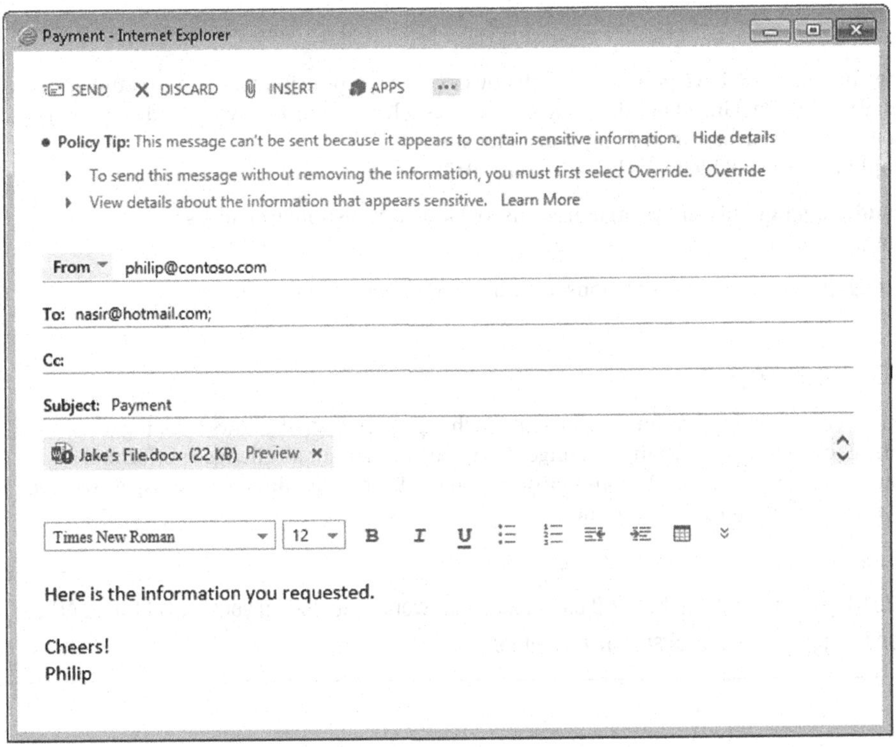

Payment - Internet Explorer

SEND ✕ DISCARD ⬜ INSERT 📱 APPS ···

● Policy Tip: This message can't be sent because it appears to contain sensitive information. Hide details

▸ To send this message without removing the information, you must first select Override. Override

▸ View details about the information that appears sensitive. Learn More

From ▾ philip@contoso.com

To: nasir@hotmail.com;

Cc:

Subject: Payment

📘 Jake's File.docx (22 KB) Preview ✕

Times New Roman ▾   12 ▾   **B** *I* <u>U</u> ≔ ≔ ≝ ≖ ▦ ⌄

Here is the information you requested.

Cheers!
Philip

Figure 9-46. DLP fingerprint policy tip in Outlook WebApp

Note that in this example NotifySender is set to "RejectUnlessExplicitOverride." This causes the message to be rejected using the message configured with RejectMessageReasonText unless the sender chooses to override this, providing a mandatory business justification, as shown in Figure 9-47.

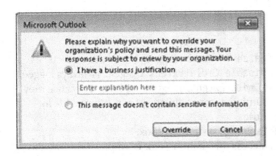

Microsoft Outlook

⚠ Please explain why you want to override your organization's policy and send this message. Your response is subject to review by your organization.

◉ I have a business justification

[Enter explanation here]

○ This message doesn't contain sensitive information

[Override] [Cancel]

Figure 9-47. Overriding DLP reject providing a business justification

■ **Tip**   If you don't see the override confirmation link in Outlook, check if you have set the DLP policy mode to Enforced. In Test mode, these interactions will not be displayed.

Auditing

Administrators in an Exchange organization have power, and with power comes responsibility. From a compliance perspective, organizations may require tracking of administrative changes, such as monitoring who made changes to a certain receive connector, or auditing the access to high-profile mailboxes.

The following auditing options are available in Exchange Server 2013:

- **Administrator audit logging** This allows organizations to audit administrative changes in their Exchange organization.

- **Mailbox audit logging** This allows organizations to audit mailbox access and changes.

Administrator Audit Logging

The administrator audit logging feature, which was introduced with Exchange Server 2010, allows auditing of who did what and where in the Exchange organization. Exchange Server 2013 can audit all changes performed by administrators in the Exchange Management Shell. Actions performed in the Exchange Admin Center are also logged because EAC constructs and runs cmdlets in the background.

■ **Tip** In Exchange Server 2013, you can view the last 500 commands that were executed on your behalf from EAC by opening up the Show Command Logging window, as shown in Figure 9-48.

Figure 9-48. *Enabling Command Logging from EAC*

"Changes" here means that view-only cmdlets like Get-* and Search-* won't be logged. Use of the cmdlets Set-AdminAuditLogConfig, Enable-CmdletExtensionAgent, and Disable-CmdletExtensionAgent is always logged, however. The cmdlets Disable-CmdletExtensionAgent and Enable-CmdletExtensionAgent are logged because they can be used to turn the administrator audit log agent on or off. The administrator audit log agent is responsible for evaluating cmdlets against the auditing configuration and logging entries.

Administrator audit logging entries are stored in the Microsoft Exchange system mailbox, SystemMailbox{e0dc1c29-89c3-4034-b678-e6c29d823ed9}. You can access this mailbox—for example, if you want to move it to a different database—by using Get-Mailbox with the Arbitration parameter; for example,

```
Get-Mailbox -Arbitration -Identity 'systemMailbox{e0dc1c29-89c3-4034-b678-e6c29d823ed9}'
```

If you want to move the system mailbox to a database named 'MDB2', for instance, you would use the following command:

```
Get-Mailbox -Arbitration -Identity 'systemMailbox{e0dc1c29-89c3-4034-b678-e6c29d823ed9}' |
New-Moverequest -TargetDatabase 'MDB2'
```

If you are concerned about the amount of logged data in the system mailbox after enabling administrator audit logging, you can check the size of the system mailbox, as follows:

```
Get-Mailbox -Arbitration -Identity 'systemMailbox{e0dc1c29-89c3-4034-b678-e6c29d823ed9}' |
Get-MailboxStatistics | Format-Table TotalItemSize
```

■ **Caution** When you are in a co-existence scenario of Exchange Server 2013 with Exchange Server 2010, you need to move the system mailbox to Exchange Server 2013. If you do not, Exchange Server 2013 tasks will not be logged in the audit log and audit log searching will not work.

Administrative auditing logging is a global setting enabled by default in Exchange Server 2013. It can be disabled using the following:

```
Set-AdminAuditLogConfig -AdminAuditLogEnable $False
```

To enable administrative audit logging, you use:

```
Set-AdminAuditLogConfig -AdminAuditLogEnable $True
```

If you want to view the current administrative audit logging settings, you use Get-AdminAuditLogConfig, as shown in Figure 9-49:

```
[PS] C:\>Get-AdminAuditLogConfig

RunspaceId                   : 2c404f92-e4ce-4f04-9958-7a0d3246ea45
AdminAuditLogEnabled         : True
LogLevel                     : None
TestCmdletLoggingEnabled     : False
AdminAuditLogCmdlets         : {*}
AdminAuditLogParameters      : {*}
AdminAuditLogExcludedCmdlets : {}
AdminAuditLogAgeLimit        : 90.00:00:00
AdminDisplayName             :
ExchangeVersion              : 0.10 (14.0.100.0)
Name                         : Admin Audit Log Settings
DistinguishedName            : CN=Admin Audit Log Settings,CN=Global Settings,CN=Litware,CN=Microsoft
                               Exchange,CN=Services,CN=Configuration,DC=contoso,DC=com
Identity                     : Admin Audit Log Settings
Guid                         : dd784880-eeb6-4544-8c8f-9c85a104fa31
ObjectCategory               : contoso.com/Configuration/Schema/ms-Exch-Admin-Audit-Log-Config
ObjectClass                  : {top, msExchAdminAuditLogConfig}
WhenChanged                  : 1/4/2014 9:47:41 PM
WhenCreated                  : 1/4/2014 5:30:10 PM
WhenChangedUTC               : 1/4/2014 8:47:41 PM
WhenCreatedUTC               : 1/4/2014 4:30:10 PM
OrganizationId               :
OriginatingServer            : AMS-DC01.contoso.com
IsValid                      : True
ObjectState                  : Unchanged


[PS] C:\>_
```

Figure 9-49. Administrator audit logging settings

As you can see from Figure 9-49, there are additional options for administrator audit logging. There are options to restrict logging to certain cmdlets or parameters, for example. These administrator audit logging options are explained next.

■ **Caution**   The administrator audit logging setting is stored in Active Directory, and depending on replication, it may not immediately be applied. Also, for any current Exchange Management Shell session, it may take up to one hour for the new setting to become effective.

Administrator Audit Logging Options

To restrict logging to only specific cmdlets or only if specific parameters are used, you use `Set-AdminAuditLogConfig` in combination with the `AdminAuditLogConfigCmdlets` and `AdminAuditLogConfigParameters` parameters. For example, to log only the cmdlets `New-Mailbox` and `Remove-Mailbox`, you would use:

```
Set-AdminAuditLogConfig -AdminAuditLogCmdlets 'New-Mailbox','Remove-Mailbox'
```

You can also choose to exclude certain cmdlets from being logged using the `AdminAuditLogExcludeCmdlets` parameters; for example,

```
Set-AdminAuditLogConfig -AdminAuditLogExcludeCmdlets 'set-Mailbox'
```

You can restrict logging when certain parameters are used. For example, to log only the name, identity, Windows email address and email addresses parameters, you would use:

```
Set-AdminAuditLogConfig -AdminAuditLogParameters 'Name', 'Identity', 'WindowsEmailAddress',
'EmailAddresses'
```

To cover a set of related cmdlets or parameters, you can use wild cards. For example, to log only cmdlets related to the mailbox and only those parameters containing "address," you would use:

```
Set-AdminAuditLogConfig -AdminAuditLogCmdlets '*-Mailbox' -AdminAuditLogParameters '*Address*'
```

The default values for `AdminAuditLogCmdlets` and `AdminAuditLogParameters` are *, which causes any cmdlet in combination with any parameter to be logged. If you want to reset these values to their default, you use:

```
Set-AdminAuditLogConfig -AdminAuditLogCmdlets '*' -AdminAuditLogParameters '*'
-AdminAuditLogExcludeCmdlets $null
```

By default, administrative audit logging is restricted to a 90-day period. After 90 days, the log entries are deleted. You can increase or decrease this limit by using the AdminAuditLogAgeLimit parameter, specifying the number of days, hours, minutes, and seconds that entries should be kept. The format to specify this parameter is dd.hh:mm:ss. For example, to set the limit to 180 days, you use:

```
Set-AdminAuditLogConfig –AdminAuditLogAgeLimit 180.00:00:00
```

Administrative audit logging only logs information like the cmdlet ran, when it ran, the context, and any specified parameters and values. By configuring the log level to Verbose, it will also log the previous values of any changes attributes: Set-AdminAuditLogConfig –LogLevel Verbose. To return to the default logging, you set the log level to None.

By default, test cmdlets are not logged. To log the test cmdlets, set TestCmdletLoggingEnabled to $true; for example,

```
Set-AdminAuditLogConfig -TestCmdletLoggingEnabled $true
```

To disable it again, set TestCmdletLoggingEnabled to $false.

Custom Logging Entries

In addition to the administrator audit logging cmdlets, you can create custom entries in the administrator audit log. This can be useful when you want to create markers for when to run scripts or for maintenance stop and starting events, for example.

To create a custom administrative audit log entry, use the Write-AdminAuditLog cmdlet, with the Comment parameter to pass the message to log. For example, to log the start of a scheduled maintenance cycle, you could use:

```
Write-AdminAuditLog –Comment 'start of scheduled maintenance'
```

▪ **Caution**   The maximum size of the comment text is 500 characters.

Auditing Log Searches

Logging information for auditing purposes would be useless if there were no ways to search through or retrieve the logged information. To search the administrator audit log using EAC, navigate to Compliance Management ➤ Auditing, and select to view the administrator audit log or to export the administrator audit log when you want to perform a search and then send the results to a mailbox.

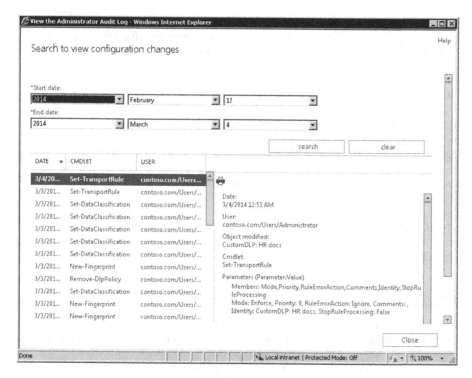

Figure 9-50. *Inspecting the administrator audit log*

EAC is a bit limited when it comes to searching the audit log, as you can only further specify the start and end dates for reports on the administrator audit log. When you want to check the administrative audit log using the EMS using additional search criteria, Exchange provides two cmdlets:

- **Search-AdminAuditLog** Use this cmdlet to search through the administrator audit log entries based on search criteria. These searches are synchronous.

- **New-AdminAuditLogSearch** This cmdlet is similar to Search-AdminAuditLog, but instead of returning the audit log entries, it can be used to send the results to a recipient. These searches run asynchronously in the background.

The search criteria you can specify with Search-AdminAuditLog and New-AdminAuditLogSearch are as follows:

- **Cmdlets** To specify which cmdlets you want to search for in the administrator audit log.

- **Parameters** Too specify which parameters you want to search for in administrator audit log.

- **StartDate** and **EndDate** To restrict the search in the administrator audit log to a certain period. When running an export using New-AdminAuditLogSearch, a start date and end date are mandatory.

- **ObjectIds** To specify the names of the changed objects to search for. This can be the name any Exchange-related configuration item, such as mailboxes, aliases, database, send connector, and the like.

- **UserIds** To search for cmlets in the administrator audit log ran by specific users.

- **IsSuccess** To restrict the search to successful or failed events.

- **ExternalAccess** When used in Exchange Online or Office 365, using $true will return audit log entries generated by Microsoft service administrators; using $false will return audit log entries generated by the tenant administrators.

- **StatusMailRecipients** Specifies the SMTP addresses of the recipients who should receive the audit log report. This parameter is only valid when using New-AdminAuditLogSearch.

- **Name** Specifies the subject of the email. This parameter is only valid when using New-AdminAuditLogSearch.

■ **Note** It can take up to 15 minutes for Exchange to generate and deliver the report. The raw information in XML format attached to the report generated by New-AdminAuditLogSearch can have a maximum size of 10 MB.

For example, to search the audit log for entries where the Remove-TransportRule cmdlet was used on an object (in this case, transport rule) named 'HR Documents' since March 3, 2014, 3:15, you would use the following:

```
Search-AdminAuditLog –Cmdlets Remove-TransportRule -ObjectIds 'HR Documents' -StartDate '3/3/2014
3:15'
```

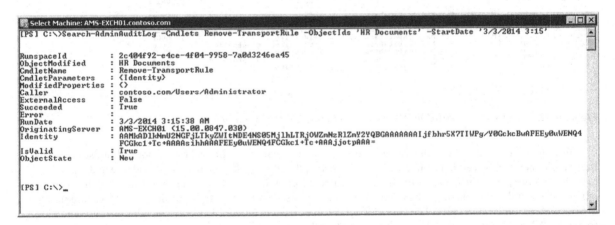

Figure 9-51. *Using* Search-AdminAuditLog *to search the administrator audit log*

■ **Tip** As with many cmdlets, only the first 1,000 entries are returned. When necessary, use -ResultSize Unlimited to return all matching audit log entries.

To return all cmdlets run by administrator against objects named Philip, you would use:

```
Search-AdminAuditLog –UserIds Administrator –ObjectIds Philip
```

To return all audit log entries where the New-ManagementRoleAssignment or Remove-ManagementRoleAssignment cmdlets were run, you would use:

```
Search-AdminAuditLog –Cmdlets New-ManagementRoleAssignment, Remove-ManagementRoleAssignment
```

To run the same query against the past 24 hours and send the results to a recipient named philip@contoso.com, you would use:

```
New-AdminAuditLogSearch –Name 'ManagementRoleAssignment Changes'
 –Cmdlets New-ManagementRoleAssignment, Remove-ManagementRoleAssignment
 -StatusMailRecipients philip@contoso.com -StartDate (Get-Date).AddDays(-1) -EndDate (Get-Date)
```

You can also search for specific parameter usage and or use ExpandProperty to get an overview of all changed values using parameters. For example, if you want to show changes in the circular logging settings of mailbox databases in the last seven days, you would use:

```
Search-AdminAuditLog –Cmdlet Set-MailboxDatabase -StartDate (Get-Date).AddDays(-7)
 -EndDate (Get-Date) | Select RunDate,CmdletName -ExpandProperty CmdletParameters
```

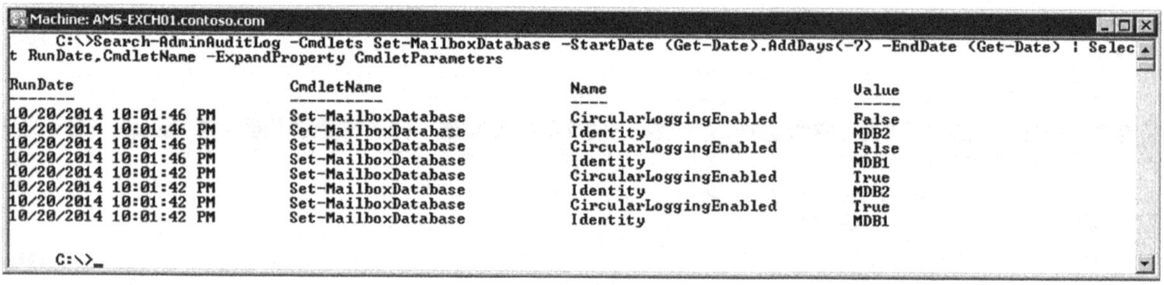

Figure 9-52. *Using* Search-AdminAuditLog *to search the administrator audit log*

You can retrieve a list of current searches using Get-AuditLogSearch. This will return both administrator audit log searches and mailbox audit logging searches. You can optionally specify "created after" and "created before" to limit the time span of the items returned. The returned information contains the name, the name of the job or email subject, and the recipients of the report. The time span used for the report is returned as an UTC time stamp in StartDateUtc and EndDateUtc. The attribute 'Type' can be used to differentiate between administrator audit log searches ("Admin") and mailbox audit log searches ("Mailbox"):

```
Get-AuditLogSearch | Format-Table Name, Type, CreationTime, StartDateUtc, EndDateUtc,
StatusMailRecipients –AutoSize
```

This cmdlet will return a list of current audit log searches, similar to the output shown in Figure 9-53.

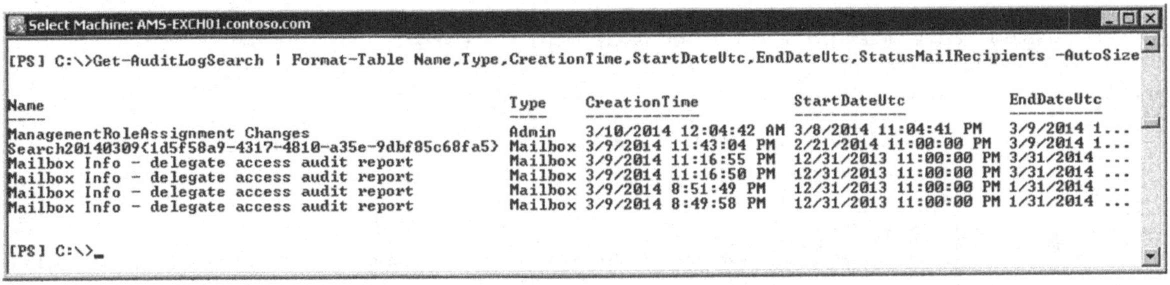

Figure 9-53. *Retrieving a list of audit log search jobs*

As shown in Figure 9-52, the audit log entries are returned as a set of objects. The structure of the returned administrator audit log entries is as follows:

- **ObjectModified** Contains the object modified.

- **CmdletName** Contains the cmdlet ran.

- **CmdletParameters** Contains the parameters specified with the cmdlet.

- **ModifiedProperties** Is only populated when the log level is set to Verbose. When set, this field will contain the modified properties of 'ObjectModified'.

- **Caller** Contains the user account that ran the cmdlet.

- **Succeeded** Reports if the cmdlet ran successfully.

- **Error** Contains the error message if the cmdlet did not run successfully.

- **RunDate** Contains the time stamp when the cmdlet ran.

- **OriginatingServer** Indicates which server ran the cmdlet.

As you can see, the CmdletParameters, as well as the ModifiedProperties when applicable, will by default only display the parameter name or the name of the attribute changed. To see the related value, expand the CmdletParameters or ObjectModified attribute.

For example, to find the last logged New-TransportRule cmdlet and view what parameters and configuration values were used, you can use the following commands:

```
$LogEntry= Search-AdminAuditLog –Cmdlets New-TransportRule | Sort StartDate -Desc | Select –First 1
$LogEntry
$LogEntry.CmdletParameters
```

In Figure 9-54, you can see that TransportRule was last used on March 3, 2014, by "Administrator" to set the mode to Audit and Notify and to set Notify Sender to Reject Unless Explicit Override.

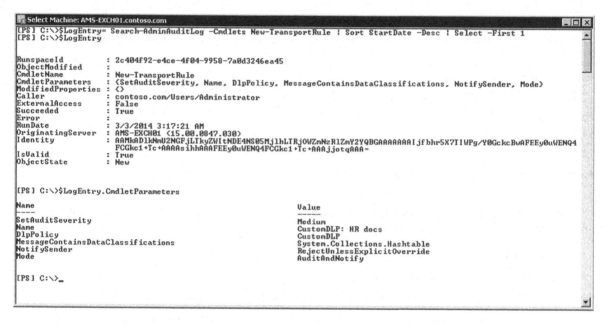

Figure 9-54. Inspecting the audit log entry using SearchAdminAuditLog

Mailbox Audit Logging

Along with the auditing administrative changes, an organization might require tracking the access or changes made to individual mailboxes, especially mailboxes potentially containing sensitive information from a business or privacy perspective. This also applies to non-personal mailboxes, which are mailboxes attached to a disabled user account and which are used by multiple mailbox users commonly referred to as "delegates."

Mailbox audit logging can audit access and changes performed by the mailbox owners, delegates, and administrators. After enabling the mailbox audit logging, you can additionally limit the audit log to record only log certain operations—for example, creation, movement, or deletion of messages. You can also specify the logon type to audit—for instance, owner, delegate, or administrator.

You cannot enable mailbox audit logging using EAC. To enable mailbox audit logging from the EMS, use the Set-Mailbox cmdlet, setting AuditEnabled to $true; for example,

```
Set-Mailbox -Identity 'Info' -AuditEnabled $true
```

To verify that the auditing is enabled and see what has been the logged use, check the audit attributes of the mailbox, as follows:

```
Get-Mailbox -Identity 'Info' | Select Name, Audit*
```

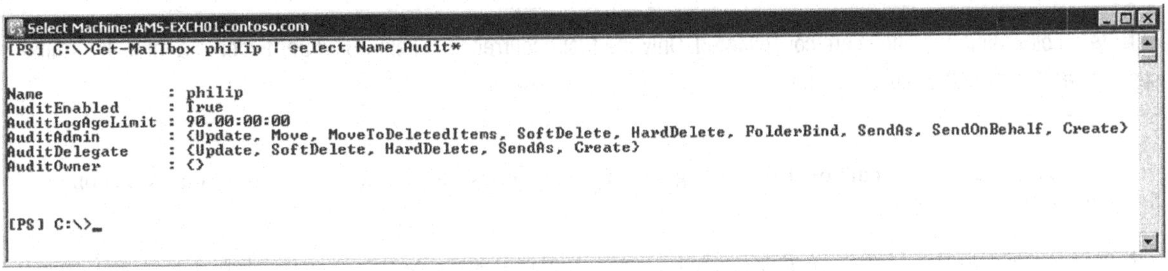

```
Select Machine: AMS-EXCH01.contoso.com
[PS] C:\>Get-Mailbox philip | select Name,Audit*

Name             : philip
AuditEnabled     : True
AuditLogAgeLimit : 90.00:00:00
AuditAdmin       : {Update, Move, MoveToDeletedItems, SoftDelete, HardDelete, FolderBind, SendAs, SendOnBehalf, Create}
AuditDelegate    : {Update, SoftDelete, HardDelete, SendAs, Create}
AuditOwner       : {}


[PS] C:\>_
```

Figure 9-55. *Verifying the mailbox audit logging settings*

To disable mailbox audit logging, you use:

```
Set-Mailbox -Identity 'Info' -AuditEnabled $false
```

Mailbox Audit Logging Options

As seen earlier when verifying the mailbox audit logging settings, there are several options that can be used to determine what is logged per type of logon—that is, owner, delegate, or administrator. Not all actions can be logged for all logon types. Table 9-1 lists the mailbox audit logging options.

Table 9-1. *Mailbox Audit Logging Options*

Action	Description	Owner	Delegate	Administrators
Copy	Item is copied to another folder	NO	NO	YES*
Create	Creation of an item (e.g., item received). Folder creation isn't audited.	YES	YES*	YES
FolderBind	Folder access	NO	YES	YES*
HardDelete	Permanent deletion of an item.	YES	YES*	YES
MessageBind	Item access	NO	NO	YES
Move	Item is moved to another folder	YES	YES	YES*
MoveToDeletedItems	An item is deleted (moved to Deleted Items)	YES	YES	YES*
SendAs	A message is sent using SendAs permissions	-	YES*	YES*
SendOnBehalf	A message is sent using SendOnBehalf permissions	-	YES	YES
SoftDelete	An item is moved from Deleted Items to Recoverable Items	YES	YES*	YES
Update	Updating of item properties	YES	YES*	YES*

* *Default option*

To log a specific action for a certain logon type, use the parameter AuditOwner for logging owner actions (this includes delegates with full access mailbox permissions), AuditDelegate for logging actions performed by delegate, and AuditAdmin for logging actions performed by administrators.

■ **Note**   FolderBind operations are consolidated. Only the first occurrence of FolderBind per folder in a three-hour time span generates a mailbox audit log entry.

For example, to enable mailbox audit logging on a shared mailbox called 'Info' and only log Send As actions for delegates, you would use:

```
Set-Mailbox -Identity 'Info' -AuditEnabled $true -AuditDelegate SendAs -AuditAdmin None -AuditOwner None
```

```
Select Machine: AMS-EXCH01.contoso.com                                                    _□X
[PS] C:\>Set-Mailbox -Identity 'Info' -AuditEnabled $true -AuditDelegate SendAs -AuditAdmin None -AuditOwner None
[PS] C:\>Get-Mailbox -Identity 'Info' | Select Audit*

AuditEnabled      : True
AuditLogAgeLimit  : 90.00:00:00
AuditAdmin        : {}
AuditDelegate     : {SendAs}
AuditOwner        : {}


[PS] C:\>_
```

Figure 9-56. Configuring mailbox audit logging

When mailbox audit logging is enabled, the audit log entries are stored in the mailbox itself, in the audits folder located in the recoverable items folder. When a mailbox is moved, the recoverable items are also moved, including any existing audit log entries.

The default retention period of mailbox audit log entries is 90 days. You can adjust that retention period by using Set-Mailbox with the AuditLogAgeLimit parameter. For example, to set the retention period of the mailbox audit log for Philip's mailbox to 180 days, you would use:

```
Set-Mailbox -Identity Philip -AuditLogAgeLimit 180
```

■ **Note**   If the mailbox is on in-place hold, the mailbox audit logs entries will not be removed after the retention period.

If you are concerned about the amount of logged audit data in the mailbox after you have enabled the mailbox audit logging, you can use the following commands to check the size of the folder mailbox:

```
Get-Mailbox -Identity Info | Get-MailboxFolderStatistics -FolderScope RecoverableItems |
  Where { $_.Name -eq 'Audits' } | Select FolderSize
```

In this command, Get-MailboxFolderStatistics retrieves statistical information on the folders. By using FolderScope, you can configure it to look into a specific well-known folder. As mentioned earlier, the mailbox audit log entries are stored in the recoverable items folder in a subfolder named "audits." So, you set the scope to Recoverable Items to only return that folder. Next, you use Where to filter the folder name "audits," of which you display its FolderSize property.

Searches of the Mailbox Audit Logging

To search a mailbox audit log using EAC, you navigate to Compliance Management ➤ Auditing. Exchange EAC provides two options for generating mailbox audit log reports:

- **Run a non-owner mailbox access report**. This option allows you to generate a report on non-owner access to mailboxes. You can select the search period, the auditing-enabled mailboxes to investigate, and the type of access.

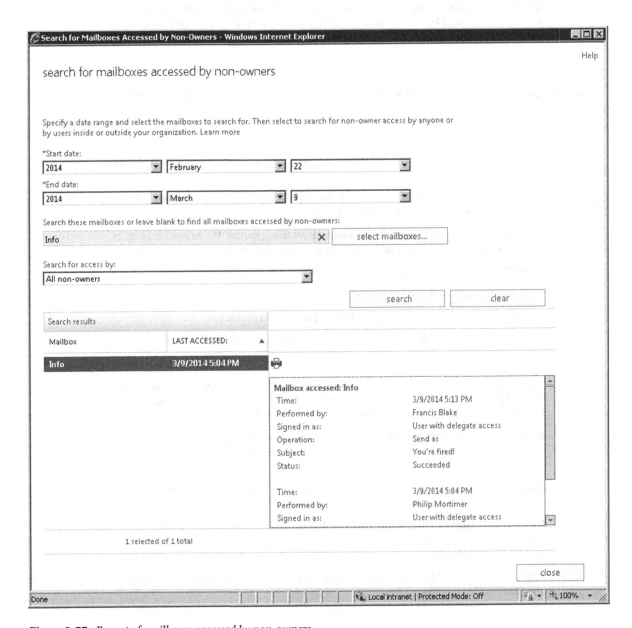

Figure 9-57. Report of mailboxes accessed by non-owners

- **Export mailbox audit logs**. This option allows you to export the mailbox audit logs and send them as an attachment to selected recipients.

As with administrator audit logging, the searching and reporting options are limited when managed through EAC. In the EMS, mailbox audit logging provides the following cmdlets for searching and reporting:

- **Search-MailboxAuditLog**. Use this cmdlet to search the mailbox audit logs based on search criteria. These searches are synchronous.

- **New-MailboxAuditLogSearch**. This cmdlet is similar to Search-MailboxAuditLog but instead of returning the audit log entries, it can be used to send the results to a recipient. These searches run asynchronously in the background.

■ **Note**   These cmdlets are similar in usage and purpose to the administrator audit logging searching cmdlets, Search-AdminAuditLog and New-AdminAuditLogSearch.

The search criteria you can specify with SearchMailboxAuditLog and New-MailboxAuditLogSearch are the following:

1. **Identity** To specify the mailboxes to search for audit log entries. This parameter is only available when using Search-MailboxAuditLog.

2. **Mailboxes** To specify the mailboxes to search for audit log entries. When neither identity nor mailboxes is specified, all mailbox auditing enabled mailboxes will be searched.

3. **LogonTypes** To specify the logon types to search. Valid logon types are:

   - *Admin* for administrator logon types.

   - *Delegate* for delegate logon types, including users with Full Access.

   - *External* for Microsoft service administrators in Exchange Online or Office 365.

   - *Owner* for primary owner.

4. **ShowDetails** to retrieve details of each audit log entry. This parameter is mandatory when LogonTypes is set to Owner and can't be used together with the mailboxes parameter. This parameter is only available when using Search-MailboxAuditLog.

5. **StartDate** and **EndDate** to restrict the search in the administrator audit log to a certain period. When running an export using New-AdminAuditLogSearch, the start date and end date are mandatory.

6. **ExternalAccess** to search for audit log entries generated by users outside of your organization such as Microsoft service administrators in Exchange Online or Office 365.

7. **StatusMailRecipients** specifies the SMTP addresses of the recipients that should receive the audit log report. This parameter is only available when using New-MailboxAuditLogSearch.

8. **Name** specifies the subject of the email. This parameter is only available when using New-MailboxAuditLogSearch.

When used without specifying parameters, `Search-MailboxAuditLog` will return all auditing-enabled mailboxes, as follows:

```
Search-MailboxAuditLog
```

To see what auditing information is returned by mailbox audit logging, let's pick a single audit log entry while specifying `ShowDetails` to include detailed information, as follows:

```
Search-MailboxAuditLog -ShowDetails -ResultSize 1
```

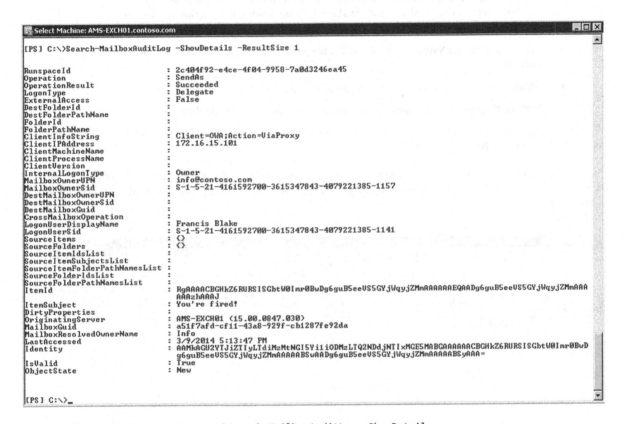

Figure 9-58. *Audit information returned* `Search-MailboxAuditLog -ShowDetails`

As you can see, a lot of information is available per audit log entry. You may notice a few unpopulated fields, which are due to the operation. In this example, folder names are not logged for SendAs operations. Here's a short list of some of the important fields:

- **LastAccessed** Contains the time stamp when the operation was performed.

- **Operation** Is one of the actions Copy, Create, FolderBind, HardDelete, MessageBind, Move, MoveToDeletedItems, SendAs, SendOnBehalf, SoftDelete, or Update.

- **OperationResult** Shows if the operation succeeded, failed, or partially succeeded.

- **LogonType** Shows who performed the operation, whether the owner, a delegate, or administrator.

- **FolderPathName** Contains the folder name that contains the item.

- **ClientInfoString** Contains information about the client or Exchange component that performed the operation.

- **ClientIPAddress** Contains the IPv4 address of the client computer used.

- **InternalLogonType** Contains the type of logon performed by the non-owner.

- **MailboxOwnerUPN** Contains the UPN of the mailbox owner.

- **DestMailboxOwnerUPN** Contains the UPN of the destination mailbox owner for cross-mailbox operations; CrossMailboxOperation contains information about whether the operation is acrossmailboxes.

- **LogonUserDisplayName** Contains the display name of the logged on user who performed the operation.

- **ItemSubject** Contains the subject line of the item affected.

- **MailboxResolvedOwnerName** Contains the display name of the mailbox.

For example, to search all auditing-enabled mailboxes for log entries generated for non-owner access by delegate or administrator logon types, you could use:

```
Search-MailboxAuditLog -LogonTypes Delegate,Admin -ShowDetails | Format-Table LastAccessed,
MailboxResolvedOwnerName, Operation, LogonType, LogonUserDisplayName, ClientIPAddress, ItemSubject
-AutoSize
```

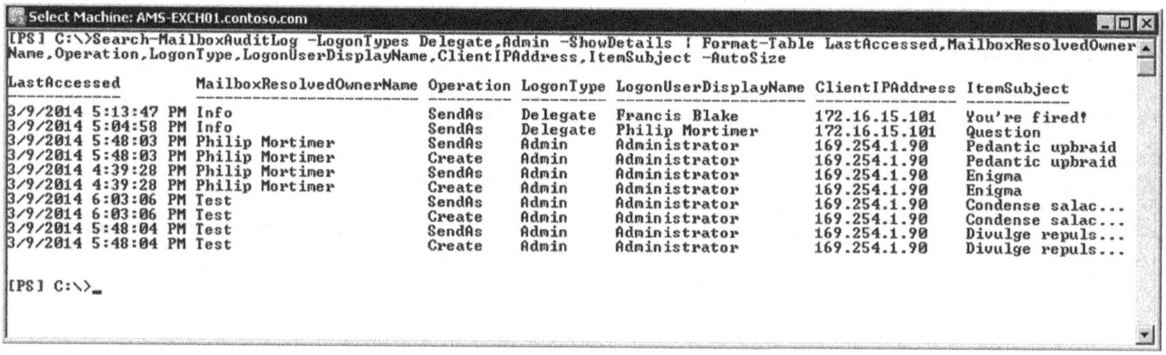

Figure 9-59. Using Search-MailboxAuditLog to search mailbox audit log entries

---

■ **Note** Use ResultSize to limit the number of entries when using Search-MailboxAuditLog.

In this example, you query the mailbox 'Info,' which is mailbox auditing enabled, for non-owners' access to a specific folder. Because you can not specify the operations to search for directly as a Search-MailboxAuditLog parameter, you can pipe the output through Where-Object, where you filter entries so that only objects where the operation is FolderBind (i.e., folder access) and the folder path name is '\Inbox.' Of the objects returned, you then select certain fields for displaying:

```
Search-MailboxAuditLog -Identity 'Info' -LogonTypes Delegate, Admin -ShowDetails | Where {
$_.Operation -eq 'FolderBind' -and $_.FolderPathName -eq '\Inbox' } | Format-Table LastAccessed,
InternalLogonType, LogonType, LogonUserDisplayName, FolderPathname
```

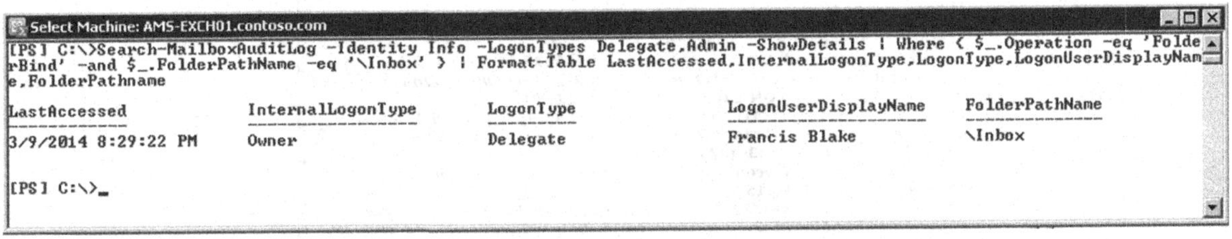

Figure 9-60. *Using Search-MailboxAuditLog to search for folder access by delegate*

When required, you can narrow your search to a certain period by specifying the start date and end date as well.

In addition to Search-MailboxAuditLog you can use New-MailboxAuditLogSearch to gather mailbox audit log information in the background and have it sent as an email attachment to specific recipients. The parameters you can use are similar to those you can use with Search-MailboxAuditLog, only you can't use identity for reporting on a specific mailbox; you need to specify the message subject (name) and recipients (status mail recipients).

That said, to create a background mailbox audit log query on delegate access to a mailbox called 'Info' from January 1, 2014 to February 1, 2014, you could use:

```
New-MailboxAuditLogSearch -StartDate '1/1/2014' -EndDate '4/1/2014' -Mailboxes 'Info'
-ShowDetails -LogonTypes Delegate -Name 'Mailbox Info - delegate access audit report'
-StatusMailRecipients philip@contoso.com
```

You can use Get-AuditLogSearch to list current audit log searches. The generated export of audit information in XML format and the accompanying email message will look similar to those shown in Figure 9-61.

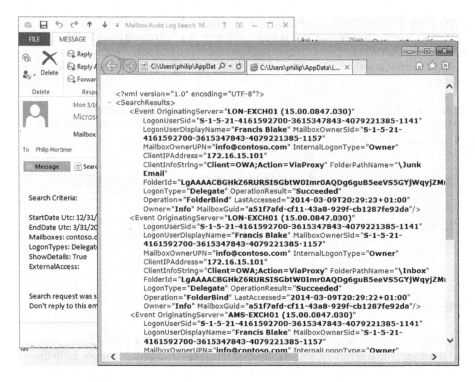

Figure 9-61. *Mailbox audit log information report with attached XML formatted data*

As visible, the XML contains the same elements as the Search-MailboxAuditLog output, allowing organizations to perform additional processing or reporting using the information contained in the XML file. For example, when you store the attached XML file locally, you can import it using PowerShell by using:

```
[xml](Get-Contents .\SearchResults.xml)
```

■ **Note**   Do not try to import an XML file using Import-CliXml. The purpose of Import-CliXml is to import serialized powerShell objects, usually generated using the Export-CliXml cmdlet.

A simple query to retrieve the information contained in SearchResults.xml and select certain information from audit log events is as follows:

```
[xml](Get-Contents .\SearchResults.xml) | Select -ExpandProperty SearchResults | Select
-ExpandProperty Event | Format-Table LastAccessed, LogonType, Operation, LogonUserDisplayName,
FolderPathName -AutoSize
```

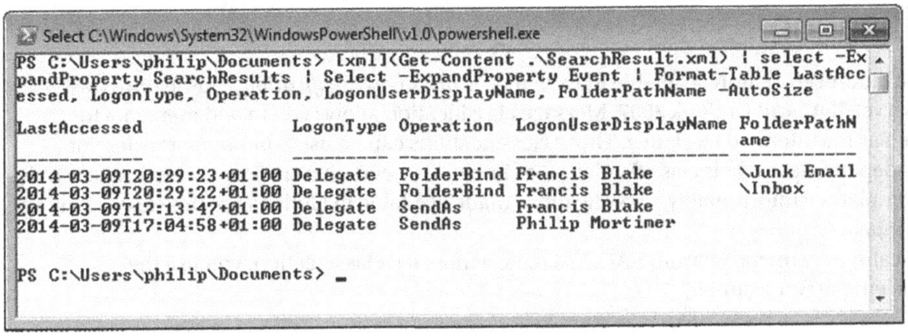

Figure 9-62. Sample of using SearchResult.xml *with audit information*

Bypass of Mailbox Audit Logging

Applications may implicitly use administrator permissions when processing mailboxes, generating excessive amounts of audit log information for mailboxes that have mailbox auditing enabled for MessageBind or FolderBind operations. Examples of such applications are backup or archiving solutions. Audit log information generated by these applications are likely not of interest to the organization with regard to compliance, and are viewed only as creating "noise" in the mailbox audit logs while also claiming valuable system resources in the process.

To create exceptions for these types of applications, Exchange Server 2013 can be configured to bypass mailbox auditing using mailbox auditing bypass associations. These bypass associations can be assigned to user or computer accounts. The cmdlet to configure bypass associations is Set-MailboxAuditBypassAssociation. To configure bypass for an account named 'BesAdmin,' for example, you would use:

```
Set-MailboxAuditBypassAssociation -Identity 'BesAdmin' –AuditBypassEnabled $true
```

To remove the bypass association for 'BesAdmin,' you set AuditBypassEnabeld to $false:

```
Set-MailboxAuditBypassAssociation -Identity 'BesAdmin' –AuditBypassEnabled $false
```

To retrieve the accounts currently associated with mailbox auditing bypass, you use:

```
Get-MailboxAuditBypassAssociation | Where { $_.AuditBypassEnabled } | Select Name
```

■ **Caution**   When configuring mailbox auditing bypass associations, bear in mind that some organizations need to closely monitor these bypass associations, as these accounts will not generate mailbox audit log information. Alternatively, organizations can leverage role-based access control to restrict those configuring bypass associations using the Exchange Management Shell. You can also monitor the msExchBypassAudit attribute of user objects in Active Directory.

Message Classification

A little-known, and therefore little-used, feature available in Exchange is *message classification*. This feature was introduced with Exchange Server 2007 and Outlook 2007. Message classification allows you to add metadata to messages using Outlook, such as the intended audience. Those classifications can be used in transport rules, for example, to act on messages depending on their classifications—as in blocking certain mail flow of "internal use only" messages or applying IRM templates. Unfortunately, classifications made available in Outlook are not easy to manage, but more on that in a short while.

Message classifications cannot be managed from EAC. To create a message classification, you use the New-MessageClassification cmdlet; for example,

```
New-MessageClassification -Name 'InternalUseOnly'
-DisplayName 'Internal Use Only' -SenderDescription 'This message is for internal use only'.
```

This cmdlet will create a message classification of Default\InternalUseOnly with a display name of 'Internal Use Only.' The text visible at the top of the message will be "This message is for internal use only."

■ **Tip** You can specify a separate recipient description to show the receiver of the message. When the recipient description is not specified, Sender Description will be used instead.

You can view the current defined message classifications using Get-MessageClassificiation, as shown in Figure 9-63.

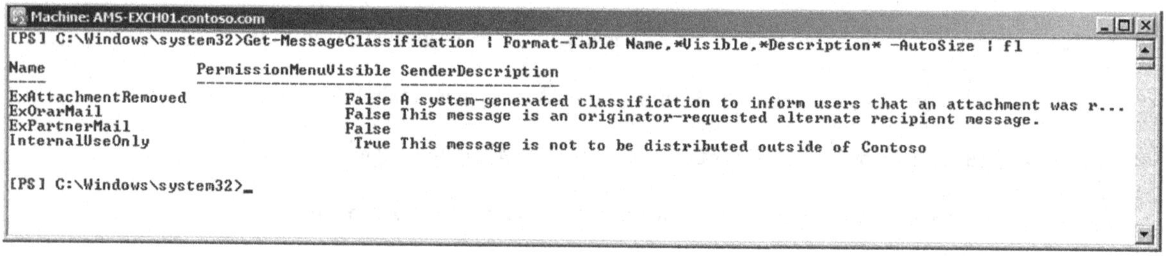

Figure 9-63. Viewing the message classification definitions

As you may spot, there are three additional message classifications: ExAttachmentRemoved, ExOrarMail, and ExPartnerMail. These are built-in message classifications that are not selectable, as their PermissionMenuVisible is set to $False, nor can they be changed or removed.

The identity of the example classification is Default\InternalUseOnly. Default is to indicate it is the default InternalUseOnly classification picked for display name and description information. You can also create localized versions of message classifications by specifying the locale parameter while using the same name; for example,

```
New-MessageClassification -Name 'InternalUseOnly' -Locale nl-NL
-DisplayName 'Intern Gebruik' -SenderDescription 'Dit bericht is uitsluitend bestemd voor intern
gebruik'.
```

■ **Tip**   When you want to use the same classification between organizations or between Exchange on-premises and Exchange Online, keep the classification IDs in sync. The ID is stored in the header field "X-MS-Exchange-Organization-Classification" when messages leave or enter the organization. You can set this ID when creating classifications or by `Set-MessageClassification` using the `ClassificationID` parameter (looks like a GUID in the Export-OutlookClassifications XML file); for example, `Set-MessageClassification-Identity 'InternalUseOnly' –ClassificationID '733d2e24-6f92-4b3e-acad-dc3674b91927'`

The identity of this classification will be nl-NL\InternalUseOnly. To view all message classifications including localized ones, use `Get-MessageClassification` with `-IncludeLocales`; for example,

```
Get-MessageClassification -IncludeLocales
```

After creating the classifications, they are selectable from the Set Permissions option:

The receiver, as well as the sender, of an email will see the configured description at the top of the message, upon opening it, as shown in Figure 9-65.

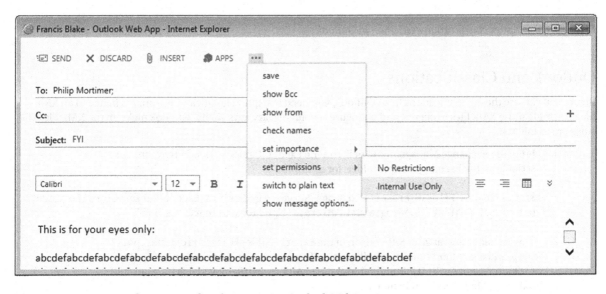

Figure 9-64. *Assigning the message classification using Outlook WebApp*

To remove an existing classification, use `Remove-MessageClassification`; for example,

```
Remove-MessageClassification -Identity 'Default\InternalUseOnly'
```

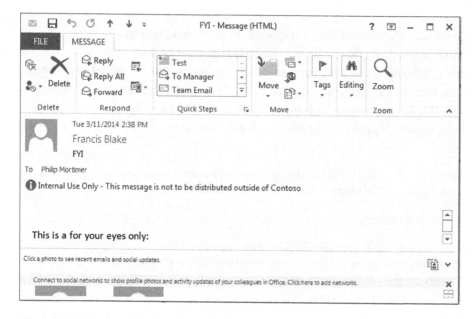

Figure 9-65. *Message classification descrption in Outlook*

Outlook and Classifications

Before you can use these classifications from Outlook, you need to export classifications from Exchange to an XML file, distribute those XML files to clients, and configure several registry keys so that Outlook picks up the XML file. The steps are as follows:

1. From the Exchange Management Shell, run the Export-OutlookClassification.ps1 script from the Exchange scripts folder; for example,

    ```
    & 'C:\Program Files\Microsoft\Exchange Server\v15\Scripts\Export-OutlookClassification.
    ps1' | Set-Content 'C:\ProgramData\Microsoft\Office\OutlookClass.xml'
    ```

2. The Exchange Server 2013 SP1 version of the Export-OutlookClassifications.ps1 script will also export built-in classifications. To prevent them from becoming options in Outlook, edit the XML file and remove the ExAttachmentRemoved, ExOrarMail, and ExPartnerMail classification items.

3. Copy the XML file to a location on the client that is readable by users.

4. On the client, make the following registry changes. For example, `C:\ProgramData\ Microsoft\Office\OutlookClass.xml` as the location of the classification XML file. Note that 15.0 is for configuring Outlook 2013; use 14.0 for Outlook 2010 and 12.0 for Outlook 2007.

```
[HKEY_CURRENT_USER\Software\Microsoft\Office\15.0\Common\Policy]
'AdminClassificationPath'='C:\\ProgramData\\Microsoft\\Office\\OutlookClass.xml'
'EnableClassifications'=dword:00000001
'TrustClassifications'=dword:00000001
```

5. Restart Outlook. Now, when composing a message, you will see the message classification options appear under Options ➤ Permission Level.

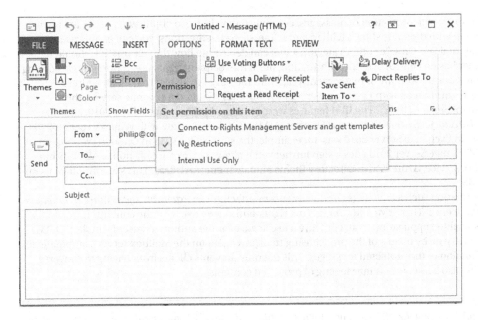

Figure 9-66. *Assigning message classification using Outlook*

Classifications and Transport Rules

As explained earlier, you can use transport rules to act upon message classifications. As a small example, create a transport rule that will apply an RMS template on messages with the classification InternalUseOnly. To select messages with this specific classification, use the `HasClassification` predicate:

```
New-TransportRule -Name 'RMS Confidential to InternalUseOnly'
-HasClassification 'InternalUseOnly'
-ApplyRightsProtectionTemplate 'Contoso-Confidential'
```

Information Rights Management

Apart from wanting to have control over the retention of information and the flow of communications, an organization may need to control what receivers of those messages can do with the information. For example, an organization may want to disallow forwarding, printing, or exporting of messages. This is where information rights management (IRM)comes into play.

▪ **Caution**   Though IRM offers advanced technologies to protect information, it cannot protect information from being reproduced using third-party screen-capture software, cell phones, or cameras. However, high-risk environments could be covered by having workplaces where, for example, cell phones are prohibited.

The purpose of IRM is to provide protection of messages, certainly online but also offline when users are traveling and carrying that information with them. As shown with regard to message classifications, you can enable users to mark information as "Internal Use Only" or other categories that can determine how the information should be treated. However, the sender has no control over the information, nor if the recipient treats the information according company policies; the recipient can, willfully or inadvertently, forward messages to an external email address.

Thus, IRM features were introduced with Exchange Server 2007 but they required a separate service, the Windows Rights Management Service (RMS). The IRM features were enhanced in Exchange Server 2010, allowing leverage use of the *Active Directory Rights Management Services* (AD RMS) role that came with Windows Server 2008 instead. A welcome feature in Exchange Server 2010 was, for example, the support for RMS in Outlook WebApp on non-Microsoft browsers. Exchange Server 2013 goes a step further yet; it allows you to not only utilize AD RMS but also use a cloud-based RMS service, Azure Active Directory Rights Management (AADRM). This section will focus on on-premises use of AD RMS.

AD RMS protects information such as messages or documents by attaching an *extensible rights markup language* (XrML)-based certificate or license. This XrML file contains the rights-authorized users for the content. To access the information, AD RMS-enabled applications must procure a use license for the authorized user from the AD RMS service. Exchange Server 2013 will, by means of the prelicensing transport agent on the Mailbox servers, automatically attach usage license information to the protected messages. This not only prevents clients from having to converse with the AD RMS server but also allows for offline viewing of protected contents.

▪ **Note**   AD RMS is supported by Outlook 2010 and up, Outlook WebApp, Windows Phone, and its predecessor Windows Mobile 6, but also many non-Windows devices. Devices supporting Exchange ActiveSync 14.1 and up (more specific supporting the RightsManagementInformaton tag) can create, read, reply to, or forward IRM-protected messages without requiring the user to connect to a computer and activate it for IRM, which was the case with Windows Mobile 6.x. Exchange ActiveSync 14.1 was introduced with Exchange Server 2010 Service Pack 1.

Exchange Server 2013 is also capable of reading IRM-protected information by means of the RMS decryption transport agent on the Mailbox servers. This transport agent decrypts received or submitted messages, enabling, for example, transport rules to check conditions against IRM-protected messages.

Configuring the Active Directory Rights Management Services

Essentially, the process of setting up a basic AD RMS server consists of the following steps:

1. Determine your AD RMS requirements. Also, if you want to add multiple AD RMS servers to the AD RMS cluster, you need Microsoft SQL Server; otherwise, you can utilize Windows Internal Database for storing information. You create prerequisites like the AD RMS service account, which can be a standard account or managed service account.

2. Determine on which server you will host the AD RMS cluster. It is best practice to run AD RMS on dedicated servers and not install it on a domain controller or an Exchange server.

3. Add the Active Directory Rights Management Services role.

For more information on configuring and managing AD RMS, visit `http://bit.ly/ADRMSVC`.

After installation of AD RMS, there remain some post-configuration steps to be performed so as to enable AD RMS support on Exchange Server 2013:

1. Grant, read, and execute permissions to the AD RMS certification pipeline (`ServerCertification.asmx`) to the Exchange servers group and AD RMS service. By default, this file is located in `'$env:SystemDrive\inetpub\wwwroot\_wmcs\ certification'` on the AD RMS server. For example, when the default location is used and the AD RMS service is named ADRMSSVC, you use the following command:

```
$File= 'C:\inetpub\wwwroot\_wmcs\certification\ServerCertification.asmx'
$Acl= Get-Acl -Path $File
$ExPerm= New-Object System.Security.AccessControl.FileSystemAccessRule(
'Exchange Servers','ReadAndExecute', 'Allow')
$SvcPerm= New-Object System.Security.AccessControl.FileSystemAccessRule(
'AD RMS Service Group','ReadAndExecute', 'Allow')
$Acl.AddAccessRule( $ExPerm)
$Acl.AddAccessRule( $SvcPerm)
Set-Acl -Path $File -AclObject $Acl
```

■ **Note** If you receive an error message when running Set-Acl, stating that it attempted to perform an unauthorized operation, use the following alternative: `[System.IO.File]::SetAccessControl( $File, $Acl)`

---

2. Add the federation mailbox `FederatedEmail.4c1f4d8b-8179-4148-93bf-00a95fa1e042` to an AD RMS super-users group on the AD RMS cluster. This allows decryption of messages in transport and journals the reports and IRM in Outlook WebApp and Exchange Search. For example:

```
New-ADGroup -Name 'ADRMSSuperUsers' -Security Security -GroupScope Global
Add-ADGroupMember -Identity 'ADRMSSuperUsers'
 -Members FederatedEmail.4c1f4d8b-8179-4148-93bf-00a95fa1e042
```

■ **Caution** Members of the super-users group can decrypt any IRM-protected contents. Monitor and auditing of this group is, therefore, highly recommended.

---

3. On the AD RMS cluster, using the Active Directory Rights Management Services console, you configure the super-users group via Security Policies ➤ Super Users. On that node, you perform "Enable Super Users." Then, you open up the properties dialog of the super-users node and configure the distribution group created earlier as the super-user group.

4. Depending on whether you configured AD RMS to use an https connection in conjunction with a self-signed certificate, you must export that self-signed certificate from the AD RMS cluster and import it on the Exchange Mailbox servers. After installation, this self-signed certificate will be valid for communications between Exchange and the AD RMS cluster.

5. Exchange must be configured for IRM, and internal recipients must IRM-enabled for them to be able to access the AD RMS templates, which are used for IRM-protected contents. To enable IRM for internal recipients, you use:

```
Set-IRMConfiguration -InternalLicensingEnable $true
```

To inspect the current IRM configuration settings, you use `Get-IRMConfiguration`, as shown in Figure 9-67.

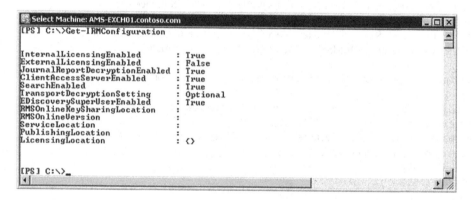

Figure 9-67. *Checking current IRM configuration settings*

As you might notice, the TransportDecryptionSetting is initially configured as Optional, meaning Exchange will deliver the message even if it cannot decrypt the message. If you do not want that, use `Set-IRMConfiguration`; in this case, you set `TransportDecryptionSetting` to Mandatory; for example,

```
Set-IRMConfiguration -TransportDecryptionSetting Mandatory
```

■ **Note**   When the transport decryption is set to mandatory, failure to decrypt a message will result in an NDR.

The other switches you may need to adjust according to the requirements of your organization are as follows:

- **JournalReportDecryptionEnabled** Determines if the journaling agent is allowed to attach a decrypted copy of an IRM-protected message to the journal reports.

- **ClientAccessServerEnabled** Determines if IRM functionality is available on Client Access servers for Outlook WebApp and Exchange ActiveSync.

■ **Note** When Exchange ActiveSync is enabled for IRM, it is recommended you use the ActiveSync policy settings Require Password and Require Device Encryption, and that you disallow non-provisionable devices.

- **SearchEnabled** Determines if Exchange search is allowed to index IRM-protected messages.
- **EDiscoverSuperUserEnabled** Determines if IRM-protected messages in the discovery mailbox can be accessed by members of the discovery management role group.

■ **Note** You cannot export IRM-protected messages from a discovery mailbox to another mailbox or PST file. Those messages can only be accessed using Outlook WebApp.

6. To verify that IRM is working properly, use Test-IRMConfiguration with two valid email addresses; for example,

```
Test-IRMConfiguration –Recipient philip@contoso.com
-Sender francis@contoso.com
```

```
Select Machine: AMS-EXCH01.contoso.com
[PS] C:\>Test-IRMConfiguration –Recipient philip@contoso.com –Sender francis@contoso.com

Results : Checking Exchange Server ...
            - PASS: Exchange Server is running in Enterprise.
          Loading IRM configuration ...
            - PASS: IRM configuration loaded successfully.
          Retrieving RMS Certification Uri ...
            - PASS: RMS Certification Uri: http://adrms.contoso.com/_wmcs/certification.
          Verifying RMS version for http://adrms.contoso.com/_wmcs/certification ...
            - PASS: RMS Version verified successfully.
          Retrieving RMS Publishing Uri ...
            - PASS: RMS Publishing Uri: http://adrms.contoso.com/_wmcs/licensing.
          Acquiring Rights Account Certificate (RAC) and Client Licensor Certificate (CLC) ...
            - PASS: RAC and CLC acquired.
          Acquiring RMS Templates ...
            - PASS: RMS Templates acquired.
          Retrieving RMS Licensing Uri ...
            - PASS: RMS Licensing Uri: http://adrms.contoso.com/_wmcs/licensing.
          Verifying RMS version for http://adrms.contoso.com/_wmcs/licensing ...
            - PASS: RMS Version verified successfully.
          Creating Publishing License ...
            - PASS: Publishing License created.
          Acquiring Prelicense for 'philip@contoso.com' from RMS Licensing Uri
          (http://adrms.contoso.com/_wmcs/licensing) ...
            - PASS: Prelicense acquired.
          Acquiring Use License from RMS Licensing Uri (http://adrms.contoso.com/_wmcs/licensing) ...
            - PASS: Use License acquired.

          OVERALL RESULT: PASS


[PS] C:\>_
```

Figure 9-68. *Verifying the IRM configuration*

Choosing AD RMS Templates

Once you have verified that IRM is set up properly, you can check the default set of RMS templates. Exchange 2013 provides, by default, one "Do Not Forward" RMS template. You can view the current set of RMS templates using Get-RMSTemplate:

Get-RMSTemplate

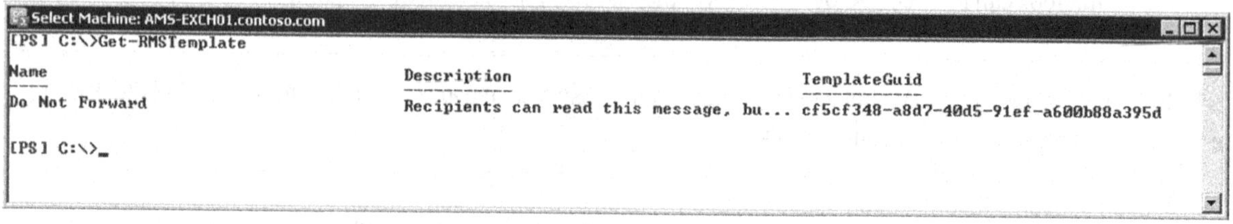

Figure 9-69. *Viewing the RMS template definitions*

You can create custom AD RMS templates depending on the needs of your organization. Per template, you can specify the Active Directory-based user or group that is allowed to use it, or you can specify that anyone can use it if it should be made generally available.

Some ideas for AD RMS templates are the following:

- *Company-wide or department-only confidential* for limiting accessibility to a selection of recipients within an organization.

- *View-only* when you want recipients to be able to only view messages but not reply, forward, or print the message.

- *Prohibit print*, where you allow all functions except the printing option.

- *Prohibit reply to all*, where you allow all functions except the reply to all option.

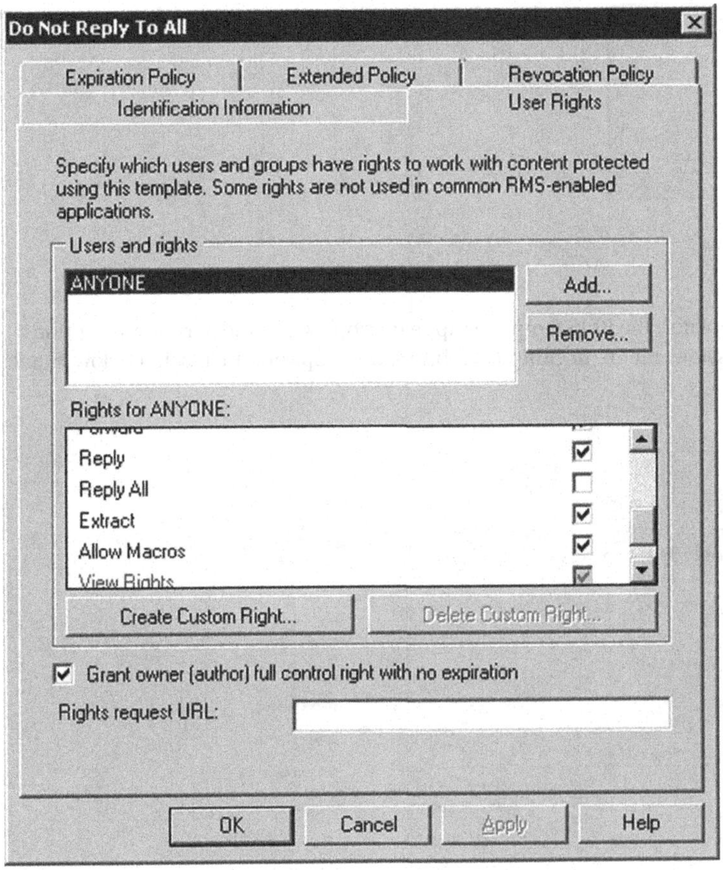

Figure 9-70. *RMS template properties*

For more information on creating and managing your own AD RMS templates, visit `http://bit.ly/ADRMSTemplates`.

Protecting Messages Using IRM

Outlook users can apply IRM-protection to messages using AD RMS templates. Despite this being a client-driven IRM-protection, Exchange can access the information provided it is using the same AD RMS infrastructure. When using Outlook 2010 or later, IRM protection can be automatic, using Outlook protection rules.

Before Outlook can use RMS to view or protect messages, though, Outlook needs to retrieve and configure the RMS templates. When you create a message and open up the Options ➤ Permission menu, you will see that, apart from any available message classifications, Outlook provides the option to "Connect to Rights Management Servers" and get templates. Select it to download the RMS templates.

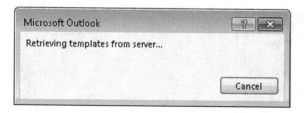

Figure 9-71. Outlook retrieving RMS templates

After Outlook has retrieved the RMS templates, the RMS templates appear as options in the permission Options ➤ Permission button or the File ➤ Set Permissions menu. In Outlook WebApp, these options are located below ➤ Set Permissions.

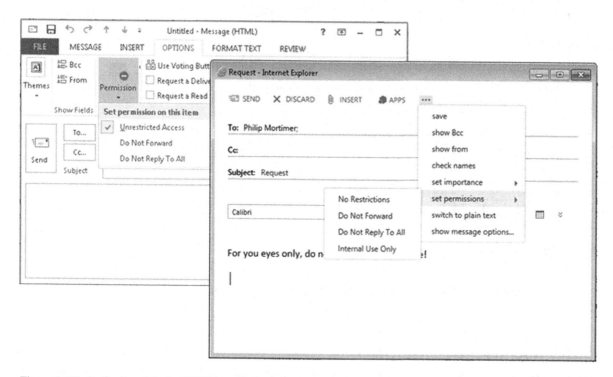

Figure 9-72. Outlook and Outlook WebApp displaying IRM options

When an IRM-protected message enters your inbox, it will be accompanied by a Stop icon to indicate its protected status. When recipients open IRM-protected messages, they are limited in their options to further process the information. For example, the Reply All and Forward options are disabled in the screen captures shown in Figure 9-73.

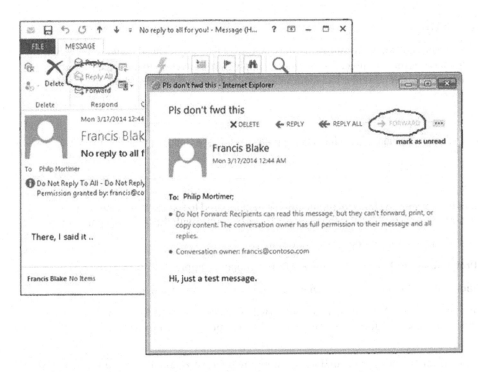

Figure 9-73. Outlook and Outlook WebApp displaying IRM-protected messages

---

■ **Note** Messages keep their original IRM-protected status, even when forwarded or responses are made on those messages.

Outlook 2013 uses RMS Client v2 for AD RMS support and automatic RMS template distribution. For earlier versions of the RMS client used by previous versions of Office, IT administrators had to deploy these templates to clients using other methods. By default, RMS Client v2 caches RMS templates for seven days in %LOCALAPPDATA%\ Microsoft\MSIPC\Templates. For Outlook, you can adjust this setting to a different number of days by using the following registry key:

```
[HKEY_CURRENT_USER\Software\Classes\Local Settings\Software\Microsoft\MSIPC]
'TemplateUpdateFrequency'=dword:00000001
```

You can also trigger immediate updating by Outlook of the RMS templates by removing the following registry key:

```
HKEY_CURRENT_USER\Software\Classes\Local Settings\Software\Microsoft\
MSIPC\<AD RMS CLUSTER NAME>\Template
```

Outlook Protection Rules

In addition to Outlook and AD RMS, you can use a complementary feature of Exchange, called *Outlook protection rules*. Outlook protection rules allow administrators to automatically apply IRM-protection to messages before they leave the client, where ransport protection rules can automatically IRM-protect messages when they enter the transport pipeline.

■ **Tip**   You can also create Outlook protection rules without using predicates. These Outlook protection rules will apply to all messages.

Outlook protection rules have a limited choice of predicates when compared to transport protection rules. To create an Outlook protection rule, use the New-OutlookProtectionRule cmdlet with the following parameters:

- **Name** Specifies the name of the Outlook protection rule.

- **ApplyRightsProtectionTemplate** Specifies the AD RMS template to apply.

- **FromDepartment** Filters the sender's department as configured in Active Directory.

- **SentTo** Specifies one or more SMTP recipients. SendTo will not accept wild cards. When multiple recipients are specified, messages sent to any of the recipients are considered a match.

- **SendToScope** Filters on the message destination. Options are InOrganization to match on messages sent to internal recipients or use All for message sent to any recipient.

- **UserCanOverride** Determines if the user is allowed to override an Outlook protection rule. The default value is $true, allowing the user to override. If the user overrides, Outlook will add an X-MS-Outlook-Client-Rule-Overridden header in the message.

- **Priority** Determines the order of processing; lower numbers are processed first.

For example, to configure an Outlook protection rule to apply the "Do Not Reply To All" RMS template to messages sent to an internal recipient, use the following:

```
New-OutlookProtectionRule -Name 'Auto Do Not Reply To All'
-SentToScope InOrganization
-ApplyRightsProtectionTemplate 'Do Not Reply To All'
```

To configure an Outlook protection rule to apply the "Do Not Forward" template to message sent to an internal recipient from the HR department, use the following:

```
New-OutlookProtectionRule -Name 'Do Not Forward from HR'
-SentToScope InOrganization -FromDepartment 'HR'
-ApplyRightsProtectionTemplate 'Do Not Forward'
```

You can disable or enable Outlook protection rules at creation time by setting the Enable parameter to $true or $false, or you can toggle them using Enable-OutlookProtectionRule and Disable-OutlookProtectionRule; for example,

```
Disable-OutlookProtectionRule -Identity 'Do Not Forward from HR'
```

To display an overview of the configured Outlook protection rules, use `Get-OutlookProtectionRule`, as shown in Figure 9-74.

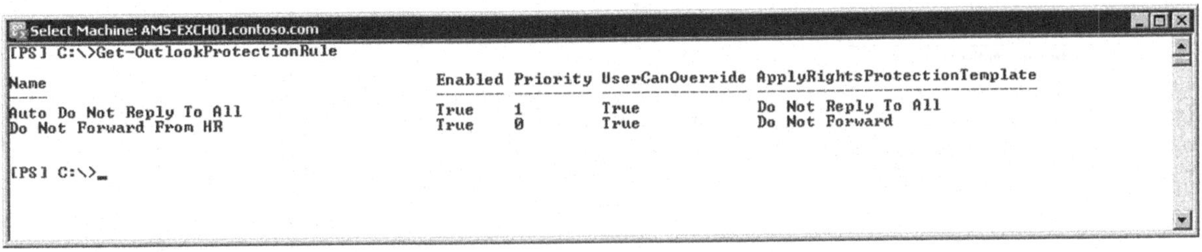

Figure 9-74. *Displaying configured Outlook protection rules*

To remove an Outlook protection rule, use `Remove-OutlookProtectionRule`, as follows:

```
Remove-OutlookProtectionRule 'Auto Do Not Reply To All'
```

Transport Protection Rules

Transport protection rules are similar to Outlook protection rules. Both can protect messages by applying RMS templates based on predicates. Transport protection rules are applied by the Transport service on the Mailbox Servers by the transport rules agent, whereas the Outlook protection rules are applied to applicable messages in Outlook as they are sent.

To create or reconfigure a transport rule to apply an AD RMS template to certain messages, you specify the `ApplyRightsProtectionTemplate` with the name of the AD RMS template. Transport rules are more versatile than Outlook protection rules and also can operate on external messages. For example, you could choose to automatically IRM-protect messages received from a selected partner with whom you have set up a mandatory secure SMTP connection, thereby allowing only certain groups of employees to access those messages.

For example, assume you want to apply an RMS template 'Do Not Forward' to messages sent by users from the HR department to other users in the organization. You can open EAC and navigate to Mail Flow ➤ Rules to create this transport rule, clicking the arrow next to the + sign and selecting "Apply Rights Protection" to the messages; or you can create one from scratch.

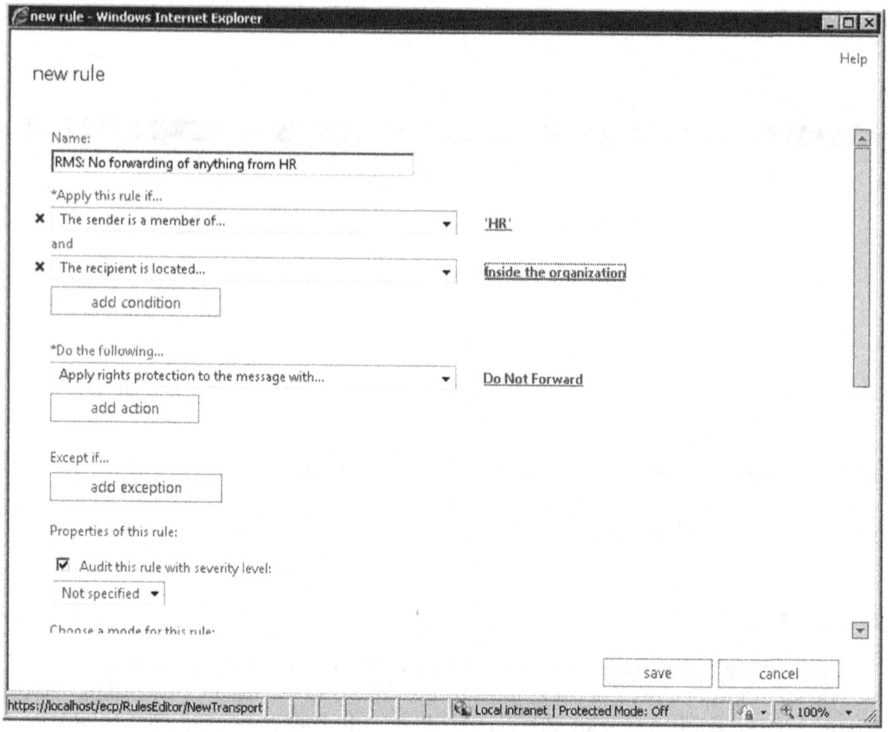

Figure 9-75. *Applying an RMS template using transport rules*

Alternatively, you can use the `New-TransportRule` cmdlet, as follows:

```
New-TransportRule -Name 'RMS: No forwarding of anything from HR'
-SentToScope 'InOrganization' -FromMemberOf 'HR@contoso.com'
-ApplyRightsProtectionTemplate 'Do Not Forward' -Mode 'Enforce'
```

You can also apply RMS templates in combination with data classification—for example, to protect messages with the 'Do Not Forward' template when a credit card is detected, and notify senders using a policy tip about sending possibly sensitive information, you can use:

```
New-TransportRule -Name 'Do not forward credit card numbers'
-SentToScope 'InOrganization' -Mode 'Enforce' -NotifySender 'NotifyOnly'
-MessageContainsDataClassifications @{'Name'='Credit Card Number'}
-ApplyRightsProtectionTemplate 'Do Not Forward'
```

In Figure 9-76, you can see that the user sent a message containing a credit card number and received a policy tip that she was about to send sensitive information. After the message was sent, the recipient received an IRM-protected message to which the 'Do Not Forward' was applied.

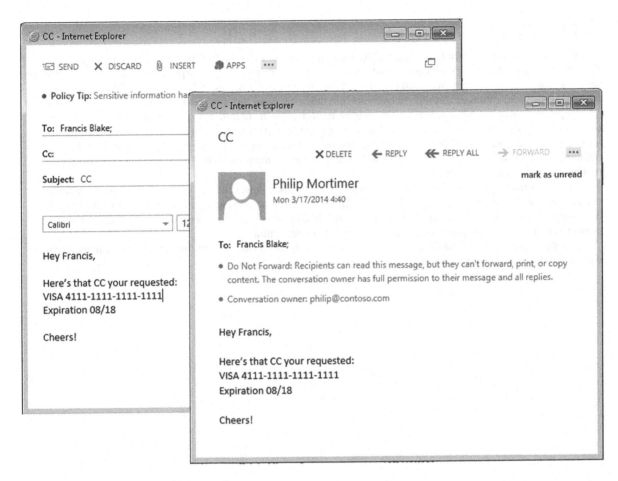

Figure 9-76. *Transport Rules applying IRM to sensitive information*

Of course, data classification can also consist of document fingerprints. These fingerprints allow you to automatically protect messages that match documents with certain fingerprints; not only can you protect information sent from a specific department but you can also protect messages with attached documents whose fingerprints match documents belonging to that department, even when they are sent by other users. However, this power could potentially lead to unwanted blocking of communications, so test these limits before you implement them. In any event, the combination of message classification, DLP fingerprinting, and IRM can be powerful tools in document and/or information protection for an organization.

Summary

This chapter surveyed the compliance features in Exchange 2013 and showed how these features can help organizations meet their business requirements stipulated by laws or regulations. In-place archiving, in combination with managed records management, can be helpful in monitoring the contents of the primary mailbox by using retention policies to automatically offload contents into the in-place archives or to remove them after a certain period.

In-place discovery can be used to search for information, allowing organizations to create exportable sets of content using discover mailboxes for external investigations. When required, organizations can make their mailboxes immutable by using in-place hold for legal investigations or other purposes. To investigate activities related to mailboxes, organizations can leverage their mailbox auditing to log mailbox access or specific operations on mailboxes, or even on specific folders.

Transport rules automatically process messages or control mail flow. Data loss prevention helps organizations control leakage of sensitive information, and Exchange Server 2013 Service Pack 1 makes this feature more powerful by adding document fingerprinting and support for additional clients. Information rights management can be used to protect contents, controlling how recipients can handle the information.

Finally, regarding the Exchange environment itself, organizations can use administrator auditing to log or report changes in the Exchange environment.

## CHAPTER 10

Security

Most organizations operating Exchange Server have it running 24/7. Yet expecting Exchange Server to run perfectly all the time is unrealistic; without proper management and without securing its components, you're going to encounter problems. Particularly, security doesn't end at the edges of your company's office building or data center. Depending on the scenario, you may need to arrange protocols and safety measures for communications with parties over the public network—communications that, by default, are open and readable to others.

Since Exchange 2007, Exchange Server has been positioned by Microsoft as "secure by default." With the *Trustworthy Computing* (TwC) initiative started in 2002, Microsoft began integrating *security development lifecycle* (SDL) principles into their development process. These efforts have involved a security review for each feature and component, during which even elementary aspects like default settings have been discussed.

This is in contrast with earlier versions of Exchange Server, for which companies developed "hardening guides" to reduce the product's potential attack surface. Effectively, this meant locking down the operating system, but doing that could be quite challenging, as Exchange Server depended on and was built upon its operating system, such as the Internet Information Server (IIS).

This "secure by default" approach not only meant changes in default settings like the POP3 service; it also instigated architectural changes or introduced features such as the Role Based Access Control (RBAC) in Exchange 2010, the Mailbox servers' self-signed certificates to secure internal communications, and reintroduction of S/MIME support in Exchange Server 2013 SP1.

Of course, implementing on-premises security measures is only part of the solution. End users nowadays expect to be able to work anywhere, including when traveling or from home, as part of the bring-your-own-device movement, whereby employees use personal devices to access corporate data. So there is needed a corporate mentality that couples access with security, as well as an awareness by all that security is vitally important.

In this chapter, we will discuss the following security-related features:

- Role-Based Access Control

- Split permissions

- Secure/multipurpose Internet mail extensions (S/MIME)

Note With a product as complex as Exchange Server, and as it is so intertwined with security matters, there's the question of how best to cover the subject in a book such as this. We chose to consider security in context with other topics rather than to handle all aspects of it in a single "security" chapter. So if you are looking for discussion of publishing Exchange, protocol authentication, or SSL offloading, those can be found in Chapter 3; the topic of mail flow is covered in Chapter 4, and message hygiene is the subject of Chapter 6.

Role-Based Access Control

Earlier versions of Exchange Server had a limited permissions and delegation model, grouped around a few security groups (three in Exchange 2003, five in Exchange 2007), and the approach was simplistic and task orientated. For finer-grained permissions, organizations had to resort to measures like using ACLs to restrict permissions in Active Directory, which in turn could lead to complications when upgrading to a newer version of Exchange. Meanwhile, the predecessor of its role-based access control saw daylight as Authorization Manager, which was made available for Windows Server 2003 and was a role-based security framework for .NET applications.

The security feature Role Based Access Control (RBAC) was introduced with Exchange 2010. It is, as the name implies, a role-based access control permissions model that continues into Exchange 2013. It allows for fine-grained control over the Exchange environment, without the need to manipulate Active Directory objects. It even goes as far as to offer the ability to control and limit access not only on the cmdlet level but on the parameter level as well.

■ **Note** Exchange servers holding the Edge Transport server role are not part of RBAC security, since it typically is not a member server in the Exchange domain.

The implementation of RBAC revolved around the Universal Security Group (USG) Exchange Trusted Subsystem. That group is effectively the Exchange ecosystem that not only has full access rights on every Exchange object in the organization but also has permission to manage objects on the Active Directory level by being a member of the administrators local security group and the Windows Permissions Security Group. All installed Exchange 2013 servers are members of the Exchange Trusted Subsystem.

■ **Note** For full reference to permissions granted to the Exchange Trusted Subsystem, visit `http://bit.ly/Ex2013DeployPerms`. As a result of the permission structure, you can not use AdminSDHolder protected accounts, such as administrator accounts, for daily operations, as the AdminSDHolder process will reset the permissions on those accounts every hour. This prevents the Exchange Trusted Subsystem from managing those accounts properly, like registering an ActiveSync device. Often, a quick fix is to enable the "Include inheritable permissions from this object's parent" setting on the object, but this is not recommended and the setting will be reset by the AdminSDHolder process. For more information on the AdminSDHolder process, see `http://bit.ly/AdminSDHolder`.

Through the RBAC system, you are effectivly proxying your actions through Exchange Server, which, based on the RBAC configuration, determines what you are allowed to do and not do. This goes not only for administrators but also for end users. An example of the latter is having the ability to manage distribution groups or modify properties, such as your display name.

The RBAC model is based on the concept of assigning who can do what and where, as follows:

- A role is a set of tasks one can perform (what).

- A role group is a collection of roles (who).

- To limit the scope of roles, one can assign scopes (where).

While Exchange 2013 contains several predefined roles and role groups that suffice for most organizations, it allows the creation of custom roles and custom role groups. These custom roles can be assigned through EAC or EMS (see Figure 10-1). Creating custom elements for RBAC can only be done through the EMS.

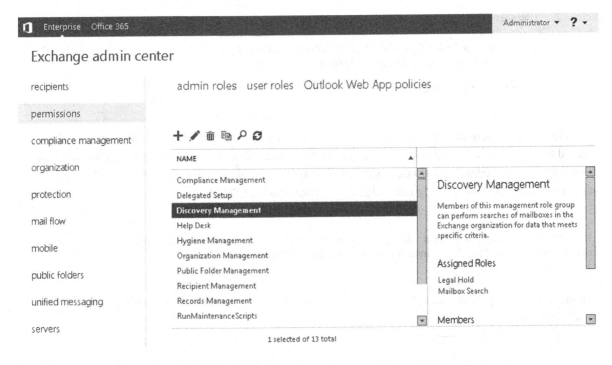

Figure 10-1. Options for role-based access control in EAC

The basic RBAC configuration of administrator or user roles employing predefined objects or changing memberships can be accomplished by using EAC. These options are located in EAC ➤ Permissions ➤ Admin Roles. User roles function to manage assignment policies, which are discussed later in this chapter.

■ **WARNING** The practice of loading the PowerShell snap-in modules directly from PowerShell or through scripts is not supported. This not only bypasses RBAC but it also may result in non-working Exchange cmdlets, since you might be missing certain permissions in your current security context when compared to the effective permissions provided by the Exchange Trusted Subsystem through RBAC.

To properly load an Exchange Management Shell that will honor the RBAC configuration, you have two options:

1. Call the RemoteExchange.ps1. You adjust the Exchange path accordingly, for example,

    "C:\Program Files\Microsoft\Exchange Server\v15\bin\RemoteExchange.ps1"

    Connect-ExchangeServer -auto

    If you want to connect to a specific Exchange server, use the parameter ServerFqdn, for example:

    Connect-ExchangeServer -ServerFqdn ams-exch01.contoso.com

2. Connect to Exchange remotely by setting up a remoting session, as follows:

```
$Session= New-PSSession -ConfigurationName Microsoft.
Exchange-ConnectionUri <Server FQDN>/PowerShell/

Import-PSSession $Session
```

■ **Caution**   Depending on the locally present PowerShell modules, data from remote PowerShell sessions may be returned as type string. This prevents you from further processing that information directly using methods provided by the PowerShell object or cmdlets; for example, mailbox sizes may return something like 3.495 MB (3,665,004 bytes), and you may not be able to directly call the conversion methods like .ToMB() or .ToGB().

After defining the management roles (what), management scopes (where), and role groups (who), you can now connect these pieces of the puzzle by using management role assignments.

■ **Caution**   RBAC objects are stored in Active Directory. Take replication latencies into account when making changes to RBAC configuration.

The Basic RBAC Components

The components used in the RBAC model and their relationships are shown in Figure 10-2. The next section discussses these components, their relationships, and how to put them into action.

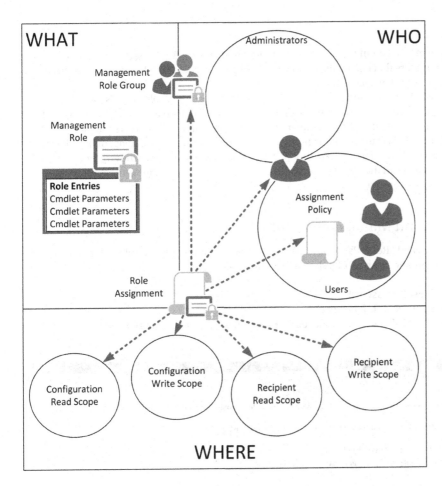

Figure 10-2. Components of the RBAC

■ **Note** To manage RBAC, with the exception of unscoped management roles, you need to be assigned the Organization Management role group. Be careful, though, as the Organization Management role group is managed by the Organization Management role group, and you could create a situation whereby you lock yourself out.

You must know the concepts, components, and possibilities before you can start customizing RBAC to meet the specific requirements of your organization. When planning for RBAC customization at a high level, keep the following in mind:

- Determine the organizational structure. In most cases, job responsibilities follow the hierarchy of the organization. Distinguish between role levels—for example, senior versus junior.

- Define the roles in the organization by detailing their responsibilities and tasks. Categorize the roles—for example, support, sales.

- Attempt to map the roles to corresponding management roles. Identify the gaps as potential new management roles.

- Document the permissions requirements for each position.

The What Component

The "what" component is set by the management roles and management role entries. A *management role* defines the job, with its set of cmdlets and parameters that can be used. Exchange 2013 SP1 has 85 predefined management roles. You can obtain a list of these by using Get-ManagementRole.

Management role entries consist of cmdlets and parameters. When the management role entry is part of a management role, that management role can use those cmdlets in combination with its parameters. Exchange 2013 SP1 has 2,005 management role entries. Note that the parameters can be a subset of the parameters that would normally be available. You can obtain a list of current management role entries for particular management roles using Get-ManagementRoleEntry -Identity "<Management Role>*". Alternatively, you can query the RoleEntries attribute of the management role. To view all the management role entries, use "*" as the management role—for example, Get-ManagementRoleEntry -Identity "**".

Using Management Roles and Management Role Entries

Let's inspect the management role named "Reset Password." We can retrieve the management role object and view its attributes by using the following command, with results shown in Figure 10-3:

```
Get-ManagementRole -Identity "Reset Password" | fl
Get-ManagementRoleEntry -Identity "Reset Password\*"
Get-ManagementRole -Identity "Reset Password" | Select -ExpandProperty RoleEntries | fl
```

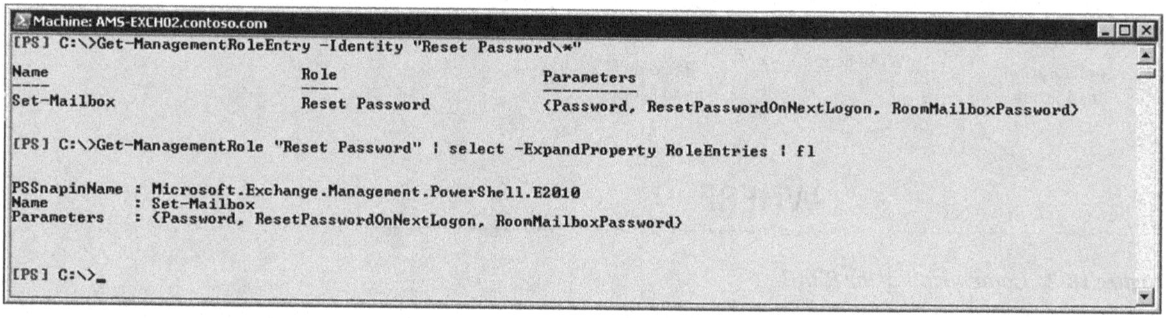

Figure 10-3. *View of the summoned management role entry*

The latter two cmdlets show that the Reset Password management role permits use of the cmdlet Set-Mailbox, together with the parameters Password, ResetPasswordOnNextLogon, or RoomMailboxPassword.

Creating Custom Management Roles

As mentioned, you can create custom management roles by using the New-ManagementRole cmdlet. In Exchange 2013, there are two types of management roles: normal and unscoped. The *normal* management role requires you to specify an existing role, termed "the parent." This can be a predefined management role or a custom management role. The parent is used as a template but also as a limiter. This means that, while you can remove any superfluous cmdlets or parameters from the custom management role, you cannot add cmdlets or parameters that are not part of the parent management role.

■ **Caution**   When you assign a Set-* cmdlet to a management role, you also need to assign the corresponding Get-* cmdlet. That is, you need to be able to view things in order to be able to configure them.

In this example, you will create a simple custom role for mail recipients. This predefined role is used for managing mail-enabled objects in the organization. You use this command:

```
New-ManagementRole -Name 'NL Mail Recipients' -Parent 'Mail Recipients'
```

You can verify the capabilities of this new custom role, which will be identical to the capabilities of the mail recipients role, by using:

```
Get-ManagementRoleEntry -Identity 'NL Mail Recipients\*'
```

Now, suppose you want to remove the capability of using one of the role entries. To do that, you use the Remove-ManagementRoleEntry cmdlet, specifying <Management Role>\<Management Role Entry>, like this:

```
Remove-ManagementRoleEntry -Identity 'NL Mail Recipients\Set-UserPhoto'
```

■ **Caution**   When stripping role entries from a custom management role that will be using EAC, be careful not to remove the Set-ADServerSettings cmdlet. This cmdlet is used during initialization of the session to enable the View Entire Forest option to discover the permissions of the currently logged-on user.

Adding or Removing Parameters

A bit contrary to the verb-noun PowerShell principle is the method of adding or removing parameters. To accomplish those tasks, you need to use the Set-ManagementRoleEntry cmdlet. Together with specifying Parameter with the parameters you want added or removed, you need to use -AddParameter or -RemoveParameter, depending on whether you wish to add or remove those parameters from the role entries. For example, if you want to remove the ability to use the preview parameter with Set-UserPhoto, you use this command:

```
Set-ManagementRoleEntry -Identity 'NL Mail Recipients\Set-UserPhoto'
-Parameter Preview -RemoveParameter
```

To reinstate this preview parameter, you use:

```
Set-ManagementRoleEntry -Identity 'NL Mail Recipients\Set-UserPhoto'
-Parameter Preview -AddParameter
```

To quickly retrieve roles that use certain cmdlets, parameters, scripts, or script parameters, you can use the Get-ManagementRole cmdlet in conjunction with the parameters Cmdlet, CmdletParameters, Script, or ScriptParameters. You can also use GetChildren to retrieve roles that are "children" of the parent role or use Recurse to return a role and all its offspring. For example, this returns all roles that allow Set-Mailbox:

```
Get-ManagementRole -Cmdlet Set-Mailbox
```

This cmdlet will return all roles allowing use of a parameter called `EmailAddresses` with any cmdlets:

```
Get-ManagementRole -CmdletParameters EmailAddresses
```

And this cmdlet will return all roles that allow running a script:

```
Get-ManagementRole -Script *
```

Unscoped Top-Level Management Roles

A special kind of management role is the *unscoped top-level* management role. This is a management role whose purpose is to provide administrators or specific user accounts with the permission to execute scripts or non-Exchange cmdlets. As the name implies, unscoped roles are scopeless, as they have no parent role attached, whereas regular management roles are attached to parent management roles.

To create an unscoped management role, you need to be assigned to the Unscoped Role Management Group. To quickly assign the administrator account to this group, you use:

```
New-ManagementRoleAssignment -Name 'Unscoped Role Management-Administrator'
-User 'Administrator' -Role 'Unscoped Role Management'
```

If you want to grant permission to the group, you use the `SecurityGroup` parameter instead of `User`, and you specify the group name; for example,

```
New-ManagementRoleAssignment -Name 'Unscoped Role Management-Organization Management'
-SeurityGroup 'Organization Management' -Role 'Unscoped Role Management'
```

Note that you need to restart the EAC of the EMS session for the new permission to become effective. It is best practice to name the management role assignment by combining the name of the management role group and the user or group you have assigned the role group to. When not specified, this combination will be used as the Management Role Assignment.

Now, you specify the switch `UnScopedTopLevel` when using the `New-ManagementRole` cmdlet; for example,

```
New-ManagementRole -Name 'Maintenance Scripts' -UnscopedTopLevel
```

Since you did not use a template, the unscoped management role will initially be empty. We have seen before how we can add role entries to management roles. Unscoped management roles are special, in that you can assign scripts or non-Exchange cmdlet permissions to them. The scripts you want to use must reside in the $exinstall\RemoteScripts folder, though. When the default Exchange installation folder is used, $exinstall\RemoteScripts will point to the location `C:\Program Files\Microsoft\Exchange Server\v15\RemoteScripts`.

■ **Note** The scripts you want to use via unscoped management roles need to reside in the $exinstall\RemoteScripts folder on each relevant Exchange server—for example, on all servers or only on those within a specific site, depending on your scenario.

To allow the execution of scripts via management role entries for an unscoped management role, you use the following syntax:

```
Add-ManagementRoleEntry -Identity '<role name>\<script filename>' -Parameters <param1, param2,..>
-Type Script -UnscopedTopLevel
```

Note   You need to specify all required parameters. You cannot use a wildcard to accept a parameter.

For example, to allow the unscoped role ExManScripts to execute the script HealthCheck.ps1 using the parameter Notify, you first make sure that HealthCheck.ps1 is present in the Remote Scripts folder. Next, you use the following cmdlet to allow it through a role entry:

```
Add-ManagementRoleEntry -Identity 'Maintenance Scripts\HealthCheck.ps1'
-Parameters 'Notify' -Type Script -UnscopedTopLevel
```

Caution   When adding scripts to role entries, know that the cmdlet only performs basic validation for the parameters specified. It is not dynamic, so any changes to the script or removal of the script will not be detected, and you need to manually correct the related role entries.

Now, assume you have a special-purpose account called sa_ExScripts, which you will use to run these scripts. For purposes of this example, you will create a role group called ExScripts with the ExManScripts management role, and you will add the sa_ExScripts account as a member:

```
New-RoleGroup -Name 'RunMaintenanceScripts' -Roles 'Maintenance Scripts'
Add-RoleGroupMember -Identity 'RunMaintenanceScripts' -Member 'sa_ExScripts'
```

The output of the previous cmdlets is shown in Figure 10-4.

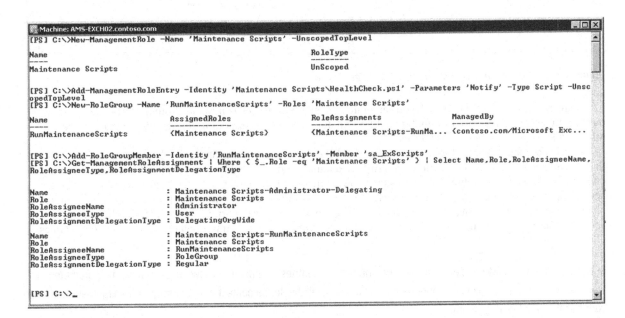

Figure 10-4. *Creating an unscoped top-level management role with script*

■ **Tip** If the user executing the Add-RoleGroupMember cmdlet is not part of the ManagedBy property of the role group (i.e., accounts that can manage their membership), you need to specify the BypassSecurityGroupManagerCheck switch. This will bypass the built-in group management checks.

You may notice that there are two assignments created, each with a different role assignment delegation type:

- The user creating the roles gets a DelegationOrgWide type assignment. This assigment is automatically created after creating the management role, and it allows the role assignee (the creator) to delegate permissions for the role.

- The assignment created using New-RoleGroup is a regular type assignment. This allows the role assignee to execute the role entries associated with that role group.

Now, when sa_ExScripts opens a remote EMS session as shown in Figure 10-5, it will have only the HealthCheck.ps1 script at its disposal. You can quickly test this using the Connect-ExchangeServer cmdlet, with the User and Prompt parameters to provide the account name, and let it prompt for the password. The Auto switch is added to make it connect to any available server.

```
Connect-ExchangeServer -Auto -User 'contoso\sa_ExScripts' -Prompt
```

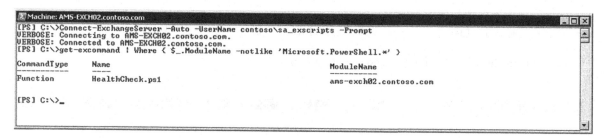

Figure 10-5. *Limited cmdlets owing to RBAC configuration*

Note that as shown in Figure 10-5, you can omit all regular PowerShell commands from the Get-ExCommand output. You accomplished this by filtering on the command ModuleName, excluding commands offered through Microsoft PowerShell* modules, as follows:

```
Get-ExCommand | Where { $_.ModuleName -NotLike 'Microsoft.PowerShell.*' }
```
Note also that you allowed only the role to execute the script. There is no single Exchange cmdlet available. If you want to be able to execute cmdlets from your script or directly, you need to allow them as well, doing so by adding them as role entries using New-ManagementRoleEntry. This may take a while to set up, as you need to go through scripts to collect information on cmdlet and parameter usage, but it grants you fine-grained control over permissions, which should make your security officer happy and may prevent disasters from occurring by powerful unscoped top-level management roles.

■ **Caution** When allowing execution of scripts through role entries, you need to allow used cmdlets and parameters as well. Otherwise, these cmdlets and parameters will not be available in the context of the unscoped management role, and your script will not work properly.

As mentioned earlier, in addition to using unscoped management roles to assign permissions to run scripts, you can use them to grant permissions to execute non-Exchange cmlets. To grant these kinds of permissions via management role entries for an unscoped management role, you use the following syntax:

```
Add-ManagementRoleEntry -Identity <role name>\<cmdlet name>
-PSSnapinName <snap-in name> -Parameters <param1, param2, ..> -Type Cmdlet -UnscopedTopLevel
```

If you want to add a non-Exchange cmdlet, you specify the cmdlet as well as the PowerShell snap-in that contains the cmdlet you want to grant permission to. For example, assume you want to grant permission to use a cmdlet named Get-QADUser with the parameter Identity. The cmdlet is part of the snap-in Quest.ActiveRoles.ADManagement. You can create a management role entry as follows:

```
Add-ManagementRoleEntry -Identity 'Maintenance Scripts\Get-QADUser' -Parameters 'Identity'
-PSSnapinName Quest.ActiveRoles.ADManagement -UnscopedTopLevel
```

■ **Caution**   To control access to non-Exchange cmdlets, the snap-ins you want to control via unscoped management roles need to be installed and registered on all relevant Exchange servers.

The cmdlet to remove the script or non-Exchange cmdlet management role entries for unscoped management roles is similar to removing normal management role entries; for example,

```
Remove-ManagementRoleEntry -Identity 'Maintenance Scripts\HealthCheck.ps1'
```

Finally, should you want to remove user-defined management roles, you use Remove-ManagementRole. Note that only user-defined management roles can be removed. But before you can remove a management role, you first need to remove any dependencies on that management role or use the Recurse parameter to perform a cascaded delete on the roles and child roles; for example,

```
Remove-ManagementRole -Identity 'My Custom Role' -Recurse
```

If you want to remove an unscoped top-level management role, don't forget to specify the parameter UnScopedToplevel as well; for example,

```
Remove-ManagementRole -Identity 'ExManScripts' -UnScopedTopLevel
```

The Where Component

The "where" component determines where the cmdlets are allowed to run from an Active Directory perspective; that is, the scope. This scope can be as broad as an organizational unit, an Active Directory site, or the entire Exchange organization. It can also be more specific, such as be only certain recipients, Exchange servers, or Exchange databases. You can limit the operational usage of cmdlets by using scopes.

RBAC defines two types of management scopes:

- *Regular* or non-exclusive scopes define which objects in Active Directory can be accessed—for example, on Organizational Unit (OU) or the server level.

- *Exclusive* scopes are like regular scopes except that they include access to Active Directory objects. Only members of groups with exclusive access can access those Active Directory objects; others will be denied access.

When defining scopes, be aware of the following:

- When you create a custom management role, it will inherit the non-exclusive scope configuration of the parent management role. These inheritable scopes are called *implicit*, as they are set by the parent.

- Custom scopes are called *explicit* scopes, as they are not inherited.

There's more on implicit and expliciet scopes later in the chapter.

■ **Note**   Unscoped top-level management roles have no scopes defined. The scope properties of these roles will state "Not Applicable."

Regular Scopes

There are two types of scopes you can configure: recipient and configuration. And for each of these, you can configure a read or a write scope. *Recipient* refers to recipient objects, such as mailboxes, distribution groups, or mail-enabled users. *Configuration* refers to Exchange configuration objects, such as Exchange servers or databases. Each role can have the following types of scopes configured:

- *Recipient Read Scope* Determines which recipient objects the assignee is allowed to read from Active Directory.

- *Recipient Write Scope* Determines which recipient objects the assignee is allowed to create or modify from Active Directory.

- *Configuration Read Scope* Determines which configuration objects the assignee is allowed to read from Active Directory.

- *Configuration Write Scope* Determines which configuration objects, such as Exchange servers or databases, the assignee is allowed to create or modify from Active Directory.

■ **Note**   The write scope cannot exceed the boundaries of the related read scope or, in other words, you cannot configure what you cannot view.

Implicit scopes are predefined for the management roles and are stored in the properties ImplicitRecipientReadScope, ImplicitRecipientWriteScope, ImplicitConfigReadScope, and ImplicitConfigWriteScope of the management role objects. Child management roles inherit the parent's management scopes. When a management role is used in a management role assignment, the implicit scopes of the management role apply to the assignment unless the assignment has explicit scopes defined (which will be explained a bit later). A configured explicit scope will override the implicit scopes, making it an uninheritable explicit scope. The only exception to this override rule is implicit read scopes, which always prevail over explicit scopes. Table 10-1 lists all the available implicit scope definitions.

Table 10-1. *Implicit Scope Definitions*

Name	Recipient	Configuration	Description
Organization	Read/Write		Recipient objects in the Exchange organization
MyGAL	Read		Read the properties of any recipient within the current user's GAL
Self	Read/Write		The current user's properties
MyDistributionGroups	Read/Write		Distribution groups managed by the current user
OrganizationConfig	Read/Write		Exchange server or database objects in the Exchange organization
None			Blocks a scope

Explicit scopes are user-configured scopes that override implicit write scopes. Explicit scopes are defined on the management role assignment level, allowing implicit roles to be used consistently and persisting through inheritance while allowing for exceptions that are configured explicit scopes.

Management role assignments have specific properties for predefined relative scopes. Those scopes are a subset of the implicit scopes that are relative to the role assignee. Possible options for predefined relative scopes are a subset of the implicit scopes, as follows:

- *Organization* allows assignees to modify recipients in the entire Exchange organization. For example, if a role allows configuration of the display name and user photo, this scope will allow configuring those properties for all recipients in the Exchange organization.

- *Self* allows assignees to modify their own properties. For example, if a role allows configuration of the display name and user photo, having this scope assigned will extend that action only to the assignee.

- *MyDistributionGroups* allows assignees to create and manage distribution groups where they are configured as owner.

Predefined relative scopes are assigned to management role assignment objects using the `RecipientRelativeWriteScope` property.

Finally, when the implicit scopes, optionally in combination with a predefined relative scope, meet your requirements, you can use a custom scope. This allows you to define specific targets, such as particular organizational units, recipients, or databases. As with predefined relative scopes, custom scopes override the implicit scopes with the exception of the read scope. To create reuseable custom scopes, you can define and assign management scope objects. This also makes them more manageable. (There's more on management scopes later in the chapter.)

You can define these types of custom scopes:

1. *OU scope* targets recipients within the configured OU. It is configured through the `RecipientOrganizationalUnitScope` property of management role assignment objects.

2. *Recipient filter scope* uses a management scope object to filter recipients based on properties such as recipient type, department, manager, or location by using an OPATH filter. The filter is configured through the `RecipientRestrictionFilter` property of the management scope object, optionally in combination with `RecipientRoot` to define the filter starting point. Then, the management scope is given to a management role assignment using the assignment's `CustomRecipientWriteScope` property.

■ **Note** When you specify an alternative root location for the recipient filter scope using `RecipientRoot`, you need to specify `RecipientRoot` in canonical form, not the distinguished name. For example, `OU=nl,DC=contoso,DC=com` *will not work*, `contoso.com/nl` *will*.

3. *Configuration scope* uses a management scope object to target specific servers based on server lists or filterable properties, such as the Active Directory site of server role, or to target specific databases based on database lists or filterable database properties.

- Server scopes on management scope objects are configured using the `SeverRestrictionFilter` parameter using an OPATH filter, or the `ServerList` parameter. Note that server configuration objects, like receive connectors or virtual directories, can be managed if the related server is in-scope.

- Database scopes on management scope objects are configured using the `DatabaseRestrictionFilter` parameter using an OPATH filter, or the `DatabaseList` parameter. Database configuration settings like quota settings, maintenance schedule, or database mounting can be managed if the related database is in-scope. Also, if the database is in-scope, the assignee can create mailboxes in that database.

■ **Caution** When you move or rename organizational units in Active Directory, make sure you process these changes in applicable scopes as well.

To create a new management scope object, you use the `New-ManagementScope` cmdlet and give it a name using the `Name` parameter. Additionaly, depending on whether you want to provide a recipient scope or server scope, you provide the corresponding parameters and the filter value itself. For example, to create a scope for all recipients who are members of a certain group named Staff and only target the recipients below a top-level OU named NL in consoto.com, you would use:

```
New-ManagementScope -Name 'NL-Staff' -RecipientRoot 'contoso.com/NL'
-RecipientRestrictionFilter {membergroup -eq 'cn=Staff,ou=Users,dc=contoso,dc=com'}
```

To create a scope for the Active Directory site London, you would use:

```
New-ManagementScope -Name 'Site London' -ServerRestrictionFilter {ServerSite -eq 'CN=London,
CN=Sites,CN=Configuration,DC=contoso,DC=com'}
```

To create a scope for a fixed set of servers using ServerList, you use:

```
New-ManagementScope -Name 'Servers Amsterdam' -ServerList AMS-EXCH01,AMS-EXCH02
```

To create a scope for a databases starting with 'NL-*', you use:

```
New-ManagementScope -Name 'Databases NL' -DatabaseRestrictionFilter {Name -like 'NL-*'}
```

▪ **Note**   Recipient or server filters use OPATH filters to define recipient or configuration—that is, server or database—restrictions. More information on scope filtering can be found at `http://bit.ly/RBACScopeFilters`.

Exclusive Scopes

As mentioned earlier, along with regular scopes there are exclusive scopes. Exclusive scopes target a specific set of recipients or configuration objects in Active Directory, which then become inaccessible for other management role assignments when accessing the same type of object. This is true even if those other assignments have that object in-scope. For example, if you define an exclusive recipient assignment for a top-level OU named NL, other assignments will be blocked from NL tree access, including assignments with the organization scope. A sample scenario would be for high-profile recipients, for which you could create a separate exclusive manage-recipient role assignment, blocking management of these recipients by others.

To create an exclusive scope, you use the `Exclusive` switch when creating or reconfiguring a management role assignment. For example, to create an exclusive scope using a recipient filter for all recipients located in the VIP OU tree, you use this command:

```
New-ManagementScope -Name 'Exec Recipients' -RecipientRoot 'contoso.com/VIP'
RecipientRestrictionFilter {Name -like '*'} -Exclusive
```

Now suppose you want to assign a group called Exec Admins the role of Mail Recipients, using the scope you've just created. You would use the `ExclusiveRecipientWriteScope` instead of the `CustomRecipientWriteScope` for the exclusive scope:

```
New-ManagementRoleAssignment -SecurityGroup 'Exec Admins'
-Role 'Mail Recipients' -ExclusiveRecipientWriteScope 'Exec Recipients'
```

The reason for using `ExclusiveRecipientWriteScope` is to confirm that you are specifying an exclusive scope. If you use `CustomRecipientWriteScope`, Exchange will notify you that the scope you have specified is exclusive. This way, Exchange not only takes care of configuring the `CustomRecipientWriteScope` with the scope you provided but it also sets the `RecipientWriteScope` to the `ExclusiveRecipientScope` type to indicate that the scope is exclusive.

You can check the assignment using `Get-ManagementRoleAssignment`, knowing that Exchange will use the <Role>-<Role Assignee Name> as the assignment name. If that name already exists, it will append sequence numbers. To check, you use this command; Figure 10-6 shows an example of the possible output:

```
Get-ManagementRoleAssignment -Identity 'Mail Recipients-Exec Admins' | fl
```

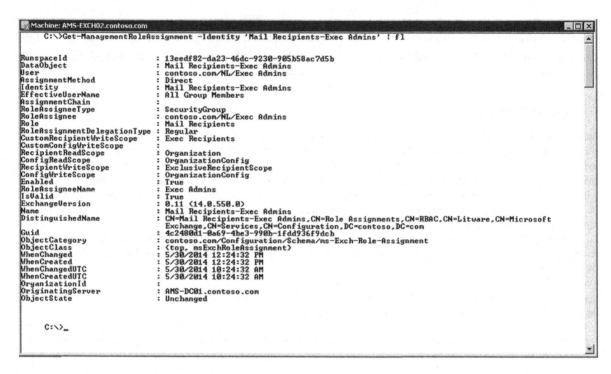

```
Machine: AMS-EXCH02.contoso.com                                                    _ □ X
    C:\>Get-ManagementRoleAssignment -Identity 'Mail Recipients-Exec Admins' | fl

RunspaceId                     : 13eedf82-da23-46dc-9230-905b58ac7d5b
DataObject                     : Mail Recipients-Exec Admins
User                           : contoso.com/NL/Exec Admins
AssignmentMethod               : Direct
Identity                       : Mail Recipients-Exec Admins
EffectiveUserName              : All Group Members
AssignmentChain                :
RoleAssigneeType               : SecurityGroup
RoleAssignee                   : contoso.com/NL/Exec Admins
Role                           : Mail Recipients
RoleAssignmentDelegationType   : Regular
CustomRecipientWriteScope      : Exec Recipients
CustomConfigWriteScope         :
RecipientReadScope             : Organization
ConfigReadScope                : OrganizationConfig
RecipientWriteScope            : ExclusiveRecipientScope
ConfigWriteScope               : OrganizationConfig
Enabled                        : True
RoleAssigneeName               : Exec Admins
IsValid                        : True
ExchangeVersion                : 0.11 (14.0.550.0)
Name                           : Mail Recipients-Exec Admins
DistinguishedName              : CN=Mail Recipients-Exec Admins,CN=Role Assignments,CN=RBAC,CN=Litware,CN=Microsoft
                                 Exchange,CN=Services,CN=Configuration,DC=contoso,DC=com
Guid                           : 4c2480d1-0a69-4be3-990b-1fdd936f9dcb
ObjectCategory                 : contoso.com/Configuration/Schema/ms-Exch-Role-Assignment
ObjectClass                    : {top, msExchRoleAssignment}
WhenChanged                    : 5/30/2014 12:24:32 PM
WhenCreated                    : 5/30/2014 12:24:32 PM
WhenChangedUTC                 : 5/30/2014 10:24:32 AM
WhenCreatedUTC                 : 5/30/2014 10:24:32 AM
OrganizationId                 :
OriginatingServer              : AMS-DC01.contoso.com
ObjectState                    : Unchanged


    C:\>_
```

Figure 10-6. *View of the management role assignment*

As Figure 10-6 shows, members of the Exec Recipients group are now the only users allowed to manage recipients in the Board OU (and below). Mail recipients on the organization level—that is, administrators with organization management membership inclusive—cannot do so.

■ **Note** Exclusive scopes can overlap. Objects that are part of multiple exclusive scopes can be managed by assignees of those scopes.

The Who Component

The "who" component defines who receives the permissions. This information is stored in the Management Role Groups, or just the Role Groups, which are the Universal Security Group (USG) with special flags to indicate they are role groups. By assigning role groups to one or more management roles, you are effectively granting those role groups the permissions that are part of the management role's list of management role entries.

■ **Note** A Management Role Group is a Universal Security Group with msExchCoManagedByLink and msExchVersion configured, and with msExchRecipientTypeDetails set to 1073741824.

Table 10-2 lists all built-in role group definitions, as well as short descriptions of the capabilities of members of those role groups.

Table 10-2. Built-in Role Groups

Name	Members of this Role Group Have/Can
Organization Management	Administrative access to the entire Exchange 2013 organization. By default, its members cannot perform mailbox searches or manage unscoped top-level management roles.
View-Only Organization Management	Read-only access to the entire Exchange organization.
Recipient Management	Administrative access to all recipients in the entire Exchange organization.
UM Management	Manage Unified Messaging (UM) features such as UM service configuration, UM mailbox properties, UM prompts, and UM Auto Attendants.
Discovery Management	Perform in-place discovery mailbox searches and manage in-place hold mailbox settings.
Records Management	Configure compliance features such as retention policy tags, message classifications, or transport rules.
Server Management	Configure server-specific features such as transport and client access, as well as mailbox features such as database copies, certificates, transport queues, receive connectors, virtual directories, and client access protocols.
Help Desk	Limited recipient access to all recipients in the entire Exchange organization and can perform tasks such as password resets.
Hygiene Management	Configure messaging hygiene features such as anti-spam and anti-malware.
Compliance Management	Manage Exchange compliance features.
Public Folder Management	Manage modern public folders.
Delegated Setup	Deploy Exchange servers using placeholder information provisioned by a member of the Organization Management Role Group.

Create a Role Group

Of course, you can create your own role group. To create a role group, you have to be a member of the Organization Management Role Group. To manage a role group, you have to be the manager of the role group, which is determined by the ManagedBy property. Alternatively, you can use the BypassSecurityGroupManagerCheck to bypass internal checks that might be blocking you from managing the role group if you are not the currently configured role group manager.

To create a role group, you use the New-RoleGroup cmdlet, giving the role group a name and optionally assigning to it one or more existing management roles using the Roles parameter, as follows:

```
New-RoleGroup -Name 'UM Mailbox Manager' -Roles 'UM Mailboxes'
```

Users or groups can be directly added to the role group at creation time using -Members; or you can manage the members of a role group by using Add-RoleGroupMember or Remove-RoleGroupMember, respectively. For example, to add a user Olrik to UM Mailbox Manager, you use:

```
Add-RoleGroupMember -Identity 'UM Mailbox Manager' -Member 'Olrik'
```

The New-RoleGroups cmdlets allows you to specify management roles using the Roles parameter, scopes using the various available Scope parameters, and desired role group members using the Members parameter. This way, you can accomplish role assignments using one cmdlet, assuming the building blocks are in place or built in, as the scope and management role definitions. It will also allow you to (re)configure the ManagedBy property of the role group, which will determine who can manage the role group membership. For example, you could use the following cmdlet:

```
New-RoleGroup -Name 'Exec Recipient Management' -Roles 'Mail Recipients','UM Mailboxes'
 -CustomRecipientWriteSope 'Exec'Recipients -ManagedBy 'Olrik' -Members 'Philip','Francis'
```

This will accomplish the following:

1. A new role group named Exec Recipient Management is created.

2. Users Philip and Francis are added as members of this role group.

3. User Olrik is configured as manager of the role group.

4. The following management role assignments are created, where each assignment will configured with Exec Recipients as CustomRecipientWriteScope:

   - Mail recipients-Exec Recipient management

   - UM mailboxes-Exec Recipient management

Linked Role Groups

When it's required in a multi-forest environment—for example, with an Exchange resource forest and an account forest where all the users and group accounts reside—you can create linked role groups. This allows you to create role groups that are linked to the Universal Security Group (USG) in the trusted forest. Two-way trusts are not required.

Assuming the trust has been set up correctly, you can create a linked role group with the following command:

```
New-RoleGroup -Name '<Role Group Name>-Linked' -LinkedForeignGroup <Name of foreign USG>
 -LinkedDomainController <foreign DC fqdn> -LinkedCredential (Get-Credential) -Roles <Roles>
```

You can then use the Roles property of the role groups to get a list of roles to assign to the linked role. For example, to create a linked role group for the Server Management Role Group, you use the following:

```
New-RoleGroup -Name 'Server Management-Linked'
 -LinkedForeignGroup 'Server Management Admins' -LinkedDomainController dc1.users.contoso.com
 -LinkedCredential (Get-Credential) -Roles (Get-RoleGroup -Identity 'Server Management').Roles
```

■ **Tip** To convert existing built-in role groups to linked role groups, use the procedure described at http://bit.ly/ConvertToLinkedRoleGroups.

Putting it All Together: Management Role Assignments

After defining the management roles (the what), the management scopes (the where), and the role groups (the who), you can now connect these pieces of the puzzle by using management role assignments. Some of the earlier examples showed how to use New-ManagementRoleAssignment to assign a user or USG to a management role. Besides direct role assignments, end users can be granted permission through role assignment policies. But before moving onto management role assignments, let's briefly look at the relevant parameters that are available. (Note that you need to assign the management role using either Computer, SecurityGroup, User, or Policy parameters as the assignee, as these are required but mutually exclusive.) Here's an overview of the possibilities:

- The optional Name parameter can be used to specify the name of the management role assignment. If a name is not provided, Exchange will use the <Role>-<Role Assignee Name> as assignment name. If that name already exists, it will start appending sequence numbers.

- The Computer parameter specifies the computer account to assign the management role to.

- The SecurityGroup parameter specifies the management role group or Universal Security Group to assign the management role to.

- The User parameter specifies the name or alias of the user to assign the management role to.

- The Policy parameter specifies the name of the management role assignment policy to assign the management role to. The IsEndUserRole property of the specified role needs to be $true, indicating it is a user role.

- The Role parameter specifies the management role to assign.

- The CustomConfigWriteScope parameter specifies the regular management scope for configuration objects. If CustomConfigWriteScope is specified, you cannot use ExclusiveConfigWriteScope.

- The CustomRecipientWriteScope parameter specifies the regular management scope for recipient objects. If CustomRecipientWriteScope is specified, you cannot use ExclusiveRecipientWriteScope or RecipientOrganizationalUnitScope.

- The delegating switch specifies if the user or USG are allowed to grant the assigned management role to other accounts.

- The ExclusiveConfigWriteScope parameter specifies the exclusive management scope for configuration objects. If ExclusiveConfigWriteScope is specified, you cannot use CustomConfigWriteScope.

- The ExclusiveRecipientWriteScope parameter specifies the exclusive management scope for the recipient objects. If ExclusiveRecipientWriteScope is specified, you cannot use CustomRecipientWriteScope or RecipientOrganizationalUnitScope.

- The RecipientOrganizationalUnitScope parameter specifies the OU to scope the role assignment. Use the canonical form when specifying the OU, for example domain/OU/subOU.

- The RecipientRelativeWriteScope parameter specifies the type of restriction to apply to the recipient scope. Valid options are Organization, MyGAL, Self, MyDistributionGroups, and None.

- The UnScopedTopLevel switch needs to be specified if the role provided is an unscoped top-level management role.

These are the most common options available with New-ManagementRoleAssignment to create management role assignments. Now let's look at a few examples to see how to create these assignments using management roles, management scopes, and role groups.

Assume you have administrators who have the task of managing recipients in the top-level OU called NL. These administrators are named in the USG NL Admins. Since you only want to filter on an OU, specifying the RecipientOrganizationUnitScope parameter will suffice for accomplishing this, as shown in Figure 10-7:

```
New-ManagementRoleAssignment -SecurityGroup 'NL Admins' -Role 'Mail Recipients'
-RecipientOrganizationalUnitScope 'contoso.com/NL'
```

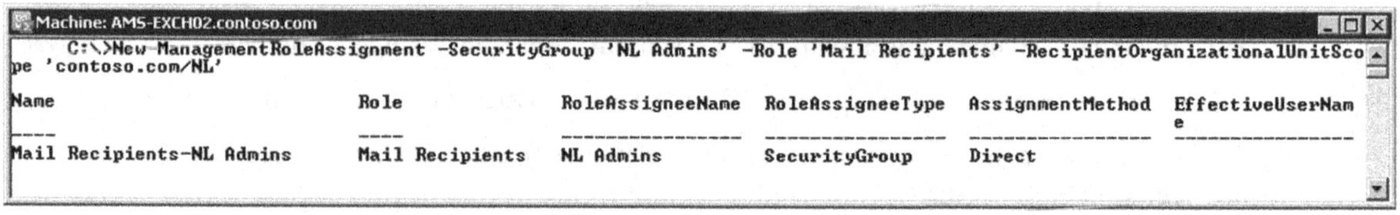

Figure 10-7. *Creating a role assignment with recipient OU scope*

Now, assume you want those NL administrators to only manage recipients in the NL OU who are located in the Amsterdam office. Before you can assign a scope to a role assignment, you need to define the scope, as follows:

```
New-ManagementScope -Name 'OU-NL_Amsterdam' -RecipientRoot 'contoso.com/NL'
-RecipientRestrictionFilter { City -eq 'Amsterdam' }
```

You can now adjust the previously created assignment and have it use the configured management scope as CustomRecipientWriteScope:

```
Set-ManagementRoleAssignment -Identity 'Mail Recipients-NL Admins'
-CustomRecipientWriteScope 'OU-NL_Amsterdam'
```

To retrieve information regarding effective permissions, you can use Get-ManagementRoleAssignment with the EffectiveUsers switch. This will return what users are granted the permissions given by a management role through the role groups, assignment policies, and USGs that are assigned to them. For example, to return all assignments where the account AdminNL has effective permissions, you would use:

```
Get-ManagementRoleAssignment -GetEffectiveUsers | Where { $_.EffectiveUserName -eq 'AdminNL' } |
Select EffectiveUserName, Role, RoleAssignee, Identity
```

In Figure 10-8, you can see that there is an assignment for the Mail Recipients role, for which the AdminNL user has permissions through the role assignee, which in this case is a USG.

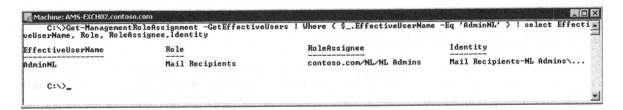

Figure 10-8. *Results showing effective permissions with* Get-ManagementRoleAssignment

---

■ **Tip** Use Get-ManagementRoleAssignment with the EffectiveUsers switch to return effective user permissions for the role assignments.

Policies for Role Assignments

End users can automatically be assigned permissions by way of role assignment policies. One policy is present by default: the default role assignment policy. This policy contains relative scopes that, when enabled, allow users to manage certain elements of their mailbox related to their Active Directory account or other items, such as distribution groups owned by the user. The default policy gets assigned when new mailboxes are created. Of course, when required, you can modify the default policy or create your own explicit role assignment policy.

These role assigment policies can be managed through the EAC, via Permissions ➤ User Roles. When opening up the default role assignment policy, as shown in Figure 10-9, you will notice several end-user roles that control what a user is or is not allowed to configure on his own mailbox or related objects like distribution groups managed by the mailbox owner.

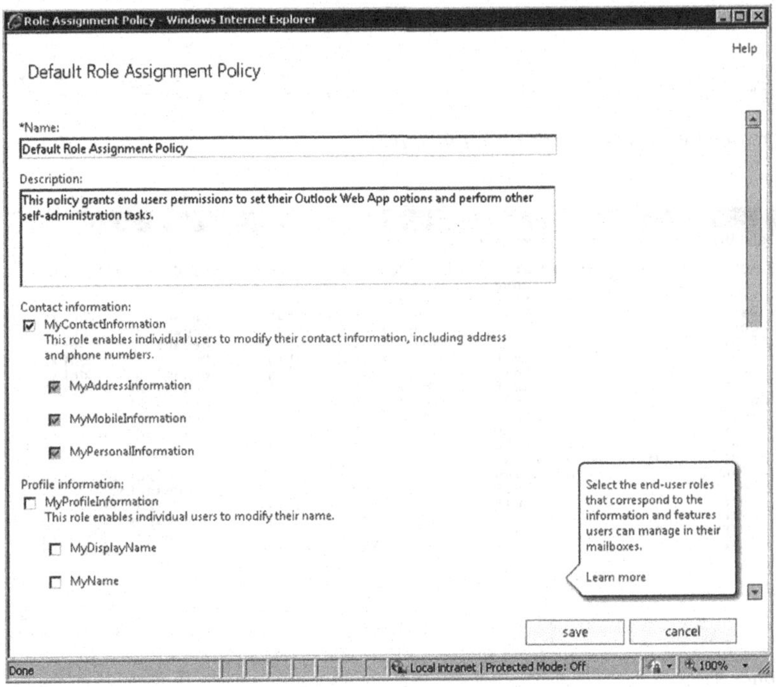

Figure 10-9. *Using the EAC to manage user roles*

To display the current default assignment policy from the EMS, use Get-RoleAssignmentPolicy; for example,

```
Get-RoleAssignmentPolicy | Where { $.IsDefault }
```

The property Roles contains the roles assigned and the property RoleAssignments has the role assignments that have been created by the policy. To inspect which assignments were created, as well as the scopes that were used in making the assignments, you store the currently configured default assignment policy in a variable. Then, you use the RoleAssignments property of that policy to perform a Get-ManagementRoleAssignment for each assignment, which will return the scope information as well:

```
$RAP=Get-RoleAssignmentPolicy | Where { $_.IsDefault }
$RAP.RoleAssignments | Get-ManagementRoleAssignment | ft Role,Recipient*Scope,Config*Scope
```

As you can see in Figure 10-10, there are some built-in roles used specifically for the assignment policy. The available user roles can easily be displayed by filtering on the IsEndUserRole property, as shown in Figure 10-11; for example,

```
Get-MangementRole | Where { $_.IsEndUserRole } | ft Name,*Scope
```

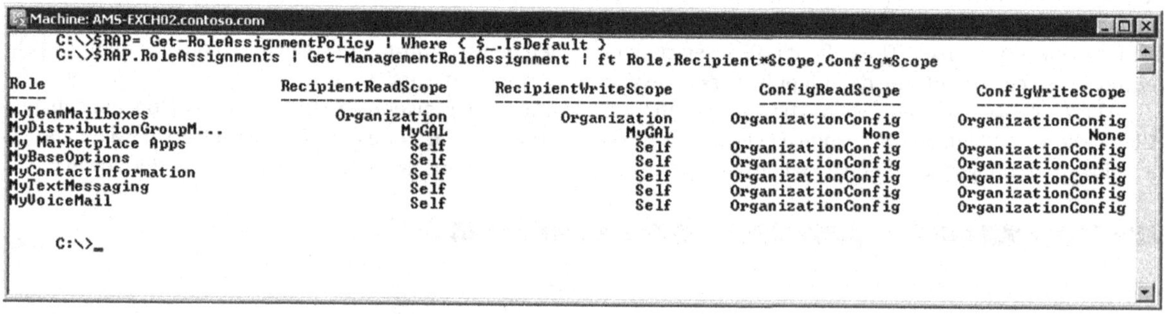

Figure 10-10. *View of role assignments created by the default role assignment policy*

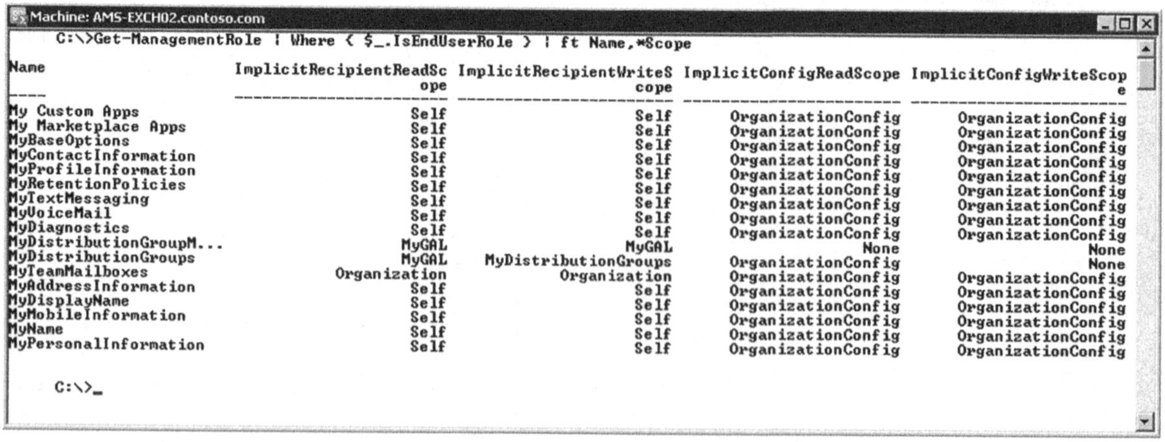

Figure 10-11. *Built-in user roles and implicit scopes*

These built-in user roles contain the role entry information that determines which cmdlets the assignee is allowed to run. However, take a look at Table 10-3 for a quick overview of these roles and their purposes.

Table 10-3. *Built-in User Roles*

Name	Permissions Granted
My Custom Apps	Allows users to view and modify their custom apps.
My Marketplace Apps	Allows users to view and modify their marketplace apps.
MyBaseOptions	Enables individual users to view and modify the basic configuration of their own mailboxes and associated settings.
MyContactInformation	Enables individual users to modify their contact information, including address and phone numbers.
MyProfileInformation	Enables individual users to modify their names.
MyRetentionPolicies	Enables individual users to view their retention tags and view and modify their retention tag settings and defaults.
MyTextMessaging	Enables individual users to create, view, and modify their text messaging settings.
MyVoiceMail	Enables individual users to view and modify their voice mail settings.
MyDiagnostics	Enables end users to perform basic diagnostics on their mailboxes, such as retrieving calendar diagnostic information.
MyDistributionGroupMembership	Enables individual users to view and modify their membership in distribution groups in the organization, provided those distribution groups allow manipulation of group membership.
MyDistributionGroups	Enables individual users to create, modify, and view distribution groups, as well as modify, view, remove, and add members to distribution groups they own.
MyTeamMailboxes	Enables individual users to create site mailboxes and connect them to SharePoint sites.
MyAddressInformation	Enables individual users to view and modify their street addresses and work telephone and fax numbers.
MyDisplayName	Enables individual users to view and modify their display names.
MyMobileInformation	Enables individual users to view and modify their mobile telephone and pager numbers.
MyName	Enables individual users to view and modify their full names and their notes field.
MyPersonalInformation	Enables individual users to view and modify their websites, addresses, and home telephone numbers.

To create a new default assignment policy, you use New-RoleAssignmentPolicy; for example,

```
New-RoleAssignmentPolicy -Name 'Limited Configuration'
-Roles MyBaseOptions,MyAddressInformation,MyDisplayName
```

The previous cmdlet created an explicit policy. To create the same assignment policy making it the default policy, you specify the IsDefault switch:

```
New-RoleAssignmentPolicy -Name 'Limited Configuration'
-Roles MyBaseOptions,MyAddressInformation,MyDisplayName -IsDefault
```

When you want to reconfigure an existing assignment policy as the new default policy, you use Set-RoleAssignmentPolicy and specify IsDefault; for example,

```
Set-RoleAssignmentPolicy -Identity 'Limited Configuration' -IsDefault
```

To add to and remove roles from an assignment policy, you use New-ManagementRoleAssignment and Remove-ManagementRoleAssignment, respectively.

To configure an assignment policy for a mailbox, you use the Set-Mailbox cmdlet with the RoleAssignmentPolicy:

```
Set-Mailbox -Identity 'Philip' -RoleAssignmentPolicy 'Limited Configuration'
```

To retrieve all mailboxes that have a specific assignment policy configured, you use the following:

```
Get-Mailbox -ResultSize Unlimited | Where { $_.RoleAssignmentPolicy -eq 'Limited Configuration'}
```

To remove an assignment policy, you use Remove-AssignmentPolicy, as follows:

```
Remove-RoleAssignmentPolicy -Identity 'Limited Configuration'
```

Monitoring and Reports

Provided administrator audit logging is enabled, you can use EAC or EMS to report on changes in role membership groups or role assignments. To verify the status of administrator audit logging, you use the following:

```
Get-AdminAuditLogConfig | Select AdminAuditLogEnabled
```

The AdminAuditLogEnabled property indicates if administrator audit logging is enabled. If it is not enabled, you can use the following cmlet to enable the administrator audit logging:

```
Set-AdminAuditLogConfig -AdminAuditLogEnabled $true
```

To report on changes in role group membership via EAC, you use the Compliance Management ➤ Auditing ➤ Run an Administrator Role Group Report option. This will bring up a dialog box, as shown in Figure 10-12, where you can enter some details to narrow the search further.

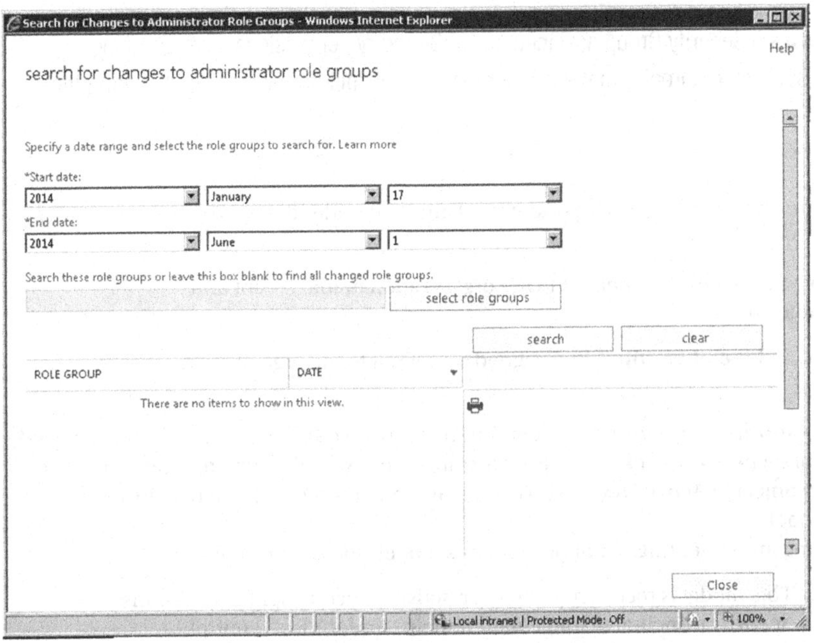

Figure 10-12. *Running a report on an administrator role group*

This EAC option only reports on changes. Alternatively, in EMS, you can search the administrator audit logs for entries related to RBAC cmdlets by using SearchAdminAuditLog. For example, to search changes related to role assignment policy that might have occurred in the last seven days, you use something like:

```
Search-AdminAuditLog -Cmdlets New-RoleAssignmentPolicy,Set-RoleAssignmentPolicy
-StartDate (Get-Date).AddDays(-7)
```

To search for role assignments created or modified in the last 24 hours, you use the following:

```
Search-AdminAuditLog -Cmdlets New-ManagedRoleAssignment,Set-ManagedRoleAssignment
-StartDate (Get-Date).AddDays(-1)
```

Note: there's more on administrator audit logging in Chapter 9.

Split Permissions

In most deployments, Exchange Server is installed using the shared permissions model that is the default installation mode. In shared permissions mode, you are able to create and manage security principals in Active Directory through EMS cmdlets. This is because Exchange Trusted Subsystem is a member of the Exchange Windows Permissions Security Group, which has permissions in Active Directory for doing such things as creating user or group objects.

■ **Note**   Having the Windows Permissions Security Group assigned Active Directory permissions, and assigning permissions to the Exchange Trusted Subsystem directly, makes implementation of split permissions or changing the mode a simple process.

More specifically, in shared mode, the following management roles are used under the hood to create security principals in Active Directory:

- **Mail recipient creation role**, assigned by default to the organization management and recipient management role groups.

- **Security group creation and membership role**, assigned by default to the organization management role groups.

However, depending on your organization's security requirements, or the way your IT infrastructure is managed, you may need stricter management of security principals in Active Directory. For example, creating a new mailbox automatically also creates a new user object in Active Directory. When that is not desired, you might consider implementing a split permissions model.

If your organization is considering implementing a split permissions model, you have two options:

- **RBAC split permissions**. This model is recommended over Active Directory split permissions. The model is flexible and security principal management remains under RBAC control. Exchange Trusted Subsystem is still member of Exchange Windows Permission USG. Exchange servers, services, and specific groups can manage security principals such as distribution groups or role groups. The Exchange tools keep working. Configuring RBAC split permissions is a manual process.

- **Active Directory Split Permissions**. This model isolates management of Exchange configuration and Active Directory security principals. Exchange Trusted Subsystem will not be a member of Exchange Windows Permission USG. This may result in your having to use separate tools for managing Exchange and Active Directory security principals, includes managing distribution groups. Finally, third-party products might not work, as they do not have (implicit) permissions on the Active Directory level. Configuring AD split permissions is an automated process.

■ **Note**   When considering split permissions, sometimes delegation of the task of installing Exchange Server is discussed, as this might be a remote worker or contractor; this is when the Delegated Setup role group comes into play. Exchange administrators can provision placeholder information in Active Directory by using `setup.exe /NewProvisionedServer:<server name>`. After that, members of the Delegated Setup role group, with local administrator permissions to install both prerequisites and Exchange Server, can deploy that server by running `setup.exe`. If you want those administrators to do some configuration on the server, you need to add them to the Server Management role group or create an assignment using a scope for confinement.

RBAC Split Permissions

Implementing split permissions on the RBAC level is relatively simple and makes good use of RBAC features. In shared permissions mode, the Mail Recipient Creation role and the Security Group Creation and Membership management roles are used to create security principals in Active Directory.

Enabling RBAC split permissions is a manual process and will effectively transfer the permission for creating security principals to a user-defined role group, rather than using the built-in Organization Management and Recipient Management role groups. Assuming you have not enabled Active Directory split permissions, you proceed as follows to configure the RBAC split permissions:

1. Create a role group that will contain AD administrators who have permission to create security principals.

2. Make regular and delegating role assignments between Mail Recipient Creation role and the new role group. You do the same for Security Group Creation and Membership role groups.

3. Remove the regular and delegating role assignments between Mail Recipient Creation and the Organization Management role groups and Recipient Management role groups. You do the same for Security Group Creation and Membership role groups.

4. Optionally, you reconfigure the ManagedBy property of the role group, as this will initially contain the creator.

For example, assuming ADAdmins is the name of the designated group as mentioned in step 1, with permissions to create and manage security principals in Active Directory, you run the following set of cmdlets to enable RBAC split permissions:

```
New-RoleGroup -Name 'ADAdmins' --Roles 'Mail Recipient Creation',
'Security Group Creation and Membership'

New-ManagementRoleAssignment -Role 'Mail Recipient Creation'
-SecurityGroup 'ADAdmins' -Delegating

New-ManagementRoleAssignment -Role 'Security Group Creation and Membership'
-SecurityGroup 'ADAdmins' -Delegating

Get-ManagementRoleAssignment -RoleAssignee 'Organization Management'
-Role 'Mail Recipient Creation' | Remove-ManagementRoleAssignment

Get-ManagementRoleAssignment -RoleAssignee 'Recipient Management'
-Role 'Mail Recipient Creation' | Remove-ManagementRoleAssignment

Get-ManagementRoleAssignment -RoleAssignee 'Organization Management'
-Role ' Security Group Creation and Membership' | Remove-ManagementRoleAssignment

Set-RoleGroup -Identity 'ADAdmins' -ManagedBy 'ADAdmins'
```

Note that now only members of the role group—that is, AD Admins—will be able to create security principals such as mailboxes (which implies creating a security principal in Active Directory). The following cmdlets become unavailable: New-Mailbox, New-MailContact, New-MailUser, New-RemoteMailbox, Remove-Mailbox, Remove-MailContact, Remove-MailUser and Remove-RemoteMailbox. Certain features in EAC or OWA/ECP might become unavailable or nonfunctioning, owing to the aforementioned cmdlets not being available.

■ **Tip**   If you want the AD Admin role group to also manage Exchange attributes on new objects, assign the Mail Recipients role.

Active Directory Split Permissions

At some point, anyone who has installed a new Exchange 2013 organization using GUI mode must have seen the dialog that is shown in Figure 10-13.

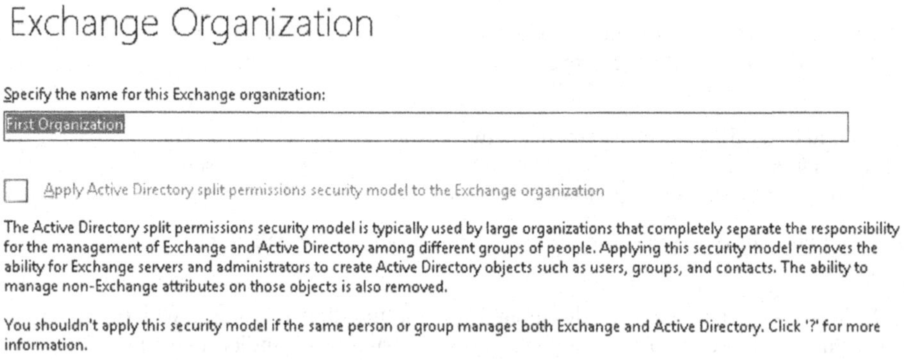

Exchange Organization

Specify the name for this Exchange organization:

First Organization

☐ Apply Active Directory split permissions security model to the Exchange organization

The Active Directory split permissions security model is typically used by large organizations that completely separate the responsibility for the management of Exchange and Active Directory among different groups of people. Applying this security model removes the ability for Exchange servers and administrators to create Active Directory objects such as users, groups, and contacts. The ability to manage non-Exchange attributes on those objects is also removed.

You shouldn't apply this security model if the same person or group manages both Exchange and Active Directory. Click '?' for more information.

Figure 10-13. Active Directory split permissions option

■ **Note**   You cannot enable Active Directory split permissions when you have installed Exchange on a domain controller, but this is generally not recommended anyway.

With Active Directory split permissions, the Recipient Management and Organization Management roles will not be able to create security principals in Active Directory, such as users (for mailboxes) or groups (for distribution lists). When configured, the Active Directory administrators are responsible for creating security principals in Active Directory. Exchange administrators, being Recipient or Organization Management group members, will be responsible for configuring and managing the Exchange attributes on those security principals, like mail-enabling an existing security principal.

■ **Note**   You can switch Active Directory split permissions mode by running `setup.exe` `/ActiveDirectorySplitPermissions:[true|false]`, specifying true or false depending on whether you want to enable or disable the split permissions, and `/PrepareAD` or `/PrepareAllDomains`, depending on your domain model and choice of wanting to prepare all domains at once.

The AD split permissions model is implemented through the Setup wizard by checking the Apply Active Directory Split Permissions mode or when running `setup.exe /PrepareAD /ActiveDirectorySplitPermissions:true` from the command line. Depending on whether you are enabling Active Directory split permissions during the initial setup of Exchange 2013 or are switching from shared permissions or RBAC split permissions mode, enabling Active Directory split permissions results in the following changes:

1. An organizational unit named Microsoft Exchange Protected Groups is created.

2. The Exchange Windows Permissions USG is created, or when it already exists, is moved to this Microsoft Exchange Protected Groups.

3. When the Exchange Trusted Subsystem USG is a member of the Exchange Windows Permissions Group, it is removed from that group.

4. When they exist, any nondelegating role assigment to the Mail Recipient Creation and Security Group Creation role groups and the Membership role group is removed.

5. Any existing access control entries (ACEs) assigned to the Exchange Windows Permissions USG are removed from the domain object—for example, CN=contoso,CN=com. This is repeated for all domains in the forest, depending on use of the `/PrepareAllDomains` switch.

After enabling the Active Directory split permissions model, the following cmdlets will be accessible, but cannot be used to create or manage distribution groups: `Add-DistributionGroupMember`, `New-DistributionGroup`, `Remove-DistributionGroup`, `Remove-DistributionGroupMember`, and `Update-DistributionGroupMember`.

You'll also find that the following cmdlets will be unavailable: `New-Mailbox`, `New-MailContact`, `New-MailUser`, `New-RemoteMailbox`, `Remove-Mailbox`, `Remove-MailContact`, `Remove-MailUser`, and `Remove-RemoteMailbox`. Certain features in EAC or OWA/ECP might become unavailable or non-functioning as well, owing to the aforementioned cmdlets not being available or not functioning, depending on the operation you are trying to run.

S/MIME

S/MIME is a standard for certificate-based signing and encryption of email messages. It is an endpoint solution, and it is built on top of *public key infrastructure* (PKI) technology. Exchange 2013 RTM lacked S/MIME support. However, the Exchange Server 2013 Service Pack 1 reintroduced support for S/MIME in Outlook WebApp (OWA). All recent versions of Outlook contain S/MIME support, and Windows Phone 8.1 adds support for S/MIME as well. There's more background information on PKI at `http://bit.ly/AboutPKI`.

By encrypting messages, you maintain confidentiality while the message is transported on the public network. The only one able to read the message is the intended recipient. However, to send someone an encrypted message, the sender must know the public certificate of the receiver. That public certificate is then used to encrypt the message. So, the only one able to decrypt that message is the one owning the private key, which normally is the intended receiver. Some mail clients allow you to always include the public key with your messages, which then enables the receiver to encrypt future messages should he or she choose to do so. The encryption and decryption process is shown in Figure 10-14.

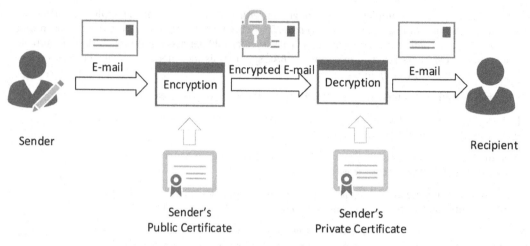

Figure 10-14. E-mail encryption and decryption process

■ **Note**   S/MIME encrypted messages are readable only for the intended receiver. Since these messages are not readable by the indexer (treated as "unknown"), they cannot be searched and cannot be discovered.

Exchange 2013 SP1 supports *triple-wrapped* messages. This means that signed messages are encrypted after the message is signed. This is the highest form of security with S/MIME, but it does increase message size.

■ **Caution**   S/MIME is an ActiveX control and is supported by Internet Explorer 9 and above. Currently, S/MIME is unsupported for Firefox, Opera, or Chrome. S/MIME is also not supported on OWA for devices.

After the sender signs a message and it is encrypted, the receiver can be sure that message was actually sent by the reported sender (non-repudiation), and that the message has not been tampered with. Signing e-mail requires owning the private key of the certificate.

■ **Caution**   Be advised that, when using non-public certificates for signing or encryption, you need to properly manage those certificates, expired ones included, as loss may result in an inability to decrypt and thus read messages.

To use S/MIME for signing messages, you must have installed a certificate on the client or device. For encrypting the messages, you need the public certificate of the receiver as well. Certificates can be installed manually or distributed through the Global Address List (GAL). For mobile devices, you can use mobile device management solutions like the Windows Phone Enterprise Feature Pack for Windows Phone 8.1 devices or the System Center Configuration Manager.

> ■ **Note** When using GAL distribution via Office 365, a hybrid configuration is required. In such a configuration, you need to set up DirSync to provision the certificates through the on-premises user certificate attribute in Active Directory to Azure Active Directory for Office 365. This setup also allows organizations with a mix of on-premises users, as well as users hosted in Exchange Online, to exchange S/MIME messages.

Configuring S/MIME in Exchange 2013 SP1

Before configuring, let's have a quick look at mobile device mailbox policies, better known through their old name, Exchange ActiveSync mailbox policies. These allow you to create a policy whereby you configure a set of options for mobile devices, which you then assign to mailboxes. After that, mobile devices configured to connect to those mailboxes can satisfy any compliance settings and will receive those settings, such as allowing use of cameras or enforcing mandatory password use for lock screens.

The mobile device mailbox policy also has options for several S/MIME-related settings:

- `AllowSMIMEEncryptionAlgorithmNegotiation` specifies whether the messaging application on the mobile device can negotiate the encryption algorithm if a recipient's certificate doesn't support the specified encryption algorithm. Possible values are `BlockNegotiation`, `OnlyStrongAlgorithmNegotiation`, and `AllowAnyAlgorithmNegotiation`.

- `AllowSMIMESoftCerts` specifies whether S/MIME software certificates are allowed.

- `RequireEncryptedSMIMEMessages` specifies whether you must encrypt S/MIME messages.

- `RequireEncryptionSMIMEAlgorithm` specifies what required algorithm must be used when encrypting. Possible values are `TripleDES`, `DES`, `RC2128bit`, `RC264bit`, or `RC240bit`.

- `RequireSignedSMIMEAlgorithm` specifies what required algorithm must be used when signing a message. Possible values are `SHA1` or `MD5`.

- `RequireSignedSMIMEMessages` specifies whether the mobile phone must send signed S/MIME messages.

The default settings of the default mobile device mailbox policy can be displayed by using the following:

```
Get-MobileDeviceMailboxPolicy | Select Name,*MIME*
```

Running this cmdlet returns the selected MIME-related pieces of information from the mobile device mailbox policy, as shown in Figure 10-15.

```
Machine: AMS-EXCH02.contoso.com

  C:\>Get-MobileDeviceMailboxPolicy | select Name,*Mime*


Name                                   : Default
RequireSignedSMIMEMessages             : False
RequireEncryptedSMIMEMessages          : False
AllowSMIMESoftCerts                    : True
RequireSignedSMIMEAlgorithm            : SHA1
RequireEncryptionSMIMEAlgorithm        : TripleDES
AllowSMIMEEncryptionAlgorithmNegotiation : AllowAnyAlgorithmNegotiation


  C:\>_
```

Figure 10-15. *Display of default mobile device mailbox policy S/MIME settings*

To change an option, use `Set-MobileDeviceMailboxPolicy -Identity <Policy Name>`, followed by the parameter and value. For example, to change the required algorithm used for encryption, you use:

```
Set-MobileDeviceMailboxPolicy -Name 'Default' -RequireEncryptionSMIMEAlgorithm RC240bit
```

You can use EAC to assign policies with SMIME options created from PowerShell. Alternatively, you can use:

```
Set-CASMailbox -Identity <Mailbox ID> -ActiveSyncMailboxPolicy <MDM Policy ID>
```

Next to the MDM policy, there is also the option to configure how SMIME operates in OWA, utilizing the `Set-SMIMEConfig` cmdlet. You can display current settings using `Get-SMIMEConfig`.

Running the `Get-SMIMEConfig` cmdlet will show you the currently configured S/MIME settings, as shown in Figure 10-16.

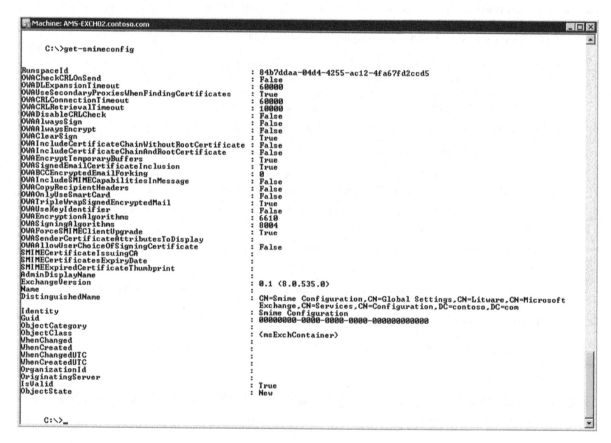

Figure 10-16. *Display of default S/MIME configuration*

■ **Note** Configuring the S/MIME options using `Set-SMIMEConfig` requires membership in the Organization Management role group.

The following options can be configured using `Set-SMIMEConfig`:

- `OWATripleWrapSignedEncryptedMail` specifies whether signed and encrypted email messages in OWS are triple-wrapped. The default is `$true`.

- `OWAAllowUserChoiceOfSigningCertificate` specifies whether to allow users to select the certificate to use when they digitally sign email messages in OWA. The default value is `$false`.

- `OWAAlwaysEncrypt` specifies whether all outgoing messages are automatically encrypted in OWA. The default is `$false`.

- `OWAAlwaysSign` specifies whether all outgoing messages are automatically signed in OWA. The default is `$false`.

- `OWASigningAlgorithms` specifies the list of signing algorithms that are used by OWA to sign messages.

- `OWAEncryptionAlgorithms` specifies a list of algorithms that are used by OWA to encrypt messages.

- `OWASignedEmailCertificateInclusion` specifies whether the sender's encryption certificate is included from a signed email message in OWA. The default value is `$true`. This means the public certificate is automatically included with signed messages, allowing the receiver to encrypt future messages for this sender.

Regarding the OWA encryption algorithms and OWA signing algrithms, you'll notice a list of algorithms separated by a semicolon. Some algorithms support multiple key lengths (strengths). For those, you need to specify the key length in the format <ID>:<key length>. Table 10-4 lists the available encryption and signing algorithms.

Table 10-4. *Supported Encryption and Signing Algorithms*

Encryption Algorithms	Signing Algorithms
RC2 (supported key: 40, 56, 64 and 128) ID:6602	CALG_SHA_512
DES (56-bit) ID:6601	CALG_SHA_384
3DES (168-bit) ID:6603	CALG_SHA_256
AES128 ID:660E	SHA1
AES192 ID:660F	CALG_MD5
AES256 ID:6610	

So, assuming you want to configure RC2 128-bit, 3DES and AES256 for encryption, you would use:

```
Set-SMIMEConfig --OWAEncryptionAlgorithms 6602:128,6603,6610
```

To configure SHA1 for signing, you use:

```
Set-SMIMEConfig --OWASigningAlgorithms SHA1
```

Outlook Web Access and S/MIME

Assuming your secure email certificate is stored and available in Active Directory, you can proceed as follows to use S/MIME in Outlook:

1. Open Outlook Web Access.

2. Create a new email message.

3. Click ... and select Show Message Options.

4. Select Encrypt This Message (S/MIME) or "Digitally Sign This Message (S/MIME), depending on what you want to achieve; see Figure 10-17.

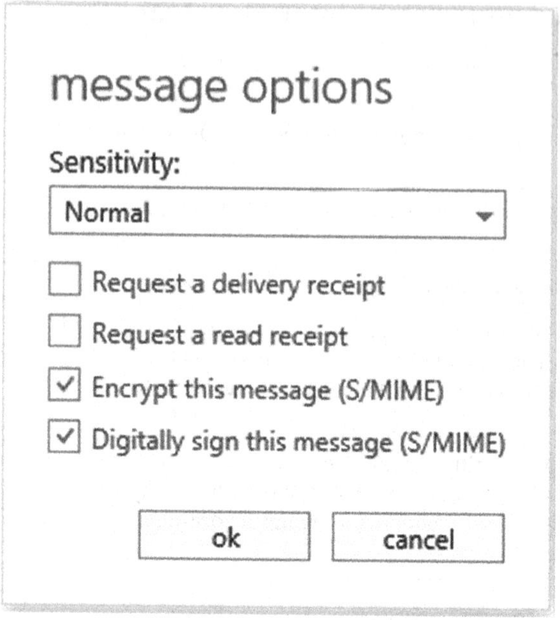

message options

Sensitivity:

| Normal ▼ |

☐ Request a delivery receipt

☐ Request a read receipt

☑ Encrypt this message (S/MIME)

☑ Digitally sign this message (S/MIME)

| ok | | cancel |

Figure 10-17. *Configuring the S/MIME options in OWA*

5. When you return to the composition window, you may receive a warning, depending on whether you have already installed the S/MIME ActiveX control. The warning states: "Tip: You can't sign or encrypt this message until you install the S/MIME control." So, to install S/MIME, click the link and install the downloaded owasmime.msi package. You must relog for the installed control to work.

6. When you compose a message and select Encrypt or Sign, you will notice a key or certificate symbol at the right of the subject line; this indicates whether encryption or signing is selected for the current message.

Outlook and S/MIME

To be able to use S/MIME in Outlook, you proceed as follows:

1. If you have not installed your secure email certificate yet, do so now. It may be automatically distributed to you or you may need to manually install it. In the latter case, you open the certificate and import it to the personal certificate store of the user.

2. Configure Outlook to use the ceryou click Trust Center Settings, after which you select the Email Security pane, as shown in Figure 10-18.

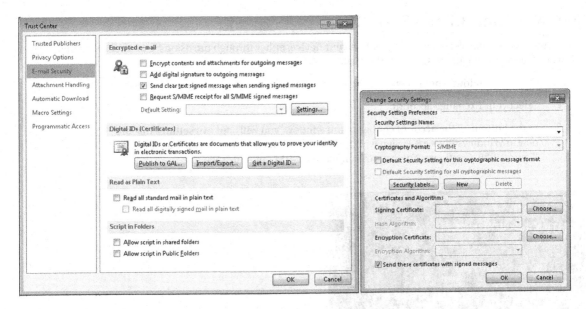

Figure 10-18. *Configuring the email security options in Outlook 2013*

3. Click Settings to open up the dialog to configure the security settings. You provide a
meaningful name for the setting you are going to create, and click Choose. A popup will
appear where you can pick the secure email certificate to use. In the Change Security
Settings window, you provide additional details like the algorithms to use and, last but
not least, select whether you want to automatically send your certificates with signed
messages so that the receiver may reply to you with encrypted messages.

When you compose an email in Outlook, you can select the Options pane and select Encrypt or Sign to encrypt or
sign the message, as shown in Figure 10-19.

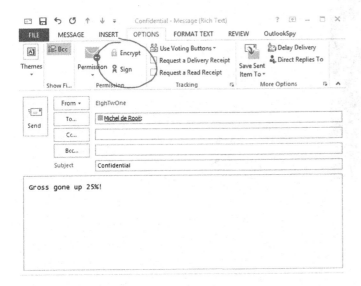

Figure 10-19. *Sending a S/MIME message using Outlook 2013*

Windows Phone 8.1 and S/MIME

Assuming the secure email certificate is present on your device, either through provisioning or after manually installing it, you then configure S/MIME on the related account:

1. On your Windows Phone device, navigate to Settings ➤ Email + Accounts.

2. Select your Exchange account.

3. At the bottom of the account configuration window, you will spot two settings that are new in Windows Phone 8.1: Sign with S/MIME and Encrypt with S/MIME, as shown in Figure 10-20. Configure. You cannot configure S/MIME per message.

Figure 10-20. *S/MIME usage in Windows Phone 8.1*

4. Depending on whether you enabled encryption or signing, you will see a "Signed and encrypted message" notification when composing a message, also shown in Figure 10-20. This same notification will be displayed when receiving signed or encrypted messages.

Summary

This chapter discussed the Role Based Access Model (RBAC)in Exchange 2013 and its components, such as management roles, management scopes, and role groups, as well as special features like unscoped top-level management groups, and how these features can help you achieve granular permissions in your Exchange and Active Directory environments using a role-based model.

The chapter also showed how to enable and utilize the split-permissions model when business requirements require strict separation of tasks formanagement of the Exchange organization and Active Directory.

Finally, Chapter 10 surveyed the purpose of S/MIME, which was introduced with Exchange Server 2013 Service Pack 1, and how to configure it using Outlook or Windows Phone.

CHAPTER 11

■ ■ ■

Office 365 and Exchange Online

Office 365 and Exchange Online are subscription-based online offerings built around Office-related software and services. While many consid'er today's Office 365 and Exchange Online programs as well established, they were officially launched as recently as June 2011. Office 365 is the succesor to Business Productivity Online Suite (BPOS). BPOS was launched in 2008 as a package of individually hosted Microsoft products, such as Exchange, SharePoint, and at that time, Live Meeting. At the time of this writing, Office 365 offers software and cloud-based services founded on the following products:

- Microsoft Exchange for email

- Microsoft Lync for communications and conferencing

- Microsoft SharePoint for social networking and collaboration

- Microsoft Office WebApps for online Microsoft Office Suite

- OneDrive for cloud file storage

- Yammer for social networking

- Microsoft Office desktop application licenses

What products and services are available to your organization depends on the subscription. The Office 365 subscriptions and packages change quite frequently; current Office 365 subscriptions are described and can be compared at `http://bit.ly/O365BusinessPlans`. This is also the location to start your Office 365 journey by selecting one of the business plans. Some plans offer the option of a trial run.

■ **Note** When there are references to Exchange Online (EXO), these are for the Exchange environment that is part of Office 365. Exchange Online is also the name of a specific Office 365 business plan, solely offering hosted Exchange email services. For clarity, we've used Office 365 to refer to the service in general and Exchange Online to mean the Exchange environment in Office 365.

At the Microsoft Exchange Conference in 2014, the Office team announced adoption of a cloud-first strategy. This means that changes and new features will be introduced in Office 365 first. This is because the high level of standardization in the Office 365 platform allows for introducing or rolling back small, gradual changes. When they are deemed suitable for on-premises usage, changes will be made available for the on-premises Exchange Server product in the form of a cumulative update or service pack. However, owing to scale, some features might never make it to the on-premises world, such as Delve (formerly known by its code name, Oslo), which went live in Office 365 in September, 2014. Delve offers personalized features to search and discover relevant contents across Office 365 by using machine learning. It searches your e-mail messages, meetings, contact information, connected social networks and documents to show the end user relevant information. Delve is available through all Office 365 subscriptions plans. More information on Delve can be found at `http://bit.ly/DelveStart`.

Because of the nature of Outlook WebApp and the Outlook client, this cloud-first strategy also means client changes will become available in Outlook WebApp first, as the Outlook client requires a hotfix or service pack to add new or changed functions. Also, the functionality of Office 365 may leverage all server products, even when you are not directly using them, making an on-premises situation more difficult—for example, SharePoint might not be present on-premises or might not be integrated with on-premises Exchange.

When considering Office 365, organizations need to make sure the platform suits their present and future business requirements, and that they can embrace the consequences of switching to a cloud-based solution, either partially or in full. For example, while you can configure some aspects of your cloud-based tenant, such as password expiration settings, cloud-based tenants are bound to retention periods that are set by the provider.

Deployment Options

Organizations can choose among three deployment options when they want to migrate to Office 365.

- **Cloud-only or all-in**, whereby companies solely utilize software and services from the cloud—in this case, Office 365 (see Figure 11-1).

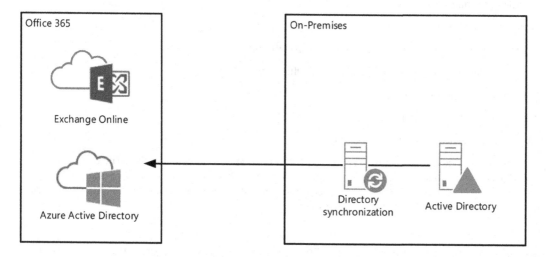

Figure 11-1. *Full cloud deployment of Exchange*

- **None**, where companies keep utilizing their on-premises software and services (see Figure 11-2).

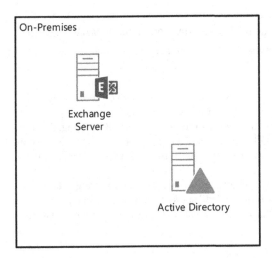

Figure 11-2. Exclusive on-premises deployment of Exchange

- **Hybrid**, where companies utilize a mixed model, using and optionally integrating on-premises software and services with Office 365 or cloud services. In this model, companies can have both on-premises mailboxes and mailboxes in Office 365 (see Figure 11-3).

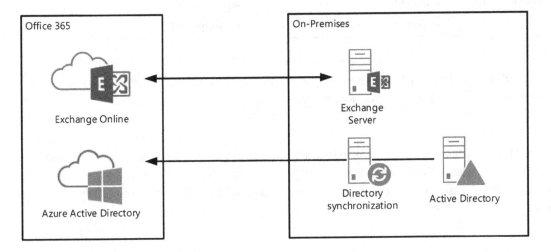

Figure 11-3. Hybrid deployment of Exchange

The depicted directory synchronization server, presently known as Windows Azure Active Directory synchronization server (WAADsync), is optional but highly recommended when using an Exchange hybrid situation. It provisions objects and synchronizes information such as email addresses in Windows Azure Active Directory, using information from the on-premises Active Directory. This is one-way traffic for the majority of attributes, and as a consequence you need to manage cloud-based mailboxes, contacts, and other mail-related objects on-premises, letting WAADsync provision the objects and propagate the attribute changes in Windows Azure Active Directory and Exchange Online. WAADsync also enables the same sign-on experience using password synchronization. (But there's more on this later in the chapter).

▪ **Caution** When using the Exchange hybrid and WAADsync, management is performed on-premises. WAADsync will handle the provisioning and synchronization of information in Windows Azure Active Directory and Exchange Online.

To assist organizations with a move to Office 365 or help to integrate cloud components with their on-premises environment, Microsoft has made available the Exchange deployment assistant. After answering a few basic questions, such as what version of Exchange is currently used and what deployment option you will be using, this tool generates step-by-step instructions for migrating or connecting to Office 365. The Exchange deployment assistant can be found at http://bit.ly/exchangeda. It gets updated regularly to reflect changes in the migration process, which may occur frequently.

Also, when you want to implement an Exchange hybrid deployment and are still running an Exchange 2007 environment, you need to use an Exchange 2010 or Exchange 2013-based hybrid server. These servers can handle client traffic for on-premises down-level servers, as well as redirect or proxy requests to Office 365. Table 11-1 lists the hybrid deployment scenarios that are supported.

Table 11-1. Hybrid Deployments Supportability Matrix

On-Premises	Exchange 2010 SP3 Hybrid Server	Exchange 2013 SP1 Hybrid Server
Exchange 2013 SP1	Not supported	Supported
Exchange 2010 SP3	Supported	Supported
Exchange 2007 SP3 RU10	Supported	Supported
Exchange 2003	Supported	Not supported

▪ **Note** If required to run an Exchange hybrid server, elegible cloud tenants can request a free product key through the Office 365 Management Portal or via http://aka.ms/hybridkey.

▪ **Caution** Cumulative updates are necessary for maintaining currency, as Exchange builds are supported for two release cycles. This also applies to Exchange hybrid and the Edge servers, meaning that when an Exchange 2013 Cumulative Update "N" is released, the support for hybrid servers running Exchange 2013 Cumulative Update "N-2" ends.

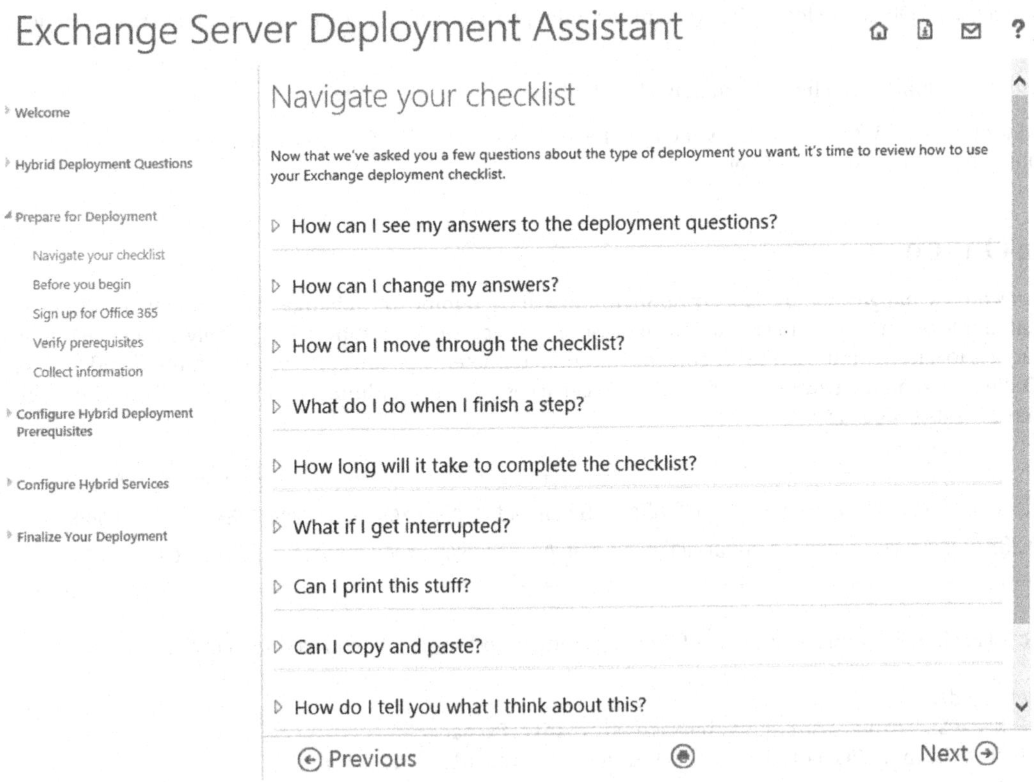

Exchange Server Deployment Assistant

⌂ ▯ ✉ ?

Navigate your checklist

▷ Welcome

▷ Hybrid Deployment Questions

◢ Prepare for Deployment

    Navigate your checklist

    Before you begin

    Sign up for Office 365

    Verify prerequisites

    Collect information

▷ Configure Hybrid Deployment
   Prerequisites

▷ Configure Hybrid Services

▷ Finalize Your Deployment

Now that we've asked you a few questions about the type of deployment you want, it's time to review how to use your Exchange deployment checklist.

▷ How can I see my answers to the deployment questions?

▷ How can I change my answers?

▷ How can I move through the checklist?

▷ What do I do when I finish a step?

▷ How long will it take to complete the checklist?

▷ What if I get interrupted?

▷ Can I print this stuff?

▷ Can I copy and paste?

▷ How do I tell you what I think about this?

⊙ Previous   ◉   Next ⊙

Figure 11-4. *Exchange Server's deployment assistant*

The initial setup and configuration of Office 365 and its related components are covered in the step-by-step instructions generated by the deployment assistant. Because of all the possible variations in deployment and the Office 365 update cadence, those instructions might easily fill a book themselves. Therefore, this chapter will focus on some of the more common topics involved in migrating to or administering Office 365 or an Exchange hybrid deployment.

■ **Tip** The Office 365 service is under constant development. To receive notifications when changes are made to Office 365-related URLs or IP addresses, subscribe to the RSS feed located at `http://go.microsoft.com/fwlink/p/?linkid=236301`.

Connecting to Office 365

Many of the examples used in the previous chapters of this book apply not only to Exchange 2013 on-premises but also to Office 365. However, your cloud tenant is subject to limitations as configured through RBAC, so cmdlets or parameters might not be available.

Most administrators will use the Exchange Control Panel (ECP) when administering Office 365 for everyday tasks. But, as with on-premises Exchange, using PowerShell sometimes proves a better option, as repetitive tasks might become tedious when performed through the ECP. In some situations, using PowerShell might even be required, such as for enabling customization of your cloud tenant using `Enable-OrganizationCustomization`.

When connecting to Office 365 for Exchange administration, be aware that there are two separate environments to connect to:

- Exchange Online, which can be managed through a remote PowerShell session.

- Windows Azure Active Directory, which can be managed using the Windows Azure Active Directory module for PowerShell.

Exchange Online

When you connect to Exchange Online using PowerShell, you will encounter an Exchange Management Shell (EMS) session that's similar to when you connect to an on-premises Exchange 2013 environment. The only difference is that you will have access to a RBAC-imposed subset of cmdlets and parameters that are appropriate for your cloud tenant, as Exchange Online is a shared environment. You will also get access to some additional cmdlets specific to Exchange Online, such as Get-InboundConnector.

■ **Note** At the time of this writing, Exchange 2013 offers 792 cmdlets while Exchange Online makes 521 cmdlets available. Only 383 of these latter cmdlets are available for both on-premises Exchange 2013 and Exchange Online.

To connect to Exchange Online, you use the following cmdlets and see the screen as shown in Figure 11-5:

```
$o365Cred= Get-Credential
$o365Session= New-PSSession -ConfigurationName Microsoft.Exchange
    -ConnectionUri https://ps.outlook.com/powershell/ -Credential $o365Cred
    -Authentication Basic -AllowRedirection
Import-PSSession $o365Session
```

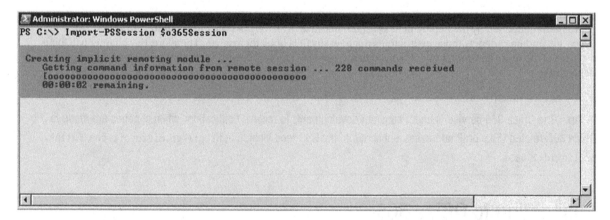

Figure 11-5. *Connecting to Exchange Online*

When prompted, you enter your cloud tenant's administrative credentials.

To make this information available in every session, you edit your PowerShell profile and include the cmdlets to connect to Exchange Online as a function. Your regular PowerShell profile is contained in the PowerShell variable $profile. You can add a function Connect-EXO, which is then available in every PowerShell session you start, as follows:

1. In PowerShell session, enter $profile. This will display the full filename of the profile file. For example,

   ```
   C:\Users\administrator.CONTOSO\Documents\WindowsPowerShell\
   Microsoft.PowerShell_profile.ps1
   ```

2. When the file does not exist, create it and optionally create the path.

3. Add the following contents to Microsoft.PowerShell_profile.ps1:

   ```
   Function Connect-EXO {
       $o365Cred= Get-Credential
       $o365Session= New-PSSession -ConfigurationName Microsoft.Exchange
        -ConnectionUri https://ps.outlook.com/powershell/ -Credential $o365Cred
        -Authentication Basic -AllowRedirection
       Import-PSSession $o365Session
   }
   ```

4. Save and close the file.

5. Open a new PowerShell session.

6. Enter the following command: Connect-EXO.

You can also extend the PowerShell integrated scripting environment with menu options to connect to various remote or local environments. An example of how to accomplish this can be found at http://bit.ly/ConnectISE.

▪ **Tip** The cmdlet Import-PSSession provides a parameter prefix that allows you to prefix cmdlets for the related session. This means you can use the same cmdlets, albeit with a prefix for the noun. This may come in handy when you are connected to multiple Exchange environments or to Office 365 tenants. For example, if you use Import-PSSession $o365Session -Prefix EXO, the noun of the imported Exchange Online-related cmdlets will be prefixed with EXO–for example, Get-EXOMailbox, Set-EXOMailbox, and Get-EXOMailUser. These cmdlets work identically to their normal counterparts—that is, Get-Mailbox, Set-Mailbox and Get-MailUser.

Windows Azure Active Directory

Connecting to Windows Azure Active Directory requires installing the related PowerShell module. You can download and install the x64 version of the module via http://bit.ly/WAADM. After installing the module, you can start the Windows Azure Active Directory module for the PowerShell shortcut. To connect to Windows Azure Active Directory, you use the following cmdlet:

Connect-MSOLService

When prompted, you enter your cloud tenant's administrative credentials. From here, you have Windows Azure Active Directory cmdlets at your disposal—for example, you can use New-MSOLUser to create user objects, Set-MSOLUserLicense to assign licenses, or cmdlets to configure federation.

Autodiscover

Chapter 3 covered Autodiscover and explained how this process works in an on-premises Exchange environment. When you're using cloud-only mailboxes, the client process is similar, but instead of pointing the public DNS record for Autodiscover to your on-premises environment, you create a CNAME record to the Office 365 environment; for example,

```
autodiscover.contoso.com          CNAME          autodiscover.outlook.com
```

When using Exchange hybrid mode, you can have mailboxes residing on-premises and also mailboxes residing in Office 365. In this situation, the Autodiscover record can point to either the on-premises environment or the Office 365, as Autodiscover supports redirection. When the mailbox is located elsewhere, the `--targetAddress` (external email address) configured attribute will be leveraged for redirection. These mail-enabled users will be created in Office 365 for on-premises mailboxes.

■ **Note** The `targetAddress` attribute is used primarily to redirect mail flow. It is essential when exchanging address book information using multiple forests in something called *global address list syncronization* (GALsync). Autodiscover will leverage this attribute to redirect lookups.

To redirect Autodiscover and mail flow, the email domain and service name space of the cloud tenant are used—for example, contoso.onmicrosoft.com, as shown in Figure 11-6.

autodiscover.contoso.com CNAME mail.contoso.com
autodiscover.contoso.onmicrosoft.com CNAME autodiscover.outlook.com

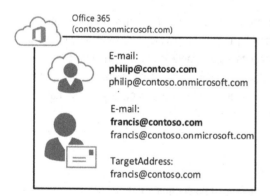

Figure 11-6. Autodiscover redirection using `targetAddress`

In Figure 11-6, Philip is a user with a mailbox in Office 365. His email address is philip@contoso.com. When Outlook does an Autodiscover lookup, it contacts contoso.com for Autodiscover. That request is processed by the on-premises Exchange Server 2013 infrastructure, which finds a mail-enabled user object with that address. It also discovers that its target address is configured as philip@contoso.onmicrosoft.com, and it will return that value to the client. The client can now try to use contoso.onmicrosoft.com for Autodiscover, and this request will successfully be processed by Office 365.

■ **Note** When moving mailboxes from or to Office 365, the `targetAddress` attribute is updated by the mailbox replication service (MRS) that coordinates the move.

DNS Checks

The DNS checker in the Office 365 Admin Center might notify you if your Autodiscover record is not pointing to autodiscover.outlook.com. However, you might not be synchronizing all the on-premises mailboxes as identities to Office 365; you may need to redirect Autodiscover for mail-enabled users yourself, or you may have Autodiscover set up for other trusted Exchange organizations. In such cases, you can leave the Autodiscover record pointing to the on-premises environment. The downside of doing this is that all Autodiscover queries related to cloud-based identities will access your environment first, including services like free/busy.

Optionally, you can turn off the DNS checks in the Office 365 Admin Center, via the `Domains` option, as shown in Figure 11-7.

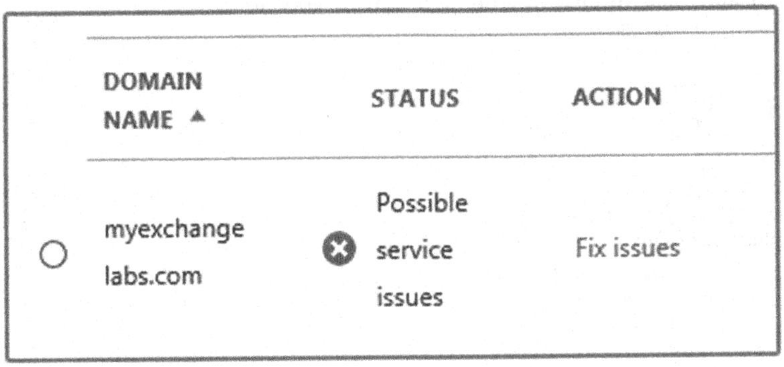

DOMAIN NAME ▲	STATUS	ACTION
⭕ myexchange labs.com	❌ Possible service issues	Fix issues

Figure 11-7. *Office 365 Admin Center DNS checks*

Federation

Your organization and users might need to exchange information with other organizations. For example, companies agreeing to a form of partnership or preparing for an upcoming merger might want to share their calendaring information. Another example is contractors or vendors who want to share product information with the organizations they work for or with.

In earlier versions of Exchange, some information could be shared between Exchange organizations by using something called the *inter-organization replication tool* (IORepl). Because it was limited to information stored in public folders, and because it was replicated information, there were some downsides to using it; for example, you could only use public folder contents such as free/busy information. Also, because replication was involved, the information was not live. Replication was MAPI-based and required forest trusts to prevent its easily traveling on the public network, which is not secure.

Exchange 2007 introduced Exchange Web Services (EWS). Together with the Availability service, it does not require setting up replication; rather, it enables a web-like exchange of information by using a secure http and a service account to authenticate the lookup in the remote organization. However, trust and provisioning of contact objects for external organizations were still required for initiating and directing the lookup.

■ **Tip** The default availability period for lookup is different from that for Exchange 2007 (42 days) or Exchange 2010 and Exchange 2013 (62 days). This may result in failed availability requests—for example, when using Exchange 2013 with Exchange 2007 in co-existence scenarios or as a hybrid server. To align these values, extend the default availability lookup period of Exchange 2007. To do this, edit the `$exinstall\ClientAccess\ExchWeb\` `EWS\web.config` file on all your Exchange 2007 CAS, and add the following item to the `AppSettings` section: `<add key="maximumQueryIntervalDays" value="62" />`.

Starting with Exchange 2010, *federation* was introduced to allow the secure sharing of information between Exchange organizations (see Figure 11-8). After configuration, the federation delegation uses organization relationships among its partners. For organizations to federate, they establish a trust relationship via the Windows Azure Active Directory authentication system. Formerly known as Microsoft federation gateway (MFG), the Windows Azure Active Directory authentication system functions as an online trust broker. This approach does away with the earlier requirement of having to configure trusts and set up accounts for sharing information. If you trust the Windows Azure Active Directory authentication system, and it has verified your domain, you are good to go.

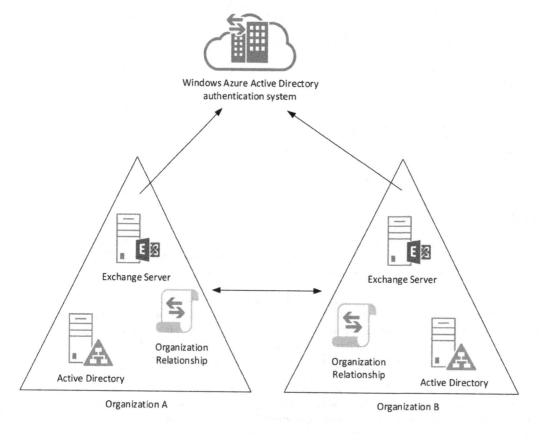

Figure 11-8. *Federation through the Windows Azure AD authentication system*

▦ **Note**   Cloud-only organizations in Office 365—those using the small business plans included—are already trusted and enabled for federation.

Before Exchange Exchange 2010 Service Pack 2, organizations were required to manually set up and configure the federation and do all the other steps that the hybrid configuration wizard (HCW) now performs to configure the mail flow, such as configuring the connectors in their on-premises environments or in their Office 365 cloud tenants, or establishing better Exchange Online protection.

When you're setting up a hybrid configuration in Exchange 2013, the supported procedure is the HCW. This tool configures the federation automatically, allowing organizations running the Exchange hybrid to share information between mailboxes in the on-premises Exchange 2013 and the cloud-based mailboxes.

▦ **Caution**   The HCW must run successfully for your Exchange hybrid deployment to be supported.

The HCW in Exchange 2013 works according to the following sequence:

1. Using the HCS, you define the desired state. Part of the process is proving ownership of the domain names you want to enable for federation by creating TXT records in the public DNS containing hash secrets. So, be prepared to make changes in the public DNS when running the HCW.

   Under the hood, the desired hybrid configuration is then stored in Active Directory using the cmdlet Set-HybridConfiguration. The location of the information is below the Configuration container at CN=Hybrid Configuration,CN=<Exchange Organization Name>,CN=Microsoft Exchange,CN=Services.

2. At the completion of the HCW, you run Update-HybridConfiguration. This triggers the hybrid configuration engine.

3. The engine reads the desired state.

4. The engine discovers the current on-premises Exchange and Office 365 configuration.

5. Based on the desired state and the current on-premises Exchange and Office 365 configuration state, the engine determines the delta and executes tasks to realize the desired state. Depending on the delta, these tasks may include:

   - Managing accepted domains for mail flow and Autodiscover requests. Your Office 365 tenant will have a domain in the form of <domain name>.onmicrosoft.com. This address space is added to the default email address policy, and secondary email addresses are stamped with this address for internal routing—that is, between the on-premises environment and Office 365.

   - Configuring an on-premises certificate for secure messaging between the on-premises environment and Office 365 using TLS.

   - Configuring the federation and defining the organizational relationships between the on-premises environment and Office 365, and vice-versa.

- Configuring the secure mail flow on on-premises CAS and Mailbox servers or Edge servers, and Exchange Online Protection (EOP) in Office 365. You also have the option to always route outbound messages through your on-premises organization using the `Enable centralized mail transport` option. (There's more on mail flow later in this chapter).

- Configuring the OAuth authentication (as of Exchange 2013 Cumulative Update 5 and up). (There's more on this later in this chapter).

■ **Note** One thing the HCW does not configure is your public MX record. If you want to direct inbound messages via Exchange Online Protection, you need to reconfigure the MX record and point it to the `< domain>.mail.protection.outlook.com`, where you replace the dot in your domain name with a dash—for example, `myexchangelabs-com.mail.protection.outlook.com`.

When the wizard is finished, your organization is ready to start federating with other trusted organizations.

When free/busy lookups are performed for federated organizations, the Availability service follows the same route as Autodiscover, as described in the Autodiscover section earlier in this chapter. In this process, the organization relationship definitions are consulted to check if one exists for the target domain. If not, no lookup is performed. If one exists, Exchange requests a token from the Windows Azure AD authentication system, which it uses in sending requests to the server handling the target domain. Of course, if the target organization does not trust the Windows Azure AD authentication system, no token is returned and the lookup fails. When successful, the Exchange server in the target domain receives the request with the authorization token, after which information is returned to the requester, following permitted sharing policies.

■ **Caution** The federation scenario for on-premises Exchange 2013 with other organizations running Exchange hybrid doesn't work for cloud-based mailboxes. Because the on-premises Exchange server performing the availability lookup has an organizational relationship with the on-premises Exchange organization of the partner, it will not proxy the request to Office 365 after receiving a `targetAddress` redirect to `@<tenant>.onmicrosoft.com address`. A workaround is to create an organizational relationship with `<tenant>.onmicrosoft.com` for partners and to use those addresses for email or to configure them as `targetAddress` on locally stored contacts objects. However, this is far from ideal, as it requires you to know which partner mailboxes are cloud-based and which are not.

Each time the HCW runs, as well as when you're updating the hybrid configuration, it logs its steps in a text file stored in `$ExInstall\Logging\Update-HybridConfiguration`. When for some reason the configuration fails, the file provides pointers to the cause of the problem. You can also use the remote connectivity analyzer (RCA) to troubleshoot connectivity issues that might be preventing your setting up Exchange hybrid. You can find the RCA at `http://exrca.com`.

After running the HCW succesfully, you can verify the federation trust configuration of your on-premises Exchange organization by running the `Test-FederationTrust` cmdlet from an on-premises EMS session. Each step of the test should result in success, as shown in Figure 11-9.

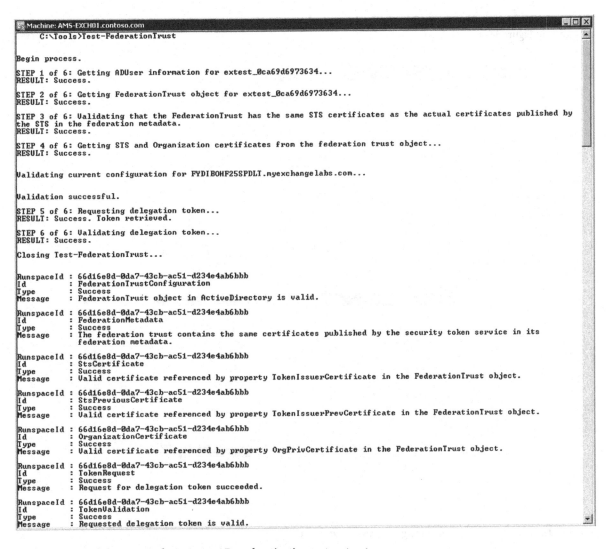

Figure 11-9. *Validating Windows Azure AD authentication system trust*

Sharing of Information

Sharing information is possible on two levels in Exchange 2013 and Office 365:

- **Organization relationships**, or organizational sharing as it is named in Office 365, allow federated organizations to share calendar information with other federated organizations.

- **Sharing policies** allow user sharing of calendar information.

Because your on-premises Exchange organization is separate from your cloud-based tenant, you will have two locations where organizational relationships and sharing policies are defined. These settings are not synchronized. Running HCW will configure the sharing policies for your on-premises organization, as well as for the cloud tenant.

You can inspect and configure the current sharing policy by using the ECP, navigating to Organization ➤ Sharing, as shown in Figure 11-10.

Figure 11-10. *Configuring your sharing policies through ECP*

As you can see in Figure 11-10, the HCW has created an on-premises organizational relationship "On-Premises to Office 365 - <GUID>" for the domain myexchangelabs.onmicrosoft.com, which is the domain of the tenant in Office 365. The GUID postfix in the name is the organization's GUID. This value matches the GUID property of Get-OrganizationConfig–for example, (Get-OrganizationConfig).Guid.

Organizational Relationships

You can view the configured organizational relationship by using the cmdlet Get-OrganizationRelationship. If you run this cmdlet in a remote EMS session, you will see the existing organizational relationships, such as the one created by the HCW wizard. This is the counterpart of the organizational relationship it has created on-premises, as shown in Figure 11-10. If you pipe the output to format-list (fl), you can inspect all its properties, using Get-OrganizationalRelationship | fl, as shown in Figure 11-11.

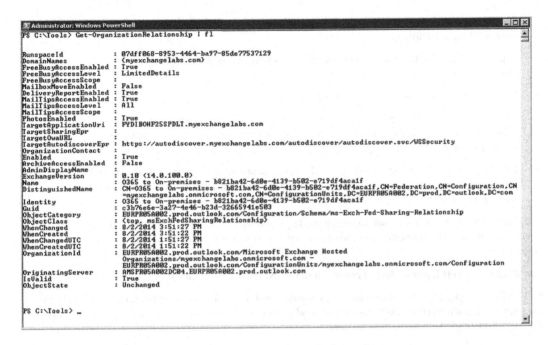

Figure 11-11. *Inspecting the configuration of organizational relationships*

In Figure 11-11, you can see that the cloud-based mailboxes can access certain shared information from the on-premises mailboxes by using the on-premises address space, myexchangelabs.com. The information that is shared with the address spaces configured through the DomainNames property is defined with the following properties:

- FreeBusyAccessEnabled sets if the organization wants to share free/busy information.

- FreeBusyAccessLevel sets the amount of detail that is shared as part of the free/busy information. Possible options are:

  - *None* when no free/busy access is shared.

  - *AvailabilityOnly* when only free/busy with time information is shared.

  - *LimitedDetails* when free/busy is shared with time, subject, and location information.

- FreeBusyAccessScope can be used to limit the information sharing to a certain security group. When this is not set, the free/busy settings in the organizational relationship apply to the whole organization.

- MailboxMoveEnabled sets if mailboxes can be moved to the external organization.

- DeliveryReportEnabled sets if the organization wants to share delivery report information. This needs to be enabled in both organizations when they want to perform cross-organization message tracking.

- ArchiveAccessEnabled sets whether the organization has been configured to provide access to remote personal archives. This needs to be enabled in your on-premises organizational relationship setting for the related tenant in Office 365 when using Exchange Online Archiving (EOA), for example.

- `MailTipsAccessEnabled` sets if the mail tips information is returned when requested by users in the external organization.

- `MailTipsAccessLevel` sets the amount of detail that is returned with the mail tips. Options are:

  - *None* when no mail tips information is to be returned.

  - *Limited* when only mail tips are to be returned that can prevent nondelivery reports (NDR) or automatic replies such as out-of-office notifications (OOF). Custom, large audience, and moderated recipient mail tips are not returned.

  - *All* when all mail tips are to be returned. The external organization is treated as external, which is important to know when setting transport rules. It also means that the external organization will receive external out-of-office notifications.

- `MailTipsAccessScope` can be used to return mail tips only for certain security groups. When this is not set, the mail tips settings in the organization relationship are applied to the whole organization.

- `PhotosEnabled` **sets if photo data is returned to the external organization.**

When the HCW is running, you are only asked to provide the level of free/busy information to be shared between the on-premises environment and Office 365. It is recommended you not change the default settings as configured, as rerunning the wizard would likely reset those values.

Custom Organizational Relationships

It is possible to create a custom organizational relationship with another federated partner. You can accomplish this through ECP, via Organization ➤ Sharing ➤ Organization Sharing. You select the New button and enter the relationship details, such as name, domain name of the organization you want to share with, and what level of information you want to share, as shown in Figure 11-12.

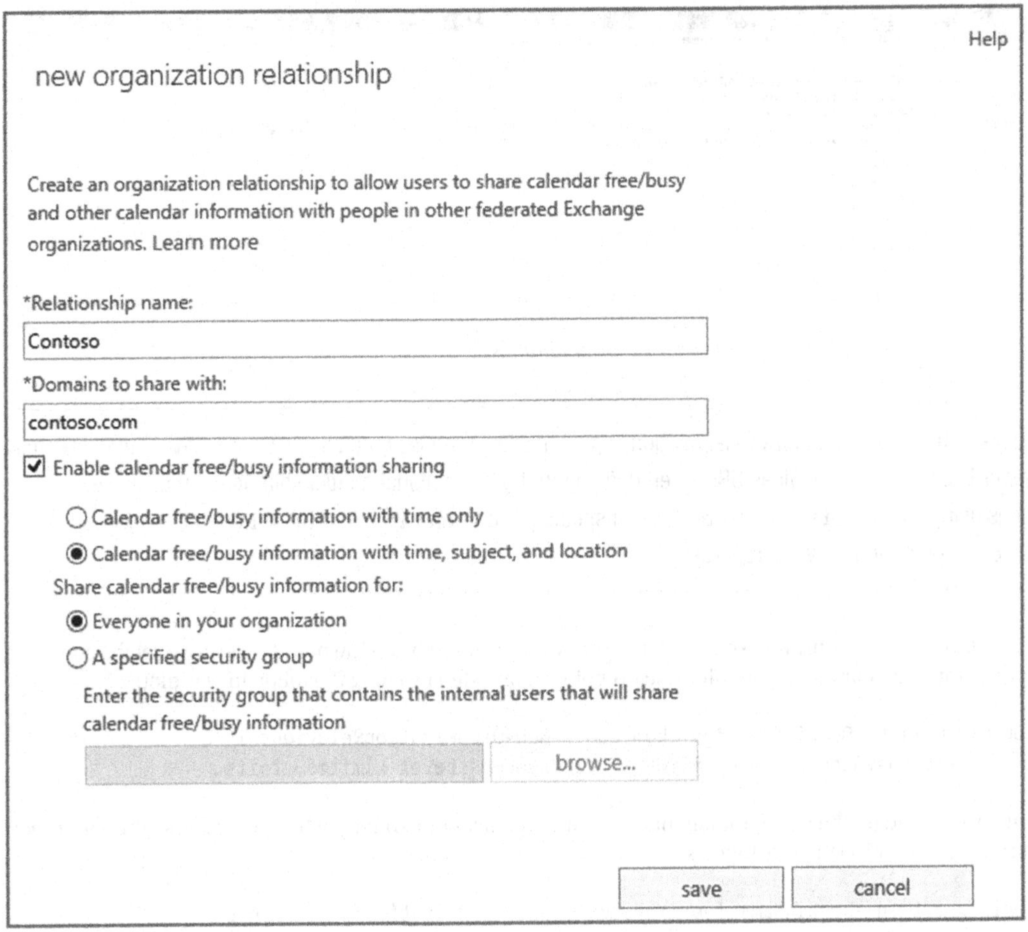

Figure 11-12. Creating a custom organizational relationship

Note Although the field caption is "Domains to share with," you can enter a single domain name. However, you can add additional domain names after you have saved the relationship.

To accomplish the same thing using the EMS, you use the `New-OrganizationalRelationship` cmdlet. The federated partner might have more than one domain name registered for federation, which you may also need to include in your organizational relationship definition.

For example, if you want to make sure you include all domain names that myexchangelabs.com has set up for federation, you can use `Get-FederationInformation`. To retrieve the domain names for a domain-named myexchangelabs.com, you use `Get-FederationInformation -DomainName myexchangelabs.com`, as shown in Figure 11-13.

```
Machine: AMS-EXCH01.contoso.com                                                                    _□✕
        C:\Tools>Get-FederationInformation -DomainName myexchangelabs.com

RunspaceId            : 72c63349-4a63-4722-934d-bdc7f8c0bdb6
TargetApplicationUri  : FYDIBOHF25SPDLT.myexchangelabs.com
DomainNames           : {myexchangelabs.com}
TargetAutodiscoverEpr : https://autodiscover.myexchangelabs.com/autodiscover/autodiscover.svc/WSSecurity
TokenIssuerUris       : {urn:federation:MicrosoftOnline}
Identity              :
IsValid               : True
ObjectState           : Unchanged


        C:\Tools>_
```

Figure 11-13. Viewing the federation information for domain names

---

■ **Note**   If you are setting up an organizational relationship with an on-premises organization, you may need to overrule the Autodiscover or Exchange Web Services URL when defining that organizational relationship. You can view the registered settings using `Get-FederationInformation`, inspecting the `TargetApplicationUri` (Web Services) and `TargetAutodiscoverEpr` (Autodiscover) properties.

In Figure 11-13, you see that only myexchangelabs.com was registered by the owner of myexchangelabs.com. You can create an organizational relationship for all these domains in one step by using the following cmdlet:

```
Get-FederationInformation -DomainName fabrikam.com | New-OrganizationRelationship
-Name 'Fabrikam' -FreeBusyAccessEnabled $true -FreeBusyAccessLevel LimitedDetails
```

Should you need to update the list of domain names in an organizational relationship, you can use the same trick with `Set-OrganizationRelationship`, as follows:

```
Get-FederationInformation -DomainName fabrikam.com | Set-OrganizationRelationship
-Identity 'Fabrikam'
```

■ **Tip**   Before you can customize sharing for your cloud tenant, you may be required to enable the tenant customization using the cmdlet `Enable-OrganizationCustomization`. To accomplish this, connect to a remote EMS session and run the cmdlet.

Should you need to alter one of the other sharing settings, you can use `Set-OrganizationRelationship` with the parameters as descibed earlier for `Get-OrganizationRelationship`. For example,

```
Set-OrganizationRelationship -Identity 'Fabrikam'
 -FreeBusyAccessEnabled:$true -FreeBusyAccessLevel AvailabilityOnly
-MailTipsAccessEnabled:$true -MailTipsAccessLevel All
```

You can also restrict the sharing to certain groups by using the `FreeBusyAccessScope` parameter. For example, to configure the organizational relationship "Fabrikam" to only share the information of a member of the group called "Fabrikam Sales," you use:

```
Set-OrganizationRelationship -Identity 'Fabrikam' -FreeBusyAccessScope 'Fabrikam Sales'
```

Note that you need to maintain these organizational relationships in your on-premises Exchange environment, as well as for your Office 365 tenant.

■ **Note** When deploying the Exchange 2013 hybrid server in a pre-Exchange 2013 environment, you need to perform one additional step, which is to define the method that the Availability service should use to look up free/busy information so that down-level CAS traffic is proxied through the Exchange 2013 hybrid server. This is done using the Add-AvailabilityAddressSpace cmdlet. For example, to define the access method for an external trusted organization using the domain fabrikam.com, which for Exchange Web Services FQDN is mail.fabrikam.com, you use:

Add-AvailabilityAddressSpace -ForestName fabrikam.com -AccessMethod InternalProxy

-UseServiceAccount:$true -ProxyUrl https://mail.fabrikam.com/EWS/Exchange.asmx.

You can configure the OWA URL when users with cloud-based mailboxes use the on-premises OWA URL to redirect to—for example, mail.contoso.com. When cloud-based mailbox users use this URL, they might receive an error message that the Outlook WebApp address is invalid. Instead, they should use something like https://outlook.com/owa/contoso.com.

To redirect those users, you configure the TargetOWAUrl property of the organizational relationship between on-premises and Office 365—for example, "On-premises to O365 - <GUID>." Here are the steps:

1. Create a CNAME record for the cloud-based OWA mail access and point it to outlook.com:

    cloudmail   CNAME   outlook.com

2. Use Set-OrganizationRelationship with TargetOWAUrl to redirect users; for example,

    Get-OrganizationRelationShip 'On-premises to O365 *' |
    Set-OrganizationRelationship
     -TargetOWAUrl http://cloudmail.fabrikam.com/owa

At some point, you may want to test your organizational relationship. To do so, you use Test-OrganizationRelationship, specifying the name of the organizational relationship object to use as Identity and the mailbox to consult as UserIdentity. For example, to test an organizational relationship named "EighTwOne" in the current Exchange organization to access a mailbox named francis@myexchangelabs.com, you use:

Test-OrganizationRelationship -UserIdentity francis@myexchangelabs.com -Identity EighTwOne

As you can see in Figure 11-14, the organizational relationship is valid, but there are warning related to a case mismatch between the configured TargetApplicationUri on the relationship and the ApplicationUri on the federation trust (Get-FederationTrust), as well as a problem verifying the relationship. In this example, you could fix that by enabling WS-Security on the Autodiscover and Web Services by running the following cmdlets:

Get-OrganizationRelationship | Set-OrganizationRelationship
 -TargetApplicationUri http://fydibohf25spdlt.myexchangelabs.com

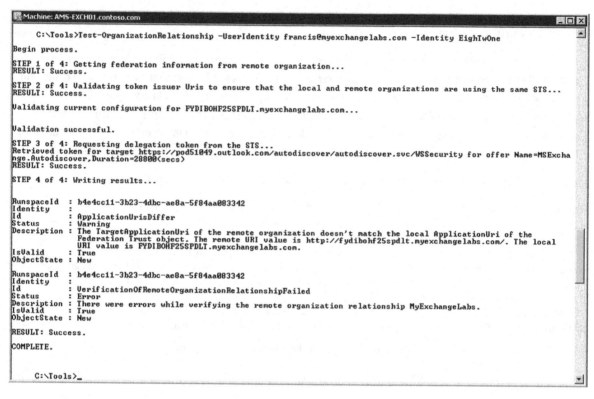

```
Machine: AMS-EXCH01.contoso.com                                                    _ □ X

      C:\Tools>Test-OrganizationRelationship -UserIdentity francis@myexchangelabs.com -Identity EighTwOne

Begin process.

STEP 1 of 4: Getting federation information from remote organization...
RESULT: Success.

STEP 2 of 4: Validating token issuer Uris to ensure that the local and remote organizations are using the same STS...
RESULT: Success.

Validating current configuration for FYDIBOHF25SPDLT.myexchangelabs.com...

Validation successful.

STEP 3 of 4: Requesting delegation token from the STS...
Retrieved token for target https://pod51049.outlook.com/autodiscover/autodiscover.svc/WSSecurity for offer Name=MSExcha
nge.Autodiscover,Duration=28800(secs)
RESULT: Success.

STEP 4 of 4: Writing results...

RunspaceId   : b4e4cc11-3b23-4dbc-ae8a-5f84aa083342
Identity     :
Id           : ApplicationUrisDiffer
Status       : Warning
Description  : The TargetApplicationUri of the remote organization doesn't match the local ApplicationUri of the
               Federation Trust object. The remote URI value is http://fydibohf25spdlt.myexchangelabs.com/. The local
               URI value is FYDIBOHF25SPDLT.myexchangelabs.com.
IsValid      : True
ObjectState  : New

RunspaceId   : b4e4cc11-3b23-4dbc-ae8a-5f84aa083342
Identity     :
Id           : VerificationOfRemoteOrganizationRelationshipFailed
Status       : Error
Description  : There were errors while verifying the remote organization relationship MyExchangeLabs.
IsValid      : True
ObjectState  : New

RESULT: Success.

COMPLETE.

    C:\Tools>_
```

Figure 11-14. *Testing the organizational relationship*

After configuring the organizational relationship and enabling the sharing of free/busy information, you can schedule meetings with recipients in that domain (see Figure 11-15). You will notice that the relationship is working when you are not confronted with the free/busy information bar of the recipient displaying an arced "No information available" bar.

Figure 11-15. *Scheduling meetings with other federated organizations*

■ **Tip**   If your free/busy lookups stop working, check if the federation trust is still okay by using Test-FederationTrust. If it reports "Failed to validater delegation token," try to refresh the metadata of the on-premises federation trust by using Get-FederationTrust | Set-FederationTrust -RefreshMetaData:$true.

Sharing Policies

Whereas organizational relationships define how information is shared, sharing policies, or individual sharing, as it is called in ECP, define the user calendar-sharing options. This includes sharing calendar or contact information with users of both federated organizations and non-federated organizations. In the latter case, Internet publishing is used instead.

The sharing policies define what users are allowed to share, and the action of sharing that information is end-user initiated. When you want to manage the sharing policies through the ECP, you navigate to Organization ➤ Sharing. In the bottom area named "**Individual Sharing,**" you will find the currently configured sharing policies, as shown in Figure 11-16.

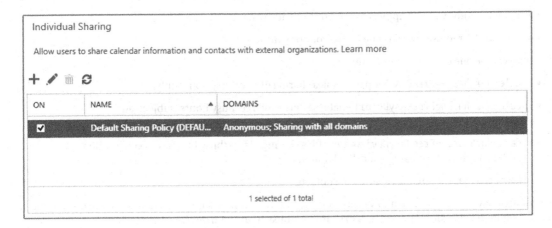

Figure 11-16. Default sharing policy for calendar information

When using the EMS, you can retrieve the list of current sharing policies by using Get-SharingPolicy. You'll see that, out of the box, there is one sharing policy already configured: the **default sharing policy**. To inspect the configuration of this policy, you use Get-SharingPolicy | fl Name, Domains, Enabled, as shown in Figure 11-17.

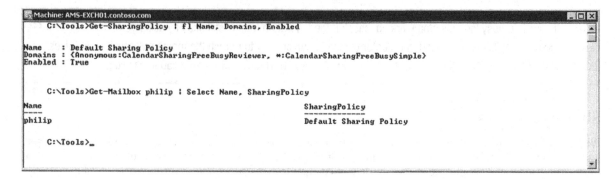

Figure 11-17. View of the sharing policies and sharing policy assignment

In Figure 11-17, you can see that there are two entries configured in the default sharing policy: Anonymous :CalendarSharingFreeBusyReviewer and *:CalendarSharingFreeBusySimple. The format of these entries is Domain:Action[,Action], whereby:

- The domain "**Anonymous**" applies to everyone outside your organization.

- The domain "*****" represents everyone inside your organization.

- Action can be one of the following values:

    - CalendarSharingFreeBusySimple enables sharing of free/busy hours only.

    - CalendarSharingFreeBusyDetail enables sharing of free/busy hours, subject, and location.

    - CalendarSharingFreeBusyReviewer enables sharing of free/busy hours, subject, location, and the body of the message or calendar item.

    - ContactsSharing enables sharing of contacts.

So, the default policy is configured to allow users to share free/busy hours, subject, location, and the body of the message or calendar item with external users, and to share free/busy hours with any internal domain.

■ **Caution** For anonymous calendar and contact sharing features to work, verify that AnonymousFeaturesEnabled is set to True on the OWA virtual directory. To enable this for all OWA virtual directories, you use Get-OwaVirtualDirectory | Set-OwaVirtualDirectory -AnonymousFeaturesEnabled $true.

Let's create a new sharing policy named "Custom Sharing Policy," and allow users to share CalendarSharingFreeBusyReviewer and contact information with the domain eightwone.com. For this you need to run New-SharingPolicy as follows:

```
New-SharingPolicy -Name 'Custom Sharing Policy'
 -Domains 'eightwone.com:CalendarSharingFreeBusyReviewer,ContactsSharing'
```

Now, suppose you want to allow `CalendarSharingFreeBusySimple` sharing with all other external domains and make this sharing policy the new default policy. You need to run `Set-SharingPolicy`, as follows:

```
Set-SharingPolicy -Identity 'Custom Sharing Policy'
 -Domains @{Add='Anonymous:CalendarSharingFreeBusySimple'} -Default:$true
```

Each mailbox is assigned one sharing policy. This will be the default sharing policy unless you have configured another sharing policy as the default. To assign a mailbox a different sharing policy, you use `Set-Mailbox` with the `SharingPolicy` parameter. For example, to assign your new "Custom Sharing Policy" to a mailbox called francis@myexchangelabs.com, you use the following, as shown in Figure 11-18:

```
Set-Mailbox -Identity francis@myexchangelabs.com -SharingPolicy 'Custom Sharing Policy'
```

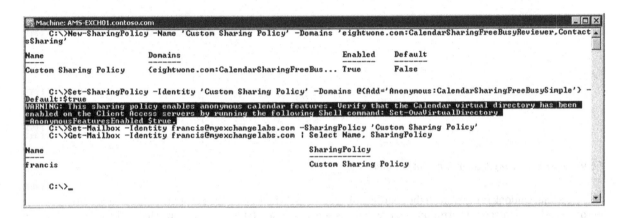

Figure 11-18. *Creating a custom sharing policy and assigning it to a mailbox*

Now, if the user wants to share his calendar or contacts folder, he can use the Share Calendar or Share Contacts folder options from Outlook. For calendar sharing, he may choose a lower level of detail than allowed by the policy by adjusting the Details option, as shown in Figure 11-19.

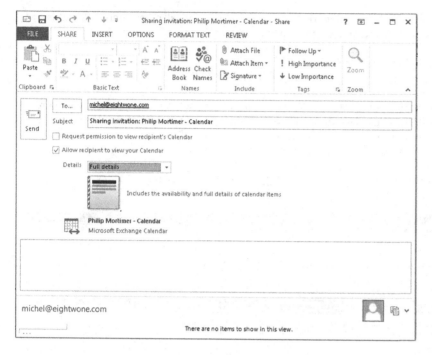

Figure 11-19. *Sharing a calendar from Outlook*

Note that Outlook is unaware of the sharing policy settings. When a user tries to share more details than permitted, she will receive an error message as soon as she tries to send the email with the sharing link. Also, when the intended recipient is not part of a trusted organization, the user is notified and she will need to use Internet Calendar Publishing instead (see next section).

■ **Note**   The link sent to recipients to access the calendar or contacts is obfuscated but is not password protected.

After sending the link to contacts in the internal organization, you can configure the permissions on the Calendar or Contacts folder by using the Calendar Permissions or Contacts Permissions button, as shown in Figure 11-20.

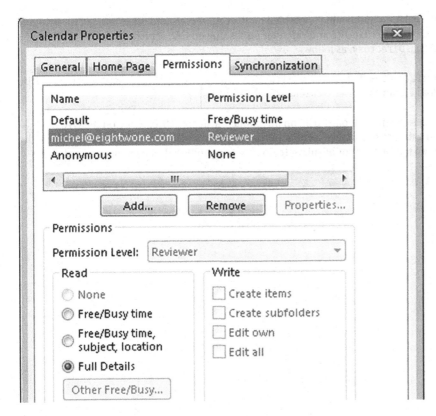

Figure 11-20. Changing the calendar sharing permissions in Outlook

Internet Calendar Publishing

To share calendar information with non-federated or non-Exchange recipients, users can be allowed to publish their calendar online, depending on the effective sharing policy configuration.

To allow outbound traffic to go from the Mailbox server through an Internet proxy, you may need to configure this proxy on your Mailbox servers so they can reach the Internet. For example,

```
Get-MailboxServer | Set-ExchangeServer -InternetWebProxy http://proxy.contoso.com
```

If your web proxy uses a different port, you can specify this as well; for example,

```
Get-ExchangeServer | Set-ExchangeServer -InternetWebProxy http://proxy.contoso.com:8080
```

You can clear the Internet web proxy setting by using $null as the value.

■ **Caution**   When configuring InternetWebProxy, make sure you use the *http* scheme in the URL, not *https*. When you specify *https*, federation-related cmdlets going through the defined proxy will not work.

Next, you need to verify that the calender publishing is enabled on the CAS servers and the external URL is configured. For example, to configure the external URL and calendar publishing on CAS servers AMS-EXCH01 and AMS-EXCH02, you use Set-OwaVirtualDirectory, as follows:

```
'AMS-EXCH01','AMS-EXCH02' | ForEach-Object { Set-OwaVirtualDirectory -Identity "$_\owa (Default Web Site)" -ExternalUrl 'https://mail.contoso.com' -CalendarEnabled $true }
```

After that, the user can publish his calendar, or parts of it, on the publicly available URL, based on the OWA external URL. When you are initiating the sharing of the calendar publishing from Outlook by using Publish Online, the OWA is opened and you can configure the calendar publishing. To do so, when prompted, you enter your credentials.

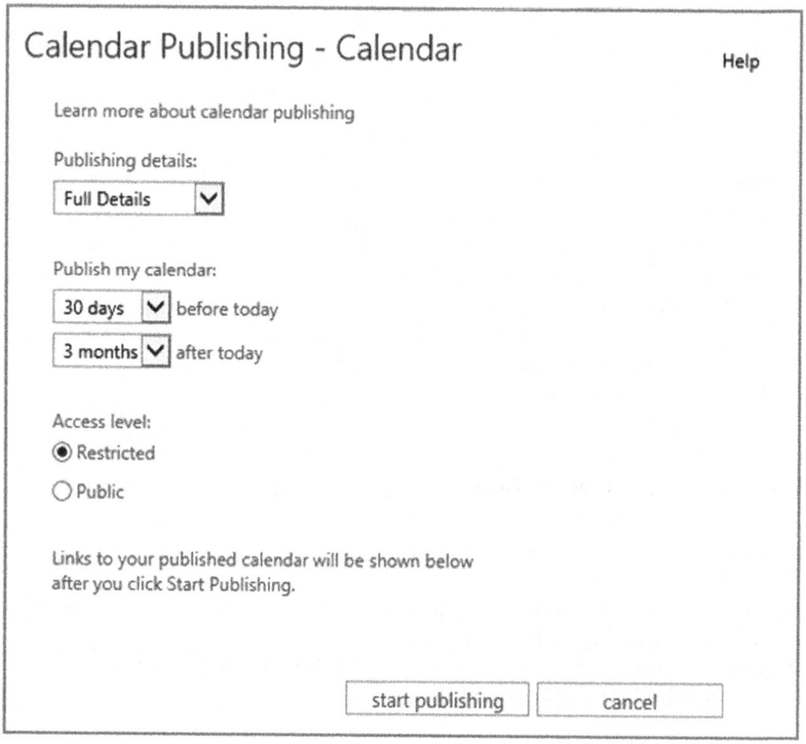

Figure 11-21. Enabling Internet Calendar Publishing

The calendar is published as an iCalendar ICS file and as an HTML page. The URL is based on the Internet web proxy setting and access level as specified. When Public is selected, the URL is relatively simple; as with Restricted, a GUID and hash are added to make the URL less obvious. However, selecting Public or Restricted does not change the permissions on the file itself. For example, the location to access the iCalendar file of philip@myexchangelabs.com would be as follows:

- Public: http://mail.myexchangelabs.com/owa/calendar/philip@myexchangelabs.com/ Calendar/calendar.ics

- Restricted (the hashes will vary): http://mail.myexchangelabs.com/owa/calendar/58b843 d23d124ae2af0fc1e338e1357f@myexchangelabs.com/865a2dcb67814672b2e9fec0240a4f9 c9679842447551712479/ calendar.ics

Although less likely to be guessed or memorized, the URL is not secure because http is used, despite your specifying https with the `Internet WebProxy` setting, and so the .ICS file remains unprotected. You could tighten security on the /owa/calendar folder on the CAS servers, or the reverse-proxy, if applicable, by disallowing anonymous access and enabling Digest or Basic authentication. Basic should be used only when SSL is required to access the ICS file, or else passwords will travel the wire in clear text.

■ **Note** ICS (iCal) is a calendar file format that is compatible with many applications, including Outlook.

Should you need to manually add ICS calendars to Outlook, you can open up the Calendar view, right-click Calendars, and select Add Calendar ➤ From Internet, as shown in Figure 11-22. Then you are asked to provide the location of the ICS file.

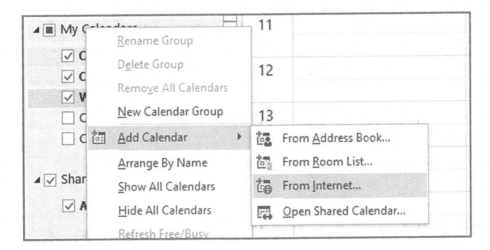

Figure 11-22. Manually adding Internet Calendar to Outlook

OAuth Authentication

OAuth is an authentication protocol that provides applications or services a secure way to delegate access to their resources. In the world of Exchange 2013, this means allowing applications such as Lync Server 2013 and SharePoint Server 2013 to authenticate to Exchange 2013 or vice-versa, using OAuth. For this purpose, those applications are configured as partner applications. Configuring OAuth enables cross-application functionality, such as cross-product In-Place eDiscovery.

Configuring OAuth in an on-premises environment involves running the `Configure-EnterpriseApplication.ps1` script, located in $exscripts folder—for example, C\Program Files\Microsoft\Exchange\v15\Scripts. For instance, to configure OAuth for Lync, you use:

```
$exscripts\Configure-EnterprisePartnerApplication.ps1
-AuthMetaDataUrl https://lync.contoso.com/metadata/json/1 -ApplicationType Lync
```

In this example, you replace the `AuthMetaDataUrl` value with the URL through which your `AuthMetaData` for Lync is published.

If you want to integrate your Exchange hybrid deployment with Office 365, you need to configure OAuth as well. OAuth enables organizations to use features across premises, such as in-place discovery or in-place archiving. For example, OAuth enables searching on-premises mailboxes with cloud-based personal archives.

Unfortunately, the HCW in Exchange 2013 Service Pack 1 did not configure OAuth between on-premises and Office 365. If you are using this version of Exchange 2013, you need to manually configure OAuth as documented at `http://bit.ly/OAuthConfig`. At the time of this writing, Exchange 2013 Cumulative Update 6 is available. The HCW of Exchange 2013 Cumulative Update 5 and later includes the steps to configure OAuth automatically (see Figure 11-23).

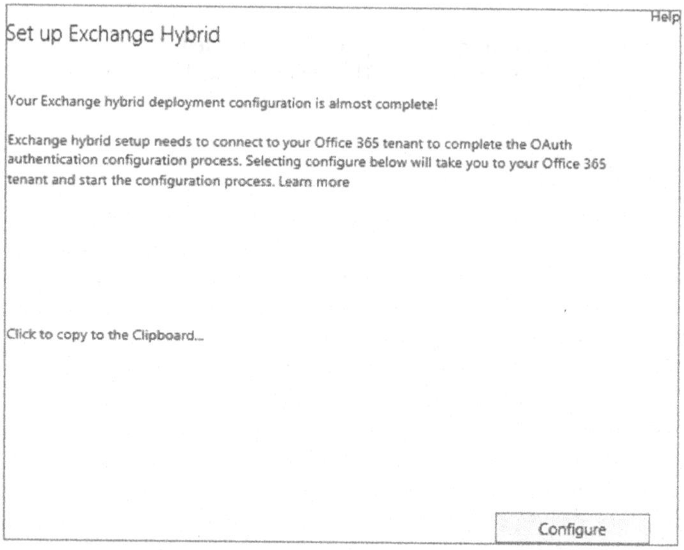

Figure 11-23. *OAuth prompt in the HCW*

This process involves redirection to a website where you will be asked to download and run two application manifests of around 20 MB each that will configure OAuth. These manifests should be run from an Exchange server, as they depend on some Exchange components. Also, you need to make sure your browser is not locked down, as you must be allowed to download and run these two applications.

Alternatively, you can follow the manual procedure; a link was provided earlier in this section.

■ **Caution**   OAuth configuration is required for organizations exclusively running Exchange 2013. Organizations running a mix of Exchange 2013 and Exchange 2010 or Exchange 2007 will not use OAuth for authentication and will rely instead on the federation trust. When this situation is detected, the wizard will skip the OAuth configuration option.

After setting up OAuth, you can test OAuth from the on-premises environment to Office 365 and vice versa by using Test-OAuthConnectivity and specifying the remote service URI, as well as a mailbox you want to use for testing. You can specify the application to test using service—for example, EWS, AutoD for Autodiscover, Sharepoint, or generic.

```
Test-OAuthConnectivity -Service EWS -TargetUri https://outlook.office365.com/ews/exchange.asmx
  -Mailbox <mailbox>-Verbose
```

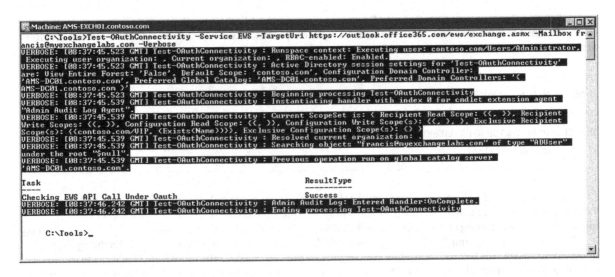

Figure 11-24. *Testing the OAuth configuration*

When testing this configuration from a remote EMS session in Office 365, you use your local service URI—for example, `https://mail.myexchangelabs.com/EWS/Exchange.asmx`–in combination with an on-premises mailbox.

Access Management

One of the consequences of operating multiple environments with separate identities is having to authenticate to each platform when accessing each's resources. When you are using a combination of on-premises Active Directory and Office 365, this situation is no different. The on-premises identity is a different one from that stored in Azure Active Directory. However, to mitigate the situation and make the end-user experience easier when alternating between on-premises and Office 365 resources, there are two options:

- **Password synchronization** (same sign-on) can be used to synchronize passwords so users can utilize the same account name and password in the on-premises environment as in Office 365.

- **Federated identities** (single sign-on) allows users to access Office 365 by using their on-premises credentials.

Windows Azure Active Directory Synchronization Tool

■ **Note** At the time of this writing, Microsoft published the next version of the WAADsync tool and rebranded it Azure Active Directory Sync (AADsync). Some enhancements in this version are support for synchronization with multiple forests, including the option for password synchronization. The new tool should provide at least the same functionality as WAADsync.

Originally, Microsoft offered a tool called DirSync to provision objects in Office 365 (or formerly, Business Productivity Online Suite), using information from on-premises environments for cloud tenants. However, password synchronization was not an option; as a result, passwords could differ and there were separate policies effective for each environment.

In February 2014, version 6382.0 of WAADsync was released, in which Microsoft introduced the password synchronization feature. Thus, the password hash from the on-premises Active Directory is sychronized with Azure Active Directory, in addition to carrying other attributes. This creates a seamless sign-in logon experience.

■ **Note** Before you implement WAADsync, it is recommended you use a tool called IdFix to identify erroneous users, contacts, and groups that may be in your Active Directory and that could lead to synchronization problems. Running IdFix upfront allows you to remediate the situation ahead of time. You can download the IdFix tool at http://bit.ly/IdFixTool.

Password policies for the on-premises environment override password policies configured in Office 365, except for cloud-only users. Be advised that the passwords of synchronized users in Office 365 are set to never expire, meaning those users can log on to Office 365 while having an expired on-premises password.

When you are configuring WAADsync, you will be asked at some point if you want to **enable Exchange hybrid deployment**. Check this box, as it will allow WAADsync to write back specific attributes from Office 365 to the on-premises environment (see Figure 11-25). This is used, for example, when deploying Exchange Online Archiving or when offboarding mailboxes.

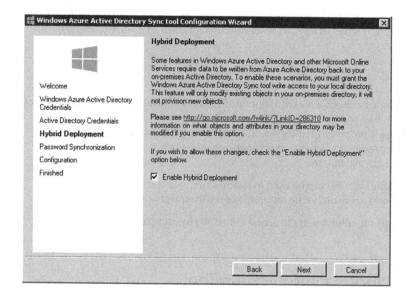

Figure 11-25. Enabling hybrid deployment in WAADsync

The attributes that are written back from Office 365 to the on-premises environment are listed in Table 11-2.

Table 11-2. *WAADsync Hybrid Deployment Write-Back Attributes*

Attribute	Purpose
msExchArchiveStatus	Personal archive status for users using cloud-based personal archives—i.e., Exchange Online Archiving.
msExchUserHoldPolicies	In-place hold status of mailboxes.
ProxyAddresses (LegacyExchangeDN as X500)	Email addresses of mailboxes to provision mail-enabled users (MEUs) on-premises. Those MEUs can be used as targets when offboarding mailboxes, but also to provision address books.
SafeSendersHash BlockedSendersHash SafeRecipientHash	Filtering and online safe and blocked sender information.
msExchUCVoiceMailSettings	Voice-mail status for users having cloud-based voice mail configured.

■ **Note**   To prevent nondelivery reports when replying to old email messages (as those messages will be using the x500 address stored in the named cache file instead of the SMTP address presented), the legacyExchangeDN is written back as a secondary x500 address on the mail-enabled user. This is the reverse of provisioning mail-enabled users for mailbox move targets, performed by WAADsync and scripts like Prepare-MoveRequest.ps1, for example. This prevents nondelivery messages when you are offboarding mailboxes.

After you've implemented WAADsync, you'll find it runs every three hours, meaning attribute changes in your local Active Directory will be synchronized with Azure Active Directory in, at most, three hours' time. The exception to this are password changes, which are replicated every two minutes.

Alternatively, you can force manual synchronization, as shown in Figure 11-26, as follows:

1. On the server running WAADsync, start a PowerShell session.

2. Import the WAADsync module using Import-Module WAADsync.

3. Execute the cmdlet Start-OnlineCoexistenceSync.

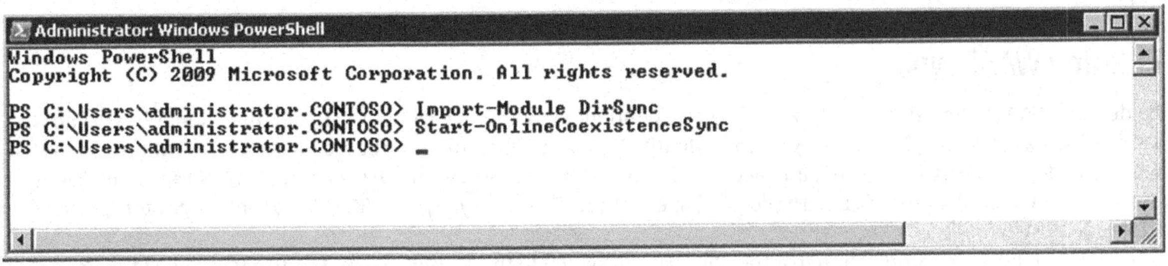

Figure 11-26. *Manually synchronizing Active Directory with Azure Active Directory*

To inspect the synchronization status in Office 365, you can check the portal at Dashboard ➤ Users and Groups ➤ Active Users in the Active Directory synchronization section, as shown in Figure 11-17.

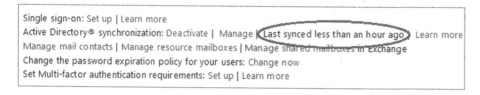

Single sign-on: Set up | Learn more
Active Directory® synchronization: Deactivate | Manage | Last synced less than an hour ago | Learn more
Manage mail contacts | Manage resource mailboxes | Manage shared mailboxes in Exchange
Change the password expiration policy for your users: Change now
Set Multi-factor authentication requirements: Set up | Learn more

Figure 11-27. Checking WAADsync status from Office 365

To inspect the status of the local agent, you check the application log by using the event viewer and watching for events generated by directory synchronization, as shown in Figure 11-28. Another option is to use a script developed by Mike Crowley, which will generate a short report on the status of the WAADsync tool. (You can download the script at http://bit.ly/WAADsyncReport).

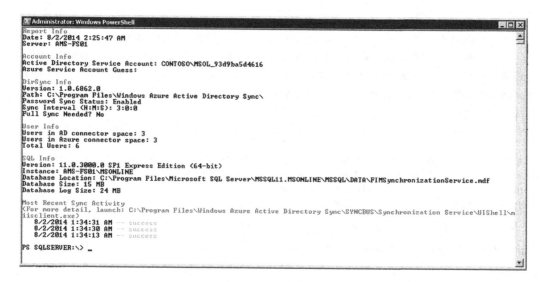

Figure 11-28. WAADsync report script output

Filtering WAADsync

By default, WAADsync will synchronize all users to Windows Azure Active Directory. Under the hood, WAADsync is a stripped-down version of Microsoft ForeFront Identity Manager. The tool to configure the synchronization is included when you deploy WAADsync, and it is called miisclient.exe. When you use the x64 version of WAADsync, miisclient.exe is located in C:\Program Files\Windows Azure Active Directory Sync\SYNCBUS\Synchronization Service\UIShell.

To limited the synchronization to a specific OU, you switch to the **Management Agents** view. Select the **Active Directory Connector** and open up the **Properties**. Select **Configure Directory Partitions**, where you can configure from which directory partitions to synchronize objects. Select **Containers**. You may be asked to enter your on-premises credentials. After that, you can select the containers that you want to synchronize with Windows Azure Active Directory, or deselect the containers you do not want to sync.

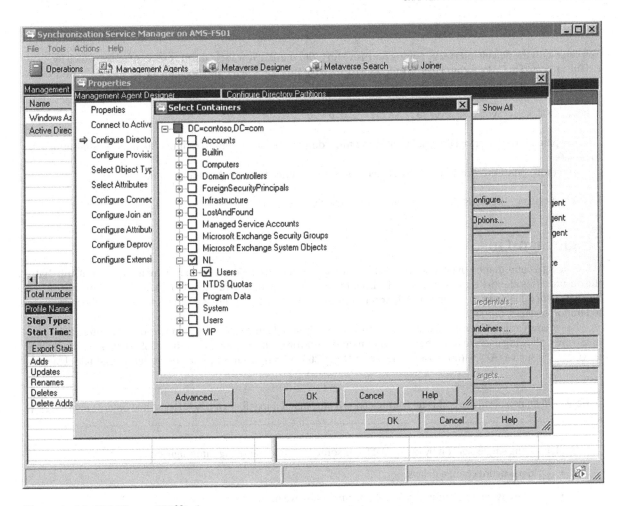

Figure 11-29. *WAADsync OU filtering*

In the **Properties** list of the management agent named **Active Directory Connector**, in the **Configure Directory Partitions** section, you can also select the domains you want to synchronize when want to filter on a specific domain.

Finally, you can filter by using attributes. In the **Properties** list of the management agent named **Active Directory Connector**, you select **Configure Connector Filter**. Scroll down and select the **user** in the **Data Source Object Type** list. There, you can add custom filters. For example, to exclude users who have their extensionAttribute1 configured, you select **New**. Then, in the Filter for the user, you select the **data source attribute** extensionAttribute1 and set the **operator** to Is Present. When you are done, you select **Add Condition** and click **OK**. When it's finished, you select the Management Agent, select **Run**, and then run **Full import Full Sync**.

■ **Caution**   Be cautious when editing the default WAADsync configuration. While modification of WAADsync configuration is supported up to certain limits, incorrectly configuring WAADsync may result in wrong objects being synchronized to your tenant.

Synchronization Interval

You can adjust the default interval by editing the `Microsoft.Online.DirSync.Scheduler.exe.config` file, which by default is located in **C:\Program Files\Windows Azure Active Directory Sync**. You open up the file in your favorite editor and change the line that reads `<add key="SyncTimeInterval" value="3:0:0" />` to your required interval—for example,

```
1 hour:<add key="SyncTimeInterval" value="1:0:0" />
```

Keep in mind the Active Directory replication time; don't go below 15 minutes, or use 30 minutes minimum just to be safe.

You then restart the Windows Azure AD syncronization service to make the change effective:

```
Restart-Service 'Windows Azure Active Directory Sync Service'
```

Single Sign-On

When using a combination of on-premises Active Directory and Office 365 such as Exchange hybrid, you'll find that the on-premises identity is a different identity from the one stored in or synchronized to Azure Active Directory. To allow Office 365 users to log on using their on-premises credentials, you can implement the Active Directory federation services, or ADFS.

As we saw earlier, WAADsync with password synchronization (same sign-on) can be used to synchronize passwords, allowing users to use the same account and password combination as in Office 365. With a security token service (STS) such as ADFS, those users can access Office 365 by using their on-premises credentials (single sign-on).

■ **Note**　When deploying ADFS, it is recommended you implement it together with WAADsync and before using the HCW.

Implementing single sign-on by using ADFS has some benefits over using same sign-on:

- No password change delays.

- Disabling an on-premises account becomes effective immediately in Office 365 as well.

- Password policy follows on-premises definition—for example, complexity, minimum length, and so on.

- Access control uses network location (IP ranges) or multi-factor authentication.

- Support for third-party software, such as interoperability with a Shibboleth-based federation solution.

The first version of ADFS came in 2005 with Windows Server 2003 R2. The availability of current versions of ADFS depends on the operating system you're using, as listed in Table 11-3.

Table 11-3. ADFS Version Overview

ADFS	Platform
2.0	Installable software for Windows Server 2008 and Windows Server 2008 R2. Download from `http://bit.ly/ADFS20DL`.
2.1	Installable server role in Windows Server 2012.
3.0	Installable server role on Windows Server 2012 R2.

■ **Note**   Like regular software, ADFS needs to be managed, and it will receive updates. For the built-in versions, these updates will come in the form of Windows update fixes. For ADFS 2.0, or actually 2.0 RTW (where RTW stands for "Release to Web" to indicate it is an installable package), update rollups are available. At the time of this writing, ADFS 2.0 Update Rollup 3 is available at `http://support.microsoft.com/kb/2790338`.

An ADFS implementation consists of one or more of the following components:

- **ADFS server,** responsible for authenticating users against Active Directory and issuing tokens or claims to requesters.

- **ADFS proxy server,** responsible for authenticating users against Active Directory via an ADFS server. This allows organizations to protect ADFS from direct Internet-based access. An ADFS proxy server is optional. An organization can also use reverse proxy solutions, existing ForeFront Threat Management Gateway (TMG) implementations included, the Web Application Proxy (WAP) role as found in Windows Server 2012 R2, or load balancing solutions like Kemp Loadmasters or F5 BIG-IP LTM to sit between the Internet and their ADFS servers.

- **ADFS configuration database,** used by ADFS servers to store information such as trusted partners, certificates, and service configurations. This information can be stored in Windows internal database (WID) for up to five ADFS servers or you can use a central Microsoft SQL server database. This decision is made at installation time.

To make the ADFS solution highly available, organizations need to implement multiple ADFS servers and ADFS proxy servers for availability and load balancing, using a load balancing solution or DNS round robin. The first is preferred, since DNS round robin is not a highly available solution.

■ **Tip**   ADFS components may be critical to your environment. When the ADFS is unavailable, users will not be able to authenticate and use the services hosted in Office 365. Therefore, it is recommended you have at least two ADFS servers and two ADFS proxy servers when applicable.

Your on-premises ADFS endpoint will be accessed through a hostname. Typical hostnames are sts.<domain name> or fs.<domain name>. This name also needs to be registered in your internal DNS when you are using split-DNS for local client lookups.

Since the SSL will be used to access your ADFS infrastructure, you need to obtain a valid third-party certificate with this hostname. This certificate needs to be installed on the ADFS servers and any ADFS proxy servers or other reverse proxy if you are doing layer-7 load balancing and use a SAN certificate for Exchange, ADFS, and perhaps other published services.

The concept of authentication using ADFS is depicted in Figure 11-30.

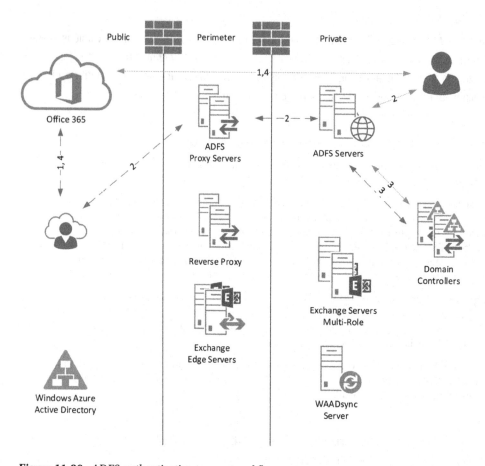

Figure 11-30. *ADFS authentication concept and flow*

The authentication flow for external users accessing Office 365 services is as follows:

1. User accesses Office 365 resource—for example, Exchange Online. Exchange Online notices the request is unauthenticated and redirects the request to the Windows Azure Active Directory authentication system. The Windows Azure AD notices the request is unauthenticated and, based on the domain name of the ID provided, redirects the request to the published ADFS URL.

2. The user needs to authenticate to the ADFS proxy server, which proxies the request to the internal ADFS server.

3. ADFS authenticates to the on-premises Active Directory. The user receives a signed security token and claim that will grant the user access to the resource.

4. The user accesses the Office 365 resource, authenticating itself using the token and claim received from ADFS.

The flow for domain users is similar, but because they are already logged on to the on-premises Active Directory, and thus have a Kerberos ticket, the Windows Azure AD authentication system directs them to the on-premises ADFS infrastructure instead of the public endpoint. (Further discussion of ADFS and claims-based authentication is beyond the scope of this book. For those looking for more information, see http://bit.ly/ADFSdocs).

When you have implemented ADFS, you can test your configuration by using the Exchange remote connectivity analyzer (ExRCA), available on `http://exrca.com`. On the tab **Office 365**, there is an option for **Office 365 Single Sign-On Test**. This will allow you to test your setup remotely, as shown in Figure 11-31.

Figure 11-31. *Testing ADFS single sign-on by using remote connectivity rnalyzer*

■ **Tip**   When running WAADsync and ADFS 3.0 with hotfix KB2919355 applied, you can configure an alternative login ID. This allows you to provision the User Principal Name in Windows Azure AD with your primary email address, permitting users to log on to AFDS-enabled applications using their email addresses instead of domain\user combinations. The procedure is described at `http://bit.ly/AlternateLoginID`.

ADFS Primary Server

When you have ADFS running and use the Windows internal database for the ADFS configuration database, one of these servers will be the primary federation server and the other servers will be secondary federation servers. The primary federation server will perform read/write operations on the database. The other servers will host read-only copies, replicating information from the primary federation server copy. Figure 11-32 shows the relationships.

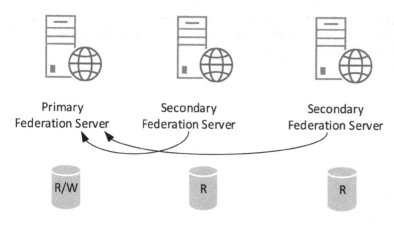

Figure 11-32. ADFS federation server database synchronization

---

■ **Note**   The default interval for secondary federation servers to replicate updates from the primary federation server is five minutes. You can configure the pulling interval on the local node using `Set-ADFSSyncproperties -PollDuration <number of seconds>`. Restarting the ADFS service will also trigger a sync request.

Should your primary server become unavailable, you may need to promote one of the secondary servers to primary. To do so, you proceed as follows:

1. Log on to the secondary sever you want to promote.

2. Open a PowerShell session.

3. Load the ADFS PowerShell module:

    ```
    Add-PSSnapIn Microsoft.ADFS.PowerShell
    ```

4. Configure the role as primary:

    ```
    Set-ADFSSyncProperties -Role PrimaryComputer
    ```

Next, you need to reorient the other secondary servers to the new primary server:

1. Log on to the secondary server.

2. Open a PowerShell session.

3. Load the ADFS PowerShell module:

    ```
    Add-PSSnapIn Microsoft.ADFS.PowerShell
    ```

4. Configure the role as secondary, assuming:

    ```
    Set-ADFSSyncProperties -Role SecondaryComputer
    -PrimaryComputer fs2.contoso.com
    ```

You also need to perform this procedure on the former primary server should it become available again.

> ■ **Note** When using SQL server for ADFS configuration database, there is no primary and secondary federation servers and all ADFS servers have read/write access to the same database.

Enabling OWA for ADFS

Exchange 2013 Service Pack 1 and later are claims-aware and include support for ADFS authentication on OWA and ECP. This allows authenticated users to seamlessly access OWA without being required to authenticate.

Assuming ADFS has been set up and configured correctly, you need to enable and configure the ADFS authentication on Exchange. On headlines, the process is as follows:

1. Set up and validate ADFS.

2. Add both OWA and ECP as relying trust parties in ADFS.

3. When not present, add claims descriptions for UPN, primary SID, and group SID.

4. Enable the Exchange organization for for ADFS.

5. Enable ADFS authentication on the OWA and ECP virtual directories.

For step-by-step instruction, visit `http://bit.ly/EX2013SP1ADFSOWA`. This site also contains instructions should you use pre-authentication software.

ADFS Service Monitoring

When using ADFS in combination with a load balancer solution, you might want to ensure that the ADFS service is responding before forwarding the traffic to the ADFS server or ADFS proxy server. This is better than the commonly used ICMP test ("ping"), which is more a matter of testing the availability of the network stack of that server than testing the service you are load balancing.

If your load balancer is capable of service monitoring, the way to implement this depends on the load balancer used. However, the building blocks are often the same:

- Use an HTTPS GET request.

- Specify the URL to use to check for "service health."

  For ADFS Servers, use: `/adfs/fs/federationserverservice.asmx`.
  For ADFS Proxy Servers, use: `/adfs/ls/idpInitiatedSignon.aspx`.

- Check if the request returns a 200 OK.

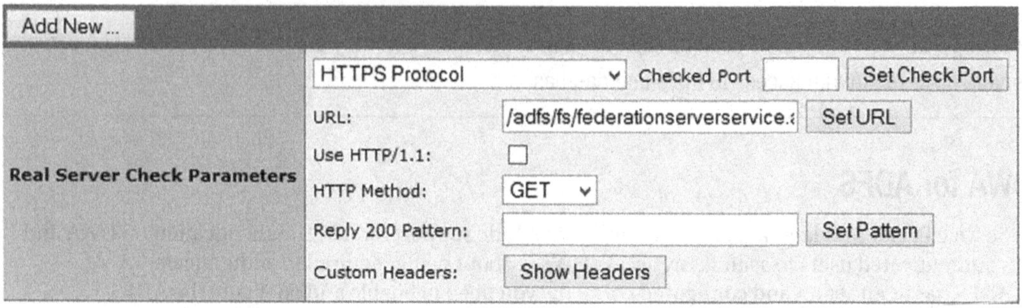

Figure 11-33. *Load balancer ADFS service monitor*

■ **Note** You can also use this information as input for regular monitoring products.

ADFS Client Access Policy Builder

ADFS contains support for claim rules that allow you to configure ADFS to restrict authentication to external network addresses. This enables organizations to block access to certain Office 365 services for particular networks or for members of certain groups.

The procedure to configure this is quite labor-intensive and prone to error owing to the regular expressions you might need to use. Fortunately, the ADFS product team publishes a graphic tool to create and configure these client access policies, baptized the "Client Access Policy Builder."

■ **Note** Office 365 currently supports only IPv4 addresses.

The first step lets you prepare the ADFS configuration database with rules for the required claim types. Next, you choose one of the five pre-configured scenarios:

- Block all external access to Office 365.

- Block all external access to Office 365 except for Exchange ActiveSync.

- Block all external access to Office 365, except for for browser-based applications.

- Block all external access to Office 365 for members of one or more groups.

- Block external access to Office 365 for Outlook clients.

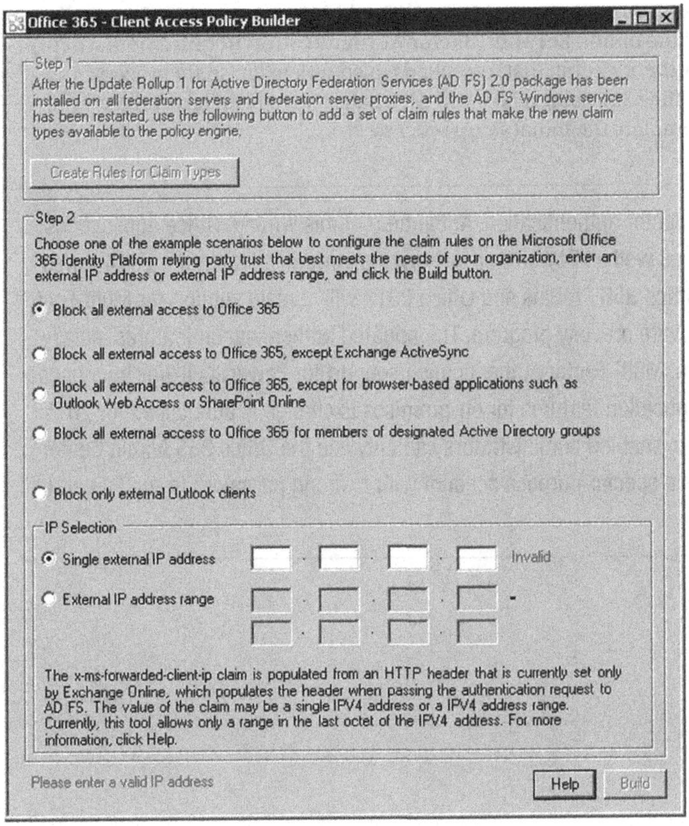

Figure 11-34. ADFS Client Access Policy Builder

Of course, these scenarios are not exhaustive. If your specific requirements are not covered by the default options, you can use the tool to create a starting point or for learning by example. For instructions related to manually creating network- or application-based restrictions in ADFS using claim rules, see `http://bit.ly/ADFSFilter`. You can download the ADFS Client Access Policy Builder at `http://bit.ly/ADFSCAPB`. The tool needs to be run on the ADFS server.

Multi-Factor Authentication

Authentication is based on something you know (e.g., your password), something you have (e.g., security token or smart card), or who you are (biometrics). By having two factors instead of one, the identities are more secure than they would be otherwise. *Multi-factor authentication* (MFA) is the form of authentication whereby the user identifies him or herself by using more than one factor. Multi-factor authentication should be considered for accessing cloud-based services, especially for administrator-type accounts. The multi-factor authentication option was added to the Office 365 service for Enterprise plans in February 2014. It is optional and does not require any additional subscription.

■ **Note** Multi-factor authentication is currently not available for Small Business and Dedicated Office 365 plans.

To enable users for multi-factor authentication, you open up the Office 365 Admin Center, and navigate to **Users and Groups ➤ Active Users**. There, you will find the option **Set Multi-factor Authentication Requirements: Setup**. When you have enabled a user for multi-factor authentication, that user needs to complete the setup process. The process is initiated when the user accesses Office 365 using a browser. Alternatively, you can direct the user to `http://aka.ms/MFASetup`, where the user can complete the initial setup process.

■ **Caution**   Not every application supports multi-factor authentication. At the time of this writing, Office applications such as Outlook, Lync, and OneDrive for Business, as well as PowerShell, are *not* supported. In November 2014 it was announced that the November 2014 updates for Office 356 ProPlus and Office 2013 will contain support for Multi-Factor Authentication when connecting to Office 365 A private preview program. The updated authentication features initially will be available through a private preview program. Multi-Factor Authentication support for PowerShell was announced for 2014. General availability of the updated authentication features for on-premises Exchange is announced for 2015. The consequence is that multi-factor authentication-enabled administrators can only use the Office 365 Admin Center for management tasks. The suggestion is to create a special-purpose account with a strong password to run PowerShell cmdlets or scripts in the Office 365 tenant.

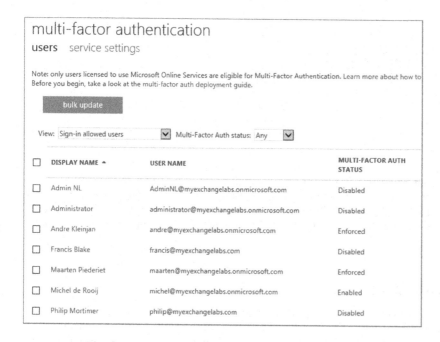

Figure 11-35. Configuring multi-factor authentication in Office 365

The way the user can authorize the logon by confirming his identity is called the *contact method*. The following contact methods are available:

- Mobile phone or office phone numbers for receiving authorization codes through calls.

- Mobile phone numbers for receiving authorization codes through text messages.

- Mobile App on smartphone.

Mobile App is available on Windows Phone, iOS, and Android. An additional benefit, apart from Mobile App being perhaps more convenient for an end user, is that it prevents additional costs that would be incurred as part of other contact methods, such as calling mobile phone or office numbers, or sending text messages.

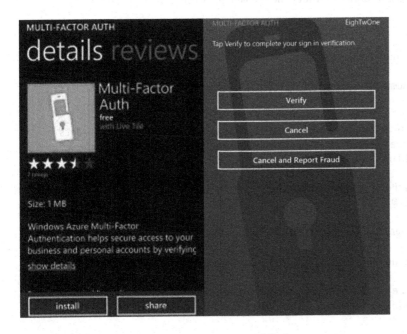

Figure 11-36. Multi-factor authentication on Mobile App

The Mobile App needs to be set up, linking the owner of the phone to the cloud identity in Windows Azure Active Directory. To accomplish this, the owner enters a verification code in the app or scans an on-screen QR code as part of the multi-factor authentication setup process. The owner is then asked to verify that the process is working by testing the verification process using the app.

■ **Note**   The multi-factor authentication app requires Internet access to receive the verification request. The on-screen six-digit number can be used as a fallback mechanism if the smartphone does not have Internet access. Also, the Mobile App is configured to receive push notifications, whereby the user is automatically prompted to verify her identity. When it is not able to receive those notifications, the user can check for pending authentication requests using "**Check for auth.**"

Of course, administrators can also manage multi-factor authentication from PowerShell by using the Windows Azure AD module for Windows PowerShell. This not only allows organizations to configure multi-factor authentication for existing users using PowerShell but also to enhance the current provisioning process with multi-factor authentication options.

By pre-configuring multi-factor authentication, administrators can prevent users from having to go through the initial setup process and hence be able to use their currently configured mobile phone or office number for verification.

Configuring MFA using the WAAD Module

To configure multi-factor authentication using the WAAD module for PowerShell, you open up a Windows Azure AD module for Windows PowerShell session and connect to your Office 365 tenant, with the following:

```
Connect-MSOLService
```

Next, you define a strong authentication object, as follows:

```
$st= New-Object Microsoft.Online.Administration.StrongAuthenticationRequirement
$st.RelyingParty= '*'
```

Now you can enable users for MFA by using `Set-MSOLUser` with the `StrongAuthenticationRequirements` parameter, passing it the strong authentication object created earlier. For example, to enable MFA for user michel@myexchangelabs.com, you would use:

```
Set-MsolUser -UserPrincipalName michel@myexchangelabs.com
 -StrongAuthenticationRequirements @($st)
```

To disable MFA, you clear the `StrongAuthenticationRequirements` attribute:

```
Set-MsolUser -UserPrincipalName michel@myexchangelabs.com -StrongAuthenticationRequirements @()
```

Administrators can also predefine the contact methods for users by configuring the `StrongAuthenticationRequirement` attribute state and providing least one contact method through the `StrongAuthenticationMethods` parameter:

```
$st= New-Object Microsoft.Online.Administration.StrongAuthenticationRequirement
$st.RelyingParty= '*'
$st.State= 'Enforced'
$m1 = New-Object -TypeName Microsoft.Online.Administration.StrongAuthenticationMethod
$m1.IsDefault = $true
$m1.MethodType = "OneWaySMS"
```

So, `$st` now contains a state of preconfigured authentication requirement and `$m1` has one contact method, in this case `OneWaySMS`. Possible values for `MethodType` are:

- `OneWaySMS` text code to mobile phone.
- `TwoWayVoiceMobile` call my mobile phone.
- `TwoWayVoiceOffice` call my office phone.
- `TwoWayVoiceAlternateMobile` call an alternate mobile phone number.
- `PhoneAppOTP` show one-time code in app—that is, six-digit number. OTP stands for "one-time password."
- `PhoneAppNotification` notify me through an app using in-app verification.

When you specify `OneWaySMS`, `TwoWayVoiceMobile`, or `TwoWayVoiceOffice` contact methods, the currently configured mobile phone or office phone number attributes on the user object will be used.

Now, to apply this to user michel@myexchangelabs.com, you use:

```
Set-MsolUser –UserPrincipalName michel@myexchangelabs.com
 -StrongAuthenticationRequirements @(st) -StrongAuthenticationMethods @($m1)
```

■ **Note** When users have configured PhoneAppNotification, by default they will also have the PhoneAppOTP contact method configured, which serves as a fallback for situations when there is no data coverage.

If you want to add another authentication contact method—for example, to have the user receive a call on his mobile phone—you add it as an element to the StrongAuthenticationMethods attribute:

```
$m2 = New-Object -TypeName Microsoft.Online.Administration.StrongAuthenticationMethod
$m2.IsDefault = $false
$m2.MethodType = "TwoWayVoiceMobile"
Set-MsolUser –UserPrincipalName michel@test.com  -StrongAuthenticationRequirements @($st)
-StrongAuthenticationMethods @($m1, $m2)
```

At some point, administrators may want to receive a report on which users are multi-factor authentication-enabled and what contact methods they have configured. The StrongAuthenticationMethods attribute contains the configured method. Using this knowledge, you can construct a cmdlet to get a list of MFA-enabled users and their configured methods; for example,

```
Get-MsolUser | Where-Object {$_.StrongAuthenticationRequirements} | Select UserPrincipalName,
@{name="MFA"; expression={$_.StrongAuthenticationRequirements.State}}, @{name="Methods";
expression={($_.StrongAuthenticationMethods).MethodType}} | ft -AutoSize
```

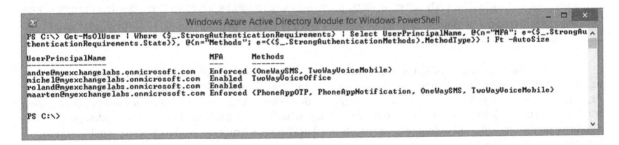

Figure 11-37. Reporting the multi-factor authentication status of users

---

■ **Tip** You can shorten the custom output field headers Name and Expression to N and E, respectively—for example, Select @{name="MFA"; expression={$_.StrongAuthenticationRequirements.State}} is identical to Select @{n="MFA"; e={$_.StrongAuthenticationRequirements.State}}.

App Passwords

Unfortunately, few applications support MFA at the time of this writing. Among those that do are Outlook, Lync, and Exchange ActiveSync clients, the Windows 8 mail app included. App passwords are service-generated passwords that you need to use just as you would a regular password when authenticating any apps to Office 365. These app passwords are 16 characters and are non-user configurable.

■ **Tip** Use a per-device app password, such as one password for all applications on your tablet and another password for all applications on your laptop. This allows you to invalidate the password that is used on a single device with one step, should the device get compromised or lost.

On the organization level, you can can disable app password usage for users. The generated password does not expire, so some organizations may require disallowing app passwords, should their security policy stipulate that.

Onboarding and Offboarding Mailboxes

Examining your Office 365 tenant, you may see that you have some mailboxes on-premises and some mailboxes in Office 365. If you just completed setting up your Office 365 tenant, all your mailboxes might still be located on-premises. So, how do you get those mailboxes to the cloud? This is *onboarding*. And what if you want to move some cloud-based mailboxes back to on-premises? That is *offboarding*.

■ **Note** This section applies to Exchange hybrid deployments. Mailbox moves oves that are part of a cutover - also known as big-bang - migration are one way and are migrated in bulk, using Exchange Online Admin Center's built-in migration feature or using third-party software. Cloud-based mailboxes might be relocated to the cloud as the host deems necessary, and should not be something for administrators to worry about—that's one of the joys of the cloud services.

Like cross-forest mailbox moves, the target environment needs to have a mail-enabled user that will function as a target for the mailbox move. In on-premises cross-forest migrations, this task is performed by a script called `Prepare-MoveRequest.ps1` or by identity management solutions like ForeFront Identity Manager, which can provision mail-enabled user objects in the target environment through what is called a *GALsync*. In a typical Exchange hybrid deployment, the mail-enabled user objects are provisioned in Windows Azure AD via the directory synchronization process done by WAADsync.

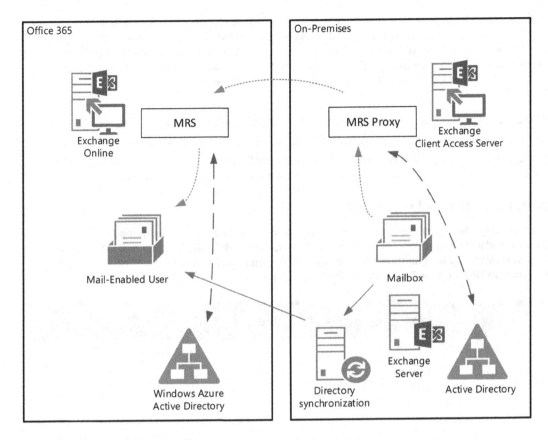

Figure 11-38. Onboarding a mailbox

When you are performing regular mailbox moves within the same organization, a service called *Microsoft Exchange mailbox replication* coordinates the move. When you are performing cross-forest moves or moves between on-premises and Exchange Online (also known as *remote* moves), something called the *MRS proxy* on the Client Access servers proxies the traffic related to the move, acting as the counterpart to the MRS. Both MRS and MRS proxy update the Active Directory in their respective environments with information such as the database hosting the mailbox, then converting the mailbox user objects to mail-enabled user objects (or vice-versa) when the move has been completed.

By default, the MRS proxy functionality is disabled, so before you can perform any remote moves, you need to enable MRS proxy from the EAC via **Servers ➤ Virtual Directories and** configure the properties of **EWS (default website)** entries. Alternatively, you can use EMS:

```
Get-WebServicesVirtualDirectory -Server <Server> |
 Set-WebServicesVirtualDirectory -MRSProxyEnabled:$true
```

To enable MRS proxy on all Client Access servers, you use:

```
Get-WebServicesVirtualDirectory | Set-WebServicesVirtualDirectory -MRSProxyEnabled:$true
```

■ **Note** The hybrid configuration wizard in Exchange 2013 Cumulative Update 5 and later will automatically configure the MRS proxy setting on the Web Services virtual directories.

Remote moves can be initiated from the source or the target environment, effecting a push or pull mailbox move. Depending on the origin of the move request, the MRS proxy is enabled on the remote end as the source Exchange Client Access servers (pull) or the "target" the Exchange Client Access servers (push). When you are moving mailboxes between Exchange on-premises and Exchange Online, the move is always initiated from Exchange Online. For this reason, you always need to enable MRS proxy for Exchange on-premises.

■ **Note** With the exception of Exchange Server 2003 as a source, mailbox moves are online and users restart their client only after the move has completed successfully. Also, because onboarding and offboarding use native Exchange mailbox moves, and the mailbox signature is preserved, there is no need to resynchronize the OST offline cache file.

Onboarding Mailboxes Using EAC

We start with onboarding, though offboarding is, in principle, the same process with the source and target environments switched and the cmdlet a little bit different. From the Office 365 Admin Center, you can initiate moves to or from Exchange Online via **Recipients ➤ Migration**. Click the + sign and you will have the option to **Migrate to Exchange Online** or to **Migrate from Exchange Online** (see Figure 11-39).

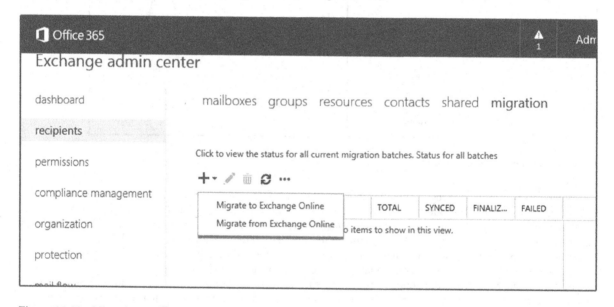

Figure 11-39. *Migrating mailboxes to or from Exchange Online using EAC*

You select the option **Remote Move Migration**. After that, you can provide the identities of the mailboxes you would like to move across, after which the remote move will be initiated. But before that, let's see what is configured on the mailbox and mail-enabled user before and after the remote move.

To do that, let's inspect the email addresses stamped on the on-premises mailbox using a sample user named Olrik. Note that, in the example that follows, the following is the case:

- myexchangelabs.com is the managed email domain.

- myexchangelabs.onmicrosoft.com is the default routing domain, created by Office 365.

- myexchangelabs.mail.onmicrosoft.com is the coexistence domain used for email routing; this domain is added when activating DirSync in your tenant.

```
[PS] >get-mailbox Olrik | fl WindowsEmail*,EmailAddr*,ExternalEmail*,legacyExchangeDN

WindowsEmailAddress         : olrik@myexchangelabs.com
EmailAddresses              : {x500:/o=ExchangeLabs/ou=Exchange Administrative Group
                              (FYDIBOHF23SPDLT)/cn=Recipients/
                              cn=f2970c513a2b49dc8de37a83766d4fda-Olrik,
                              smtp:olrik@myexchangelabs.mail.onmicrosoft.com,
                              smtp:olrik@myexchangelabs.onmicrosoft.com,
                              SMTP:olrik@myexchangelabs.com}
EmailAddressPolicyEnabled : True
LegacyExchangeDN            : /o=Litware/ou=Exchange Administrative Group
                              (FYDIBOHF23SPDLT)/cn=Recipients/
                              cn=1caf9bcc4ccd4e2db9ced9192c87736b-Olrik
```

The mail-enabled user in Windows Azure Active Directory, as provisioned by WAADsync, is as follows:

```
[PS] >get-mailuser Olrik | fl WindowsEmail*,EmailAddr*,ExternalEmail*,legacyExchangeDN

WindowsEmailAddress         : olrik@myexchangelabs.com
EmailAddresses              : {SMTP:olrik@myexchangelabs.com,
                              smtp:olrik@myexchangelabs.mail.onmicrosoft.com,
                              smtp:olrik@myexchangelabs.onmicrosoft.com}
EmailAddressPolicyEnabled : False
ExternalEmailAddress        : SMTP:olrik@myexchangelabs.com
LegacyExchangeDN            : /o=ExchangeLabs/ou=Exchange Administrative Group
                              (FYDIBOHF23SPDLT)/cn=Recipients/
                              cn=f2970c513a2b49dc8de37a83766d4fda-Olrik
```

As you can see, each entry has a unique legacyExchangeDN and the mailbox already contains an x500 address pointing to the legacy Exchange domain name of the mail user. The external email address (targetAddress) of the mail-enabled user points to the on-premises mailbox.

Now, you define the remote move request further by providing the credentials of an on-premises account with sufficient privileges to access and read the mailbox. Then, you will be asked to confirm the migration endpoint. When you have multiple regions publishing Exchange, you select the public FQDN of the endpoint closest to the mailbox.

■ **Tip**   When you have a KEMP load balancer and you get an error message stating, "The connection to the server <endpoint> could not be completed" while you are defining the migration batch, check if the KEMP support article at http://bit.ly/KempCont100Err applies to your situation (my thanks to Michael van Horenbeeck for this tip).

You are then asked to name the batch, which allows for easy reference when grouping multiple move requests. You are also asked to provide the target delivery domain. This is the email address currently configured on the mailbox and that contains the specified domain name, which will be configured as targetAddress (external email address) on the mail-enabled user. This is the mail-enabled user that remains after the mailbox has been moved successfully and the mailbox user has been converted to a mail-enabled user. In this step, you also have the option of only moving the personal archive (when you are moving to an Exchange Online Archiving plan, for example).

■ **Caution**   You need to remove any secondary email addresses from the mailbox that are using a domain name that is not part of the accepted domains in your Office 365 tenant. This includes local addresses, such as <alias>@contoso. local. If you do not do this, the move will fail and the error report will say "You can't use the domain because it's not an accepted domain for your organization."

On the final screen, you have the option of configuring a recipient who will receive the migration report. Additionally, you can select if you want the batch to run immediately or on demand. You can also choose to suspend the move when the contents have been copied but before finalizing the move by updating Active Directory (SuspendWhenReadyToComplete). The batch can then be resumed at a later time, copying over the last deltas and finalizing the move.

Via the Migration menu, you can monitor the progress of the migration batch. Via the **Details option**, you can check the progress of the individual mailbox moves and view the results of the move.

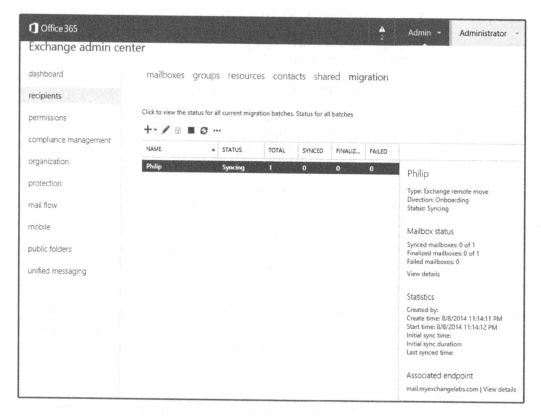

Figure 11-40. Migrating mailboxes to or from Exchange Online using EAC

When the move is successful, you are prompted to restart the Outlook client, after which users can access their mailboxes from the new location. If you keep getting this dialog box when starting Outlook, and you are running the Lync client, close the Lync because it may keep a session open to your mailbox, preventing updates to your Outlook profile from propagating.

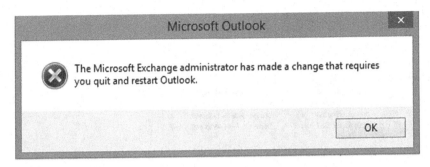

Figure 11-41. *Exchange configuration change prompt in Outlook*

You may also be required to re-enter your credentials when you are not using a single sign-on solution. The reason for this is that when you are saving the password in Outlook, it is stored for the endpoint being used for mailbox access. With the mailbox onboarding, the endpoint used to access the mailbox is switched from an on-premises FQDN to `office365.outlook.com` for Office 365, so the password must be provided.

If you follow the Autodiscover process, the on-premises Exchange environment is consulted, but Autodiscover gets instructed to look up **olrik@myexchangelabs.mail.onmicrosoft.com** instead. This leads to Exchange Online, which is where you just moved this mailbox to.

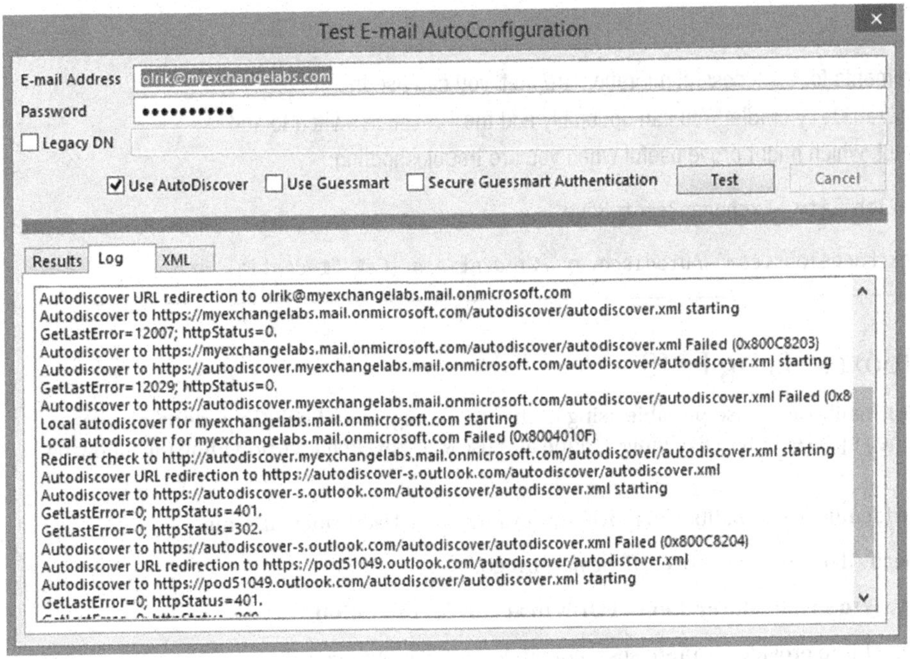

Figure 11-42. *The Autodiscover redirect after onboarding a mailbox*

You can also verify that Outlook is connected to Exchange Online by opening up the Outlook connection status window, right-clicking the Outlook system tray icon, and selecting **Connection Status**, as shown in Figure 11-43.

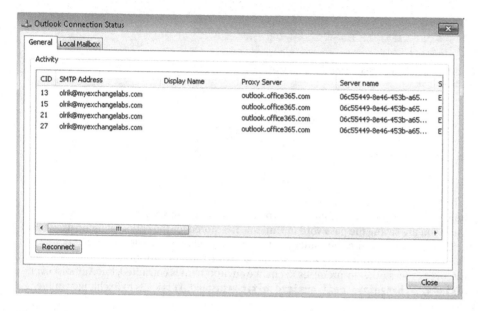

Figure 11-43. *Window for Outlook connection status*

■ **Tip** To test if the requirements for a successful migration are met, you can use the Test-MigrationServerAvailability cmdlet. You can optionally add the -Verbose switch to add extra information to the output, which might prove useful when you are troubleshooting:

Test-MigrationServerAvailability -ExchangeRemoteMove

-EmailAddress olrik@myexchangelabs.com -Autodiscover -Credentials (Get-Credential)

Onboarding Mailboxes Using EMS

Onboarding and offboarding mailboxes is also possible using Exchange Management Shell. To perform a cross-forest mailbox move, you open up a session to Exchange Online and use New-MoveRequest providing the following parameters:

- Identity is the identity of the mailbox to move—for example, the UserPrincipalName.

- Remote is to specify that a remove move will be performed.

- RemoteHostName **is to specify the endpoint FQDN to access for migration**.

- RemoteCredential is to provide on-premises credentials with mailbox access.

- TargetDeliveryDomain is to specify the email domain name of the secondary address to stamp as the external email address (targetAddress) to route traffic from the mail-enabled user to the mailbox. A typical value would be <tenant name>.mail.onmicrosoft.com.

- SuspendWhenReadyToComplete (optional) is to indicate the move should be suspended when the mailbox contents have been copied successfully and the move can be finalized.

- `BadItemLimit` (optional) increases the tolerance for bad items by allowing migration to skip this maximum number of corrupt items.

- `LargeItemLimit` (optional) allows migration of a certain number of messages that are larger than the current message size limit. The current message size limit in Office 365 is 35 MB (25 MB + MIME overhead).

- `PrimaryOnly` (optional) allows you to move only the primary mailbox. When not specified, any configured personal archive mailboxes are moved as well.

- `ArchiveOnly` (optional) allows you to move only the personal archive of the mailbox.

So, in an Exchange Management Shell session, to move a mailbox to Exchange Online, the cmdlet you need to use is:

```
$cred= Get-Credential
New-MoveRequest -Identity <Identity> -Remote -RemoteCredential <Credentials>
 -RemoteHostName <On-Premises Endpoint> -TargetDeliveryDomain <Domain>
```

For example, to onboard a mailbox called philip@myexchangelabs.com through endpoint mail.myexchangelabs.com, you use the following cmdlet:

```
$cred= Get-Credential
New-MoveRequest -Identity olrik@myexchangelabs.com -Remote -RemoteCredential $cred
 -TargetDeliveryDomain myexchangelabs.mail.onmicrosoft.com
 -RemoteHostname mail.myexchangelabs.com
```

When prompted, you provide on-premises credentials with sufficient access.

To track the progress of the move, you use `Get-MoveRequest` and `Get-MoveRequestStatistics`, as shown in Figure 11-44.

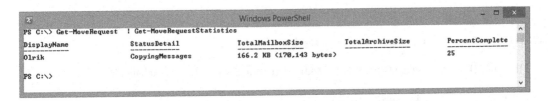

Figure 11-44. *Inspecting the mailbox move status*

■ **Tip** Exchange Online client access is throttled, including mailbox moves. When planning mailbox moves, use an average 0.3-1 GB/hour rate per mailbox, but an exact number is impossible owing to the many variables (e.g., MRS proxy hardware, available bandwidth, or number of items). To enhance throughput, increase the number of concurrent moves. When the MRS proxy server becomes the bottleneck, add more MRS proxy servers. In addition, you can use the `SuspendWhenReadyToComplete` option when you need to plan the time of completion. To make a reasonable estimate of the time, perform some trial migrations and check those reports for throughput rates.

After waiting for the WAADsync cycle, again check the email addresses stamped on the on-premises mail-enabled user, as updated by the WAADsync write-back actions:

```
[PS] >Get-RemoteMailbox Olrik | fl WindowsEmail*,EmailAddr*,ExternalEmail*,legacyExchangeDN

WindowsEmailAddress      : olrik@myexchangelabs.com
EmailAddresses           : {x500:/o=Litware/ou=Exchange Administrative Group
                           (FYDIBOHF23SPDLT)/cn=Recipients/
                           cn=1caf9bcc4ccd4e2db9ced9192c87736b-Olrik,
                           X500:/o=ExchangeLabs/ou=Exchange Administrative Group
                           (FYDIBOHF23SPDLT)/cn=Recipients/
                           cn=f2970c513a2b49dc8de37a83766d4fda-Olrik,
                           smtp:olrik@myexchangelabs.mail.onmicrosoft.com,
                           smtp:olrik@myexchangelabs.onmicrosoft.com,
                           SMTP:olrik@myexchangelabs.com}
EmailAddressPolicyEnabled : True
LegacyExchangeDN         : /o=Litware/ou=External (FYDIBOHF25SPDLT)/cn=Recipients/
                           cn=ae9c9a3bcc0d4c10ab593fb6a622c239
```

The cmdlet Get-RemoteMailbox will not show the **external email address**, as Get-MailUser would. However, you can inspect its value using, for example, the Get-ADUser cmdlet from the Active Directory module:

```
[PS] >Get-ADUser Olrik -Properties targetAddress | select TargetAddress

SMTP:olrik@myexchangelabs.mail.onmicrosoft.com
```

■ **Note**   targetAddress is not one of the default properties returned by Get-ADUser, so you need to have it returned using Properties.

The mailbox user in Office 365 contains the following addresses:

```
[PS] >Get-Mailbox Olrik | fl WindowsEmail*,EmailAddr*,ExternalEmail*,legacyExchangeDN

WindowsEmailAddress      : olrik@myexchangelabs.com
EmailAddresses           : {x500:/o=Litware/ou=External (FYDIBOHF25SPDLT)/cn=Recipients/
                           cn=ae9c9a3bcc0d4c10ab593fb6a622c239,
                           SMTP:olrik@myexchangelabs.com,
                           smtp:olrik@myexchangelabs.mail.onmicrosoft.com,
                           smtp:olrik@myexchangelabs.onmicrosoft.com
                           X500:/o=Litware/
                           ou=Exchange Administrative Group (FYDIBOHF23SPDLT)/cn=Recipients/
                           cn=1caf9bcc4ccd4e2db9ced9192c87736b-Olrik}
EmailAddressPolicyEnabled : False
LegacyExchangeDN         : /o=ExchangeLabs/
                           ou=Exchange Administrative Group (FYDIBOHF23SPDLT)/cn=Recipients/
                           cn=f2970c513a2b49dc8de37a83766d4fda-Olrik
```

As you can see, the `legacyExchangeDN` of the mail-enabled user has been added as the secondary x500 address to the mailbox and the `targetAddress` of the mail-enabled user is now set and pointing to the namespace used by Exchange Online for internal email routing, ending in .mail.onmicrosoft.com.

After the mailbox is onboarded, the on-premises mail-enabled user is called a "remote mailbox," or an on-premises mail-enabled user with an associated Office 365-based mailbox. It functions identically to a mail-enabled user and its recipient type is also `MailUser`. Remote mailboxes should be managed using `Get-Command -Noun RemoteMailbox` cmdlets—for example, `Get-RemoteMailbox`. `Get-MailUser` will not work and will result in a "recipient not found" error.

In the on-premise EAC, these remote mailboxes appear as in **Recipients ➤ Mailboxes** as mailboxes of the type **Office 365**. This could be confusing, but may simplify management of on-premises and Office 365-based mailboxes by using a single Admin Center.

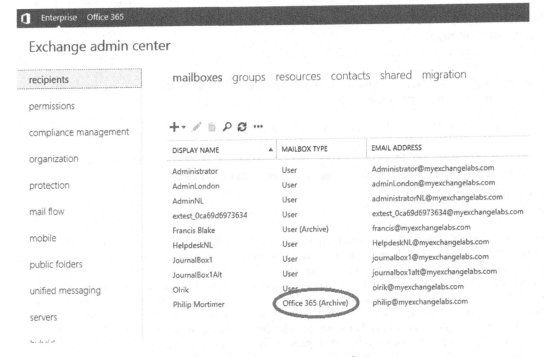

Figure 11-45. *Remote mailboxes show up in Exchange on-premises listings*

■ **Caution**   Like on-premises mailbox moves, you need to clean up the move requests by using `Remove-MoveRequest`. For example, to clear out all completed move requests, use `Get-MoveRequest -MoveStatus Completed | Remove-MoveRequest`.

Onboarding Multiple Mailboxes

Of course, you can move multiple mailboxes at once by selecting multiple mail-enabled users and piping them to New-MoveRequest or by using CSV files containing identities. For example, to move all mailboxes where the customAttribute1 (extensionAttribute1) contains "YES," you select all mail users satisfying that criterion, after which you can pipe those objects to New-MoveRequest, as follows:

```
$cred= Get-Credential
Get-MailUser -Filter { customAttribute1 -eq 'YES'} | New-MoveRequest -Remote
 -RemoteCredential $cred -TargetDeliveryDomain myexchangelabs.mail.onmicrosoft.com
 -RemoteHostname mail.myexchangelabs.com -BatchName 'Attr1Yes'
```

■ **Note**   The credential you need to provide with New-MoveRequest -RemoteCredential is that of an on-premises account with sufficient permissions.

In the example just given, BatchName was used. This puts a common label on all these move operations, allowing you to address all related move requests by specifying the batch name; for example,

```
Get-MoveRequest -BatchName 'Attr1Yes' | Get-MoveRequestStatistics
```

■ **Tip**   For a complete overview of all possible properties you can use with Filter, see http://bit.ly/ExFilterProperties.

As mentioned earlier, with Office 365, the move request is initiated from Exchange Online. Consequently, you are limited in the way you can select mailboxes to move by using on-premises criteria, such as organizational unit, because you depend on the attributes synchronized by WAADsync.

One way to tackle this problem is to create a CSV in the source environment that contains the identities of all mailbox users in a specific organizational unit or some other criterion. You can then use this CSV with the Office 365 Admin Center to create a migration batch, or use it with New-MoveRequest to move all these mailboxes at once.

To use a CSV file holding the identities of all mailboxes from a certain organizational unit (OU), including subcontainers, you first get the mailboxes specifying the organizational unit to filter on OU, and export those entries to a CSV file named Users.csv. You then use the canonical name when specifying OrganizationalUnit and export the alias as Identity, since New-MoveRequest will not take Alias as pipeline input for identity:

```
Get-Mailbox -OrganizationalUnit contoso.com/NL | Select @{name='Identity';expression={$_.Alias}}
 | Export-CSV .\Users.csv -NoTypeInformation
```

Now, you switch to an Exchange Online session and use the CSV file as input:

```
$cred= Get-Credential
Import-CSV .\users.csv | New-MoveRequest -Remote
 -RemoteCredential $cred -TargetDeliveryDomain myexchangelabs.mail.onmicrosoft.com
 -RemoteHostname mail.myexchangelabs.com -BatchName 'UsersNL'
```

Another way to approach this is to connect to on-premises Exchange and Exchange Online at the same time, and use session prefixes to alternate between them. As mentioned earlier in "Connecting to Office 365," you can use prefixes when importing sessions, which are added in front of the cmdlet nouns—for example, Get-CloudMailbox.

To do this, you open up an on-premises Exchange Management Shell session and connect to Office 365. You use a noun prefix of Cloud for all cmdlets related to this Exchange Online session:

```
$o365Cred= Get-Credential
$o365Session= New-PSSession -ConfigurationName Microsoft.Exchange
    -ConnectionUri https://ps.outlook.com/powershell/ -Credential $o365Cred
    -Authentication Basic -AllowRedirection
Import-PSSession $o365Session -Prefix Cloud
```

You can now repeat the above move operation, this time using the Cloud cmdlets instead of a CSV file:

```
$Aliases= Get-Mailbox -OrganizationalUnit contoso.com/NL | Select @{name='Identity';expression=
{$_.Alias}}
$cred= Get-Credential
$Aliases| New-CloudMoveRequest -Remote
 -RemoteCredential $cred -TargetDeliveryDomain myexchangelabs.mail.onmicrosoft.com
 -RemoteHostname mail.myexchangelabs.com -BatchName 'UsersNL'
```

Keep in mind that all cmdlets now need to use Cloud as well; for example,

```
Get-CloudMoveRequest -BatchName 'UsersNL' | Get-CloudMoveRequestStatistics
```

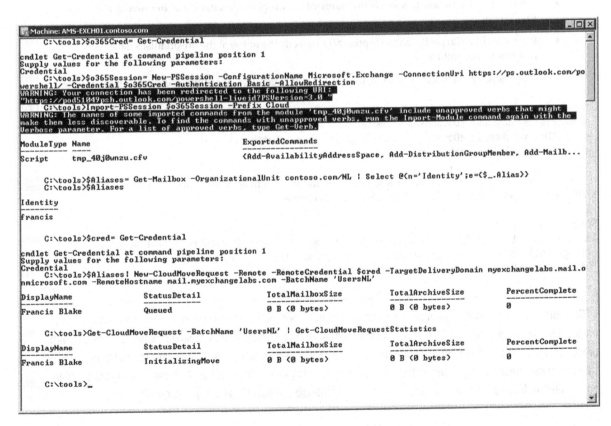

Figure 11-46. Moving mailboxes based on organizational unit information

■ **Tip**   There are two ways to filter identities: using the `Filter` parameter or piping the output through a filter—that is, `Where-Object` (or one of its aliases, `Where` or `?`). It is recommended you filter as early as possible, limiting the resulting set returned from Active Directory by having `Get-MailUser` utilize an LDAP-based query. When you do not use `Filter`, but filter through `Where` instead, all mail-user objects from Active Directory are returned and processed, which is less efficient and less friendly for Active Directory. However, the `Filter` parameter is limited, and using `Where` allows you to create more complex filters, so pick a method that suits your needs.

Offboarding Mailboxes

As mentioned earlier, the process of offboarding mailboxes is similar to onboarding. In the Office 365 Admin Center, you select **Migrate** *from* **Exchange** Online instead of **Migrate** *to* **Exchange Online**. The dialogs that follow are similar to those for onboarding, with the following differences:

- `TargetDeliveryDomain` to specify the on-premises target delivery domain. This will be stamped on the mail-enabled user in Office 365, which will remain.

- `Outbound` **to indicate that the move is going outbound (from the perspective of Exchange Online)**

- `RemoteTargetDatabase` **to specify the name of the on-premises database to move the mailbox to.**

- `RemoteArchiveTargetDatabase` (optional) to specify the name of the on-premises database to move personal archives to.

When using Exchange Management Shell, the cmdlet you need to use for offboarding is as follows:

```
New-MoveRequest -Identity <Identity> -Outbound -RemoteCredential <Credentials>
  -RemoteTargetDatabase <Database> -RemoteHostName <On-Premises Endpoint>
  -TargetDeliveryDomain <Domain> -RemoteTargetDatabase <Database>
  -RemoteArchiveTargetDatabase <Database>
```

Let's offboard the olrik@myexchangelabs.com user and move him back to on-premises. In this example, you use MDB1 as the target database and MDB2 as the archive database:

```
$cred= Get-Credential
New-MoveRequest -Identity olrik@myexchangelabs.com -Outbound -RemoteCredential $cred
  -TargetDeliveryDomain myexchangelabs.com -RemoteHostname mail.myexchangelabs.com
  -RemoteTargetDatabase MDB1 -RemoteArchiveTargetDatabase MDB2
```

■ **Caution**   When onboarding or offboarding mailboxes, there will be a significant amount of traffic between your on-premises environment and Office 365. Take note that if you have network devices sitting between MRS and MRS proxy that have some form of intrusion or detect some denial of service, after which they start to throttle or even block traffic, you may need to disable this to keep the process working at maximum speed. A classic example of software with such a built-in feature is ForeFront Threat Management Gateway, with its Flood Mitigation option.

Incrementally Managing Mailbox Moves

To stage your mailbox moves, you can specify the -SuspendWhenReadyToComplete switch when creating the move request. When the transfer of mailbox contents is complete and if SuspendWhenReadyToComplete was specified, the move will get suspended automatically and the **status detail** will display "**Auto Suspended.**"

You can resume any suspended moves by using Resume-MoveRequest. When specified like that, the last changes of the move are copied, after which the mailbox is briefly locked to finalize the move with adjustments to Active Directory attributes that are related to the mailbox user and mail-enabled user.

You can also use Resume-MoveRequest to resume a suspended move request and specify -SuspendWhenReadyToComplete again. This will copy the last changes, after which the move request changes to AutoSuspended again. This provides a convenient way to provision mailboxes and periodically perform incremental copies of the mailbox contents, which will keep the final delta to a minimum when you are actually planning to finalize the mailbox move.

■ **Caution** From the store's point of view, mailboxes being staged are disconnected. Therefore, they are subject to mailbox deletion retention time, which is 30 days in Office 365. After this period, mailboxes for which the move has not been completed will be removed. When a mailbox is removed, it is re-created when the move is resumed. In this case, all items that were already transferred are copied again.

Exchange Online Archiving

With the potential mix of on-premises mailboxes and mailboxes in Office 365 comes the flexibility for organizations to find cost-effective business solutions. The personal archive feature introduced with Exchange 2010, called *in-place archive* in Exchange 2013 and Office 365, adds that flexibility, as an organization can choose to host its mailboxes on-premises while also hosting its in-place archive in Office 365. Some of the Exchange Online plans and Office 365 Enterprise plans offer *unlimited* storage in the user's in-place archive for a small additional fee; alternatively, organizations can pick the standalone Exchange Online Archiving subscription, as shown in Figure 11-47.

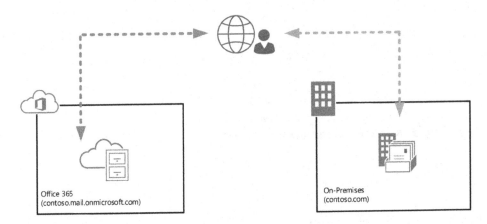

Figure 11-47. Exchange Online Archiving

To use Exchange Online Archiving, you need to deploy Exchange hybrid with WAADsync. In discussing the WAADsync tool earlier, it was mentioned that by checking the **Hybrid Deployment** option during WAADsync configuration, you would allow WAADsync to write back several attributes to the on-premises environment.

One of those attributes is msExchArchiveStatus. When an on-premises mailbox user has msExchArchiveStatus set to 1, that is an indication there is an in-place archive configured in Office 365.

Creating an Exchange Online Archive is a two-stage process. First, the on-premises mailbox gets enabled for an Exchange Online Archive. This is made effective in the next WAADsync cycle, which picks up the on-premises configuration change and provisions an in-place archive in Office 365. This archive is not immediately present, but when it has been created, the msExchArchiveStatus is set. In the next WAADsync cycle, that attribute is written back to the on-premises Active Directory and the user is able to access his in-place archive.

To enable an in-place archive in Office 365, you can use the Offic e 365 Admin Center, or use Enable-Mailbox with RemoteArchive from the Exchange Management Shell. You also need to specify ArchiveDomain, which functions similar to TargetDeliveryDomain when moving mailboxes, and it points to the environment hosting the archive. For this purpose, you can use your coexistence domain; the cmdlet to trigger creation of a remote archive for user Francis, for example, would be the following:

```
Enable-Mailbox Francis -RemoteArchive -ArchiveDomain myexchangelabs.onmicrosoft.com
```

Now, you wait for the WAADsync cycle or you manually run it to trigger creation of the in-place archive. When you consult the archive-related properties of the mailbox, you can see that the **archive status** has changed from None to Hosted Pending, indicating that msExchArchiveStatus is still not set:

```
Get-Mailbox Francis | ft DisplayName, ArchiveGuid, ArchiveStatus,
  ArchiveDomain, ArchiveState -AutoSize
```

After the second WAADsync cycle, the on-premises msExchArchiveStatus becomes 1. You can take a peek at the WAADsync by using miisclient.exe. On the Operations pane, wait for the last **Active Directory Connector | Export**, log entry and check if there have been **updates** in the **Export Statistics** pane. The entry is clickable, allowing you to identify the actual write-back of msExchArchiveStatus:

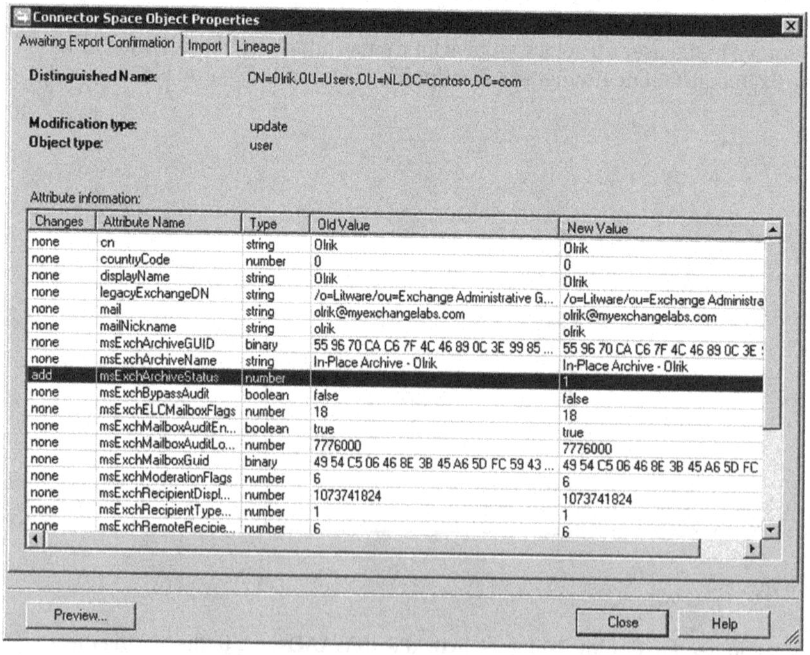

Figure 11-48. *Write-back status of the in-place archive*

When you are getting the archive properties of the on-premises mailbox, you will see the archive status now show as Active, indicating the completed provisioning of the archive, as shown in Figure 11-49.

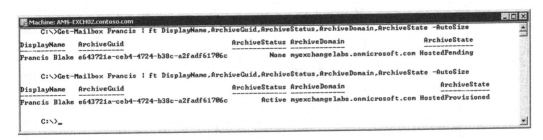

Figure 11-49. Remote archive status changes following WAADsync cycles

The end user with an Exchange Online Archive will notice that, if the Outlook Connection Status window is opened, it will show that his or her Outlook client is connected to his on-premises Exchange environment, as well as to Exchange Online. To make the user experience seamless, it is recommended you employ the same sign-on or single sign-on.

Mail Flow

Mail flow describes how email is routed in an organization and between the organization and external destinations, such as the Internet or partners. With Office 365, you need to configure routing between your organization and Office 365, especially with Exchange hybrid deployments where you want communications between on-premises mailboxes and cloud-based mailboxes to be secure.

Chapter 4 discussed mail flow and how to configure it for Exchange on-premises deployments by using send and receive connectors. In Office 365, you also can define connectors, but only on the Exchange Online Protection (EOP) level, and you need to use the Set-OutboundConnector and Set-InboundConnector cmdlets. When using these cmdlets in Exchange Online, you are actually configuring the connectors on the Edge servers that are part of Exchange Online Protection.

■ **Note**   Exchange Online Protection (EOP) was formerly known as ForeFront Online Protection for Exchange (FOPE) and is a hosted message hygiene service offered by Microsoft. Depending on your Office 365 plan, EOP may or may not be included.

The Exchange hybrid configuration wizard will take care of configuring the mail flow between your Exchange on-premises and Exchange Online. What it does not do is reconfiguring your public MX record, which determines if inbound messages will land on-premises or in Exchange Online. However, both inbound mail flows will work, as both environments are set up to accept the same managed domain name and the connectors are configured to transport mail between the on-premises and the Exchange Online organization. Exchange Online depends on the mail-enabled users in Exchange on-premises to redirect the email to the coexistence domain, as shown in Figure 11-50.

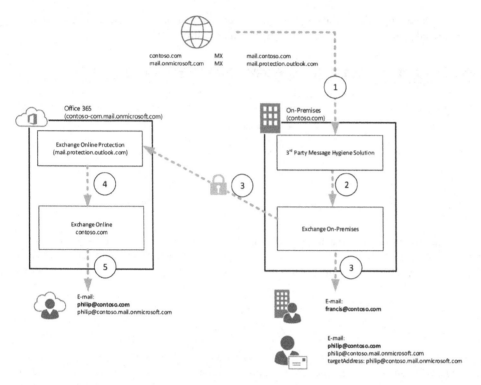

Figure 11-50. *Inbound email routed via on-premises*

■ **Note** One benefit of routing your email through Exchange Online Protection is that the email with other Exchange Online Protection users (also those from other organizations) is traveling securely within the EOP infrastructure.

All you need is a quick walkthrough for when Exchange hybrid is configured, and you'll keep the inbound email entering your on-premises organization. In this example, the sender is contoso.com and the recipient is either philip@contoso.com, who has his mailbox in Exchange Online, or francis@contoso.com, who has his mailbox on-premises. Here's how it works:

1. The mail transfer agent that wants to deliver the mail looks up the MX record for contoso.com. This points to **mail.contoso.com**, so it hands it off to the on-premises third-party gateway.

2. The gateway processes the message and delivers it to Exchange on-premises.

3. Exchange on-premises knows the mailbox francis@contoso.com and delivers the message. For philip@contoso.com, however, it finds a matching mail-enabled user. This has a targetAddress directing the message to philip@contoso.mail.onmicrosoft.com. For that address space a send connector is present, **Outbound to Office 365**, which is configured to securely deliver messages. Exchange looks up the MX record for contoso.mail.onmicrosoft.com, which points to the **mail.protection.outlook.com** (Exchange Online Protection), where it delivers the message.

4. Exchange Online Protection uses an internal connector for the internal address space `mail.onmicrosoft.com` domain, and hands off the message to Exchange Online.

5. The message is delivered to philip@contoso.mail.onmicrosoft.com—that is, `philip@contos.com`.

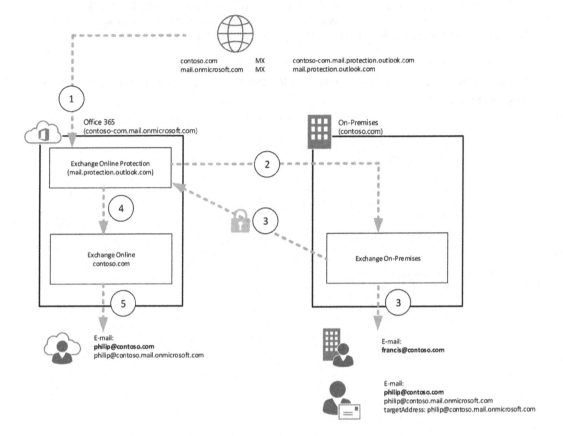

Figure 11-51. *Inbound email delivered via EOP*

When the MX record is configured to deliver inbound mail to Exchange Online Protection, the following occurs:

1. The mail transfer agent that wants to deliver the mail looks up the MX record for contoso. com. This points to `mail.protection.outlook.com` (EOP), so it hands it off to the EOP.

2. Exchange on-premises has a matching outbound connector for domain *, **Outbound to <Organization GUID>**, which is configured to securely delivers message to a smart host, **mail.myexchangelabs.com**. It delivers the message to this smart host.

3. Exchange on-premises knows mailbox `francis@contoso.com` and delivers the message. For `philip@contoso.com`, it will again use the configured `targetAddress` `philip@contoso.mail.onmicrosoft.com` and use the send connector **outbound to Office 365**. After the MX lookup, Exchange delivers the message to **mail.protection.outlook.com** (EOP).

4. Exchange Online Protection delivers the message destined for the internal address space mail.onmicrosoft.com to Exchange Online.

5. The message is delivered to philip@contoso.mail.onmicrosoft.com—that is, philip@contos.com.

Regarding outbound traffic, organizations must decide if they want to let all outbound email traffic flow through their Exchange on-premises organization. This is configured by selecting the **Centralized Mail Transport** option when configuring your Exchange hybrid deployment using the hybrid configuration wizard.

■ **Note**   In the hybrid configuration wizard, the **centralized mail transport** is hidden from view, and you need to make it visible by selecting **More Options**.

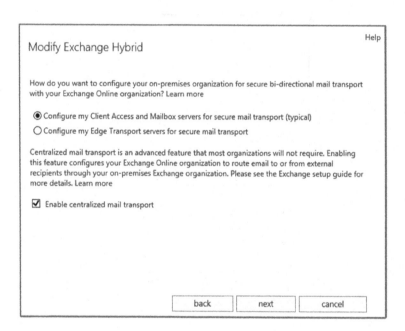

Figure 11-52. Configuring the centralized mail transport

One scenario in which the centralized mail transport is beneficial is when you want to secure transport with partners. By forcing the traffic to flow through your organization, you create a single point of administration for secure email transport with those partners.

Now, let's look at the mail flow of both situations—when using the decentralized mail transport and when using the centralized mail transport. In both scenarios, philip@contoso.com is sending mail to an external recipient—say, joe@fabrikam.com—from his mailbox in Exchange Online. Since outbound mail from Exchange on-premises is not affected by the centralized mail transport setting, that is not shown, as illustrated in Figure 11-53.

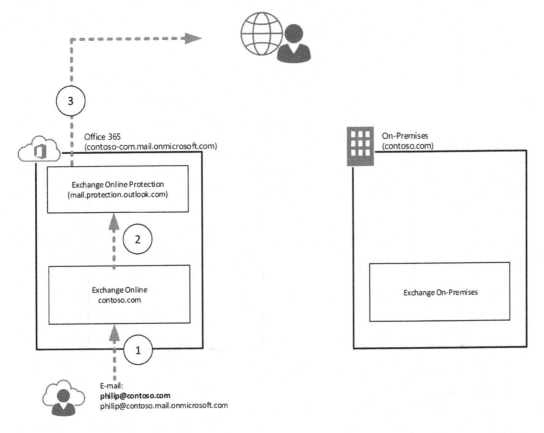

Figure 11-53. *Decentralized mail transport*

When your Exchange hybrid is configured to not use the centralized mail transport, here's what happens:

1.   The user philip@contoso.com submits a message to joe@fabrikam.com in Exchange Online.

2.   Exchange Online sees that it is not authorized for fabrikam.com and routes the message to Exchange Online Protection for delivery.

3.   Exchange Online Protection determines that fabrikam.com is external, does an MX lookup, and delivers the message to the configured host, as shown in Figure 11-54.

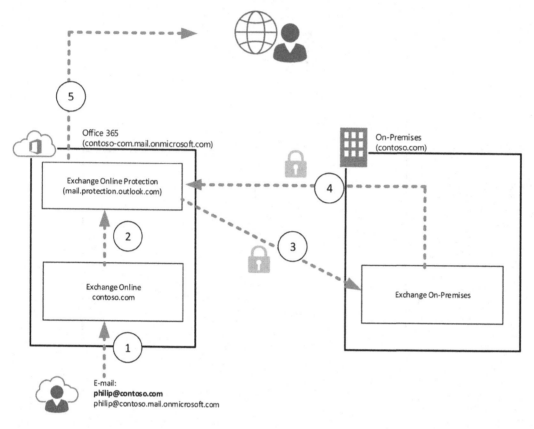

Figure 11-54. *Centralized mail transport*

■ **Note** If the recipient is someone with an Exchange on-premises mailbox—for example, @contoso.com—then Exchange Online Protection routes those messages through a connector "Outbound to <Organization Guid>," which is configured to securely deliver messages to smarthost mail.contoso.com for contoso.com.

When your Exchange hybrid is configured to use central mail transport, the following occurs:

1. The user philip@contoso.com submits a message to joe@fabrikam.com in Exchange Online.

2. Exchange Online sees it is not authorized for fabrikam.com and hands off the message to Exchange Online Protection for delivery.

3. Exchange Online Protection finds a matching connector "**Outbound to <Organization Guid>**," which is configured to always route all messages via on-premises (Get-OutboundConnector property RouteAllMessagesViaOnPremises), using smart host **mail.contoso.com**.

4. Assuming you have configured outbound email to be deliverd to Exchange Online Protection and there is no connector for fabrikam.com, the message is delivered to Exchange Online Protection.

5. Exchange Online Protection determines fabrikam.com is external, does an MX lookup, and delivers the message.

■ **Tip** The connectors configured by the hybrid configuration wizard to securely transport messages between Exchange on-premises and Exchange Online use *transport layer security* (TLS). If the mail transport does not work, verify that there are no appliances sitting between your Exchange on-premises and the Internet that may tamper with SMTP traffic, such as fixup/mailguard by Cisco PIX. Your SMTP logs will show a line similar to : **220** *******, where it is supposed to be given the **STARTTLS** command. More information on this at `http://bit.ly/MailGuard`.

Reporting

Office 365 has some built-in report-generating capabilities. Unfortunately, these reports are not available for on-premises usage. You can find the reports in the Office 365 Admin Center under "**Reports**," but there are some specific PowerShell-based reporting cmdlets as well. Note that whether you have reporting capabilities depends on your Office 365 plan and role—for example, password administrators in Office 365 have reporting options that are diferent from those global administrators have.

Service Health

The *service health* dashboard in Office 365 offers an overview of the current status of the Office 365 service and all its underlying components. It also provides historical information, which is helpful when users do not report problems immediately, but instead say things along the line of "I could not access my mailbox last Saturday." The information icons are clickable and lead to getting background information on problems. See Figure 11-55.

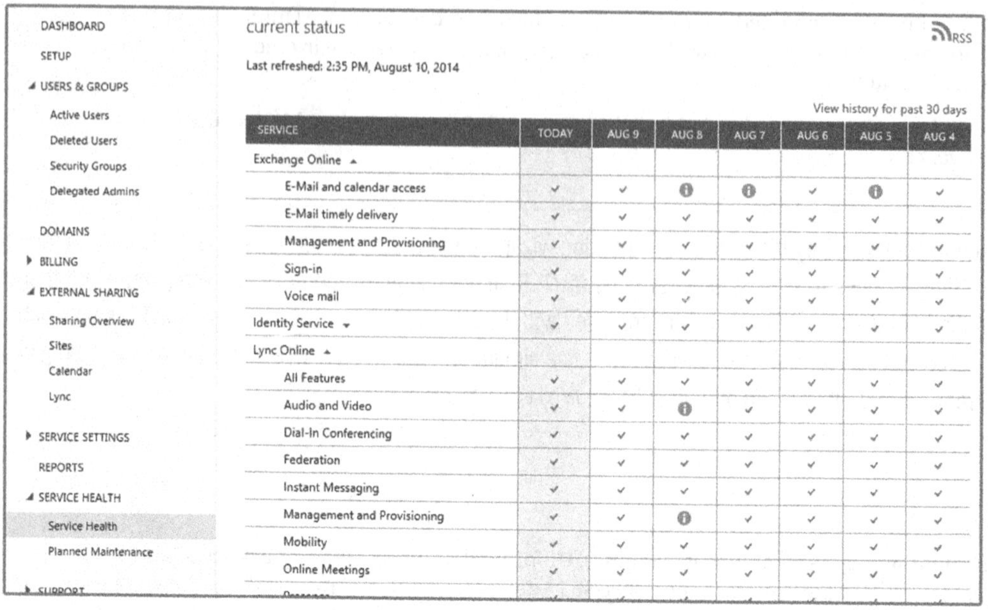

DASHBOARD

SETUP

⊿ USERS & GROUPS

  Active Users

  Deleted Users

  Security Groups

  Delegated Admins

DOMAINS

▶ BILLING

⊿ EXTERNAL SHARING

  Sharing Overview

  Sites

  Calendar

  Lync

▶ SERVICE SETTINGS

REPORTS

⊿ SERVICE HEALTH

  Service Health

  Planned Maintenance

▶ SUPPORT

current status

Last refreshed: 2:35 PM, August 10, 2014

View history for past 30 days

SERVICE	TODAY	AUG 9	AUG 8	AUG 7	AUG 6	AUG 5	AUG 4
Exchange Online ▲							
E-Mail and calendar access	✓	✓	ℹ	ℹ	✓	ℹ	✓
E-Mail timely delivery	✓	✓	✓	✓	✓	✓	✓
Management and Provisioning	✓	✓	✓	✓	✓	✓	✓
Sign-in	✓	✓	✓	✓	✓	✓	✓
Voice mail	✓	✓	✓	✓	✓	✓	✓
Identity Service ▼	✓	✓	✓	✓	✓	✓	✓
Lync Online ▲							
All Features	✓	✓	✓	✓	✓	✓	✓
Audio and Video	✓	✓	ℹ	✓	✓	✓	✓
Dial-In Conferencing	✓	✓	✓	✓	✓	✓	✓
Federation	✓	✓	✓	✓	✓	✓	✓
Instant Messaging	✓	✓	✓	✓	✓	✓	✓
Management and Provisioning	✓	✓	ℹ	✓	✓	✓	✓
Mobility	✓	✓	✓	✓	✓	✓	✓
Online Meetings	✓	✓	✓	✓	✓	✓	✓

Figure 11-55. Office 365 service health report

You can subscribe to an RSS feed that will contain updates on the service status using the RSS button shown in Figure 11-55. If you want to know if there is any maintenance planned, check the Planned Maintenance option. It's helpful to give yourself or your end users a heads-up on possible service interruptions.

Tenant Reports

Table 11-4 is a list of currently (as of this writing) available Exchange Online-related reports available in Office 365 Admin Center. As Office 365 is under constant modification, the list may be subject to change.

Table 11-4. Office 365 Reports

Category	Reports
Mail	Active and inactive mailboxes
	New and deleted mailboxes
	New and deleted groups
	Mailbox usage
	Types of mailbox connections
Devices	Browser used
	Operating system used
Auditing	Mailbox access by non-owners
	Role group changes
	Mailbox content search and hold
	Mailbox litigation holds

(continued)

Table 11-4. *(continued)*

Category	Reports
Protection	Top senders and recipients
	Top malware for mail
	Malware detections
	Spam detections
	Sent and received mail
Rules	Top rule matches for mail
	Rule matches for mail
DLP	Top DLP policy matches for mail
	Top DLP rule matches for mail
	DLP policy matches by severity for mail
	DLP policy matches, overrides, and false

Some reports offer the option of exporting the information to a CSV file, allowing you to further process the information.

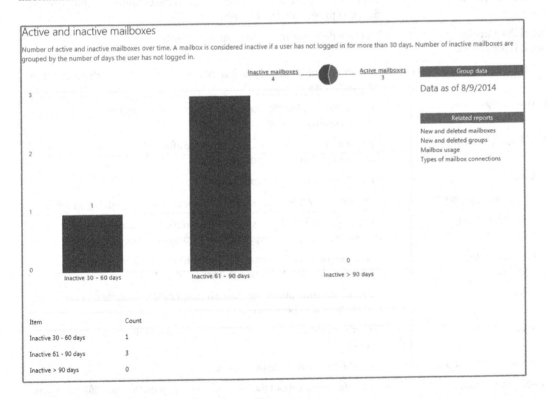

Figure 11-56. *Office 365 active and inactive mailboxes report*

When connected to Exchange Online in Office 365, you have additional reporting and tracking commands at your disposal. These are listed in Table 11-5.

Table 11-5. *Office 365 Reporting Commands*

Command	Description
Get-ConnectionByClientTypeReport/ Get-ConnectionByClientType DetailsReport	View details about the different types of clients that are connected to mailboxes in your organization. The client types indicate different protocols; for example, Outlook WebApp, MAPI, POP3, IMAP4, Exchange ActiveSync, and Exchange Web Services.
Get-GroupActivityReport	View the number of distribution groups that were created and deleted.
Get-LastLogonStats	Connect to Office 365 and export a list of all your Office 365 mailbox-enabled users' last logon date/time to a CSV file. The script can be downloaded from http://bit.ly/GetLastLogonStats.
Get-MailboxActivityReport	View the number of mailboxes that were created and deleted.
Get-MailboxUsageReport/ Get-MailboxUsageDetailReport	View the number of mailboxes in your organization that are within 25% of the maximum mailbox size, and the number of mailboxes that are over the maximum size.
Get-MailDetailDlpPolicyReport	View the details of messages that matched the conditions defined by any data loss prevention (DLP) policies.
Get-MailDetailMalwareReport/ Get-MailDetailSpamReport	View the details of malware or spam messages.
Get-MailDetailTransportRuleReport	View the details of messages that matched the conditions defined by any transport rules.
Get-MailFilterListReport	View possible values for various parameters that can be supplied to other reporting cmdlets.
Get-MailTrafficPolicyReport	View statistics about messages that were affected by data loss prevention (DLP) policies and transport rules.
Get-MailTrafficReport	View details about message traffic.
Get-MailTrafficSummaryReport	View summary information about message traffic in your organization.
Get-MailTrafficTopReport	View a report of the highest volume senders, recipients, malware recipients, and spam recipients in your organization.
Get-MessageTrace/ Get-MessageTraceDetail	Trace messages as they pass through the Office 365 tenant; show additional details for a message trace event.
Get-MxRecordReport	View information about the mail exchanger (MX) records that are configured for a specified domain.
Get-OutboundConnectorReport	View the outbound connectors that are used to deliver mail to specific domains.
Get-RecipientStatisticsReport	View the recipient statistics report.
Get-ServiceDeliveryReport	View information about the message delivery path for a specified recipient.
Get-StaleMailboxReport/ Get-StaleMailboxDetailReport	View the number of mailboxes that haven't been accessed for at least 30 days.

For example, Get-MailTrafficReport will output traffic summary, as shown in Figure 11-57.

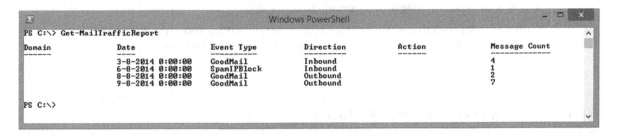

Figure 11-57. *Mail traffic report for Office 365*

Don't forget that while Office 365 has some nice built-in reporting features and cmdlets that, alas, are not available for Exchange on-premises, you can build your own such reports using PowerShell.

■ **Note**   Developers can utilize the Office 365 reporting web service to create custom reports. More on this can be found at http://msdn.microsoft.com/en-us/library/jj984321.aspx.

Message Tracking

In Exchange on-premises, you can use the Get-MessageTrackingLog cmdlet to track messages processed in the Exchange on-premises environment. Of course, in Office 365, your tenant is part of a shared infrastructure and therefore tracking could raise privacy issues. Also, Exchange Online uses Exchange Online Protection (EOP) for secure messaging and message hygiene. Without adjustments to the built-in message tracking functionality, email would always be received or delivered to Exchange Online, which makes troubleshooting more difficult. This is where the Exchange Online-only cmdlet Get-MessageTrace comes into play. This command extends message tracking to EOP, and it is to be used for message tracking in Exchange Online. Get-MessageTrackingLog is not available, however.

Here's a short list of the possible parameters you can use with Get-MessageTrace and how they compare to the parameters you can use with Get-MessageTrackingLog:

- StartDate and EndDate work identically; they enable you to restrict the results to a specific date range.

- RecipientAddress filters results on recipient email address. You can specify multiple values using a comma, and you can use wildcards such as *@myexchangelabs.com.

- SenderAddress is similar to RecipientAddress, but filters on sender email address instead. Like RecipientAddress, you can use wildcards.

- FromIP is new. For inbound messages, it filters on the source IP address—that is, the public IP address of the SMTP server delivering the message. For outbound messages, the trace would return a blank value.

- MessageTraceID can be used in combination with RecipientAddress to uniquely identify a message trace and obtain more details. A message trace ID is generated for every message processed.

- MessageId filters works identical, and filters on the Message-ID header field of the message.

- Status filters on the delivery status of the message—that is, None, Failed, Pending, Delivered, or Expanded. This is similar to Get-MessageTrackingLog's EventId parameter. It is not identical, as internal routing of messages will be obfuscated.

- ToIP is new. For outbound messages, this filters on the public IP address of the resolved MX record for the destination domain. For inbound messages, the trace would return a blank value.

■ **Note**   You can only track messages from the last 30 days.

For example, to retrieve all message traces of messages received through an SMTP host homed at 131.107.35.27, between November 1, 2014, and November 30, 2014, sent to philip@myexchangelabs.com, you would use something like this:

```
Get-MessageTrace -StartDate 11/1/2014 -EndDate 11/30/2014 -FromIP 131.107.35.27 -Recipient philip@
myexchangelabs.com | Format-Table -AutoSize Received, SenderAddress, RecipientAddress, Subject
```

To see all the messages traces of email coming from an email domain named "microsoft.com" in the past seven days, showing only the last ten trace events, you would use:

```
Get-MessageTrace -StartDate (Get-Date).AddDays(-7) -EndDate (Get-Date)
 -SenderAddress '*@microsoft.com' | Select Received, MessageId, Status |
Sort Received -Descending | Select -First 10 | Format-Table -AutoSize
```

The output of these examples is shown in Figure 11-58.

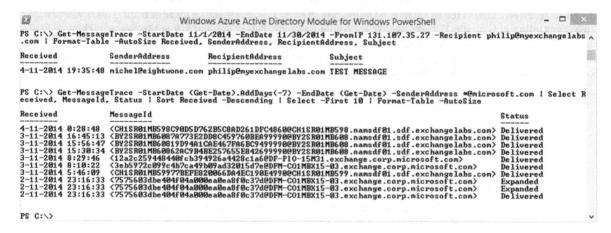

Figure 11-58. Office 365 report on message trace

Summary

This chapter guided you through the deployment options for Office 365 and how to connect to Office 365. It discussed the importance of setting up Autodiscover, and showed features like federated organizations, as well as how to configure organization-wide settings that determine what information can be shared between federated organizations. It also showed how to publish calendaring information for non-federated scenarios and how to set up OAuth to provide cross-product authentication.

In this chapter also was how to set up and configure directory synchronization to Azure Active Directory, how to configure Active Directory federation services in Exchange, and how to enable multi-factor authentication for users.

Next, we showed how to onboard and offboard mailboxes from Exchange on-premises to/from Office 365, how to deploy Exchange Online Archiving, and how to configure mail-flow options when deploying Exchange hybrid.

The chapter concluded with a survey of reporting options and advice on using message tracking in Office 365.

Index

■ H

■ I

Get the eBook for only $10!

Now you can take the weightless companion with you anywhere, anytime. Your purchase of this book entitles you to 3 electronic versions for only $10.

This Apress title will prove so indispensible that you'll want to carry it with you everywhere, which is why we are offering the eBook in 3 formats for only $10 if you have already purchased the print book.

Convenient and fully searchable, the PDF version enables you to easily find and copy code—or perform examples by quickly toggling between instructions and applications. The MOBI format is ideal for your Kindle, while the ePUB can be utilized on a variety of mobile devices.

Go to www.apress.com/promo/tendollars to purchase your companion eBook.

Apress®
THE EXPERT'S VOICE™